W9-BFZ-519

Natural Supernaturalism

TRADITION AND
REVOLUTION IN
ROMANTIC LITERATURE

Natural Supernaturalism

TRADITION AND REVOLUTION IN ROMANTIC LITERATURE

M. H. ABRAMS

W · W · NORTON & COMPANY

New York · London

W. W. Norton & Company, Inc.
500 Fifth Avenue, New York, N.Y. 10110
www.wwnorton.com

W. W. Norton & Company Ltd.
Castle House, 75/76 Wells Street, London W1T 3QT

Books That Live
The Norton imprint on a book means that in the publisher's
estimation it is a book not for a single season but for the years.
W. W. Norton & Company, Inc.

Library of Congress Cataloging in Publication Data

Abrams, Meyer Howard.
    Natural supernaturalism: tradition and revolution in
romantic literature.

    (Norton library)
    Includes bibliographical references.
    1. Romanticism. I. Title.
[PN603.A3   1973]   809'.9'14   73–7855

ISBN 0-393-00609-3

Printed in the United States of America
        7 8 9 0

For Jane
and
For Judy

Contents

Preface

"The literature of England," Shelley wrote in *A Defence of Poetry*, "has arisen as it were from a new birth." "We live among such philosophers and poets as surpass beyond comparison any who have appeared since the last national struggle for civil and religious liberty," and these men have in common "the spirit of the age." In a letter to Charles Ollier of October 1819, he further remarked that the great poets derive "from the new springs of thought and feeling, which the great events of our age have exposed to view, a similar tone of sentiment, imagery, and expression," and that such similarity in the "best writers" of an age attests to "the spirit of that age acting on all." Some of Shelley's contemporaries, as we shall see, made similar assertions. Suppose that we abstract the factual claims in Shelley's pronouncements and restate them as follows: A number of major poets, who differed markedly from their eighteenth-century predecessors, had in common important themes, modes of expression, and ways of feeling and imagining; the writings of these poets were part of a comprehensive intellectual tendency which manifested itself in philosophy as well as in poetry; this tendency was causally related to the drastic political and social changes of the age. It seems to me that the claims, so stated, are valid; and I would add that they are valid not only for English but also for German literature and philosophy during the lifetime of Shelley.

My aim in this book is to substantiate these claims by specifying some of the striking parallels, in authorial stance and persona, subject matter, ideas, values, imagery, forms of thought and imagination, and design of plot or structure, which are evident in a number of the prominent poets, post-Kantian philosophers,

11

writers of romances, authors of partly fictional autobiography, and exponents of the related form the Germans called *Universalgeschichte*—a philosophical scheme of the human past, present, and predictable future—in both England and Germany during that remarkable period of creativity, the three or four decades following the outbreak of the French Revolution. Within the great variety of literary, philosophical, and historical forms that fall within this purview, each has its own premises and principles of organization, while each major writer has his distinctive preoccupations and voice; in dealing with a particular work or a particular writer, I have tried to do justice to such differences in formal intention and individual utterance. Nevertheless, these writers shared a concern with certain human problems, and an identifiable way of considering and moving toward the resolution of these problems, which justify Shelley and his contemporaries in distinguishing what they called "the spirit of the age," and what I, for economy of discussion, have chosen to call by the conventional though ambiguous term "Romantic."

The title *Natural Supernaturalism* indicates that my recurrent, but far from exclusive, concern will be with the secularization of inherited theological ideas and ways of thinking. In England and Germany, two great Protestant nations with a history of theological and political radicalism, the Biblical culture fostered collateral developments of response to what Shelley called "the great events of the age," by which he meant above all the French Revolution, its unbounded promise and its failure, and the revolutionary and counter-revolutionary shock waves it had set up in that era of the turbulent emergence of the modern political, social, and industrial world. Philosophers such as Fichte, Schelling, and Hegel, imaginative writers from Blake and Wordsworth to Shelley and the young Carlyle in England, and Hölderlin and Novalis in Germany, as well as others who, like Schiller and Coleridge, were equally metaphysicians and bards, conceived themselves as elected spokesmen for the Western tradition at a time of profound cultural crisis. They represented themselves in the traditional persona of the philosopher-seer or the poet-prophet (in England, the chief model was Milton, the great "bard" of what Shelley called "the last national struggle for civil and religious liberty"), and they set out, in various yet recognizably parallel ways, to reconstitute the grounds of hope and to announce the certainty, or at least the possibility, of a rebirth in which a renewed mankind will inhabit a renovated earth where he will find himself thoroughly at home.

It is a historical commonplace that the course of Western thought since the Renaissance has been one of progressive secularization, but it is easy to mistake the way in which that process took place. Secular thinkers have no more been able to work free of the centuries-old Judeo-Christian culture than Christian theologians were able to work free of their inheritance of classical and pagan thought. The process—outside the exact sciences at any rate—has not been the deletion and replacement of religious ideas but rather the assimilation and reinterpretation of religious ideas, as constitutive elements in a world view founded on secular premises. Much of what distinguishes writers I call "Romantic" derives from the fact that they undertook, whatever their religious creed or lack of creed, to save traditional concepts, schemes, and values which had been based on the relation of the Creator to his creature and creation, but to reformulate them within the prevailing two-term system of subject and object, ego and non-ego, the human mind or consciousness and its transactions with nature. Despite their displacement from a supernatural to a natural frame of reference, however, the ancient problems, terminology, and ways of thinking about human nature and history survived, as the implicit distinctions and categories through which even radically secular writers saw themselves and their world, and as the presuppositions and forms of their thinking about the condition, the milieu, the essential values and aspirations, and the history and destiny of the individual and of mankind.

This book does not undertake to be an inclusive survey of thought and literature in the early nineteenth century. Even in the writers who are my primary concern, I deal largely with selected works written in the prime of their powers, while some major writers of the age are marginal to my focus. Keats, for example, figures mainly insofar as he represented in some of his poems a central Romantic subject: the growth and discipline of the poet's mind, conceived as a theodicy of the individual life (what Keats called "a system of Salvation") which begins and ends in our experience in this world. Byron I omit altogether; not because I think him a lesser poet than the others but because in his greatest work he speaks with an ironic counter-voice and deliberately opens a satirical perspective on the vatic stance of his Romantic contemporaries.

The book is organized as a sequence of movements out of and back to various passages in the programmatic statement, first written at the turn of the century, which Wordsworth put forward in his Preface to *The Excursion* as "a kind of *Prospectus* of the design and scope" of his intended masterpiece, *The Recluse,* and of the entire corpus of his lesser poems. My rationale is that Wordsworth (as his English contemporaries acknowledged, with whatever qualifications) was the great and exemplary poet of the age, and his Prospectus stands as the manifesto of a central Romantic enterprise against which we can conveniently measure the consonance and divergences in the writings of his contemporaries. In each section I also look before and after—back to the Bible, to Christian exegetic, devotional, and confessional literature, and to relevant aspects of both exoteric and esoteric philosophy, and ahead as far as some prominent writers in our own time. I do so in order to show that Romantic thought and literature represented a decisive turn in Western culture. The writers of that age, in reinterpreting their cultural inheritance, developed new modes of organizing experience, new ways of seeing the outer world, and a new set of relations of the individual to himself, to nature, to history, and to his fellow men. This fact has been obvious to most of the important writers from the mid-nineteenth century to the present time, and many of these writers have defined their own literary enterprise by either a positive or a negative reference to the forms and inherent ethos of the Romantic achievement. These topics and materials, I realize, are extremely diverse; at times, in the refractory work of putting them together, I have ruefully remembered Coleridge's comment as to why he took so long over his projected *Magnum Opus*—that it dealt *de omne scibile quibusdamque aliis.*

An early version of this book was delivered as the Addison L. Roache Lectures at the University of Indiana in April and May of 1963, and a revised version as the Alexander Lectures at the University of Toronto in May of the following year. I take this occasion to express my thanks for the many kindnesses extended to me at both these universities, and to pay tribute to the late Professor A. S. P. Woodhouse, whose scholarly concerns touched in many ways on the matter of this work and who was closely associated with the Alexander Lectures from their inauguration in 1929 until his retirement at the end of the term in which I had the honor to participate in this distinguished series. I have expanded the text for this book, to the extent that four lectures have burgeoned into eight chapters. The topics and general argument, however, remain those of the Alexander Lectures. The additions are mainly a more comprehensive treatment of the post-Kantian philosophers and cultural historians in Germany, and a large increase in the citations of illustrative passages. My justification for the latter procedure is the principle that in such matters authors, so far as feasible, should be allowed to speak for themselves; I take comfort in the thought that a reader, unlike a captive audience, has the liberty to linger or leap over, as his interests dictate.

While this work was evolving, I was aided by a Guggenheim Fellowship in the spring of 1960, by a research grant and term's leave of absence from Cornell University in 1965, and by a very pleasant year, 1967-8, at the Center for Advanced Study in the Behavioral Sciences at Stanford, California. At the Center I profited especially from conversations with Professors Morton Bloomfield, Donald MacRae, Gregory Vlastos, and Maurice Mandelbaum; the last, by a happy chance, turned out to be writing a book, related to my own subject, on the philosophy of history and of the social sciences in the nineteenth century. It was also my good fortune to have Professor Harold Bloom, once my student, for a colleague this year as a distinguished Fellow from Yale at the Cornell Society for the Humanities; he read through the manuscript, and the text has at numerous points been improved by his remarkable command of the Romantic and post-Romantic literary tradition. Several undergraduate and graduate research assistants, especially Ira Nadel and Arthur Gross, Jr., and Mrs. Berniece Roske and the secretarial staff of the Cornell Department of English, helped greatly in the onerous task of preparing the manuscript for publication. And my wife, as always, performed cheerful and yeomanly service, with no more than a stimulating modicum of complaint that this book, so long in the making, got in the way of other scholarly and domestic plans.

In the third book of *The Prelude,* describing his residence at Cambridge, Wordsworth projected his vision of an ideal university —as A. C. Bradley remarked, instead of working at his studies, he imagined a university in which he would have worked. Suppose one were now to imagine an ideal place for writing a work on Romantic literature. He might envision a study in a commodious old university building surrounded by the studies of scholars, generous of their learning, whose provinces include both ancient and modern literatures and philosophy; a minute's stroll distant there would be a major research library with a notable collection in the age of Wordsworth, reached by a path commanding a Wordsworthian prospect of hill, wood, lake, and sky. This was in fact my situation in 171 Goldwin Smith Hall, where this book was planned, worked out in lectures and discussions, and largely written. My debt to some of my colleagues and former students I have occasion to acknowledge in the notes; let me express here my obligation to all the others.

M. H. ABRAMS

Cornell University
January 1, 1969

ONE

"This Is Our High Argument"

Das Bekannte überhaupt ist darum, weil es bekannt ist, nicht erkannt.

> —G. W. F. Hegel,
> Preface, *Phenomenology of the Spirit*

A picture held us captive, and we could not get outside it, for it lay in our language and language seemed to repeat it to us inexorably. . . .

We are not contributing curiosities, but observations which no one has doubted, but which have escaped remark only because they are always before our eyes.

> —Ludwig Wittgenstein,
> *Philosophical Investigations*

ONE

On Man, on Nature, and on Human Life,
Musing in solitude . . .

Wɪᴛʜ these words Wordsworth announced the gen-
esis of *The Recluse,* the work to which he planned "to devote
the Prime of my life and the chief force of my mind" [1] and on
which he staked his claim to be ranked with the greatest poets.
This project was perhaps the most remarkable, and certainly
one of the most grandiose, ever undertaken by a major writer.
As Wordsworth described his plan in 1814, *The Prelude,* itself
an autobiography of epic dimension, was to serve merely as
"preparatory poem" to a trilogy in which each part, to judge
by *The Excursion* (which may itself be incomplete), was intended to be a good deal longer than the standard epic.[2] In
spite of persistent and anguished effort Wordsworth accomplished, in addition to *The Prelude,* only Book I of Part I
(*Home at Grasmere*), Part II (*The Excursion*), and none of
Part III; so that, as Helen Darbishire has remarked, all we
have of *The Recluse* is "a Prelude to the main theme and an
Excursion from it." These writings were finished by 1814.
From then almost until his death in 1850 Wordsworth suffered
from the proddings of his well-meaning family and friends, as
well as from his own sense that he had fallen short in a mission
for which, he claimed, he had been granted the vision of a
seer.[3]

In his Preface to *The Excursion* Wordsworth declined "formally to announce a system" for *The Recluse,* declaring that
from the completed poem "the Reader will have no difficulty
in extracting the system for himself." As an interim statement,
however, he appended a verse passage of 107 lines to serve "as
a kind of *Prospectus* of the design and scope of the whole

Poem." This passage is our indispensable guide to understanding the design informing Wordsworth's poetry—including not only the completed parts of *The Recluse* but *The Prelude* and the shorter poems of the great period between 1798 and 1814 as well.

The first existing version of Wordsworth's poetic statement was probably written at some time between 1800 and 1806.[4] This manuscript was expanded to serve as the announcement, at the end of *Home at Grasmere*, of the "theme" of the new poetry Wordsworth felt it was his special mission to sing. A decade or so later, in the Preface to *The Excursion* (1814), Wordsworth still chose to reprint this radical statement of his poetic intentions, with only slight adjustment to more orthodox views, as a "Prospectus" to the whole of *The Recluse*. In that Preface he also likened the design implicit in all his writings to the structural plan of "a gothic church," in which the "preparatory poem" we now call *The Prelude* is "the ante-chapel," the tripartite *Recluse* is "the body," and all his "minor Pieces," when "properly arranged," are equivalent to "little cells, oratories, and sepulchral recesses, ordinarily included in those edifices." [5] In the following year, moreover, he invited the readers of his *Poems* of 1815 to regard the separate pieces "under a two-fold view; as composing an entire work within themselves, and as adjuncts to the philosophical Poem, 'The Recluse.' " [6] Wordsworth could not have been more precise or insistent: he envisaged all his poems as one immense work, a poem made up of poems, written in accordance with a single comprehensive design.

Of this grand structural scheme Wordsworth's Prospectus is his one explicit and detailed exposition.[7] It asks, then, for our closest attention. The Prospectus is an instance of the visionary style in which, according to a view until recently current, Wordsworth is held to indulge his penchant for resounding sublimities by hiding logical evasions behind vague phrasing and lax syntax. But let us assume that in a crucial passage so long meditated, so often rewritten, and so emphatically stated, Wordsworth knew what he was saying and meant what he said, and let us examine it to see what Wordsworth claimed to be doing as a poet. His claim turns out to be an astonishing one, but that should not faze us. A. C. Bradley long ago laid down an essential rule for understanding Wordsworth: "The road into Wordsworth's mind must be through his strangeness and his paradoxes, and not round them." [8]

1. WORDSWORTH'S PROGRAM
FOR POETRY

In the verse preceding the Prospectus in its original place at the end of *Home at Grasmere*, Wordsworth announces his discovery that he has been chosen to be a poet-prophet for his age. He has been granted "an internal brightness" that is "shared by none" and that compels him, "divinely taught," to speak "Of what in man is human or divine."

> I would impart it, I would spread it wide,
> Immortal in the world which is to come.

He must bid farewell to his earlier scheme of playing a warrior's role in the world of action, as well as to his long-standing plan to write a traditional epic—"the hope to fill/ The heroic trumpet with the Muse's breath." Nevertheless in this remote and peaceful Vale of Grasmere "A Voice shall speak, and what will be the Theme?" [9] The answer to this question is the passage he later called the *"Prospectus* of the design and scope" of his work as a poet.

The first verse-paragraph of this passage ends: "I sing:—'fit audience let me find though few!'" Wordsworth adds, "So prayed, more gaining than he asked, the Bard—/ In holiest mood." [10] That Bard, of course, is Milton. Almost every sentence of the Prospectus rings with echoes of Milton's voice in *Paradise Lost*, beginning with the phrase at the opening, "Musing in solitude," which recalls Milton's assertion that he sings with unchanged voice, though "with dangers compast round,/ And solitude"; this passage Milton used to introduce Raphael's account of the creation of the world, and as in Wordsworth, it closely precedes his prayer that he "fit audience find, though few." [11] The unparalleled density of the Miltonic reminiscences suggests what the explicit argument of the

Prospectus confirms, that Wordsworth is setting out to emulate his revered predecessor—and rival—by writing the equivalent for his own age of the great Protestant English epic.

In the manuscript version of a passage in *The Prelude,* Wordsworth explained his feeling at Cambridge that "I was not for that hour/ Nor for that place" by the fact that it was his destiny to be "a chosen Son,"

> A youthful Druid taught in shady groves
> Primeval mysteries, a Bard elect. . . .[12]

That is, in the line of inspired British poets (what Harold Bloom has called "the Visionary Company"), he has been elected as the successor to Milton. Wordsworth remarked to Henry Crabb Robinson that "when he resolved to be a poet, [he] feared competition only with Chaucer, Spenser, Shakespeare, and Milton."[13] Of these poets, however, Chaucer and Shakespeare exemplify what Wordsworth called "the human and dramatic Imagination"; while it is Spenser, and above all Milton, who exemplify the "enthusiastic and meditative Imagination" against which Wordsworth persistently measured his own enterprise.[14] Early in 1801, in a mood between exasperation and laughter, Charles Lamb described a monitory letter from Wordsworth,

> with a deal of stuff about a certain Union of Tenderness and Imagination, which in the sense he used Imagination was not the characteristic of Shakspeare, but which Milton possessed in a degree far exceeding other Poets: which Union, as the highest species of Poetry, and chiefly deserving that name, "He [Wordsworth] was most proud to aspire to."[15]

Wordsworth's belief that he had inherited the poetic mode and office of Milton was an enduring one. Thirteen years later he described *The Recluse* as a poem "which, if I live to finish it, I hope future times will 'not willingly let die.' These you know are the words of my great Predecessor, and the depth of my feelings upon some subjects seems to justify me in the act of applying them to myself."[16]

The greater part of Wordsworth's echoes originate in the invocations with which Milton opens the first, third, seventh, and ninth books of *Paradise Lost,* and it is evident that the Prospectus has the same function as these great passages, in which Milton specifies his subject and his theme, measures it against the traditional epic subjects, alludes to his personal circumstances, and justifies his fitness for the immense endeavor by invoking and claiming divine inspiration. Wordsworth announces that he is "intent to weigh/ The good and evil of our mortal state" (lines 8–9). As Milton indicates in his opening synopsis, he had set out to weigh the good against the evil—in his theological terms, to "justify the ways of God to men"—by specifying the implications of the Biblical revelation of the first to the last things, including (by direct narrative, retrospect, and prediction) the creation of "the Heav'ns and Earth . . . out of Chaos," the fall of man "With loss of Eden," the coming of "one greater Man" to "restore us, and regain the blissful Seat," and the culmination of the providential plan in the apocalyptic end of the old world, which "shall burn, and from her ashes spring/ New Heav'n and Earth" wherein the just shall "see golden days" (III, 334–7). In the Prospectus Wordsworth patently sketches out his emended version of Milton's argument. He undertakes, that is, to represent what he calls (line 69) a "creation"; and if he does not explicitly set forth his version of a fall and a loss of Eden (though Coleridge later claimed that this had been his intention),[17] he at least proposes a resurrection from the "sleep/ Of death" and the way to the instauration of an earthly paradise —transferred, however, from a supernatural to a natural frame of reference, for this paradise will be "A simple produce of the common day," and is described by words "Which speak of nothing more than what we are."

Wordsworth preempts Urania, the pagan muse whom Milton, following earlier Christian precedent, had baptized and equated with the "heav'nly Muse" who had inspired Moses and the Biblical prophets and had associated with the Holy Spirit who moved upon the face of the waters at the beginning of all created things. Wordsworth calls upon the "prophetic Spirit," the "primal source/ Of all illumination," to descend upon him. As Milton's Spirit prefers "before all Temples th' upright heart and pure," so Wordsworth's Spirit, which inspires "The human Soul of universal earth," possesses also "A metropolitan temple in the hearts/ Of mighty Poets." Milton had grandly proclaimed that his "advent'rous Song" will soar

> Above th' *Aonian* Mount while it pursues
> Things unattempted yet in Prose or Rhyme

—that is, in its Christian subject his song will exceed in originality, boldness, and sublimity the Greek and Roman epics of arms and the man, "hitherto the only Argument/ Heroic deem'd." [18] Wordsworth calmly requisitions a greater muse than Milton's, for he must undertake a poetic enterprise which is more novel, more adventurous, and of even greater dimension. In his epic flight Milton had claimed, with the help of the Muse, only to have ventured "down/ The dark descent" to the *"Stygian* Pool" and *"Chaos* and *Eternal Night,"* and then, "Up led by thee," to have ascended "Into the Heav'n of Heav'ns . . . and drawn Empyreal Air" (III, 13–21; VII, 12–14). The cosmos of Wordsworth's poem, however, is of larger extension, and requires an imaginative journey that must descend deeper and rise higher than Milton's flight:

> Urania, I shall need
> Thy guidance, or a greater Muse, if such
> Descend to earth or dwell in highest heaven!
> For I must tread on shadowy ground, must sink
> Deep—and, aloft ascending, breathe in worlds
> To which the heaven of heavens is but a veil.
> All strength—all terror, single or in bands,
> That ever was put forth in personal form—
> Jehovah—with his thunder, and the choir
> Of shouting Angels, and the empyreal thrones—
> I pass them unalarmed. Not Chaos, not
> The darkest pit of lowest Erebus,

—in an earlier manuscript Wordsworth had written, "The darkest pit/ Of the profoundest hell"—

> Nor aught of blinder vacancy, scooped out
> By help of dreams—can breed such fear and awe
> As fall upon us often when we look . . .

Higher than the eternal heaven beyond the visible heavens,[19] more awesome than Jehovah with his thunder and shouting angels, deeper and more terrifying than the realms of chaos and hell; what is to be the prodigious setting of this poem?

> . . . when we look
> Into our Minds, into the Mind of Man—
> My haunt, and the main region of my song.

William Blake, who respected Wordsworth enough to read him closely and take his claims seriously, told Henry Crabb Robinson, in whimsical exasperation, that this passage "caused him a bowel complaint which nearly killed him." "Does Mr. Wordsworth think his mind can surpass Jehovah?" [20] To which the answer is, "No, he did not," any more than he thought himself a greater poet than Milton. What Wordsworth claims is that the mind of man is a terra incognita which surpasses in its terrors and sublimities, hence in the challenge it poses to its poetic explorer, the traditional subject matter of Milton's Christian epic. Blake took offense at Wordsworth's literary enterprise because it paralleled his own, but deviated on the crucial issue of naturalism. For in his *Milton* (1804–10) Blake too had undertaken, as the epigraph said, "To Justify the Ways of God to Men" by his own imaginative revision of the doctrines of *Paradise Lost;* but what Wordsworth in the Prospectus calls "this goodly universe" is to Blake the illusory result of the fall of man. After politely hearing out Robinson's loyal defense of that poet, Blake, with his engaging mixture of candor and generosity, finally set Wordsworth down "as a Pagan, but still with great praise as the greatest poet of the age." [21]

According to the Prospectus, then, the heights and depths of the mind of man are to replace heaven and hell, and the powers of the mind are to replace the divine protagonists, in Wordsworth's triple (or, counting *The Prelude,* quadruple) successor to Milton's religious epic. Following his model, Wordsworth at once goes on to identify the supreme power of that mind, whose function is to restore to us "the blissful Seat" of the lost paradise.

In the course of his flight from hell to earth Satan had discerned the newly created stars which, upon nearer view,

> seem'd other Worlds,
> Or other Worlds they seem'd, or happy Isles,
> Like those *Hesperian* Gardens fam'd of old,
> Fortunate Fields, and Groves and flow'ry Vales,
> Thrice happy Isles. . . .   (III, 566–70)

Again when Satan, perched on the Tree of Life, achieved his first prospect of paradise and the Garden of Eden, Milton pillaged the pagan legends of the golden age, the Elysian Islands, the Gardens of the Hesperides, and other fabulous pleasances, in order to adumbrate the supernal beauty and blessedness of the true paradise, *"Hesperian* Fables true,/ If true, here only . . ."* (IV, 250–1).[22] And when this residence shall be restored to man by one greater Man, its location may be either on earth or in heaven, no matter which, for then, Milton says, the earth "shall all be Paradise" (XII, 463–5). Wordsworth makes it clear that his concern is limited to the green earth, but that to his visionary gaze this present reality exceeds in beauty all the imaginative constructions of poets who have portrayed a golden age. The point is especially explicit in his earliest manuscript version:

> Beauty, whose living home is the green earth
> Surpassing far what hath by special craft
> Of delicate Poets, been call'd forth, & shap'd
> From earth's materials, waits upon my steps
> Pitches her tents before me as I move
> My hourly neighbour.

He goes on to say, repeating Milton's very phrases, that the pagan Elysium and Islands of the Blest need not be limited to the realm of fantasy, nor need the Christian paradise be a paradise lost:

> Paradise, and groves
> Elysian, Fortunate Fields—like those of old

Sought in the Atlantic Main—why should they be
A history only of departed things,
Or a mere fiction of what never was? [23]

For such realms are available on this earth, to each of us, as an ordinary possibility of every day. We need only to unite our minds to the outer universe in a holy marriage, a passionate love-match, and paradise is ours.

For the discerning intellect * of Man,
When wedded to this goodly universe
In love and holy passion, shall find these
A simple produce of the common day.

That Wordsworth commits himself deliberately to this figure of a culminating and procreative marriage between mind and nature he makes unmistakable by expanding upon it with pomp and circumstance. "I, long before the blissful hour arrives,/ Would chant, in lonely peace, the spousal verse/ Of this great consummation. . . ." The plot envisioned by the aid of the "prophetic Spirit," then, will end in the marriage of the protagonists, and Wordsworth's song is to be the "spousal verse," or sustained prothalamion, of its anticipated "consummation." This song will be an evangel to effect a spiritual resurrection among mankind—it will "arouse the sensual from their sleep/ Of death" [24]—merely by showing what lies within any man's power to accomplish, as he is here and now. For the poet will proclaim how exquisitely an individual mind—and perhaps the developing mind of generic man as well—is fitted to the external world, and the external world to the mind,[25] and how the two in union are able to beget a new world:

And the creation (by no lower name
Can it be called) which they with blended might
Accomplish:—this is our high argument.

That is, this is *our* high argument, as distinguished from the one Milton had defined in his opening announcement:

* In the MS, "mind."

> That to the highth of this great Argument
> I may assert Eternal Providence,
> And justify the ways of God to men.

Here, in short, is Wordsworth's conception of his poetic role and his great design. The author, though a "transitory Being," is the latest in the line of poets inspired by the "prophetic Spirit," and as such has been granted a "Vision" (lines 97–8) which sanctions his claim to outdo Milton's Christian story in the scope and audacious novelty of his subject. The vision is that of the awesome depths and height of the human mind, and of the power of that mind as in itself adequate, by consummating a holy marriage with the external universe, to create out of the world of all of us, in a quotidian and recurrent miracle, a new world which is the equivalent of paradise.

In a passage in the third book of *The Prelude* Wordsworth, looking back from maturity upon his youthful experience, is able to recognize the early signs of his election into the society of poet-prophets, as well as early evidences of the divinely creative interaction between his mind and the visible universe which was to be his destined theme:

> I was a chosen son.
> For hither I had come with holy powers
> And faculties, whether to work or feel:
> To apprehend all passions and all moods
> Which time, and place, and season do impress
> Upon the visible universe, and work
> Like changes there by force of my own mind. . . .
> I had a world about me; 'twas my own,
> I made it; for it only liv'd to me,
> And to the God who look'd into my mind. . . .
> Some call'd it madness: such, indeed, it was . . .
> If prophesy be madness; if things view'd
> By Poets of old time, and higher up
> By the first men, earth's first inhabitants,
> May in these tutor'd days no more be seen
> With undisorder'd sight.
>   . . . Of Genius, Power,
> Creation and Divinity itself

I have been speaking, for my theme has been
What pass'd within me. . . .
This is, in truth, heroic argument,
And genuine prowess; which I wish'd to touch
With hand however weak; but in the main
It lies far hidden from the reach of words.[26]

It is noteworthy that in the line, "This is, in truth, heroic argument," Wordsworth echoes, in order to supersede, Milton's claim in the introduction to Book IX of *Paradise Lost* that his was "argument/ Not less but more Heroic than the wrath/ Of stern Achilles." And in this instance it is unmistakable that what Wordsworth vaunts is the height of his given argument, not the adequacy of his powers to accomplish a task which may require more than even poetry can manage.

An extraordinary theme, surely, for a more-than-heroic poem! Yet the more we attend to the central claims of some of Wordsworth's major contemporaries, in Germany as well as in England, the less idiosyncratic do Wordsworth's pronouncements seem. For a number of these writers also put themselves forward as members of the small company of poet-prophets and bards; they measured their enterprise against the earlier revelation of present, past, and future things, either as presented in the Bible itself or as represented by Milton or other Biblical poets; and they undertook, either in epic or some other major genre—in drama, in prose romance, or in the visionary "greater Ode"—radically to recast, into terms appropriate to the historical and intellectual circumstances of their own age, the Christian pattern of the fall, the redemption, and the emergence of a new earth which will constitute a restored paradise. Take even Wordsworth's startling figure for this last event, the renovative marriage between mind and nature whose annunciation will arouse "the sensual from their sleep/ Of death." In his *Dejection: An Ode* Coleridge wrote that the inner condition of total vitality he called "Joy,"

is the spirit and the power,
Which, wedding Nature to us, gives in dower
A new Earth and new Heaven,
Undreamt of by the sensual and the proud.[27]

Blake prefaced the concluding chapter of *Jerusalem* with the voice of the Bard arousing Albion from his "sleep of death," so that he may unite with his separated female emanation:

> England! awake! awake! awake!
>   Jerusalem thy Sister calls!
> Why wilt thou sleep the sleep of death?
>   And close her from thy ancient walls. . . .
>
> And now the time returns again:
>   Our souls exult & London's towers,
> Receive the Lamb of God to dwell
>   In Englands green & pleasant bowers.

The poem closes with the dawn of "the Eternal Day" of a universal resurrection in a restored paradise, illuminated by an etching of Albion and Jerusalem in an embrace of love.[28] At the conclusion of Shelley's *Prometheus Unbound* the regeneration of man in a renovated world has for its central symbol the union of Prometheus and Asia, an act in which all the cosmos sympathetically participates.

Comparable are two German works which were written in the latter 1790s, almost contemporaneously with the earliest version of Wordsworth's Prospectus. In a climactic passage of Hölderlin's *Hyperion* the young poet-hero, inspired, cries out to "holy Nature":

> Let all be changed from its Foundations! Let the new world spring from the root of humanity! . . . They will come, Nature, thy men. A rejuvenated people will make thee young again, too, and thou wilt be as its bride. . . . There will be only one beauty; and man and Nature will unite in one all-embracing divinity.[29]

Novalis' unfinished romance, *Heinrich von Ofterdingen,* incorporates a *Märchen* which epitomizes the theme of the whole. At the end of this complex allegory it is announced that "the old times are returning," in which the Gardens of the Hesperides "will bloom again and the golden fruit send forth its fragrance," and that "out of suffering the new world is born" in which there will be no more woe. The event symbolizing this consummation is the nuptial embrace of the king and queen, which becomes epidemic:

> In the meantime the throne had imperceptibly changed into a magnificent bridal bed. . . . The king embraced his blushing beloved, and the people followed the example of the king and caressed one another.[30]

In one of his Fragments Novalis also stated flatly that all "the higher philosophy is concerned with the marriage of Nature and Mind." [31] The philosopher Schelling looks forward to just such a union between intellect and nature, as well as to the poet-seer adequate to sing this great consummation in an epic poem:

> Now, after long wanderings [philosophy] has regained the memory of nature and of nature's former unity with knowledge. . . . Then there will no longer be any difference between the world of thought and the world of reality. There will be one world, and the peace of the golden age will make itself known for the first time in the harmonious union of all sciences. . . .
>
> Perhaps he will yet come who is to sing the great heroic poem, comprehending in spirit what was, what is, what will be, the kind of poem attributed to the seers of yore.[32]

It begins to be apparent that Wordsworth's holy marriage, far from being unique, was a prominent period-metaphor which served a number of major writers, English and German, as the central figure in a similar complex of ideas concerning the history and destiny of man and the role of the visionary poet as both herald and inaugurator of a new and supremely better world.

This book is organized as a commentary—at times a freely discursive commentary—on these and other matters set forth in Wordsworth's Prospectus to his poetry. I shall range over the more prominent antecedents of these concepts in intellectual and literary history, the political and social circumstances in Wordsworth's age which help to account for their emergence, and their relevance to the subject matter and form of a number of Wordsworth's poems. Since Wordsworth is not only a highly

innovative but also a very representative poet, I shall emphasize the striking analogues to Wordsworth's program and practice in the writings of some major contemporaries—metaphysicians and philosophers of history as well as poets and novelists—in Germany as well as in England. This procedure will
bring out important elements of both continuity and change
between characteristic Romantic ways of thinking, imagining,
and valuing, and the theological, philosophical, and literary
traditions of which Romantic writers were legatees. I intend
also to look before as well as after, in order to indicate the
extent to which works that we think of as distinctively modern
continue to embody Romantic innovations in ideas and design,
although often within a drastically altered perspective on man
and nature and human life.

2. THE DESIGN OF BIBLICAL HISTORY

"The grand store-house of enthusiastic and meditative Imagination," Wordsworth tells us—that kind of imagination which
he trusted he had himself demonstrated "in these unfavorable
times"—"is the prophetic and lyrical parts of the holy Scriptures, and the works of Milton." [33] Behind Wordsworth's program for poetry was *Paradise Lost,* and behind *Paradise Lost*
were the Holy Scriptures. We pay inadequate heed to the
extent and persistence with which the writings of Wordsworth
and his English contemporaries reflect not only the language
and rhythms but also the design, the imagery, and many of the
central moral values of the Bible, as well as of Milton, the great
poet of Biblical history and prophecy. Blake identified the
Hebrew Prophet with the British Bard, and in *Milton* he
whimsically figured that poet as entering into his left foot, in
order to project the entirely serious notion that he was carrying
out, by his imaginative endeavor, Milton's unfinished task of
redeeming the English people.[34] In his own person, Blake
"warmly declared" to Henry Crabb Robinson that "all he
knew was in the Bible," and his long poems tell one story and
one story only, according to his own interpretation, and in

various episodes and renderings: "The Old & New Testaments," he wrote, "are the Great Code of Art." [35]

The German writers of the time were steeped in Biblical literature and exegesis. Theology had been Schiller's favorite study in his early youth, and he developed some of his leading ideas in the form of a commentary on the Pentateuch. Fichte, Schelling, and Hegel (like the poet Hölderlin) had all been university students of theology, and explicitly undertook to translate religious doctrine into their conceptual philosophy. And for Novalis, as for Blake, the Bible was the great code of art.

We need to keep in mind that Wordsworth had been given religious training at Hawkeshead, which was a Church of England foundation under a clerical headmaster, and had been early destined to take holy orders. Coleridge, who aspired to be the Milton of his age before resigning that task to Wordsworth, was (in his own phrase) a "tolerable Hebraist," an inveterate philosopher-theologian, and a lay preacher who came within a hair of accepting appointment to a Unitarian pulpit. Keats was much less directly and persistently Biblical than any of his great fellow-poets; but he had studied carefully Wordsworth's Prospectus as well as his poems, and with his usual acumen, he recognized that Wordsworth had set himself to go beyond Milton's enterprise by humanizing Milton's "hintings at good and evil in the Paradise Lost" and by freeing them from Milton's "remaining Dogmas and superstitions." Keats envisaged his own destiny as a poet to be the exacting one of going beyond Milton, and Wordsworth as well, in order to develop "a system of Salvation which does not affront our reason and humanity." [36] Shelley, although an agnostic and vigorous anti-Jahwist, idolized "the sacred Milton"; Thomas Medwin tells us that "so far above all other Poems indeed did he class the *Paradise Lost,* that he even thinks it a sacrilege to name it in speaking of any other Poem. . . ." [37] We also know from Mary Shelley that "the Bible was his constant study"; [38] the list of books he gave to Medwin as adequate to make a good library consisted only of Milton and fourteen other titles, including, as he said, "last, yet first, the Bible." [39]

Last, yet first, the Bible. Let us begin, then, at the beginning and look to the Bible for the light it can throw on the argument and imagery in Wordsworth's Prospectus and in the many other writings of the period which reflect and transpose, in their various ways, the design, concepts, and images of Biblical history and prophecy.

The canonical books of the Old and New Testament, from Genesis to Apocalypse, constitute an account of the world and man from the literal beginning to the literal end. This account has assimilated elements from various environing cultures, but in its totality, and in accordance with the way that the earlier events are successively recalled and interpreted in the later books, it embodies a pattern of history which is profoundly distinctive. In classical antiquity, for example, philosophies of history fall chiefly into two categories. (I use "philosophy of history" in the elementary sense of the term, as a view of the overall distribution of value, especially of human well-being and happiness, through time.) One of these, the primitivist view, which was confined mainly to myth and poetry, held that the best time was at the beginning, or in the very distant past, and that there has been an overall decline ever since. The second view, which was widespread in the sophisticated thinking of philosophers, historians, and political theorists, as well as poets, was the theory of cycles: the overall course of events is from bad to better to best to worse to worst to better, and so on, time without end. Some proponents of this theory held a view of eternal recurrence, maintaining that the kinds of things that have happened before will happen again, as time brings the world back to the corresponding phase in the cycle of human values, or even that each individual being will recur and each particular event will in due course be reenacted. According to the version of individual recurrence proposed by Chrysippus, for example, every historical cycle will end in an *ekpyrosis*, or total conflagration, followed by a renewal, and

> again there will exist Socrates and Plato and every man, with the same friends and fellow citizens, and he will suffer the same fate and will meet with the same experiences and undertake the same deeds. . . . And there will be a complete restoration of the whole . . . and the same things will be restored without end.[40]

The paradigm of history implicit in the Biblical canon, which was made explicit by early Christian commentators, exhibits radical differences from these classical forms—differences which were fateful for post-classical thought and culture, and for the course of history itself. As against Greco-Roman views, the Christian pattern of history has these distinctive attributes: it is finite; it has a clearly defined plot; it is providential; it is right-angled; and it is symmetrical.

1) Biblical history is finite. It represents events as occurring once and once for all, in a single closed temporal span. Hence the early and repeated Christian assaults against the chief competing doctrine of the *circuitus temporum,* in which there is supposed to be "a constant renewal and repetition of the order of nature" and "cycles will ceaselessly recur." "Far be it . . . from us to believe this," St. Augustine cried. "For once Christ died for our sins; and, rising from the dead, He dieth no more. . . . And we ourselves after the resurrection shall be 'ever with the Lord.' " [41]

2) The design of Biblical history constitutes a sharply defined plot with a beginning, a middle, and an end, and a strongly accented sequence of critical events. These events are summarized in the opening lines of Milton's *Paradise Lost,* which invoke the Heavenly Muse, who had taught Moses how "In the Beginning . . . the Heav'ns and Earth/ Rose out of *Chaos,*" to sing "Of Man's First Disobedience . . . With loss of *Eden,*" and then of the coming of "one greater Man" and how he will one day "Restore us, and regain the blissful Seat." The degree to which all of history was viewed as a drama turning on a very few key agents and actions is indicated by the striking tendency of Christian exegetes to read the myriad intervening events as either echoes or prophecies of the nodal episodes—that is, as reflections of man's first disobedience; as either prefigurations or later reminiscences of the Incarnation and Passion; or as prefigurations of the ultimate redemption. There soon developed various schemes for periodizing history, dividing the procession of events into three, or four, or six ages; but these were for the most part attempts to order the fortunes and vicissitudes of nations and institutions in the temporal course of the fallen world—vicissitudes which shrink into in-

significance when put into comparison with the radical change in the fortunes of all mankind which had occurred at the fall or at the Incarnation, or which was to occur at the second Advent.

3) The plot of history has a hidden author who is also its director and the guarantor of things to come. God planned it all before it began, and He controls its details, under the seemingly casual or causal relations of events, by His invisible Providence. The inherent distinction in the Biblical account between the apparent order and connections of things, available to human inspection, and the prepotent but hidden order of Providence, soon emerged in theology as the distinction between secondary causes and the first cause, which is the invisible and immutable working of the purpose of God. As Thomas Burnet summarized the traditional distinction, the "ordinary Course of Nature" is "a Disposition or Establishment of second Causes" which "produce the most regular Effects, assisted only with the ordinary Concourse of the first Cause," which is God's "Providence." [42] From its early stages Christian thought thus manifested a strong and persistent tendency—to which the assimilation of Platonic dualism gave added impetus —toward a dual or multiple interpretation of persons, objects, and events as both manifest and covert, literal and figurative. Whether in Scriptures, history, the natural sciences, or just ordinary observation, everything tended to be looked upon as endowed with a divine duplicity, functioning both as surface and as symbol.

4) While the main line of change in the prominent classical patterns of history, whether primitivist or cyclical, is continuous and gradual, the line of change in Christian history (and this difference is pregnant with consequences) is right-angled: the key events are abrupt, cataclysmic, and make a drastic, even an absolute, difference. Suddenly, out of nothing, the world is created by divine fiat. There is a precipitous fall from a deathless felicity into a mortal life of corruption and anguish in a stricken world. The birth of the Redeemer, at a precise instant in time, is the crisis, the absolute turning point in the plot which divides the reign of law and promise from the reign of grace and fulfillment and assures the happy outcome. The

visible dénouement of the plot, however, awaits Christ's second Advent,[43] which will bring an immediate restoration of lost happiness on earth. His reign will be followed, at the unknown but appointed moment, by the abrupt termination of this world and of time and their replacement, for all who shall be deemed worthy in the Last Judgment, by a heavenly kingdom in eternity.

5) The Biblical scheme is symmetrical. It begins with the creation of the heaven and the earth and ends with the creation of "a new heaven and a new earth"; the history of man begins with his felicity in an earthly paradise and ends with his felicity in an equivalent paradise,[44] first on earth, then in a heavenly city which will reproduce the conditions of Eden, including the "river of water of life," the "tree of life," and man's original innocence, for "there shall be no more curse" (Revelation 22:1–3). The pattern of Christian history, as Karl Löwith puts it, thus constitutes "one great detour to reach in the end the beginning." [45] And in this pattern it is the terminal and not the initial felicity that really matters, for the finish is also the goal, the *telos,* of the entire providential plan. Hence, as Paul and other early propagandists pointed out, the immense advantage of the Christian scheme as against competing schemes: paganism is hopeless, but Christianity gives man hope; hope is not only an obligation but also a reward of Christian faith. Despite its emphasis on a lost paradise in the distant past, and however thoroughgoing the contempt for life in this world among some of its apologists, the persistent pressure of the Christian view of history is not retrospective but strongly prospective; for always, the best is yet to be.

3. THE SHAPE OF THINGS TO COME: THE APOCALYPTIC MARRIAGE

Over the centuries Biblical prophecies of the last act of the drama of history have powerfully and insistently shaped the intellection and imagination of Western man. The most detailed, terrifying, and compelling of all the descriptions of the last days, the Book of Revelation, has attracted commentary by numerous nonprofessionals, including, in more recent times, such assorted exegetes as Isaac Newton, Joseph Priestley, D. H. Lawrence, and Paul Claudel.[46] Lawrence tells us that, as a nonconformist child, by the time he was ten "I am sure I had heard, and read, that book ten times over"; he adds that "down among the uneducated people you will still find Revelation rampant," and expresses the plausible judgment that "it has had, and perhaps still has more influence, actually, than the Gospels or the great Epistles." [47] "The imagery and themes of the Apocalypse," Michael Fixler has remarked, so "permeated the depths of [Milton's] imagination" that he derived as many literary images from the Book of Revelation as from the three Synoptic Gospels together.[48] A similar claim can be made for Spenser, and the preoccupation with Apocalypse in these two poets had important consequences for their Romantic successors in the prophetic tradition. Even in the English Neoclassic Age the apocalyptic end of the world remained a favorite subject for set-pieces in prose and verse. Following the examples of Milton's descriptive passages in *Paradise Lost* and of Thomas Burnet's elaborate and eloquent elaboration upon the events of Revelation in his *Sacred Theory of the Earth,* the last days were graphically rendered—to name only some of the better-known instances—by Dryden in the conclusion of *Anne Killigrew,* John Pomfret in his Pindaric odes *On the General Conflagration* and *Dies Novissima,* Pope in *The Messiah,* James Thomson in the conclusion of *The Seasons,* James Hervey in his *Meditations among the Tombs,* Edward Young in his ode *The Last Day* and in the ninth book of *Night Thoughts,* and William Cowper in the sixth book of *The Task.*

In its late and developed form an apocalypse (Greek *apokalypsis,* "revelation") is a prophetic vision, set forth in arcane and elaborate symbols, of the imminent events which will bring an abrupt end to the present world order and replace it by a new and perfected condition of man and his milieu. The root elements of the form occur in the evolving concern, among Old Testament prophets, with eschatology, "the latter end of the days"; in the related preoccupation with "the day of Jahweh" and the convulsions and disasters to be visited upon the enemies of Israel, and upon Israel itself, "in that day"; and in the emergence of the expectation of a Messianic deliverer.[49] These elements are all to be found collected under the name of the prophet Isaiah, with a particular stress, after the visitation of God's wrath upon Israel, on the advent of a new world of ease, plenty, unalloyed rejoicing, and universal peace.

> For, behold, I create new heavens and a new earth: and the former shall not be remembered, nor come into mind. . . .
> And I will rejoice in Jerusalem, and joy in my people: and the voice of weeping shall be no more heard in her, nor the voice of crying. . . .
> The wolf and the lamb shall feed together, and the lion shall eat straw like the bullock.
>
> (65:17–25; also Chapters 2, 9, 11, 24–27)

Eschatological prophecies and expectations abounded in the century and a half that preceded and that followed the birth of Christ. Apocalyptic passages were incorporated into the Synoptic Gospels and the Epistles of Paul, and the two greatest of the fully developed apocalypses of that period (a number of others survive as apocrypha) were adopted into the Biblical canon—the Book of Daniel into the Old Testament, and the Book of Revelation into the New. These works embody the visions of a desperately oppressed minority with a proud record of election who, despairing of history and the possibility of effecting a recovery by their own efforts, seek (in the words of Rufus Jones) "the fierce comfort of an apocalyptic relief expedition from the sky." [50] The dreams in Daniel include a vision of the four beasts (signifying four successive kingdoms) in which the fourth beast, "dreadful and terrible, and strong exceedingly . . . devoured and brake in pieces, and stamped the residue with the feet of it"; and when "the thrones were cast down" there appeared "the Ancient of days" on a fiery throne; then "one like the Son of man came with the clouds of heaven," and was brought before the Ancient of days.

> And there was given him dominion, and glory, and a kingdom, that all people, nations, and languages, should serve him: his dominion is an everlasting dominion, which shall not pass away, and his kingdom that which shall not be destroyed.
>
> (7:1–14)

A later revelation in Daniel adds the prophecy of a resurrection, when "many of them that sleep in the dust of the earth shall awake, some to everlasting life, and some to shame and everlasting contempt" (12:2).

The author of the Book of Revelation took up the concepts, phrases, and imagery of Isaiah, Daniel, and other Jewish prophecies and eschatologies, adapted them to Christian Messianism, and developed them into the intricately ordered symbolism of the most awesome and influential of all apocalyptic visions. In the course of his vision ("I John saw these things and heard them") a series of parallel but progressive symbolic events— the opening of seven seals, the sounding of seven trumpets, the pouring out of seven vials—signalize natural catastrophes and plagues, as well as the conflict between the forces of Christ and of Anti-Christ. In the course of this prodigious violence stars fall like ripe figs, the heavens are rolled up like a scroll, and the harvest of the earth is reaped and cast "into the great winepress of the wrath of God . . . and blood came out of the winepress, even unto the horse bridles, by the space of a thousand and six hundred furlongs" (6:13–14; 14:14–20; *cf.* Isaiah 34:4; 63:1–4). But the fierce destruction is a cleansing one, preparatory to the chaining up of the Dragon and the establishment of the Kingdom of Christ and his resurrected Saints. In Isaiah and Daniel the restoration of felicity under the dominion of God was to take place in this world and to endure everlastingly. In the Book of Revelation the prediction of God's kingdom on earth is retained, but with the qualification that it is to be temporary, lasting only one thousand years, "the Millennium." [51] After that period the Dragon will be loosed again and defeated finally. Then will occur the universal resurrection and the Last Judgment, after which the old heaven and earth, their function in the divine plot accomplished, will pass away, to be replaced by a new heaven and earth and by a new and eternal Jerusalem which will reconstitute, for those who merit it, the conditions of the lost Eden. "And God shall wipe away all tears from their eyes: and there shall be no more death, neither sorrow nor crying, neither shall there be any more pain: for the former things are passed away" (21:4). And all these things, the prophet emphasizes, are immediately imminent. "And, behold, I come quickly." "Surely I come quickly." (22:12, 20).

Because they recur persistently in later writings, whether theological or secular, which derive from Biblical Apocalypse, I want to stress two key images in the Book of Revelation which mark the consummation of the historical plot. The first of these is, "And I saw a new heaven and a new earth: for the first heaven and the first earth were passed away; and there was no more sea." "And he that sat upon the throne said, Behold, I make all things new" (21:1, 5). These were precisely the terms in which Isaiah had earlier described the coming peaceable kingdom in this world. "For behold," the Lord had said to him, "I create new heavens and a new earth"; and again, "the new heavens and the new earth, which I will make, shall remain before me" (65:17; 66:22). The concept, and often the phrasing, are recurrent in both Biblical and extra-Biblical eschatology.[52] In 2 Peter 3:10–13 we find it joined to the notion, widely adopted thereafter, that this world will end in fire.

> But the day of the Lord will come as a thief in the night; in which the heavens shall pass away with a great noise, and the elements shall melt away with fervent heat, the earth also and the works that are therein shall be burned up. . . .
> Nevertheless we, according to his promise, look for new heavens and a new earth, wherein dwelleth righteousness.

The term "apocalypse" has come into increasing vogue in recent literary criticism, where it is often applied loosely to signify any sudden and visionary revelation, or any event of violent and large-scale destruction—or even anything which is very drastic. I shall restrict "apocalypse" to the sense used in Biblical commentary, where it signifies a vision in which the old world is replaced by a new and better world. It should be noted that, even when applied to Biblical visions of the events of the last days, the term is equivocal and can signify the expectation of either an earthly or a heavenly paradise. For the book called the Apocalypse includes the episode of the millennial reign of God on earth; so that the term "apocalyptic" sometimes signifies a coming state of felicity on this earth after it shall have been renewed (which is the final state of things in Isaiah and Daniel, but only a passing state in Revelation), and sometimes signifies a transcendental new earth, or else a city in heaven and eternity (in Revelation, "the holy Jerusalem, descending out of heaven from God," 21:10), which will be the residence of the redeemed after this earth has been obliterated. To compound the ambiguity, the promise of the ultimate new earth in the Apocalypse itself was interpreted by some commentators to signify not a transcendent location in the eternity of heaven, but merely a purged and renovated form of the earth we now inhabit. Milton dismissed these alternatives as insoluble and of minor importance. When "this world's dissolution shall be ripe," Christ will come with glory and power "to reward/ His faithful and receive them into bliss"; it does not matter in what location,

> Whether in Heav'n or Earth, for then the Earth
> Shall all be Paradise. . . .[53]

In the Apocalypse the approach of the last things is heralded by "as it were the voice of a great multitude," announcing that "the marriage of the Lamb is come, and his wife hath made herself ready" (19:6–7). This is the second distinctive image for the last things; the coming of the new heaven and new earth is signalized by the marriage between Christ and the heavenly city, his bride. "And I John saw the holy city, new Jerusalem, coming down from God out of heaven, prepared as a bride adorned for her husband"; there follows a detailed description of the shining glories of "the bride, the Lamb's wife . . . that great city, the holy Jerusalem, descending out of heaven from God" (21:2, 9–10). The longing of mankind for apocalypse is appropriately expressed as an urgent invitation to the wedding: "And the Spirit and the bride say, Come. And let him that heareth say, Come. And let him that is athirst come" (22:17); while those who are destined for the new heaven and earth are represented as guests who have been invited to the wedding feast: "And he saith unto me, Write, Blessed are they which are called unto the marriage supper of the Lamb" (19:9).

This insistent and haunting image of the consummation of

all things as the celebration of a sacred marriage had its roots in the ancient Old Testament concept of marriage as a form of covenant, and the consequent representation of the Lord's particular covenant with Israel by the metaphor of a marriage between the people and the Lord (Proverbs 2:17; Malachi 2:4–14). By easy metaphoric inference, the violation of this marriage covenant by Israel was figured as her sexual infidelity, adultery, or whoredom with idols and strange gods, of which the condign penalty for the bride is to be divorced from God and sent into exile; although with the promise of a future reunion between the repentant and purified nation (or by metonymy, the purified land, or the renovated city of Jerusalem) and the divine Bridegroom. Striking elaborations of this great Biblical trope are to be found in Ezekiel 16, in Hosea 2–6, and in Jeremiah 3:

> For all the causes whereby backsliding Israel committed adultery I had put her away, and given her a bill of divorce. . . . And it came to pass through the lightness of her whoredom, that she defiled the land, and committed adultery with stones and with stocks. . . . Turn, O backsliding children, saith the Lord; for I am married unto you . . . and I will bring you to Zion.

The most memorable passages depicting the reunion of God with his redeemed bride, after he shall have wreaked his wrath on the day of Jahweh, occur in Isaiah. "How is the faithful city become an harlot!" (1:21). "Thus saith the Lord, Where is the bill of your mother's divorcement, whom I have put away?" (50:1). But "Awake, awake; put on thy strength, O Zion; put on thy beautiful garments, O Jerusalem, the holy city. . . . For the Lord hath comforted his people, he hath redeemed Jerusalem" (52:1, 9). "For thy Maker is thine husband . . . and thy Redeemer the Holy One of Israel" (54:5). Of many passages the most profoundly influential was that in which Isaiah figured forth the final redemption as a holy marriage between Zion (renamed Hephzibah, "my delight is in her") together with its land (renamed Beulah, "a married one") and the people of Israel, under the auspices of God, who in this context is represented not as the bridegroom, but as one who rejoices like a bridegroom over his bride:

> Thou shalt no more be termed Forsaken; neither shall thy
> land any more be termed Desolate: but thou shalt be called
> Hephzibah, and thy land Beulah: for the Lord delighteth in
> thee, and thy land shall be married.
>
> For as a young man marrieth a virgin, so shall thy sons
> marry thee: and as the bridegroom rejoiceth over the bride, so
> shall thy God rejoice over thee.   (62:2–5)

Some recent commentators explain the pervasive Biblical
imagery of marriage and whoredom as an assimilation of the
myths, associated with ritual marriage and the rite of sacred
prostitution, which celebrated the death and resurrection of
vegetational deities in the agricultural societies of the ancient
Middle East.[54] Whether or not this is a tenable hypothesis, it
is not in the least necessary to explain the Biblical figure, for
the long evolution of the figure, from its rudimentary form in
the early books of the Old Testament through the prophets to
the Book of Revelation, is coherent, full, and explicable without reference to anything outside the Biblical texts themselves.
After many centuries of such evolution the author of Revelation—following the traditional procedure of both Old and
New Testament authors to collocate, merge, elaborate, reinterpret, and play metaphoric variations upon passages from
earlier texts—concentrated the concept of idolatry as whoredom in the person of the false bride, "the great whore," "Babylon the Great, the Mother of Harlots and abominations of the
earth"; focused on one of the many existing specifications of
the true bride as a new, or purified, Jerusalem; [55] transferred
the role of the bridegroom from Jehovah to Christ, the Lamb;
and represented the culminating union of the Lamb and the
New Jerusalem as fulfilling the prediction in Isaiah and other
prophets of a final redemption in the figured form of a divine
marriage.

In the Gospels, as well as in the Book of Revelation, the
image of the bridegroom and of marriage is repeatedly applied
to Christ, at both His first and second Advent. "And Jesus said
unto them, Can the children of the bridechamber mourn, as
long as the bridegroom is with them? But the days will come,
when the bridegroom shall be taken from them, and then shall

they fast." And during the time when the five foolish virgins had
gone out to buy the oil they had neglected to provide, "the
bridegroom came; and they that were ready went in with him
to the marriage: and the door was shut. . . . Watch therefore;
for ye know neither the day nor the hour wherein the Son of
man cometh." [56] So thoroughly was the figure of Christ the
Bridegroom interinvolved with the concept of Christ the Redeemer, that commentators early inaugurated the tradition
that Christ's words on the cross (*"consummatum est"* in the
Vulgate, John 19:30) signified that Christ mounted the cross as
a bed on which to consummate the marriage with humanity
inaugurated at the Incarnation, in the supreme act of sacrifice
which both certified and prefigured His apocalyptic marriage
at the end of time. As it was vividly put, in a sermon attributed
to Augustine:

> Like a bridegroom Christ went forth from His chamber. He
> went out with a presage of His nuptials into the field of the
> world. . . . He came to the marriage bed of the cross, and
> there, in mounting it, He consummated his marriage. And
> when He perceived the sighs of the creature, He lovingly gave
> himself up to the torment in the place of His bride . . . and
> He joined the woman to Himself for ever.[57]

The deep-rooted Scriptural image of marital union representing God's reconciliation with His redeemed people and with
the land, the city of Jerusalem, and the holy temple helped to
justify the hotly disputed inclusion of the Song of Songs in
both the Jewish and Christian Biblical canon, by pointing the
way to interpret its songs of sexual passion and union as an
allegory signifying the love and marriage of the Lord to Israel,
or of *Christus* to *Ecclesia,* or any of a large number of alternative
relationships.[58] In some exegeses the union celebrated in the
Song of Songs is interpreted as prefiguring the marriage of the
Lamb at the end of time—a kind of prothalamion, to which the
Book of Revelation is the epithalamion. The canonizing of
Canticles, with its candid, detailed, and erotic physicalism,
opened up a rich stock of sensuous imagery on which later
writers could draw to embellish the austerely abstract marital

symbolism of the other books of the Bible. The result of these complex developments is the paradox that Christianity, which under the powerful influence of Pauline theology has been mainly ascetic in its doctrines and attitudes, has often employed sexual union as its central symbol for the crucial events of Biblical history, and for several of the churchly sacraments as well.[59]

Resort to the Song of Songs for detailed erotic imagery reached its height in the later Middle Ages, among commentators whose concern was less with theology than with private devotion. These pious explorers of the inner world transferred the locus of the marriage of the Lamb from the apocalyptic conclusion of history to the individual soul, which they held to be capable of achieving, even in this fallen life, the acme of experience, the mystic union with Christ the Bridegroom. This topic introduces a new and important dimension of the traditional renderings of the Biblical plot.

4. CHRISTIAN HISTORY AND CHRISTIAN PSYCHO-BIOGRAPHY

Christian thought readily extended the reference of Biblical eschatology from the last day of the human race to the last day of the redeemed individual, whose soul, at the time of his bodily death, is translated to heaven as the bride of the Lamb, or at least as a festive participant in the nuptials of the Lamb, while awaiting the larger company of those who shall be deemed worthy at the Last Judgment.[60] It is to this tradition that the mourning father in the fourteenth-century elegy *Pearl* owes his comfort in the dream-vision of his daughter among the redeemed virgins in the New Jerusalem, who are already spouses of the heavenly Bridegroom. Hence also the possibility of the soaring climax of Milton's *Lycidas,* in which the elegiac singer achieves the vision—described in words echoing the Book of Revelation—of the dead shepherd alive again, where he

hears the unexpressive nuptial Song,
In the blest Kingdoms meek of joy and love.

There entertain him all the Saints above,
In solemn troops and sweet Societies
That sing, and singing in their glory move,
And wipe the tears forever from his eyes.

A more important and dramatic phenomenon was the tendency, grounded in texts of the New Testament itself, to internalize apocalypse by transferring the theater of events from the outer earth and heaven to the spirit of the single believer, in which there enacts itself, metaphorically, the entire eschatological drama of the destruction of the old creation, the union with Christ, and the emergence of a new creation—not *in illud tempus* but here and now, in this life.

And when he was demanded of the Pharisees, when the kingdom of God should come, he answered them and said, The kingdom of God cometh not with observation:
Neither shall they say, Lo here! or lo there! for, behold, the kingdom of God is within you. (Luke 17:20–21)

The concluding phrase is now often translated, "the kingdom of God is among you"; but the words of Christ have in the past been widely interpreted to mean that the coming universal kingdom may achieve an immediate realization in the spirit of each believer. And in the Gospel of John a present and spiritual passage through death to a new life, achievable now and by each individual through an act of absolute faith, all but displaces reference to an historical apocalypse and a racial Last Judgment:

He that heareth my word, and believeth on him that sent me, hath everlasting life, and shall not come into condemnation; but is passed from death unto life.
Verily, verily, I say unto you, The hour is coming, and now is, when the dead shall hear the voice of the Son of God: and they that hear, shall live.[61]

The first man to give personal testimony as to what it is like to undergo the abrupt transition to this new life was St. Paul, who was struck blind on the road to Damascus that he might see a new world, and so became the endlessly influential exemplar of the central Christian experience of conversion. Paul's allusions to his experience are in metaphoric parallel with the historical prophecies of the annihilation of the old creation and its replacement by a new heaven and new earth. "Therefore if any man be in Christ, he is a new creature: old things are passed away; behold all things are become new" (2 Corinthians 5:17; see also Ephesians 4:21–25, Colossians 3:1–10). The individual reborn lives as though in a world re-created; and his new life is figured by Paul as a death to the old marriage covenant in the form of laws and a rebirth to spiritual marriage with the divine Bridegroom: "Wherefore, my brethren, ye also are become dead to the law by the body of Christ; that ye should be married to another, even to him who is raised from the dead, that we should bring forth fruit unto God." [62]

Some three and a half centuries later, in the account of his spiritual crisis in the eighth book of *The Confessions,* Augustine followed the established tradition of conversion reaching from St. Paul through Athanasius' recent *Life of St. Antony,*[63] and added an extensive analysis of his spiritual agonies, modeled both on the conflict in the Apocalypse between the forces of Christ and Anti-Christ and on the description of God's destructive violence during the *dies irae,* preparatory to bringing forth a new creation. The result is the emergence in Augustine, fully developed, of the distinctively Christian spiritual autobiography. Its moral psychology is very different from representative classical treatments of self-reliance, self-continuity, and the rational weighing of alternatives; [64] it is, however, entirely consonant with the crises, cataclysms, and right-angled changes of the Christian pattern of history. For the mental experience in *The Confessions* is one of chiaroscuro, discontinuity, and sudden reversals, of "two wills" locked in internecine conflict—Armageddon translated into psychomachia—and of a savage, persistent, and self-destructive suffering which culminates in the abrupt interposition of God to effect, at a specific point in time (Augustine's phrases are *punctum ipsum temporis, confestim, statim*), a new identity, described metaphorically as the end of the old creature and the beginning of the new: "dying unto death and living unto life." [65]

A striking index to the psycho-historical parallelism in Christian thinking is the early appearance and elaborate development of the distinction between the "letter" and the "spirit" of Biblical narrative, the same text being taken to signify, in its literal sense, an outer event of sacred history, and in one of its several "spiritual" or "allegorical" senses, an inner event which may occur within the soul of every man.[66] This poly-semantics of simultaneous reference to the outer history of mankind and the spiritual history of the individual—extended from the Scriptures to secular authors, and with a shift of the literal sense from providential history to fictional narrative—shaped the design and component details of many literary allegories in the Middle Ages and early Renaissance. I shall mention one late example because it is by a man whom Wordsworth put below only Milton as a poet of the "enthusiastic and meditative Imagination" with whom he sought and feared comparison,[67] and also because it incorporates a number of the events and images that I have been discussing. The poet is Spenser, and the work is one of Wordsworth's great favorites, Book I of *The Faerie Queene*.[68] The prototype for the plot and symbolic elements of this work is the Book of Revelation.[69] The Red Cross Knight escapes the wiles of the false bride, Duessa, the Whore of Babylon; is granted a vision of the New Jerusalem, "Where is for thee ordained a blessed end"; assaults and, after a long struggle, slays the "old Dragon," thereby lifting the long siege of the king and queen (Adam and Eve) and reopening access to the land called Eden; and at the end is ceremoniously betrothed to the true bride, Una, radiant with "heavenlie beautie." In one of its dimensions this "continued Allegory, or darke conceit" signifies the historical Advent of Christ, whose coming victory over the dragon and marriage to the bride will herald the restoration of Eden to all elected mankind; in another dimension, however, it signifies the quest, temptation, struggle, triumph, and redemptive marriage to the one true faith which is acted out within the spirit of each believing Christian.

The most detailed development of spiritual eschatology, however, is to be found not in the allegorists, but among the writers whom we know as Christian "mystics," who represented the soul's pilgrimage toward its private apocalypse both as an inner *imitatio* of the passion and resurrection of Christ and as an inner preenactment of the events of the latter days in the Book of Revelation—an enactment in which the culmination is figured as a holy marriage and is rendered, often, in sensuous imagery suggested by the Song of Songs. Authors of commentaries on the Canticles from Origen to Richard of St. Victor, followed by a long sequence of later contemplatives, charted the mystic way as a sustained and arduous spiritual journey and quest, which is beset by a powerful and wily enemy and is subject to violent shifts and sudden reversals. The goal of the inner journey is the death and renovation of the old self by means of a "spiritual marriage" of the soul as *sponsa Dei* to Christ as Bridegroom, in a *unio passionalis* which sometimes is set forth in metaphors of physical lovemaking, or even of violent sexual assault, that disconcert a modern reader by their candor and detail.[70]

As one product of a millennium and a half of these developments, here is a familiar devotional sonnet by John Donne:

> Batter my heart, three-personed God; for You
> As yet but knock, breathe, shine, and seek to mend;
> That I may rise and stand, o'erthrow me, and bend
> Your force to break, blow, burn, and make me new.
> I, like an usurpèd town, to another due,
> Labor to admit You, but O, to no end;
> Reason, Your viceroy in me, me should defend,
> But is captived, and proves weak or untrue.
> Yet dearly I love You, and would be lovèd fain,
> But am betrothed unto Your enemy.
> Divorce me, untie or break that knot again;
> Take me to You, imprison me, for I
> Except You enthrall me, never shall be free,
> Nor ever chaste, except You ravish me.

The insistent paradoxes and figurative shock tactics are characteristically Donne's, but behind the diversity of Donne's metaphors we can make out the root-images of the latter days as described in the Book of Revelation, translated to a personal and spiritual application. The violence of a wrathful but loving

God, the conflict with the forces of evil embodied in one adversary, the destruction of the created world in an immense *conflagratio* (a detail from 2 Peter 3:10) in order to make it new (Revelation 21:5, "Behold, I make all things new"), and the ultimate marriage with the Bridegroom, represented as a rape of the longingly reluctant soul [71]—all these elements, which had long since become commonplaces of Christian devotion, Donne compresses into fourteen virtuoso lines of serious wit.

The same tradition of historical and spiritual correspondences provided Milton the opportunity for a number of the serious conceits upon which he plays throughout *Paradise Lost.* Thus Satan brings with him into Eden "the hot Hell that always in him burns,/ Though in mid Heav'n" (IX, 467–8; *cf.* IV, 19–23). Conversely, as Michael tells the fallen but now penitent Adam, if he adds to his hard-won wisdom answerable deeds and the Christian virtues,

> then wilt thou not be loath
> To leave this Paradise, but shalt possess
> A paradise within thee, happier far—

a psychological state which, in degree of felicity, is precisely equivalent to the historical state of the outer world after apocalypse which Michael had just foretold:

> for then the Earth
> Shall all be Paradise, far happier place
> Than this of *Eden,* and far happier days.[72]
> (XII, 585–7; 463–5)

Such spiritual overreadings of the literal texts of Scripture are in the mainstream of Christian thought. Especially germane to our enquiry, however, is a mode of interpretation applied by left-wing, Inner Light Protestants which effected a radically heterodox reading of Biblical history and apocalyptic prophecy. The greatest representative of this hermeneutic tradition is Jacob Boehme; but I shall present by way of example an English writer, Gerrard Winstanley, leader of a radical splinter group during the Puritan Revolution, who developed a theory of Christian communism and in 1649–50 set up a short-lived community of "Diggers" in Surrey.[73]

Winstanley's pamphlets extend the correspondence between the spiritual history of the individual and the Biblical history of mankind back from the last to the first things, so as to establish a parallel between the innocence of Adam in Eden and that of each man at birth: "a childe that is new borne, or till he growes up to some few yeares . . . is innocent, harmelesse . . . And this is *Adam,* or mankinde in his Innocency." [74] Winstanley, moreover, drastically alters the age-old procedure of retaining the literal meaning of the Biblical text as the base for the spiritual overmeanings. Not only does he attach a spiritual sense to the key personages, places, events, actions, and doctrines represented in the Bible, but he systematically invalidates the literal sense. As a result, Biblical history is completely internalized and the entire text becomes no more than a sustained metaphoric vehicle for the powers, states, conflicts, and processes of individual minds in the course of their experience on earth. All doctrinal divinity, Winstanley asserts, is based on the interpretation of Scripture by those who "think they are wise and learned, and the only men sent of God to preach the Gospel," but it is in fact nothing other than "that great Dragon, that hath deceived all the world, for it draws men from knowing the Spirit, to own bare letters, words and histories for spirit." [75]

Here are representative passages from Winstanley, most of them cited from his central declaration of belief, *The New Law of Righteousnes,* which he wrote in 1648: "All that which you call history, and have doted upon it, and made it your idol, is all to be seen and felt within you." All its component elements, including Adam, Cain and Abel, Abraham, Moses, Israel, the Land of Canaan, Judas, the commanders of the Jews, the good and bad angels—all are "to be seen within you" (p. 215). And the heaven and hell of orthodox divinity are no more than externalized fantasies of a disturbed mind—"a Doctrine of a sickly and weak spirit, who hath lost his understanding . . . of the temper of his own Heart and Nature, and so runs into fancies, either of joy or sorrow"; "indeed it is not knowledg, but imagination" (pp. 567–8).

Whosoever worships God by hear-say, as others tels them, knowes not what God is from light within himselfe; or that thinks God is in the heavens above the skyes; and so prayes to that God which he imagines to be there and every where . . . this man worships his owne imagination, which is the Devill.   (p. 107)

Therefore you Preachers, do not tell the people any more, that a man called *Adam*, that disobeyed about 6000 years ago, was the man that filled every man with sin and filth, by eating an apple. . . . For assure yourselves, this *Adam* is within every man and woman; and it is the first power that appears to act and rule in every man.   (p. 176)

Jesus Christ at a distance from thee, will never save thee; but a Christ within is thy Saviour. (p. 113) [For the spirit] which is the light and life of Christ within the heart, discovers all darknesse, and delivers mankind from bondage; *And besides him there is no Saviour.*   (p. 214)

No less than its beginning and middle, the apocalyptic end of the Biblical text signifies a personal and inner experience, not a generic and outer event. "Now the second *Adam* Christ, hath taken the Kingdom my body, and rules in it; *He makes it a new heaven, and a new earth, wherein dwells Righteousnesse*" (pp. 173–4). "And this is to be made a new creature, in whom old corrupt lusts are passed away, and every power in him is a new power" (p. 176). When in the fullness of time this power shall triumph in the spirit of all individuals, then shall the prophecies of Revelation be fulfilled: "And when this universall power of Righteousnesse is spread in the earth," the world shall be *"a Land flowing with milke and honey,* plenty of all things, every one walking righteously in the Creation one to another . . . as it was in the beginning" (p. 181). "And that prophesie will not generally be fulfilled till this time. *Rev.* 12:9" (p. 184). "Wel: this wil be a great day of Judgment; the Righteous Judge wil sit upon the Throne in every man and woman" (p. 206). Consonantly, the restored paradise of the Apocalypse will not be a location outside this world to which we will be transferred after death; it will be this world itself, as experienced by our redeemed and glorified senses in our earthly existence. "And now in this new heaven and new earth, he himself who is the King of Righteousnesse doth dwel and rule . . . O ye hear-say Preachers, deceive not the people any longer, by telling them that this glory shal not be known and seen, til the body is laid in the dust. I tel you, this great mystery is begun to appear, and it must be seen by the material eyes of the flesh: And those five senses that is in man, shall partake of this glory" (p. 170; cf. p. 153).

Winstanley sounds uncommonly like William Blake, who claimed that a literal-minded "Priesthood" had caused men to forget that "All deities reside in the human breast," and for whom heaven, hell, and paradise were not outward places but states of mind. We recognize the similarity in passages such as this in *Jerusalem* 77, although Blake rehabilitates the term "Imagination" to signify not a sickly fantasy, but the faculty of vision and eternal truth:

> I know of no other Christianity and of no other Gospel than the liberty both of body & mind to exercise the Divine Arts of Imagination. . . . What is the Divine Spirit? is the Holy Ghost any other than an Intellectual Fountain? . . . What are the Treasures of Heaven which we are to lay up for ourselves, are they any other than Mental Studies and Performances? What are all the Gifts of the Gospel, are they not all Mental Gifts? . . . What is the Joy of Heaven but Improvement in the things of the Spirit? What are the Pains of Hell but Ignorance, Bodily Lust, Idleness & devastation of the things of the Spirit[?] . . . To labour in Knowledge is to Build up Jerusalem.

Winstanley's God who is externalized and worshiped "in the heavens above the skyes," and is therefore really "the Devill," is kin to Blake's Nobodaddy, the sky god whom he later incorporated into Urizen:

> Why art thou silent & invisible
> Father of Jealousy,
> Why dost thou hide thyself in clouds
> From every searching Eye?

And Winstanley's insistence that the apocalyptic new heaven and new earth will be the existing world as perceived by the

glorified "five senses that is in man" suggests Blake's conten-
tion that, while "the ancient tradition that the world will be
consumed in fire" is true, it is true in the sense that "this will
come to pass by an improvement of sensual enjoyment," for
"if the doors of perception were cleansed every thing would
appear to man as it is, infinite." [76]

This parallelism between Blake and Winstanley (we shall
find in a later chapter that it extends to Blake's central myth
of the fall as a splintering of the primal man) should not surprise us. When Blake had warmly declared that "all he knew
was in the Bible," he at once added, H. C. Robinson tells us,
that "he understands by the Bible the spiritual sense"; [77] and
Blake's "spiritual sense" was derived from the native English
tradition of radical Inner Light hermeneutics, which had already assimilated Behmenist and other esoteric doctrines, and
which continued to be propagated by one or another of the
extreme dissenting sects in the London of Blake's younger days.
But notice that Winstanley's drastic internalization of the
powers of divinity also approximates—not as explicit creed but
as a way of thinking—Wordsworth's announcements of his high
poetic theme:

>   Of Genius, Power,
>   Creation and Divinity itself
>   I have been speaking, for my theme has been
>   What pass'd within me. . . .
>   This is, in truth, heroic argument.
>   (*Prelude* III, 171–82)

And when we turn back to Wordsworth's Prospectus for his
poetry, we find that what at first seemed singular in his statement now has a familiar ring. The main region of his song is
"the Mind of Man," but in exploring that internal realm the
poet will pass, unalarmed, the externalized Deity—"all terror
. . . That ever was put forth in personal form"—who is the
wrathful and thundering Jehovah of the Apocalypse, enthroned
in the empyrean amidst his "choir of shouting angels." Our
ears are attuned now to the echoes in Wordsworth's passage of
the Book of Revelation:

> And immediately I was in the spirit and, behold, a throne
> was set in heaven, and one sat on the throne. . . . And round
> about the throne were four and twenty seats. . . . And out of
> the throne proceeded lightnings and thunderings and voices.
> . . . And I heard the voice of many angels round about the
> throne and the beasts and the elders: and the number of them
> was ten thousand times ten thousand, and thousands of thou-
> sands.[78]

Nor can an externalized hell or any "blinder vacancy scooped
out/ By help of dreams," Wordsworth says, match the fear and
awe we feel when we look into the depths of the human mind.
As the poet moves through the region of the mind, beauty (in a
Biblical phrase) "pitches her tents" hourly before him. All
points toward "the blissful hour" which is Wordsworth's version of the holy marriage at the end of time. This event, however, is transported from the indefinite future to the experiential present, and translated from external intervention to an
act of unaided vision, in which the Lamb and the New Jerusalem are replaced by man's mind as the bridegroom and nature
as the bride. But this "great consummation" will nevertheless
suffice to create the restored paradise predicted in the Apocalypse—although Wordsworth's syntax leaves it suspended
whether the original paradise was a true "history . . . of departed things/ Or a mere fiction of what never was." Furthermore, that re-creation of the world which an individual mind
can accomplish here and now, "the progressive powers . . ./
Of the whole species," will perhaps some day accomplish universally. In the meantime the poet's prophetic annunciation of
high human possibility will effect, in those who heed and believe him, the spiritual correlate of the resurrection at the last
day—a revival from the "sleep/ Of Death." "This," Wordsworth grandly proclaimed, "is our high argument."

5.   ALTERNATIVE WAYS TO
THE MILLENNIUM: PROGRESS
AND REVOLUTION

Not only did Gerrard Winstanley in 1648 foresee a future
when the general triumph of the Spirit in individual minds

would inaugurate a new earth; he also announced that the Puritan Revolution even then under way marked the beginning of that glorious time in England, and that this event, by world-wide contagion, would effect the universal millennium prophesied in Daniel and in Revelation. The new David, which is the "new Law of righteousnesse,"

> is now coming to raign, and the Isles and Nations of the earth shall all come in unto him; he will rest every where, for this blessing will fill all places: All parts of the Creation in whom the curse remains shall be shaken and moved.   (pp. 152–3)
> But now it is done, it is done, it is done, time shal be no more to thee. . . . O rejoyce, rejoyce, for the time that the Lord God omnipotent wil raign in al the earth is beginning.
> (pp. 207–9)

We shall find that in the early 1790s Wordsworth, together with Blake and a number of other contempararies, rejoiced in a similar assurance that the revolution of their epoch would issue in an earthly paradise, and also that the early millennial expectations of these writers influenced the themes of their later imaginative productions. To indicate the complex interrelations among these various matters I shall need to turn briefly from spiritual interpretations of the Apocalypse to some literal and historical interpretations of the events that it promised.

The pervasive and persisting expectation that history will end once and for all in a new heaven and new earth is unique to Judeo-Christian civilization,[79] and it has had a powerful and irremissive effect in forming secular as well as religious thinking. The explosive element in apocalyptic prophecy was the millennium. The anticipation of a heavenly kingdom, to be achieved only after the end of the creation, posed no threat to the established order of the world. But in its millennial (or in the Greek term, chiliastic) component, the Biblical text denounced the present state of the world as unrelievedly evil and promised God's early intervention to annihilate all existing states and institutions in order to set up His kingdom, not in heaven, but on earth; and this constituted a patent menace to the status quo. Over the centuries of delay in the arrival of what had at first been an imminently expected second Advent,[80] the Church itself moved from its situation as a small persecuted sect to the dominant position of power, and the capital of Christianity became that very Rome which had been the unholy and obscene Babylon of the Book of Revelation. Early in the fifth century St. Augustine in *The City of God,* following some earlier precedents, construed the Biblical promise of the millennium as an allegory which signified the invisible, spiritual Kingdom of God that had in fact been inaugurated by Christ's first Advent. Thereafter the figurative interpretation of the earthly kingdom became the established doctrine of the Church, and literal millennialism was looked upon as an aberration.

The concept, nevertheless, of a final state of literal felicity on this earth, equal to or (in a fairly common opinion) better than the lost paradise at the beginning, continued to be a subject for learned commentary and abstruse arithmetic computation; it also remained vigorously alive in popular thought and art, and broke out repeatedly into feverish expectations of the imminent return of Christ the King. And in the increasingly secular period since the Renaissance, no less than in earlier Christian eras, we have continued to live in an intellectual milieu which is oriented, in Tennyson's phrase, toward "one far-off divine event to which the whole creation moves"— an assumption so deep and pervasive, and often so transformed from its Biblical prototype, that it has been easy to overlook both its distinctiveness and its source. The pressure of this millennial orientation has helped to shape important elements of Western thought which lack close parallels in cultures that developed outside the Hebrew-Christian orbit.

One of these elements is the theory of general, continuing, and unlimited historical progress, in the moral as well as the intellectual and material realms. Historians such as J. B. Bury were wont to attribute the inauguration and rapid expansion of this idea after the Renaissance to the conspicuous advances in science, technology, and the practical arts, and to the optimism engendered by geographical discoveries, foreign colonization, and commercial and economic expansion.[81] Recently, however, revisionist historians of the idea of progress—among them Carl Becker, Ronald S. Crane, and latterly Ernest Tuveson in convincing detail—have emphasized the important fact that the concept of inevitable and all-comprehensive progress evolved within the existing frame of Christian prospectivism, in a culture long predisposed to expect an inevitable future of absolute moral and material well-being on earth.[82] It seems clear that the modern development of the idea of general progress had multiple causes, and that the great post-Renaissance advances in the sciences and the applied arts entered into a preexisting scheme of historical expectation, but at the same time altered that scheme drastically. For the first time men seemed to have developed ways to achieve the anticipated state of plenty and happiness gradually and peacefully instead of abruptly and catastrophically, and by human and material means, without the need for a sudden relief expedition from the sky.

In this context Francis Bacon's views on progress are especially relevant, because he was held in extraordinary esteem by Wordsworth, and by Coleridge and Shelley as well. (Wordsworth classified Bacon, with Milton and Shakespeare, as a man in whom was enshrined "as much of the divinity of intellect as the inhabitants of this planet can hope will ever take up its abode among them." [83]) Like the early Christian apologists, Bacon saw the cyclical theory as the specific enemy of his mission: "By far the greatest obstacle to the progress of science" is the despair engendered by the supposition "that in the revolution of time and of the ages of the world the sciences . . . at one season . . . grow and flourish, at another wither and decay, yet in such sort that when they have reached a certain point and condition they can advance no further." He undertakes, on the contrary, "to give hope"; in this task "the beginning is from God," as is its destined end—he reads the prophecy of Daniel "touching the last ages of the world: 'Many shall go to and fro, and knowledge shall be increased' " as signifying that the exploration of the globe "and advancement of the sciences, are destined by fate, that is, by Divine Providence, to meet in the same age." [84]

Bacon's scheme is that of the readily possible (or as he suggests in the passage I have quoted, the providentially necessary and inevitable) advance in man's mastery over nature and over the material conditions of his well-being by the application of experimental science. In this scheme, however, the basic *don-*

nées remain those of Biblical history, although in a special interpretation of its crucial episodes, past and future. The fall, Bacon says, had a double aspect, one moral and the other cognitive, for man "fell at the same time from his state of innocency and from his dominion over creation. Both of these losses however can even in this life be in some part repaired: the former by religion and faith, the latter by arts and science." [85] Man's cognitive fall was occasioned by the loss of "that pure and uncorrupted natural knowledge whereby Adam gave names to the creatures according to their propriety," and this loss represented a divorce and separation of mind from nature, or (in terms of the mental powers involved) of the empirical senses from reason. The aim of Bacon's *Great Instauration* is to investigate "whether that commerce between the mind of man and the nature of things . . . might by any means be restored to its perfect and original condition," through establishing "forever a true and lawful marriage between the empirical and the rational faculty, the unkind and ill-starred divorce and separation of which has thrown into confusion all the affairs of the human family." [86] Such a marriage will herald our entrance into the "kingdom of man," which is closely equivalent to our entrance into the moral Kingdom of God promised to us in the latter days; for it will be a return to the condition of the original Eden by way of man's resumption of the "purity and integrity" of the mind of a child: with "the understanding thoroughly freed and cleansed, the entrance into the kingdom of man, founded on the sciences," is "not much other than the entrance into the kingdom of heaven, whereinto none may enter except as a little child." [87] This purgation and reintegration of the mind is to be achieved by eliminating, or at least controlling, the "idols, or phantoms," either innate or acquired from false philosophy, which distort the relations between the mind and the world. In a climactic passage of *The Great Instauration* Bacon proclaims his work to be no other than a prothalamion which celebrates the coming marriage of the redeemed mind (that is, the mind which has recovered its original purity and integrity in perception) to the universe without:

The explanation of which things, and of the true relation between the nature of things and the nature of the mind, is as
the strewing and decoration of the bridal chamber of the mind
and the universe, the divine goodness assisting, out of which
marriage let us hope (and be this the prayer of the bridal song)
there may spring helps to man, and a line and race of inventions that may in some degree subdue and overcome the necessities and miseries of humanity.[88]

Unexpectedly, then, we find in Bacon's "bridal song" a close
formal equivalent to Wordsworth's "spousal verse" in the
Prospectus, which celebrates the wedding of man's mind "to
this goodly universe" and the "creation" of the paradisal world
to be accomplished by their "blended might." My intent is not
to claim that Wordsworth derived his concept and imagery
from Bacon's prose—these things lie in the public domain of
Western culture—but only to show how the persistent Biblical
association of the fall and infidelity of man with separation and
divorce, and of the redemption of man and his world with the
union of bridegroom and bride, fostered striking metaphoric
parallels in thinkers concerned with secular ways to the coming
kingdom of man, even if those ways are as diverse as Bacon's
purged scientific understanding and Wordsworth's liberated
poetic imagination. And whatever the relation between these
two writers, the Baconian parallel highlights the fact that in
the Prospectus Wordsworth tentatively commits himself to the
idea of the gradual progress of all mankind toward the great
consummation—

> my voice proclaims
> How exquisitely the individual Mind
> (And the progressive powers perhaps no less
> Of the whole species) to the external World
> Is fitted. . . .

In *The Great Instauration,* moreover, only a few pages after
announcing his "bridal song," Bacon goes on to describe the
valid relation of the investigative eye to nature (preparatory to
achieving a scientific apocalypse of nature) in words notably

similar to Wordsworth's statements of the need of the poet to keep his eye steadily on its object:

> And all depends on keeping the eye steadily fixed upon the facts of nature and so receiving their images simply as they are. For God forbid that we should give out a dream of our own imagination for a pattern of the world; rather may he graciously grant to us to write an apocalypse or true vision of the footsteps of the Creator imprinted on his creatures. . . . Wherefore if we labor in thy works with the sweat of our brows, thou wilt make us partakers of thy vision and thy sabbath.[89]

More relevant to our concerns, however, than the theory of rectilinear general progress is a way of historical thinking which is much more primitive, yet one which in recent times has been given an elaborate and sophisticated understructure of theoretical sanctions. This is the belief in an imminent revolution, of which the effect on the well-being of humanity will be sudden, absolute, and universal. The concept and conduct of local rebellion against an oppressive individual or group or nation have doubtless occurred at all times and in all places. But peculiarly Western, and relatively recent, are the doctrine and trial of a total revolution, which is conceived to possess many, or all, of these attributes: (1) the revolution will, by an inescapable and cleansing explosion of violence and destruction, reconstitute the existing political, social, and moral order absolutely, from its very foundations, and so (2) bring about abruptly, or in a remarkably short time, the shift from the present era of profound evil, suffering, and disorder to an era of peace, justice, and optimal conditions for general happiness; (3) it will be led by a militant élite, who will find ranged against them the forces dedicated to preserving the present evils, consolidated in a specific institution or class or race; (4) though it will originate in a particular and critical time and place, it will by irresistible contagion spread everywhere, to include all mankind; (5) its benefits will endure for a very long time, perhaps forever, because the transformation of the institutional circumstances and cultural ambience of man will heal the intellectual and spiritual malaise which has brought him to his present plight; and (6) it is inevitable, because it is guaranteed either by a transcendent or by an immanent something, not ourselves, which makes for the ineluctable triumph of total justice, community, and happiness on earth.

In its most recent and fateful forms this doctrine has usually claimed to base its predictions on valid reasoning from historical experience. But the course of history provides no valid grounds for large-scale certainty about the future; [90] or at any rate, if the history of unhappy man demonstrates anything at all, it demonstrates that we have no reason to expect radical perfection either in man's moral nature or in his political, economic, and social institutions. The doctrine of absolute revolution has not an empirical but, ultimately, a theological basis; its certainty is a faith in Providence—a Providence converted into its secular equivalent of an immanent teleology, or dialectical necessity, or the scientific laws compelling historical events; and its prototype is the deeply ingrained and pervasive expectation in the Western world, guaranteed by an infallible text, of an abrupt, cataclysmic, and all-inclusive change which, after an indispensable preliminary of fierce destructiveness, will result in the perfection of an earthly paradise for a redeemed mankind. Its roots, that is to say, are in the Biblical scheme of apocalyptic history.

The attempt to translate Scriptural prophecy into revolutionary action has been a recurrent phenomenon; especially, as Norman Cohn has shown in *The Pursuit of the Millennium*, in Protestant countries, at a time of rapid commercial or industrial development, and where there exists a large and oppressed class of workers.[91] The fifteenth and sixteenth centuries in northern Europe—the age of the Taborites, of Thomas Müntzer, and of John of Leyden, the "Messiah of the Last Days"—was a time of diverse movements to expedite the imminent divine kingdom by a struggle against the established powers of evil.[92] Another such period was that of the civil wars in seventeenth-century England, when we find fervent eschatological expectations among various radical sects in the parliamentary armies, especially the "Fifth Monarchy Men" (a name derived from the apocalypse of Daniel) who, as saints in the army of

Christ "the General," undertook to play their part in the violent preliminaries to founding His kingdom on earth.[93] Gerrard Winstanley, as we know, called on England to rejoice that "the time that the Lord God omnipotent will raign in al the earth is beginning"; and Oliver Cromwell himself expressed his persuasion that "I am one of those whose heart God hath drawne out to waite for some extraordinary dispensations, according to those promises that hee hath held forth of thinges to bee accomplished in the later time, and I cannott butt thinke that God is beginning of them." [94] The sense of an imminent earthly kingdom also inflamed the imagination of Milton, who confidently awaited the advent on England's green and pleasant land of "the Eternall and shortly-expected King" who shall "open the Clouds to judge the severall Kingdomes of the World . . . proclaiming thy universal and milde *Monarchy* through Heaven and Earth"; on that day "some one" (doubtless himself) will be heard chanting songs appropriate to this great consummation—"high *strains* in new and lofty *Measures* to sing and celebrate thy *divine Mercies,* and *marvelous Judgments* in this Land throughout all Ages." In *Animadversions* Milton reiterated his expectation in the traditional figure of the apocalyptic marriage:

> Thy Kingdome is now at hand, and thou standing at the dore. Come forth out of thy Royall Chambers, O Prince of all the Kings of the earth . . . for now the voice of thy Bride calls thee, and all creatures sigh to bee renew'd.[95]

To return to the era of our primary concern: the later eighteenth century was another age of apocalyptic expectation, when the glory and promise of the American Revolution and, much more, of the early years of the French Revolution, revived among a number of English Nonconformists the millenarian excitement of Milton and other seventeenth-century predecessors. And at the formative period of their lives, major Romantic poets—including Wordsworth, Blake, Southey, Coleridge, and later, after his own fashion, Shelley—shared this hope in the French Revolution as the portent of universal felicity, as did Hölderlin and other young radicals in Germany.

Though these writers soon lost confidence in a millennium brought about by means of violent revolution, they did not abandon the form of their earlier vision. In many important philosophers and poets, Romantic thinking and imagination remained apocalyptic thinking and imagination, though with varied changes in explicit content. This provenance is reflected in the ideas, design, and imagery of many characteristic writings of the age, including the work whose argument Wordsworth announced in his Prospectus as the possibility of an earthly paradise which would be a simple produce of the common day. The details of this widespread shift in the bases of hope from political revolution to the powers inherent in human consciousness will be a matter for later discussion.

6. NATURAL SUPERNATURALISM

I began with Wordsworth's *"Prospectus* of the design and scope" of his intended masterwork and went on, by way of Wordsworth's chief model, *Paradise Lost,* into what must seem an inordinate excursion on the design and imagery of Biblical history and on the diverse later interpretations of the crucial events between the first and last things. This background of Biblical text and exegesis, however, will prove of repeated relevance to our understanding of the Romantic achievement. For the fact is that many of the most distinctive and recurrent elements in both the thought and literature of the age had their origin in theological concepts, images, and plot patterns which were translated, in Wordsworth's terms, to men "as natural beings in the strength of nature," living in "the world/ Of all of us, the place in which, in the end,/ We find our happiness, or not at all" *(Prelude,* III, 194; X, 726 ff.). The phenomenon is conspicuous, and has not escaped the attention of critics and historians. If we nonetheless remain unaware of the full extent to which characteristic concepts and patterns of Romantic philosophy and literature are a displaced and reconstituted theology, or else a secularized form of devotional experience, that is because we still live in what is essentially, although in derivative rather than direct manifestations, a Biblical culture, and readily mistake our hereditary ways of organizing experience for the conditions of reality and the universal forms of thought. Pierre Proudhon, himself a militant advocate of "humanitarian Atheism," long ago recognized his helplessness to escape religious formulas which, since they are woven into the fabric of our language, control the articulation of our thinking:

> [I am] forced to proceed as a materialist, that is to say, by observation and experience, and to conclude in the language of a believer, because there exists no other; not knowing whether my formulas, theological despite myself, ought to be taken as literal or as figurative. . . . We are full of the Divinity, *Jovis omnia plena;* our monuments, our traditions, our laws, our ideas, our languages, and our sciences—all are infected with this indelible superstition, outside of which we are not able either to speak or act, and without which we simply do not think.[96]

The assimilation of Biblical and theological elements to secular or pagan frames of reference began with the establishment of Christianity, and it was immensely accelerated from the Renaissance through the eighteenth century. What is exceptional in the period beginning in the 1790s is the scope of this undertaking, and the deliberateness with which it was often carried on. A conspicuous Romantic tendency, after the rationalism and decorum of the Enlightenment, was a reversion to the stark drama and suprarational mysteries of the Christian story and doctrines and to the violent conflicts and abrupt reversals of the Christian inner life, turning on the extremes of destruction and creation, hell and heaven, exile and reunion, death and rebirth, dejection and joy, paradise lost and paradise regained. (Looking about the contemporary scene, Carlyle remarked sardonically that men cannot do for very long without the devil.) But since they lived, inescapably, after the Enlightenment, Romantic writers revived these ancient matters with a difference: they undertook to save the overview of human history and destiny, the experiential paradigms, and the cardinal values of their religious heritage, by reconstituting them in a way that would make them intellectually acceptable, as well as emotionally pertinent, for the time being.

This general enterprise is apparent in almost all the major metaphysicians and poets of the period, qualified to the extent that a particular writer was Christian, theist, agnostic, or atheist. The early philosophical writings of Schiller, Fichte, Schelling, and above all Hegel, set out, often quite explicitly, to retain what was valid in the myths, or what Hegel called the "picture-representation," of the Biblical account, by translating them into the concepts and scheme of speculative philosophy. William Blake's archetypal poet, Los, laboring at the construction of the imaginative city of Golgonooza, declared that he "must create a System" or be enslaved by the ready-made system of the current Christian creed, institutions, and morality (*Jerusalem* I. 10). Contemporary writers in Germany also announced the need for what Friedrich Schlegel called a "new mythology," to be formed "out of the uttermost depth of the spirit," which would serve as the unifying ground for all modern poetry; he looked to its imminent development out of a synthesis between the revolutionary inwardness of philosophical idealism and the revelations of contemporary physical science.[97] Friedrich Schelling agreed that at the present moment "each truly creative individual must invent a mythology for himself," and saw in contemporary *Naturphilosophie* the adumbration of a universal mythology that would harmonize Greek myth and the seemingly antithetic claims of Christianity.[98] Coleridge, who from the time of his maturity was a professing Christian, carried on a lifetime's struggle to save what seemed to him the irreducible minimum of the Christian creed within an essentially secular metaphysical system; while on his side Shelley, who declared that "the *Divina Commedia* and *Paradise Lost* have conferred upon modern mythology a systematic form," [99] set out to assimilate what seemed intellectually and morally valid in this mythology to his own agnostic and essentially skeptical world-view. John Keats, whose philosophical stance was that of humanistic naturalism, undertook to project his own "system of Salvation" [100] in the form of the modified classical myths of *Hyperion* and *The Fall of Hyperion*. "The Mythus of the Christian Religion," Carlyle's protagonist observed in *Sartor Resartus,* "looks not in the eighteenth century as it did in the eighth," and he announced as the great need of the age "to embody the divine

Spirit of that Religion in a new Mythus." Carlyle's statement of the early 1830s precisely defines a cardinal endeavor of the preceding generation; to its results we can apply another phrase from *Sartor Resartus*—"Natural Supernaturalism" [101]—for the general tendency was, in diverse degrees and ways, to naturalize the supernatural and to humanize the divine.

T. E. Hulme recognized this tendency and appraised it, in his blunt way, a half century ago: "Romanticism, then, and this is the best definition I can give of it, is spilt religion." [102] Hulme, who thought it an act of courage to take one's dogma straight, scorned the Romantic endeavor as a failure of nerve. But the historian of the period need not accept this evaluation, nor that of other orthodox commentators who look upon it not as a sign of weakness, but as a display of overweeningness. The Romantic enterprise was an attempt to sustain the inherited cultural order against what to many writers seemed the imminence of chaos; and the resolve to give up what one was convinced one had to give up of the dogmatic understructure of Christianity, yet to save what one could save of its experiential relevance and values, may surely be viewed by the disinterested historian as a display of integrity and of courage. Certainly the greatest Romantic writers, when young and boldly exploratory, earned the right to their views by a hard struggle. Wordsworth, announcing in *Home at Grasmere* his discovered mission "divinely taught . . . to speak as I have felt/ Of what in man is human or divine," insisted that "the undaunted quest" involved its high challenges and risks—

> of foes
> To wrestle with, and victory to complete,
> Bounds to be leapt, darkness to be explored.[103]

And in a manuscript of the Prospectus he described himself, the "transitory being that beheld/ This vision," as

> In part a Fellow-citizen, in part
> An outlaw, and a borderer of his age.

These lines indicate how audacious Wordsworth esteemed his undertaking to shift his haunt and the main region of his song from heaven, Jehovah, and hell to "the Mind of Man" in the act of finding what will suffice.

My last phrase deliberately echoes Wallace Stevens, as a reminder that the Romantic endeavor to salvage traditional experience and values by accommodating them to premises tenable to a later age has continued to be a prime concern of post-Romantic poets. Stevens expressly identified the aim "of modern poetry" as the attempt to convert the setting and agents and language of Scripture into

> The poem of the mind in the act of finding
> What will suffice. It has not always had
> To find: the scene was set; it repeated what
> Was in the script.
> > Then the theatre was changed
> To something else. Its past was a souvenir.
> It has to be living, to learn the speech of the place.[104]

Among modern poets none stays so close to some of Wordsworth's formulations as Stevens does, so that his departures from his predecessor stand out with special prominence. Wordsworth, we know, did not think of *The Recluse* as an epic but as a poem for which he renounced his earlier hope to blow "the heroic trumpet," [105] but in taking up Milton's role he often echoed Milton's heroic voice and the idiom of Biblical prophecy as well. Stevens deliberately rejected both the prophetic stance and the epic voice:

> To say more than human things with human voice,
> That cannot be; to say human things with more
> Than human voice, that, also, cannot be;
> To speak humanly from the height or from the depth
> Of human things, that is acutest speech.[106]

In place of the tradition Wordsworth had inherited from Milton, we find in Stevens qualities closer to the naturalism, the unillusioned resignation, and the Epicureanism of a more ancient cosmic poet, Lucretius. But within the altered frame and tone of Stevens' meditations there remains a notable continuity with Wordsworth. Shall she not find, he enquires about his protagonist in *Sunday Morning,*

In any balm or beauty of the earth,
Things to be cherished like the thought of heaven?
Divinity must live within herself. . . .
Shall our blood fail? Or shall it come to be
The blood of paradise? And shall the earth
Seem all of paradise that we shall know? . . .
There is not any haunt of prophecy,
Nor any old chimera of the grave,
Neither the golden underground, nor isle
Melodious, where spirits gat them home,
Nor visionary south, nor cloudy palm
Remote on heaven's hill, that has endured
As April's green endures; or will endure
Like her remembrance of awakened birds,
Or her desire for June and evening, tipped
By the consummation of the swallow's wings.

Stevens represents the musing in solitude of a modern woman as she savors the luxuries of her Sunday breakfast in a brilliant un-Wordsworthian setting of sun, rug, coffee and oranges, and a green cockatoo. In these subdued lines, however, we recognize something approximating the high argument of the Romantic poet who (while "Beauty—a living Presence of the earth" waited upon his steps) proclaimed the power of the mind of man to realize an equivalent of "Paradise, and groves/ Elysian, Fortunate Fields," by the "consummation" of a union with the common earth which will require of us "nothing more than what we are."

TWO

Wordsworth's "Prelude" and the Crisis-Autobiography

They are as a creation in my heart;
I look into past time as prophets look
Into futurity. . . .
                —Wordsworth, MS Fragment

Are the true Heroic Poems of these times to be written
with the *ink of Science?* Were a correct philosophic Biography of a Man (meaning by philosophic *all* that the name
can include) the only method of celebrating him? The true
History . . . the true Epic Poem?—I partly begin to sur-
mise so.

                Thomas Carlyle, *Two Notebooks*

What is left to say when one has come to the end of writing
about one's life? Some kind of development, I suppose,
should be expected to emerge, but I am very doubtful of
such things, for I cannot bring life into a neat pattern. If
there is a development in my life—and that seems an idle
supposition—then it has been brought about more by
things outside than by any conscious intention of my own.

                —Edwin Muir, *An Autobiography*

TWO

Having announced in the Prospectus to *The Recluse* his high argument, Wordsworth goes on to pray to the "prophetic Spirit" that

> if with this
> I mix more lowly matter; with the thing
> Contemplated, describe the Mind and Man
> Contemplating; and who, and what he was—
> The transitory Being that beheld
> This Vision; when and where, and how he lived;—
> Be not this labour useless.

In this way Wordsworth designated and justified the personal narrative which makes up the part of *The Recluse* he called *Home at Grasmere*, as well as the entire poem that his wife later named *The Prelude*. Wordsworth described the latter work as a "tributary" and also "as a sort of portico to the Recluse, part of the same building." [1] The time taken to compose *The Prelude* straddled the writing of the Prospectus, and the completed work was conceived as an integral part of the overall structure whose "design and scope" Wordsworth specified in that poetic manifesto. "The Poem on the growth of your own mind," as Coleridge recalled the plan in 1815, "was as the ground-plat and the Roots, out of which the Recluse was to have sprung up as the Tree"—two distinct works, but forming "one compleat Whole." [2] The role of *The Prelude*, as Wordsworth himself describes his grand design, is to recount the circumstances and mental growth of a "transitory Being," culminating in his achievement of a "Vision" and in the recognition that his mission is to impart the vision in the public and enduring form of an unprecedented kind of poem:

> Possessions have I that are solely mine,
> Something within which yet is shared by none . . .
> I would impart it, I would spread it wide,
> Immortal in the world which is to come.[3]

1. THE IDEA OF "THE PRELUDE"

In this era of constant and drastic experimentation with literary materials and forms, it is easy to overlook the radical novelty of *The Prelude* when it was completed in 1805. The poem amply justified Wordsworth's claim to have demonstrated original genius, which he defined as "the introduction of a new element into the intellectual universe" of which the "infallible sign is the widening the sphere of human sensibility." [4]

The Prelude is a fully developed poetic equivalent of two portentous innovations in prose fiction, of which the earliest examples had appeared in Germany only a decade or so before Wordsworth began writing his poem: the *Bildungsroman* (Wordsworth called *The Prelude* a poem on "the growth of my own mind" [5]) and the *Künstlerroman* (Wordsworth also spoke of it as "a poem on my own poetical education," and it far surpassed all German examples in the detail with which his "history," as he said, was specifically "of a *Poet's* mind").[6] The whole poem is written as a sustained address to Coleridge—"I speak bare truth/ As if alone to thee in private talk" (X, 372–3); Coleridge, however, is an auditor *in absentia,* and the solitary author often supplements this form with an interior monologue, or else carries on an extended colloquy with the landscape in which the interlocutors are "my mind" and "the speaking face of earth and heaven" (V, 11–12). The construction of *The Prelude* is radically achronological, starting not at the beginning, but at the end—during Wordsworth's walk to "the Vale that I had chosen" (I, 100), which telescopes the circumstances of two or more occasions but refers primarily to his walk to the Vale of Grasmere, that "hermitage" (I, 115) where he has taken up residence at that stage of his life with which the poem concludes.[7] During this walk an outer breeze, "the sweet breath of Heaven," evokes within the poet "a corresponding mild creative breeze," a prophetic *spiritus* or inspiration which assures him of his poetic mission and, though it is fitful, eventually leads to his undertaking *The Prelude* itself; in the course of the poem, at times of imaginative dryness, the revivifying wind recurs in the role of a poetic leitmotif.[8]

Wordsworth does not tell his life as a simple narrative in past time but as the present remembrance of things past, in which forms and sensations "throw back our life" (I, 660–1) and evoke the former self which coexists with the altered present self in a multiple awareness that Wordsworth calls "two consciousnesses." There is a wide "vacancy" between the I now and the I then,

> Which yet have such self-presence in my mind
> That, sometimes, when I think of them, I seem
> Two consciousnesses, conscious of myself
> And of some other Being.   (II, 27–33)

The poet is aware of the near impossibility of disengaging "the naked recollection of that time" from the intrusions of "after-meditation" (III, 644–8). In a fine and subtle figure for the interdiffusion of the two consciousnesses, he describes himself as one bending from a drifting boat on a still water, perplexed to distinguish actual objects at the bottom of the lake from surface reflections of the environing scene, from the tricks and refractions of the water currents, and from his own intrusive but inescapable image (that is, his present awareness).[9] Thus "incumbent o'er the surface of past time" the poet, seeking the elements of continuity between his two disparate selves, conducts a persistent exploration of the nature and significance of memory, of his power to sustain freshness of sensation and his "first creative sensibility" against the deadening effect of habit and analysis, and of manifestations of the enduring and the eternal within the realm of change and time.[10] Only intermittently does the narrative order coincide with the order of actual occurrence. Instead Wordsworth proceeds by sometimes bewildering ellipses, fusions, and as he says, "motions retrograde" in time (IX, 8).

Scholars have long been aware that it is perilous to rely on the factual validity of *The Prelude,* and in consequence Wordsworth has been charged with intellectual uncertainty, artistic ineptitude, bad memory, or even bad faith. The poem has suffered because we know so much about the process of its composition between 1798 and 1805—its evolution from a constituent part to a "tail-piece" to a "portico" of *The Recluse,* and Wordsworth's late decision to add to the beginning and end of the poem the excluded middle: his experiences in London and in France.[11] A work is to be judged, however, as a finished and free-standing product; and in *The Prelude* as it emerged after six years of working and reworking, the major alterations and dislocations of the events of Wordsworth's life are imposed deliberately, in order that the design inherent in that life, which has become apparent only to his mature awareness, may stand revealed as a principle which was invisibly operative from the beginning. A supervising idea, in other words, controls Wordsworth's account and shapes it into a structure in which the protagonist is put forward as one who has been elected to play a special role in a providential plot. As Wordsworth said in the opening passage, which represents him after he has reached maturity: in response to the quickening outer breeze

> to the open fields I told
> A prophecy: poetic numbers came
> Spontaneously, and cloth'd in priestly robe
> My spirit, thus singled out, as it might seem,
> For holy services.   (I, 59–63)

Hence in this history of a poet's mind the poet is indeed the "transitory Being," William Wordsworth, but he is also the exemplary poet-prophet who has been singled out, in a time "of hopes o'erthrown . . . of dereliction and dismay," to bring mankind tidings of comfort and joy; as Wordsworth put it in one version of the Prospectus,

> that my verse may live and be
> Even as a light hung up in heaven to chear
> Mankind in times to come.[12]

The spaciousness of his chosen form allows Wordsworth to introduce some of the clutter and contingency of ordinary experience. In accordance with his controlling idea, however, he selects for extended treatment only those of his actions and experiences which are significant for his evolution toward an inherent end,[13] and organizes his life around an event which he regards as the spiritual crisis not of himself only, but of his generation: that shattering of the fierce loyalties and inordinate hopes for mankind which the liberal English—and European—intellectuals had invested in the French Revolution.

> Not in my single self alone I found,
> But in the minds of all ingenuous Youth,
> Change and subversion from this hour.
>
> (X, 232–4)

The Prelude, correspondingly, is ordered in three stages. There is a process of mental development which, although at times suspended, remains a continuum; [14] this process is violently broken by a crisis of apathy and despair; but the mind then recovers an integrity which, despite admitted losses, is represented as a level higher than the initial unity, in that the mature mind possesses powers, together with an added range, depth, and sensitivity of awareness, which are the products of the critical experiences it has undergone. The discovery of this fact resolves a central problem which has been implicit throughout *The Prelude*—the problem of how to justify the human experience of pain and loss and suffering; he is now able to recognize that his life is "in the end/ All gratulant if rightly understood" (XIII, 384–5).

The narrative is punctuated with recurrent illuminations, or "spots of time," and is climaxed by two major revelations. The first of these is Wordsworth's discovery of precisely what he has been born to be and to do. At Cambridge he had reached a stage of life, "an eminence," in which he had felt that he was "a chosen Son" (III, 82 ff., 169), and on a walk home from a dance during a summer dawn he had experienced an illumination that he should be, "else sinning greatly,/ A dedicated Spirit" (IV, 343–4); but for what chosen, or to what dedicated, had not been specified. Now, however, the recovery from the crisis of despair after his commitment to the French Revolution comprises the insight that his destiny is not one of engagement with what is blazoned "with the pompous names/ Of power and action" in "the stir/ And tumult of the world," but one of withdrawal from the world of action so that he may meditate in solitude: his role in life requires not involvement, but detachment.[15] And that role is to be one of the "Poets, even as Prophets," each of whom is endowed with the power "to perceive/ Something unseen before," and so to write a new kind of poetry in a new poetic style. "Of these, said I, shall be my Song; of these . . ./ Will I record the praises": the ordinary world of lowly, suffering men and of commonplace or trivial things transformed into "a new world . . . fit/ To be transmitted," of dignity, love, and heroic grandeur (XII, 220–379). Wordsworth's crisis, then, involved what we now call a crisis of identity, which was resolved in the discovery of "my office upon earth" (X, 921). And since the specification of this office entails the definition, in the twelfth book, of the particular innovations in poetic subjects, style, and values toward which his life had been implicitly oriented, *The Prelude* is a poem which incorporates the discovery of its own *ars poetica*.

His second revelation he achieves on a mountain top. The occasion is the ascent of Mount Snowdon, which Wordsworth, in accordance with his controlling idea, excerpts from its chronological position in his life in 1791, before the crucial experience of France, and describes in the concluding book of *The Prelude*.[16] As he breaks through the cover of clouds the light of the moon "upon the turf/ Fell like a flash," and he sees the total scene as "the perfect image of a mighty Mind" in its free and continuously creative reciprocation with its milieu, "Willing to work and to be wrought upon" and so to "create/ A like existence" (XIII, 36–119). What has been revealed to Wordsworth in this symbolic landscape is the grand locus of *The Recluse* which he announced in the Prospectus, "The Mind of Man—/ My haunt, and the main region of my song," as well as the "high argument" of that poem, the union between the mind and the external world and the resulting "creation . . . which they with blended might/ Accomplish." The event which Wordsworth selects for the climactic revelation in *The Prelude,* then, is precisely the moment of the achievement of "this Vision" by "the transitory Being" whose life he had, in the Prospectus, undertaken to describe as an integral part of *The Recluse.*

In the course of *The Prelude* Wordsworth repeatedly drops the clue that his work has been designed to round back to its point of departure. "Not with these began/ Our Song, and not with these our Song must end," he had cried after the crisis of France, invoking the "breezes and soft airs" that had blown in the "glad preamble" to his poem (XI, 1 ff. and VII, 1 ff.). As he nears the end of the song, he says that his self-discovery constitutes a religious conclusion ("The rapture of the Hallelujah sent/ From all that breathes and is") which is at the same time, as he had planned from the outset, an artistic beginning:

> And now, O Friend; this history is brought
> To its appointed close: the discipline
> And consummation of the Poet's mind.
>   . . . we have reach'd
> The time (which was our object from the first)
> When we may, not presumptuously, I hope,
>   Suppose my powers so far confirmed, and such
> My knowledge, as to make me capable
> Of building up a work that should endure.
>   (XIII, 261–78)

That work, of course, is *The Recluse,* for which *The Prelude* was designed to serve as "portico . . . part of the same building." *The Prelude,* then, is an involuted poem which is about its own genesis—a prelude to itself. Its structural end is its own beginning; and its temporal beginning, as I have pointed out, is Wordsworth's entrance upon the stage of his life at which it ends. The conclusion goes on to specify the circular shape of the whole. Wordsworth there asks Coleridge to "Call back to mind/ The mood in which this Poem was begun." At that time,

> I rose
> As if on wings, and saw beneath me stretch'd
> Vast prospect of the world which I had been
> And was; and hence this Song, which like a lark
> I have protracted. . . .   (XIII, 370–81)

This song, describing the prospect of his life which had been made visible to him at the opening of *The Prelude,* is *The Prelude* whose composition he is even now concluding.[17]

2. PROUST'S GOTHIC CHURCH

Such features of Wordsworth's poem bring to mind the subject matter, aim, and structural experiments in the chief enterprise of some of our best modern writers. This is the "creative auto-biography"—the more-or-less fictional work of art about the development of the artist himself, which is preoccupied with memory, time, and the relations of what is passing to what is eternal; is punctuated by illuminated moments, or "epiph-anies"; turns on a crisis which involves the question of the meaning of the author's life and the purpose of his sufferings; is resolved by the author's discovery of his literary identity and vocation and the attendant need to give up worldly involve-ment for artistic detachment; and includes its own poetic, and sometimes the circumstances of its own genesis. Above all *The Prelude* points toward one of the most influential literary achievements of the present century, *A la recherche du temps perdu.*

Like Wordsworth's poem, Proust's great novel opens with a preamble at a time of his life when the narrator, falling asleep, has already experienced the events he is about to unfold. The narrative proper then begins with memories of the author's childhood at Combray, of which the central scene is Marcel waiting for his mother to come upstairs after the family had entertained M. Swann for dinner. It then makes a quick leap in time to a moment of illumination in the author's middle life—the tasting of the *madeleine* dipped in tea—from which unfolds the whole "vast structure of recollection." All of his past is rendered not by direct narration, but as the emergence of his past self and experiences within the context of his drastically altered present self and consciousness; and the narrator, moving bewilderingly back and forth through time, is persistently concerned with the nature of voluntary and involuntary memory, the importance of the seemingly trivial or banal perception, the attempt to establish a single identity from his multiplex consciousness, the "anaesthetic" quality of the intellect and of habit (so needful for life, but so deadly to freshness of perception and the truth of recollection), and above all, with time and the possibility of breaking free of time. The narrative is woven together by recurrent motifs and is lit by repeated illuminations; and it ends, after a profound mental and physical crisis, with the event to which all the huge work has been pointing—the event of its own beginning.

Irrecoverably ill, exhausted, despairing of the validity of his life and of art itself, the narrator attends the reception of the Princess de Guermantes. But "sometimes at the moment when everything seems lost the monition occurs which is capable of saving us." [18] In a sequence of illuminations, involving events from the past involuntarily called forth by present impressions, he experiences a "felicity," "a state of ecstasy," which is in effect a conversion to the religion of art. In his ultimate revelation the narrator learns the significance of his earlier partial illuminations, and is finally able to answer the questions raised but left unanswered by the initial illumination when he had tasted the *madeleine:* "This potent joy. . . . Whence did it come? What did it mean?" [19] In such a recovery of former experience he not only has the power to live and enjoy the essence of things "entirely outside of time," but also to create a new world, an eternal world of art, out of the "resurrection" of his fugitive time-bound past. Only now is he able to recognize that an implicit design had been silently governing his seemingly haphazard and wasted past, so that "all my life up to that day could have been . . . summed up under this title: 'A vocation.'" [20] This vocation is to be an aesthetic evangelist for the age, announcing his discovery of a theory of art within the work which exemplifies the theory. "The true paradises are the paradises we have lost." Nevertheless art is "the genuine

Last Judgment," [21] for by extricating essence from time, it is able to recover the past in a new creation—an aesthetic world which is a regained paradise, because it is purged from impurity and is "extra-temporal," out of time. At the close of *The Prelude* Wordsworth had called on Coleridge to join him in making for men "a work . . . of their redemption" (XIII, 439–41). Marcel's vocation is also a work of redemption; not the redemption of men, however, but of time.

In the course of his final, cumulative revelation, the author also discovers that all the sorrows and sufferings of life, for the artist who "has finally achieved his true vocation," are ultimately for the artistic best, and end in aesthetic joy. "Happiness alone is beneficial for the body, but it is grief which develops the powers of the mind." "In the end, sorrow kills," but "the instant sorrows are turned into ideas . . . the transformation itself releases joy." The inescapable cost of creation is suffering, of which creativity is the priceless reward, and the artist must die to involvement with the world in order to be reborn to the detachment of the artist.

> My illness, in forcing me, like a stern spiritual adviser, to die to this world, had done me a service, for except a corn of wheat fall into the ground and die, it abideth alone; but if it die, it bringeth forth much fruit.[22]

But "it was time to begin." "I must at once set myself to this work. It was high time." One of Proust's favorite analogues for his work, like that of Wordsworth for *The Recluse*, was architectural—the intricate structure and disposition of stresses of "une église," a "grande Cathédrale." [23] At the end of his elaborately ordered narrative Marcel is haunted by the book *François le Champi* that his mother had read to him as a child, and he hears still reverberating, "shrill, sharp, and inexhaustible," the "iron tinkling of the little bell which told me that at last M. Swann had gone and Mama was about to come upstairs" [24]—memories of the central scene in his childhood at Combray with which, immediately after the proem, Marcel had begun his novelistic quest for time lost. A further refinement confirms the rondure of the whole. The initial word of the proem itself had been *longtemps,* repeating the *temps perdu* in the title and echoed by *temps* in each of the two sentences following. So in the coda: "In the long last sentence of the book," as Edmund Wilson has said, "the word 'Time' begins to sound, and it closes the symphony as it began it" [25]— in the concluding phrase, "dans le Temps."

Such similarities in works otherwise so unlike—Wordsworth after all is the heir of Milton and of the moral severity of English Puritanism, while Proust, although he took a lively interest in the Wordsworthians George Eliot and John Ruskin, manifests the influence of Symbolism, the Decadence, and *l'art pour l'art*—such similarities are the less surprising when we realize that these works are cognate, and that their ultimate source (as the densely religious vocabulary of both writers indicates) is not secular, but theological. This source is the fifteen-hundred-year-old tradition of religious confessional writings, and within the tradition the first and greatest example, and one of the most influential of all books, in Catholic as in Protestant Europe, was the *Confessions* of St. Augustine.

3. THE ART OF AUGUSTINE'S "CONFESSIONS"

Augustine's work, written at the close of the fourth century, is on the one side a culmination of the classical mode of giving an account and justification of one's life. But it converts the classical procedure of putting oneself forward as the representative of a cultural ideal, performing overt deeds on a public stage, into a circumstantial narrative of the private events of the individual mind.[26] It is thus the first sustained history of an inner life and deserves, as much as any book for which the claim has been made, to be called the first modern work. It is modern, however, precisely because it is thoroughly Christian. Augustine expanded in great and fine detail the tendency (already evident, as we have seen, in the New Testament) to individualize and internalize the pattern of Biblical history; in so doing, he imposed on the flux of experience, the randomness of events, and the fugitive phenomena of memory the enduring plot-form and the standard concepts and imagery of that unique and characteristic genre of Christian Europe, the spiritual autobiography.

The book, like its many successors, is not the presentation of an individual life for its inherent interest, but is written from a special point of view and for a given purpose. The whole is an extended "confession" addressed to God, who overhears the meditation that the author conducts in solitude, but renders in the rhetorical mode of colloquies with himself, with God, and with the natural creation. One of Augustine's aims is to know himself better and so to strengthen his private will; but he also sees himself in a public role as one of God's chosen sons whose life has been transformed, and upon whom has been imposed the mission to bring good tidings to other Christian wayfarers:

> I confess not only before You . . . but also in the ears of the
> believing sons of men, companions of my joy and sharers of my
> mortality, my fellow citizens, fellow pilgrims. . . . These are
> Your servants, my brethren, whom You have chosen that they
> should be Your sons, my masters whom You have commanded
> me to serve.[27]

The *Confessions* begins in the present time, with a meditation and prayer by the mature writer on the relations of God to His creation and to His creature, man, before it proceeds to the narrative proper, which opens with events in the author's infancy, and even with speculations about his prenatal condition. There are two distinct selves in the book—"what I once was" and "what I now am"—and between these two identities lies the crucial occasion when Augustine's "past sins" were "forgiven and covered up, giving me joy in You, changing my life by faith and Your sacrament" (X.iii). Throughout the book Augustine evokes his life explicitly as the present recollection of the past, in which Augustine as he was is co-present with Augustine as he is:

> All this I do inside me, in the huge court of my memory. . . .
> And in my memory too I meet myself—I recall myself, what
> I have done, when and where and in what state of mind I was

when I did it. . . . And upon them all I can meditate as if they were present.[28]

Looking back after the outcome, the regenerate Augustine is able to discern the silent workings of God's providential plan from the beginning of what at the time had seemed the random contingencies of his unregenerate life. In defining these hidden workings he adumbrates the concept of what we now call unconscious motivation, by internalizing the distinction, common in the Christian view of history, between the secondary causes which are available to human observation and the omnipresent but invisible First Cause. You "were then acting in me by the hidden secret of Your Providence" (V.vi); there is a difference between "Your action upon me" and "my reason" for my actions (V.viii); "You brought it about through me, and without my being aware of it" (VI.vii), for "there is something of man that the very spirit of man that is in him does not know" (X.v). Augustine uses God's latterly discovered plan as a controlling idea, to give retrospective form to the raw data of his remembered experience. (The discrepancy between Augustine's account of the crucial events of his inner life in his *Confessions* and what he had written at the time of those events has occasioned a debate about the "truth" of Augustine's autobiography exactly parallel to the debate about the factual validity of Wordsworth's *Prelude*.[29]) All is ordered around the great scene of his conversion in the garden at Milan. Before this he had been torn by the conflict of "my two wills, one old, one new, one carnal, one spiritual" (VIII.v), compelling him simultaneously to the goods of this sensible world and to the good beyond sense and the world. In the garden he undergoes the anguish of the annihilation of that old self and the travail of the birth of the new, "dying unto death and living unto life"—an account which has shaped the experience of innumerable men since Augustine's time, yet (as Augustine's own comments indicate) was itself modeled, even in detail, upon conventions which had been established in a sequence of works from Paul's account of his conversion through Athanasius' *Life of St. Anthony*.[30]

Throughout the *Confessions* the haunt and main region of

his narrative is not outer events and actions but what Augustine calls the "inner life" of "the interior part." From the multitude of the *res gestae et visae* of his past, therefore, he selects, orders, and dwells upon only those few which are heavy with spiritual significance, as indices of a stage in his toilsome journey from attachment to the things of this world toward detachment and the transference of his allegiance to a transcendental kingdom. His youthful *acte gratuit* in stealing some pears, for example (we recall Wordsworth's youthful theft of a rowboat), reveals to him his participation in the theft of an apple from Eden (II.iv–x). And in a seemingly fortuitous meeting with a drunken and happy beggar at a time of "utter misery" he now recognizes that "You acted to bring home to me the realization of my misery" (VI.vi). So Wordsworth in *The Prelude* comes at a critical time upon a blind beggar, upon whom he stares "as if admonish'd from another world" (VII, 621–2). "As if admonish'd"—Wordsworth's experience is an as-if providentialism, a translated grace. And in another of his poems shaped in retrospect from an actual experience, Wordsworth in deepest dejection comes suddenly upon an old leech-gatherer who, in a manner of speaking, saves him.

Augustine's own experiences, together with the course of general human history, pose what is for him the central problem, *"Unde malum?"* "Whence then is evil since God who is good made all things good?" (VII.v). The question is answered by his discovery that evil issues in a greater good, in his own life as in the history of mankind. By his intense self-scrutiny Augustine achieved an astonishing subtlety in discriminating the variety and nuance of man's "affections and the movements of his heart" (IV.xiv), of the complex interaction between what the altering mind brings to its perceptions and what is given to it in perception, of the difficulty of separating the pure fact in memory from the intrusive presence of the self that remembers, and of the slow and obscure growth of convictions and values which burst suddenly into awareness in the quantum leap of a moment of insight; in these passages Augustine established the spiritual vocabulary for all later self-analyses and treatments of self-formation and the discovery of one's identity. Augustine also opened out, in the mode of a philosophy of lived experience, the topics which have since engaged the close study of professional philosophers up to that fervent admirer of the *Confessions,* Ludwig Wittgenstein.[31] These topics have also become the preoccupation of writers of secular confessions, from Rousseau and Wordsworth through Proust and Joyce. They include the question of "the vast recesses, the hidden and unsearchable caverns, of memory," that "inward place, which yet is no place" (X.viii–ix). Most prominent and persistent is the problem "What is time?". Augustine's attempt to solve the problem entails the distinction between the "three times, a present of things past, a present of things present, a present of things future" (XI.xx), as well as analyses of the difference between subjective time and the time measured by the movements of external bodies, of the relation of time and change to what is eternal and immutable (XI.xiii ff.), and of the significance of recurrent moments of illumination *in ictu trepidantis aspectus,* "in the thrust of a trembling glance" (VII.xvii), which occur in time and pass away, yet serve as portents of the ultimate escape from time into eternity.

In the induction to the *Confessions* Augustine had meditated on the relations of the Creator to the creation and of the timeless to that which exists in time. In the final book he rounds back to the genesis of all things, in a review of the significance of the creation at the beginning of time, and goes on to the uncreation of all things at the apocalyptic end of time—the word begins to toll as we approach the conclusion:

> For this gloriously beautiful order of things that are very good will pass away when it has achieved its end: it will have its morning and its evening. But the seventh day is without evening. . . .
> But You, Lord, are ever in action and ever at rest. You do not see in time nor move in time nor rest in time. Yet You make the things we see in time, and You make both time while time is and rest when time is no more.[32]

4. THE TRANSACTIONS OF MIND AND NATURE

Under the similarities between the *Confessions* and *The Prelude* there lies, of course, a profound disparity. To get at the crux of this difference I shall put side by side passages from each work which have a common vocabulary and a related subject. The passage in Augustine represents him in a colloquy with the "heaven and earth"; it reminds us that to conduct a conversation with the landscape is by no means a Romantic innovation, and that Wordsworth's "speaking face of earth and heaven" is a lineal descendant of the ancient Christian concept of the *liber naturae,* whose symbols bespeak the attributes and intentions of its author.[33]

> And what is this God? I asked the earth and it answered: "I am not He"; and all things that are in the earth made the same confession. I asked the sea and the deeps and the creeping things, and they answered: "We are not your God; seek higher." . . . I asked the heavens, the sun, the moon, the stars, and they answered: "Neither are we God whom you seek." And I said to all the things that throng about the gateways of the senses: "Tell me of my God, since you are not He. Tell me something of Him." And they cried out in a great voice: "He made us." My question was my gazing upon them, and their answer was their beauty. And I turned to myself and said: "And you, who are you?" And I answered: "A man." Now clearly there is a body and a soul in me, one exterior, one interior. From which of these two should I have enquired of my God? . . . The inner man knows these things through the ministry of the outer man: I the inner man knew them, I, I the soul, through the senses of the body.   (X.vi)

This is what Wordsworth wrote, in describing an "eminence" that his life had reached during his residence at Cambridge University:

> For hither I had come with holy powers
> And faculties, whether to work or feel:

To apprehend all passions and all moods
Which time, and place, and season do impress
Upon the visible universe, and work
Like changes there by force of my own mind.
                           . . . All
That I beheld respired with inward meaning.
Thus much for the one Presence, and the Life
Of the great whole; suffice it here to add
That whatsoe'er of Terror or of Love,
Or Beauty, Nature's daily face put on
From transitory passion, unto this
I was as wakeful, even, as waters are
To the sky's motion. . . .
I had a world about me; 'twas my own,
I made it; for it only liv'd to me,
And to the God who look'd into my mind.
                     . . . Of Genius, Power,
Creation and Divinity itself
I have been speaking, for my theme has been
What pass'd within me. . . .
O Heavens! how awful is the might of Souls,
And what they do within themselves, while yet
The yoke of earth is new to them. . . .
Points have we all of us within our souls,
Where all stand single; this I feel, and make
Breathings for incommunicable powers.
                        . . . there's not a man
That lives who hath not had his godlike hours,
And knows not what majestic sway we have,
As natural beings in the strength of nature.
                               (III, 83–194)

The passage in Augustine has three points of reference, which serve as the premises and prime functional terms throughout the *Confessions:* God, the natural creation, and man—or more precisely, since man's body and senses are a part of nature, the human soul. Of the three, God (figured here as speaking through His creation) retains all initiative, as the first, efficient, and final cause of nature and soul. In Wordsworth's passage God has not quite dropped out, but He is mentioned only after the fact, and given nothing to do except to be spectator of a completed action—"for it only liv'd to me,/ And to the God who look'd into my mind." But if God has become a nonparticipant, it is with this peculiar result: His traditional attributes and functions (the "holy powers," "Creation," and "Divinity") survive, to be inherited (together with the appropriate sentiments of wonder and awe) by the two remaining components of Augustine's triad, nature and the human "soul," or "mind."

My concern is not with the valid autobiographical question: "What was Wordsworth's creed—pantheist, panentheist, Christian?" in the sense of "What propositions about God would Wordsworth have been prepared to assert outside the poem?" [34] With respect to the conceptual scheme of *The Prelude,* the relevant question is: "What role does God play within the poem itself?" To answer this question it is not enough to list the passages in which reference is made to God; for the essential matter is, "What does God *do* in the poem?" And to this the answer is patently, "Nothing of consequence." In *The Prelude* of 1805 (and this fact is only thinly overlaid with pious phrases in Wordsworth's later revisions and additions) [35] God is at intervals ceremoniously alluded to, but remains an adventitious and nonoperative factor; if all allusions to deity were struck out of *The Prelude,* there would be no substantive change in its subject matter or development. God is the purely formal remainder of His former self, because His traditional offices have for all practical purposes been preempted by the other two elements of the triad—in Wordsworth's phrase in the passage I quoted, by men "as natural beings in the strength of nature." Whatever his beliefs—and it seems likely that Wordsworth did not greatly trouble himself about the question of orthodoxy until incited to do so by Coleridge's alarm and the remonstrances of friends and reviewers—the interesting thing is that Wordsworth described the process of his spiritual development within a system of reference which has only two generative and operative terms: mind and nature. As Hazlitt, with his usual acumen, observed even of Wordsworth's later and much more traditional *Excursion* (1814): "It is as if there were nothing but himself and the universe." [36]

In this manner of proceeding *The Prelude* participates in

the large movement of Romantic philosophy.[37] In its central tradition Christian thought had posited three primary elements: God, nature, and the soul; with God of course utterly prepotent, as the creator and controller of the two others and as the end, the telos, of all natural process and human endeavor. The tendency in innovative Romantic thought (manifested in proportion as the thinker is or is not a Christian theist) is greatly to diminish, and at the extreme to eliminate, the role of God, leaving as the prime agencies man and the world, mind and nature, the ego and the non-ego, the self and the not-self, spirit and the other, or (in the favorite antithesis of post-Kantian philosophers) subject and object. Fichte, Schelling, and Hegel, for example, begin with an undifferentiated principle which at once manifests itself in the dual mode of subject and object, whose interactions (in and through individual human selves) bring into being the phenomenal world and constitute all individual experience, as well as all the history of mankind. The notable fact, however, is that this metaphysical process does not delete but simply assimilates the traditional powers and actions of God, as well as the overall pattern of Christian history; now, however, subject and object, in their long interworking, are adequate to account for the whole story, from the metaphysical equivalent of the creation, through the fall and redemption, to the apocalyptic consummation at the end of the providential plot. As Hegel, who of all his contemporaries was most clearly aware of his procedure, put the matter: "Philosophy is thus identical with religion, but the distinction is that it is so in a peculiar manner, distinct from the manner of looking at things which is commonly called religion as such."[38] This retention of traditional Christian concepts and the traditional Christian plot, but demythologized, conceptualized, and with all-controlling Providence converted into a "logic" or dialectic that controls all the interactions of subject and object, gives its distinctive character and design to what we call "Romantic philosophy." In this grandiose enterprise, however, it is the subject, mind, or spirit which is primary and takes over the initiative and the functions which had once been the prerogatives of deity; that is why we can justifiably call Romantic philosophy, in its diverse forms, by the generic term "Idealism."

We shall have occasion in the next two chapters to look more closely at the typical plot-form of post-Kantian philosophical systems. Now notice how this metaphysics of subject-object interaction parallels the exemplary lyric form which Wordsworth, following the instance of Coleridge's *Frost at Midnight,* established in *Tintern Abbey:* an individual confronts a natural scene and makes it abide his question, and the interchange between his mind and nature constitutes the entire poem, which usually poses and resolves a spiritual crisis.[39] *The Prelude,* too, begins with the poet alone in an open prospect, responding in spirit to the attributes and alterations of the landscape, and it proceeds by recurrent passages in which the mind is made aware of a new stage in its growth by coming to a new accounting with the natural scene. In the intervening sections *The Prelude* represents the people, actions, and events of Wordsworth's quotidian life; otherwise it would not be an autobiography (even a spiritual autobiography) but something more like Hegel's *Phenomenology of Spirit*—a work which manages the feat of epitomizing the cultural history of the maturing spirit entirely in terms of the diverse separations, conflicts, and incremental reconciliations of subject and object. We find in *The Prelude,* then, although with parsimony in number and detail, the account of people other than the poet himself, including his mother and father, various playmates, "my old Dame, so motherly and good," old beggars, and Beaupuis the revolutionary, as well as descriptions of Wordsworth's literal actions and experiences at Hawkeshead and in Cambridge, London, and France.

By a triumph of invention, however, Wordsworth supplements his literal story of a real life in this variegated world with the correlative account of the growth of the poet's mind as a direct transaction between that mind and nature. In many passages, for example, nature is endowed with the attributes and powers of a mother, father, nurse, teacher, lover, as well as a deity (or deities) who seek out, incite, guide, and discipline the individual whom "Nature" had selected to "frame/ A favor'd Being, from his earliest dawn/ Of infancy" (I, 363–5).

(That in the earliest version of this passage it was not "Nature," but first "genii," then "spirits," which performed this role indicates that Wordsworth's locutions about the "soul" and "spirit," or "spirits," of nature are not meant to assert a creed, but to constitute a poetic manner of speaking, or serious conceit.[40]) Wordsworth manages, in passages that alternate with the literal exposition, to assimilate even the recalcitrant materials of the later books of *The Prelude* to the nature and agency of landscape. In London, for example, still "the Spirit of Nature was upon me," and the place

> Was throng'd with impregnations, like those wilds
> In which my early feelings had been nurs'd,
> And naked valleys, full of caverns, rocks,
> And audible seclusions.   (VII, 735; VIII, 791–4)

In the section of *The Prelude* devoted to "Books," the greatest of these works of man are similarly naturalized, to the reader who "with living Nature hath been intimate," for their power over him springs

> From the great Nature that exists in works
> Of mighty Poets. Visionary Power
> Attends upon the motions of the winds
> Embodied in the mystery of words.
>   (V, 612–21)

The account of his heightening response to the existence of men outside himself, and of his growing identification with them, is entitled "Love of Nature Leading to Love of Mankind," and its central episode is the sudden appearance of the shepherd as "a Power/ Or Genius, under Nature, under God,/ Presiding," with his form "glorified" and "like an aerial Cross" —an epiphany which Wordsworth analyzes as an epiphenomenon of the mist and the setting sun (VIII, 393–410). The poet's deepening experience of human suffering and mortality is systematically translated into an altering relationship between his eye and its object: the natural scene articulates and reflects back the inchoate sentiments which are brought to it by the apperceptive mind, so that the correlate of his coming to look upon men "with another eye" is his coming to perceive natural objects as suffused by a different light and shade. He felt

> A dawning, even as of another sense,
> A human-heartedness about my love
> For objects hitherto the gladsome air
> Of my own private being, and no more . . .
> A new-born feeling. It spread far and wide;
> The trees, the mountains shared it, and the brooks. . . .
> Whatever shadings of mortality
> Had fallen upon these objects heretofore
> Were different in kind; not tender: strong,
> Deep, gloomy were they and severe; the scatterings
> Of Childhood.[41]

And in the series of revelations with which *The Prelude* draws to a close, we remember, the first is of a landscape seen as the mind of man, the main region of his song, and the last is of the secondary region of his song, the life which he himself had lived, seen as a landscape.

On the recurrent level of narration in which mind and nature must suffice to generate the plot of *The Prelude,* a heavy requisition is placed on nature, but a still heavier one is placed on mind, which in Wordsworth, as in the German Idealists, is the prior and preeminent power. For it is not nature but "the Mind of Man" which is "the main region of my song"; and in the passage in which Wordsworth speaks of "Power,/ Creation and Divinity itself," he speaks "not of outward things," but of "what pass'd within me" and of "my youthful mind." [42] In the final analysis the view that informs *The Prelude* is not naturalism, but humanism, in which man is "of all visible natures crown . . ./ As, more than anything we know instinct/ With Godhead" (VIII, 634–9); and if Wordsworth develops in *The Prelude* what Harold Bloom calls a "myth of Nature," this is incorporated within a higher and more comprehensive myth of mind.

5. THE THEODICY OF THE PRIVATE LIFE

In the Prospectus to *The Recluse* and its associated poems Wordsworth announced his intent "to weigh/ The good and evil of our mortal state." This was his version of Milton's undertaking to "justify the ways of God to men." Wordsworth's argument, like Milton's, is a theodicy which locates the justification for human suffering in the restoration of a lost paradise. In Milton's view, this event will not occur "till one greater Man/ Restore us, and regain the blissful Seat." Wordsworth's paradise, however, can be achieved simply by a union of man's mind with nature, and so is a present paradise in this world, capable of being described "by words/ Which speak of nothing more than what we are"—without recourse, that is, either to an intervenient deity or to a heavenly kingdom to redress any imbalance between the good and evil of our mortal state.

In Wordsworth's *Prelude,* the autobiographical preliminary to *The Recluse,* the ultimate goodness governing the course of his life is brought into question by his suffering and crisis of spirit, then is established by the outcome of his experience, which is represented as prototypical for the men to whom he addresses himself. Wordsworth's assumption, like that of all writers of theodicies, whether of universal scope or of the private life, is that if life is to be worth living there cannot be a blank unreason or mere contingency at the heart of things; there must be meaning (in the sense of a good and intelligible purpose) in the occurrence of both physical and moral evils. The Christian theodicy of the private life, in the long lineage of Augustine's *Confessions,* transfers the locus of the primary concern with evil from the providential history of mankind to the providential history of the individual self, and justifies the experience of wrongdoing, suffering, and loss as a necessary means toward the greater good of personal redemption. But Wordsworth's is a secular theodicy—a theodicy without an operative *theos*—which retains the form of the ancient reason-

ing, but translates controlling Providence into an immanent
teleology, makes the process coterminous with our life in this
world, and justifies suffering as the necessary means toward the
end of a greater good which is nothing other than the stage of
achieved maturity:

> Ah me! that all
> The terrors, all the early miseries
> Regrets, vexations, lassitudes, that all
> The thoughts and feelings which have been infus'd
> Into my mind, should ever have made up
> The calm existence that is mine when I
> Am worthy of myself! Praise to the end!
> Thanks likewise for the means!   (I, 355–62)

In other words, the Wordsworthian theodicy of the private
life (if we want to coin a term, we can call it a "biodicy"),
belongs to the distinctive Romantic genre of the *Bildungsgeschichte,* which translates the painful process of Christian
conversion and redemption into a painful process of self-
formation, crisis, and self-recognition, which culminates in a
stage of self-coherence, self-awareness, and assured power that
is its own reward.

On the one level Wordsworth tells this story in terms of
his literal experiences of terror, pain, error, and misery, climaxed by his crisis of doubt and despair after the failure of
the French Revolution; and he justifies these experiences (as
he says in a revision of the passage just quoted) as "bearing a
part,/ And that a needful part" in making him a man, in
making him a poet, and in making him exactly the kind of
man and poet he was. But throughout *The Prelude* there is a
double story being told—a story of Wordsworth's life in the
world and a correlative story of his life in nature. And on this
second narrative level Wordsworth incorporates the problem
of suffering within his overarching myth of the interaction between mind and nature, in which fostering nature conducts the
mind through successive stages of growth, while speaking nature
defines and communicates to the mind that degree of self-
knowledge which its stage of cumulative experience has prepared it to receive.

6. THE THEODICY OF THE LANDSCAPE

No sooner does Wordsworth begin the story of his life as a child engaged in the ordinary activities of bathing, basking in the sun, and running through the fields and woods, than he turns to the correlative presentation of his soul in direct engagement with nature, as it is formed by contrary influences of the external scene:

> Fair seed-time had my soul, and I grew up
> Foster'd alike by beauty and by fear.
>
> (I, 305–6)

Throughout the earlier books of *The Prelude* Wordsworth repeatedly represents his mind as developing by a sustained interchange with "these two attributes," the "sister horns that constitute [nature's] strength," whose "twofold influence . . . of peace and excitation" instills in the mind a union of "emotion" and "calmness," of "energy" and "happy stillness." [43] Of one type are the gentle and "fearless" aspects of nature—the calm and ordered prospect, small-scale objects, "quiet Heavens," "tranquil scenes," "gentle breezes," "a garden with its walks and banks of flowers," all of which manifest "love" and "tenderness," act by effecting "pleasure and repeated happiness," and move the mind "by feelings of delight." But "Nature . . . when she would frame/ A favor'd Being" alternates her "gentlest visitation" with "severer interventions, ministry/ More palpable." Of this opposite type are the awe-inspiring and terrifying aspects of nature—vast scenes of wildness and majesty, the "awful" and the "grand," elements "in tumult," "the midnight storm," "the roaring ocean and waste wilderness," which act on the mind by "terror" and by "pain and fear" and manifest not nature's "love" but her punitive actions: her "impressive discipline of fear." [44]

In this natural polarity of "beauteous forms or grand," or of "forms sublime or fair," [45] as Samuel Monk pointed out more than three decades ago, Wordsworth adapted the two primary categories—that of the beautiful and that of the sublime—into which earlier eighteenth-century theorists had apportioned the aesthetic qualities of the natural scene.[46] By and large the beautiful is small in scale, orderly, and tranquil, effects pleasure in the observer, and is associated with love; while the sublime is vast (hence suggestive of infinity), wild, tumultuous, and awful, is associated with pain, and evokes ambivalent feelings of terror and admiration. But behind this familiar eighteenth-century aesthetic dichotomy lay centuries of speculation about the natural world—speculation whose concerns were not aesthetic but theological and moral, and which in fact constituted a systematic theodicy of the landscape. For on the Pauline ground that "the invisible things of Him from the creation of the world are clearly seen," the problem had early arisen, how to justify the goodness of an omnipotent Creator who has brought into being an earth which, in many of its aspects, is not beautiful and beneficent, but wild, waste, ugly, perilous, and terrifying?

This is precisely the question put to God by Dorigen in Chaucer's *Franklin's Tale* when, her husband away on a distant voyage, she looks with terror from the brink of a cliff upon the sea and its "grisly feendly rokkes blake,"

> That semen rather a foul confusion
> Of werk than any fair creacion
> Of swich a parfit wys God and a stable,
> Why han ye wroght this werk unresonable? . . .
> I woot wel clerkes wol seyn as hem leste,
> By argumentz, that al is for the beste—

But having thus displaced the burden of theodicy from human evil and suffering, with its backdrop of Eden, Calvary, and the New Jerusalem, to the ugly and terrifying aspects of what should be the best of all possible physical worlds, Dorigen helplessly resigns all disputation on the matter "to clerkes," while her friends, to distract her from the "disconfort" of the wild sea, escort her to conventional places of ordered and agreeable beauty:

They leden hire by ryveres and by welles,
And eek in othere places delitables.

(lines 856–99)

The "clerkes" proposed a variety of answers to this question, but a standard one was that a perfect, wise God had originally created a perfectly smooth, orderly, useful, and beautiful world. Mountains and other wild, waste places were the product not of divine benevolence but of human depravity, for they had been wreaked by the wrath of a just God at the original fall of man in Eden, or alternatively (in some commentators, additionally), they had been effected by the devastating flood with which He punished the all-but-universal corruption of mankind at the time of Noah. Henry Vaughan expressed the common opinion in his poem *Corruption;* when Adam sinned

> He drew the Curse upon the world, and Crackt
> The whole frame with his fall.

Mountains, therefore, and other vast, chaotic and frightful aspects of nature, as Marjorie Nicolson has said, were looked upon as "symbols of human sin" and of the consequent wrath of a justly punitive God.[47]

A late and circumstantial document in this tradition was Thomas Burnet's *The Sacred Theory of the Earth,* of which the first Latin version was published in 1681–89. On the one side, this immensely popular book fostered the development of "physico-theology," which undertook to demonstrate the existence and attributes of God, and especially the justice of His ways to men in the creation, entirely by reasoning from the phenomena of nature; on the other side, it served as an influential model for translating theological and moral concepts into an aesthetics of landscape. Burnet was often compared to Milton (Coleridge described *The Sacred Theory* as "a grand Miltonic Romance" [48]), and not merely because of the baroque magnificence of his style. As Burnet's subtitle to the expanded version in English describes his subject, it is "an Account of the Original of the Earth, and of all the General Changes which it hath already undergone, or is to undergo, till the Consummation of all Things." The span of his work, then, from creation to apocalypse, coincides with that of the plot of *Paradise Lost;* and although Burnet tells the story primarily in terms of changes in the physical universe which were effected by natural law, or "second Causes," these causes operate in preestablished harmony with what he calls the "first Cause"— that is, with the underlying purpose and providence of Milton's God.[49]

According to Burnet the perfect God had originally brought into being a perfectly beautiful world; and this, by Burnet's Palladian standards of beauty, was a world "smooth, regular, and uniform; without Mountains, and without a Sea" (I, 72). Earliest mankind dwelt in perfect innocence and ease in an unchanging springtime, in a region of the flawless world which was even more perfect than the rest. This region was the paradise which is described in Genesis and is also dimly remembered in pagan myths of *"Elysian* Fields, Fortunate Islands, Gardens of *Hesperides, Alcinous,* etc."—a passage Wordsworth may well have recalled when he wrote in the Prospectus of "Paradise, and groves Elysian, Fortunate Fields. . . ."[50] The providential cause of the destruction of this perfect world was God's wrathful judgment on "the Wickedness and Degeneracy of Men" at the time of Noah, when "the Abyss was open'd" and "the Frame of the Earth broke and fell down into the *great Abyss";* the resulting flood and cataclysm transformed all nature into its present state, "wherein it must continue till the Redemption and Restitution of all Things." The world we now inhabit therefore is only the wreck of paradise, with some remains indeed of its original beauty, yet overall "the Image or Picture of a great Ruin . . . the true Aspect of a World lying in its Rubbish" (I, 130, 90, 223, 148).

Toward the ruinous parts of the present world Burnet exhibits the complex attitudes which helped form the new aesthetics of the following century. For he finds positive values in those aspects of the landscape which are vast, misproportioned, terrifying, and by traditional aesthetic standards, ugly; but these values are both aesthetic and quasi-theological, for in them the speaking face of earth declares the infinity, the power, and the wrath of a just deity.

> As to the present Form of the Earth, we call all Nature to Witness for us; the Rocks and the Mountains, the Hills and the Valleys, the deep and wide Sea, and the Caverns of the Ground: Let these speak, and tell their Origin: How the Body of the Earth came to be thus torn and mangled? (II, 331–2)

Yet these same phenomena, "the greatest Objects of Nature," the "boundless Regions where Stars inhabit . . . the wide Sea and the Mountains of the Earth," seem to him "the most pleasing to behold."

> There is something august and stately in the Air of these things, that inspires the Mind with great Thoughts and Passions; we do naturally, upon such Occasions, think of God and his Greatness: And whatsoever hath but the Shadow and Appearance of INFINITE, as all Things have that are too big for our Comprehension, they fill and over-bear the Mind with their Excess, and cast it into a pleasing kind of Stupor and Admiration.
> And yet these Mountains . . . are nothing but great Ruins; but such as shew a certain Magnificence in Nature.
>
> (I, 188–9)

Inherent in precisely those ruined elements of landscape which manifest the terrifying wrath of God are the highest aesthetic values, because they also express God's infinite power, and so evoke from Burnet attitudes and emotions which men had earlier felt for almighty God Himself.

Burnet's distinction between the beautiful and the "great" aspects of nature was developed by later theorists (with the help of a term imported from Longinus' treatise on the elevated style) into the distinction between the beautiful and the "sublime." Even in later naturalistic treatments of these categories, we recognize a consonance with the earlier theological context, in which the beautiful elements in nature are the enduring expression of God's loving benevolence, while the vast and disordered in nature express his infinity, power, and wrath, and so evoke a paradoxical union of delight and terror, pleasure and awe. Edmund Burke, for example, in his greatly influential *Philosophical Enquiry into . . . the Sublime and Beautiful,* bases the sense of beauty on the passion of love and associates it with pleasure, while "whatever is fitted in any sort to excite the ideas of pain, and danger, that is to say, whatever is in any sort terrible . . . is a source of the *sublime*." [51] The sublime also has its source in the associated qualities of "power," "vastness," "infinity," and "magnificence," and its characteristic effects on the beholder are the traditional ones aroused by the conception of the infinite power of a stern but just God: "terror," "astonishment," "awe," "admiration," and "reverence." [52]

William Wordsworth, who in his writings showed an early and continuing interest in the antithetic categories of the beautiful and the sublime,[53] thus inherited a long tradition of finding moral and theological meanings in the aesthetic qualities of the landscape, as well as of conducting an inquiry into cosmic goodness and justice by reference to the contrary attributes of the natural world. From such hints he constructed his account of an individual mind in its developing capacity to respond to and interpret "whatso'er of Terror or of Love,/ Or Beauty, Nature's daily face put on" (III, 132–3)—an achievement which in its subtlety and insight had no precedent either in the physico-theology, the aesthetics, or the psychology of his day.

We can most clearly follow Wordsworth's procedure in the biography of the Pedlar which he interpolated into the 1798 version of his greatest narrative poem, *The Ruined Cottage.* Wordsworth told Isabella Fenwick that he represented in the Pedlar "chiefly an *idea* of what I fancied my own character might have become in his circumstances," [54] and he later transferred a number of passages from this description into *The Prelude.* The biography of the Pedlar, then, is the first sketch of what I have called the controlling "idea" of *The Prelude,* and in it Wordsworth, in some 250 packed lines, describes the growth of the Pedlar's mind from early childhood, through a spiritual crisis (experienced "before his twentieth year was pass'd," in which "his mind became disturbed" and he turned "in vain . . ./ To science for a cure" in order "to mitigate the fever of his heart") to the time in which he discovered his role in life and "assumed/ This lowly occupation." But though his outer occupation was that of a pedlar, he had also been born to be a mute inglorious poet, for

> he was a chosen son
> To him was given an ear which deeply felt
> The voice of Nature in the obscure wind
> The sounding mountain and the running stream.
>   . . . In all shapes
> He found a secret and mysterious soul,
> A fragrance and a spirit of strange meaning.[55]

The compactness of this biography allows Wordsworth to sustain the narrative mode of the transaction between mind and nature in a way not possible in the extended autobiography of *The Prelude*. In early childhood the Pedlar's mind had been fostered by his solitary experiences with the terror, power, and grandeur of the natural sublime:

> So the foundations of his mind were laid
> In such communion, not from terror free.
> While yet a child, and long before his time
> He had perceived the presence and the power
> Of greatness, and deep feelings had impressed
> Great objects on his mind.   (lines 77–82)

Though even at this time, in the "fixed and steady lineaments" of the face of the landscape, he had "traced an ebbing and a flowing mind," he had not yet been ready for a later stage of nature's teaching, "the lesson deep of love" enciphered in the gentle aspects of the outer scene.

> In his heart
> Love was not yet, nor the pure joy of love,
> By sound diffused, or by the breathing air,
> Or by the silent looks of happy things.

The passage to that stage at which he learns to decipher the lesson of love in nature is precisely fixed in time: it occurred "ere his ninth summer," when having for the first time been sent out alone to tend his father's sheep, he beheld the beauty of a mountain dawn.

> He looked,
> The ocean and the earth beneath him lay
> In gladness and deep joy. The clouds were touched
> And in their silent faces did he read
> Unutterable love. . . .
> His mind was a thanksgiving to the power
> That made him. It was blessedness and love.
>
> (lines 106–41)

Such were the experiences which fostered the development of his mature mind which, "in a just equipoise of love," had the psychic strength to participate with human wretchedness—"He could afford to suffer/ With those whom he saw suffer."[56]

In a revealing passage Wordsworth says that the boy "had learned to read/ His bible" while at school, before he came to discover the same meanings written more distinctly and impressively in the *verba visibilia,* the symbolic language of the landscape:

> But in the mountains did he *feel* his faith
> There did he see the writing—All things there
> Looked immortality, revolving life,
> And greatness still revolving, infinite;
> . . . nor did he *believe*—he saw.
>
> (lines 54–6, 146–55)

But it would appear that the Pedlar learned to transfer the divine attributes from the Book of Scripture to the Book of Nature with some help from the physico-theology of Burnet's *Sacred Theory;* for one of the revelations he found encoded in a scene of bleak sublimity was that of the cosmic vengeance which had loosed the mountain-making deluge in the age of Noah—in

> some peak
> Familiar with forgotten years, which shews,
> Inscribed, as with the silence of the thought,

Upon its bleak and visionary sides,
The history of many a winter storm,
Or of the day of vengeance, when the sea
Rose like a giant from his sleep, and smote
The hills, and when the firmament of heaven
Rained darkness which the race of men beheld
Yea all the men that lived and had no hope.[57]

In *The Prelude* (which also contains echoes of Burnet's *Sacred Theory*,[58] as well as of various eighteenth-century treatises on the aesthetics of landscape), after Wordsworth moves from the rural milieu of his boyhood into the variegated life of Cambridge, London, and France, he represents himself as coming to terms with his experience in periodic accountings with the natural scene. The mind finds in the scene what it has become ready to find, and what it finds is its own aspect. As Wordsworth put it, "from thyself it is that thou must give,/ Else never canst receive" (XI, 333–4). And what the mind at such moments brings to nature is the hitherto inchoate product of its experience of men and the world since it had last come to an understanding with nature.

A central instance of this recurrent tactic constitutes a notable passage in Book VI of *The Prelude*. There Wordsworth describes his first pedestrian trip through France in the summer of 1790, when he participated joyously in that festival period of the Revolution. On his way through the Alps from France to Italy he crosses the Simplon Pass and descends into the narrow and gloomy ravine of the Gondo, there to read, inscribed in the physical properties of the scene, a revelation about man and nature and human life.

Burnet had long before incorporated in *The Sacred Theory* reminiscences of his trip across the "great Ruins" of the Alps,[59] and the description of Alpine sublimity had become a standard *topos* among eighteenth-century connoisseurs of pleasing horror, including John Dennis, Shaftesbury, Addison, and Thomas Gray, who had vied in representing prospects where, as Gray said, "not a precipice, not a torrent, not a cliff, but is pregnant with religion and poetry." [60] Wordsworth's description of the ravine below Simplon thus epitomizes a century of commentary on the religion and poetry in the sublime Alpine landscape, brought together by a poet of genius and endowed with an ominous life:

> The immeasurable height.
> Of woods decaying, never to be decay'd,
> The stationary blasts of water-falls,
> And everywhere along the hollow rent
> Winds thwarting winds, bewilder'd and forlorn,
> The torrents shooting from the clear blue sky,
> The rocks that mutter'd close upon our ears,
> Black drizzling crags that spake by the way-side
> As if a voice were in them, the sick sight
> And giddy prospect of the raving stream. . . .

The grimness of the lesson this scene bespeaks is made even more emphatic in a manuscript addition which suggests Burnet's view that mountains and rocks are the ruins left by the wrathful destruction of the pristine world, and also indicates the implicit relevance of the prospect to the violent contingencies of human life:

> And ever as we halted, or crept on,
> Huge fragments of primaeval mountain spread
> In powerless ruin, blocks as huge aloft
> Impending, nor permitted yet to fall,
> The sacred Death-cross, monument forlorn
> Though frequent of the perish'd Traveller. . . .

Integral to Wordsworth's description of terrifying sublimity, however, is a contrary aspect of the scene: the light and serenity of beauty, exhibited in "the clear blue sky" and in "the unfetter'd clouds, and region of the Heavens." And this *coincidentia oppositorum* suddenly expresses a revelation which Wordsworth equates with the showing forth of the contraries of God in the Apocalypse, the Book of Revelation itself. There the Lamb of the gospel of love had manifested Himself as the terrifying deity of the *dies irae*, while men cried "to the mountains and rocks, Fall on us and hide us . . . from the wrath of the Lamb: For the great day of his wrath is come"; but the opening and closing chapters had insistently reiterated that the

God of wrath and destruction is one and coeternal with the God who manifests his love in the creation at the beginning and in the redemption at the end of time: "I am Alpha and Omega, the beginning and the ending"; "Fear not; I am the first and the last"; "I am Alpha and Omega, the beginning and the end, the first and the last." [61] In Wordsworth's version:

> Tumult and peace, the darkness and the light
> Were all like workings of one mind, the features
> Of the same face, blossoms upon one tree,
> Characters of the great Apocalypse,
> The types and symbols of Eternity,
> Of first and last, and midst, and without end.
>
> (VI, 551–72)

In consonance with Wordsworth's two-term frame of reference, the Scriptural Apocalypse is assimilated to an apocalypse of nature; its written characters are natural objects, which are read as types and symbols of permanence in change; and its antithetic qualities of sublimity and beauty are seen as simultaneous expressions on the face of heaven and earth, declaring an unrealized truth which the chiaroscuro of the scene articulates for the prepared mind—a truth about the darkness and the light, the terror and the peace, the ineluctable contraries that make up our human existence.

This recognition, however, is not the end but only a midstage in the evolution of the poet's mind. Book IX, which will begin the fateful record of his second visit to France and its aftermath, opens with a statement of Wordsworth's human reluctance to face the crisis of maturity, as he winds and doubles back like a river which fears the way "that leads direct to the devouring sea"; the passage ominously echoes Milton's invocation to his ninth book, which narrates the fall of man and his expulsion from paradise into "a world of woe,/ Sin and her shadow Death, and Misery." [62] After the failure of the limitless initial promise of the French Revolution, the growing divisions and conflicts in a world gone mad are reflected in Wordsworth's inner divisions and conflicts, until the integrity of his spiritual development is shattered in what seems incipient madness. He suffers from Kafka-esque nightmares, pleading

> Before unjust Tribunals, with a voice
> Labouring, a brain confounded, and a sense
> Of treachery and desertion in the place
> The holiest I knew of, my own soul.
>
> (X, 378–81)

He makes a desperate attempt to reestablish on abstract premises, and by logical analysis and reasoning, what had originally
been his spontaneous confidence in life and his hope for man,
but the attempt leads only to utter perplexity about "right and
wrong, the ground/ Of moral obligation," until he breaks
down completely. In the context of our discussion it is significant that Wordsworth describes his crisis as involving, explic-
itlý, his despair about a solution to the problem of the good
and evil of our moral state:

>   I lost
> All feeling of conviction, and, in fine,
> Sick, wearied out with contrarieties,
> Yielded up moral questions in despair.
> This was the crisis of that strong disease,
> This the soul's last and lowest ebb.[63]

The account of the dark night of his soul—"I was benighted
heart and mind" (XII, 21)—is at once correlated, in Wordsworth's double narrative, with an account of the paralysis of
the earlier reciprocative relation between his mind and nature.
For his heart "had been turn'd aside/ From nature by external
accidents" (X, 886–7), and the habit of "logic and minute analysis," infecting even his perceptions, replaced the attitude of
total receptiveness to all that nature had to give—"I never
thought of judging, with the gift of all this glory filled and
satisfied"—by an attitude in which the mind sat "in judgment"
on nature,

>   disliking here, and there,
> Liking, by rules of mimic art transferr'd
> To things above all art.   (XI, 126–55)

That is, he evaluated the scene according to the fixed and formal aesthetic categories of the picturesque which had been
abstracted from the principles of composition in the art of

landscape painting.[64] And in place of the earlier freedom in its negotiations with nature, his mind, thus weakened, became a slave to "the eye . . ./ The most despotic of our senses," which rejoiced "to lay the inner faculties asleep" (XI, 171–99). The poet had succumbed to the "sleep/ Of death" from which, in the Prospectus (60–61), he undertook to "arouse the sensual" by his evangel of the creative power of the liberated mind.

Wordsworth's eleventh book, which begins the systematic account of his "Imagination . . . Restored," opens with another extended parallel to *Paradise Lost,* this time echoing Milton's relief, in his invocation to the third book, at escaping the realms of hell, "though long detain'd/ In that obscure sojourn." In Wordsworth's version:

> Long time hath Man's unhappiness and guilt
> Detain'd us; with what dismal sights beset
> For the outward view, and inwardly oppress'd . . .
> And lastly, utter loss of hope itself,
> And things to hope for. Not with these began
> Our Song, and not with these our Song must end:
> Ye motions of delight, that through the fields
> Stir gently, breezes and soft airs that breathe
> The breath of Paradise, and find your way
> To the recesses of the soul!

Thus having traversed his personal hell, he turns to the correspondent breeze which had blown in the glad preamble of his song—now specified as "the breath of Paradise" that finds its way "to the recesses of the soul"—to assist him in restoring the paradise within.[65] Wordsworth narrates the process of this recovery by his customary alternation between the details of his outer life (the influence of Dorothy, of Coleridge, and of the "uncouth Vagrants" and "lowly men" with whom he talked in his solitary wanderings) and his private intercourse with "Nature's Self, by human love/ Assisted," which ultimately brings his mind back to what it had earlier been, but on the level now of deepened awareness, wider breadth, and firm stability. Nature's self

> Conducted me again to open day,
> Revived the feelings of my earlier life,

> Gave me that strength and knowledge full of peace,
> Enlarged, and never more to be disturb'd.

In a manuscript version of this passage Wordsworth remarks that in saying this much he feared "to encroach upon a theme/ Reserv'd to close my Song." [66] This ultimate resolution of his crisis is reserved for the concluding book of *The Prelude,* and follows from the climactic revelation on Mount Snowdon in which, in a sudden burst of natural illumination, the poet sees the landscape as "the perfect image of a mighty Mind." Like the ravine below Simplon Pass, the prospect unites the contraries of tumult and peace, the darkness and the light—the terrifying dark chasm, "a deep and gloomy breathing-place through which/ Mounted the roar of waters," while overhead the moon "naked in the Heavens . . . look'd down upon this shew/ In single glory." Above all, the give and take of influence between the moon and the mist-shrouded scene shows forth the radical power of human minds to confront nature in a creative and life-giving interchange, "Willing to work and to be wrought upon," so that "in a world of life they live." From this power, Wordsworth says, follows "sovereignty within and peace at will," "truth in moral judgments and delight/ That fails not in the external universe," as opposed to the tendency, from which he has finally freed himself, of "habit to enslave the mind . . . by laws of vulgar sense," and so to

> substitute a universe of death,
> The falsest of all worlds, in place of that
> Which is divine and true.
>
> (XIII, 39–143)

That is, his mind has escaped back to "a world of life" from its experiential equivalent of the hell which Milton had described (in the phrase Wordsworth here dramatically echoes) as "a Universe of death, which God by curse/ Created evil, for evil only good/ Where all life dies, death lives" (*Paradise Lost,* II, 622–4).

There immediately follows the first part of Wordsworth's resolution of his long dialectic of good and evil:

To fear and love,
To love as first and chief, for there fear ends,
Be this ascribed; to early intercourse,
In presence of sublime and lovely Forms,
With the adverse principles of pain and joy,
Evil as one is rashly named by those
Who know not what they say. From love, for here
Do we begin and end, all grandeur comes,
All truth and beauty, from pervading love,
That gone, we are as dust.

And this love is a "higher love," a "love more intellectual" than maternal and sexual love, which are "human merely," for this "proceeds/ More from the brooding Soul, and is divine" (XIII, 143–65). Patently Wordsworth's statement is in the traditional idiom of Christian theodicy, and is exactly equivalent in its place and function to Adam's climactic statement in the last book of Milton's epic when, upon hearing Michael foretell Christ's birth, death, resurrection, and return to an earth which then "shall all be Paradise," he acknowledges the justice of the ways of God to men:

O goodness infinite, goodness immense!
That all this good of evil shall produce,
And evil turn to good; more wonderful
Than that which by creation first brought forth
Light out of darkness! Full of doubt I stand,
Whether I should repent me now of sin
By me done and occasion'd, or rejoice
Much more, that much more good thereof shall spring,
To God more glory, more good will to Men
From God, and over wrath grace shall abound.
(XII, 469–78)

In the passage in *The Prelude* of 1805, however, there is no mention of the Incarnation, Crucifixion, or Second Coming, nor even of a deity. The recognition Wordsworth describes is the end product of a sustained intercourse between mind and nature, and in defining it he collects and resolves the contrary qualities of the natural scene—aesthetic, moral, and quasi-theological—with which he has been weaving the complex design of his theodicy since his opening statement that he grew up fostered alike by beauty and by fear. On the one side is the "sublime" and its near-synonym, "grandeur"; and on the other the "lovely Forms" of nature (the identification is sharpened in the later revision of line 146, "In presence of sublime or *beautiful* forms"). With the sublime are aligned "fear" and "pain," hence what is mistakenly supposed to be "evil"; with the beautiful are aligned the "adverse principles," which are "joy" and "love." And whereas in the poet's earlier revelation in the Alpine ravine he had envisioned the contraries of peace and fear to be equal as well as coeternal attributes of the "first and last, and midst, and without end," he now has progressed to the higher realization that love is "first and chief, for there fear ends," and therefore is the last as well as the first ("from love . . ./ Do we begin and end"), so that in this final accounting not only the beautiful but the sublime turns out to issue from love: "From love . . . all grandeur comes,/ All truth and beauty." Such is Wordsworth's naturalistic equivalent, in a theodicy transacted between mind and nature, of the Miltonic doctrine that God's love not only subsumes and justifies, but necessitates the pain and fear imposed on man by God's wrath —a paradox put by Dante with a starkness beyond Milton when he inscribed over the eternal gates of his ghastly hell that primal love had made it:

> Fecemi la divina potestate
> La somma sapienza e'l primo amore.[67]

Not all readers of *The Prelude* attend to its conclusion with the care they devote to the earlier sections, and to some of those who do it has seemed that Wordsworth's shift from pain and evil to love and good has been managed by logical sleight of hand. A main undertaking in the later parts of the poem, John Jones has said, is to marshal "into consequential argument 'the history of a poet's mind,'" and the "optimism . . . of the late *Prelude* is a determined end towards which the poem must be manipulated, like the plot of a bad play." [68] But Wordsworth does not undertake to prove that good subsumes ill by consequential argument; in fact, he has told us that it was the attempt to apply "formal proof" to moral matters that precipitated the breakdown in which he "yielded up moral questions in despair." What Wordsworth attempts is to represent a mode of experience, in which the recovery from his spiritual crisis yields the vision of a nature transformed, and in which, conversely, what he now sees in nature is correlative with a radical change in himself.[69] "His attainment of intellectual love," Francis Christensen has said, is "a kind of secular conversion" marking "the poet's entrance into his maturity" and involving (as Wordsworth goes on to describe in some detail) "the taming of the daring, the turbulent, the violent, the wilful in his nature." [70] That is, it involves the taming of the equivalent in Wordsworth's inner nature to the sublime aspects of external nature; for his own "soul," as he puts it, had been framed at birth to be "a rock with torrents roaring" (XIII, 221–32). It is possible to read the slackened power of these passages as a sign that Wordsworth feels less than the total assurance to which he aspires, and it is also possible to infer, from our knowledge of his later fate as a poet, that he has given up too much for too little. The conclusion of Wordsworth's theodicy, however, is not an extemporized argument, but is grounded in the beginning. And if this conclusion exhibits "optimism," it is of a kind which, far from denying the reality of pain, terror, and suffering, insists not only that they are humanly inevitable but that they are indispensable conditions for developing the calm, the insight, and the power that is ours when, as Wordsworth put it, we are worthy of ourselves.

In *The Prelude,* then, the justification of seeming evil turns on a crisis and inner transformation, parallel to Augustine's agony and conversion in the garden at Milan. An important difference is that in Augustine's account, although his spiritual preparation has been long, the conversion is instant and absolute, an accession of grace which takes place at a precise point in time, *"punctum ipsum temporis,"* and effects at a stroke the destruction of the old creature and the birth of the new. In Wordsworth's secular account of the "growth" of his mind, the process is one of gradual recovery which takes three books to tell in full; and for the Christian paradigm of right-angled change into something radically new he substitutes a pattern (the typical Romantic pattern, we shall see in the next chapter) in which development consists of a gradual curve back to an earlier stage, but on a higher level incorporating that which has intervened. "Behold me then," Wordsworth says, "Once more in Nature's presence, thus restored," although now "with memory left of what had been escaped" (XI, 393–6). But if in the overall accounting, by Wordsworth's calculation, the gain outweighs the loss, he does not deny that growth is change, and change entails loss. Nature, he says, "I seem'd to love as much as heretofore," and yet this passion

> Had suffer'd change; how could there fail to be
> Some change, if merely hence, that years of life
> Were going on, and with them loss or gain
> Inevitable, sure alternative.   (XI, 36–41)

There remains a second stage in Wordsworth's elaborate resolution, in the concluding book of *The Prelude,* of the problem of human suffering. Having recognized the general truth that love is first and last, he turns to the evaluation of the particular life that he has lived. Typically, as we have seen, he transforms that life into a landscape over which he soars in metaphoric flight; and from this high perspective he is able to discern that all its parts are centered in love, and that all its earthly sorrows are ultimately for the best:

>   Call back to mind
> The mood in which this Poem was begun,
> O Friend! the termination of my course
> Is nearer now, much nearer; yet even then
> In that distraction and intense desire
> I said unto the life which I had lived,
> Where art thou? Hear I not a voice from thee
> Which 'tis reproach to hear? Anon I rose
> As if on wings, and saw beneath me stretch'd
> Vast prospect of the world which I had been
> And was; and hence this Song, which like a lark
> I have protracted, in the unwearied Heavens
> Singing, and often with more plaintive voice
> Attemper'd to the sorrows of the earth;

> Yet centring all in love, and in the end
> All gratulant if rightly understood.[71]

This was, he says, the vision given him at the beginning of the poem, although what he now assays is his life as represented in his just-completed song, the work of art which is *The Prelude* itself. If we turn back to the poem's beginning, we find in its fifteenth line the first prominent instance of Wordsworth's carefully chosen and allocated allusions to *Paradise Lost*—a very striking instance, because in his opening he echoes the closing lines of Milton's epic, when Adam and Eve, between sadness and expectancy, leave paradise to take up their journey in this world of all of us:

> The World was all before them, where to choose
> Their place of rest, and Providence their guide:
> They hand in hand with wand'ring steps and slow,
> Through *Eden* took their solitary way.

"The earth is all before me," Wordsworth too says; but his mood is joyously confident, and he entrusts his guidance not to Providence but to nature:

> The earth is all before me: with a heart
> Joyous, nor scar'd at its own liberty,
> I look about, and should the guide I chuse
> Be nothing better than a wandering cloud,
> I cannot miss my way   (I, 15–19)

Critics who have noted this parallel interpret it to signify that *The Prelude* as a whole is a kind of sequel to *Paradise Lost;* "as if," Elizabeth Sewell has said, "Wordsworth meant to dovetail his epic directly into the very place where the Miltonic epic ends." [72] This, I think, is a mistake (although an easy one to make) for it overlooks the fact that, though the preamble comes first in the structural order of the *Prelude,* it inaugurates the stage of the narrator's life which comes last in its temporal order. It is not, then, *The Prelude* which Wordsworth meant to dovetail into the place in Milton's poem at which man, having lost paradise, sets out on his pilgrimage to recover it again, but the narrative which follows *The Prelude;* namely, the opening book of *The Recluse* proper, *Home at Grasmere,* in which the poet takes up the place of rest he has selected at the end of the preamble, when "I made a choice/ Of one sweet Vale whither my steps should turn" (I, 81–2).

On his first glimpse of this happy valley when, as a "roving schoolboy," he had overlooked it from the verge of a "steep barrier," it had appeared as a "paradise before him" (*Home at Grasmere,* lines 1–14), and now that he has returned to this "dear Vale,/ Beloved Grasmere," he describes it in terms which repeatedly echo Milton's description of Eden in *Paradise Lost* (e.g., lines 126 ff.). By "surpassing grace," however, his is an Eden happier far than Adam's original paradise, because it possesses an attribute which "among the bowers/ Of blissful Eden . . . was neither given,/ Nor could be given": it is a felicity that incorporates the memory of what it was to have lacked it (lines 103–9). Above all, his is a higher paradise than Milton's because it is inhabited by man as he is, exhibiting the mixed state "of solid good/ and real evil"; that is, it possesses the solid advantage of reality over "all golden fancies of the golden Age," whether located "before all time" or in some distant future "ere time expire" (lines 405–6, 625–32). The point that Wordsworth repeatedly makes in *Home at Grasmere* is his personal experience of a truth which, in the Prospectus concluding that poem, he announces as the argument for all *The Recluse:* that in our life in this actual world, with its ineradicable evil and suffering, lies the possibility, and the only possibility, of achieving a paradise which serves him, as it did Milton, to justify the evil of our mortal state.

At the conclusion of *The Prelude* itself, in justifying the sorrows which had fostered the growth of his mind as "in the end all gratulant," Wordsworth has completed his private "history" of "the discipline/ And consummation of the Poet's mind." But this poet, as he had said in the opening preamble, is a poet-prophet, "singled out, as it might seem,/ For holy services." He has, that is, a public role; and at the close Wordsworth calls upon his fellow poet Coleridge, to whom the whole account has been addressed, to serve with him in a recreant age as, quite explicitly, an evangelist of a new redemption. Though "this Age fall back to old idolatry," we shall be to men

> joint-labourers in a work
> (Should Providence such grace to us vouchsafe)
> Of their redemption, surely yet to come.
> Prophets of Nature, we to them will speak
> A lasting inspiration. . . .

But the prophet of nature at once proceeds to a coda which is a *gloria in excelsis* not to nature but to the mind of man. We will

> Instruct them how the mind of man becomes
> A thousand times more beautiful than the earth
> On which he dwells, above this Frame of things . . .
> In beauty exalted, as it is itself
> Of substance and of fabric more divine.
>
> (XIII, 431–52)

Thus he announces the end of his long preparation for writing his masterpiece. But in describing that preparation Wordsworth, no less than Proust, has achieved the masterpiece itself.

7. THE REDEMPTIVE IMAGINATION

I have reserved for separate consideration a crucial element in Wordsworth's theodicy of the mind in nature. During the revelation which precipitates the resolution of the argument, when in the prospect from Mount Snowdon the mind discovers itself in its highest workings, the poet discerns "a fracture in the vapour . . . through which/ Mounted the roar of waters, torrents, streams/ Innumerable."

> In that breach
> Through which the homeless voice of waters rose,
> That dark deep thoroughfare had Nature lodg'd
> The Soul, the Imagination of the whole.

And in the passage which follows, justifying fear, pain, and seeming evil as stemming from pervading love, he goes on to say that this love can neither exist nor triumph over evil except through the imagination as its complement and intermediator. "This love more intellectual cannot be/ Without Imagination" (or, more clearly by later revision, "This spiritual Love acts not nor can exist/ Without Imagination"),

> which, in truth,
> Is but another name for absolute strength
> And clearest insight, amplitude of mind,
> And reason in her most exalted mood.

Abruptly, Wordsworth now discloses that in his account of the transactions of mind and nature, the protagonist had in fact been this power of his mind, so that what he has all along been narrating is the story of the birth, growth, disappearance, and resurrection of imagination. He represents this faculty in the metaphor of a stream, which flows intermittently above and under ground:

> This faculty hath been the moving soul
> Of our long labour: we have traced the stream
> From darkness, and the very place of birth
> In its blind cavern, whence is faintly heard
> The sound of waters; follow'd it to light
> And open day, accompanied its course
> Among the ways of Nature, afterwards
> Lost sight of it, bewilder'd and engulph'd,
> Then given it greeting, as it rose once more
> With strength . . .
> And lastly, from its progress have we drawn
> The feeling of life endless, the great thought
> By which we live, Infinity and God.[73]

The crisis narrated in *The Prelude,* then, has been a crisis of imagination. "This History," as Wordsworth says, "hath chiefly told/ Of intellectual power, from stage to stage/ Advancing,"

> And of imagination teaching truth
> Until that natural graciousness of mind

Gave way to over-pressure of the times
And their disastrous issues.

(XI, 42–8)

Hence Wordsworth entitled the central Books XI and XII, on his crisis and recovery, "Imagination, How Impaired and Restored." Now, in the last book, he concludes his natural theodicy by describing imagination and intellectual love as two-in-one, distinct yet undivided entities:

Imagination having been our theme,
So also hath that intellectual love,
For they are each in each, and cannot stand
Dividually.—Here must thou be, O Man!
Strength to thyself; no Helper hast thou here. . . .

(XIII, 185–9)

If my explication of Wordsworth on imagination has been complicated, that is in part because—whether from the difficulty of what he had to say or from prudence in the way he chose to say it—Wordsworth's own account has been uncommonly abstruse. The immediate context, however, together with the overall pattern in *The Prelude* of insistent and coherent parallels with crucial passages in *Paradise Lost,* makes its tenor clear enough. The faculty of imagination is born, then goes underground, but only to rise "once more/ With strength"; it is distinct from, yet "each in each" with, the intellectual love which is "the first and chief" and in which "we begin and end"; and it is also the indispensable mediator by which love manifests that it abounds over pain and apparent evil, by saving the poet from "a universe of death" and opening the way to an earthly paradise. It is apparent, then, that in Wordsworth's sustained myth of mind in its interchange with nature, the imagination plays a role equivalent to that of the Redeemer in Milton's providential plot. For in Milton's theodicy it is the birth, death, and return of the risen Christ to save mankind and to restore a lost paradise which serves to demonstrate the "goodness infinite . . ./ That all this good of evil shall produce,/ And evil turn to good."

I do not mean to propose a strict correlation but only an

overall functional parallel between Milton's sacred story of
mankind and Wordsworth's secular account of the growth of
an individual mind; nor can we be certain that Wordsworth
deliberately assigned to imagination the Redeemer's role in his
asserted enterprise, as one of the "Prophets of Nature," to write
a poetic work "Of [men's] redemption, surely yet to come."
Yet as late as 1812, after he had adopted some Christian tenets,
Wordsworth remarked to Henry Crabb Robinson that "he
could not feel with the Unitarians in any way. Their religion
allows no room for imagination, and satisfies none of the crav-
ings of the soul. 'I can feel more sympathy with the orthodox
believer who needs a Redeemer.' " But then he added, "I have
no need of a Redeemer"—a declaration which so startled the
usually liberal-minded Robinson that he veiled it in the decent
obscurity of his private shorthand.[74] At any rate, the high
argument of *The Prelude* of 1805 had no need for an external
Redeemer, because in that poem the function had been vested
in a power of the unaided mind of man. As Wordsworth goes
on to say, with extraordinary emphasis and iteration:

> Here must thou be, O Man!
> Strength to thyself; no Helper hast thou here;
> Here keepest thou thy individual state:
> No other can divide with thee this work,
> No secondary hand can intervene
> To fashion this ability; 'tis thine,
> The prime and vital principle is thine
> In the recesses of thy nature, far
> From any reach of outward fellowship,
> Else 'tis not thine at all.   (XIII, 188–97)

In this aspect Wordsworth's *Prelude* participates, however
guardedly, in a major intellectual tendency of his age, and of
ours. In the seventeenth century the radical spiritualist Gerrard Winstanley had looked forward to the "latter dayes" when
such outer fictions as "the Lamb held forth at a distance to be
our Mediatour, should all cease"; for "Christ within the heart
. . . delivers mankind from bondage; *And besides him there
is no Saviour.*" [75] William Blake, who placed his faith in the
redemptive power of man's divine creativity, characteristically

put a concept, implicit in *The Prelude,* in the startling form of an express identification: "Imagination . . . is the Divine Body of the Lord Jesus, blessed for ever." [76] In Germany, Novalis, speaking of art, declared that "in his works and in his acts and failures to act," man "proclaims himself and his evangel of nature. He is the Messiah of nature." [77] Goethe looked upon his works of imagination as a mode of redemption not of nature, but of himself; in writing *Götz von Berlichingen* and *Clavigo,* he said, "I carried on the poetic confession which I had already begun, so that by this self-tormenting penance I might become worthy of an inner absolution." [78] "The tragedy," declared a later heir of Romantic thought, Friedrich Nietzsche, "is that we cannot believe the dogmas of religion and metaphysics" yet continue to "need the highest kind of means of salvation and consolation"; and by a drastic exercise of the principle of parsimony, he canceled the role of nature as well as God, leaving only one agent to play out the ancient spiritual plot:

> Just take one step farther; love yourself through Grace; then you are no longer in need of your God, and the whole drama of fall and redemption is acted out in yourself.[79]

Modern poetry, Wallace Stevens said, is "the poem of the mind in the act of finding/ What will suffice." It turns out that nothing less will suffice than the crucial experience for which earlier poets had relied on an intervenient deity: "After one has abandoned a belief in god, poetry is that essence which takes its place as life's redemption." Stevens draws a conclusion which is formally equivalent to that of Blake: "We say God and the imagination are one." His claim for the efficacy of that imagination, however, is a good deal more modest than Blake's: "How high that highest candle lights the dark." [80] W. B. Yeats saw all of modern literature moving along the path laid out by Nietzsche:

> The individual soul, the betrayal of the unconceived at birth, are among her principal themes, it must go further still; that soul must become its own betrayer, its own deliverer, the one activity, the mirror turn lamp.[81]

Some of Yeats's own poems exhibit the sufficiency of the individual soul to act out the whole drama of fall and redemption, until "all hatred driven hence,/ The soul recovers radical innocence." In Yeats's chief poem of autonomous grace, Wordsworth's two terms have been reduced to one, so that the colloquy is no longer between mind and nature but between antithetic aspects of the single mind: "A Dialogue of Self and Soul." Deaf to the soul's summons to reject life for beatitude, Yeats's Self reviews his life of error and suffering, in a passage comparable to Wordsworth's visionary flight over his remembered life near the close of *The Prelude:*

> I am content to follow to its source,
> Every event in action or in thought;
> Measure the lot; forgive myself the lot!
> When such as I cast out remorse
> So great a sweetness flows into the breast
> We must laugh and we must sing,
> We are blest by everything,
> Everything we look upon is blest.[82]

Yeats sees his life and the world he looks upon as all gratulant, although not by a Wordsworthian but by a Nietzschean act of heroic self-forgiveness and self-redemption.

8. THE NEW MYTHUS: WORDSWORTH, KEATS, AND CARLYLE

Both the genre of *The Prelude* and its representative character were more obvious to some discerning Victorian readers than to many readers of our own time. The Reverend F. D. Maurice wrote to Charles Kingsley in 1851:

> I am sure that you are right, Wordsworth's Prelude seems to me the dying utterance of the half century we have just passed through, the expression—the English expression at least—of all that self-building process in which, according to their different schemes and principles, Byron, Goethe, Wordsworth, the Evangelicals (Protestant and Romanist), were all engaged, which their novels, poems, experiences, prayers, were setting

forth, in which God, under whatever name, or in whatever aspect, He presented Himself to them, was still the agent only in fitting them to be world-wise, men of genius, artists, saints.[83]

Since *The Prelude* had been published only the year before, Maurice makes the natural error of putting it at the end rather than at the beginning of the tendency he describes (and deprecates), but he is right about the currency of the Christian confession converted into the form of a *Bildungsgeschichte* which, whether ostensibly religious or openly secular, long or short, in verse or in prose, points toward a culmination which is comprehended within life itself. The major lyric innovation of the Romantic period, for example, the extended poems of description and meditation, are in fact fragments of reshaped autobiography, in which the poet confronts a particular scene at a significant stage of his life, in a colloquy that specifies the present, evokes the past, and anticipates the future, and thereby defines and evaluates what it means to have suffered and to grow older. In some of these poems the confrontation occurs at a time of spiritual crisis which is called "dejection" (the *acedia, deiectio,* or spiritual aridity of the Christian experts of the interior life); and the ancient struggle for the blessedness of reconciliation with an alienated God becomes the attempt to recover in maturity an earlier stage of integrity with oneself and the outer world, in a mode of consciousness for which the standard name is "joy."

We shall later observe how pervasive, in longer works of philosophy, fiction, drama, and narrative poetry, was the Romantic theme of the justification of evil and suffering, represented in the plot-form of a circuitous yet progressive self-education, self-discovery, and the discovery of vocation, in a life which terminates in this world. Now, in the context of Wordsworth's *Prelude,* I want to glance at two other English instances of the crisis-autobiography represented in a fictional form, Keats's *Fall of Hyperion* and Carlyle's *Sartor Resartus;* for the disparities among these three works, written over a period of more than three decades, throw into bold relief the attributes, both in concept and design, which are their common possession.

Keats did not have access to *The Prelude,* but he studied carefully *Tintern Abbey* and the *Intimations Ode,* as well as Wordsworth's program in the Prospectus published with *The Excursion,* and the long and superficially Christianized debate on "Despondency" and "Despondency Corrected" in *The Excursion* itself. By that leap of insight familiar to the readers of his letters, Keats recognized that Wordsworth's persisting concern was to justify the experience of loss and suffering in terms of a purpose that is immanent in the mind's growth into maturity. He also recognized that Wordsworth had deliberately elected to take up this problem where Milton had left it off.

"The Burden of the Mystery" Keats called the problem of the justification of suffering, in a phrase taken from *Tintern Abbey;* and in a letter of May 1818, he undertook to explore the problem as a secular theodicy of the individual life as it moves through successive stages of experience and insight. In his version of the great trope of life as a journey, he posits "a large Mansion of Many Apartments" in which we move from "the infant or thoughtless Chamber" to "the Chamber of Maiden-Thought"; but then, by a sharpened vision into the human heart and by "convincing ones nerves that the World is full of Misery and Heartbreak," we arrive at a stage of darkness, when "we see not the ballance of good and evil." "To this point was Wordsworth come . . . when he wrote 'Tintern Abbey.' " But even in going so far "I must think Wordsworth is deeper than Milton" because he has profited from the general "advance of intellect"; and this advance, Keats makes clear, is the movement from Christian supernaturalism to agnostic humanism. For Milton's "hintings at good and evil in the Paradise Lost" were grounded still on the "remaining Dogmas and superstitions" which survived the Protestant Reformation; thus "he did not think into the human heart, as Wordsworth has done." [84]

In a letter he wrote a year later, Keats sketched his own scheme for validating suffering as a necessary discipline toward a greater good. His metaphor now is of the world as "the vale of Soul-making," in which the function of suffering is to subject the native human "intelligence or Mind" to the knowledge and stresses (the phrasing is strikingly modern) which gradually

form its "identity." "Do you not see how necessary a World of
Pains and troubles is to school an Intelligence and make it a
soul?"—in the sense that intelligences are merely unformed and
unindividuated egos: "are not Souls till they acquire identities,
till each one is personally itself." Such a theodicy of the individual life on earth, as opposed to the Christian view of the
world as a place "from which we are to be redeemed by a certain arbitrary interposition of God and taken to Heaven,"
Keats says, is "a faint sketch of a system of Salvation which
does not affront our reason and humanity." [85] In this way Keats,
like the contemporary German philosophers and poets whom he
had not read, explicitly translated the theological system of
salvation into a secular system of progressive education.

In estimating where Wordsworth stood relative to Milton in
exploring "those dark Passages," Keats had promised that "if
we live, and go on thinking, we too shall explore them." [86] Just
this is what he undertook to do in the poem *Hyperion*, some
five or six months after writing the first of his two remarkable
letters; it is apparent that as Wordsworth had set out to emulate
and pass beyond Milton in his intention "to weigh/ The good
and evil of our mortal state," so Keats set out to emulate and
pass beyond Milton and the "deeper" Wordsworth as well, in
gauging what he called "the ballance of good and evil."

Hyperion is a Miltonic epic, but it embodies its inquiry into
the rationale of evil in a Greco-Roman myth, substituting for
Milton's "loss of Eden" its pagan analogue, the loss of the
Saturnian Golden Age. As it opens "Saturn is fallen" (I, 234),
the god who had exercised his "influence benign" in "all those
acts which Deity supreme/ Doth ease its heart of love in"; so
that now "the days of peace and slumberous calm are fled" (I,
108–12; II, 335). Again and again Saturn asks the question,
Why? Who? How? What justification can there be in the course
of things for the destruction of the easy felicity of the Golden
Age, through the overthrow of its blameless deities?—and he
answers despairingly that he cannot "find reason why ye should
be thus:/ No, no-where can unriddle" (1, 112 ff., 227 ff.; II,
128 ff.). Oceanus proffers a solution which is in accord with
pagan Stoicism: "we fall by course of Nature's law" that "first
in beauty should be first in might," and this truth must simply

be faced and accepted, for "to bear all naked truths . . . all calm,/ That is the top of sovereignty" (II, 181–229). This answer, however, though not invalid, is insufficient, and the narrative moves toward the revelation that suffering, even when undeserved, is explicable not merely by a natural law, but by a moral principle as well. Saturn and his fellow Titans had ruled in high and unfeeling simplicity, "solemn, undisturb'd/ Un-ruffled, like high Gods" (I, 330–1); and though they now suffer humanlike passion and anguish, it is without human under-standing, in the absence of what Keats, in his letter on the "Mansion of Many Apartments," had called "the human heart." Thea can only press her hand

> upon that aching spot
> Where beats the human heart, as if just there,
> Though an immortal, she felt cruel pain.
> (I, 42–4)

As soon as Apollo makes his delayed appearance he reveals why he deserves his preeminence over Hyperion, for though he too lives "in aching ignorance," he feels "curs'd and thwarted" by his ignorance and is avid and active in his desire for knowledge. Suddenly he reads in the face of Mnemosyne, goddess of memory—who is to be mother of the muses and so of all the arts—the history of the undeserved defeat of the Titans, and discovers the knowledge he seeks. This knowledge is the knowledge of good and evil, in a sudden expansion of consciousness to the recognition that all process entails loss, and that there can be no creative progress except through the painful destruction, however unmerited, of the preceding stage:

> Knowledge enormous makes a God of me.
> Names, deeds, gray legends, dire events, rebellions,
> Majesties, sovran voices, agonies,
> Creations and destroyings, all at once
> Pour into the wide hollows of my brain,
> And deify me. . . .   (III, 91–118)

Apollo becomes truly a god (and so, by the grim justice of the immanent rationale of things, unintentionally effects the overthrow of the innocent Hyperion) only by willingly assuming humanity and its burden of the mystery that through loss and suffering alone can we rise from simple and ignorant innocence to the higher identity of a more inclusive, complex, and integral awareness. As the fragment breaks off Apollo experiences the application of this principle to himself, in the ordeal of dying to the stage of ignorance in order to be born to the stage of mature knowledge, like one who should "with fierce convulse/ Die into life." And since Apollo is "the Father of all verse" (III, 13), he is reborn not only as god of the sun, successor to Hyperion, but also as the god of tragic poetry, the high genre which, in this very poem, displaces the simple pastoralism of the Golden Age.

Between dropping this work in April of 1819 and taking it up again late that summer, Keats had clarified his "system of Salvation" in his second letter, on the Vale of Soul-making. *The Fall of Hyperion* transfers the locus in which the burden of the mystery is unriddled from the ordeal of the growing mind of the god of poetry to the ordeal of the growing mind of the poet himself, as he moves through stages of experience to the discovery of his poetic identity and status. Keats does this by assimilating his Miltonic epic to the form of an earlier theodicy, Dante's dream-vision, *The Divine Comedy,* which had reconciled evil and suffering with God's justice not in a third-person narrative, but in an allegorical account of the narrator's own progress through hell and purgatory to heaven. In a creative application of the medieval convention, Keats begins *The Fall of Hyperion* with a long Induction in which he presents himself, the narrator, as the sentient center of the poem, who is transformed by experiencing a vision within the double dream that he narrates. The initial dream is that of a garden in which the poet eats and drinks of a feast which "seem'd refuse of a meal/ By angel tasted or our Mother Eve" (I, 29–30), falls asleep, and awakens into a second dream in which the garden has vanished, and has been replaced by an ancient sanctuary, within which a flight of stairs leads up to the altar of Moneta (who incorporates and replaces Mnemosyne, the Titaness of the earlier poem). The narrator goes on to justify his loss of Eden as in some sense a fortunate fall, but he

translates the theodicy of his private life into the form of a
pagan mystery-ritual of death, rebirth, and salvation by means
of an initiation into *gnosis,* a secret knowledge.

As he approaches, then touches, the lowest stair, the poet
feels "what 'tis to die and live again before/ Thy fated hour."
The colloquy with Moneta that follows serves to epitomize and
to project in dramatic form an extended process of self-formation, self-analysis, and self-discovery in the poet's inner life.
Moneta's evolving challenges, in the form of charges against
his deficiencies, and the responses he makes to these charges,
recapitulate the progressive stages of his development and
manifest his expanding awareness of what it is to be a poet
instead of a dreamer, then to be a poet who feels "the giant
agony of the world," and then one who, instead of simply
venoming all his days, aspires to be "a sage;/ A humanist,
Physician to all men." Thus tested, he wins to the stage at
which he is able to endure, "without stay or prop/ But my own
weak mortality," the vision that Moneta finally grants him of
the fallen and innocently suffering Titans (I, 145–210; 388–9).
By demonstrating his readiness and capacity to endure the
burden of the tragic knowledge that human growth and creativity entail correspondent loss and suffering, the narrator has
established his identity as a poet and defined the kind of poet
that he is, and so earned the power, though remaining a mortal
man (line 304), "to see as a God sees"; that is, with compassion,
yet with aesthetic distance. By that fact he has also earned
the right to essay his epic poem of tragic suffering.[87]

The Induction to *The Fall of Hyperion* is much closer to
Wordsworth's achievement than Keats could know, for it is a
Prelude in miniature which sets forth, immediately preparatory
to his major poetic undertaking, the discipline and consummation of the poet's mind. It represents these events not as autobiography, but in the fiction of a *rite de passage.* In Keats's
condensed and ritual form, however, as in Wordsworth's expanded and realistic account, the growth of the poet's mind
turns on a crisis in which he achieves and recognizes his poetic
identity and mission; incorporates the justification of pain as
indispensable to his coming of age both as a man and as a
poet of suffering humanity; involves the clarification to him of

his own poetics and of the great poet's high office as sage, humanist, and physician to all men; and issues in the genesis of the epic poem that the poet envisions and goes on, at the end, to narrate. And while there is more than one compelling reason why Keats gave up this latter enterprise, it is a probable conjecture that, just as Wordsworth found that he had absorbed into the *Prelude* to *The Recluse*—his account of "the transitory Being that beheld/ This Vision"—the material which was to have been the vital center of *The Recluse* itself, so Keats, in setting forth the growth of the poet's own mind by way of Induction to his epic, found that he had expended his material for the central element of the epic proper: the growth to tragic understanding of Apollo, the father of all verse.

Carlyle's *Sartor Resartus* recounted the "self-building process" of one of the spirits F. D. Maurice ironically denominated "men of genius," as distinguished from "artists." It is much more fictional than Wordsworth's *Prelude,* but also much closer to their common theological prototypes, in the abundant genre of spiritual histories in the seventeenth and eighteenth centuries, as well as in the exemplary *Confessions* of Augustine himself.[88] Carlyle set out, very explicitly, to salvage the primary forms of Christian experience in a world which had to make do without the traditional Creator and Redeemer. "The Mythus of the Christian Religion looks not in the eighteenth century as it did in the eighth," so that he must undertake, in an iron age, "to embody the divine Spirit of that Religion in a new Mythus, in a new vehicle and vesture, that our Souls, otherwise too like perishing, may live." This new mythus, whose "one Bible" is that which is "felt in my own heart," [89] is a mythus without a creed, and aims at a salvation which is the stage of mature consciousness: the achievement of the secure spiritual stance toward oneself and the universe that Carlyle calls "the Everlasting Yea."

Sartor is also a radical experiment in artistic form; but unlike *The Prelude,* whose innovations are unobtrusive and easily overlooked, it is so blatantly eccentric that it is readily misestimated as a freak in the history of prose narrative. In literary genealogy it is a cross between Augustine's *Confessions* and that progenitor of all anti-novels, Sterne's *Tristram Shandy;* for it is a serious parody of the spiritual autobiography which plays with and undercuts the conventions it nonetheless accepts. Augustine's two selves, and Wordsworth's "two consciousnesses," are split by Carlyle into separate literary personae. One is Diogenes Teufelsdroeckh, German author of an enigmatic work on *Die Kleider, ihr Werden und Wirken;* the other is his British editor and biographer, who knows the outcome of the life from the outset, but must, in honest bewilderment, struggle to interpret the book and to construct a coherent total biography from the only available data, the almost illegible autobiographical scribblings which Teufelsdroeckh had penned at various stages and had left, in chronological confusion, in "Six considerable PAPER-BAGS, carefully sealed, and marked successively, in gilt China-ink, with the symbols of the Six southern Zodiacal Signs" (pp. 77–9). *Sartor* had no close equivalent until such serio-perverse manipulations of the self-reflexive work of fiction as André Gide's *The Counterfeiters,* which (in Harry Levin's succinct description) is "the diary of a novelist who is writing a novel about a novelist who is keeping a diary about the novel he is writing." [90] A more recent and pre-eminently complex exponent of the genre is Vladimir Nabokov. *Pale Fire,* for example, is the bizarre revelation of his own life by a demented editor who ostensibly recounts the life of a poet in the process of editing the poet's autobiographic poem; it is a work in which everything is done with mirrors—an indefinite regress of mutually reflective and fantastically distorting mirrors.

The devices of the double authorship, the work-within-the-work, and the paper bags provide Carlyle with the literary excuse to violate calendar time in the life of Teufelsdroeckh by leaps and returns which seem random but in fact bring out its immanent and evolving design. Through the shifting perspectives, the temporal oscillations, and the tenebrous rhetoric, we make out a familiar Romantic metaphysic and life history.[91] An I confronts the not-I: "You are alone with the Universe, and silently commune with it, as one mysterious Presence with another" (p. 53). In this subject-object transaction the mind is primary and prepotent, and is sometimes represented as the sole ground of experience; "our ME," as Teufelsdroeckh says, "the only reality: and Nature, with its thousandfold production and destruction, but the reflex of our own inward Force" (p. 55). Despite its subsidiary status, however, nature is described as "thousand-voiced," a "God-written Apocalypse" which "speaks" to the prepared spirit by means of "symbols." [92] Existence begins in the stage of "Happy Childhood" for which "Kind Nature . . . a bountiful mother" has provided "a soft swathing of Love and infinite Hope" in a "fair Life-garden" (pp. 90–1). From this Eden the protagonist is expelled by the perfidy of his beloved Blumine; and this experience is followed by the erosion of all his inherited certainties, as a consequence of succumbing to the analytic procedure and skeptical rationalism of eighteenth-century thought. Having lost all traditional supports, the mind moves into the "Everlasting No" of what Carlyle calls its "Fever-crisis" (p. 157), taking a spiritual beating whose savagery has rarely been equaled in the long history of Christian soul-crises. "Falling, falling, towards the Abyss" (p. 146), the protagonist "turns pilgrim" and carries out an "extraordinary world-pilgrimage" (pp. 146–7, 152), which is the outer correlate of an agonized inner journey and quest. The first stage of this journey is through a spiritual hell, a "Gehenna . . . within," which correspondently transforms the outer universe, "God's fair living world," into "a pallid, vacant Hades and extinct Pandemonium" (pp. 148, 114). In such a lifeless world, as in a "Golgotha, and Mill of Death," he "walked solitary; and (except as it was my own heart, not another's, that I kept devouring) savage also, as the tiger in his jungle" (p. 164). Like his late-Romantic contemporary, Kierkegaard, Teufelsdroeckh experiences the *Angst* of existence—"I lived in a continual, indefinite, pining fear . . . apprehensive of I knew not what . . . as if the Heavens and the Earth were but boundless jaws of a devouring monster" (p. 166)—as well as spiritual nausea, "the fordone soul drowning slowly in quagmires of Disgust!" (p. 164).

The "turning-point of the battle" (p. 185) occurs without forewarning, in a sudden breakthrough in the "dirty little *Rue Saint-Thomas de l'Enfer,*" when the thought of defiance "rushed like a stream of fire over my whole soul; and I shook base Fear away from me forever." "It is from this hour that I incline to date my Spiritual New-birth"—a crisis and recovery which he equates with dying to youth to be reborn to early maturity: "Perhaps I directly thereupon began to be a Man" (pp. 166–8, 185). After a series of "Temptations in the Wilderness," the process culminates in a spiritual event of self-destruction and re-creation, described in explicit analogy to the Biblical Apocalypse. In a deep and healing sleep the "Annihilation of Self" was finally accomplished, and "I awoke to a new Heaven and a new Earth." But this new earth is simply the old earth redeemed by the mind of man, whom Carlyle, following Novalis, calls "the 'Messias of Nature'" (pp. 186, 220). Like other writers in the tradition of the Augustinian confession, Carlyle has throughout been occupied with the relation of time to eternity; now he is able to discern that eternity lies all about us, if we but succeed in piercing through the perceptual illusions, or cognitive "Thought-forms," of "Space and Time" (pp. 260–6).

These events raise the problem of what is "at present called Origin of Evil," an ever-recurring question which each age must resolve anew, "for it is man's nature to change his Dialect from century to century; he cannot help it though he would." Carlyle's solution is very much in the dialect of his own age, for it transfers the problem of theodicy to the private life, and justifies sorrow and suffering as the necessary conditions for achieving the wisdom, resignation, and power of insight which are the attributes of maturity. But where Wordsworth's justification of the discipline of suffering had its roots in Christian Stoicism, Carlyle's is a secular version of the ancient recourse to the Passion of Christ as paradigm. To Carlyle the wisdom of maturity is based on the recognition of the sacredness of suffering and "Divine Depth of Sorrow," and also on the renunciation of "pleasure" and the "Love of Happiness" in order instead to "find Blessedness" through a salutary and self-validating "Worship of Sorrow."

To the *"Worship of Sorrow"* ascribe what origin and genesis thou pleasest, *has* not that Worship originated, and been generated; is it not *here?* Feel it in thy heart, and then say whether it is of God! (pp. 189–94)

Despite his reversion to the Augustinian conversion in an instant of time, Carlyle sees the overall history of his protagonist in accordance with the Romantic model of stages of growth to maturity. We have "followed Teufelsdroeckh through the various successive states and stages of Growth . . . into a certain clearer state of what he himself seems to consider as Conversion," in which his "spiritual majority . . . commences" (pp. 198–9). And this spiritual majority, we are told, had to be achieved "before his apostolic work . . . could begin." His crisis thus turns out to have been a crisis of identity, resolved in the discovery that there had been a hidden design shaping his life toward the vocation of "Authorship as his divine calling." "Awake arise! Speak forth what is in thee," in an "Art" which is also a "Priesthood"; for it is an art used, as the editor says near the end, to marshal the "Happy few! little band of Friends" to join with him in the "highest work of Palingenesia," of which the aim is nothing less than the "Newbirth of Society" (pp. 185, 198–200, 268–70).

All this while the editor has been more and more assuming the ideas and accent of his author. The book closes with the ironic hint that its two personae, the unruly protagonist and his dogged biographer, may in fact be one, and that this one may even now be in London, laboring at his apostolic work of man's spiritual redemption. In "these dark times" of the Paris revolution of 1830, Teufelsdroeckh has disappeared from his haunt in the coffee-house *Zur Grünen Gans* in the town of Weissnichtwo, leaving as his last cryptic words *"Es geht an* (It is beginning)"—that is, the French Revolutionary song, *Ça ira.* He is "again to all appearance lost in space!" but

our own private conjecture, now amounting almost to certainty, is that, safe-moored in some stillest obscurity, not to lie always still, Teufelsdroeckh is actually London!

(pp. 292–7)

Carlyle wrote his remarkable book in 1830–31, twenty-five years after *The Prelude* was completed, but twenty years before it was published. In dwelling on the parallels between these two works, we must not forget how wide is the division between the Romantic poet-seer and the Victorian prophet. As an indication of their difference, we might note that Wordsworth's evangel centers in a visionary quietism—"the calm mood of holy indolence/ A most wise passiveness"—but that Carlyle's issues in a strenuous economic activism: "Up and work!" "Produce! Produce!" [93]

9. WORDSWORTH AS EVANGELIST

Admirers of Wordsworth who hold the modern view of poetry as poetry and not another thing go counter to his claim in the Prospectus to sing "of blessed consolations in distress," in the prayer that his verse may "chear/ Mankind in times to come." [94] But for the most sensitive critics in the generation or so after Wordsworth's death, it was precisely his extraordinary success in bringing consolation to a "time of dereliction and dismay" that gave him a status below only Shakespeare and Milton. Matthew Arnold asked in *Memorial Verses,*

> Where will Europe's latter hour
> Again find Wordsworth's healing power?

Leslie Stephen held that "Wordsworth is the only poet who will bear reading in times of distress," and that his persistent concern with the possibility of transmuting sorrow into strength is "the single topic which . . . can really be called consolatory." What he does, said John Morley, "is to assuage, to reconcile, to fortify . . . to give us quietness." [95] More than this: Wordsworth in the Prospectus had undertaken to "arouse the sensual from their sleep/ Of death" (echoing Psalm 13, in which awakening from "the sleep of death" is paralleled to "salvation"); and *The Prelude* begins with the claim that he is "singled out, as it might seem,/ For holy services" and ends with the behest to Coleridge to carry on with him, as a prophet of nature and of the mind of man, the work of men's "redemption, surely yet to come." It is interesting to inquire: to what extent did Wordsworth succeed as an evangelist of nature and mind?

Wordsworth's first recorded success was with Coleridge himself, on whom he called to be the Virgil of his pilgrimage through his inner life:

> A Traveller I am,
> And all my Tale is of myself. . .
> . . . And Thou, O honor'd Friend!
> Who in my thoughts art ever at my side,
> Uphold, as heretofore, my fainting steps.[96]

But it was Coleridge who faltered—in fact, he had begun to falter even before Wordsworth asked him to uphold his fainting steps. And when in January 1807 Coleridge, sunk in spiritual torpor, first heard the poet read his *Prelude* through, he recorded the event in the ode *To William Wordsworth*, a remarkable summary of that "more than historic, that prophetic lay" as it appeared to one who had played an important part in its genesis. Coleridge called it an "Orphic song" (line 45), and given Coleridge's interest in the Orphic mysteries and his precision in language, Professor Stallknecht may be right in taking the phrase to imply that the poet has been revived from spiritual death by his own song.[97] As Coleridge listened, at any rate, it effected in him an unmistakable, if temporary, passage from the sleep of death back to life:

> Ah! as I listened with a heart forlorn,
> The pulses of my being beat anew:
> And even as Life returns upon the drowned,
> Life's joy rekindling roused a throng of pains—
> Keen pangs of Love, awakening as a babe
> Turbulent, with an outcry in the heart.

And when the reading was over, "I found myself in prayer."

John Stuart Mill's *Autobiography* is an austerely secular account of his intellectual development—the autobiography of a steam engine, Carlyle called it. Yet its fifth chapter, "A

Crisis in My Mental History. One Stage Onward," shows that even a steam engine can break down. The title of the chapter also indicates that Mill, like Carlyle himself, adapted the Augustinian crisis-pattern to the contemporary design of life as ascending stages of self-formation. Mill compared the sudden and total apathy and anomie into which he fell at the age of twenty to the state "in which converts to Methodism usually are, when smitten by their first 'conviction of sin.' . . . I seemed to have nothing left to live for"; and he illustrated his condition by lines from Coleridge's crisis-poem, *Dejection: An Ode:* "A grief without a pang, void, dark and drear." The first relief from his "dry heavy dejection" came with the reading of a scene from Marmontel's *Mémoires*—significantly, for a son dominated by an autocratic father, the scene in which young Marmontel, his father newly dead, gives his family to feel, as Mill says, that he "would supply the place of all that they had lost." But even more decisive for his recovery was his introduction to Wordsworth's collective *Poems* of 1815. These were "a medicine," says Mill, "for my state of mind," because they represented the interchange between nature and mind; or in Mill's associationist terms, because "they expressed, not mere outward beauty, but states of feeling, and of thought colored by feeling, under the excitement of beauty." Especially important was the *Intimations Ode,* in which Mill recognized the design of crisis, loss, and compensatory gain attendant upon the growth from youth into maturity. In the *Ode*

> I found that he too had had similar experience to mine; that he also had felt that the first freshness of youthful enjoyment of life was not lasting; but that he had sought for compensation, and found it, in the way in which he was now teaching me to find it. The result was that I gradually, but completely, emerged from my habitual depression, and was never again subject to it.[98]

Wordsworth's poetry also played a role in the genre of Victorian confessions of despair and recovery, of conversion and deconversion. *The Autobiography of Mark Rutherford* is the semi-fictional account of his own life by William Hale White, one of the numerous men of the age who broke free from evangelicalism by a reverse form of the conversion experience which was central to evangelical piety. The book, like Mill's *Autobiography,* was written before *The Prelude* was published, and the immediate agency for White's experience was an encounter with Wordsworth's *Lyrical Ballads.* These poems hardly seem radical to us, but only because Wordsworth's revolutionary program for poetry has been so thoroughly successful. On William Cullen Bryant, for example, *Lyrical Ballads* had something of the effect Wordsworth intended, to arouse the reader from the sleep of death and reveal a new heaven and earth. "I shall never forget," wrote Richard Henry Dana in 1833, "with what feeling my friend Bryant, some years ago, described to me the effect produced upon him [when still young] by his meeting for the first time with Wordsworth's Ballads. . . . He said, that upon opening Wordsworth, a thousand springs seemed to gush up at once in his heart, and the face of nature, of a sudden, to change into a strange freshness and life." [99] On William Hale White the effect of these poems was a conversion from the Christianity of his childhood, in an experience which he defined by reference to the prototype of all conversions to Christianity: "It conveyed to me no new doctrine, and yet the change it wrought in me could only be compared with that which is said to have been wrought on Paul himself by the Divine apparition" on the road to Damascus. In Wordsworth, White said, "God is nowhere formally deposed"; yet the deity in a personal form has faded away, leaving his attributes to be assimilated by nature, which is then confronted by a mind with an appropriately altered attitude:

Instead of an object of worship which was altogether artificial, remote. . . God was brought from that heaven of the books, and dwelt on the downs in the far-away distances, and in every cloud-shadow which wandered across the valley. Wordsworth unconsciously did for me what every religious reformer has done,—he re-created my Supreme Divinity.[100]

Wordsworth, as we know, declared that all his poems relate to the high argument he set forth in the Prospectus. Which of Wordsworth's writings has in fact served his prophetic enterprise has varied with the temper and needs of the individual reader, as well as with the works available to him. When John Stuart Mill "looked into the Excursion" he "found little in it." [101] But when William James fell into a spiritual crisis, it was "the immortal Wordsworth's *Excursion*" [102] which helped rescue him. The symptoms of his soul sickness, which began in the autumn of 1869, are familiar to us—"a disgust for life," the loss of all feeling of conviction, the ebbing of the will to carry on, and a weariness with the burden of the mystery which tempts him to yield up moral questions in despair. "Today I about touched bottom, and perceive plainly that I must face the choice with open eyes: shall I *frankly* throw the moral business overboard, as one unsuited to my innate aptitudes, or shall I follow it and it alone. . . ?" "Can one with full knowledge and sincerely ever bring one's self so to sympathize with the total process of the universe as heartily to assent to the evil that seems inherent in its details?" By March of 1873, however, the father was able to report to Henry James his brother's spiritual rebirth:

> He came in here the other afternoon when I was sitting alone, and . . . exclaimed "Dear me! What a difference there is between me now and me last spring this time. . . . It is the difference between death and life." . . . I ventured to ask what specially in his opinion had promoted the change. He said several things: the reading of Renouvier (specially his vindication of the freedom of the will) and Wordsworth, whom he has been feeding upon now for a good while.[103]

That the power of Wordsworth's evangel has not in our time been exhausted is shown by an autobiography published in the 1950s, Bede Griffiths' *The Golden String*. "One of the decisive events of my life," the author tells us in his Prologue, occurred on an evening of his last term at school, when the chorus of birds, the sight of hawthorns in full bloom, the soar and song of a lark struck him with a surprise as great as though he "had been brought suddenly among the trees of the Garden of Paradise." "It was as though I had begun to see and smell and hear for the first time. The world appeared to me as Wordsworth describes it with 'the glory and the freshness of a dream,' " and nature "began to wear a kind of sacramental character for me."

> As time went on this kind of worship of nature began to take the place of any other religion. . . . I had begun to read the romantic poets, Wordsworth, Shelley and Keats, and I found in them the record of an experience like my own. They became my teachers and my guides, and I gradually gave up my adherence to any form of Christianity.[104]

Among these Romantic "prophets" of a "new religion," he later makes clear, Wordsworth was *facile princeps*. "The religion of Wordsworth, as I found it expressed in the 'Prelude' and in the 'Lines Written Above Tintern Abbey' had a deeper meaning for me than anything else I had ever known, because it came nearer to my own experience." Later in his development, however, came a time when "the splendour of St. Augustine's *Confessions* broke upon me" and "penetrated into the depths of my soul."

> It is only now after thirty years that the full meaning of that which was revealed to me that day at school has become clear to me. That mysterious Presence which I felt in all the forms of nature has gradually disclosed itself as the infinite and eternal Being, of whose beauty all the forms of nature are but a passing reflection. . . . I know now the meaning of St. Augustine's words, "O thou Beauty, so ancient and so new, too late have I loved thee, too late have I loved thee." . . . I had sought him in the solitude of nature and in the labour of my mind, but I found him in the society of his Church and in the Spirit of Charity. And all this came to me not so much as a discovery but as a recognition.[105]

All process, Romantic thinkers believed, moves forward and also rounds back. Wordsworth's absorption of the personal God into a sacramental nature in communion with an apotheosized faculty of mind, which had resolved his own crisis and assisted other men to resolve theirs, and which had converted Mill from Benthamism and William Hale White from Augustinianism, now helped put Bede Griffiths on the way back to the prototype of the mind's religious colloquy with nature. You will recall the passage in which Augustine addressed himself to the speaking face of earth and heaven:

> And I said to all the things that throng about the gateways of the senses: "Tell me of my God, since you are not He." . . . And they cried out in a great voice: "He made us." My question was my gazing upon them, and their answer was their beauty.

THREE

The Circuitous Journey: Pilgrims and Prodigals

In the circumference of a circle beginning and end coincide.
—Heraclitus

Hoc tantum notantum esse admoneo, quomodo omnis theologia circularis et in circulo posita existit.
—Nicholas of Cusa, *De docta ignorantia*

The true is its own becoming, the circle that presupposes its end as its aim and thus has it for its beginning.
—Hegel, Preface, *Phenomenology of the Spirit*

The common end of all *narrative*, nay, of *all*, Poems is . . . to make those events, which in real or imagined History move on in a *strait* Line, assume to our Understandings a *circular* motion—the snake with its Tail in its Mouth.
—Coleridge, Letter to Joseph Cottle, 1815

THREE

It was a matter of jocular remark in Wordsworth's day, as it is in ours, that he was a conspicuously asexual poet. "One would suppose, from the tenor of his subjects," Hazlitt said, "that on this earth there was neither marrying nor giving in marriage." [1] In *Peter Bell the Third* Shelley, tempering with malice his just rendering of Wordsworth's virtues, remarked that

> from the first 'twas Peter's drift
> To be a kind of moral eunuch,
> He touched the hem of Nature's shift,
> Felt faint—and never dared uplift
> The closest, all-concealing tunic
>
> (IV, xi)

It is notable that so ascetic a poet should use the image of a passionate marriage to formulate the "high argument" of his poetry—

> the discerning intellect of Man
> When wedded to this goodly universe
> In love and holy passion

—and the fact testifies to the power and persistence of the Biblical use of marriage as a figure for redemption, both in the individual and in the human race. There is, however, a novel circumstance in Wordsworth's eloquent restatement of the traditional image: he represents the "great consummation" as a marriage, specifically, between mind and nature—between "the individual Mind/ (And the progressive powers perhaps no less/ Of the whole species)" and "the external World." What did Wordsworth intend to signify by a culminating marriage, individual and generic, between mind and nature?

An important clue is contained in the letter Coleridge wrote to Wordsworth in May 1815, just after he had, with considerable disappointment, read *The Excursion,* together with the Prospectus to *The Recluse* which Wordsworth had included in his Preface. *The Excursion,* Coleridge says, suffers by comparison with *The Prelude;* and he reminds Wordsworth of what he had understood, from their earlier discussions, to have been the intended argument of *The Recluse* as a whole:

> I supposed you first . . . to have laid a solid and immoveable foundation for the Edifice by removing the sandy Sophisms of Locke, and the Mechanic Dogmatists. . . . Next, I understood that you would take the Human Race in the concrete . . . to have affirmed a Fall in some sense, as a fact, the possibility of which cannot be understood from the nature of the Will, but the reality of which is attested by Experience & Conscience . . . to point out however a manifest Scheme of Redemption from this Slavery, of Reconciliation from this Enmity with Nature . . . in short, the necessity of a general revolution in the modes of developing & disciplining the human mind by the substitution of Life, and Intelligence . . . for the philosophy of mechanism which in every thing that is most worthy of the human Intellect strikes *Death.*[2]

The full passage, in its abstractness and system, is manifestly the formulation of Coleridge the metaphysician, but it parallels some problematic statements in Wordsworth's own Prospectus and points the way toward interpreting them. As Coleridge interpreted Wordsworth's poetic design, the fall of man, a doctrine valid "in some sense, as . . . attested by Experience," was conceived to involve a falling out, an "Enmity," between man and nature; "the sensual" whom Wordsworth undertook in the Prospectus to arouse "from their sleep/ Of death"[3] were those who had fallen into such division and conflict with nature, through becoming enslaved to Lockean sensationism and its "philosophy of mechanism," which (like the fall of man) "strikes *Death*"; while Wordsworth's annunciation of a paradise to be achieved by a union between mind and nature was equivalent to what Coleridge called a "Scheme of Redemption from this Slavery, of Reconciliation from this Enmity with Nature." In one of many passages in which Coleridge expressed similar concepts, the basic distinction is that between the "intuition of things which arises when we possess ourselves, as one with the whole," which is the fullness of life and joy, and the mode of experience when "we think of ourselves as separated beings, and place nature in antithesis to the mind, as object to subject, thing to thought, death to life." [4]

In this and the two chapters that follow I hope to make it clear that it was indeed a cardinal concern of Wordsworth as bard, and of Coleridge as both metaphysician and bard, to help redeem man by fostering a reconciliation with nature, which, because man has severed himself from his earlier unity with it, has become alien and inimical to him. I also propose to show that this concern was an element in a set of interrelated concepts which had wide currency in the age of Wordsworth and Coleridge—concepts which have evolved into the reigning diagnosis of our own age of anxiety: the claim that man, who was once well, is now ill, and that at the core of the modern malaise lies his fragmentation, dissociation, estrangement, or (in the most highly charged of these parallel terms) "alienation." The individual (so runs the familiar analysis) has become radically split in three main aspects. He is divided within himself, he is divided from other men, and he is divided from his environment; his only hope for recovery (for those writers who hold out hope) is to find the way to a reintegration which will restore his unity with himself, his community with his fellow men, and his companionability with an alien and hostile outer world. These ideas are shared in our time by theologians, philosophers, economists, sociologists, psychologists, artists, writers, critics, and readers of *Life* magazine and *The Reader's Digest,* and the copious writings on this theme have been assembled into widely-read anthologies.[5]

Such a view of the plight of modern man was an integral part of the overall scheme of history to which many Romantic philosophers and men of letters subscribed. But the Romantic writers in their turn had merely elaborated and adapted one of the oldest theses about radical good and evil, and one of the most persistent of the ordering designs by which men have tried to come to terms with their nature and destiny—a design which explained where civilization had gone wrong, provided the sanction for a workable rule of life, and pointed the way toward possible recovery. This way of thinking had roots in both pagan and Biblical culture, and existed in both mythic and conceptual formulations. The several decades beginning with the 1790s constituted a genuine epoch in intellectual and cultural history; not, however, by absolute innovation but by a return to a mode of hereditary wisdom which was re-defined, expanded, and applied to the emerging world of continuous political, industrial, and social revolution and disorder which is the world we live in today.

Let me say before I begin this highly selective survey that a similar conceptual scheme is recognizable in writings which range from positions near the lunatic fringe of thought to some of the most subtle attempts in our literature to assess man and his place in nature and in the historical process; so that its presence is not in itself an index to the quality or adequacy of the world view of which it is a part. In addition, the fact that the concept of divided and alienated man is one of the oldest of commonplaces does not controvert either its general relevance to the human condition or its special usefulness as a speculative instrument for examining our own greatly troubled era, which was inaugurated by the new science and the new philosophy of the seventeenth century and which reached its first great crisis in the age we conventionally call Romantic. But as we shall see, the problem is that various diagnosticians offer entirely opposed views about the causes and cure of the human malaise, whose symptoms they describe in the same general categories of essential good and evil, human health and disorder.

1. THE GREAT CIRCLE: PAGAN AND CHRISTIAN NEOPLATONISM

Since the philosophical history of this way of thinking has in the main been a long series of footnotes to Plotinus, we can start with the *Enneads* and then touch upon some later developments which were of special importance for distinctive Romantic views of the nature, present condition, and destiny of man.

Plotinus formulated a radical monism which holds that the first principle is the One, and that the One is identical with the Good; [6] so that in his thought absolute unity functions both as the source and supreme mode of all existence and as the locus and criterion of all value. Whence then the patent multiplicity and evil in the world? Plotinus' solution to this problem follows from the concept traditionally named "emanation"—perhaps the most seminal of the radical metaphors of metaphysical thinking. The categories of emanation are derived from analogy with the spring which overflows, or the fire which radiates heat and light, or (in Shelley's fusion of both of Plotinus' figures) the "burning fountain" from which everything flows and which is "the fire for which all thirst." According to Plotinus, the undifferentiated One, by virtue of the very fullness of its perfection, overflows (without diminution of itself) into an other, and so on into all existing things, through a series of stages, or "hypostases"—first, mind (including the totality of the fixed Platonic forms), then soul (including all levels of individual souls), and at the farthest possible limit, the material universe. These hypostases descend along a scale of ever increasing "remoteness" from the One which, *ipso facto,* is a scale of increasing division and multiplicity.

Evil appears in the final and most remote stage, that of matter; but not, as in the theory of the Manicheans and some Gnostics (whom Plotinus scornfully attacked), because matter is in itself a positive evil; [7] for like all other existing things, matter proceeds from the primal Good. In Plotinus, evil is a negative attribute which supervenes upon matter by reason of its distinctive location in the scale of hypostases: its ultimate distance from, hence utter antithesis to, the One and the Good. For "things utterly sundered, having nothing in common, standing at the remotest poles, are opposites in nature" (I. viii. 3–6; II. iv. 16). Physical evil, then, is in effect identified with the farthest state of division, separateness, and multiplicity, or the ultimate "privation" of unity;

while moral evil, or vice, which is manifested by souls that
are immured in the matter of the body, is held to be the result
of a "fall" or "descent," in which the individual human soul,
in its severed and partial condition, turns its desires from the
One to the material manifold, becomes self-centered and self-
concerned, and undertakes to be self-sufficient. There comes
a state at which individual souls

> become partial and self-centred; in a weary desire of standing
> apart they find their way, each to a place of its very own. This
> state long maintained, the Soul is a deserter from the All;
> its differentiation has severed it; its vision is no longer set in
> the Intellectual; it is a partial thing, isolated, weakened, full of
> care, intent upon the fragment; severed from the whole . . .
> it nestles in one form of being; for this, it abandons all else,
> entering into and caring for only the one, for a thing buffeted
> about by a worldful of things. . . . It has fallen.
>
> (IV. viii. 4)

To this eternal "procession" from the One, Plotinus opposes
a counter-process of "epistrophe," or return to the source:
"To Real Being we go back, all that we have and are; to that
we return as from that we came" (VI. v. 7). Such a return is
achievable during this life, but only if a man by long discipline
succeeds in turning from the outer world inward, and then
only passingly, in an ecstasy of union in which all division
vanishes (VI. 9. 9). At times Plotinus makes graphic the longing of the separated part for its source, in the figure of the
soul as lover and the One as the beloved (VI. v. 10); and
this metaphor is elaborated into a distinction between the
errant soul (which has fixed its desire on the things of the
material world) as a harlot and the faithful soul as the heavenly
Aphrodite:

> So long as it is There, it holds the heavenly love; here its
> love is the baser; There the soul is Aphrodite of the heavens;
> here, turned harlot, Aphrodite of the public ways: yet the soul
> is always an Aphrodite.   (VI. ix. 9)

Alternating with this erotic figure for the relation of the
separated soul to the One is a familial figure, in which the

soul is a daughter who "takes up with another love, a mortal, leaves her father and falls. But one day coming to hate her shame, she puts away the evil of earth, once more seeks the father, and finds her peace" (VI. ix. 9; also V. 1. 1). The child-father analogue for the individual soul and its one source, extended, becomes the parable of an internal spiritual journey in quest of a lost home (VI. v. 3); and in this application Plotinus proposes an allegoric reading of Homer's epic narrative which was destined to have a long and prolific life in European thought. "But what must we do? How lies the path? How come to vision of the inaccessible Beauty?" He cites the *Iliad*, II. 140:

> "Let us flee then to the beloved Fatherland": this is the soundest counsel. But what is this flight? How are we to gain the open sea? For Odysseus is surely a parable to us when he commands the flight from the sorceries of Circe or Calypso— not content to linger for all the pleasure offered to his eyes and all the delight of sense filling his days.
>
> The Fatherland to us is There whence we have come, and there is The Father.   (I. vi. 8; *cf.* V. ix. 1)

In the fifth century Proclus undertook to reduce Plotinus' thought to systematic form in his *Elements of Theology*. In this highly influential work Proclus represents procession and epistrophe as a circular movement, in which the smaller circles of emanation and return to their secondary principles are comprehended within the single great circle of all things, as they depart from primal unity and subdivide, then reconverge in a return to their point of departure:

> *All that proceeds from any principle and reverts upon it has a cyclic activity.* For if it reverts upon that principle whence it proceeds, it links its end to its beginning, and the movement is one and continuous, originating from the unmoved and to the unmoved again returning. Thus all things proceed in a circuit, from their causes to their causes again. There are greater circuits and lesser, in that some revert upon their immediate priors, others upon the superior causes, even to the beginning of all things. For out of the beginning all things are, and towards it all revert. . . .

> *In any divine procession the end is assimilated to the be-*
> *ginning, maintaining by its reversion thither a circle without*
> *beginning and without end.* . . . . This reversion of the end
> upon the beginning makes the whole order one and determin-
> ate, convergent upon itself and by its convergence revealing
> unity in multiplicity.[8]

Here, in formal rendering, is the radical image of a tenacious
metaphysical (and metaphorical) vision of man and the cosmos.
For convenience of discussion, let us call it "the great circle":
the course of all things is a circuit whose end is its beginning,
of which the movement is from unity out to the increasingly
many and back to unity, and in which this movement into and
out of division is identified with the falling away from good to
evil and the return to good.[9] Notice that in Proclus this circle is
a circulation, a closed, continuous, and eternally revolving
process. Similarly, in the later version of the great circle in
Dionysius the Areopagite, "Goodness draweth all things to
Itself, and is the great Attractive Power which unites things
that are sundered":

> And herein the Divine Yearning showeth especially its be-
> ginningless and endless nature, revolving in a perpetual circle
> for the Good, from the Good, in the Good, and to the Good,
> with unerring revolution, never varying its centre or direction,
> perpetually advancing and remaining and returning to It-
> self.[10]

This world scheme, wherever and however it came to be
known, exerted a profound attraction upon both Hebrew and
Christian theologians, and it altered in many ways and to
various degrees the creeds drawn from Scriptural revelation.
There were, to be sure, various Biblical passages which provided *points d'appui* for Neoplatonic interpretation and expansion—the recurrent figure, for example, of Israel's divorce and
exile from the one God, but with the promise of future reunion; the prayer of Jesus "that they may be one, even as we
are one . . . that they may be made perfect in one" (John
17: 21–3); or the repeated statements in Revelation, "I am
Alpha and Omega, the first and the last." Taken overall, how-

ever, Neoplatonism, with its abstract and impersonal first principle and unending circling of procession and epistrophe, is
radically alien to the Christian *Heilsgeschichte,* with its personal God and its plot, which occurs in time and only once
for all time, and begins with a creation, moves through a fall,
incarnation, passion, and second coming, and comes to an end
in an apocalypse. We can recognize the impact of Neoplatonism by the strains it imposed on the essential Christian categories as these were modified, and in extreme cases transformed, by the assimilation of a historical religion to a timeless
pagan metaphysic. Let me suggest, very summarily, three characteristic aspects of a Neoplatonized Christianity that are most
relevant to our present topic.

First, the personal God the Father tends to become an impersonal first principle, or absolute, whose perfection is equated
with his self-sufficient and undifferentiated unity. Evil, correspondingly, is held to be essentially a separation from unity,
or a division, fragmentation, estrangement from the One,
which is reflected in a division within the nature of man. As
Leone Ebreo wrote in his influential *Dialogues on Love:*

> Sin is truly that which causes division in man and cuts his
> nature in twain, just as righteousness makes a man to be single
> and preserves the unity of his nature. . . . Sin and division in
> man are almost one and the same thing, or at least two in-
> separable things, the one always implying the other.[11]

Second, the fall of man is conceived to be primarily a falling-
out-of and falling-away-from the One, into a position of remoteness and a condition of alienation from the source. Consonantly, the original human sin is identified as self-centered-
ness, or selfhood, the attempt of a part to be sufficient unto
itself; while the primary consequence of the fall—death—is
described as a state of division from the one Being. Some
thinkers, adopting without qualification the view that all
separation is evil, pursued this view to its ultimate implication
by moving the fall back from Eden to the event of the creation
itself—a creation regarded as that original and disastrous
splintering of the primal unity which inaugurated both the
material universe and sundered man. In all versions of the fall

as a falling out of unity, redemption is regarded as a process of reintegration; and this view, in its extreme form, manifested itself as the heresy of "apocatastasis," the doctrine that there is no eternal damnation, since all creatures and creation will participate in the redemptive return to the divine unity. This final event is often symbolized by the sacred marriage in the Book of Revelation—a figure which is now employed to signify the reunion of all fragmented separates into their initial undivided condition.

Third, the Neoplatonic circle of emanation and return manifested itself most widely in the concept of *circuitus spiritualis,* a powerful current of "love," or cohesive and sustaining supernatural energy, which flows ceaselessly from God down through the successive levels of ever remoter being and circles back to God—the force that holds the universe together and manifests itself to human awareness as the yearning to return to an undivided state.[12] We also find, however, a much more radical and comprehensive application of the circular design. In some thinkers the Christian pattern of history—finite, linear, right-angled in its abrupt reversals, and symmetrical in its balance between the paradise created at the beginning and the kingdom to be recovered at the end—is modulated into the pattern of the Neoplatonic circle; but the Neoplatonic circle in its turn, when thus assimilated to Christian history, is temporalized and given a specific historical beginning and end. That is, the eternal circulation becomes a single circle, which begins in unity and perfection and then, in a given span of time, moves around and down into division and evil and around and back up again to unity and perfection, and there it stops. This design of a temporal and finite great circle is applied not only to the world and all mankind (whose history is conceived as a long circuitous detour to reach its origin) but also to the life of each redeemed individual (whose "conversion" is conceived to occur at the moment at which his direction changes from a movement out to a movement back to his lost integrity).

As early as the third century Origen manifestly Neoplatonized the Christian scheme of history when he described the fall as a lapse into dispersion from the divine One, and, linking the Apocalypse to Genesis, interpreted "the end or consummation" of all things as a rotation back to their primal unity. "For the end is always like the beginning," and in the coming world "that dispersion and separation from the one beginning" will undergo "a process of restoration to one and the same end and likeness." [13] Elements of the Neoplatonic world view were incorporated into the doctrinal categories of many bulwarks of Western orthodoxy, including Augustine, Aquinas, and Dante. In these writers, however, by virtue of their firm distinction between the literal and allegorical meanings of Scripture, Neoplatonism was limited to the status of a metaphysical superstructure upon a creed which remained fixed in the literal story. On the other hand, the writings of John Scotus Erigena, a thinker of the ninth century who, in intellectual isolation, built a metaphysical system on the grand scale, show how drastically the Christian plot of history is transformed by a wholesale application of circular emanationism to a freely allegorical reading of the Biblical narrative.

In his *De divisione naturae* Erigena assimilates the crucial events of sacred history, from creation to apocalypse, to the primary categories of *processio, divisio, reditus,* and *adunatio* —a going forth which is also a division, and a return which is also a reunion. God, "the source and cause and goal" of all things,[14] is one and undivided; and man, as originally created in God's own image, was also one and undivided, and hence exhibited no sexual differentiation. All division in nature was the result of the fall of man, which occurred with very little or no lapse of time after the creation (IV. xv) and resulted in the separation of man from God, as well as the split of primal man into male and female sexes. Since man is the microcosm in whom all the creation is epitomized, the fall of man involved simultaneously the separation of heaven from earth and of the world from paradise, and effected the divisions of eternity into the existing world of quality and quantity, space and time (II. vii). Redemption is made possible by Christ, who in His risen form, like man before the fall, "united the masculine and feminine in his single person" (II. x). As evil is the principle of division, so redemption is the principle of reintegration; and the process of redemption is a return which reverses the results of the fall, in a cumulative reunion of male to female, paradise to the world, and heaven to earth, until man, having reunited in himself all the divisions of nature and having become again spiritualized, is rejoined with the Creator in a perfect unity in eternity. In this restored unity, however, differentiation and individuation are not lost, although they survive not in their material embodiments but in their essence (V. xiii).

This course of procession and return constitutes a vast cycle, which is illustrated by the circling of the heavenly bodies and is reflected (according to Erigena's proto-Hegelian system) in the structure of dialectic, mathematics, and the other arts, all of which manifest a design that begins with unity and rounds through division back to unity. And so also with the entire cosmic process:

> For the end of the entire movement is its beginning, and it terminates at no other end than its own origin, from which it began to be moved and to which it strives ceaselessly to return, in order to stop and find rest therein. And the same is to be understood not only for the parts of the sensible world but also for the world as a whole. For the end of this is its beginning, toward which it strives and in which, when it has been found again, it will rest; not in such a way that its substance will perish, but in such a way that it will return to the causes from which it has proceeded. (V. iii)

And to signify the return of mankind to the unity of his origin Erigena employs the figure of the apocalyptic marriage. As God in the *De divisione* summarizes His divine plan, this is "that most intimate and secret marriage of my divinity and humanity, which I had prepared purely in my thoughts before the world began, and to which I will lead you when the world is ended" (V. xxxviii).

2. DIVIDED AND REUNITED MAN: THE ESOTERIC TRADITION

Erigena is an impressive metaphysician; but in his doctrine of primal man as the epitome in whom "everything which follows from God is contained," so that all created nature participates in his fall into sexual and other divisions and will participate in his destined return to unity,[15] we detect a myth which has been only partially conceptualized. The myth is that of primordial man as a cosmic androgyne, who has disintegrated into the material and bisexual world of alien and conflicting parts, yet retains the capacity for recovering his lost integrity. In its Western form this myth has roots in Plato's *Symposium* (Aristophanes' story of the halving of bisexual man), in Gnosticism, and in the Orphic and other mysteries; [16] it has been the major pictorial medium for embodying and sustaining the doctrine that perfection is identical with simple unity and that the cosmic course is from the One and the Good into evil and multiplicity and back to the One; and it has demonstrated remarkable tenacity, persisting into our day as the central component of the esoteric *philosophia perennis*.[17] Two forms of this traditional wisdom were so widespread and so deeply influential as to justify particular comment. Both these traditions had a double origin—in the Bible, and also in various forms of Neoplatonism and of Gnostic and pagan mythology. One tradition is the Hebrew Kabbala, and the other the Christian version of Hermetic lore.

You will recall the recurrent Old Testament figure of Israel as a woman, the beloved but faithless, and therefore divorced and exiled, bride of the Lord, to whom is held out the promise, when she shall repent, of reunion with the Bridegroom. This figure—together with passages such as the allusion in Proverbs 8 to a female heavenly wisdom whom "the Lord possessed . . . or ever the earth was," and who was "daily his delight, rejoicing always before him"—provided access for a feminine component into the austere male-monotheism of Hebrew theology. Over the post-Biblical centuries there developed a line of Jewish commentary which wove such suggestions together with strands of non-Biblical philosophy and myth, and elaborated them into a radically "mystical" or figurative reinterpretation of the letter of the Old Testament which, by the thirteenth century, had become identified as Kabbala, "the Tradition." [18] Of these esoteric doctrines the documents collected as *Sefer Ha-Zohar,* "The Book of Splendor," written in the latter thirteenth century, were a highly developed exposition which after some time, and for several centuries' duration, became for many Jews a canonical text on a level with the Bible and the Talmud.

For our purpose two cardinal principles of these complex and unordered exegeses of the Bible are especially relevant. First, among a people for whom the central and repeated tragedy had been the *Galut*—exile and dispersion from the holy city and the holy land, and thereafter from a number of temporary homes—original and essential evil is understandably identified with the exile of man and of his world from their source in the unity of the divine Being. Second, in the *Zohar* sexuality enters into the very nature of God, and the sacred union becomes a central and pervasive symbol which accounts for the origin and sustainment of all life, while the vicissitudes of this union are used to explain the course of history, from the literal genesis, through multiform and continued division and dispersion, to the enduring reunion of all things that will occur at the end of time.

Thus, within *En-Sof,* the infinite and hidden One, emanate ten manifestations—the *Sefiroth,* constituting the "world of union"—which are represented mythically as composing the body of Adam Kadmon, the primordial One Man. Immanent within these manifestations of deity is the *Shekhinah*, "the divine presence," the feminine principle which is both antithesis and complement to the masculine principle within the divine unity, and which is referred to figuratively as "Princess," "Matrona," "Queen," "Bride." [19] Originally there had been a perfect and unintermitted union between God and the Shekhinah, binding all the worlds of creation into unity with the life of God. This union was disrupted by the sin of Adam, which struck a breach in the divine unity, in an event described as "the exile of the Shekhinah." The effect was to splinter the initial purely spiritual integer into "the world of separation" —the scattered parts of the material universe, isolated from one another and from God, including the corporeal embodiments of individual human selves, who strive to maintain their self-sufficiency yet feel a longing to return to their one source. As Gershom Scholem says, "Moral evil, according to the *Zohar,* is always either something which becomes separated and isolated, or something which enters into a relation for which it is not made. Sin always destroys a union. . . ." [20] Although in the present world this division can be partially healed by the pious acts of individual men, the total reachievement of unity is possible only in the spiritual vision of the mystic. But the ultimate redemptive goal of the divine will is to return all separates completely and permanently to their starting place in primal unity—a consummation which is figuratively described as the resumption of the originally continuous marital union between the archetypal male and female polarities, the queen and the king, or God and His Shekhinah.[21]

> Thus Moses was a new beginning in the world. And if you ask, Who is the termination? the answer is, the King Messiah, for then there shall be such perfection in the world as had not been for all generations before. For then there shall be completeness above and below, and all worlds shall be united in one bond [literally, "shall be one by coupling"—Aramaic *ziwwūgā:* "coupling," "wedlock"] as it is written, "On that day the Lord shall be one and his name one" (Zech. XIV. 9). . . .
>
> In time to come God will restore the Shekhinah to its place, and there will be a complete union ["the whole will exist in one coupling"] as it is written: "On that day the Lord shall be one and his name one" (Zech. XIV. 9). It may be said: Is He not now one? No; for now through sinners He is not really one; for the Matrona is removed from the King and they are not united [coupled]. . . . Therefore, as it were, He is not one. But when the Matrona shall return to the place of the temple, and the King shall be wedded with her ["coupled with her in a single coupling"], then all will be joined together without separation.[22]

There was some interchange between Kabbalism and European Hermeticism—that body of writings, evolving over many centuries of speculation, which existed both as an independent body of esoteric philosophy and as the metaphysical foundation of the science of alchemy—and though the one mode of wisdom undertakes to explicate the secret meaning of Scriptures and the other to expound a secret practice, they share certain principles. These principles are common also to many of the esoteric and illuministic cults which have developed from Eastern, Neoplatonic, and Gnostic sources, in the environment of a Biblical culture.

The body of Hermetic literature is large, varied, and written in a fantastic symbolism which is designed to conceal its potent mysteries from the uninitiate; we are, nevertheless, to make out a reiterative conceptual pattern.[23] The basic ontology is broadly biological, and specifically anthropomorphic. That is, Hermeticism did not draw the modern sharp division between the animate and the inanimate but applied the categories of living things to all of nature; it also posited a correspondence between the human and the nonhuman, but in such a way that the human serves as the paradigmatic form. With reference to Hermetic writings, therefore, it is more accurate to speak of the cosmos as a macro-anthropos than to speak of man as a micro-cosm. In this scheme there is a strong emphasis on polarity, conceived on the model of sexual opposites and regarded as the force that compels all natural processes. In addition, the overall course of things is envisioned as a circular movement from unity into multiplicity and, ultimately, back to unity. Thus "The Poimandres," the first book among the documents of the *Corpus Hermeticum* (dating from the second and third centuries A.D.), expounds the doctrine that the first Mind, "which is Life and Light," is bisexual, and that when he "gave birth to Man, a Being like to Himself," man was also bisexual. But man fell in love with nature and matter and took up his abode there, and so, together with all living creatures, was divided into two sexes, which proceeded to multiply according to their kind. Nevertheless, if men learn to know that state which was their origin, their minds, after the death of the body, will mount back through the spheres and "enter into God. This is the Good; this is the consummation, for those who have got *gnosis*." [24]

Some thirteen hundred years later Paracelsus, writing at the high tide of Hermetic philosophy during the Renaissance, proposed an elaborate and Christianized form of the doctrine, in which, however, we recognize a similar cosmic design.[25] The world is an emanation or expansion from the first principle, which is conceived as a simple and eternal unity and is sometimes identified as the *Mysterium Magnum*. The creation is effected by the principle of *separatio*. A series of manifestations, which are compelled by a creative conflict of opposing powers and involve the emergence of the three basic elements of sulfur, mercury, and salt, results in the totality of all separate existences, including man. Since this separation from unity constituted the fall of Lucifer, the creation of the world, according to Paracelsus, coincides with its fall: "the creation of the whole of nature is the fall of nature, and the curse which followed on account of it." [26] As originally created the primal Adam—who represented in himself the cosmic whole—had a nonphysical body and was androgyne; but his fall plunged him into the gross material world of separated and conflicting physical and sexual elements, in which each individual part attempts to be self-sufficient. The cosmic movement of descent into division is matched, however, by the complementary movement of return to the source. This transformation of the physical back to the spiritual, and the simultaneous return of separates into unity, was made possible for man by Christ, the God-man; correspondingly, in the realm of metallic nature, the inherent tendency to return to the one origin is expedited by the Philosopher's Stone, the principle of transformation and unification which it is the task of the alchemist to disengage and purify. In the ultimate transformation, man will be transfigured and will circle back to his point of departure, together with all the creation of which man is the microcosm. For "each thing that has been created naturally desires to be again that which it was before the creation. That is the ground of all our philosophy." "All things will return to their beginning and only that will remain which was before the *Mysterium Magnum*, and is eternal. . . . We come out of the *Mysterium Magnum*, and not *procreato*." [27]

In its period of full development alchemy, as F. S. Taylor has said, was "at once a craft and a creed." [28] For the initiate who, unlike Paracelsus, was a practicing alchemist rather than a Hermetic philosopher, the *magnum opus* was to produce by physical manipulations in the laboratory the Philosopher's Stone, which had the power to expedite the slow process of nature by transmuting base metals into their primordial perfection as gold. But since matter and spirit were held to be related by a system of correspondence, and since the aim of all alchemy was to transform each thing, whether material or human, to the perfection of its own nature, the languages of physical and of spiritual alchemy were interchangeable; so that the description of the laboratory operation served as objective correlative for the human regimen of religious redemption. Furthermore, since the opposing yet generative powers in this fallen physical world were conceived on the model of sexual opposites, chemical union was equated with a sexual coupling; and the culmination of the entire physical *operatio* was frequently imaged as the *coniunctio,* or "chymical wedding," of the prototypical male and female opposites—identified in alchemical symbolism as sulfur and mercury, or Sol and Luna, or king and queen.[29] This *mysterium coniunctionis,* leading to a new alchemical birth, was equated in the realm of mind with the event of spiritual death and rebirth, and the conjunction was often pictured in Hermetic literature by a male and female figure in a sexual embrace.[30] (As a clue to one source of the Romantic theme of the symbolic love of brother and sister, it is noteworthy that in alchemy, on the grounds that the male and female opposites had a common genetic source, the *coniunctio* was often represented as an incestuous brother-sister union.) From the chymical wedding issues the Philosopher's Stone, figured as a "rebis," or androgyne, who reunites the two sexes into the unitary form they had exhibited before their separation. In Christian alchemy the Philosopher's Stone was held to correspond to Christ, the Messiah of Nature, who has the apocalyptic function of restoring both fallen and divided man and the fallen and fragmented universe to the perfection of their original unity. And from the early period of Hermetic philosophy, the cosmic design of departure from and return to the source was sometimes pictured as the Ouraboros, the circular serpent who is eating his own tail.

In recent decades a number of scholars have made us aware how extraordinarily prevalent, among even the leading thinkers of the European Renaissance, were Hermetic ideas, as well as Christianized versions of Kabbalist doctrines.[31] This occult tradition was in turn communicated to later thinkers by various theorists, including Giordano Bruno, but above all, by Jacob Boehme.[32] In Boehme, for example, we find still the ancient myth of primal and spiritual man, the microcosmic androgyne, who fell into sexual as well as into material and psychological division, and whose redemption—the recovery of his lost integrity—is made possible by Christ who, like unfallen Adam, unites the attributes of both sexes in himself.[33] But in Boehme this myth is part of a metaphysical system which, although expressed in an outlandish idiom, is a remarkably subtle and extremely influential innovation upon the Christian form of the Neoplatonic circle of emanation and return. In his interpretation of the creation story in the Book of Genesis, Boehme poses as the primal source an eternal unity which, in its absolute lack of determinateness or distinctions, is literally a Nothing, *ein ewig Nichts,* the *Ungrund.* But this *Ungrund* possesses an inner nisus, *eine Sucht,* which in its striving for self-realization effects within itself an opposing force, *den Willen,* thus establishing the contraries of impulsion and opposition which set the otherwise static unity into a motion like that of a turning wheel, and so transform the Nothing into a Something—indeed, into the source of all existing things.[34] The coincidence of opposites in the one God manifests itself in the opposition of positive and negative forces that constitute all of nature. For

> there is a single God; He is himself all existence, He is evil
> and good, heaven and hell, light and darkness, eternity and
> time, beginning and end; where His love is hidden in a being,
> just there is His anger apparent.[35]

The origin of cosmic evil was the fall of Lucifer, which coincided with the creation of the material world we now inhabit. This event was followed by the fall—more precisely, by a sequence of falls—of Adam which was effected by the principle of selfhood (*Selbheit*), that is, by Adam's turn away from God to nature, in the attempt to be sufficient unto himself. The result of these successive falls has been that man has plunged ever deeper into the material and animal world, and so has moved ever farther from unity into division, until he has become a fragment (*Bruchstück*), utterly separated from God in an isolation from which he can only be rescued by the intervention of that grace which gave him his Redeemer.

Boehme left to philosophy a first principle which becomes creative by generating its own contrary, which it then proceeds to reconcile to itself. He left also the compelling vision of a fallen universe which is constituted throughout by an opposition of quasi-sexual contraries, at once mutually attractive and repulsive, whose momentary conciliations give way to renewed attempts at mastery by the opponent powers, in a tragic conflict which is at the same time the very essence of life and creativity as well as the necessary condition for sustaining the possibility of progression back to the strenuous peace of the primal equilibrium.[36] The motion into which all things are thus compelled is a circular one, composing a design like that of the self-devouring serpent: "For all beings move onward until the end finds the beginning; then the beginning again swallows [*verschlingt*] the end, and is as it was eternally, without any model remaining." According to Boehme the creation described in the Book of Genesis ensued from the primordial division of forces in the *Ungrund* and manifested the shape of a circle, for "the eternal rest found the beginning of creation in the afternoon of the sixth day" in which the Sabbath began; "then did beginning and end turn back into unity, and there was revealed what God had made in the intervening days."[37] The course of the created world through time is destined to repeat the circular design figured in Genesis, in the ratio of one thousand years for each creative day; for just as the creation began as a single order [*Regiment*], "but divided itself . . . into the many in time, so does the many seek to return to unity."[38] Furthermore, Boehme announces, the closure of the circle in the unity of the paradise which was its origin is at hand, and the Bridegroom is even now preparing for His holy marriage in the Sabbath of history:

> Now the end has found the beginning again, and you shall see, feel, and find, all those of you born in God, what paradise was. For that paradise has been born again . . . and stands revealed to the children of God in the spirit and in the soul. . . . For the end has found the beginning, there is

no stopping it, the power and the falsehood are shattered, and it is only a matter of awaiting the coming of the Bridegroom.[39]

Various doctrines of this remarkable cobbler of Goerlitz soon worked their way into radical Christian theology, especially among the Pietists in Germany and a number of Inner Light Puritans in seventeenth-century England. You may recall my citing Gerrard Winstanley in the first chapter as an extreme exemplar of the reading of the Bible entirely as spiritual allegory. Here are some passages frcm Winstanley's *The New Law of Righteousness* (1648) which represent the currency, in a popularized form, of the myth of the microcosmic and androgynous Adam who falls into division and so effects the material creation. They express also the associated view that the history both of the cosmos and of each fallen and redeemed individual describes a circle from unity into division and back.

> In the beginning of time the whole Creation lived in man, and man lived in his Maker . . . there was no opposition between him and the beast, fowls, fishes, or any creature in the earth: so that it is truly said, The whole Creation was in man, one within. . . . And man lived in his Maker the Spirit, and delighted in no other.

Man, however, "led by the powers of the curse in flesh, which is the *Feminine* part, not by the power of the righteous Spirit which is Christ, the *Masculine* power,"

> began to fall out of his Maker . . . and sought content from creatures and outward objects, then he lost his dominion, and the creature fell out of him, and became enemies and apposers of him, and then rise up mountaines, and valleys, and hils, and all unevennesse, both in mans heart, and in mans actions. And as the man is become selfish; so are all the beasts and creatures become selfish. . . .
>
> And this now is the curse, Man is gone out of his Maker, to live upon objects; and the creatures are gone out of man. . . .
>
> But now the time is come, that the Spirit will draw all things into man againe, to live and be at rest in him . . . and so man returning to his Maker, to rest in peace in none but him. . . . And all bondage, curse and tears shall be done away.[40]

3. THE PRODIGAL'S RETURN

The theological design exemplified in the life of man was
readily convertible into the characters and plots of Christian
works of literature, according to a procedure which was demonstrated in the writings of the theologians themselves. Plotinus,
as we saw, had illustrated his abstract doctrine of the circular
course of the soul by an allegoric reading of Homer's epic, in
which the counsel of Agamemnon, "Let us flee then to the
beloved Fatherland," is applied to mankind, and the return of
Odysseus to his native land is interpreted as a parable of the
return of the many to the One. In *The City of God* Augustine
did not scruple to apply this pagan figure to the Christian life:

> Is that sentiment of Plotinus forgotten?—"We must fly to our
> beloved fatherland. There is the Father, there our all. What
> fleet or flight shall convey us thither? Our way is, to become
> like God." [41]

There was also available to Augustine in the Scriptures themselves an alternative analogue for life as a journey in quest of
a distant place. The primary passage is Hebrews 11:8–16, where
Paul declared that Abraham sojourned "in the land of promise,
as in a strange country," for he lived in faith of a city "whose
builder and maker is God." And so his seed "all died in faith,"

> not having received the promises, but having seen them afar
> off, and were persuaded of them, and embraced them, and con-
> fessed that they were strangers and pilgrims on the earth.
> For they that say such things declare plainly that they seek a
> country. And truly, if they had been mindful of that country
> from whence they came out, they might have had opportunity
> to have returned. But now they desire a better country, that
> is, an heavenly: wherefore God is not ashamed to be called
> their God: for he hath prepared for them a city. [42]

In Augustine and countless other writers this passage inspired the radical Christian figure (used in condensed form as

a homiletic topic and in expanded form as a literary plot), in which post-Adamic man is an exile and wayfarer in an alien land and the course of his life is a toilsome *peregrinatio* in quest of a better city in another country, which is where he truly belongs.[43] In its usual form, as in the founding passage in the Epistle to the Hebrews, this figure differs from the circular journey of Odysseus in that its design is linear. The model Christian life, whether individual or generic, pursues a course from here to there, which has its ups and downs, its catastrophes and reversals, but points toward a goal which, although it is its birthright, is another and higher place than that whence it departed. This central trope of life as a pilgrimage attracted into its orbit various Old Testament stories of exiled wanderers, especially the account of the exodus of the chosen people from their bondage in Egypt and of their long wanderings in the wilderness before the entry into the promised land. The goal of the journey was usually imaged as the New Jerusalem, which is both a city and a woman; and the longing for the goal was frequently expressed, following Revelation 22:17, as an insistent invitation to a wedding: "And the Spirit and the bride say, Come. And let him that heareth say, Come. And let him that is athirst come."

The Bible also contained an apt, detailed, and impressive figure for life as a circular rather than a linear journey, which had been uttered explicitly as a parable of man's sin and redemption, and by the authoritative voice of Jesus himself. This was the story of the Prodigal Son (Luke 15:11–32), who collected his inheritance and "took his journey into a far country, and there wasted his substance with riotous living"; then, remorseful, made his way back to his homeland and the house of his father, who joyously received him, clothed him in the best robe, a ring, and shoes, and ordered the fatted calf that they might "eat, and be merry: For this my son was dead, and is alive again; he was lost, and is found." This parabolic journey offered analogues of detail, which were exploited by the commentators, between the Prodigal's plunge into riotous living "with harlots" and the Old Testament image of the violation of God's marital covenant as fornication and harlotry, and also between the gift of the ring by the forgiving father and God's pledge of remarriage with a repentant Israel at the triumphant close of the history of mankind.[44]

The apologue of the Prodigal Son was a special favorite among Neoplatonic theologians. Erigena, for example, who envisioned all history as a movement from the One into division and back to the One, expanded at length upon this story as figuring fallen man, who "strays from his Creator" but "after a time will return to his Father." [45] By many commentators the parable was employed as a supplement to the image of the *peregrinatus* in Hebrews. The allusion was one of Augustine's favorites in his *Confessions;* Roy Battenhouse in fact proposes that throughout the book "Augustine sees his own life in terms of the parable of the Prodigal Son." [46] "I fell away," Augustine says, "into vanity and went so far from Thee, My God," like "Thy prodigal son" when he went "to that far country" whence "he returned, all poor and stripped" (I. xviii). This falling away from God is a turn to harlotry, for "the soul is guilty of fornication when she turns from You" to seek what she will nowhere find "unless she returns to You" (II. vi). It is at the same time a fall from unity into self-dividedness and dispersion, for it is only "by continence" that "we are all collected and bound up into unity within ourself, whereas we had been scattered abroad in multiplicity" (X. xxix). Indeed, all of our life in this world is inescapably an experience of fragmentation and conflict that will cease only with our reunion to the One. "I am divided up in time . . . and my thoughts and the deepest places of my soul are torn with every kind of tumult until the day when I shall be purified and melted in the fire of Thy love and wholly joined to Thee" (XI. xxix). And the course of the life of faith, Augustine declares, will end where it began, in a marital union with the Bridegroom from whom, in our wandering, we departed: we "rejoice with joy for the voice of the bridegroom, returning to the Source of our being. Thus it is that He is the Beginning: unless He remained when we wandered away, there should be no abiding place for our return" (XI. viii).

An unspoken precept of Biblical typology was that images which signify the same thing are interchangeable with each other; hence the drastic condensation and displacement of metaphor in Christian devotional literature. By way of example, here are two related passages in which Augustine represents his life as a journey from scatteredness and evil to unity and goodness. By a fusion of the pilgrimage in Hebrews, the circular journey of the Prodigal Son, the culmination of the Book of Revelation, and the imagery of the Song of Songs, the goal of the composite journey is at once a country and a city and a home, both a place and a person, both male and female, and a father who is also the mother, the bridegroom, and the spouse:

> Let me *enter into my chamber* and sing my songs of love to Thee, groaning with inexpressible groaning in my pilgrimage, and remembering Jerusalem with my heart stretching upwards in longing for it: Jerusalem my Fatherland, Jerusalem which is my mother: and remembering Thee its Ruler, its Light, its Father and Tutor and Spouse . . . the sum of all ineffable good because Thou alone art the one supreme and true Good. So that I shall not turn away but shall come to the peace of that Jerusalem, my dear mother, where are the first-fruits of my spirit . . . and there Thou shalt collect from my present scatteredness and deformity all that I am, and Thou shalt re-form me and confirm me into eternity. . . .
>
> For that City the friend of the bridegroom sighs . . . *waiting for adoption, the redemption of his body.* He sighs for it, for he is a member of the Spouse of Christ; and he is jealous for it, for he is the friend of the bridegroom.
>
> (XII. xvi; XIII. xiii)

In such passages Augustine's *Confessions,* which fathered the enduring genre of literal spiritual histories, also pointed the way toward that abundant form of Christian fiction in which the significance is not literal but allegorical, the action is a journey in quest of a land or city which is the dwelling of a woman of irresistible erotic charm, the conclusion is often signalized by a betrothal or marriage, and the protagonist is usually not a particular person but someone called Christian, or Pilgrim, or Everyman, or Mankind. The greatest instance of this pilgrimage-and-quest plot introduces in the opening line its root-metaphor of the *cammin di nostra vita,* and it unites spiritual autobiography with generic allegory; for Dante is both his

individual self and the type of the successful Christian wayfarer, in his descent through hell and ascent through purgatory
to a vision of paradise which is proleptic of the experience of
all the redeemed *all' ultima giustizia* (*Paradiso,* XXX. 45).
The poem also infuses the bridal symbolism of the Old and
New Testaments with the eros doctrine of pre-Renaissance
Neoplatonism, so as to transform the creaturely Beatrice into
the female focus of all desire, whose beauty lures the pilgrim
by degrees back up to the *fons et origo* of all love, light, and
joy (XXX. 28–42; XXXI. 79–87), in the "true kingdom"
which is also "our city," and where at his appointed time
Dante too shall sup at the wedding feast both as a friend of
the Bridegroom and as a member of the Spouse (XXX. 98,
130–5; XXXI. 1–3).

The chivalric romances of the Middle Ages, with their
standard plot of literal travel, quest, and trial by combat and
by moral temptation, were readily convertible into the Christian "Allegory, or darke conceit," of which Spenser's *Faerie
Queene* was a late and complex instance. The poem overall
represents Arthur's journey in search of the Faerie Queene,
whom he had seen in a vision before the opening of the narrative and, by her "excellent beauty ravished," had upon
awaking "resolved to seeke her out"; [47] the successful conclusion
of this search is prefigured by the first canto, which closes with
the ceremonious betrothal of the Red Cross Knight to Una in
the delivered Land of Eden. As complement to this aristocratic
allegory of the quest of the knight on horseback, there developed the tale of the working-class pilgrim who shoulders his
pack and trudges sturdily over stile and through mire in search
of the Celestial City. John Bunyan, who in *Grace Abounding*
wrote the liveliest of many seventeenth-century instances of
the literal Augustinian personal history,[48] also wrote in *Pilgrim's Progress* the immortal allegory of the pedestrian quest.
Even in this Puritan and proletarian version, the land and
city which is the goal is represented in a bluff rendering of the
language of sexual desire.

Now I saw in my dream, that by this time the Pilgrims were
. . . entering into the country of *Beulah,* whose air was very

sweet and pleasant. . . . Here they were within sight of the
city they were going to. . . . In this land also, the contract
between the bride and the bridegroom was renewed. . . . By
reason of the natural glory of the city, and the reflection of
the sunbeams upon it, *Christian* with desire fell sick; *Hopeful*
also had a fit or two of the same disease. Wherefore, here they
lay by it a while, crying out, because of their pangs, *If ye find
my beloved, tell him that I am sick of love.*

But, being a little strengthened, and better able to bear
their sickness, they walked on their way. . . . [49]

4. FORMS OF ROMANTIC IMAGINATION

The procession and epistrophe of Neoplatonic metaphysics and
of a Neoplatonized theology, the myth of sexual division, opposition, and reconjunction which is at the center of occult
thought, the persistent Christian metaphor of life as the exile's
pilgrimage toward the home and bride he has faithlessly abandoned—what have these to do with the philosophy and literature of the Romantic generation?

In the first place we can answer—if we are indulged the
convenience of sweeping initial generalizations—that the basic
categories of characteristic post-Kantian philosophy, and of
the thinking of many philosophical-minded poets, can be
viewed as highly elaborated and sophisticated variations upon
the Neoplatonic paradigm of a primal unity and goodness, an
emanation into multiplicity which is *ipso facto* a lapse into
evil and suffering, and a return to unity and goodness. "If we
are to speak of anyone at all as a 'key' to the understanding of
Romanticism," Paul Reiff declared, "one man only merits the
term, Plotinus." [50] This statement is acceptable, but only as
an initial approximation, and only if we include, together with
Plotinus, the variants of emanation-metaphysics which were
developed by Christian thinkers, and if we make appropriate
allowance for the changes imposed on the inherited paradigm
by the diverse premises and operative concepts of individual
Romantic thinkers. In the second place, a number of German
thinkers, and a few English ones as well, took seriously the

esoteric concepts which they found in Giordano Bruno and other Renaissance philosophers, in Jacob Boehme, and in German Pietists and Inner Light theologians in England. In his *Lectures on the History of Philosophy* Hegel gave detailed and respectful attention to Neoplatonic philosophers, to Giordano Bruno, and to Boehme—to the last writer he devoted a special section in which he put him, together with Francis Bacon, under the heading, "Modern Philosophy in Its First Statement." Boehme, said Schelling, "was a miraculous phenomenon in the history of mankind. . . . As popular mythologies and theogonies preceded science, so did J. Boehme, in the birth of God, as he describes it for us, precede all the scientific systems of modern philosophy." [51] And all students of Coleridge are aware of his keen interest in Neoplatonism, in the esoteric thinkers of the Renaissance, and in the speculations of Jacob Boehme—a keen but carefully qualified interest; for as he said of Boehme, that "theosophist" was at times "so far deluded, as to mistake the tumultuous sensations of his nerves, and the co-existing spectres of his fancy, as parts or symbols of the truths which were opening on him." [52]

It would be an error to regard elements derived from the esoteric tradition as, *ipso facto,* aberrations which discredit the writings in which they occur. From Ficino through the Renaissance, Hermetism—not in its lunatic fringe of goldmakers, practicing magicians, and spiritual libertines, but in its central premises and outlook—had been a reputable, indeed an almost universally accepted part of the intellectual universe. During the course of the seventeenth century this mode of thought had been displaced by philosophies based on the new science, whose immensely effective working hypotheses were forthwith translated from a convenient fiction into a blueprint of the actual universe. In the several decades beginning with the 1780s, however, a number of the keenest and most sensitive minds found radically inadequate, both to immediate human experience and to basic human needs, the intellectual ambiance of the Enlightenment, with (as they saw it) its mechanistic worldview, its analytic divisiveness (which undertook to explain all physical and mental phenomena by breaking them down into irreducible parts, and regarded all wholes as a collocation of such elementary parts), and its conception of the human mind as totally diverse and alien from its nonmental environment. Renaissance vitalism had envisioned an integral universe without absolute divisions, in which everything is interrelated by a system of correspondences, and the living is continuous with the inanimate, nature with man, and matter with mind; a universe, moreover, which is activated throughout by a dynamism of opposing forces which not only sustains its present existence but also keeps it moving along the way back toward the unity of its origin. In this way of thinking some Romantic philosophers detected intimations of a viable counter-metaphysic to contemporary mechanism, elementarism, and dualism; provided that (as Schelling said with respect to Boehme in the passage I just quoted) the mythical elements are translated into philosophical concepts, and these are ordered into a "scientific," that is, a coherent conceptual system. As Coleridge explained the importance to him of this esoteric tradition, in the philosophical milieu of his youth:

> For the writings of these mystics . . . contributed to keep alive the *heart* in the *head;* gave me an indistinct, yet stirring and working presentiment, that all the products of the mere *reflective* faculty partook of DEATH. . . . If they were too often a moving cloud of smoke to me by day, yet they were always a pillar of fire throughout the night, during my wanderings through the wilderness of doubt.[53]

Incidentally, it is now becoming apparent that the esoteric view of the universe as a plènum of opposed yet mutually attractive, quasi-sexual forces—which was discredited and displaced by Cartesian and Newtonian mechanism, but was revived, in a refined form, in the *Naturphilosophie* of Schelling in Germany and of Coleridge in England—proceeded, by a peripety of intellectual history, to feed back into scientific thought some of the most productive hypotheses of nineteenth-century and modern physics.[54]

One other preliminary point. Certain major poets of the Romantic Age, as we shall see, incorporated into their writings myths and imagery which are recognizably esoteric in origin. They used such elements, however, as symbolic conveniences, "metaphors for poetry." The older view of the world helped them to define the malaise of their own time, and they sometimes adopted its mythology to project and dramatize their feeling that they did not belong in the intellectual, social, and political milieu of their oppressive and crisis-ridden age. This sense of being an alien in a world which had been made by man's own unhappy intellect also manifested itself in a widespread revival of the traditional plot-form of the wanderings of an exile in quest of the place where he truly belongs; although, we shall see, with differences that demarcate sharply the various Romantic quests both from the Plotinian odyssey and the Christian pilgrimage.

I propose in the next two chapters to examine some prominent developmental patterns, and the concepts associated with them, which were widely manifested both in the structure of individual metaphysical systems and in the design of individual works of literature by major writers, German and English, in the four decades after 1790. In this overview of a large and very diverse body of materials, it may help us to keep our bearings if I end this chapter with some general observations about the characteristic philosophies of the age, and also about the relations between philosophy and literature which help to explain the remarkable parallels between these Romantic forms of thought and imagination.

i   The self-moving and self-sustaining system.   Post-Kantian philosophers called their organized thought a "system," by which they signified that it was self-generative, self-determinative, all-inclusive, and self-contained. That is, its first premise by an immanent necessity evolves into everything essential in the universe—including even itself, by virtue of the fact that its conclusion returns to and implicates the premise, so that the completed system stands free of reliance on any principle outside itself. Such a system differs essentially from the metaphysical structures of most of their great predecessors; for these, whatever the nature of the world they described, had themselves, in theory, been composed of fixed concepts ordered by rational connections into a stable structure of enduring truths. The remarkable thing is that the system of Romantic philosophy—in a fashion adumbrated by Fichte, developed by Schelling, and carried to its ultimate by Hegel—is itself represented as a *moving* system, a dynamic process which is driven by an internal source of motion to its own completion. As Schelling defined the deficiency of the philosophy of Spinoza, whom he nevertheless acknowledged as his "teacher and predecessor":

> Spinoza knows that powerful equilibrium of the primordial powers which he opposes to one another as extended . . . and thinking. . . . But he knows only the equilibrium, not the strife arising from their equipollence; the two powers are in inactivity beside each other, without mutual excitement or enhancement [*Steigerung*]. . . . Hence the deficiency in his system with regard to life and development.

For, Schelling says, "Contradiction is life's mainspring and core. . . . If there were only unity, and if everything were at peace, then truly nothing would want to stir, and everything would sink into listlessness." [55] As the quotation reveals, Schelling regards the nisus which drives the universe as the energy inherent in polarities—conceived as antitheses, contraries, contradictions—which manifests itself as a tension of repulsion and attraction, of centrifugal and centripetal forces. But it is not only the universe that philosophy describes which manifests perpetual motion: the philosophical system is itself conceived as an immanently propelled and ever evolving process of oppositions, reconciliations, and renewed oppositions, moving toward a final state in which all oppositions will be reconciled.

Fichte's *Wissenschaftslehre,* Coleridge said, "by commencing with an *act,* instead of a *thing* or *substance* . . . supplied the *idea* of a system truly metaphysical . . . (i.e., having its spring and principle within itself)." [56] Fichte's *Science of Knowledge* begins with the concept of the ego, which is a pure activity that posits itself to itself as the non-ego merely that it may have a field in which it can realize itself, by an "infinite striving" against a resisting non-self toward an approachable yet inaccessible goal of absolute freedom. The relation of opposition and conflict between ego and non-ego is the generative energy in Fichte's universe. In a consonant fashion Fichte's own conceptual system evolves by posing a thesis, opposing this by an antithesis, and resolving the opposition in a synthesis which becomes in turn the thesis which is opposed by a new antithesis.

Schelling, Coleridge went on to say, was "the most successful *improver* of the Dynamic System." Schelling's *System of Transcendental Idealism,* to take an early example, is set and sustained in motion by the compulsion to closure of the basic opposition between the concepts of subject and object, and this primal opposition involves the oppositions between intelligence and nature, between the conscious and unconscious, between freedom and necessity. "If all knowledge has, as it were, two poles, which reciprocally presume and demand each other, then these poles must seek each other in all sciences; there must therefore necessarily be two basic sciences; and it must be impossible to start out from the one pole without being driven to the other." [57] The compulsion in the processes of nature to convert object to subject, nature to intelligence, has its reciprocal in the dynamic compulsion within the conceptual scheme of his own philosophy to resolve the contradiction between subject and object. This resolution, in the *Transcendental Idealism,* Schelling locates in the concept of the "imagination" of the productive artist, the one faculty by which we are able both "to think and to reconcile contradictions," and which annuls, by uniting in a single activity and product, the ultimate contradiction working "at the roots of the artist's whole being," between nature and intelligence, conscious and unconscious, subject and object.[58]

The self-starting, continuously evolving, all-inclusive, and self-sufficient philosophic system reached its culmination in the dialectic of Hegel. Wherever you engage with Hegel's thought, you find yourself in immediate motion. The elemental units of his system, the "Concepts" [*Begriffe*], are themselves "self-movements, circles . . . spiritual entities." "The Concept is the object's own self which presents itself as its becoming . . . that moves itself and takes its determinations back into itself," and passes over into its own complement, or antithesis.[59] "In science the Concept develops itself out of itself, and is merely an immanent progression and production of its own determinations"; this "moving principle of the Concept . . . I call dialectic." And the same dialectic—of immanent movement and the self-induced passage of each element into its own contraries and contradictions, which in turn press for reconciliation or synthesis—manifests itself in the phenomenal world of objects, of people, and of institutions, just as it does in the systematic thinking of the philosopher.

> Wherever there is movement, wherever there is life, wherever anything is carried into effect in the actual world, there Dialectic is at work. . . . Everything that surrounds us may be viewed as an instance of Dialectic . . . by which the finite, as implicitly other than what it is, is forced beyond its own immediate or natural being to turn suddenly into its opposite.[60]

The totality of the movements of the component concepts is philosophy, or "science"; and truth in this energetic and integral philosophic system does not inhere in any propositions severed from the whole (for by severance they are at once rendered "dead and positive") but in the entirety of the dynamic process itself: "this whole movement constitutes the positive and its truth." And the dialectic in which no part is at rest, yet which in its totality constitutes the truth which is timeless and therefore at rest, Hegel describes in a famous oxymoron: "The true is thus the bacchanalian whirl in which no member is not drunken; and because each, as soon as it detaches itself, dissolves immediately—the whirl is just as much transparent and simple repose." [61]

In both Hegel and Schelling the persistent reference, both in defining the nature of their system and in establishing its superior truth over alternative philosophies, is to "life" as against "death." The recurrent metaphors in Hegel's exposition reveal that the paradigm from which he derives his categories is a biological one, and that his metaphysical system is in fact systemic—conceived on the analogue of the growth of a living organism, in which the parts are in ceaseless self-generated motion, die when severed from their organic milieu, and constitute a whole which, by an immanent energy, evolves toward its own completed form. "The idea," Hegel says, is like a flower, "a unity of leaves, of form, of color, of smell, something living and growing." "The true," accordingly, "has the drive to *develop*. . . . The idea, concrete in itself and developing, is thus an organic system." [62]

Within this inclusive biological perspective, the dynamic principle—that of the creative power of contraries which are antithetic yet complementary, exhibit a tension of opposition and attraction, and conjoin in a union that generates a new existence—seems, in the final analysis, to have acquired its attributes by analogy with bisexual reproduction. This dialectic is sometimes represented in terms that reveal its affinity to the prototype (central to earlier esoteric thought) of sexual division, opposition, and procreative reunion. To define the essential polarity underlying "the production of the first parts of the world-system," Schelling refers to human procreation, "the single instance in which we are to a certain extent permitted to be witnesses of an original creation." [63] "The two Primary Poles of Nature," Coleridge wrote to C. A. Tulk, "the two correlatives and correspondent Opposites, by and in which the Unity is revealed" are "(to borrow your happy and most expressive Symbol) the Male and female of the World of Time, in whose wooings, and retirings and nuptial conciliations all other marriages and births are celebrated inclusively." [64]

In an early manuscript on love as the principle which overcomes oppositions, Hegel advances a more complex parallel, which exploits the conceptual possibilities in the phenomenon that bisexual union between human lovers begets a monosexual child, who then repeats his parents' function in the unbroken genealogical chain of union and procreation:

> What in the first instance is most the individual's own is united into the whole in the lovers' touch and contact; consciousness of a separate self disappears, and all distinction between the lovers is annulled. The mortal element, the body, has lost the character of separability, and a living child, a seed of immortality, of the eternally self-developing and self-generating [race], has come into existence. What has been united [in the child] is not divided again; [in love and through love] God has acted and created. . . .
>
> Everything which gives the newly begotten child a manifold life and a specific existence, it must draw into itself, set over

against itself, and unify with itself. The seed breaks free from its original unity, turns ever more and more to opposition, and begins to develop. Each stage of its development is a separation, and its aim in each is to regain for itself the full riches of life [enjoyed by the parents]. Thus the process is: unity, separated opposites, reunion. After their union the lovers separate again, but in the child their union has become unseparated.

This union in love is complete, but it can remain so only as long as . . . each separate lover is one organ in a living whole.[65]

In Hegel's cryptic fragment we see a constitutive analogue in the process of yielding what were to be the essential categories of his mature dialectic. In the sexual opposition and union of the parents inheres the concept of complementary antitheses which, by mutual attraction, are drawn into a synthesis in which "all distinction . . . is annulled." In the resulting generation of a child who unites the traits of both parents but immediately begins its independent development into a new monosexual individual who proceeds to find and unite with his own sexual contrary, we find the emergent concept of a synthesis which passes over to a new opposition that leads to a new generative synthesis. Finally, in the fact of the cumulative genealogical inheritance of all the component unions between individuals in "the eternally self-developing and self-generating [race]," we find the germ of Hegel's primary dialectical innovation over Fichte's method of sequential but segmented theses and antitheses, and over Schelling's concept of multiple polarities: the notion of a single unbroken and all-inclusive chain of self-renewing and accumulative, hence progressive, syntheses. As Hegel describes the process, all the successive oppositions are successively *aufgehoben;* that is (in that triple German equivoque which he made into one of the most influential of metaphysical ideas), they are at the same time annulled, preserved, and raised to a higher level.

ii Immanent teleology. The inherent movement of post-Kantian systems of thought is in no way random, nor does it permit any essential options to the initiative of the metaphysician. The systems are represented as moving toward a built-in goal, or end state, by a process in which each stage arises from the preceding one in a self-determined order, constituting a sequence which the philosophers sometimes call "deductive." The process, in other words, as it manifests itself in the systematic thinking of the philosopher, moves by an immanent teleology. The dialectical movement within the timeless philosophic system, accordingly, constitutes a kind of preordained plot, and a similar plot exhibits itself, spread out in time, in the agents and events of the outer world. In Hegel's fully developed form of this way of thinking, the dialectical evolution of systematic reason in philosophy has its phenomenal and temporal correlative in the process of the physical universe, and in the course of all human experience and human history. The world, said Hegel, is "Objective Thought," or conversely, "Reason is in the world: which means that Reason is . . . its immanent principle, its most proper and inward nature, its universal." Hence the same self-evolving "spirit" which realizes itself in the total system of philosophy (*Wissenschaft*) also manifests itself as "nature," and in another aspect, when it is "spirit given over into time," it manifests itself as history.[66]

This concept of the ineluctable working-out of an implicit design in systematic thought, in nature, and in the history of human actions and consciousness is very like the theological concept of the universal but hidden working of divine Providence, transferred from an external personal God as planner and controller to the immanent operation (in Hegel's repeated phrase) of "the cunning of Reason." And we find, in fact, that these philosophical systems are, as Novalis said of Fichte's philosophy, "perhaps nothing else than applied Christianity." [67] That is, they assimilate into their overall design and conceptual details the plot pattern and crucial events of Biblical history, from the creation (which, as transposed into philosophical terms, does not occur in time but in the timeless conceptual priority of that "moment" at which the ego, or absolute, or spirit sets itself off as object to itself as subject) to a last far-off divine event toward which both speculative thought and the universe inevitably move.[68] In some part, doubtless, this procedure was the unwitting result of the retention in philosophical thought of inherited cultural prepossessions. In large part, however, the persistent tendency of post-Kantian thinking (in the words of the historian of philosophy, Frederick Copleston) "to demythologize Christian dogmas, turning them in the process into a speculative philosophy," [69] was a deliberate enterprise, on the stated assumption that Christianity embodies in its design of history and in its particular fables and doctrines an advanced, although imperfectly refined, stage in the evolution of truth. Hegel repeatedly describes his philosophy as knowledge which transcends Christian theology, but only by assimilating it into a higher order of conceptually articulated and systematic truth. "For, though philosophy must not allow herself to be overawed by religion," Hegel said, "or accept the position of existence on sufferance, she cannot afford to neglect these popular conceptions" and "the tales and allegories of religion." [70] As we shall see in the next chapter, prominent among the popular conceptions which Fichte, Schelling, and Hegel explicitly undertook to translate into their philosophies were the story of the fall and the prophecy of the redemption of mankind.

iii   Unity lost and unity regained.   The theological design, as transposed into the metaphysical systems of the German Idealists, is an extraordinarily complex, but nonetheless recognizable, version of the great circle of Neoplatonic Christianity, according to which the process of emanation ends in its beginning, and the beginning and ending are the One. Kant, Fichte remarks, "proceeds from the assumption that a manifold is given, as something to be collected into the unity of consciousness." But the true "science of knowledge, which has to encompass the entire system of the human spirit," must take the opposite way, and lead down from the unity of the absolute ego, which posits the non-ego in itself and then continues in a sequence that comprehends the manifold of particulars, "until we arrive at the highest theoretical fact; namely, at that through which the ego consciously posits itself as determined through the non-ego. Thus the theoretical science of knowledge closes with its first principle, returns into itself, and accordingly becomes, by its own agency, completely closed [*Beschlossen*]." [71]

And in the conclusion to his *Foundations of the Total System of Knowledge* Fichte writes:

> The circle has now been completed. . . . And that which guarantees the completeness of our deduction of the chief compulsions of the ego is the fact that it rounds off and closes the circle of the system of those compulsions.[72]

In an early essay Schelling proposed, in opposition to Kant's nonsystematic procedure, that

> all science in its highest perfection and unity must become possible insofar as the first principle of philosophy is precisely also its last principle—when that with which all philosophy, including theoretical philosophy, begins is itself also the last result of practical philosophy, in which all knowledge comes to its conclusion.

Schelling begins his own *Transcendental Idealism* with the premise of an absolute unity—the "identity" or "indifference" (the utter lack of differentiation)—of subject and object. This "eternal and original unity" is "sundered by the process of thought," and it manifests itself in its divided subject-object form both in the realm of nature and of mind. But "a system is completed when it returns to its starting point"; and thus is it with his system, whose process of demonstration has led back at the end "to that original ground of all harmony of the subjective and objective which, in its original identity, could only be represented through an intellectual intuition [*Anschauung*]." [73]

"The true," Hegel said, "is its own becoming, the circle that presupposes its end as its aim and thus has it for its beginning." [74] Hegel claimed that Fichte and Schelling had succeeded no more than Kant before them in achieving their stated aim of rounding their systems back from division to the beginning in "the perfected, real unity of subject and object, or Ego and Non-Ego." [75] Hegel's own system undertakes to remedy this deficiency. As he summarizes the design of his philosophy in the shorter *Logic:*

The very point of view, which originally is taken on its own evidence only, must in the course of the science be converted to a result,—the ultimate result in which philosophy returns into itself and reaches the point with which it began. In this manner philosophy exhibits the appearance of a circle which closes with itself, and has no beginning in the same way as the other sciences have.[76]

Thus his philosophical system, having generated everything, returns at the end to swallow its own generative premise, leaving nothing outside itself.

When the history of mankind is envisioned as this circular design manifested in time, the Christian view of the lost and future paradise assumes the form of unity, unity lost, and unity-to-be-regained. In Romantic as in Neoplatonic thought, division, separateness, externality, isolation are equated with evil, as well as with that other consequence of the Biblical fall of man, death. "So long as I myself am *identical* with nature," said Schelling, "I understand what a living nature is as well as I understand my own life. . . . As soon, however, as I separate myself . . . from nature, nothing more is left for me but a dead object." [77] "The activity of differentiating" by the understanding, Hegel wrote, effects the dismembered "unactuality" that we call "death"; while "the life that endures and preserves itself through death is the life of the spirit." [78] As Novalis summarized what was a Romantic commonplace: "All evil and wickedness is isolating (it is the principle of separation)." [79]

In consonance with this outlook, Romantic thinkers regard philosophical reflection, the very act of taking thought (since it necessarily seeks understanding by the analytic division of one into many) as in itself, in Schelling's words, "a spiritual sickness of mankind . . . an evil," because once begun, it continues inexorably to divide everything "which nature had permanently united." And the radical and cardinal malaise of man, because it is both the initial cause and the continuing manifestation of his evil and suffering, is the separation with which consciousness and reflection begins when "man sets himself in opposition to the outer world" [80]—in the split, as it was variously expressed, between ego and non-ego, subject and object, spirit and the other, nature and mind. The primal fracture which results when man begins to reflect, and so to philosophize, is usually conceived as having two dimensions, one cognitive and the other moral. The first of these manifests itself in a split between his mind and outer nature, and the second manifests itself in a split within the nature of man himself. In its cognitive dimension, this division consists in the loss of the original unity of mind with nature, through man's emergent awareness of a separation of the subject that knows from that object, or "nature," that is known. In its moral dimension, it consists in the loss of the mind's original unity with itself (its primogenial harmony of impulse and action) through man's emergent awareness of an opposition and conflict between that "nature" which is the substratum of his human nature (man's natural instincts, desires, and compulsions which constitute the realm of "necessity") and his subjective "reason" (the capacity to distinguish alternative choices which are right or wrong) together with his subjective realm of "freedom" (the capacity to choose what is right and reject what is wrong). Man's self-consciousness thus alienates him from his world and also imposes on him the terrible burden of freedom of choice in the knowledge of good and evil. But this initial, two-dimensional fission between mind and outer nature, and between the mind and its own natural impulses, although it is in itself an evil, is the very act which releases the energy that sets in motion the speculative philosophy whose basic aim (as Schelling goes on to say in the passage I quoted) is to cancel all cognitive and moral separation and opposition in a restored and enduring unity. Without the "original separation . . . we would have no need to philosophize," and "true philosophy" sets out from the primal separation "in order to annul and sublimate [*aufzuheben*] that separation forever."

Romantic philosophy is thus primarily a metaphysics of integration, of which the key principle is that of the "reconciliation," or synthesis, of whatever is divided, opposed, and conflicting. It is in this context that we are to understand Schelling's claim that "all philosophizing consists in recalling the condition in which we were at one with nature"; [81] and it is within this philosophical tradition that we are able to understand the vehemence of Coleridge's decrial, cited early in this chapter, of the act of "the mere understanding" by which "we think of ourselves as separated beings, and place nature in antithesis to the mind, as object to subject, thing to thought, death to life." [82] And for Hegel, the inherent goal of the total process of spirit, as manifested in the course of human thought, is finally and completely to reclaim for consciousness the world from which it had been alienated by the initial act in which it became conscious:

> The spirit is this movement of becoming something other for itself, i.e., an object for its self, and then to sublimate this otherhood. . . . [It] becomes estranged and then returns to itself from estrangement . . . and becomes the property of consciousness.[83]

iv Progress by reversion: the Romantic spiral.   The typical Romantic design differs from the circular monism of the Neoplatonists in two chief aspects; and these differences are all-important, for they entail an outlook on life and a set of values which are entirely opposed to those most characteristic in philosophical Neoplatonism. In the first place, the early systems of post-Kantian philosophy transferred the unity which is the beginning and goal of all process, and the locus and criterion of ultimate value, from the Plotinian other-realm to this world of man and nature and human experience. As a goal, such unity might be regarded by Romantic philosophers either as accessible to mankind or else (by Fichte, for example) as infinitely recessive, and so only progressively approximable by mankind. In either case, however, the history of the race and of the individual—which had in Neoplatonism been a passing episode of absence from felicity, a regrettable deviation into this-worldly existence—became the sole realm in which, in the end, we either find our happiness or not at all: the aim of our life in this world can be nothing else than to enhance the quality of that life itself. In the second place, in the most representative Romantic version of emanation and return, when the process reverts to its beginning the recovered unity is not, as in the school of Plotinus, the simple, undifferentiated unity of its origin, but a unity which is higher, because it incorporates the intervening differentiations. "We have now returned," as Hegel said in a comment which was added to the conclusion of his shorter *Logic,* "to the notion of the Idea with which we began," but "this return to the beginning is also an advance." [84] The self-moving circle, in other words, rotates along a third, a vertical dimension, to close where it had begun, but on a higher plane of value. It thus fuses the idea of the circular return with the idea of linear progress, to describe a distinctive figure of Romantic thought and imagination—the ascending circle, or spiral. Hugo von Hoffmannsthal's later description of this design is terse and complete: "Every development moves in a spiral line, leaves nothing behind, reverts to the same point on a higher turning." [85]

According to this view, the reunion or synthesis which follows after any division into contraries constitutes a "third thing" which is higher than the original unity because it preserves the distinction that it has overcome. Goethe's description of what he calls "spiral" development uses the alchemical term *Steigerung* (enhancement) for this result: "The two great drive-wheels of all nature" are "the concept of polarity and of enhancement." Every phenomenon must separate itself in order to manifest itself as a phenomenon, but "the separate seeks itself again" and if "the separate first enhances itself it brings forth through the union of the enhanced parts a third, new, higher, totally unexpected thing." [86] "In Life, and in the view of a vital philosophy," as Coleridge put the concept, "the two component counter-powers actually interpenetrate each other, and generate a higher third, including both the former, 'ita tamen ut sit alia et major.' " [87] In the process of systematic knowledge, according to Hegel's view, "the abundance of the content, simplified into determinateness, returns into itself . . . and develops into its higher truth"; with the result that "the last stage of philosophy is the product of all earlier philosophy, nothing is lost, all principles are preserved." [88]

In the central tradition of Neoplatonic thought the absolutely undifferentiated One had been the absolute good, perfection itself, the *primum exemplar omnium,* and the end to which all existence aspires. In this distinctive Romantic innovation, on the contrary, the norm of truth, goodness, and beauty is not the simple unity of the origin, but the complex unity of the terminus of the process of cumulative division and reintegration. William James once remarked of the Neoplatonic One that "the stagnant felicity of the absolute's own perfection moves me as little as I move it." [89] James's recoil from the traditional apotheosis of static, uniform, and self-sufficient simplicity overpasses that of most thinkers of our period, who acknowledged the strong attraction of the primal unity of being; but they view such an attraction, we shall see, as a hopeless nostalgia for a lost condition to which civilized man can never return, and ought not to return if he could; for what makes him civilized, and a man, is his aspiration toward a harmony and integrity which is much higher than the unity he has lost. And it is higher, these thinkers point out, not only because it preserves diversification and individuality, but also because, instead of being a condition which has merely been given to man, it is a condition which he must earn by incessant striving along an inclined circuitous path. The typical Romantic ideal, far from being a mode of cultural primitivism, is an ideal of strenuous effort along the hard road of culture and civilization.

A. O. Lovejoy has said that the shift from "uniformitarianism" to "diversitarianism"—the preference for maximum diversity, for the fullness of individuality, and for particularity, as against the earlier preference for the uniform, the simple, and the general—emerged in "the generation of German writers who came to maturity between the seventies and the nineties," and that this diversitarianism constitutes "the most significant and distinctive feature of the Romantic revolution." [90] This is true, but it is not the whole truth; one must add that what was most distinctive in Romantic thought was the normative emphasis not on plenitude as such, but on an organized unity in which all individuation and diversity survive, in Coleridge's terms, as distinctions without division. It is well, as Coleridge put the matter, if "the understanding" operative in abstract knowledge "distinguish without dividing," and so prepare the way "for the intellectual re-union of the all in one" in the "eternal reason." [91] The norm of the highest good was thus transferred from simple unity, not to sheer diversity as such but to the most inclusive integration. At the highest point of culture, Schiller said, "man will combine the greatest fullness of existence with the highest autonomy and freedom, and instead of losing himself to the world, will rather draw the latter into himself in all its infinitude of phenomena, and subject it to the unity of his reason"; and as in life, so in art, the unity and definiteness of beauty "does not reside in the exclusion of certain realities, but in the absolute inclusion of all realities." This complex attribute Coleridge called "multeity in unity"; it served him, as it did Schiller, as the norm both for life and for beauty; and he tended, like many of his German contemporaries, to rank all living things and all human achievements, moral and aesthetic, according to the double criterion of inclusiveness and organization: the multiplicity and diversity of the component parts together with the degree of their integration into a unified whole.[92]

To shift the location of the highest truth and the highest value from the simple beginning to the complex end of an extended process is to transform Plotinus' emanation into evolution, and so to convert Plotinus' derogation of the movement from the One to the many as a descent from perfection to its laudation as an indispensable stage in the ascent toward perfection. To Jacobi's traditional view that "the ground" from which we educe anything is necessarily of a higher order of reality and value than that which is educed from it, Schelling retorted in an essay of 1812 that "the true method of philosophizing is ascending, not descending." "Always and necessarily the ground from which anything evolves is lower than that which evolves from it." Or in the traditional language of theology, the one God at the end of the spiral of development, because He will have evolved into a unity that includes all diversity, is immeasurably greater than He was in His undifferentiated unity at the beginning of the process.

> I posit God as the first and the last, as Alpha and Omega, but as Alpha he is not what he is as Omega; and insofar as he is the first . . . he cannot, strictly speaking, be called God; unless one were to say expressly "the undeveloped God," *Deus implicitus,* since, as Omega, he is *Deus explicitus.*[93]

Hegel similarly insisted that the philosophical absolute is "not an original unity as such, or an immediate unity as such," which "in itself is . . . unstained sameness and unity with itself" and therefore "is not serious about otherness, estrangement, and the overcoming of this estrangement." The absolute which is the criterion-principle of philosophic truth and value is to be found not at the beginning but at the end of the developmental process: "the absolute is to be comprehended essentially as result." As usual, Hegel does not hesitate to formulate the extreme position to which this way of thinking points. The true, he says, is no other than the achieved actualization of the entire circle of becoming.

> The true is the whole. But the whole is only the essence perfecting itself through its development. Of the absolute it should be said that it is essentially result, that it is only in the end what it is in truth, and precisely in this consists its nature: to be actual, subject, or that which becomes itself.[94]

The absolute in which Hegel's dialectic of spirit and its alienated others culminates is an all-in-one: that undivided unity which, having overcome yet preserved all preceding individuation, incorporates in itself not less than everything.

v Redemption as progressive self-education. I remarked earlier the extent to which post-Kantian philosophical thought incorporated a conceptualized version of the design of Christian history. In this process the redemptive goal of the history of mankind was shifted from the reconciliation and reunion of man with a transcendent God to an overcoming of the opposition between ego and non-ego, or a reconciliation of subject with object, or a reunion of the spirit with its own other, and this culmination was represented as occurring in the fully developed consciousness of men living their lives in this world: the justification for the ordeal of human experience is located in experience itself. Accordingly, the history of mankind, as well as the history of the reflective individual, was conceived not as a probation for an other-worldly heaven but as a process of the self-formation, or self-education, of the mind and moral

being of man from the dawn of consciousness to the stage of
full maturity. The mind of man, whether generic or individual,
is represented as disciplined by the suffering which it experiences as it develops through successive stages of division, conflict, and reconciliation, toward the culminating stage at which,
all oppositions having been overcome, it will achieve a full and
triumphant awareness of its identity, of the significance of its
past, and of its accomplished destiny. The course of human life
(in the economy of statement made possible by German com-
pounds) is no longer a *Heilsgeschichte* but a *Bildungsgeschichte;*
or more precisely, it is a *Heilsgeschichte* translated into the
secular mode of a *Bildungsgeschichte.*

In this philosophy the primacy and initiative lies in the principle of mind, and in the Western tradition the distinctive attribute of the mind is "consciousness," and its distinctive activity is "knowing." Hence the extraordinary degree to which
these metaphysical systems—even though they undertook to
account for the totality of the universe—were primarily
epistemological and cognitive systems. For everything essential
that exists and happens is referred, ultimately, to the "becoming," the evolving history, of human consciousness. In his
Transcendental Idealism Schelling defined "the whole of
philosophy" as "the progressive history of self-consciousness,"
and Hegel described the subject of the *Phenomenology of
the Spirit* as "the becoming of knowledge," or "the detailed
history of the education [*Bildung*] of consciousness to the
level of science." [95] In this philosophical context the Christian
history of the creation, fall, and redemption was translated
to the realm of human consciousness as stages, or "moments,"
in its evolving knowledge. In the initial act of self-conscious
knowledge which separates the knower from the known
consists both the creation of a world conceived as external
to the knowing mind and also the fall of man from his
primal innocence (equated with self-unity) into the knowledge of evil (equated with self-division and conflict). But
if knowledge is initially analytic and divisive, it is also,
in its higher manifestation, unifying and integrative; for
the mind, when it fully succeeds in grasping and comprehending the thing it knows, assimilates that thing and makes it its

own. In consequence, the redemptive goal of human life is envisaged as that ultimate stage of the collective consciousness of mankind when, by the fullness and perfection of its power of organized knowing, it will utterly repossess everything which it has, in its earlier stages of imperfect and partial knowledge, separated and alienated as object to itself as subject. Only in that point, as Schelling put it, "of total coincidence of the world as known by us with the world of nature" at which "the world of thought has become the world of nature . . . lies the last and supreme appeasement and expiation of cognition, and only in this can the fulfillment of the demands of morality be achieved." [96]

The transformation of theological history into the process of human education shows itself even in the titles of some of the numerous writings on "universal history" of the latter eighteenth century, from Lessing's *Die Erziehung des Menschengeschlechts* (1780) to Schiller's *Über die ästhetische Erziehung des Menschen* (1795). Hegel made it clear that he considered the plot of history to be the self-realization and self-education of the spirit, and that the result of this process constitutes the justification of God's ways to men; it is in this sense that "the history of the world," as the "developmental process and realization of the spirit," is "the true *Theodicaea,* the justification of God in History." [97] In his *Phenomenology of the Spirit,* Hegel declared, "the general individual, the self-conscious spirit, has to be considered in its education [*Bildung*]," of which "the aim is the spirit's insight into what constitutes knowledge." [98] "The general fall of man," Schelling wrote in 1803, which occurred when Greek paganism gave way to Christianity, was "the breaking away of man from nature," and "the consciousness of this fact puts an end to innocence." Correspondingly, then, redemption from the fall will occur in the "conscious reconciliation which takes the place of the [original] unconscious identity with nature, as well as of the estrangement from fate, and reinstates unity on a higher level"; and it is the recognition of this process—the fall from innocence which will lead to a higher innocence—which "is expressed in the idea of Providence." [99]

This is a theory of progress—or more precisely, a theory of

the progressive education of the mind of man—but it is not a philosophy of optimism, except insofar as the Christian view of history is itself optimistic in holding that the best is yet to be, and that the end of human history justifies the means of Providence. These philosophers did not deny the reality of evil but conceived it (in Schelling's phrase) as "a necessary evil"; [100] nor did they minimize the agonies of the human condition. On the contrary, the essential role that Schelling and Hegel assigned to estrangement, conflict, and death in each successive stage of a developmental process brought into high relief the inescapability of suffering, loss, and destruction in human life and history. Physical and moral pain as well as dread [*Angst*], Schelling wrote in *The Ages of the World,* is "something universal and necessary in all life." Since it is God Himself who evolves through history, He undergoes the suffering necessarily "involved in development" and in the progressive education of the consciousness of mankind:

> God leads human nature through no other course than that through which his own nature must pass. Participation in everything blind, dark, and suffering of God's nature is necessary in order to raise him to highest consciousness.[101]

Contemplating "the ills, the evil, the destruction" and the "unspeakable misery" of the human spectacle, it appeared to Hegel that history was, overall, a vast "slaughter bench." In his *Phenomenology* he described the stages of the educative process of the generic human mind as "stations," equivalent to the Stations of the Cross; and he concluded the book, in his persisting mode of Biblical parallelism, by describing his preceding account of the sufferings of human consciousness evolving toward its goal of "absolute knowledge" as the conceptual reality of the story of the Passion—as "the recollection and the Golgotha of the absolute spirit." [102]

vi The spiral journey back home.   In Hegel, and also in Schelling, then, the timeless metaphysical system, as it evolves through time in the mode of history, has a clearly defined plot: the painful education through ever expanding knowledge of the conscious subject as it strives—without dis-

tinctly knowing what it is that it wants until it achieves it—
to win its way back to a higher mode of the original unity with
itself from which, by its primal act of consciousness, it has inescapably divided itself off. When described in metaphysical
terms, the basic categories for this process, as we have seen,
tended to be derived from the model of biological genesis,
growth, and development; a process which was in turn interpreted as the sequential reconciliation of recurrent contraries,
or else as the reconciliation with itself of a concept which has
evolved to an extreme at which it "passes over," in Hegel's
term, to its own antithesis or "negation." But in addition the
historical process was often represented by these philosophers
in an allegorical or pictured form; and for this imaginative
mode, the most apt and available vehicle was the traditional
one of the history of mankind as a circuitous journey back
home. So represented, the protagonist is the collective mind or
consciousness of men, and the story is that of its painful pilgrimage through difficulties, sufferings, and recurrent disasters
in quest of a goal which, unwittingly, is the place it had left
behind when it first set out and which, when reachieved, turns
out to be even better than it had been at the beginning. Thus
redemption, even after it has been translocated to history and
translated into the self-education of the general mind of mankind, continues to be represented in the central Christian trope
of life as a pilgrimage and quest: the *Bildungsgeschichte* of the
Romantic philosophy of consciousness tends to be imagined in
the story form of a *Bildungsreise* whose end is its own beginning.

One of Schelling's favorite figures for the course of all things
was Plotinus' analogue of the circular voyage of the Homeric
hero; the human process, he said, is a two-part epic of departure and return, in which "the first part is the *Iliad*, the
second the *Odyssey* of history." [103] Discussing "the PHILOS-
OPHY of History," Coleridge said that if we see that "the
nurture and evolution of humanity is the final aim," we recognize that its course is that of a circuitous journey: "Man sallies
forth into nature," only to learn "at last that what he *seeks* he
has *left behind*." [104] Hegel's reiterative image for the self-educative process of consciousness, whether collective or individual,

is that of a *Weg*—a road, or journey. "To become true knowledge," the spirit "has to work its way through a long journey
[*Weg*]"; and every "individual must also pass through the
contents of the educational stages of the general spirit, but . . .
as stages of a way [*Weg*] that has been prepared and evened for
him." [105] In his systematic translation of the Christian process
of redemption into the process of human history, which he
conceived as "The Education of the Human Race," Lessing
had earlier represented the course which is determined by an
immanent Providence as the *Weg*, or *Bahn*, of mankind as a
whole, which must also be trodden by each single man: "The
very path [*Bahn*] upon which the race reaches its perfection,
every individual man (some sooner, others later) must first
have traveled over." [106] Lessing's path exhibits the design of
the linear progress of the Enlightenment which, however it
may waver, nonetheless moves steadily onward as well as upward. Hegel's path, on the other hand, is the Romantic way
along an inclined plane back toward the point of origin. And
we shall see that the figure of the circuitous journey homeward,
which in other Romantic philosophers is a recurrent but passing allusion, Hegel developed into the sustained vehicle for his
Phenomenology of the Spirit, which recounts the vicissitudes
of the spirit at the crucial stages of its laborious educational
journey, from its "moment" of departure from its own alienated
self, around and up and back, until it finds itself "at home
with itself in its otherness." [107]

vii   Philosophical system and literary plot.   At no other
place and time have literature and technical philosophy been
so closely interinvolved as in Germany in the period beginning
with Kant. The major German poets and novelists (as well as
Coleridge, and later Carlyle, in England) avidly assimilated the
writings of the philosophers; many of them wrote philosophical
essays; and all incorporated current philosophical concepts and
procedures into the subject matter and structure of their principal works of imagination. And on their part philosophers
remained closely in touch with literature; Schelling and Hegel
themselves wrote poetry, and both these thinkers gave literature
and the arts a prominent—Schelling, in his central period, the

cardinal—place in their metaphysical systems.[108] It is not by chance nor by the influence of a mysteriously noncausal *Zeitgeist*, but through participation in the same historical and intellectual milieu, through recourse to similar precedents in the religious and cultural tradition, and by frequent interaction, that the works of philosophy and literature of this age manifest conspicuous parallels in ideas, in design, and even in figurative detail.

Much of English Romantic literature, Bernard Blackstone has said, is "a literature of movement," [109] in which the protagonist is a compulsive wanderer; and the generalization can be applied equally to German literature. Some of these wanderers are guilt-driven sinners, on the model of Cain or the Wandering Jew; others are like Ishmael, who is born an alien and exile even in his native land. Especially common, however, is the story form of the pilgrimage and quest—the journey in search of an unknown or inexpressible something which gradually leads the wanderer back toward his point of origin.

The two chapters that follow will deal with some notable examples, both in philosophy and literature, of the Romantic plot of the circular or spiral quest, and also with the concepts of which this fictional form is the imaginative correlative and vehicle. Such plots may be literal and realistic, with the progress of the individual pilgrim represented as typical of all artists, or all philosophical minds, or all mankind; or they may be cast in an allegorical and symbolic mode, or else in that type of invented myth, incorporating a philosophy of life and of history, which the Germans called the *Märchen*. In any case they embody an implicit theodicy, for the journey is a spiritual way through evil and suffering which is justified as a necessary means to the achievement of a greater good; and usually, although with greater or less explicitness, this process is conceived as a fall from unity into division and into a conflict of contraries which in turn compel the movement back toward a higher integration.

The chief antecedent of this narrative form is the Christian allegory of the journey of life. The wayfaring Christian on his laborious pilgrimage to heaven-haven, however, is converted into a hero whose journey is an education in experience through stages of awareness which culminate on the level of intellectual maturity—a stage of integrity, power, and freedom in which the protagonist finally learns who he is, what he was born for, and the implicit purpose of all that he has endured on the way. Behind many Romantic versions of the internal circuitous quest we can recognize the chief prototype of the circular variant of the ancient Christian *peregrinatio,* that is, the parable of the Prodigal Son interpreted as the type of the journey of all mankind out of and back toward its original home; and in Romantic as in Christian literature, this parable is frequently conflated with the apocalyptic marriage that signalized the restoration of Eden in the Book of Revelation. Accordingly, the yearning for fulfillment is sometimes expressed as *Heimweh,* the homesickness for the father or mother and for the lost sheltered place; [110] or else as the desire for a female figure who turns out to be the beloved we have left behind; or sometimes, disconcertingly, as the desire for father, mother, home, and bride all in one.

We shall also find, however, that in a number of Romantic writers the journey in quest of an earthly consummation is qualified by the realization that the goal is an infinite one which lies forever beyond the reach of man, whose possibilities are limited by the conditions of a finite world. As Schiller presented the human dilemma in his fine lyric, *Der Pilgrim:* in the spring of his life the prodigal poet leaves his father's house and inheritance, takes up his pilgrim's staff, and sets out confidently on the ascending path toward that golden gate, somewhere out there, where the earthly is indistinguishable from the heavenly—

> Denn das Irdische wird dorten
> Himmlisch, unvergänglich sein.

But his pilgrimage leads only to the conclusion that the there is never here:

> Ach, kein Steg will dahin führen,
> Ach, der Himmel über mir
> Will die Erde nie berühren,
> Und das dort ist niemals hier.

By some poets, as by Schiller himself, the antinomy between human need and human possibility was resolved by substituting approximation for attainment, making success in life depend on man's sustaining his infinite aspiration throughout the course of his finite existence. In other poets (Blake is the supreme example) the goal of life is represented as attainable, but only by a sudden and radical alteration of consciousness. For to Blake "the lost Traveller's Dream under the Hill" is a wish-fulfilling fantasy, and the Romantic yearning that he attributes to his sunflower, "seeking after that sweet golden clime/ Where the traveller's journey is done," [111] is a hopeless nostalgia. Man must, by a triumph of imagination, break out of the cycle of his present existence into the enduring vision of an integral and entirely human world which is alone adequate to the reach of his desire.

In one of his *Fragments* Novalis brings into focus a philosophical analogue to the literary plot of the Romantic quest: "Die Philosophie ist eigentlich Heimweh—Trieb überall zu Hause zu sein." He also proposes an alternative description of the goal of the philosophical way: "Die höhere Philosophie behandelt die Ehe von Natur und Geist." [112] The easy shift from the metaphor of the search for a lost spiritual home to the metaphor of a marriage between mind and nature is typical and instructive. It serves also as a reminder that the beginning of our own devious pilgrimage was my undertaking to explicate in what way, and with what significance, Wordsworth came to formulate the high argument of his poetry as the possibility of a wedding between the mind of man and "this goodly universe." But to that point of departure I shall finally return.

FOUR

The Circuitous Journey: Through Alienation to Reintegration

"Wo gehn wir denn hin?"
"Immer nach Hause."
                    Novalis, *Heinrich von Ofterdingen*

On the one hand . . . [consciousness] alienates itself and
in this alienation sets itself off as object. . . . On the other
hand there is in this very process the other moment in
which [self-consciousness] has equally transcended this
alienation and objectification and taken it back into itself,
and so is at home with itself in its otherness as such.—This
is the movement of consciousness. . . .
                    —Hegel, *Phenomenology of the Spirit*

All "homes" are in finite experience; finite experience as
such is homeless. Nothing outside the flux secures the issue
of it. It can hope salvation only from its own intrinsic
promises and potencies.
                    —William James, *Pragmatism*

FOUR

No THINKER was of greater consequence than Friedrich Schiller in giving a distinctive Romantic formulation to the diagnosis of the modern malaise, to the assumptions about human good and ill which controlled this diagnosis, and to the overall view of the history and destiny of mankind of which the diagnosis was an integral part. Schiller's mature thought on these matters assimilated the contributions of many predecessors and contemporaries. He shows, for example, the continued influence of his early enthusiasm for the Pietist theology current in his native Swabia, with its emphasis on the resolution of the ills of the world in the fullness of time; and this influence included, probably, the theories of the Behmenist F. C. Oetinger, who developed a sophisticated version of the myth of the fall of the primal man into warring contraries which press toward an ultimate reunification in a *Wiederbringung aller Dinge*.[1] Like most intellectuals of his time, Schiller felt strongly the force of Rousseau's paradox of civilization: that human progress in intellection and in the sciences, arts, and social institutions, after an early optimal stage, involves a correlative decline in human happiness by imposing a growing burden of complication, conflict, oppression, and instinctual renunciation; and he thoroughly understood Rousseau's nostalgia for a unified life in which man is in complete harmony with himself and with other men. Schiller exhibits the powerful impact of Kant's ethics, with its basic concept of man "as belonging to two worlds"—the noumenal and phenomenal worlds—and its consequent view that to be civilized involves a continuous tension, which can never be completely resolved, between the categorical demands of the noumenal ego, or moral will, which assumes absolute freedom, and the inescapable limitations of the phenomenal ego, or man as a part of nature, and therefore subject both to his instinctual and sensual drives and to the laws of strict causal necessity.[2] We find also in Schiller the influence of Herder's thought, with its ruling norm of the whole man functioning as an integral part of an organic social whole, its epochal explorations, as Isaiah Berlin has said, "of what it is to belong" to a time, a place, and a group, and its exposition of the "notion of being at home" in a social unity—that is, in a community.[3]

Whatever the varied sources of his ideas, it seems to me highly significant that Schiller presented his early formulation of the pattern of individual and racial development (a formulation which remained the frame for all his later, more subtle thinking on these matters) in the mode of an exegesis upon the symbolic meaning of the Biblical story of the fall and promised restoration of man: *Something Concerning the First Human Society, according to the Guidance of the Mosaic Records* (1790). In thus correlating the outline of providential history with a secular *Universalgeschichte*, in which man works out his destiny independently of supernatural interposition, Schiller was entirely in accord with the major philosophers of his age, who also treated the Biblical narrative as a mythical or figurative representation of valid insights into the nature and history of mankind. We are apt to dismiss this procedure as a *pro forma* bow to orthodoxy and authority, or else as the use of a theological parallel to illustrate a view of history which had been developed independently of the Biblical account. It is instructive, however, to take seriously the claim of these philosophers to have found their philosophical truth embodied in the image-thinking of religion, and to investigate the extent to which the providential design may have been not merely an illustrative, but a constitutive analogue, which helped give a distinctive shape to Romantic philosophies of history.

In the first Chapter I suggested that the millennial prospectivism in Christian thinking had fostered the development of a secular theory of historical progress, which emerged at a time when spectacular advances in the sciences provided a conceptual model of secular progress, while the new technology seemed to provide the material means, and the new psychology of the school of Locke seemed to provide the educational means for achieving the long-expected goal. The detailed recurrence to the Biblical model of human history and prophecy, among German thinkers in the latter eighteenth and early nineteenth centuries, came at a time when the course of events had dramatically raised the question whether advances in science, rationality, and culture might be exacting too high a price— whether, in fact, instead of being a good in itself and a warrant of perfection to come, divisive intellection might be itself an evil and the root of all evils. A number of these thinkers adapted the Christian fable of a lost and future paradise into a theory which neatly fused the alternative views of human history as either decline or progress. This they accomplished by representing man's fall from happy unity into the evil of in- creasing division and suffering as an indispensable stage on his route back toward the lost unity and happiness of his origin, but along an ascending plane that will leave him immeasurably better off at the end than he was in the distant beginning.

1. THE PARADOX OF THE FORTUNATE DIVISION: SCHILLER AND UNIVERSAL HISTORY

G. E. Lessing's terse essay on *The Education of the Human Race* (1780) was an influential work in the genre that the Germans called *Universalgeschichte;* the ground idea of this form, as Blaise Pascal expressed it, is that we can "consider the entire sequence of human beings, during the entire course of the ages, as a single man who lives perpetually on and learns something all the time." [4] Lessing translated the Scriptural revelation of man's fall and redemption into a secular history of mankind's progressive education in reason and morality, assimilated external Providence to an immanent historical principle, equated the stages of civilization to stages in the maturation of an individual, and represented the educational process in the persistent metaphor of a laborious journey on the long road toward perfection. This perfection will be the earthly equivalent of the heavenly kingdom prophesied in Scripture, and will serve to justify the deficiencies and pains that man suffers en route.

"What education is for the individual, revelation is for the human race as a whole." [5] Biblical revelation merely gave humanity the truths which unaided reason would later have discovered for itself. In the Bible, however, these rational truths had been embodied in a story form which was accommodated to the stage of educational development that humanity had reached at a particular era, from the childish stage in the era of the ancient Hebrews, through the period of the youth of mankind at the time of the New Testament. Only in our time have we reached that stage of early maturity at which by degrees we "begin to be able to dispense with the doctrine . . . of the New Testament"; and indeed "the development of revealed truths into truths of reason is absolutely necessary, if the human race is to be helped onward by them" (Sects. 73, 76). The prime truth of which reason now assures us is that there is in human nature an inherent teleology of educational progression, which will lead inevitably to a "time of perfection" when man "will do the good because it is the good"—"the time of a *new everlasting Gospel*," or "third age of the world" which, Lessing says, had been prematurely glimpsed by "certain visionaries of the thirteenth and fourteenth centuries" (Sects. 85-7, 89); that is, in the theory of an earthly millennium which had been proclaimed by Joachim of Flora and his followers. And he bids the immanent Providence to "go its imperceptible pace! . . . You have to take so many with you on your eternal journey [*Weg*]! so many bypaths to traverse!" For "the very path [*Bahn*] upon which the race reaches its perfection, every individual man . . . must first have travelled over" (Sects. 91-3).

Four years earlier, in the second volume of *The Oldest Documents of the Human Race* (1776), Herder had already translated the Biblical account of Eden, the fall, and the restoration into his version of universal history; for the Scriptural story, he said, though told with a simplicity appropriate to children, embodies the true history both of the entire human race and of each member of the race.[6] Man's state of innocence in Eden signifies his one-time condition of freedom and peace under the absolute commandment of God. The eating of the fruit of the knowledge of good and evil signifies man's first awareness that he has a choice between better and worse alternatives; so construed, the fall coincides with the beginning of philosophical thought, at that stage of human development when "the child is no longer child, but a philosopher, metaphysician, and almost perhaps a knave" (VII, 25). This initial fall was also from innocence into the state of nature, in which man's "freedom" was equivalent to the freedom of animals; that is, men became "slaves of desire, bondmen to the senses" (VII, 113, 126–8). But "precisely from this poison did God bring forth honey," for all God's "punishments are benefits." "So does God lead, educate, and develop . . . in Adam's very lapse the well-being of the entire race, and the continuation of the chain of events" which will some day end in that destiny when "the poor caterpillar will again become a butterfly in a better Paradise" (VII, 118, 132).

In his *Ideas on the Philosophy of the History of Mankind* (1784–5), written after the publication of Lessing's essay, Herder altered and expanded the details within this pattern of human history, in which man's double fall (both into bondage to sensual desire and instinct, and into rationality) is viewed as a necessary step toward the higher good of an earned and fully developed freedom, humanity, and intellectual power. Human history is now specified as a *Bildungsgeschichte:* the "aim of our earthly existence" is "the education of humanity," in the course of which "our capacity for reason will be formed into reason, our finer senses into art, our instincts into genuine freedom and beauty, our natural impulses into love of mankind." [7] In his present condition man lives "in two intersecting systems of creation," for he is both natural and rational, bondman and freeman, animal and man, and in this "duplicity of being" he is a divided creature who "is in contradiction with himself and with the earth." But man's destiny is "to earn for himself by practice this degree of light and certainty, by means of which, under the guidance

of his Father, he may become a noble freeman by his own
effort; and he will become one" (XIII, 189–91, 194–6).

Immanuel Kant, who reviewed Herder's *Ideas on the Philosophy of the History of Mankind* in 1785, produced in the
following year his own essay on the *Conjectural Origin of the
History of Man*. Warning us of the inherent uncertainty of such
conjectural history, based as it must be on a union of imaginative speculation with reasoning from human experience, Kant
says that he will avail himself of the story in the Book of
Genesis as "a chart," and bids us to follow the Biblical text
"step by step" in order to see "whether the way which philosophy takes according to concepts coincides" with the narrative in Scripture.[8] The original state of man, as the Biblical
text says, was indeed innocent, but this was in conceptual fact
the innocence of ignorance and of absolute obedience to "instinct, this voice of God." "So long as inexperienced man
obeyed this call of nature, all was well with him." But man's
reason soon awakened and proffered him the possibility of a
free choice among infinite alternatives; and "once this condition of freedom was tasted, it became impossible for him to
return again to the condition of servitude under the dominion
of instinct." Reason also opened to man the view which looks
beyond the present moment to anticipate and plan for the
future; it thereby imposed on him the need to work and gave
him the knowledge of death, in addition to the knowledge of
good and evil (which, interpreted into its conceptual equivalent, is the awareness that he has a free choice between good
and evil alternatives). The story of the Garden of Eden and
its loss thus becomes, to Kant's view, an as-if rendering, in
imaginative form, of a probable historical truth: the development of his rational faculty drove man "out of the harmless
and secure condition of the nurtured child, as if from a garden
which took care of his wants without effort on his part, and
thrust him into the wide world, where so much sorrow, toil,
and unknown evil await him." In the future man will often
long for "a Paradise, the creature of his imagination," but
between him and "that imagined place of felicity is encamped,"
like the Biblical angel guarding the gate, the "irresistibly compelling reason, [which] doesn't allow him to return into that

condition of crudity and simplicity out of which it has dragged him" (VIII, 111–15).

What in the Biblical story form is "represented," then, as "the exit of man . . . from Paradise" was in historical fact his "passage . . . from the tutelage of instinct to the condition of freedom" (VIII, 115)—the burden of free choice in the knowledge of good and evil. And Kant expressly faces up to the question, which had been dramatically raised by Rousseau, whether this historical development was one of gain or loss, progress or decline. His answer, characteristically, is in the form of an antinomy: it is both gain and loss, depending on the perspective one assumes. (It was Rousseau's unspoken shift between the two perspectives, Kant remarks, which made his diverse evaluations of nature as against culture seem to be contradictory.) From the standpoint of the individual man, the replacement of instinctual behavior by rational thought, which opened up the possibility of free will and so inaugurated moral duties and prohibitions, inescapably led to "evils, and —what is even worse, in association with the refined reason— vices, which were entirely foreign to the condition of ignorance, and consequently, of innocence." To an individual, therefore,

> the first step out of this condition was, on the moral side, a fall, and on the physical side the result of this fall was a host of evils in life (consequently, a mode of punishment) never known before.

But if we assume the standpoint of the human race as a whole, the emergence from the state of nature and instinct to that of culture and reason is seen to be gain, not loss. For the "destiny" of the race "consists of nothing other than a progress toward perfection," in which man's transgression to rationality was the indispensable first step.

> [The individual] therefore has cause to ascribe all the evils he endures and all the bad that he enacts to his own guilt, at the same time, however, that he, as a member of the whole—the human race—has cause to admire and extol the wisdom and the ordering of means to the end of the total arrangement.
>
> (VIII, 115–16)

Kant's secular theodicy is therefore one of private evils, public benefits. Human evil and suffering are justified by a way of thinking he elsewhere called "philosophical chiliasm"; that is, by conceiving them as inevitable conditions of man's progress toward an ultimate high civilization, predicted on purely empirical and rational grounds, which Kant identifies as the secular equivalent to the Christian faith in a millennium by divine intervention.[9] In one casual sentence Kant puts the matter in a way which points toward the dialectic of the historical process which was soon to be developed by his younger contemporaries. The course of history, in Rousseau's terms, has been from the state of nature to the state of culture, or "art"; in our present stage, Kant says, the tendencies of nature survive in a condition of "rupture" [*Abbruch*] and "conflict" with the opposed requirements of culture; this division and opposition, however, will some day be resolved in a higher third stage, in which (the terminology implies) there will be a return to the initial condition of nature, but without loss of the values of the intermediate stage of art. In Kant's words, the opposition will survive "until perfect art again becomes nature [*bis vollkommene Kunst wieder Natur wird*], which is the ultimate goal of the moral destiny of the human race" (VIII, 117–18).

By the time, then, that Schiller lectured at Jena as professor of history in 1790, he had ample and distinguished precedent for his conjectural treatment of history in *Something Concerning the First Human Society, according to the Guidance of the Mosaic Records.* There is not a great deal of substantive novelty in Schiller's essay—even its subtitle, "The Transition of Man to Freedom and Humanity," conjoins the major emphases of Kant and Herder—but in his brief introductory section, by making explicit and detailed what his predecessors had passingly implied, he reformed the pattern and reformulated the process of universal history. When he was introduced into the world, Schiller says, man was entirely the creature of instinct, as "reasonless animals" still are, and, placed in a mild and fruitful climate, he looked upon everything with "a happy eye" and "a cheerful spirit." But man had to fulfill his destiny by converting instinctual behavior (in which his inclination immediately translates itself into action) into "acts of freedom and morality," in which he must consider and choose between alternatives under the rule of a moral law. Man's rebellion against "the voice of God in Eden, which forbade him the tree of knowledge" is therefore to be interpreted in naturalistic terms as "a fall [*Abfall*] from his instinct, and so as the first manifestation of his autonomous activity, the first venture of his reason, the beginning of his moral existence." Compelled by an inner drive, of which he was himself unconscious, man "tore himself loose from the leading-strings of nature . . . and threw himself into the wild game of life, set himself upon the dangerous road [*Weg*] to moral freedom."

The overall course of history, Schiller clearly indicates, can be figured as a circuitous journey out of paradise and back to paradise—that is, to a future condition in which free and rational action according to the moral law has itself become spontaneous, hence equivalent to the spontaneous instinctual behavior of man's original and undivided condition:

> Man was destined to learn to seek out, by means of his own reason, the condition of innocence which he now lost, and as a free, reasonable spirit, to return to that place whence he had started out as a plant and creature of instinct: from a paradise of ignorance and bondage he was to work up, even if it should be after thousands of years, to a paradise of knowledge and freedom; one in which he would obey the moral law in his heart just as constantly as he in the beginning had obeyed instinct, and as plants and animals still obey it.

In Schiller, furthermore, the concept of a fall, or historical decline, has been fused with the idea of progress so as to give history a spiral form; for the unity with himself to which man will return is not only as good as the unity he has forfeited; it is far better. "The teacher of the people," says Schiller, "is entirely right in treating this event as a fall of primal man . . . for instead of an innocent creature man became a guilty one, instead of a perfect pupil of nature an imperfect moral being, from a happy instrument an unhappy artist." But "the philosopher," as against the religious teacher, "is also right in wishing good fortune to this important step of human nature in general toward perfection" and in calling it "a giant-step of humanity," for by it man "first put his foot upon the ladder which after the course of many millennia will lead him to become master of himself." [10]

Schiller's text makes it plain that even this portentous concept, which converts the circular return of Neoplatonic Christianity into a spiral ascent, is a translation into his philosophical terms of a traditional theological concept—the paradox of the *felix culpa*. According to this ancient and persisting doctrine, the primal sin of Adam was a fortunate fall because out of this evil comes a greater good: "Felix ruina," as St. Ambrose exclaimed, "quae reparatur in melius!" [11] In the succinct version of this paradox voiced by Adam in *Paradise Lost,* not only was his fall the essential condition of the Incarnation, thus of the demonstration of God's abounding grace, but also of the eventual recovery by the elect of a paradise which will be a great improvement upon the paradise which Adam has lost. For at His Second Coming, the Archangel Michael tells Adam, Christ shall reward

> His faithful, and receive them into bliss,
> Whether in Heav'n or Earth, for then the Earth
> Shall all be Paradise, far happier place
> Than this of *Eden,* and far happier days.

At which Adam, like Kant in assaying whether the fall from instinct into reason was man's loss or gain, is suspended in an antinomy of contradictory perspectives:

> Full of doubt I stand,
> Whether I should repent me now of sin
> By mee done or occasion'd, or rejoice
> Much more, that much more good thereof shall spring,
> To God more glory, more good will to Men
> From God, and over wrath grace shall abound. [12]

In Schiller's secular version of the fortunate fall, all such doubt dissipates: "This fall [*Abfall*] of man from instinct—which to be sure brought moral evil into the creation, but only in order to make moral good therein possible—is, without any contradiction, the most fortunate and greatest event in the history of mankind." [13]

Schiller's later writings play changes, although with increasing distinctions and dialectical elaboration, upon this paradigm of a circular return which is also an advance. The design is apparent in the characteristic strategy of Schiller's own thinking which (as Professors Wilkinson and Willoughby remark in their excellent edition of the *Aesthetic Letters*) in "overall movement . . . is not linear but circular," [14] as well as in the way he envisions the course both of universal human history and of each individual life. And prominent among his additions to the design he had sketched in *The First Human Society* is an explicit and detailed account of the initial state of man as one of simple self-unity, which has fallen into multiplicity, fragmentation, and opposition, but in its divided state contains an inherent dialectic which presses on toward a higher unity which will incorporate the intervening multiplicity and resolve all conflicts.

The structure of Schiller's *On the Aesthetic Education of Man* (published 1795) is remarkably intricate. It begins with a series of partial statements of oppositions and resolutions, which are subsumed in a succession of more comprehensive statements, to be finally incorporated in a synthesis of all the partial syntheses. In his history of culture as the educational process of mankind, however, we recognize familiar traits. Man began as a subject of nature under "the dominion of blind necessity," from which he turned to freedom in the use of his analytic intellect and the exercise of choice, for "in the process of civilization" all men "must fall away from Nature by the abuse of Reason before they can return to her by the use of Reason." In the course of this return, however, reason "must beware of damaging the variety [*Mannigfaltigkeit*] of Nature," for it must effect a higher unity in the mode of "wholeness of character [*Totalität des Charakters*]." [15] The highest mode of wholeness hitherto achieved by man, after the initial division within human nature, was the culture of classical Greece. But if "all-unifying Nature" bestowed upon

Greece its characteristic form, it is "all-dividing Intellect" that gives to modern man his fragmented nature (pp. 31–3).

Schiller had available an incisive and detailed statement of the divisiveness which is inherent in the economic and social arrangements of an increasingly industrial and commercial age. In the mid-eighteenth century the Scottish philosopher and pioneer sociologist Adam Ferguson had grown up in a region of Perthshire where very few miles separated the integral clan-community of his native Highlands from the developed commercial society of the Scottish Lowlands. As early as 1767, in his remarkable *Essay on the History of Civil Society*, Ferguson pointed out the price that civilized man and society must pay —in division, isolation, conflict, and psychological distortion— for the efficiency and affluence made possible by the operation of the profit motive and by the ever increasing division of labor and specialization of function in a manufacturing and commercial economy. As opposed to the integrity of a community in a rude society, Ferguson says, in the modern "commercial state"

> man is sometimes found a detached and a solitary being: he has found an object which sets him in competition with his fellow-creatures, and he deals with them as he does with his cattle and his soil, for the sake of the profits they bring. The mighty engine which we suppose to have formed society, only tends to set its members at variance, or to continue their intercourse after the bands of affection are broken.[16]

The division of economic roles, although necessary for increased efficiency, results in the division of social classes between a small élite and a large number of depressed workers (p. 186); and the division of labor, although it effects a huge increase in productivity, makes the industrial workman into a mindless automaton: "Manufactures, accordingly, prosper most, where the mind is least consulted, and where the workshop may . . . be considered as an engine, the parts of which are men" (pp. 182–3). And to divide the primary social functions among specialized classes is to fragment the individual mind: "To separate the arts which form the citizen and the statesman, the arts of policy and war, is an attempt to dismember the human

character, and to destroy those very arts we mean to improve"
(p. 230).

Schiller knew and greatly admired Ferguson's writings.[17]
In his sixth *Aesthetic Letter* he assimilated Ferguson's socio-
logical analyses, together with relevant statements by Rousseau
and Herder, to his own complex dialectic of human history,
and developed them into what remains a classic diagnosis of
the ills of modern society in terms of division, fragmentation,
isolation, conflict, and distortion. He applies this analysis to
the mind of the individual, to the relations between individuals
and among classes, and also to each social, industrial, and
political institution. In our society individuals are "fragments"
of a whole and, "one might almost be tempted to assert, the
various faculties appear as separate in practice as they are distinguished by the psychologist in theory, and we see . . . whole
classes of men, developing but one part of their potentialities."
With the "sharper divisions between the sciences" and the
"more rigorous separation of ranks and occupations . . . the
inner unity of human nature was severed too, and a disastrous
conflict set its harmonious powers at variance." In place of an
"organic" system of government we have "an ingenious clock-
work, in which, out of the piecing together of innumerable
but lifeless parts, a mechanical kind of collective life ensued."
"State and Church, laws and customs were now torn asunder;
enjoyment was divorced from labour, the means from the end,
the effort from the reward"; while, "everlastingly chained to a
single little fragment of the Whole, man himself develops into
nothing but a fragment." "The State remains for ever a stranger
to its citizens," and finally "positive society begins . . . to
disintegrate into a state of primitive morality"; while the spirit
of business, having become habituated to "judging all experience whatsoever by one particular fragment of experience,"
tries "to make the rules of its own occupation apply indis-
criminately to all others" (pp. 33–9).

"It was civilization [*Kultur*] itself," Schiller dramatically
announces, "which inflicted this wound upon modern man"
(p. 33). But (*O felix divisio!*) the self-division and "fragmentary
specialization of human powers" by which "individuals . . .
suffer under the curse of this cosmic purpose" is the indis-

pensable way to a greater generic good; for "little as individuals might benefit from this fragmentation of their being, there was no other way in which the species as a whole could have progressed." If we pursue the only road of progress open to civilized man, the cultural way down will turn out to be the way back and up. "It must be open to us to restore by means of a higher Art [*eine höhere Kunst*] the totality of our nature which the arts themselves have destroyed [*welche die Kunst zerstört hat*]" (pp. 39–43).

This higher art turns out to be the art of the beautiful, or the fine arts. Schiller thus inaugurates the concept of the cardinal role of art, and of the imaginative faculty which produces art, as the reconciling and unifying agencies in a disintegrating mental and social world of alien and warring fragments—a concept which came to be a central tenet of Romantic faith, manifested in various formulations by thinkers so diverse as Schelling, Novalis, Blake, Coleridge, Wordsworth, and Shelley. This unifying function of art Schiller expounds by way of a complex train of reasoning, involving an initial opposition of the *Formtrieb* and the *Stofftrieb*, which are united and reconciled (according to Schiller's distinctive version of what became the dialectical procedure of the age) in a third thing, the *Spieltrieb*, of which the correlative phenomenon is beauty. Beauty unites "freedom" and "supreme inner necessity" in a "harmony of laws," not by "the exclusion of certain realities, but in the absolute inclusion of all realities." Beauty is also a "middle state" which unites the "diametrically opposed" contraries of matter and form, passivity and activity.

> Beauty unites these two opposed conditions and thus destroys the opposition [*hebt also die Entgegensetzung auf*]. Since, however, both conditions remain everlastingly opposed to each other, there is no other way of uniting them except by destroying them [*als indem sie aufgehoben werden*]. . . . Both these conditions totally disappear in a third without leaving any trace of division behind in the new whole that has been made.
>
> (pp. 123–5)

In this passage Schiller introduces the use of *aufheben* in the multiple dialectical sense (which Hegel later annexed) in which it signifies both the annulment and preservation, and suggests also the elevation, of contraries in a synthesis, or third thing.

In Schiller's *Aesthetic Letters* the long history of civilization is envisioned as the educational journey of the human race, through which each individual too must pass if he is to complete his education into maturity. The route leads through three major stages, from the natural through the aesthetic to a third thing, a moral state that will preserve the values of both nature and aesthetics:

> We can, then, distinguish three different moments or stages of development through which both the individual and the species as a whole must pass [*durchlaufen müssen*], inevitably and in a definite order, if they are to complete the full cycle of their destiny [*Kreis ihrer Bestimmung*]. . . . Man in his physical state merely suffers the dominion of nature; he emancipates himself from this dominion in the aesthetic state, and he acquires mastery over it in the moral. (p. 171)

Schiller's second major and immensely influential essay on aesthetics, *On Naive and Sentimental Poetry* (1795), is controlled by similar ideas and plays variations upon a similar design of human development and destiny. The intense feeling we have for the inanimate world and landscapes, for children, rural people, and aborigines, reveals our attraction to "naive" nature and expresses our recognition that all these instances manifest an "existence according to its own laws, its inner necessity, its eternal unity with itself." This is the place from which man set out on the long road of civilization, and to which he shall one day return:

> They are, what we were; they are, what we are to become again. We were, like them, nature, and our culture shall lead us, by the road [*Weg*] of reason and freedom, back to nature again.[18]

In this essay Schiller's emphasis is on the primary split in the mind's unity with itself which converts unself-consciousness into self-consciousness—the awareness of the self as a subject distinct from the object it perceives, and the intervention of reflection and choice between instinct and action. Thus the "naive" poet, who is "pure nature," composes not by reflection and rule but by an inner necessity, as "an undivided sensuous unity, and as a harmonizing whole" (p. 504). The sentimental, or characteristically modern, poet, on the other hand, is self-divided because self-conscious, and so composes in an awareness of multiple alternatives, and characteristically represents not the object in itself, but the object in the subject. He deals always "with two conflicting ideas and feelings, with the actual as a limit and with his idea as the infinite"; and in reading his poetry, our mind is "in a state of tension, and oscillates between conflicting feelings" (pp. 509, 543).

If the way of civilization and culture is envisioned as a painful journey into self-division and inner conflict, the discontents of the journeyer readily evoke the figures of exile and homesickness, which Schiller incorporates into a variant form of the parable of the Prodigal Son. In understandable moods of oppression,

> we see in non-rational nature only a more fortunate sister who remained at home in her mother's house, out of which we stormed into an alien land in the arrogance of our freedom. The moment we begin to feel the oppression of culture, we desire with painful longing to go back home, and hear, far-off in the alien country of art, the moving voice of the mother. So long as we were mere children of nature, we were both happy and perfect; we have become free, and have lost both.

But, Schiller says, you can't go back again. We must struggle onward toward an ultimate unity which is not simple but complex, and is not a condition we have inherited but one that we have earned.

> Strive for unity, but seek it not in uniformity; strive for repose, but by means of the equilibrium and not of the cessation of your activity. That nature which you envy in the non-rational is unworthy of your respect or longing. It lies behind you, it must ever lie behind you.   (pp. 494–5)

In Schiller's essay, as in the Christian tradition, the figure of the traveler sick for home is interchangeable with man's nostalgia for "a paradise, a state of innocence, a golden age." In addition, the analogue of life and civilization as a journey falls into ready coincidence with that of life and civilization as a process of education for maturity. Schiller exhorts the modern poet "not to lead us back to our childhood" but to "lead us onward to our coming of age, in order to allow us to feel the higher harmony which rewards the fighter and blesses the conqueror. Let him set himself the task of an idyll . . . which will lead mankind, for whom the way back to Arcadia is closed forever, onward toward Elysium" (pp. 537–42).

The way of the poet, the individual, and the race alike is thus imaged as a circuitous journey from self-unity through multiplex self-consciousness back to self-unity. The unity we seek at the end, however, is higher than the unity we abandoned at the beginning—infinitely higher, it now turns out, so that although it can be ever more closely approached, it can never be completely attained:

> This road [*Weg*] upon which the modern poets are travelling is the same which mankind must take, collectively and as individuals. Nature makes him in unity with himself; art divides and cuts him in two; through the Ideal he returns to unity. But because the Ideal is an infinite which he can never reach, so the cultivated man can never become perfect in his mode, as the natural man is able to become in his. . . . The goal toward which man strives by means of culture, however, is infinitely higher than that which he reaches by means of nature. The latter achieves his value by the absolute achievement of a finite, the other achieves his value through approximation to an infinite greatness. . . . Insofar as the final goal of mankind is not otherwise to be reached than by such progress, and the [natural man and natural artist] can progress in no other way than by cultivating himself, and consequently passing over into the other type, there is no question which of the two, with respect to that final goal, deserves the higher status.
>
> (pp. 505–6)

The goal of man's secular journey, like the heavenly city of the Christian wayfarer, remains somewhere on the far side of this world; but that goal is now rendered forever inaccessible by an outlook which limits human possibilities to this finite world. In terms of Kant's moral metaphysics, which Schiller had assimilated, the infinite demands of man's noumenal ego drive him through an "endless progress from lower to higher stages," toward an end from which he is inescapably cut off by the finite bounds of his phenomenal ego. Or in Fichte's terms in *The Vocation of the Scholar,* "the ultimate goal of man . . . is utterly unattainable," so that "his way to it must be endless" —that is, he can only "approximate this goal unto infinity." The result of this way of thinking is to locate the goal of the journey of life in the experience of the journey itself. As Schiller put it in his *Aesthetic Letters:* "In the eyes of a Reason which knows no limits, the Direction is at once the Destination, and the Way is completed from the moment it is trodden."

The continued trust in human aspirations to which no worldly object is adequate, together with a disbelief in the reality of any objects of human aspiration beyond those which fail to satisfy them—this is the paradox behind the formulation of what became a prominent Romantic norm: the elevation of the boundless over the bounded, the setting of man's proper aim as a *Streben nach dem Unendlichen,* and the measure of man's dignity and greatness by the very discrepancy between his infinite reach and his finite grasp. As Hölderlin put it, in an early draft of *Hyperion:* "No action, no thought can reach the extent of your desire. That is the glory of man, that nothing ever suffices." In Wordsworth's version in *The Prelude,* the "glory" of the human soul is that "our home/ Is with infinity," and therefore with "something evermore about to be"; and in Blake's extreme application in *There Is No Natural Religion,* "The bounded is loathed by its possessor. . . . Less than All cannot satisfy Man." Applied, as Schiller in his essay *On Naive and Sentimental Poetry* applies it, to the aesthetic as well as to the moral realm, this norm becomes the preference for the impossible attempt at an artistic aim beyond human capacity, over the perfect achievement of an accessible, because finite, aim. As Coleridge states this reversal of the classical ideal: in Sophocles, for example, "there is a completeness, a satisfying, an excellence, on which the mind can rest," while in Shakespeare there is "a dissatisfying, or falling short of perfection, yet so promising of our progression, that we would not exchange it for that repose of the mind which dwells on the forms of symmetry in acquiescent admiration of grace." [19]

2. ROMANTIC PHILOSOPHY AND THE HIGH ROMANTIC ARGUMENT

After Kant and Schiller it became a standard procedure for the major German philosophers to show that the secular history and destiny of mankind is congruent with the Biblical story of the loss and future recovery of paradise; to interpret that story as a mythical representation of man's departure from the happiness of ignorance and self-unity into the multiple self-divisions and conflicts attendant upon the emergence of self-consciousness, free decision, and the analytic intellect; to equate the fall, so interpreted, with the beginning of speculative philosophy itself; and to evaluate the fall as a fortunate self-division, because it was the necessary first step upon the educational journey by which thinking and striving man wins his way back toward his lost integrity, along a road which looks like a reversion but is in fact a progression.

Writing to Jacobi in 1795 about his own *Wissenschaftslehre,* Fichte declared that man's exclusive concern with practical thinking gave way to speculative philosophy when he distinguished between the particular ego, or empirical individual, and the "absolute" or "pure Ego" which, when it is posited as subsisting outside of all individuals, is equivalent to what has traditionally been called "God." The beginning of this speculative philosophy was the metaphysical fall of man:

> If mankind had never tasted this forbidden fruit, it could have dispensed with all philosophy. [But an innate tendency made this step inescapable] and the first man who raised a question about the being of God broke through the bounds, convulsed mankind in his deepest foundations, and set him into a conflict with himself which has not yet been settled, and which can only be settled by a bold progress up to that highest point, from which the speculative and the practical appear united into one. We began to philosophize through pride, and so de-

stroyed our innocence; we discovered our nakedness, and since then we philosophize out of the need for our redemption.[20]

Some ten years later Fichte undertook to deduce all of universal history out of "the unity of a first principle," by proceeding "purely as a philosopher"—that is, by "paying no attention to any experience whatever, and absolutely *a priori*." His starting point is to posit the idea of a "world-plan," which is that "the goal of the life of men on earth" is to achieve a "final state" when they will "order all their relations with freedom according to reason." From this premise Fichte deduces five necessary epochs in the history of mankind, moving from the stage of "the unconditional dominion of instinct over reason" up to the ultimate "epoch of the art of reason [*Vernunftkunst*]." But this five-act drama of logically deduced history, it turns out, coincides with the five stages of Christian theology, from "the state of the innocence of the human race" to "the state of completed justification and sanctification"; and these several stages, furthermore, constitute way stations on man's circuitous journey from a paradise unearned to a paradise which shall be earned:

> But the collective journey [*Weg*], which, according to this view, mankind pursues here below, is no other than a way back to that point upon which it stood at the very beginning, and has no other goal but to return to its origin. Only mankind must make this journey on his own feet; by his own strength he must make himself again that which he had once been without any effort on his part, and for this very purpose did he depart from that condition. . . . In paradise (to make use of a well-known image), in the paradise of right action and being, without knowledge, labor, or art, man awakens to life. But hardly has he gained the courage to dare lead his own life, when the angel comes with the fiery sword of compulsion to righteousness and drives him out of the seat of his innocence and peace . . . until, by effort and knowledge, he builds his paradise for himself according to the model of the one he has lost.[21]

Schelling inaugurated his philosophical career at seventeen with a master's essay in Latin *On the Origin of Human Evils in the Most Ancient Philosophy of Genesis, Chapter III* (1792).

His frequent references to the writings on the beginnings of culture by Lessing, Herder, and Kant reveal the tradition he follows. The Biblical account of the fall of man is a myth which embodies philosophical truth under the guise of historical narration. Philosophically speaking, Eden, like the equivalent pagan myth of a golden age, represents the dominion within man of nature (his senses, instinct, and the rule of necessity). From this state of nature man was driven by the urgency of his reason which, by distinguishing between good and evil, established the possibility of freedom of the will. The fall was one from innocent ignorance into knowledge, and from happy obedience to instinct into the misery of being confronted with multiple moral choices; and this primal division between the impulsions of the *homo sensibilis* and the demands of the *homo intelligibilis* puts us "into a strange discord," in which "we are in inner dispute with ourselves." [22] Yet even if we could return to Eden, we would not choose to do so (p. 32). For the evils of man's condition, philosophically considered, lead to great goods, since by these evils "the human race is educated, so to speak," toward the achievement of its ultimate goal, when, "to express the matter in a word, the times will return to the gold of their prime . . . but now solely under the guidance and care of the reason." [23] Five years later, after the publication of Schiller's *Aesthetic Letters* and *On Naive and Sentimental Poetry*, Schelling developed the concept of evil as essentially division and conflict, both within man and between man and nature, and he evaluated man's initial division as a fortunate fall which set him in motion on what he now regarded as a spiral course toward the greater good of a merited unity, which is a synthesis in which all divisions are *aufgehoben*. Man, striving to make himself free, left "the (philosophical) state of nature" in which "he was still at one with himself and the environing world," and this initial severance led to a progressive fragmentation of "the whole man." "Pure reflection, therefore, is a spiritual sickness . . . it is an evil." From the standpoint of "genuine philosophy," however, it is "a necessary evil" because an unavoidable means by which man "as a conqueror, and through his own merit," can knowingly return to his lost, but originally ignorant, condition of unity with himself and outer nature. For philosophical reflection

begins with that original separation, in order through freedom
again to unite what had been originally and necessarily united
in the human spirit; that is, in order to annul [*aufzuheben*]
that separation forever.[24]

Hegel offered an elaborate exposition of the consonance
between the Scriptural account of the fall of man and the
philosophical view of the development of intellection and culture, in the course of the lectures with which he supplemented
the outline of logic in his *Encyclopedia of the Philosophical
Sciences*. Of the three methods for ascertaining truth, he says,
that of mere "experience," or "immediate knowledge," includes "everything which the moralists term innocence"; but
the two other methods, that of "reflection" and that of "philosophical cognition, must leave that unsought natural harmony
behind."

> So far as they have this in common, the [two] methods which
> claim to apprehend the truth by thought may naturally be re-
> garded as part and parcel of the pride which leads man to
> trust to his own powers for a knowledge of the truth. Such a
> position involves a thorough-going disruption, and, viewed in
> that light, might be regarded as the source of all evil and wick-
> edness—the original transgression. Apparently therefore the
> only way of being reconciled and restored to peace is to sur-
> render all claims to think and know.[25]

"The Mosaic legend of the Fall of Man," Hegel remarks, "has
preserved an ancient picture [*Vorstellung*] representing the
origin and consequences of this disunion"—a "Mythus vom
Sündenfall" whose power of survival over thousands of years
is a sign that it incorporates a content which the philosopher
"cannot afford to neglect." He proceeds to a circumstantial interpretation of the myth of the fall, in which the central points
are that "the hour when man leaves the path of mere natural
being marks the difference between him, a self-conscious agent,
and the natural world"; that this opposition between the conscious self and nature was a necessary stage toward "the final
goal of man"; and that the path traced by the history of culture,
not only in the race but "in every son of Adam," is a circuit
from an instinctual self-unity, which "is a gift from the hand

of nature," through self-opposition and self-division, to a higher harmony which "must spring from the labour and culture of the spirit."

> In its instinctive and natural stage, spiritual life wears the garb of innocence and confiding simplicity: but the very essence of spirit implies the absorption of this immediate condition in something higher. The spiritual . . . sunders itself to self-realisation. But this position of severed life [*Entzweiung*] has in its turn to be suppressed [*ist . . . aufzuheben*], and the spirit has by its own act to win its way to concord again [*zur Einigkeit zurückführen*].

"The principle of restoration," says Hegel (in a patent echo of Schiller's figure that "it was civilization itself that inflicted this wound upon modern man"), "is found in thought, and thought only. The hand that inflicts the wound is also the hand which heals it." [26]

By the time, then, that Heinrich von Kleist, writing in 1810, formulated his famous figure of the great-circle route back to paradise, he merely epitomized what had become one of the most familiar of philosophical commonplaces. He uses the figure to support his paradox (derived from Schiller) [27] that puppets, acting by pure necessity, exhibit a grace beyond the reach of human dancers, since these latter are inescapably self-divided and self-conscious. The key to this disparity between puppet and dancer, says the expositor, lies in a just understanding of the third chapter of Genesis:

> We have eaten from the tree of knowledge. Now paradise is bolted shut, and the angel stands behind us. We must journey around the world and see whether perhaps it is open again somewhere on the yonder side. . . .
> "Then we would have to eat again of the tree of knowledge, in order to fall back again into the state of innocence?"
> "To be sure," he answered. "That is the last chapter in the history of the world." [28]

Nature, Schelling wrote in 1806, as the self-revelation of the Absolute, or "God," is a living identity of unity and multeity, of the infinite and the finite, and to know it as such "is the sole thing that can be called waking"; any other way of perceiving it "is dream, picture, or the utter sleep of death [*Todesschlaf*]." How then are we to explain the claim of some philosophers that nature appears to their consciousness "as a lifeless, finite, and absolute set of particulars"?

> It is not at all because of their science [*Wissenschaft*], but entirely because of their guilt, that such a finite world exists for them, and it can only be ascribed to their own will, which turned away from unity in the desire to make itself self-sufficient. . . . [This is] a truly Platonic fall of man, the condition in which that man finds himself who holds that the world, which he conceives to be dead, absolutely manifold, and separated, is in fact the true and actual world. . . . We have shown that the fact of the existence of such a world in the consciousness of mankind is exactly as widespread as the fact of sin—indeed, that it is this very fact of sin itself—and just as we can be redeemed from sin, so is that mode of consciousness neither absolutely necessary, unresolvable, nor eternal.[29]

The Neoplatonic tradition, persisting from the Church Fathers to the German Idealists, which equates the fall from paradise with a splintering of primal unity, lies behind Schelling's extraordinary claim that the perception of an alien and lifeless nature, correlative with a *Zwiespalt* (p. 95) in the mind of the perceiver, is a result of the fall of man, and constitutes the essential nature of evil itself; and his corresponding claim that redemption, "the last and supreme appeasement and atonement [*Versöhnung*] of cognition," is the state of reunified consciousness at which "the world of thought becomes the world of nature" (p. 32). Schelling's statements, in their turn, approximate Wordsworth's enterprise, announced in his Prospectus to *The Recluse,* to "arouse the sensual from their sleep/ Of Death" (compare Schelling's *Todesschlaf*) by proclaiming a union between mind and nature which will restore an experiential paradise; they also throw light on Coleridge's explanation that Wordsworth's plan had been to affirm "A Fall in some sense, as a fact," and then to present "a scheme of Redemption" which will be "a Reconciliation from this Enmity with Nature."[30]

Schelling, whose great influence on the German literary movement extended by way of Coleridge into England, helps us in other ways to see the relations of Wordsworth's poetic role and theme to a general tendency of thought in his age. Like many of his contemporaries, Schelling figured redemption, mankind's return to a lost unity, as a journey back home; for his favored analogue of the circuitous journey, however, he turned not to the Bible, but to a pagan source. Plotinus, we recall, had likened the search of the sundered soul for its unitary source to the voyage of Odysseus out to Ilium and back to "the Fatherland . . . whence we have come, and there is The Father." In his *Transcendental Idealism* (1800) Schelling said that nature "is a poem" which, if we could unriddle its secret script, would disclose itself as "the Odyssey of the spirit which, wonderfully deluded, in seeking itself, flees itself"; it reaches its goal only when it "returns completely to itself," as a subject which recognizes that it is its own object, in its own highest product, the mind of man.[31] By the time he wrote *Philosophy and Religion,* four years later, Schelling had assimilated considerable esoteric theology, especially from Boehme, to his earlier metaphysical system. He now posits, within the undifferentiated subject-object which is the absolute, a timeless cosmic fall—an *Abfall* or *Abbrechen*—which is the metaphysical equivalent of the creation of the fragmented phenomenal world, and which reaches its limit in the finite "selfhood" [*Ichheit*] of man, "the point of the extremest alienation [*Entfernung*] from God." But at this very point of utmost remoteness the process of redemption, or turning back toward the source, begins. Schelling represents the general course of human history, so conceived, as a circuitous journey which constitutes the plot of a double Homeric epic:

> History is an epic composed in the mind of God. Its two main parts are, first, that which represents the departure of humanity from its center out to its furthest alienation [*Entfernung*] from this center, and second, that which represents the return.

The first part is, as it were, the *Iliad,* the second the *Odyssey* of history. In the first part the movement was centrifugal, in the second it becomes centripetal. . . . Ideas, spirits, had to fall away from their center and introduce themselves into separateness in nature, the general sphere of the fall, in order that afterward, as separates, they might return into the Undifferentiated and, reconciled with it, remain in it without disturbing it.[32]

Now mankind, Schelling wrote in *The Ages of the World* (1811), awaits the new Homer who, speaking once again in the undivided language of mythology, but of a higher mythology which has incorporated the discoveries of modern philosophy, will sing the new epic of a reunified age. "What holds back the anticipated golden age when truth again becomes fable and fable truth?" Like a dark image, there slumbers in every soul "the archetype" of "the primordial beginning of things," and the poet and the philosopher periodically "rejuvenates himself . . . by feeling the unity of his nature." Men have not hitherto been able to sustain "this state of vision," for "what was indivisibly together in the origin unfolds and is spread out piece by piece in this present life." Now, however,

after long wanderings, [the systematic science of philosophy] has regained the memory of nature and of nature's former unity with knowledge. . . . The most supersensible thoughts now receive physical power and life, and, conversely, nature becomes more and more the visible impress of the highest concepts. In a short time . . . there will no longer be any difference between the world of thought and the world of reality. There will be one world, and the peace of the golden age will make itself known for the first time in the harmonious union of all sciences. . . .

Perhaps he will yet come who is to sing the greatest heroic poem, comprehending in spirit what was, what is, what will be, the kind of poem attributed to the seers of yore. But this time has not yet come. . . . The goal of the search is not yet reached.[33]

Schelling heralds the poet-prophet who will sing the greatest of all epics, of which the theme will be the journey back to the lost paradise, or golden age, which is the restoration of a lost unity of the human intellect with itself and with nature. This is very like the prophetic role that Wordsworth had assumed in his Prospectus and *Prelude,* and it approximates the "high argument" of the more-than-heroic poem that, as a chosen son who has been granted this "vision," he felt it was his destined office to compose. Schelling's judgment that the time was not entirely ripe for such a poem may reflect the circumstance that he had himself begun a nature epic, but then had given it up.[34] And Wordsworth, we shall see, was far from alone in assuming the persona of a bard who present, past, and future sees, and who undertakes the theme of mankind's journey back toward his spiritual home, which will be at once a paradise and golden age of peace after conflict, and of integration after severance.

3. HEGEL'S "PHENOMENOLOGY OF THE SPIRIT": METAPHYSICAL STRUCTURE AND NARRATIVE PLOT

In Chapter II I discussed some English examples of a distinctive Romantic genre, the life story of the poet or creative spirit in his painful growth toward maturity and poetic power. I then went on to indicate the consonance of this literary form to the self-generating systems of subject-object philosophy, as well as to the contemporary form of "universal history," which represented the history of mankind as an educational process in which the unitary self falls into suffering self-consciousness, on its circuitous way back toward a unification of its fragmented being. Hegel's *Phenomenology of the Spirit* (1807) stands squarely at the intersection of these diverse but collateral genres, for it is a work which explicitly fuses the modes of the circuitous and self-implicating *Bildungsbiographie,* of systematic philosophy (*Wissenschaft*), and of *Universalgeschichte.* This complex nature of the *Phenomenology* will be clarified if we consider its relation to the overall structure of Hegel's metaphysical system.

We remember Hegel's assertion, in the shorter *Logic,* that "philosophy exhibits the appearance of a circle which closes with itself." [35] It turns out, as it always does with Hegel, that the matter is not quite that simple. He also says:

> Each of the parts of philosophy is a philosophical whole, a circle rounded and complete in itself. In each of these parts, however, the philosophical Idea is found in a particular specificality or medium. The single circle, because it is a real totality, bursts through the limits imposed by its special medium, and gives rise to a wider circle. The whole of philosophy in this way resembles a circle of circles.[36]

Very schematically, this is what Hegel apparently means. The Idea (or to put it in an alternate way, anyone's mind thinking its way through philosophy) evolves through its component aspects, the "fluid" thoughts, or "concepts" [Begriffe], which inevitably move out of themselves to the extreme of their own antitheses, only to return into themselves on a higher level so as to constitute "self-movements, circles." [37] The total system of his philosophy, he tells us, falls into three major parts: logic, the philosophy of nature, and the philosophy of spirit. The logic begins with the concept "Being," which evolves, by a successive dialectical spiraling of concept into antithesis and back into higher concept, until it achieves its highest and final conceptual form, "the Absolute Idea." This form represents "a return to the [concept] of the Idea" with which the logic began, but in an achieved "unity with itself" which is higher than the initial unity of simple Being *per se,* because it retains and incorporates all the self-divisions, or differentiations, through which that concept has passed on its dialectical way. In consequence, "this return to the beginning is also an advance. We began with Being, abstract Being: where we now are we also have the Idea as Being: but this Idea which has Being is Nature." [38] We thus pass over from the first into the second major circle of his system, that of the philosophy of nature, "the science of the Idea in its otherness," and by a similar dialectical process we move on and up into a "higher circle," which is the third region of Hegel's systematic philosophy, the philosophy of spirit, "the science of the Idea come back to itself out of that otherness." This last dialectical circle begins with the emergence of subjective spirit out of nature

and closes with "Absolute Spirit"; but the final stage now constitutes a recovered unity of spirit with itself that "comprehends" (in the double sense that it incorporates and systematically understands) the totality of the differentiations which
have evolved during the process of all three circuitous stages.
As such the concluding stage rounds back, on its own higher
level, upon the primitive concept of Being which has inaugurated the entire system—it is "the ultimate result in which
philosophy returns into itself and reaches the point in which
it began." [39] The intricate total design of the vast Hegelian
system thus asks to be imaged as an immanently compelled
evolution of small dialectical circles which compose a continuum in the shape of three large circles, spiraling upward and
widening outward until they constitute one great *Kreis von
Kreisen* that comprehends everything, by reaching the end
which (though only implicitly) was in the beginning, and so
returning to the beginning which (now become explicit, "comprehended," and thus "concrete") is the end.[40]

This is *Wissenschaft,* the complete, self-generating, and self-
involving "circle" of systematic philosophy as a timeless and
eternally valid dialectic of true knowledge. But Hegel's dialectic of thought is also a dialectic of history, and of human
consciousness as well. For spirit does not merely unfold itself
timelessly in "pure thought" as "Idea." It also unfolds itself
in, and as, the evolving consciousness of the race and of each
individual, so as to constitute all of human experience. This
latter manifestation is the subject matter of the *Phenomenology
of the Spirit:* the development of *das werdende Wissen*—that
is, the evolution of human consciousness through various stages,
or "forms," on its way toward its ultimate achievement of the
total system of *Wissenschaft (Phänomenologie,* pp. xxxvii–
viii).

The *Phenomenology* is one of the most original, influential,
and baffling books ever written. A common mistake is to try
to read it as a work of systematic philosophy, against Hegel's
explicit warning that it is not philosophy—or rather that it is,
yet is not, philosophy. And in fact, although the book is informed throughout by Hegel's systematic thought, it is deliberately composed not in the mode of philosophic exposition or

demonstration, but in the mode of a literary narrative, as the growth of human awareness toward the discovery of "science," or the timeless systematic truth. As Hegel puts it, "this becoming of science in general [*der Wissenschaft überhaupt*] or of knowledge is what this phenomenology of the spirit represents." The narrative mode is thus one of a progressive self-education toward the stage of maturity, as "the spirit that educates itself matures slowly and quietly toward [its] new form"; and Hegel embodies this spiritual and intellectual history of mankind in the prevailing metaphorical vehicle of the *Bildungsweg,* the educational journey: "To become true knowledge . . . [spirit] has to work its way through a long journey [*Weg*]." [41]

The *Phenomenology,* however, is by no means the abstract *Universalgeschichte,* the standard history of the educational journey of mankind, that was current in Hegel's time. Instead, as the Preface and Introduction make plain, it is organized primarily in accordance with literary principles of structure, and persistently deploys typically literary devices. Hegel's narrative has a protagonist, whom he denominates as *das allgemeine Individuum* or *der allgemeine Geist*—"the general individual" and "the general spirit"; that is, the collective human consciousness figured as a single agent. The story he tells also applies, however, to particular minds, for each reflective individual is able to recapitulate the educational journey in his own consciousness, up to that stage which the generic human consciousness has reached in his lifetime:

> The task of leading the individual from his uneducated [*ungebildeten*] standpoint to knowledge had to be taken in its general sense, and the general individual, the self-conscious spirit, had to be considered in its education [*Bildung*]. . . .
>
> The [particular] individual must also pass through the contents of the educational stages of the general spirit, but as . . . stages of a way that has been prepared and evened for him. . . . In the boy's pedagogical progress we recognize the history of the education of the world. . . .
>
> Science [*Wissenschaft*] represents this educational movement both in its detail and necessity. . . . The aim is the spirit's insight into what constitutes knowledge. . . .
>
> The world spirit has had the patience to pass through these

forms in the long expanse of time, taking upon itself the tre-
mendous labor of world history.[42]

As Hegel says in his Introduction, such an account, "since it
has only the evolution of phenomenal knowledge [*das erschein-
ende Wissen*] for its object," does not exhibit the timeless
structure of systematic philosophy (of the "free, self-moving
form belonging exclusively to science") but exhibits instead
the structure of the journey and quest: "the way [*Weg*] of the
natural consciousness, which presses on to true knowledge."
But this way, he also indicates, is equivalent to the Christian
journey of the spirit through suffering in quest of redemption
and rebirth:

> Or it may be regarded as the way of the soul, which travels
> through the sequence of its forms, like stations [*Stationen*]
> marked out for it by its own nature, in order that it may pu-
> rify itself into pure spirit in reaching, through the complete ex-
> perience of itself, the knowledge of what it is in itself.[43]

Hegel uses the phrase *Stationen des Weges,* "stations of the
way," in his newspaper announcement of the *Phenomenology;*[44] and the submerged allusion in both these passages to
Leidenstationen—the "Stations of the Cross"—surfaces in the
next paragraph of the Introduction. Since this *Weg* involves,
for the "natural consciousness," its own negation and destruction, "it can on that account be looked upon as the way of
doubt, or more properly as the way of despair." But the spirit's
journey through death and rebirth instead turns out, in philosophical retrospect, to be the way to the triumphant fulfillment
of the educational quest: "The series of its forms, through
which consciousness travels on this way, is rather the detailed
history of the education [*Bildung*] of consciousness itself to the
level of science."

Josiah Royce passingly remarked a half-century ago that
Hegel's *Phenomenology* was akin to the contemporary *Bildungsroman.*[45] We can be more precise and more circumstantial. By a remarkable feat of invention, Hegel composed the
Phenomenology as a *Bildungsbiographie* which is in a literal
sense a spiritual history. It is, in other words, a biography of

the "general spirit," representing the consciousness of each man and Everyman, the course of whose life is a painfully progressive self-education, rendered in the plot-form of a circuitous journey from an initial self-division and departure, through diverse reconciliations and ever renewing estrangements, conflicts, reversals, and crises of spiritual death and rebirth. This plot turns out to be the unwitting quest of the spirit to redeem itself by repossessing its own lost and sundered self, in an ultimate recognition of its own identity whereby, as Hegel says in his concluding section, it can be "at home with itself in its otherness" (p. 549; B., 790).

This may serve for a preliminary outline of Hegel's design. But the closer one looks the more extraordinary does the work appear in its details. It remains unmatched for the intricate accomplishment of an impossible artistic undertaking, even in an age which takes *Finnegans Wake* in its stride; and like Joyce, Hegel has to invent a language to accommodate his special vision of the history of mankind. Since Hegel's references are persistently multiple, this language is allusive rather than denominative, and many of its operative terms are equivoques; the key dialectical term, *aufheben* (to annul, preserve, and transcend), is the most consequential pun since Christ said, "Thou art Peter, and upon this rock I will build my church." The *Phenomenology* is Hegel's first full-length book, and he writes it with vigor and high humor, entirely aware of the ironic and sometimes comic aspects of the remarkable story he has undertaken to tell. It is full of private jokes and narrative traps, and in fact constitutes a sustained and serious put-on for the unwary reader.

For example, the spirit, the protagonist of the story, maintains no one phenomenal identity, but passes through bewildering metamorphoses in the form of outer objects and phenomenal events, or "shapes of consciousness" [*Gestalten des Bewusstseins*], as well as multiple human personae, or particular "spirits"—"a slow procession and sequence of *Geister,* a gallery of pictures, each of which is endowed with the entire abundance of the *Geist*" (pp. 562–3; B., 805–7). This protagonist, the spirit, is also his own antagonist, who appears in a correlative multitude of altering disguises, so that the one actor plays all the roles in the drama; as Hegel says of one stage of the evolution, "the I is We, and the We is I" (p. 140; B., 227). It eventuates, in fact, that the one spirit is all there is in the story. It constitutes not only all the agents, but also the shifting setting in the phenomenal world of nature and society which it sets up as object against itself as conscious subject or subjects, and since the spirit's being involves all of its own ceaseless development, it constitutes the totality of the plot as well. In a sustained dramatic irony, however, the spirit carries on this astonishing performance all unknowingly. We are privileged to watch this process, as Hegel puts it, in which "consciousness doesn't know what is happening to it," as though "it goes on, so to speak, behind its back" (p. 74; B., 144)—until, that is, the process discovers itself to consciousness in its own latest manifestation, the thinking of the philosopher Hegel, in an on-going revelation with which our own consciousness is privileged to participate as we read. For the reader, no less than the author and the subject matter of the *Phenomenology,* is one of the *Geister* in which the spirit continues to manifest itself. The *Bildungsbiographie* thus turns out to have been a concealed first-person narrative—in the fullest possible sense of the term, an autobiography—and one that is told, explicitly, in the mode of a double consciousness. For the spirit at the end of the process narrated in the *Phenomenology* has experienced a rebirth into a new identity [*das neue Dasein*], which "preserves" its former identity as a "sublimated identity" [*dies aufgehobene Dasein*]—it is its "former identity, but new-born out of knowledge" (pp. 563–4; B., 807). And from the vantage of this new and enlightened self (the systematic self-awareness it now possesses in the consciousness of Hegel) the spirit proceeds to remember and represent itself to itself as it was during its own earlier stages of development, from blank nescience through ever decreasing ignorance of its identity and destiny.

In detailing the metamorphoses by which the one spirit passes over into its various objects and personae, Hegel employs many terms in reference to the process of *Trennung* ("division") between consciousness and its other; the most portentous of these is "estrangement" or "alienation" [*Entfremdung*]—a term which since Hegel has become indispensable to analyses of the human condition. His starting point is the state of "immediate knowledge," which is a unitary act of simple perception, free of all conceptualization, hence of any distinction between subject and object. This state is sundered [*entzweit*] by reflection, in which consciousness becomes an object to itself in the experience of "self-consciousness," or "consciousness of itself in its otherness" (p. 128; B., 211). At a later stage (I pick up only some critical points in the history) two human beings, as separate self-consciousnesses, confront each other in a life-and-death struggle for domination, which passes into a master-servant relation between conqueror and conquered; only to undergo, by dialectical necessity, an ironic reversal in which the servant becomes the master of its master. The master-servant antithesis, in that higher dimension in which it has been internalized in a single consciousness, reappears as "the unhappy consciousness," or "the consciousness of self as of a doubled and merely contradictory being," of which medieval Christianity is the prime historical instance (p. 158; B., 251). In the succeeding phase of conscious life, that of the ethical realm, spirit divides itself again to become *der sich entfremdete Geist*. (In this section Hegel has profited from Diderot's remarkable study of a disorganized temperament, *Le Neveu de Rameau*, which he read in Goethe's translation while writing the *Phenomenology*.) This "self-alienated condition" characterizes especially the sophisticated, disintegrated minds of eighteenth-century Europe, for whom art and culture stand in opposition to all that is natural, and in whom consciousness, knowing the "self-fragmenting nature of all relationships," rises to awareness of "its own tattered condition," and in this knowledge "raises itself above that condition" (pp. 347, 376; B., 509, 547–8). This stage evolves into the climax of estrangement in "absolute freedom and terror" (represented at its historical extreme by the French Revolution), which is capable only of a purely "negative action," and so "is merely the fury of annihilation" (pp. 414, 418; B., 599, 604).

The course of these metamorphoses is represented as a recurrent peripety, or ironic reversal [*Umkehrung des Bewusstseins*] (p. 74), in which a particular shape of consciousness is inescapably impelled to an extreme that converts it into its conflicting opposite. But each conflict moves on to a temporary reconciliation in an *anagnorisis,* a recognition scene, in which, as Hegel puts it—in one of the homely locutions that emerge engagingly from the dance of his abstractions—"each of the absolute opposites recognizes itself in its other, and this recognition breaks out as the 'Yes!' between the two extremes" (p. 547; B., 782–3).

In the outcome the ever renewing division, conflict, and suffering of the wayfaring spirit are recognized to have been evils which are justified because they lead to a greater good, and are indispensable conditions for the emergence of that good. The recognition of this truth is adumbrated in the penultimate stage of the spirit's self-education, the emergence of revealed Christianity, with its "image-representation" in "the form of objectivity" (p. 549; B., 789) of the fall, Incarnation, and redemption. The truth is not rationally grasped, or "comprehended," however, until the final stage, the achievement of genuine philosophy, which supersedes, while preserving its substance, the image-thinking of revealed religion. From this ultimate vantage the spirit recognizes that all the mysteries of religion are intrinsic to itself, as moments in its own educational development: [46] human consciousness becomes aware that it has been its own betrayer, and can be its own redeemer. It is in this respect that the end product, the story that Hegel has been relating, which is history that has been "comprehended," as he says, under the aspect of systematic philosophy, is the equivalent of the Passion—at once "the recollection and the Golgotha of the absolute spirit" (p. 564; B., 808).

Hegel describes the plot-form of his history of the questing consciousness (in a close parallel to Aristotle's description of an integral literary plot) as having an end that follows necessarily from the beginning and middle, but yields a satisfaction that requires nothing beyond itself:

> The goal of knowledge is set for it with the same necessity as the sequence of its progression. It is reached at the point at which knowledge is no longer compelled to go out beyond itself, and at which it finds itself. . . . The movement to this goal, therefore, is neither capable of stopping nor of finding satisfaction [*Befriedigung*] at any earlier station.
>
> (pp. 68–9; B., 137–8)

The denouement that concludes Hegel's narrative he calls the stage of "absolute knowledge," and he represents it as a climactic recognition scene in which spirit becomes fully "self-conscious spirit" by finding itself, comprehending itself, and so entirely repossessing its alienated self, in everyone and everything that has ever happened and is happening now. The goal of the spirit's unknowing quest (in Hegel's traditional metaphor of the pilgrimage of life) is the return to the home it has left at the beginning; its home, however, turns out to be where the spirit has been all along, without knowing it. This return occurs at the ultimate "moment" of the process of consciousness in which "it has annulled and transcended [aufgehoben] and taken back into itself this alienation [Entäusserung] and objectification, and so is at home with itself [bei sich ist] in its otherness as such" (pp. 549–50; B., 789–90). Or as Hegel describes the end of the spiritual quest again in his History of Philosophy, it is both a homecoming and a reunion—a homecoming to itself, and a reunion with itself:

> This being-at-home-with-itself [Beisichsein], this coming-to-itself of the spirit may be described as its highest, absolute goal. It is this only that it desires, and nothing else. Everything that happens in heaven and on earth—eternally happens—the life of God and everything that is done in the course of time, are nothing other than the striving to the end that the spirit may recognize itself, make itself objective to itself, find itself, become for itself, and unite itself with itself [sich mit sich zusammenschliesse]. It is division, alienation [Verdoppelung, Entfremdung], but only so that it can find itself, so that it can return to itself.[47]

This last "shape of the spirit" as absolute knowledge, Hegel says, in which the spirit finally appears to its own consciousness in the "form of objectivity," is Wissenschaft; but this science, although eternally valid, "does not make its appearance in time and in reality until the point at which spirit has arrived at this consciousness regarding itself" (pp. 556–7; B., 797–8). Now, Wissenschaft is no other than the total dialectic of truth which is embodied in Hegel's own philosophical system, so that the tortuous educational journey of the spirit ends in the event toward which it has been unknowingly pointing from the beginning: its accomplished shape in the consciousness of the philosopher Hegel. But Hegel also says the way by which consciousness reaches this goal of total self-knowledge, or "the knowledge of [the object] as itself," is by recollecting, reliving, and so "grasping," its own temporal past from the beginning up to the present, "in the form of shapes of the consciousness" (p. 550; B., 790–1). (Hegel hyphenates the first occurrence of the word for recollection, *Er-Innerung,* p. 564, in order to bring out the pun on "remembering" and "internalizing.") And this process by which consciousness recollects, reparticipates in, assimilates, and so comes to comprehend its identity in its own past, as Hegel shows in a concluding reprise of his entire book, is precisely the history of evolving consciousness that has just been recollected and narrated in the *Phenomenology* itself, in the mode of a spiritual journey. "Thus," as Hegel says in his conclusion,

> the goal, which is absolute knowledge, or spirit knowing itself as spirit, has for its road [*Weg*] the recollection [*Erinnerung*] of the spirits [*Geister*], as they are in themselves, and as they carry out the organization of their realm.   (p. 564; B., 808)

The paradox, however, is that for consciousness to "recollect" its own past stages not as the mere succession of events in time, but as "comprehended history"—history which has been incorporated by consciousness, and so is understood in all its necessary dialectical organization—it must have reached the *Wissenschaft* at the end of its educational journey before it can set out upon that journey from its beginning. As Hegel puts it in his Introduction, "the road [*Weg*] to *Wissenschaft* is itself already *Wissenschaft;* by the nature of its content, it is the *Wissenschaft* of the experience of consciousness" (p. 74; B., 144). The educational journey of the general consciousness is therefore of necessity a circuitous one: "It is a circle that returns into itself, that presupposes its beginning, and reaches its beginning only in its end" (p. 559; B., 801). And that end— which, in the unity with itself reachieved by "the spirit that knows itself," is "the beginning from which we set out," although now "at a higher level"—we are told in the sentence that terminates the book, is the spirit's recollection of its own history in the mode of "comprehended organization . . . the science of evolving phenomenal knowledge [*die Wissenschaft des erscheinenden Wissens*]" (pp. 563–4; B., 806–9). That is, the end of the *Phenomenology of the Spirit* is the beginning of the organized recollection which constitutes the *Phenomenology of the Spirit* itself.

The constitution of the book, however, is further complicated by the fact that its end is not only its own beginning but the beginning also of Hegel's written exposition of systematic *Wissenschaft,* of which the three main phases, we know, are the logic, the philosophy of nature, and the philosophy of spirit. G. R. Mure, the expositor of Hegel, describes the complex relationship of the *Phenomenology* to the body of Hegel's philosophical writings:

> As the history of man's self-education to philosophy it is a propaedeutic prelude to Hegel's system. But Hegel's dialectical view forbids sheer severance of prelude from performance. Philosophy is a result containing and preserving the whole self-educative process which it cancels but includes and crowns. Hence the *Phenomenology* is also an integral part of the system. . . . [The difference in form is that] between the genetic aspect and the aspect of full-grown scientific system.[48]

Hegel's book, taken as a literary form, is thus one of the earliest, yet at the same time the most intricate and extreme, of modern involuted works of the imagination. It is a self-contained, self-sustained, and self-implicative puzzle-book, which is enigmatic in the whole and deliberately equivocal in all its parts and passing allusions. But it is evident that in general content and overall design the work is notably parallel to Wordsworth's exactly contemporary poem on the growth of his own mind. (Wordsworth finished writing *The Prelude* in 1805, the year before Hegel completed his *Phenomenology.*) That is, it is the representative autobiography of a spiritual education, told explicitly in the mode of two consciousnesses (the enlightened spirit's present recollection of things past); it justifies evil and suffering as necessary conditions to the achievement of maturity and the recognition of one's identity and aim, is climaxed by the discovery of the implicit principles governing its own organization, evolves both into its own genesis and into the masterwork to which it serves as prelude, and reaches at its end the very stage in time at which the *Phenomenology* in fact begins—"that point" in the progressive "experience of consciousness," as Hegel specifies in the last sentence of his Introduction, at which "its exposition [*Darstellung*] . . . falls into coincidence with the genuine *Wissenschaft* of the spirit" (p. 75; B., 145).

4. SOME OTHER EDUCATIONAL TRAVELERS: HÖLDERLIN'S "HYPERION," GOETHE'S "FAUST," THE ROMANCES OF NOVALIS

As a student at the theological seminary at Tübingen, the poet Hölderlin had been the close friend of Schelling and Hegel and had showed himself to be their peer in philosophical interest and acumen. Late in 1795 he drafted a Preface to his novel-in-progress *Hyperion,* which summarized the intention of the work as it then stood. Its central idea is one that we have been describing: the course of human *Bildung,* in the individual as in the race, is a fall from the paradisal unity of being into division and conflict between the self and the outer world, which turns out to have been a necessary departure on the way back to a higher reunion with alienated nature. Hölderlin's figure for the circuitous journey of life is that of an eccentric path, *eine exzentrische Bahn:*

> We all pass through an eccentric path, and there is no other way possible from childhood to consummation [*Vollendung*].
> The blessed unity, Being (in the only sense of that word) is lost to us, and we had to lose it if we were to gain it again by striving and struggle. We tear ourselves loose from the peaceful *en kai pan* of the world, in order to restore it through ourselves. We have fallen out with nature, and what was once one, as we can believe, is now in conflict with itself, and each side alternates between mastery and servitude. . . . Hyperion too was divided between these two extremes.[49]

There has been much discussion of the literal reference of the metaphoric phrase, *exzentrische Bahn*. An "eccentric circle" had been a technical term in Ptolemaic astronomy for the orbit around the earth of a planet whose center has been displaced from the center of the earth itself; the eccentric path of a planet, therefore, is one which takes it first closer, and then farther, from its true center.[50] It would seem that Hölderlin intended to represent the course of life as an approach to its center in the initial unity of being, followed by a swing back out into estrangement, conflict, and a master-slave relationship between the self and nature.[51] It is apparent from Hölderlin's statement, however, that the unity to be earned "by striving and struggle" is of a higher order than the inherited unity we have lost. The Preface goes on to say:

> To end that eternal conflict between our self and the world, to restore the peace that passeth all understanding, to unite ourselves with nature so as to form one endless whole—that is the goal of all our striving.

But as in Schiller, so in Hölderlin, absolute unity between the self and severed nature is an infinite goal which is asymptotic to finite human endeavor, so that it can be ever more closely approached but never entirely achieved:

> Neither our knowledge nor our action, however, in any period whatever of existence, attains that point at which all conflict ceases and all is one: the determinate line unites with the undeterminate one only in infinite approximation. . . .
>
> [But that infinite reunion of man and nature] is actually at hand—in the form of Beauty; to speak as Hyperion does, a new Kingdom awaits us, where Beauty is queen.—
>
> I believe we shall all say, in the end: Holy Plato, forgive us! grievously have we sinned against you.

In its final version of 1797–9, *Hyperion* is a *Bildungsroman* in the form of letters addressed by a young eighteenth-century Greek to his friend Bellarmin. The initial letters are written at the time of his life immediately after the conclusion of the events which Hyperion, in response to a request from Bellarmin, proceeds in the third letter to narrate. "I thank you," he wrote, "for asking me to tell you about myself, and for bringing the former times back into my memory." [52] As the statement indicates, the substance of the book consists of the events of the past as recollected in the present, so that Hyperion presents himself in a double awareness—the self that he is and the self that he was when untutored by the experiences he now recollects. (In one of his letters, however, Hyperion encloses his earlier correspondence with his beloved Diotima; in this instance we find him standing forth as he was, independent of his present consciousness.)

In the course of his narrated life from infancy into manhood, Hyperion moves through stages of experience in which he periodically seems to approach a lost consonance with himself and with the outer world; at each stage, however, the equilibrium proves unstable and at once divides into opposites that press in turn toward a new integration. Hyperion passes through the Edenic self-unity of childhood, in the peace and happiness before the child "has come to be at odds with itself," and before "Nature drives it out of its Paradise." With the help of his teacher Adamas, he next experiences the harmonious world of Greek antiquity; there follows his experience of the highest male friendship with Alabanda, then of bisexual love for Diotima, who is an earthly woman, yet also a *figura* of "the consummation that we place beyond the stars, that we put off to the very end of time." Diotima is "beauty" itself, and her role is equivalent to that of Beatrice in Dante's pilgrimage, for she "shows him the way" to his earthly equivalent of the heavenly city, "the new Kingdom of the new divinity" (III, 52–3).

When Diotima urges Hyperion to seek his goal by translating ideal into action among his native Greeks, who are suffering under foreign oppression, Hyperion kindles to a vision of an apocalyptic new world, represented in the figure of a marriage between man and nature: "Let the new world spring from the root of humanity! . . . Nature! A rejuvenated people will make thee young again too, and thou wilt be as its bride" (III, 89–90). A sudden plea from Alabanda leads Hyperion to throw himself prematurely into the violence of the Greek political revolution against the Turks. The collapse of his hope in revolution, followed by his rejection by his father and the death of Diotima, plunge Hyperion into a crisis of despair in which, barred from the garden of his origin, he feels divided from his earlier self and estranged both from nature and from mankind.

> But the world to which I return is no longer the world as it was. I am an alien [*Fremdling*], like the unburied dead when they come up from Acheron. And even if I were back on my native island, in the gardens of my youth, which my father bars to me, oh! even then, even then, would I be an alien on earth and no god would bind me to my past again.
>   Yes, all is over!

His disillusion is completed by a sojourn in Germany, where he seeks consolation in the modern home of learning and philosophy but finds no human wholeness, only a nation of barbaric "fragmented" people who are not men but merely workers, thinkers, priests, masters, slaves, "like the shards of a discarded pot," or "as on a battlefield where hacked-off hands and arms and all bodily members lie in a heap, while the life blood pours out to disappear into the sand" (III, 150, 153).

From this farthest point of his eccentric orbit Hyperion is turned back, in an experience he describes in his final letter, by a revelation in the reviving landscape in springtime, in which he recognizes that his sufferings have made him capable of a deeper insight into the life of things, and accepts mortality as the necessary condition for ever renewing life. "A new joy springs up in the heart when it perseveres and survives the midnight of suffering, and . . . only then, in our deep pain, does the world's song of life sound out divinely to us." "Men fall from thee, O Nature, like rotten fruits; oh, let them perish, for thus they return to thy root; so may I too, O tree of life, that I may grow green again with thee." [53] In the great surge of renewal, the hitherto dead and alien hills, sun, natural creatures, and the moving air not only come alive again but manifest themselves as human forms to which he can join himself as one who has come back to his family and home:

"O sun, O you breezes," I cried out then, "only among you
does my heart still live, as among brothers." . . . And O you
loved ones, you who are far away, you who are dead and you
who live, how intimately were we at one! . . .

Sweet breezes blew . . . and the light smiled silently in the
aether, its home. . . .

You springs of the earth, you flowers, you woods and you
eagles and thou, brotherly light! how old and new is our
love! . . . For all of us love the aether, and in the deepest
recesses of our inmost being we are all alike.[54]

Hyperion ends, then, in a Wordsworthian way, after a mental
crisis and the discovery of a rationale for seeming evil, with a
union between the disalienated mind and a rehumanized
nature. And in a striking structural parallel with *The Prelude,*
the novel also ends at the threshold of its own origin, which is
the time of Hyperion's return from Germany to his native
Greece; as he says in the opening sentence of the first letter, he
has just arrived in his "dear Fatherland" which "once again
gives me joy and sorrow." "In this sense," as Lawrence Ryan
remarks in his extensive commentary, the novel has a circular
shape "and turns back to its beginning"; [55] and this beginning
is the home and fatherland that Hyperion had left. In the two
introductory letters which precede the chronological narration
of his recollected life, we also find Hyperion experiencing again
a union with a humanized nature, like the earlier experience
which he was to recount in his concluding letter. For it is still
that same springtime, and in "the fullness of the all-living
world" Hyperion stands with tears of desire, "the loved one
before his beloved," and it seems to him as if she, "a kindred
spirit, were opening her arms to me, as if the pain of loneliness
were dissolving in the life of the divinity" (III, 8–9). Nature,
which had been familial, now assumes a feminine form; as in
the long tradition of these figures for the reunion of long disparted separates, the metaphor of the return home modulates
easily into the metaphor of a sexual embrace.

There is, however, an important difference between the
state of the protagonist at the opening of *Hyperion* and the
state of Wordsworth at the opening of *The Prelude.* Hyperion

has made the mistake of trying to reachieve the *en kai pan,* the one life, by rejecting the long and painful course of *Bildung* toward maturity, in an endeavor to revert to the innocent peace of infancy and the inconscient unity of the infant with itself and nature. As he had said in his concluding letter:

> How gladly would I have become a child again, in order to be nearer to [Nature], how gladly would I have known less and become like the pure rays of light, in order to be nearer to her! oh, to feel myself for one instant in her peace and in her beauty—how much more it would mean to me than years full of thought, than all the endeavors of all-endeavoring mankind! All I had learned, all I had done in my life, dissolved like ice, and all the projects of my youth faded away in me.[56]

But as Schiller had said, civilized man can't go back again, and "that nature which you envy in the non-rational . . . lies behind you, it must ever lie behind you." Or in the terms of Hölderlin's own Preface, the way back is the way on, for the only lasting way to regain the integrity we have lost is "by striving and struggle." The result of Hyperion's attempted short-cut back to his primitive harmony with nature is therefore unstable and unenduring. As he says in the second of his initial letters, the instant he begins (as an adult and civilized man inevitably must) once more to take thought, the garden dies, and he is again the self-divided and alienated man, the outcast Adam—and the Prodigal Son:

> On this height I often stand, my Bellarmin. But an instant of reflection hurls me down. I think, and find myself as I was before—alone, with all the griefs of mortality; and my heart's refuge, the world in its eternal oneness, is gone; Nature closes her arms, and I stand like an alien [*Fremdling*] before her and understand her not.
>
> Ah! had I never gone to your schools! . . . Among you I became so utterly reasonable, learned so thoroughly to distinguish myself from that which is around me, that now I am solitary in the beautiful world, and so am an outcast from the garden of Nature, where I grew and flowered. . . . [Man] stands, like a worthless son whom his father has driven out of his house, and stares at the miserable pence that pity has given him for the road.   (III, 9)

But although this passage, which terminates the latter of the two introductory letters, is uttered by Hyperion at the latest point of time represented in the novel, it is not the conclusion of the novel itself. For there is a discrepancy between the time of his life which he represents in his narrative letters and the time of his life in which he composed those letters. And between the writing of the two introductory letters and the writing of the concluding letter about his remembered past, there has in fact intervened the act of composing the whole of the autobiographical narrative; and in the course of this composition, as Ryan notes,[57] Hyperion has recollected, faced up to, and to a degree comprehended his own past. The act of writing *Hyperion* is thus a functional part of the autobiography itself, on which its conclusion turns. Of the five short sentences that terminate his final letter, the first three express the insight that Hyperion, in the course of his recollection of things past, has gained into the conflict and reconciliation of quasi-sexual contraries which compel man along the circuitous path from childhood to reunified maturity:

Like the strife of lovers are the dissonances of the world. In the midst of conflict is reconciliation, and all things that are parted find one another again.

The veins separate from and return into the heart, and all is one eternal glowing life.

Hyperion's life will go on after the novel ends, to a succeeding stage which will incorporate all that he has experienced before; and it is likely that Ryan is right in his claim that this is to be the stage of Hyperion's achieved vocation as an artist— for has he not just completed his first artistic product, the epistolary novel *Hyperion* itself? If so, the *Bildungsroman* turns out to have been a *Künstlerroman*. But as artist, Hyperion must continue to experience and render the dissonances which are the inescapable condition of life; for as Hölderlin had said in the Preface, we can only approach but never attain the point "at which all conflict ceases and all is one." The shape of the novel, then, like that of the human life it represents, is circuitous yet open-ended; and its coda terminates appropriately on an unresolved chord: "So dacht' ich. Nächstens mehr." "So did I think. More in my next."

Goethe, who in *Wilhelm Meister's Lehrjahre* wrote the seminal instance of the *Bildungsroman,* also achieved in *Faust* a masterpiece of the *Bildungsgedicht.* Most Romantic versions of the educational journey, as we have seen, incorporate a displaced theodicy, in which error and suffering are justified as indispensable to the self-formation and self-realization of the mature individual, in a span of reference coterminous with his life in this world. The two parts of *Faust* are of particular interest because, instead of assimilating the Christian supernatural into a naturalistic account, it adopts, but in order radically to reinterpret, the Christian supernatural itself. Goethe employs the traditional frame, from a "Prologue in Heaven" to an "Ascension" at the end, but only as a narrative *donnée* to express an entirely secular scheme of salvation. For Faust, all deities reside in the human breast:

> Der Gott, der mir im Busen wohnt . . .
> Er kann nach aussen nichts bewegen.
>
> (I. 1566–9)

The compulsion to Faust's spiritual and geographical journey is objectified as a person who represents the "great drive-wheels" of *Polarität* and *Steigerung,* which are Goethe's version of the contrariety and sublimation in the dialectic of his philosophical contemporaries. Mephistopheles is explicitly "der Geist der stets verneint," whose negations appear to us as "sin, destruction, in short, evil," but in fact serve to compel man into progressive activity, who otherwise "all too readily prefers unconditional rest." Accordingly, Mephistopheles "excites and works and must create, in his very nature as Devil," in a cosmic irony, as Mephistopheles himself ruefully acknowledges, that makes him the unwilling agent of theodicy, as "a part of that power/ Which always wills the bad and always effects the good" (I. 338–44; 1335–44).

After the betrayal and death of Gretchen, Part II begins with Faust's sleep of self-purgation, after which "des Lebens Pulse schlagen frisch lebendig," and he awakens to a world which has

become *ein Paradies* (II. 4679-94). This spiritual rebirth, however, is correlative with the reviving life of nature in the spring,
from which Faust arises as a secular new Adam, to resume his
unwitting pilgrimage toward a redemption in this life. His
goal, symbolized in the final lines of the drama as a female
figure—"Das Ewig-Weibliche/ Zieht uns hinan"—is an infinite
beyond attainment, so that his triumph consists simply in the
experience of sustaining a desire which never relaxes into the
stasis of a finite satisfaction.

Hölderlin had expressed with unmatched economy the Romantic ideal of infinite aspiration: "Das ist die Herrlichkeit
des Menschen, dass ihm ewig nichts genügt." [58] Hölderlin's
glory of man is in Goethe's rendering the salvation of man;
as the angel says in the concluding scene:

> Wer immer strebend sich bemüht,
> Den können wir erlösen.

Goethe adopts the concept of salvation as a triumph of aspiration toward an infinite God, but alters it in a fashion that
shears away Christian supernaturalism and transvalues Christian morality. The final ascension of Faust does not signify
his rejection of the possibilities of this world in order to achieve
an other-worldly good, but his success in maintaining a desire
for a totality of experience that is infinitely beyond the possibilities of the world to satisfy, in an errorful and suffering striving which is its own reward, by making him that which he becomes and could not have been without it. The salvation of
Faust is a judgment rendered on the life that he has already
lived.

I shall conclude this sketch of a recurrent pattern in German
literature at the turn of the nineteenth century with an author
who conveniently brings together almost all the elements I
have been detailing—the Scriptural story of Eden and the
apocalypse; pagan myths and mystery cults; Plotinus, Hermetic
literature, and Boehme; the philosophical and historical doctrines of Schiller, Fichte, Schelling, and contemporary *Naturphilosophie;* the exemplary novel of education, *Wilhelm Meis-*

ter's Lehrjahre—and fuses them into the subject-matter of all his major writings. The remote and fluctuant half-world of Novalis' fantasy is *sui generis*, but behind what Novalis called his *Tropen-und-Rätselsprache* we make out a familiar complex of ideas, imagery, and design. In Novalis' romances the process of representative human experience is a fall from self-unity and community into division, and from contentment into the longing for redemption, which consists of a recovered unity on a higher level of self-awareness. This process is represented in the plot-form of an educational journey in quest of a feminine other, whose mysterious attraction compels the protagonist to abandon his childhood sweetheart and the simple security of home and family (equated with infancy, the pagan golden age, and the Biblical paradise) to wander through alien lands on a way that rounds imperceptibly back to home and family, but with an accession of insight (the product of his experience en route) which enables him to recognize, in the girl he has left behind, the elusive female figure who has all along been the object of his longing and his quest. The protagonist's return home thus coincides with the consummation of a union with his beloved bride.

Die Lehrlinge zu Sais (written 1798–9) deals with novitiates who are being educated into the mysteries of the veiled goddess Isis, whose sanctuary is at the ancient Egyptian city of Sais. The opening section begins, "Various are the ways [*Wege*] of men," and it closes with the behest of the sage who is the teacher of the novices that "each of us follow his own way, because each new way goes through new countries, and each in the end leads back to these dwellings, to this sacred home." "I too will inscribe my figure," declares the student narrator, whose search is for "the way to where, deep in sleep, the maiden dwells for whom my spirit yearns." [59]

There follow the musings and monologues of the teacher and of his students, all of which play variations—according to the way of life and depth of insight of each speaker—on a single theme, that of a unitive relationship within a man, as well as between man and nature and between an individual and other men, which has been lost and will be found again. In the "old, simple, natural condition" of integral man, "every-

thing must have seemed human, familiar, and companionable."
But thereafter it occurred to men "to signify the manifold objects of their senses by a common name, and to set themselves
in opposition to them," and this was the reason that gradually
"our inner being split into so great a variety of powers, and
with the continuation of this procedure this fragmentation will
even increase." As a result of the divisiveness inaugurated by
man's analytic understanding, nature turned into a "strange, cold
being," and to some men it became "a terrifying mill of death,"
a "gigantic machine." But artists, as well as the practitioners of
the utilitarian arts of agriculture and civilization, gradually
taught alienated nature "more friendly ways again," and she
resumed her ancient colloquy and community with man: "She
became again sociable, and gladly gave answer to the friendly
questioner, and so the old age of gold seems gradually to be
coming back again, in which she was the friend, consoler,
priestess, and miracle-worker to men." And the time will indeed
be when "all races of the world, after long separation, will
come together again." [60]

One novice describes the interchange which the poet attains
with nature as the achievement of an I-Thou relationship:
"Does not the cliff become a specific Thou, the moment I
address it?" [61] A more ardent enthusiast represents the poet's
reconciliation with nature as a sexual embrace: "When that
mighty emotion for which language has no other name than
love and voluptuousness expands within him like a powerful,
all-dissolving vapor and, trembling in sweet terror, he sinks
into the dark, alluring womb of nature, his poor individuality
consumes itself in the overwhelming waves of desire, and
nothing remains but a focus of immeasurable procreative force,
an engulfing whirlpool in the mighty ocean." In a more con-
templative mood, the poet "blends himself with all the creatures
of nature, one might say feels himself into them [*sich gleichsam
in sie hineinfühlt*]." The novice translates the mystic's marriage
of the soul with Christ into a marriage between the poet and
nature. "In nature he feels as at the bosom of his modest bride,"
and she permits him "to behold her in her duality, as a power
that engenders and gives birth, and in her unity, as an infinite,
everlasting marriage." [62]

Into these meditations Novalis inserts a light-hearted *Mär-chen* which serves as the type for the romance as a whole. The story tells how Hyazinth, enticed by the tales of a strange man "from foreign lands," abandons both his home and Rosenblüte, his childhood sweetheart, "to go forth into foreign lands," whither he knows not, to seek "the mother of things, the veiled maiden. For her is my heart aflame." After long wanderings he reaches the shrine, falls asleep, and dreams that he enters the holy of holies, the abode of Isis.

> All seemed so familiar, yet with a splendor such as he had never seen; the last trace of earth vanished as though absorbed in air, and he stood before the heavenly maiden. Then he raised the light, shimmering veil—and Rosenblüte sank into his arms. A faraway music closed off the secrets of the loving reunion, the outpourings of longing, and excluded all that was alien from this enchanting place. Afterward Hyazinth lived long with Rosenblüte among his happy parents and play-mates. . . .[63]

Die Lehrlinge was left incomplete by its author, but some fragmentary notes suggest the probable outcome. The story is a nature myth: "Isis—maiden—veil—secret treatment of natural science." In one note a "favorite of fortune" enters the Temple of Isis to find there "his bride, who received him with smiles." In another:

> One was successful—he raised the veil of the goddess of Sais—
> But what did he see? he saw—wonder of wonders—himself.

The end of the circular journey, it would seem, was to be a repossession of nature which is also the repossession of man's alienated self. His ultimate model, Novalis' notes also indicate, was the marriage of Christ and the New Jerusalem in the Apocalypse, signalizing the advent of a new heaven and new earth. Man, Novalis implies, is both his own evangelist and his own redeemer: he "proclaims himself and his evangel of nature. He is the Messiah of nature." Accordingly, after Isis has finally made her appearance, in company with the Messiah of nature, the note reads: *"New* Testament—and new nature—as *New Jerusalem."* [64]

Novalis' *Heinrich von Ofterdingen* (written 1799–1800) is a symbolic narrative of the growth of a poet's mind, represented in the vehicle of a sustained journey through the realms of experience. The stimulus to undertaking the journey is Heinrich's "inexpressible longing" for a blue flower which he sees in a dream, of which the corolla is the face of a girl. From the beginning he has the presentiment that the immanent design of his quest is a circular one:

> Henry left his father and his native city with sorrow in his heart. Now for the first time it became clear to him what separation means. . . . His familiar world was torn from him and he was washed up as it were on a foreign shore. . . .
>
> The magic flower was before him, and he gazed over into Thuringia, which he was just leaving, with the strange premonition that after long wanderings he would return to his native land [*Vaterland*] from distant regions toward which they were now traveling and hence with the feeling that it was really his native land he was approaching.[65]

The underlying motif, it is repeatedly implied, is the fall of man from the "primeval golden age and its sovereigns—love and poetry," to be followed by "the rejuvenation of nature, and the return of an everlasting golden age." "If your eyes are steadfastly turned to heaven," Heinrich is exhorted, "you will never miss your way home." [66]

At the center of this romance, too, is a *Märchen*, told by the master poet Klingsohr—this time a very elaborate one which assimilates the imagery of Revelation, Canticles, contemporary metallurgy and galvanism, and the Hermetic quest for the Philosopher's Stone, into the story of the prince who wakens the sleeping princess; the result transforms the familiar fairy tale into a cosmic myth. In the notes he wrote for an intended poetics, Novalis indicated the centrality of this form to his visionary concept of the nature and function of poetry. "The *Märchen* is as it were the canon of poetry—everything poetic must be *märchenhaft*." And the writer of the *Märchen* is the bard who present, past, and future sees, and who sees the future as a return to a bettered past:

In the future world everything is as it was in the former world—yet everything is quite different. The future world is chaos which has been rationalized [*das vernünftige Chaos*]. . . .

The genuine *Märchen* must be at the same time prophetic representation—ideal representation—absolutely necessary representation. The genuine composer of the *Märchen* is a seer into the future. . . .

With the passage of time, history must become a *Märchen* —it becomes again what it was in the beginning.[67]

Klingsohr's tale opens immediately after the fall. "The long night had just begun," and nature has become a frozen wintry world in which all trees, flowers, and fruits are the mimic work of pure artifice. Eros is seduced by Ginnistan (that is, Fantasy) who, in the incestuous fashion common to myth, alchemy, and modern psychoanalysis, assumes the form of Eros' own mother. In their absence the Scribe (characterized by Novalis in a letter as "petrifying and petrified reason")[68] takes over the household and by his divisive influence brings matters to their nadir of evil in fragmentation, strife, and death. But Fable (the Spirit of Poetry) undertakes a redemptive journey through the three realms of being, the nether world, the middle world (which is earth, the human sphere of home and the family), and the upper world. In her descent to the underworld, Fable solves the riddle of the sphinx—"What is the eternal mystery?" "Love." At once the denouement begins, in a grand conflation of pagan, occult, scientific, and eschatological imagery. The giant Atlas is revivified by a jolt of galvanic current, and is able once more to take up the burden of the earth. "The old times are returning," and soon the Garden of the Hesperides "will bloom again and the golden fruit send forth its fragrance." After a sequence of quasi-alchemical operations, the fallen world is redeemed: "The new world is born of pain, and in tears the ashes are dissolved into a drink of eternal life." In this all-inclusive reunification the Scribe, principle of division, his occupation gone, simply disappears. "A mighty springtime had spread over the earth," and there is a universal regeneration in which all things are "lifted and moved" and take on a human form; even in the "whirlwinds of dust . . . familiar figures seemed to form." "In this peaceable kingdom" the animals "approached the wakened people with friendly nods" and "the plants served them with fruits and fragrances." With the assistance of electrical forces, Eros wakens the sleeping princess Freya (Peace); "she opened her large dark eyes and recognized her beloved," and "a long kiss sealed the eternal union"; while Sophie (Wisdom) bids the happy couple to "toss the bracelet of your union into the air, so that the people and the world may remain united with you." There ensues an allegorical procession of "the stars and the spirits of nature," after which "the old moon came in with his fantastic retinue," leading the bridal procession to celebrate the union of Ginnistan with the father.

Even this sparse précis may have brought out the similarities of this little myth to symbolic inventions of Blake, Shelley, and Keats; it is as though a script writer had fused elements from *Jerusalem, Prometheus Unbound,* and *Endymion* into the scenario for a Walt Disney fantasia. The *Märchen* ends, *mutatis mutandis,* as does *Prometheus Unbound,* with the marital embrace of the king and queen (Arcturus and Sophie), which becomes universally epidemic:

> In the meantime the throne had imperceptibly changed into a magnificent bridal bed, over whose canopy the Phoenix hovered with little Fable. . . . The king embraced his blushing beloved, and the people followed the example of the king and caressed one another. One heard nothing but words of endearment and a whisper of kisses.[69]

Novalis lived to finish only the beginning of the second part of *Heinrich von Ofterdingen,* in which Heinrich, his beloved Mathilda having died, takes up his wanderings again, now in the specific character of "a pilgrim." But the contour of his way remains that of a long detour back to its beginning. When Heinrich inquires, "Wo gehn wir denn hin?" he is answered, "Immer nach Hause." Novalis' notes for the continuation indicate that when nature shall once again be humanized and resume her communication with man, his pilgrim will be at home in the presently alien world:

The book closes just the reverse of the *Märchen*—with one simple family.

All becomes quieter, simpler, and more human toward the end.

It is at the end the primal world, the golden age.

Men, beasts, plants, stones and stars, flames, tones, colors must at the end act and speak together as a single family or society, as a single race.[70]

The third of Novalis' major works, *Hymnen an die Nacht* (1800), is a feat of invention which broke ground for the Symbolists in nineteenth-century France. Many of its components, however, we recognize: the spiritual journey in search of the beloved, who has vanished into the darkness of death; the parallel between the loss of the beloved and the fall of the blessed world, when "rivers and trees, flowers and beasts, had human sense," into one in which "nature stood, lifeless and alone"; the use of the union of lover and beloved as the figural type for the consummation of all things. At the conclusion of the *Hymns,* when the loved one becomes a feminine *figura Christi,* the circuitous quest candidly reverts to its ancient prototype in the Christian pilgrimage through exile back home, where one who is at once the father, the bridegroom, and the bride stands waiting.

> Die Lust der Fremde ging uns aus,
> Zum Vater wollen wir nach Haus. . . .
>
> Wir müssen nach der Heimat gehn,
> Um diese heilge Zeit zu sehn. . . .
>
> Hinunter zu der süssen Braut,
> Zu Jesus, dem Geliebten . . .
> Ein Traum bricht unsre Banden los
> Und senkt uns in des Vaters Schoss.

So Augustine long ago had said, "groaning in my pilgrimage" in the longing for "Jerusalem my Fatherland" and for "its Father and Tutor and Spouse." "For that City the friend of the bridegroom sighs . . . for he is a member of the Spouse of Christ." [71]

FIVE

The Circuitous Journey:
From Blake to
D. H. Lawrence

O soul, repressless, I with thee and thou with me,
Thy circumnavigation of the world begin,
Of man, the voyage of his mind's return.

To reason's early paradise,
Back, back to wisdom's birth, to innocent intuitions,
Again with fair creation.
                         —Whitman, *Passage to India*

A human pest cycling (pist!) and recycling (past!) about the
sledgy streets, here he was (pust!) again!
                         —Joyce, *Finnegans Wake*

We shall not cease from exploration
And the end of all our exploring
Will be to arrive where we started
And know the place for the first time.
                         —Eliot, *Little Gidding*

FIVE

Here, in summary, are the interrelated concepts and images which, as a whole or in substantial part, were shared by a number of German poets, romance writers, and philosophers in the three decades after 1790. The poet or philosopher, as the avant-garde of the general human consciousness, possesses the vision of an imminent culmination of history which will be equivalent to a recovered paradise or golden age. The movement toward this goal is a circuitous journey and quest, ending in the attainment of self-knowledge, wisdom, and power. This educational process is a fall from primal unity into self-division, self-contradiction, and self-conflict, but the fall is in turn regarded as an indispensable first step along the way toward a higher unity which will justify the sufferings undergone en route. The dynamic of the process is the tension toward closure of the divisions, contraries, or "contradictions" themselves. The beginning and end of the journey is man's ancestral home, which is often linked with a female contrary from whom he has, upon setting out, been disparted. The goal of this long inner quest is to be reached by a gradual ascent, or else by a sudden breakthrough of imagination or cognition; in either case, however, the achievement of the goal is pictured as a scene of recognition and reconciliation, and is often signalized by a loving union with the feminine other, upon which man finds himself thoroughly at home with himself, his milieu, and his family of fellow men.

Similar elements and a similar design were prevalent also in the major literature of contemporary England. Coleridge and Carlyle were familiar with German models, but Blake, Wordsworth, and Shelley knew little or nothing of them. The concurrence in topics and design among these very diverse writers was less the result of mutual influence than it was of a common experience in the social, intellectual, and emotional climate of the post-Revolutionary age, and of a grounding in a common body of materials—above all in the Bible, especially as expounded by radical Protestant visionaries, many of whom had assimilated a modicum of Neoplatonic lore.

1. UNITY LOST AND INTEGRITY EARNED: BLAKE AND COLERIDGE

"Perhaps he will yet come," Schelling wrote in 1811, "who is to sing the greatest heroic poem, comprehending in spirit what was, what is, what will be." [1] Schelling's prophecy had already been realized by William Blake, who composed his epic poems in the persona, or what he called the "voice," of the bard "Who Present, Past, & Future sees." "Such," Blake later pronounced in *Jerusalem,* "is my awful Vision. . . . I see the Past, Present & Future existing all at once/ Before me." [2] Schelling had also put forward the related claim that "each truly creative individual must create his mythology for himself." Similarly Los, Blake's archetypal artist, cries as he labors, "I must Create a System, or be enslav'd by another Man's." [3]

"That which can be made Explicit to the Idiot," Blake roundly declared, "is not worth my care." [4] The mythical system which Blake created is complex and cryptic, and he kept altering its details and its multiple relevance both to general human history and to the personal and public affairs of his own life and age. But he described the broad and durable outline of his system, quite explicitly, as the argument of his earliest full-scale epic *The Four Zoas:*

> Four Mighty Ones are in every man: a Perfect Unity
> Cannot Exist but from the Universal Brotherhood of Eden,
> The Universal Man. To Whom be Glory Evermore Amen. . . .
> Los was the fourth immortal starry one, & in the Earth
> Of a bright Universe Empery attended day & night,
> Days and nights of revolving joy; Urthona was his name

In Eden; in the Auricular Nerves of Human Life,
Which is the Earth of Eden, he his Emanations propagated,
Fairies of Albion, afterwards Gods of the Heathen; Daughter
of Beulah Sing
His fall into Division & his Resurrection to Unity.   (I, 3–4)

For Blake "The Old & New Testaments are the Great Code of Art," [5] so that all of his prophetic epics represent—each with a different focus and area of primary reference—the overall Biblical plot of the creation and fall of man, the history of man in the fallen world, and the coming redemption of man in a restored Eden. Like the German authors of *Universalgeschichte,* however, Blake interprets the ancient fable in his own way. His mythical premise, or founding image, is not a transcendent God, but "The Universal Man" who, as "the Human Form Divine," incorporates deity in himself. A number of German writers, as we have seen, recount the past, present, and speculative future as the actions and experiences of a generic being they call "mankind" (representing the collective experience of individual men) who "falls" into self-division and is capable of being redeemed by self-reintegration. In a parallel way Blake's prophetic books narrate various stages of the division and reintegration of the Universal Man, whose life story is the collective representation of the history and potential future of "every man"—that is, of each human individual. Since Blake, however, is writing not philosophical history but imaginative myth, he embodies these concepts in the visualizable agents he calls his "Giant Forms," who act out the historical process. His Universal Man, accordingly, is not that convenient grammatical device, a collective noun (*der Mensch, die Menschheit*), but a specific *dramatis persona* whom he elsewhere names "Albion."

In its complex purport and in the fullness of its astonishing invention, Blake's myth has neither prototype nor parallel; but his founding image is recognizably in the lineage of that ancient mythical being, the primal man or Ur-Adam, who falls into fragmentation.[6] And Blake's underlying premise, which he shares with other writers in this tradition, equates essential good with unity and essential evil with separateness. Blake's

Eden, as he says, is the ideal mental state of "Perfect Unity" (which is correlative with the ideal human community of "Universal Brotherhood"), and in this original state his Universal Man, like the primal Adam of his predecessors, was sexually undivided, and incorporated all of mankind and the cosmos as well. His fall was a falling apart, a "fall into Division"; and since this is a fragmentation of unitary man both into isolated individuals and into an alien external world, the fall coincides with the creation of man and nature, as we ordinarily experience these entities. Again in traditional fashion, the original sin in this fall was what Blake elsewhere calls "Selfhood," the prideful attempt of a part of the whole to be self-sufficient and to subordinate other parts to its own desires and purposes.

From this point on, however, Blake's story is the product of his own mythopeic imagination. The process of this "dreadful state/ Of Separation" [7] he conceives as a progressive dissociation of the collective human psyche into alien and conflicting parts, each of which strives for domination. In the picture-form of myth, the Universal Man divides into the "Four Mighty Ones," the Zoas, or primary faculties and powers constituting the integral mind, and the Zoas in turn divide off from their feminine Emanations, and may subdivide again from the male remnants, or Spectres. These Giant Forms, and those which are the product of still further divisions, are portrayed as mental travelers through the realms of generation and the endless cycles of history, suffering the torment of inadequacy, isolation, and ever recurrent conflict, in the restless quest for fantasied satisfaction—"that sweet golden clime/ Where the traveller's journey is done"—which their splintered condition cannot provide.

As the fall of man is "his fall into Division" and death, so his redemption, reversing the process, is "his Resurrection to Unity." The unifying principle is Jesus, who in Blake's myth of mind is identified with the human imagination, which retains, however dimly, and even at the farthest limit of the fall (Ulro, Blake's hell-on-earth, the ultimate state of divisive rationality, tyranny, and isolated selfhood), the saving vision of the primal unity and the potentiality of re-creating it once again. "All Things," Blake says, "are comprehended in their

Eternal Forms in the Divine body of the Saviour . . . The Human Imagination." [8] This vision impels Los, who is the fallen form of Urthona, the imaginative faculty, to struggle to realize its form in the mode of art, which will serve as an evangel to annihilate all selfhood, and so to bring disparted humanity together again. Such a universal reintegration constitutes the jubilant apocalypse represented in the Ninth Night of *The Four Zoas;* it is heralded by man's dawning recognition that even outer nature is his own estranged and dehumanized self:

> So Man looks out in tree & herb & fish & bird & beast
> Collecting up the scatterd portions of his immortal body.
>   . . . wherever a grass grows
> Or a leaf buds The Eternal Man is seen is heard is felt.

In the traditional way, this recollection of the Eternal Man's scattered portions into unity is also rendered in the alternative mythical form of a marriage between the severed male and female opposites:

> Thus shall the male & female live the life of Eternity
> Because the Lamb of God Creates himself a bride & wife
> That we his Children evermore may live in Jerusalem
> Which now descendeth out of heaven a City yet a woman.

And as in all Romantic visions of the reunion of man with himself, with other men, and with his milieu, the dead of the winter of the world bursts into the joyous life of an enduring spring:

> I shall cast off my death clothes & Embrace Tharmas again
> For Lo the winter melted away upon the distant hills
> And all the black mould sings. . . .
> Joy thrilld thro all the Furious form of Tharmas humanizing
> Mild he Embracd her whom he sought.[9]

As Northrop Frye points out, since in Blake's myth "all things have proceeded from a divine Man . . . and will be reabsorbed into him . . . the total vision of life must have a circular form." [10] Blake's redemption is thus figured as a circling back of divided man to his original wholeness; he breaks out of his ceaseless round of wandering in what Blake calls "the circle of Destiny" [11]—the cyclical recurrences of pagan history—into a "Resurrection to Unity" which is the full and final closure of the Christian design of history. The dynamic of this process is the energy generated by the division of unity into separate quasi-sexual contraries which strive for closure. In Blake's version of this Romantic commonplace, as specified at the beginning of *The Marriage of Heaven and Hell:* "Without Contraries is no progression. Attraction and Repulsion, Reason and Energy, Love and Hate, are necessary to Human existence." These active contraries are to be distinguished from those artifacts of division which Blake calls "negations," for since negations lack a true opposite, they are inert and incapable of reunion into a higher organization. His Spectre which divides off from him, Los says, is a negation, and

> Negations are not Contraries: Contraries mutually Exist:
> But Negations Exist Not: Exceptions & Objections & Unbeliefs
> Exist not: nor shall they ever be Organized for ever & ever.

Los adds, "my Emanation, Alas! will become/ My Contrary." [12] The central type of the contrary is the severed female Emanation; but all contraries, in Blake, operate as opposing yet complementary male-female powers which, in their energetic love-hate relationship, are necessary to all modes of progression, organization, and creativity, or procreativity.

Like his German contemporaries, Blake views the course of human history and the normative individual life as a return which is also a "progression." It is only by an extreme historical injustice that Romanticism has been identified with the cult of the noble savage and the cultural idea of a return to an early stage of simple and easeful "nature" which lacks conflict because it lacks differentiation and complexity. On the contrary, all the major Romantic writers, and Blake most emphatically, set as the goal for mankind the reachievement of a unity which has been earned by unceasing effort and which is, in Blake's term, an "organized" unity, an equilibrium of opponent forces which preserves all the products and powers of intellection and culture. Like his contemporaries, Blake recognized the strength of civilized man's yearning for the simple self-unity of the life of infants and of instinctual creatures, and he made a place for it in his geography of the mind: the state he called "Beulah," the lower paradise of unorganized innocence "where no dispute can come." But Beulah is a peaceable kingdom only in the negative sense that it lacks conflicting contraries, and its inhabitants enjoy only such primitive security as "the beloved infant in his mothers bosom round incircled/ With arms of love & pity & sweet compassion." This mental state has value to the Sons of Eden as a vacation resort which they can visit for "a mild and pleasant rest"; but it is dangerous, in its languor and sterility, because it can become an habitual refuge from "intellectual war," that creative strife of contraries in the strenuous life of intellect and of imagination.[13]

Schiller, we recall, had said that the "nature which you envy in the nonrational is unworthy of your respect and longing," that our only possible road is not "back to Arcadia" but "onward to Elysium," and that we must struggle on until we "restore by means of a higher Art"—the imaginative creations of poetry and the fine arts—"this wholeness in our nature which Art has destroyed." This is formally close to the doctrine that Blake embodied in his myth of the active existence by which man, exhibiting the cardinal virtue of "energy," must earn his way from simple innocence back and up to a higher paradise of "organized innocence"; and in this process Blake, like Schiller, assigns the crucial function to imagination and the arts. Los labors stubbornly at his furnace with hammer and anvil in the task of building the city of Golgonooza. In Northrop Frye's terse and lucid explanation of Blake's image-representation of the social role of art: "When this structure is finished, nature, its scaffolding, will be knocked away and man will live in it. Golgonooza will then be the city of God, the New Jerusalem which is the total form of all human culture and civilization."[14]

The central subject of *The Four Zoas*, the reader sees in retrospect, has in fact been the fall of man's imaginative faculty and its education in experience to the stage at which it is capable of the highest and most comprehensively human art; and since Los, as the type of all imaginative artificers, incorporates Blake, the subject has also been the discipline and consummation of Blake's own mind and poetic power. So, as the work had begun with the epic announcement of Urthona's "fall into Division" in the form of Los, it concludes with Los's recovery of self-unity, in the acquisition of "Science":

> Urthona is arisen in his strength no longer now
> Divided from Enitharmon no longer the Spectre Los
> . . . Urthona rises from the ruinous walls
> In all his ancient strength to form the golden armour of science
> For intellectual War. The war of swords departed now
> The dark Religions are departed & sweet Science reigns.[15]

The unity which Blake thus figures at the end of the artist's redemptive course retains the fruits of the experience it has acquired en route. "The war of swords" (conflict in the fallen world) has departed, yet survives in a higher form as the equilibrium of opposing forces in "intellectual War"—that is, the "mental fight" which, in the words of Blake's great hymn, must go into the poet's building of Jerusalem "in England's green and pleasant land." The innocence of ignorance has been disciplined to "Science"; and Blake's "Science," which replaces "the dark Religions," is not so diverse as might at first appear from the unifying "knowledge" in the "aesthetic state" which concludes Schiller's account of *The Aesthetic Education of Man*—nor, for that matter, from the *Wissenschaft* which, in Hegel's *Phenomenology*, preserves but transcends orthodox religion, at the culmination of the educational journey of the spirit through the evolution of intellection and culture. For the arrival of Urthona (Blake's redeemed imagination) at its ancestral home is not simply a return to Eden-garden, but the entrance into a perfected human community in the great city of civilization, intellect, and the arts.

In Blake's last and greatest epic, *Jerusalem*, the Preface to the final chapter is a paean to "the Divine Arts of Imagination," to "Mental Studies & Performances," and to "the labours of Art & Science"; for as "the Pains of Hell" are nothing "but Ignorance," so "to Labour in Knowledge, is to Build up Jerusalem." He ends the Preface by addressing England:

> England! awake! awake! awake!
> Jerusalem thy Sister calls!
> Why wilt thou sleep the sleep of death?
> And close her from thy ancient walls.

Like Wordsworth, who in his Prospectus to *The Recluse* set himself to "arouse the sensual from their sleep/ Of Death," Blake undertakes to resurrect England (or Albion) from spiritual death by the evangel of a marriage. Wordsworth's "spousal verse," however, celebrates the wedding of man's mind to the natural world, whose "Beauty—a living Presence of the earth," he says in the Prospectus, excels the utmost human art:

> Surpassing the most fair ideal Forms
> Which craft of delicate Spirits hath composed
> From earth's materials.

This statement defines Wordsworth's essential difference from Blake; it is the chief reason that reading Wordsworth's Prospectus caused Blake—as he said in the comic hyperbole with which he delighted to confound Henry Crabb Robinson—"a bowel complaint which nearly killed him." [16] This difference is epitomized in the episode of *Jerusalem* in which Albion, the fallen Universal Man, is seduced by Vala, who is the illusory beauty of the fallen and estranged natural world. Albion embraces Vala only under a delusion, duped by her lies that she, not Jerusalem, "was Albion's Bride & Wife in great Eternity," and that she, as "Nature, Mother of all," is both the material source of imaginative form and the superior to it in beauty:

> Know me now Albion: look upon me I alone am Beauty
> The Imaginative Human Form is but a breathing of Vala.[17]

It is only when the regenerate form of Vala is reunited with Jerusalem—the true beauty which is the feminine complement of man's imaginative creativity, and of whom Vala, or natural beauty, is only the "shadow" [18]—that she can play her essential but ancillary role in consummating the apocalyptic marriage with the Universal Man.

In this great denouement the powers of the human mind,

their selfhood annihilated, are reunited as the unitary but four-fold Albion, the conflicts of the contraries (destroying, yet preserving) are sublimated into the creative and life enhancing "Wars of Love," and all the environing world, which in its divorce from man had seemed stony, dead, and alien, reveals itself to be alive and human. In conceptual terms, the world is experienced as a milieu in which man recognizes his own humanity, and so can feel thoroughly at home. Blake's rendering of the apex of human experience parallels that which was put forward by many of his contemporaries, however diverse their premises, forms, and idiom: Wordsworth's paradise effected by the marriage of mind and the outer world; Schelling's subject which, after its long odyssey, finds itself in its object; Hegel's ultimate *Gestalt des Bewusstseins,* in which consciousness repossesses and comes to be at home with itself in its otherness; Hölderlin's supreme moments (proleptic of a potentially enduring human condition) when Hyperion realizes his living community with a hitherto alien and lifeless milieu; and Novalis' vision of a recovered age of gold, ceremonialized by a ritual marriage, in which "men, beasts, plants, stones and stars . . . act and speak together as a single family or society." In Blake's mythical representation, all natural objects not only become human themselves, but reunite, without loss of individuation, into the Human Form Divine from which, at the beginning of experience, they had fallen into severance:

All Human Forms identified even Tree Metal Earth & Stone. All
Human Forms identified, living going forth & returning wearied
Into the Planetary lives of Years Months Days & Hours, reposing
And then Awaking into his Bosom in the Life of Immortality.
And I heard the Name of their Emanations, they are named
  Jerusalem.[19]

Blake's emblem for this consummation, on the last page of *Jerusalem,* is an etching of the primal contraries, Albion and his emanation Jerusalem, in their marital embrace.

When Coleridge came upon Blake's *Songs of Innocence and of Experience* in 1818, he hailed him (with remarkable insight, unless he knew more about Blake than this one publication) as "a man of Genius—and I apprehend, a Swedenborgian—certainly, a mystic *emphatically*. You perhaps smile at *my* calling another Poet, a *Mystic;* but verily I am in the very mire of commonplace common-sense compared with Mr. Blake, apo- or rather ana-calyptic Poet, and Painter!" [20] By "mystic" Coleridge usually meant a man who was receptive to esoteric doctrines, as Coleridge himself had been and continued to be. Lamb tells us that Coleridge, while a boy at the Bluecoat School, had discoursed eloquently on the mysteries of Iamblichus and Plotinus, and we know that soon thereafter he studied, with great although carefully qualified admiration, the writings of Giordano Bruno, John Scotus Erigena, Boehme, and other Neoplatonic and Hermetic philosophers.

Coleridge's *Religious Musings,* his first long blank-verse poem, is dated Christmas Eve, 1794. It is exactly contemporary with Blake's *Europe: A Prophecy;* and like Blake's work, it is modeled on Milton's ode *On the Morning of Christ's Nativity* and undertakes to adapt Milton's celebration of Christ's First and Second Coming to the current era of revolutionary and counterrevolutionary violence. *Religious Musings* is turgid and declamatory, yet it is an interesting poem, for it provides an index to Coleridge's interpretation of the fall and redemption before he had read German metaphysics. It also manifests the extent to which, in his early Miltonic period, Coleridge resembled Blake both in poetic persona and general imaginative enterprise.

Coleridge writes as an aspirant to the status of the "Philosophers and Bards" who are able, "with plastic might," to mold the chaos of a disintegrating culture "to such perfect forms" as they perceive in their "bright visions of the day." [21] For Coleridge is himself a visionary poet—"as I muse,/ Behold a VISION gathers in my soul"—who present, past, and future sees, and who recounts the history of mankind, from the primeval past through the revolutionary present to the millennial future, as a brief theodicy in which "all the sore ills" become "the immediate source/ Of mightier good." [22] These events Coleridge construes, in a strange amalgam of Neoplatonic Christianity and Hartleian philosophy, according to a meta-

physic of unity, division, and unity regained. Man's highest
state is to experience his familial participation in the One:

> 'Tis the sublime of man,
> Our noontide Majesty, to know ourselves
> Parts and proportions of one wondrous whole!
> This fraternises man. . . . But 'tis God
> Diffused through all, that doth make all one whole.
>
> (lines 127–31)

Essential evil consists in man's attempt to be self-sufficient,
which shatters the whole into a chaos of disinherited, solitary,
sensual, and mutually alienated selves. "The moral world's
cohesion" lost,

> we become
> An Anarchy of Spirits! Toy-bewitched,
> Made blind by lusts, disherited of soul,
> No common centre Man, no common sire
> Knoweth! A sordid solitary thing,
> Mid countless brethren with a lonely heart
> Through courts and cities the smooth savage roams
> Feeling himself, his own low self the whole.
>
> (lines 143–52)

Conversely when man, "all self-annihilated," shall repossess
the alienated parts in an act of all-comprehensive sympathy, he
will effect the redemption prophesied in the Second Coming.

> When [man] by sacred sympathy might make
> The whole one Self! Self, that no alien knows! . . .
> Self, spreading still! Oblivious of its own,
> Yet all of all possessing! This is Faith!
> This the Messiah's destined victory!
>
> (lines 43, 153–8)

In accordance with this philosophy of community and division,
when the "blest future rushes on my view," the poet's millennial vision of "the renovated Earth" is that of a familial society
living in a communist economy, in which

> the vast family of Love
> Raised from the common earth by common toil
> Enjoy the equal produce.
>
> (lines 340–3, 356–66)

From his youth to his old age Coleridge was a compulsive monist whose mind, as he said, "feels as if it ached to behold & know something *great*—something *one & indivisible*." [23] To feel cut off, isolated, estranged from other men and from the surrounding world—"to be betrayed into the wretchedness of *division*"—was for Coleridge intolerable, and he repeatedly describes all division as death dealing, beginning with the primal error of the intellect by which, instead of possessing "ourselves, as one with the whole . . . we think of ourselves as separated beings, and place nature in antithesis to the mind, as object to subject, thing to thought, death to life." To the materialists, accordingly, nature is "the natural alien of their negative eye," and the mechanical philosophy, in separating off phenomena from the living mind, "strikes death through all things visible and invisible." [24]

But if irredeemable division is the essential evil, what Coleridge calls "distinction" is not only redeemable but the necessary condition for progressive development, for to "distinguish without dividing" is the only way to "prepare for the intellectual re-union of the all in one." [25] Against lethal division, in all areas of human perception, intellection, and invention, Coleridge sets the concept of "life," and for him, as for Goethe, Schelling, Hegel, and Blake, "to the idea of life victory or strife is necessary." [26] Thus, in living things the "most general law" is "*polarity*, or the essential dualism of Nature," which manifests itself in the tendency "at once to individuate and connect," in a process by which "thesis and antithesis, position and counterposition" necessarily "unite in a synthesis."

> In the identity of the two counter-powers, Life *sub*sists; in their strife it *con*sists: and in their reconciliation it at once dies and is born again into a new form.[27]

Coleridge's basic opposition is between a sterile juxtaposition of divided, and therefore dead and inert, elements (equivalent

to Blake's "negations"), and a living process in which true polarities (equivalent to Blake's "contraries") depart from one
another, but only in order to remarry and so to generate a new
entity in which both components survive, but on a higher level
of organization. The mechanic philosophy, for example, knows
only of "composition . . . and decomposition,"

> the relations of unproductive particles to each other. . . . In
> life, much more in spirit, and in a living and spiritual philos-
> ophy, the two component counter-powers actually interpene-
> trate each other, and generate a higher third, including both
> the former, *ita tamen ut sit alia et major.*[28]

This is the root-principle throughout Coleridge's thought: all
self-compelled motion, progress, and productivity, hence all
emergent novelty or "creativity," is a generative conflict-in-
attraction of polar forces, which part to be reunited on a higher
level of being, and thus evolve, or "grow," from simple unity
into a "multeity in unity" which is an organized whole. It is in
this way that Coleridge conceives, for example, the process of
cosmogony ("the eternal act of creation in the infinite I Am,"
or "absolute self"), of epistemology (the "repetition" of this
creation in "the primary Imagination," or act of perceiving in
each individual mind), and of the poetic creation effected by
"the secondary Imagination" (an "echo" of the primary imagination which, like that faculty, is a "synthetic . . . power"
that "reveals itself in the balance or reconciliation of opposite
or discordant qualities").[29]

For Coleridge, as for many German contemporaries, to take
thought is inescapably to separate that which is one in primal
consciousness, so that the beginning of human rationality can
be equated with the Biblical account of the fall of man.

> The rational instinct, therefore, taken abstractedly and un-
> balanced, did, in itself, (*ye shall be as gods,* Gen. iii. 5) and in
> its consequences . . . form the original temptation, through
> which man fell: and in all ages has continued to originate the
> same, even from Adam, in whom we all fell.[30]

Coleridge's prime concern was to expedite a "Reconciliation
from [the] Enmity with Nature" into which philosophy, and

especially the contemporary philosophy of mechanism, had fallen, when it replaced a vital and productive antithesis with an absolute and unsalvageable division between subject and object, mind and alienated nature.[31] In accordance with this way of thinking, he represents the cultural history of mankind, in the recurrent Romantic apologue of the circular educational journey, as man's quest for unity between his mind and nature, which ends in the discovery that the goal of the search was its point of departure:

> Where . . . the nurture and evolution of humanity is the final aim, there will soon be seen a general tendency toward, an earnest seeking after, some ground common to the world and to man. . . . Disturbed as by the obscure quickening of an inward birth . . . man sallies forth into nature—in nature, as in the shadows and reflections of a clear river, to discover the originals of the forms presented to him in his own intellect. Over these shadows . . . Narcissus-like, he hangs delighted: till . . . he learns at last that what he *seeks* he has *left behind*, and but lengthens the distance as he prolongs the search.[32]

For Coleridge a cardinal value of the arts was that they humanized nature and so helped to repossess it for the mind from which it had been alienated. Art, he says, "is the mediatress between, and reconciler of, nature and man. It is, therefore, the power of humanizing nature, of infusing the thoughts and passions of man into every thing which is the object of his contemplation." "To make the external internal, the internal external, to make nature thought, and thought nature,—this is the mystery of genius in the Fine Arts." [33]

Coleridge, then, was a philosophical monist, but a diversitarian monist, for whom the intellectual, cultural, and moral aim of man is not to return to the undifferentiated unity at the beginning of development, but to strive toward the multiety-in-unity at its end. His consonance on this point with Schiller (and with Blake) comes out clearly in a remarkable passage in which, like Schiller in his *Naive and Sentimental Poetry*, he pays poignant tribute to the nostalgia which civilized and self-divided man feels toward the inconscient innocence and simple self-harmony that infants share with the subhuman world of living, growing things. This nostalgia, however, eventuates in an aspiration toward a higher integrity which man must earn, by the full exercise of all the faculties which make him human, civilized, and adult.

> I have at this moment before me, in the flowery meadow, on which my eye is now reposing, one of [nature's] most soothing chapters, in which there is no . . . one character of guilt or anguish. For never can I look and meditate on the vegetable creation without a feeling similar to that with which we gaze at a beautiful infant that has fed itself asleep at its mother's bosom. . . . The same tender and genial pleasure takes possession of me, and this pleasure is checked and drawn inward by the like aching melancholy, by the same whispered remonstrance, and made restless by a similar impulse of aspiration. It seems as if the soul said to herself: From this state hast thou fallen! Such shouldst thou still become, thyself all permeable to a holier power! . . . But what the plant is by an act not its own and unconsciously—that must thou make thyself to become. . . .

"That must thou *make* thyself to become." Coleridge goes on to say that in the unconscious activity by which a plant assimilates outer elements "to itself and to each other" and so effects "its own secret growth," we find an equivalent, at the lowest stage of the biological scale, of the "undivided reason" at the opposite extreme; for the highest human reason reachieves at the end of the scale the unity of the beginning, but in a functioning that incorporates all the intervening stages of differentiation. "Lo!" says Coleridge of the growing plant,

> how . . . it becomes the visible *organismus* of the entire silent or elementary life of nature and, therefore, in incorporating the one extreme becomes the symbol of the other; the natural symbol of that higher life of reason, in which the whole series . . . is perfected, in which, therefore, all the subordinate gradations recur, and are re-ordained *in more abundant honour.* . . . We . . . now recognize them all as coexisting in the unity of a higher form, the crown and completion of the earthly . . . series.[34]

Coleridge conceives that all living process, in the realm of mind as well as in the realm of nature, moves along a circular and ascending course. As he puts it, everything that is vital, rather than merely mechanical, is organized, and by the action of its inherent counter-tendencies "organization has no other meaning than a power which instead of moving in a straight line as the mechanism does, moves round upon itself in a circle." [35] For Coleridge, as for contemporary German philosophers, the "Science of Method" which governs all valid intellection exhibits the same spiral course; the process of reasoning, Coleridge says, begins with a self-grounded proposition which it reaches and validates only at the end, and so constitutes an all-inclusive and self-sustaining whole:

> From this we started (or rather seemed to start: for it still moved before us, as an invisible guardian and guide), and it is this whose re-appearance announces the conclusion of our circuit, and welcomes us at our goal.[36]

The process of the imagination, too (since this faculty "is essentially vital," as opposed to the mechanical "fancy," which "has no other counters to play with, but fixities and definites" [37]), describes a course which ends where it began. "The principle of the imagination," as Hazlitt in a balance of irony and admiration quotes Coleridge as saying, "resembles the emblem of the serpent . . . with undulating folds . . . for ever flowing into itself,—circular, and without beginning or end." [38] And the vital product, no less than the process, of the poet's imagination has the shape of an *ouroborous;* in this way Coleridge justifies, in terms of his total metaphysic, the circular poem whose end is in its beginning.

> The common end of all *narrative,* nay of *all,* Poems is to convert a *series* into a *Whole:* to make those events, which in real or imagined History move on in a *strait* Line, assume to our Understandings a *circular* motion—the snake with it's Tail in it's Mouth.[39]

Coleridge goes on to explain that all history, both of the race and of each human being, although it seems linear to short-sighted man, manifests itself to him who sees present, past, and future in one purview as a great circle from the One back to the One by way of the many. A poem achieves its perfected form by organizing its imagined segment of linear history into a small-scale version of the circular design of the total drama, as viewed under the aspect of eternity:

> Doubtless, to *his* eye, which alone comprehends all Past and all Future in one eternal Present, what to our short sight appears strait is but a part of the great Cycle. . . . Now what the Globe is in Geography, *miniaturing* in order to *manifest* the Truth, such is a Poem to that Image of God, which we were created into, and which still seeks that Unity, or Revelation of the *One* in and by the *Many*, which reminds it, that tho' in order to be an individual Being it must go forth *from* God, yet as the *re*ceding from *him* is to *pro*ceed towards Nothingness and Privation, it must still at every step turn back toward him in order to *be* at all—Now a straight Line, continuously retracted forms of necessity a circular orbit.[40]

Coleridge's view of man's fall as division and isolation and of redemption as a reconciliation, together with his related conception of the circuitous movement of the organizing imagination and the circular shape of an organic poem, are consonant with the subject matter, imagery, and ordonnance of a number of his own writings. Consider, for example, Coleridge's highest achievement in each of his two major genres: the poem of the supernatural and the poem of ordinary life.

The Ancient Mariner is neither an allegorical fable nor a symbolist poem. The persistent religious and moral allusions, however, both in the text and in the glosses which Coleridge added to assist the bewildered readers of the first published version, invite us to take the Mariner's experience as an instance of the Christian plot of moral error, the discipline of suffering, and a consequent change of heart. The Mariner's literal voyage, then, is also a spiritual journey; it is, furthermore, a circular journey in which, amid cheerful communal ceremony, he departs from his native land—

> The ship was cheered, the harbour cleared,
> Merrily did we drop

> Below the kirk, below the hill,
> Below the lighthouse top

—to come back at the close, as the prose argument emphasizes, "to his own Country." This narrative is set within the frame of a Christian sacrament which is the great type of the ultimate consummation: the celebration of a wedding. The Mariner selects one of three guests who (as in the Biblical parable) has been "bidden" to the "wedding-feast" as kinsman to the bride-groom but who, as the Mariner's instinct tells him (ll. 587–90), needs to be instructed in the full significance of love and union; and this is the purport of the tale the Mariner proceeds to relate.

A lone albatross appears in a desolate setting of ice and snow "where no living thing was to be seen." The sailors hail it "as if it had been a Christian soul" and, in the ancient ritual of acceptance into the family, give it food; but the Mariner, "in contempt of the laws of hospitality," kills the albatross. Killing "the bird that loved the man" is an act which expresses the Mariner's prideful self-sufficiency, his readiness to cut himself off from the universal community of life and love. His punishment is to experience the full measure of his elected isolation, in a world in which all his companions have died and nature has become alien and inimical to him.

> Alone, alone, all, all alone,
> Alone on a wide wide sea! [41]

The phrase, when later repeated, has become a metaphor for experience on a spiritual journey:

> O Wedding-Guest! this soul hath been
> Alone on a wide wide sea.

Only "a thousand thousand slimy things/ Lived on; and so did I." "He despiseth," the gloss says, "the creatures of the calm."

The reversal announces itself in the lines, "The moving Moon went up the sky,/ And no where did abide." In Coleridge's matchless gloss on these lines the hitherto alien moon and stars have become humanized; and the very rhythm of the poignant description of their circuitous journey bespeaks how profoundly the Mariner has learned what it means to belong to a place, a native land, a family, and a home:

> In his loneliness and fixedness he yearneth towards the journeying Moon, and the stars that still sojourn, yet still move onward; and every where the blue sky belongs to them, and is their appointed rest, and their native country and their own natural homes, which they enter unannounced, as lords that are certainly expected and yet there is a silent joy at their arrival.

The lesson of community thus achieved, the Mariner is prepared to recognize, by the light of the same journeying moon, the beauty of the life that he shares with what he had looked upon as the loathsome water snakes, and in an unpremeditated burst of fraternal love, he blesses them.

> O happy living things! no tongue
> Their beauty might declare:
> A spring of love gushed from my heart,
> And I blessed them unaware.

At once the terrible spell snaps, the dead natural elements "burst into life" and, benign again, move the Mariner along on his own circular journey, amid oblique but insistent revelations of his homesickness: the sails made "A noise like of a hidden brook/ In the leafy month of June," and the wind fanned his cheek

> Like a meadow-gale of spring—
> It mingled strangely with my fears,
> Yet it felt like a welcoming.

Having completed his literal and spiritual circumnavigation of the globe, the Mariner ends his voyage at the point of its origin, the harbor of "his native country." The three objects he had last sighted at his departure—the kirk, the hill, and the lighthouse—now reappear, but with their order reversed.

> Oh! dream of joy! is this indeed
> The light-house top I see?

> Is this the hill? Is this the kirk?
> Is this mine own contree? . . .
>
> And now, all in my own countree,
> I stood on the firm land!

—but only to carry on what the gloss calls his "penance of life," by passing "like night, from land to land," and talking, talking, talking.

Coleridge's *Dejection: An Ode* is the most impressive instance of another circuitous form which he inaugurated in *The Eolian Harp,* perfected in *Frost at Midnight,* and repeated in several other "conversation poems." [42] Typically this type of lyric begins with a description of the landscape, moves into a sustained meditation which involves the speaker's past, present, and future, and ends in a return to the outer scene, but on a higher level of insight. In *Dejection: An Ode* this meditation constitutes a brief crisis-autobiography which parallels the two books of Wordsworth's *Prelude* on "Imagination, How Impaired and Restored," except that Coleridge both begins and ends in the state of imagination impaired, and foresees no possibility of recovery from his personal crisis of isolation, apathy, and creative sterility.

In the course of the opening description the poet reveals himself to be static and self-enclosed (like the Ancient Mariner becalmed at the equator), for he lacks any "natural outlet" and is cut off from all emotional interchange with the natural world of the sky, cloud, stars, and the "fixed," unmoving moon.

> And still I gaze—and with how blank an eye! . . .
> I see them all so excellently fair,
> I see, not feel, how beautiful they are!

In a summary review of his life he ascribes this condition to recurrent afflictions which have compelled him to turn to "abstruse research," in the attempt to cut off "from my own nature all the natural man." But this inveterate and divisive analysis has now "almost grown the habit of my soul" and, having severed the mind from its objects, it leaves the poet isolated, his inner fountains of "the passion and the life" dried up and his "shaping spirit of Imagination suspended," in a nature which—since

> we receive but what we give,
> And in our life alone does nature live

—has been rendered alien and dead, like "that inanimate cold world allowed/ To the poor loveless ever-anxious crowd."

The necessary condition for overcoming this lethal division within himself and from the outer world is the state which he calls "joy,"

> Joy that ne'er was given,
> Save to the pure, and in their purest hour,
> Life, and Life's effluence. . . .

"Joy" is a central and recurrent term in the Romantic vocabulary which often has a specialized meaning. In Coleridge's philosophy of the one and the many, in which a central concern is reconciliation of subject and object in the act of perception, "joy" signifies the conscious accompaniment of the activity of a fully living and integrative mind. As he defines the term in his *Philosophical Lectures,* it is the state of abounding vitality —necessary to the working of the creative power of genius— which, by breaking down the boundaries of the isolated consciousness, relates the self both to other human selves and to an outer nature which it has inanimated, and so made compatible with itself:

All genius exists in a participation of a common spirit. In joy individuality is lost and it therefore is liveliest in youth . . . [before] the circumstances that have forced a man in upon his little unthinking contemptible self, have lessened his power of existing universally. . . . To have a genius is to live in the universal, to know no self but that which is reflected not only from the faces of all around us, our fellow creatures, but reflected from the flowers, the trees, the beasts, yea from the very surface of the [waters and the] sands of the desert. A man of genius finds a reflex to himself, were it only in the mystery of being.[43]

Thus in *Dejection,* joy, the necessary condition for "the shaping spirit of Imagination," is described as the inner power which unites the living self to a living outer world. Like Hölderlin, Novalis, and Wordsworth, Coleridge represents this union by the figure of a marriage. He also manifests his awareness of the Biblical significance of this figure, for he attributes to the marriage between mind and nature the redemption of the old world and its replacement—in a phrase he echoes from Isaiah and the Apocalypse—by "a new heaven and a new earth."

> Joy, Lady! is the spirit and the power,
> Which, wedding Nature to us, gives in dower
>   A new Earth and new Heaven,
> Undreamt of by the sensual and the proud—
> Joy is the sweet voice, Joy the luminous cloud—
>   We in ourselves rejoice!
> And thence flows all that charms or ear or sight,
>   All melodies the echoes of that voice,
> All colours a suffusion from that light.

Dejection concludes, after a brief return to the natural scene described in its opening, with a passage that expresses the poet's triumph over his exclusive self-concern, in the hope that the absent friend to whom the poem is addressed may forever retain the joy which the speaker has forever lost, and so sustain her interchange with an outer world which is thus made humanly congenial. This interchange is expressed in a Neoplatonic figure for the circulation of emanation and return [44]—in Coleridge's superb version, the metaphor of an eddy, whose end merges into its beginning, in the flow of a shared life between the elemental polarity of mind and nature.

> Joy lift her spirit, joy attune her voice;
> To her may all things live, from pole to pole,
> Their life the eddying of her living soul!
>   O simple spirit, guided from above,
> Dear Lady, friend devoutest of my choice,
> Thus mayst thou ever, evermore rejoice.

2. WORDSWORTH: THE LONG JOURNEY HOME

I have "never read a word of German metaphysics, thank Heaven!" Wordsworth wrote to Henry Crabb Robinson.[45] This claim is no doubt the literal truth; yet as Robinson several times remarked, Wordsworth's thinking frequently parallels that of his philosophical German contemporaries. Prominent in Wordsworth, for example, is his version of the great commonplace of the age: unity with himself and his world is the primal and normative state of man, of which the sign is a fullness of shared life and the condition of joy; analytic thought divides the mind from nature and object from object, and this division, if absolute, kills the object it severs and threatens with spiritual death the mind from which it has been severed. In the second book of *The Prelude* Wordsworth praises Coleridge as one to whom "the unity of all has been reveal'd," and who is therefore free from the slavery "Of that false secondary power, by which,/ In weakness, we create distinctions" that we mistake for real divisions. He goes on to oppose to "analytic industry" his own "observations of affinities/ In objects where no brotherhood exists/ To common minds," with the eventual result that "in all things/ I saw one life, and felt that it was joy." In a manuscript passage he adds that "by such communion" he was "early taught" that the separate "forms and images" evident to passive perception, as well as the divisive processes of active "thought/ Prospectiveness, intelligence or will," seem but "relapses"—that is, a falling away—from the undifferentiated oneness of self with nature, and of both these with God:

> Such consciousnesses seemed but accidents
> Relapses from the one interior life
> Which is in all things, from that unity
> In which all beings live with God, are lost
> In god and nature, in one mighty whole
> As undistinguishable as the cloudless east

> At noon is from the cloudless west when all
> The hemisphere is one cerulean blue.[46]

Some two years earlier, in a passage intended for *The Ruined Cottage*, Wordsworth's Pedlar had denounced the false kind of "science" which, instead of serving "the cause/ Of order and distinctness" (that is, by distinction without division), murders, by disconnecting, both the objects seen and the self that sees:

> For was it meant
> That we should pore, and dwindle as we pore . . .
> On solitary objects, still beheld
> In disconnection dead and spiritless,
> And still dividing and dividing still,
> Break down all grandeur . . .
> waging thus
> An impious warfare with the very life
> Of our own souls?

"Let us rise," he cries, "From this oblivious sleep"—patently this is the "sleep of Death" from which Wordsworth undertook to waken "the sensual" in his Prospectus—and reunite the severed parts in a resurrective interchange in which (as Coleridge was to phrase it in his *Dejection*) the life of all things will be the eddying of our living soul:

> Thus disciplined
> All things shall live in us and we shall live
> In all things that surround us. . . .
> For thus the senses and the intellect
> Shall each to each supply a mutual aid . . .
> And forms and feelings acting thus, and thus
> Reacting, they shall each acquire
> A living spirit and a character
> Till then unfelt.[47]

In *The Fountain* (1799) Wordsworth gave to the old man Matthew a memorable statement about the unhappy consciousness of self-divided and knowingly mortal man and the happy self-unity of creatures who act by instinct, and without memory or anticipation:

> The blackbird amid leafy trees,
> The lark above the hill,
> Let loose their carols when they please,
> Are quiet when they will.
>
> With Nature never do *they* wage
> A foolish strife; they see
> A happy youth, and their old age
> Is beautiful and free.

Like Schiller and Coleridge, Wordsworth here expresses, through the medium of an invented character, man's discontent with being human and civilized. When he speaks in his own person, however, Wordsworth conceives the mature mind as an integrity of disparate elements which is the product of a growth that necessarily involves self-division and conflict. His general norm is a unity which retains individual identity, and his particular ideal of life (as John Jones has put it) [48] is to sustain solitude in relationship. Thus Wordsworth proclaimed, in one version of his Prospectus,

> Of the individual mind that keeps its own
> Inviolate retirement, and consists
> With being limitless, the one great Life
> I sing.[49]

The great distinction of Wordsworth's *Prelude* in its age is that it is not (as Coleridge tried to make it) a philosophical poem, nor an extended cosmic myth, nor a symbolic or allegorical fable, but the presentation of a particular person, unique yet humanly representative, as he develops from infancy to maturity through his evolving experience with his natural environment, with other men, and with the great public events of his time. Wordsworth nevertheless claimed that his poetry possessed a systematic intellectual ground; as he said of *The Recluse* of which *The Prelude* was a part, while "it is not the Author's intention formally to announce a system . . . the Reader will have no difficulty in extracting the system for himself." [50] His confidence in the reader is perhaps excessive; but our present point of vantage enables us to discern in *The Prelude* a coherent understructure of ideas and a sustained evolution of images which mark its consonance with the thought and design of a number of other, and very diverse, Romantic works of literature and philosophy.

I remarked in Chapter Two that, on one recurrent level of narrative, Wordsworth undertakes to represent the growth of a poet's mind—just as German philosophers undertook to construct the development of generic and individual consciousness—within the limits of a two-term scheme of reference: the interactions between subject and object, mind and nature. Unlike the German Idealists, however, Wordsworth does not posit an initial One, or absolute, which subdivides into the knowing mind and the object known, but instead begins, as he says in the Prospectus, with a "Mind" which is fitted to "the external World" and an "external World" which is "fitted to the Mind." In the early books of *The Prelude* he sets out to show the slow and complex workings of "those first-born affinities that fit/ Our new existence to existing things" (I, 582–3), in the process by which the mind of the child, through the mediation of its senses, grows into community with its environing world. Natural objects enter, flow, are received, and sink down into the mind, while the mind dwells in, feeds on, drinks, holds intercourse with, and weaves, intertwines, fastens, and binds itself to external objects, until the two integrate as one. These are Wordsworth's recurrent metaphors, the essential lexicon he developed to enable him to say, about the development of man's cognitive and emotional involvement with the milieu into which he is born, what had never been explicitly said before, and with a subtlety that has not been exceeded since. In the crowning figure of this metaphoric complex the babe, in the security of his mother's arms, evolves into awareness of a world which is so thoroughly humanized that the pull of gravity is experienced as a familial relationship. "In one beloved presence,"

                    there exists
    A virtue which irradiates and exalts
    All objects through all intercourse of sense.
    No outcast he, bewilder'd and depress'd;
    Along his infant veins are interfus'd
    The gravitation and filial bond
    Of nature, that connect him with the world.
                                    (II, 255–64)

The dynamic element in the growth of the mind in nature is a play of polarities which is not, in Wordsworth, a systematic dialectic, but instead operates, as Charles J. Smith has said, as "a very strong habit of thinking in terms of paired opposites or contrarieties. Everywhere in nature, in individual man and in society, [Wordsworth] saw a constant interplay of opposing forces."[51] Chief among the contraries in nature, we already know, are those which Wordsworth introduces in his opening lines on his interaction with the natural scene: "I grew up/ Foster'd alike by beauty and by fear" (I, 305–6). Related to this opposition between incitation by beauty and discipline by terror are other contraries which constitute the poles between which flow the forces of "this active universe." "Calmness" and "emotion," "peace and excitation," "stillness" and "energy" —"these two attributes/ Are sister horns that constitute her strength."

In Wordsworth's account, his community with the natural milieu precedes, and is instrumental to, his development of a community with other men: "Love of Nature" leads to "Love of Mankind." The integrity of mind that he has achieved receives its first serious test in London, both on his first brief visit, when he "felt in heart and soul the shock/ Of the huge town's first presence" (1850; VII, 66–7), and during the period of his later residence there. The "blank confusion" of the metropolis terrified Wordsworth by a double threat to his sense of individuation-in-unity: by fragmenting community into an anarchy of unrelated parts, and by assimilating the parts into a homogeneity in which no individuality survives,

                    melted and reduced
    To one identity, by differences
    That have no law, no meaning, and no end.

But the strength of the integral fabric of consciousness wrought by his earlier education in nature enabled him to manage even this "unmanageable sight," as one who "sees the parts/ As parts, but with a feeling of the whole." "The forms/ Perennial of the ancient hills," changeless in "the changeful language of their countenances," had provided him with a model for reconciling "multitude,/ With order and relation"; and now "the Spirit of Nature" remained "present as a habit," and served to diffuse through

> the press
> Of self-destroying, transitory things
> Composure and ennobling harmony.
> (VII, 695–740)

This development "Of intellectual power, from stage to stage/ Advancing, hand in hand with love and joy,/ And of imagination," is shattered by the "over-pressure of the times/ And their disastrous issues" (XI, 42–8). Wordsworth describes the process of his breakdown as the cumulative fragmentation and conflict of once integral elements. He turned to abstract reason to furnish support for his failing hopes, but this was in effect to foster a divisive inner "war against myself," in the attempt "to cut off my heart/ From all the sources of her former strength" and to unsoul by logic "those mysteries of passion which have made . . . / One brotherhood of the human race" (XI, 74–88). Analytic reason divides, but it cannot reunify, for it sets up the kind of inert contraries which cannot be resolved: "Sick, wearied out with contrarieties," I "Yielded up moral questions in despair. This was the crisis of that strong disease" (1850; XI, 304–6). At the same time the "life of nature," which should have sustained and guided him, had itself succumbed to the same work of "logic and minute analysis." Hitherto he had rejoiced in its passion and its life, in which he had participated because he had confronted nature with unified and cooperative faculties and feelings,

> now all eye
> And now all ear; but ever with the heart
> Employ'd, and the majestic intellect.

But inner division became inner conflict and resulted in a state in which "the eye was master of the heart" and "often held my mind in absolute dominion" (XI, 96–180). The consequence of such division between mind and nature, and the resulting enslavement of the mind by "the laws of vulgar sense," was to destroy "a world of life" and transform it into "a universe of death" (XIII, 102–3, 138–41).

The poet's recovery, correspondingly, is represented as a gradual reintegration of all that had been divided: his faculties, senses, and feelings, his past and present self, and his mind and outer nature. My sister, Wordsworth says, "Maintained for me a saving intercourse/ With my true self," while "Nature's self . . . led me back" to the earlier "counsels between head and heart" (1850; XI, 335–54); the persistence in memory of "spots of time" helped him to reestablish continuity between the self that he is and the self that he was; and he finally reachieved the integrity of being that he had lost, although now on a level of consciousness which preserved the critical experiences through which he had passed.

> Behold me then
> Once more in Nature's presence, thus restored
> Or otherwise, and strengthened once again
> (With memory left of what had been escaped).[52]

It is time to notice that Wordsworth's account of unity achieved, lost, and regained is held together, as various critics have remarked, by the recurrent image of a journey: like a number of works by his contemporaries, Wordsworth's "poem on my own poetical education"[53] converts the wayfaring Christian of the Augustinian spiritual journey into the self-formative traveler of the Romantic educational journey. The poem in fact opens, as Elizabeth Sewell has said, "with the poet in a prospect of wide landscape and open sky," on a literal walk which serves as "the great over-all poetic figure or trope of a journey which he is about to undertake."[54] In the course of this episode the aimless wanderer becomes "as a Pilgrim resolute" who takes "the road that pointed toward the chosen

Vale," and at the end of the first book the road translates itself into the metaphorical way of his life's pilgrimage:

> Forthwith shall be brought down
> Through later years the story of my life.
> The road lies plain before me. . . .
>   (1850; I, 91–3, 638–40)

The Prelude is replete with "the Wanderers of the Earth," [55] and after the period of childhood, its chief episodes are Wordsworth's own wanderings through the English countryside, the Alps, Italy, France, and Wales—literal journeys through actual places which modulate easily into symbolic landscapes traversed by a metaphorical wayfarer. This organizing figure works in two dimensions. In one of these, *The Prelude* represents the life which the poet narrates as a self-educative journey, "from stage to stage/ Advancing," in which his early development had been "progress on the self-same path," the crisis following the French Revolution had been "a stride at once/ Into another region," and the terminus was his achievement of maturity in "the discipline/ And consummation of the Poet's mind." [56] In the second application, the poet repeatedly figures his own imaginative enterprise, the act of composing *The Prelude* itself, as a perilous quest through the uncharted regions of his own mind.

At times the vehicle for this latter poetic journey is a voyage at sea, connoting the wanderings of Odysseus in his search for home:

>   What avail'd,
> When Spells forbade the Voyager to land,
> The fragrance which did ever and anon
> Give notice of the Shore? . . .
> My business was upon the barren sea,
> My errand was to sail to other coasts.[57]

Elsewhere Wordsworth's implied parallel is to Dante, who "Nell mezzo del cammin di nostra vita" had been granted a visionary journey, with a relay of guides, through hell and the earthly paradise to heaven:

> A Traveller I am,
> And all my Tale is of myself; even so,
> So be it, if the pure in heart delight
> To follow me; and Thou, O honor'd Friend!
> Who in my thoughts art ever at my side,
> Uphold, as heretofore, my fainting steps.
>
> (III, 196–201)

At the beginning of the ninth book, "as a traveller, who has gained the brow/ Of some aerial Down" and "is tempted to review/ The region left behind him," Wordsworth turns back to his earlier youth, before he moves reluctantly on into the discordant "argument" that begins with his residence in France —"Oh, how much unlike the past!" [58] The eleventh book, narrating the process of Wordsworth's recovery, opens in a parallel to Milton's description of his epic journey back from hell to the realms of light (XI, 1–7; see *Paradise Lost*, III, 13–20). And through all these regions the imagined presence of Coleridge serves both as auditor and guide, heartening the exhausted poet in his pilgrimage and quest:

> Thou wilt not languish here, O Friend, for whom
> I travel in these dim uncertain ways
> Thou wilt assist me as a Pilgrim gone
> In quest of highest truth.
>
> (XI, 390–3)

The last book of *The Prelude*, in symmetry with its first book, also opens with a literal walk which translates itself into a metaphor for the climactic stage both of the journey of life and of the imaginative journey which is the poem itself. This time the walk is not a movement along an open plain but the ascent of a mountain, the traditional place for definitive visions since Moses had climbed Mount Sinai. As in Hegel's *Phenomenology* the spirit, at the close of its educational journey, recognizes itself in its other, so Wordsworth's mind, confronting nature, discovers itself in its own perfected powers:

> A meditation rose in me that night
> Upon the lonely Mountain . . .
>   and it appear'd to me
> The perfect image of a mighty Mind.

In the earliest stage of its development Wordsworth's "Babe,/ Nurs'd in his Mother's arms" had not only acquired "The gravitation and the filial bond . . . that connect him with the world," but had also, as "inmate of this *active* universe," established the beginnings of the reciprocative power by which

> his mind . . .
> Creates, creator and receiver both,
> Working but in alliance with the works
> Which it beholds.—Such, verily, is the first
> Poetic spirit of our human life.
>
> (II, 265–76)

On Mount Snowdon, in an evident parallel and complement to this early passage, his mind recognizes, in that image of itself "which Nature thus/ Thrusts forth upon the senses" the same power, which has now developed into "the fulness of its strength." As mist and moonlight transform the natural scene, so higher minds by a similar "Power"

> can send abroad
> Like transformation, for themselves create
> A like existence, and, whene'er it is
> Created for them, catch it by an instinct . . .
> Willing to work and to be wrought upon

by the works which they behold. An essential alteration, however, is that the mature poetic mind, whose infant perception had been a state of undifferentiated consciousness, has acquired self-consciousness, and is able to sustain the sense of its own identity as an individuation-in-unison with the objects it perceives. In Wordsworth's terse rendering,

> hence the highest bliss
> That can be known is theirs, the consciousness
> Of whom they are habitually infused
> Through every image, and through every thought,
> And all impressions.
>
> (XIII, 84–111)

I have already remarked (Chapter Two, Section 1) that *The Prelude* has a circular organization. This circularity of its form, we now see, reflects the circularity of its subject matter. In the opening passage of *The Prelude* the narrator is confirmed in his vocation as a poet-prophet and, in response to an impulse from the autumnal wood, chooses as his goal "a known Vale, whither my feet should turn," in the assurance "of some work of glory there forthwith to be begun." "Keen as a Truant or a Fugitive,/ But as a Pilgrim resolute," and also (in a complementary pedestrian metaphor) "like a home-bound labourer," he then pursued his way until a three days' walk "brought me to my hermitage" (1850; I, 71–80, 90–107). At the end of *The Prelude* Wordsworth, having taken up his "permanent abode" (XIII, 338) in this hermitage, calls "back to mind" the occasion of its beginning. But *The Prelude* has a complex function, for it is designed not only as a poem in itself, but also as a "portico" to *The Recluse*. The spiritual journey thus circles back at its conclusion to the literal journey with which it had originated; but this beginning at once turns over into the opening book of Wordsworth's "work of glory," *The Recluse* proper, which describes his way of life in the chosen vale.[59] Only now does he identify the aspect of the vale which had all along made it the goal of his tortuous literal, spiritual, and poetic journey. That goal, as in all the ancient genre of the circuitous pilgrimage, is home—*Home at Grasmere.*

The initial passage of *Home at Grasmere* makes it clear that the place to which the poet has returned is not his literal home but one which, on his first overview of the "Vale below" when, solitary, he had chanced across it as "a roving School-boy," he had recognized to be his spiritual home. "Perfect was the Spot . . . stirring to the Spirit"; and he had immediately felt that "here/ Must be his Home, this Valley be his World." Throughout his youth the vale had lingered in memory, "shedding upon joy/ A brighter joy," and now the home of his imagining has become his actual home (the word reverberates through the opening passage):

> And now 'tis mine, perchance for life, dear Vale,
> Beloved Grasmere (let the Wandering Streams
> Take up, the cloud-capt hills repeat, the Name),
> One of thy lowly Dwellings is my Home.[60]

The place in which, "on Nature's invitation" (line 71), Wordsworth's literal and metaphoric wanderings have terminated is identified, after the venerable formula, as a home which is also a recovered paradise. In his Pisgah-sight of it as a schoolboy he had looked upon it as a "paradise before him" (line 14); and it remains, after he takes up his abode in it, an "earthly counterpart" of heaven (line 642), which he describes in terms echoing Milton's description of the Garden of Eden, and in which Wordsworth and Dorothy, "A solitary pair" (line 255) are somewhat incongruously the Adam and Eve. The journey to this ultimate stage has taken him through "the realities of life so cold," but this had been a fortunate fall into experience, for "the cost" of what he has lost from the earlier stage of his life is greatly outweighed by "what I keep, have gain'd/ Shall gain," so that

> in my day of Childhood I was less
> The mind of Nature, less, take all in all,
> Whatever may be lost, than I am now.

For him, man's ancient dream of felicity has been brought down from a transcendent heaven and located in this very world—

> the distant thought
> Is fetch'd out of the heaven in which it was.
> The unappropriated bliss hath found
> An owner, and that owner I am he.
> The Lord of this enjoyment is on Earth
> And in my breast.[61]

Here he dwells, therefore, as a second and more fortunate Adam, because unlike his predecessor he possesses an Eden which has been gained:

> The boon is absolute; surpassing grace
> To me hath been vouchsafed; among the bowers
> Of blissful Eden this was neither given,
> Nor could be given, possession of the good
> Which had been sighed for, ancient thought fulfilled

> And dear Imaginations realized
> Up to their highest measure, yea and more.[62]

As in comparable passages in Hölderlin and Novalis (in Blake the parallel is more with Beulah than with the New Jerusalem), all the natural scene becomes alive, human, and feminine, and encloses the poet in an embrace of love:

> Embrace me then, ye Hills, and close me in. . . .
> But I would call thee beautiful, for mild
> And soft, and gay, and beautiful thou art,
> Dear Valley, having in thy face a smile
> Though peaceful, full of gladness.
>
> (lines 110–7)

And when the solitary pair had first entered this valley together in the winter season, its elements had addressed them as fellow beings:

> "What would ye," said the shower,
> "Wild Wanderers, whither through my dark domain?"
> The sunbeam said, "be happy." When this Vale
> We entered, bright and solemn was the sky
> That faced us with a passionate welcoming,
> And led us to our threshold

—a threshold which in an earlier version of the text had been that of "a home/ Within a home, which was to be" (lines 168–73, and footnote).

This terminus of all the poet's journeyings is not only home and paradise, but also a recovered unity and wholeness which he had experienced nowhere else except "as it found its way into my heart/ In childhood"; for this "blended holiness of earth and sky" is

> A termination, and a last retreat,
> A Centre, come from wheresoe'er you will,
> A Whole without dependence or defect,
> Made for itself; and happy in itself,
> Perfect Contentment, Unity entire.
>
> (lines 135–51)

And only here does he find a genuine human community. Man "truly is alone" only in the "vast Metropolis," where he is "doomed/ To hold a vacant commerce . . . / With objects wanting life, repelling love," and where "neighbourhood serves rather to divide/ Than to unite." In this rural place, however, all is on a human scale, a multeity-in-unity in which individuality is preserved in a society which is a family writ large, and which finds itself thoroughly at home in its natural milieu.

> Society is here
> A true Community, a genuine frame
> Of many into one incorporate. . . .
> One household, under God, for high and low,
> One family, and one mansion . . .
>   possessors undisturbed
> Of this Recess . . . their glorious Dwelling-place.
>   (lines 592–624)

The poet's spiritual home, however, remains ineluctably a paradise of this earth, for in the vale man differs "but little from the Man elsewhere" and exhibits the common qualities of "selfishness, and envy, and revenge . . . / Flattery and double-dealing, strife and wrong" (lines 347–57). But, he asks, is there not a strain of words that shall be "the acknowledged voice of life," and so speak "of solid good/ And real evil" in a higher poetic harmony than that of the unalloyed pastoral fantasy—

> More grateful, more harmonious than the breath,
> The idle breath of softest pipe attuned
> To pastoral fancies?
>   (lines 401–9)

For this poetry of real life he dismisses the poetry of wish-fulfillment, "All Arcadian dreams/ All golden fancies of the golden Age" engendered by man's "wish to part/ With all remembrance of a jarring world" (lines 625–32). Confident of "an internal brightness," he assumes "his office" as a mature artist and announces his manifesto: in this "peaceful Vale . . . / A Voice shall speak, and what will be the Theme?" (lines 660–90, 751–3).

Home at Grasmere concludes with the answer to this question, in the passage Wordsworth later excerpted to serve as the Prospectus to the subject and argument of *The Recluse* and all its related poems. This statement in fact epitomizes, and proclaims as valid for other men, what the poet himself has learned from the long and arduous journey of his life that has terminated in Grasmere Vale. The subject, he tells us, will incorporate the narrative of that life itself, in the account of "the transitory Being" who had beheld the "Vision" which constituted his poetic credential, and which it was his unique mission to impart. This vision is of "the Mind of Man," through which he will undertake a poetic journey that must ascend higher than Milton's heaven and sink deeper than Milton's hell. Of this audacious poetic enterprise it will be the high argument that we can re-create the experienced world, and that this new world, despite the inescapable fact of evil and anguish—no less evident in the solitude of "fields and groves" than when they are "barricadoed . . . / Within the walls of cities"—will provide a sufficient paradise to which we have immediate access. Here we return to Wordsworth's central figure whose complex genealogy, widespread currency, and personal significance I undertook, two chapters back, to explicate. Only let a man succeed in restoring his lost integrity, by consummating a marital union between his mind and a nature which, to the sensual in their sleep of death, has become a severed and alien reality, and he shall find "Paradise, and groves Elysian . . . A simple produce of the common day."

3.   R O M A N T I C   L O V E

One cannot leave the great Romantic subject of the divided and reunited mind without reference to *Prometheus Unbound,* and Shelley's masterpiece gives occasion for specifying the conditions which fostered this pervasive view of radical good and evil. The Romantic era was one of technical, political, and social revolutions and counter-revolutions—of industrialization, urbanization, and increasingly massive industrial slums; of the first total war and postwar economic collapse; of progressive specialization in work, alterations in economic and political power, and consequent dislocations of the class structure; of competing ideologies and ever-imminent social chaos. To such a world of swift and drastic change, division, conflict, and disorder, the inherited pieties and integrative myths seemed no longer adequate to hold civilization together. In this age the ancient view that evil is the fragmentation of a once harmonious whole into alien and embattled parts was refined and expanded to express the general sense that

> Things fall apart; the center cannot hold;
> Mere anarchy is loosed upon the world.

Long before Yeats thus analyzed the modern condition in *The Second Coming,* Schiller, as we have seen, characterized the sickness of his time as the fracture of individuals, activities, and institutions into isolated and conflicting fragments; Hölderlin described the German people of his day as *disjecta membra* of integral men; and Hegel represented the intellectual, economic, and cultural condition of his century as that of "the self-alienated spirit" and of man's growing awareness that "all relationships, by their own nature, are tearing themselves apart." In England Coleridge indicted the era as "an Anarchy of Spirits! . . . disherited of soul," and lacking a "common centre"; Wordsworth lamented "these times of fear," of "indifference and apathy," when "good men,/ On every side fall off . . . to selfishness," "this time/ Of dereliction and dismay"; Blake represented his milieu by the myth of a disintegration of humanity into partial and self-centered beings locked in savage conflict; and Shelley (in a passage that Yeats remembered when he wrote *The Second Coming*) diagnosed society in terms of a psychopathic division among its component mental powers:

> The good want power, but to weep barren tears.
> The powerful goodness want: worse need for them.
> The wise want love; and those who love want wisdom;
> And all best things are thus confused to ill.[63]

If essential evil is equated with the aggregate of what drives things apart, then essential good will be equated with the aggregate of what pulls the sundered parts together; and for this centripetal force the most eligible general name is "love." The inclusive application of the term to all the cohesive forces in the human and nonhuman universe had been common among the Neoplatonists, for whom dispersion and integration, as we have seen, had been primary metaphysical categories. In Proclus, as Anders Nygren points out in *Agape and Eros, "Eros is the bond of union in existence,"* the *"universal force of cohesion* in the most comprehensive sense of the term"; and for the Pseudo-Dionysius it is similarly the general "unifying and cohesive force." [64] "Amor," declared John Scotus Erigena, "is the bond and chain which joins together all things in the universe in an ineffable friendship and an insoluble unity." [65]

Many Romantic writers adopted the term in this universal extension. "Love," as Shelley put it, "is the bond and the sanction which connects not only man with man but with everything which exists." [66] Schiller and Hegel who, like Shelley, wrote early essays on "Love," agreed on an inclusive application of the word. "Genuine love," Hegel said, "excludes all oppositions." He expanded upon this concept in terms of his view that all development is a spiral movement from unity through incremental severance and opposition to a higher unity:

> Here life has run through the circle of development from an immature to a completely mature unity: when the unity was immature, there still stood over against it the world and the possibility of a cleavage between itself and the world; as development proceeded, reflection produced more and more oppositions . . . until it set the whole of man's life in opposition [to objectivity]; finally, love completely destroys objectivity and thereby annuls and transcends reflection, deprives man's opposite of all foreign character. . . . In love the separate does still remain, but as something united and no longer as something separate.[67]

In this sense of love as, in Aquinas' phrase, the *virtus unitiva,* not only Shelley but all the major Romantics are primarily poets of love. Even Wordsworth is more a love poet than he is a nature poet—by lexical statistics, at any rate: H. J. C. Grierson has calculated that in his writings the ratio of the word "love" to "nature" is thirteen to eight.[68] The sovereign function of poetry for Wordsworth is to sustain and propagate connectedness, which is love; the poet, as he said in the Preface to *Lyrical Ballads,* "is the rock of defence of human nature; an upholder and preserver, carrying everywhere with him relationship and love." [69]

Throughout the long history of this way of thinking, the antithesis and opponent of unitive love had been self-love, selfhood, egocentrism—the condition of Plotinus' "self-centered" soul, which transfers the center of reference from the whole to its individual and acquisitive self. The Renaissance humanist Vives summarizes with admirable clarity the view of Neoplatonic Christianity that love is the integrative force and that self-love is the separative force:

> We must return to [God] by the same way we came forth from him. Love was the cause of our being created. . . . From that love we have been separated, forsooth by the love of ourselves. . . . By love, i.e., by our love to God, we are to return to our source, which is also our end; for nothing else is able to bind together spiritual things, nothing is able to make one out of many, except love; but knowledge must precede love.[70]

This radical cause of separation, hence of evil, Boehme called *Selbheit,* Winstanley the "selfish" aspect of fallen and fragmented man, and Schelling the finite *Ichheit* which is "the point of the extremest alienation from God." "Evil generally," Hegel said, when it is expressed as concept rather than in the image-thinking of religion, is "the self-centered being-for-itself [*das insichseiende Fürsichsein*] and good is selfless simplicity [*das selbstlose Einfache*]." [71] For Blake the cancellation of "Selfhood" is the essential act which effects a redeemed, or reintegrated, humanity. Pursuing his "great task" he prays to the Saviour—"the Human Imagination" which is the repository of the unitive vision—to "Annihilate the Selfhood in me, be thou all my life!" For "Man liveth not by Self alone," but "by Brotherhood & Universal Love"; and in his "offering of Self for Another," Jesus manifests that "This is Friendship & Brotherhood; without it Man is Not." [72] For Coleridge the opposite condition to that of the man who feels "himself, his own low self the whole," is to make "the whole one Self! Self, that no alien knows! . . . Oblivious of its own"; and this latter condition, when it becomes general, will effect the universal redemption.[73]

In the mature thought of Shelley, what he called "the dark idolatry of self," together with the equally destructive but opposite extreme, the paralyzing contempt of oneself, constitute that mental state which is the only hell—"self-love or self-contempt" inscribes on the human brow "as o'er the gate of hell/ 'All hope abandon ye who enter here.'" The opposite of self-love Shelley denominates alternatively as "love" and "poetry" ("poetry and the principle of self . . . are the God and Mammon of the world"); for as he says in *A Defence of Poetry,* poetry is "the expression of the imagination," and the imagination for Shelley is the faculty by which man transcends his individual ego, transfers the center of reference to others, and thus transforms self-love into, simply, love:

> The great secret of morals is love, or a going out of our own nature and an identification of ourselves with the beautiful which exists in thought, action, or person, not our own. A man, to be greatly good, must imagine intensely and comprehensively; he must put himself in the place of another and of many others; the pains and pleasures of his species must become his own. The great instrument of moral good is the imagination. . . . Poetry enlarges the circumference of the imagination.[74]

Even Keats sets up in his *Endymion,* as "a kind of Pleasure Thermometer" calibrated by "the gradations of Happiness," a Platonic ladder of love. Keats's ascent, however, culminates not in an escape from this world to a contemplation of the Platonic forms, but in the annihilation of the limits of the self in a "fellowship with essence," of which the final stages are friendship, then selfless love. We begin the process with an escape from selfhood by means of an identification with sensuous objects outside ourselves. But there are

enthralments far
More self-destroying, leading, by degrees,
To the chief intensity: the crown of these
Is made of love and friendship, and sits high
Upon the forehead of humanity.
          . . . But at the tip-top,
There hangs by unseen film, an orbèd drop
Of light, and that is love . . .
Melting into its radiance, we blend,
Mingle, and so become a part of it.[75]

In the broad Romantic application of the term "love," as in recent depth-psychology, all modes of human attraction are conceived as one in kind, different only in object and degree, in a range which includes the relations of lover to beloved, children to parents, brother to sister, friend to friend, and individual to humanity. The orbit of love was often enlarged to include the relationship of man to nature as well. The perception that dead nature is really alive, Schelling said, is the result of "the attraction of inner love and relationship between your own spirit and that which lives in nature." Or as Wordsworth wrote:

Love, now a universal birth,
From heart to heart is stealing.
From earth to man, from man to earth. . . . [76]

Furthermore, not only in the conceptual scheme of the *Naturphilosophen* but also in the imaginative usage of some of the poets, the term "love" was extended beyond the human realm to all modes of cosmic connectivity, including the natural forces of gravitation and electromagnetism.

While Romantic poets agree in the use of "love" to signify the spectrum of attraction and relationship, they differ markedly in their choice of the specific type of relationship which serves as the paradigm for all the other types. In Coleridge, for example, friendship tends to be the paradigmatic form, and he represents sexual love as an especially intense kind of confraternity. Wordsworth's favored model is maternal love, and the development of relationship in *The Prelude* is from the babe in his mother's arms to the all-inclusive "love more intellectual," which is higher than any love that "is human merely." In Hölderlin all human relations, including sexual love, are largely subsumed under the *agape,* or primitive Christian love feast, as the elemental form. "A vision that haunts all Hölderlin's poetry," Ronald Peacock has said, is that of "the community, a people having common bonds and a common speech, gathered together to celebrate in a poetic festival its gods." [77] Consonantly, the redeemed world that Hölderlin foresees, as he says in his poem *Die Liebe,* is "ein beseeltere,/ Vollentblühende Welt," in which

> Sprache der Liebenden
> Sei die Sprache des Landes,
> Ihre Seele der Laut des Volks!

What makes the fusion of all affinities into love especially conspicuous in Shelley (as, among German poets, in Novalis) [78] is that his persistent paradigm is sexual love, with the result that in his poetry all types of human and extrahuman attraction—all forces that hold the physical, mental, moral, and social universe together—are typically represented, both in myth and in metaphor, by categories which are patently derived from erotic attraction and sexual union. This procedure, which gave scandal to the Victorians, has provided more recent critics with grounds for reducing much of Shelley's poetry to the expression of regressive sexual fantasies. It may well be that Shelley's choice of a paradigmatic relation (and equally, the alternative choices of his contemporaries) was rooted in his private preoccupations and emotional complexes. But whatever its motivation, Shelley's procedure was not in the least an unconscious one, for he was aware that he was putting a part, which he assessed as a salient but relatively lesser part, for the whole:

> That profound and complicated sentiment which we call love
> . . . is rather the universal thirst for a communion not merely
> of the senses but of our whole nature, intellectual, imaginative,
> and sensitive. . . . This want grows more powerful in proportion to the development which our nature receives from
> civilization, for man never ceases to be a social being. The

sexual impulse, which is only one and often a small part of these claims, serves from its obvious and external nature as a kind of type or expression of the rest, as common basis, an acknowledged and visible link.[79]

Shelley was also aware of the risk to which this procedure exposed his poetry:

In the human world one of the commonest expressions of love is sexual intercourse, & in describing the deepest effects of abstract love the author could not avoid the danger of exciting some ideas connected with this mode of expression, & he has exposed himself to the danger of awakening ludicrous or unauthorized images.[80]

4. SHELLEY'S "PROMETHEUS UNBOUND"

None of Shelley's longer poems is irrelevant to his theme of the human need for love to fulfill what is incomplete and to reintegrate what has been divided, both in the individual psyche and in the social order; but I shall discuss only his most detailed and successful rendering of this theme, *Prometheus Unbound.* Like Keats in his exactly contemporary *Hyperion,* Shelley in this poem explored the problem of evil and suffering in terms of the classical myth of the loss of the Golden Age when Saturn was displaced by Jupiter (see II, iv. 32 ff.). And like many other contemporaries Shelley fused the pagan myth of a lost Golden Age with the Biblical design of a fall, redemption, and millennial return to a lost felicity, and gave special prominence to the associated Biblical figure of the exile, return, and marriage of the bride. In his Preface Shelley also tells us that he chose the Titan Prometheus for his protagonist over Satan, "the hero of *Paradise Lost,*" because Prometheus has Satan's heroic virtues of courage and firm "opposition to omnipotent force," but without the moral defects which, in Milton's "magnificent fiction," engender "in the mind a pernicious casuistry which leads us to weigh his faults with his wrongs, and to excuse the former because the latter exceed

all measure." [81] *Prometheus Unbound*, then, like Wordsworth's
Prelude and *Home at Grasmere*, Blake's *Milton*, and Keats's
Hyperion, can be looked upon as a deliberate attempt by a
Romantic Miltonist—in his Preface Shelley called his predecessor "the sacred Milton"—to revise Milton's great but no
longer adequate imaginative conception of the nature, justification, and mitigation of the evils and agonies of human experience.

Many critics of Shelley's poem assert that Prometheus is an
allegorical figure, but they disagree as to what he allegorizes.
Earl Wasserman, for example, in a recent and often enlightening monograph, has argued that "Prometheus is the personifi-
cation of Shelley's concept of the One Mind," as this concept
is represented in Shelley's system of metaphysics, and that "the
drama is the history of the One Mind's evolution into perfection." [82] In his Preface, however, Shelley himself asserts that
Prometheus "is, as it were, the type of the highest perfection
of moral and intellectual nature." Shelley's hero, then, is close
kin to the agent called "Man" or "Mankind" who is the protagonist in the popular eighteenth-century genre of universal
history—a genre which, in its French and English versions,
ranked high in Shelley's favorite reading matter. In universal
history "Man" is the collective representative (in Shelley's
word, "the type") of the intellectual and moral vanguard
among human beings, who develops through history toward
his perfected human condition. In *Prometheus Unbound* Shelley renders the universal history of man in the dramatic form
of visualizable agents and their actions, and he represents man's
accession to an earthly paradise not (in the usual eighteenth-
century pattern) as the terminus of a long and gradual progress but (by a reversion to the Biblical design of history) as a
sudden, right-angled breakthrough from misery to felicity.

Within the frame of Shelley's dramatic fiction Prometheus,
like Blake's Albion, is also a descendant of a familiar mythical
figure: the one man who was once whole, has fallen into division, and proceeds to redeem his lost integrity. Throughout the
work, however, Shelley sustains the bodily separateness of Prometheus and Asia, his divided feminine complement, so that
their reunion is not represented as a reintegration of the primal

man, but as a culminating marriage. In his drama, further-more, Shelley clearly distinguishes between his *dramatis per-sonae* proper—Prometheus and the other "Giant Forms" (as Blake would call them) who act out the mythical plot—and the world that these mythical personages and actions figure forth: the real world of ordinary men and women, who are never directly presented in the action of the dramatic poem but whose experiences are reported to us by the Spirit of the Earth and the Spirit of the Hour in the third act, and whose spiritual alteration and accession to an earthly paradise are correlative with the conversion of Prometheus and his reunion with Asia.

When the play begins, Prometheus has already fallen into disunity and conflict as a consequence of his moral error in having succumbed, in response to tyranny and injustice, to the divisive passion of hate; the result is that Asia has been exiled from him. Asia is the soul's counterpart which, in his "Essay on Love," Shelley calls the "anti-type." [83] In the play she is characterized as an Aphrodite figure who embodies the uni-versally integrative and life-restoring power which Shelley called "love." "Most vain all hope but love; and thou art far, Asia!"—in "that far Indian vale," as Panthea explains,

> The scene of her sad exile; rugged once
> And desolate and frozen, like this ravine;
> But now invested with fair flowers and herbs
>   . . . from the aether
> Of her transforming presence, which would fade
> If it were mingled not with thine.
> (I, 808–9, 826–33)

Her separation has left Prometheus as the male remnant who manifests the power of the will in the highest masculine vir-tues of resistance and endurance, but remains "eyeless in hate," an isolated and immobilized Samson, in a natural setting which has become alien and lifeless to him:

> Nailed to this wall of eagle-baffling mountain,
> Black, wintry, dead, unmeasured; without herb,
> Insect, or beast, or shape or sound of life.
> (I, 9–22)

Prometheus is represented as having been chained and tortured by Jupiter. We soon learn, however, that all of Jupiter's power has been vested in him by his victim. The implication is that Jupiter is mankind's own worst potentiality—the corruption of affiliative love into self-love, with its concomitant lust for dominion and tyranny—which has been projected by the mind of man in the fantasy of a cruel tyrant-god who dwells aloof in his distant heaven. But if Jupiter is a pseudo-person, he is not the less psychologically real and effective: "I gave all/ He has; and in return he chains me here" (I, 381–2). Various clues in the text, moreover, invite us to regard all the *dramatis personae,* except one, as externalized correlatives of the powers, aspects, and activities of Prometheus' own divided and conflicting self, and to regard even the altering natural setting as projections of Prometheus' mental states.[84] The one clear exception is Demogorgon, the "mighty darkness" and shapeless form (II, iv. 2–7) who is the principle, or power, behind all process. This ultimate reason for things not only lies outside of man's mind and its activities but also, Shelley skeptically insists, lies irretrievably outside the limits of man's knowledge, by virtue of the fact that it exceeds the bounds of possible human experience. Accordingly, Demogorgon is simply postulated—like the cognitively inaccessible "Power in likeness of the Arve" in Shelley's great lyric, *Mont Blanc*—as the course of events which is in itself purposeless and amoral, but carries out the ineluctable consequences of man's decisions or acts; whether for good or ill depends on the condition of the human will which makes neutral process the instrument of its own moral purposes. Read in this way *Prometheus Unbound,* like Blake's prophetic poems, is a psycho-drama of the reintegration of the split personality by that annihilation of selfhood which converts divisive hate into affiliative love, in which the action is equally relevant to the mind of each and all of us. And by any valid reading of Shelley's myth, it is plain that man is ultimately the agent of his own fall, the tyrant over himself, his own avenger, and his own potential redeemer; as H. N. Fairchild has described Shelley's intention, justly though disapprovingly, "the mind of man is liberated from its dark delusions solely by the mind of man." [85]

The plot of *Prometheus Unbound* has no precedent in the drastic asymmetry of its construction. It begins not *in medias res* but at the end, for the reversal occurs in the opening soliloquy when Prometheus, his arrogance suddenly dissipating after his long discipline of suffering, substitutes a unifying sentiment for the separative sentiment: pity for hate. (As Blake had put it, "They have divided themselves by Wrath, they must be united by/ Pity . . . in terrors of self annihilation." [86]) Prometheus at once proceeds to "recall"—in the double sense of bringing into the full light of consciousness, and by that very fact revoking—the implications of the curse he had called down upon Jupiter, which serves in the play as the central emblem of his moral flaw. These feet, he cries to Jupiter, might trample thee,

> If they disdained not such a prostrate slave.
> Disdain! Ah no! I pity thee. . . .
>   I speak in grief,
> Not exultation, for I hate no more,
> As then ere misery made me wise. The curse
> Once breathed on thee I would recall. . . .
> Though I am changed so that aught evil wish
> Is dead within; although no memory be
> Of what is hate. . . .
>
>   (I, 51–72)

This is all Prometheus, by the reversal of his unaided masculine will, can do, except to remain indomitable against Jupiter's continuing demands for submission. But by substituting compassion for hate Prometheus, although unknowingly, has released his feminine complement, the full power of love, from her long exile.

From the end of the first act on, the plot consists almost entirely of Asia's journey to her reunion with Prometheus. She and Panthea (her sister and lesser self, through whom she has retained some relation to Prometheus in exile) obey the reiterative "Follow! Follow!" which expresses the sweet and irresistible compulsion that has been put in process by Prometheus' change of heart; this is Shelley's version of the yearning toward the apocalyptic bridal union in Revelation: "And the

Spirit and the bride say, Come. And let him that heareth say, Come." Asia's movement toward reunion is a spiritual journey which, in consonance with the great Romantic trope, is specifically a *Bildungsreise,* in the course of which she acquires essential knowledge that leaves her radically altered. Prometheus' change from hate to pity had been unpremeditated and instinctive, and, before his reformation can be complete and stable, the principle implicit in this moral act must be brought out as conscious knowledge. But since, by the conditions of Shelley's inherited story, Prometheus must remain fixed to his precipice, the function of the self-educative journey is given over to his alter ego, Asia. In obedience to her inner compulsion Asia descends to Demogorgon's underworld at the dark bases of existence and puts to him the ultimate questions about the "why" of the way things are—the rationale of all human history and experience. In the Induction to Keats's *The Fall of Hyperion,* as the poet ascends the stairs his evolving awareness is educed from him by the progressive alteration of Moneta's charges and comments. Asia's developing insight is similarly projected and dramatized in the form of a colloquy; for Demogorgon, who simply acts as he must without knowing why, responds to her queries with riddling utterances that merely stimulate her to answer her own questions, by specifying as knowledge what she had already possessed as obscure presentiment.

Accordingly it is not Demogorgon but Asia who tells us the prehistory of the drama in which, during the Golden Age under Saturn men had lived in felicity, but a felicity of ignorance, then had suffered under the tyranny of Jupiter, but had been relieved by Prometheus, who brought men science, culture, and the arts. Yet for this act of benevolence Prometheus hangs bound and tortured, and civilized man is become "The wreck of his own will, the scorn of earth/ The outcast, the abandoned, the alone." At this point Asia raises the question central to the Romantic, as to the earlier Christian spiritual journey: *unde malum?* "But who rains down/ Evil, the immedicable plague?" To Shelley's skeptical empiricism, this question oversteps the limits of possible human experience. Demogorgon does not know the answer, nor does Asia, nor can any man, for as Demogorgon says, "the deep truth is imageless." He can give her only as much knowledge as she already possesses, below the level of distinct awareness; but this knowledge turns out to be all we need to know—that to "Fate, Time, Occasion, Chance, and Change . . . / All things are subject but eternal Love." To which Asia replies

> So much I asked before, and my heart gave
> The response thou hast given; and of such truths
> Each to itself must be the oracle.
>
> (II, iv. 32–123)

Asia's educational journey, then, like Wordsworth's in *The Prelude,* terminates in the lesson that love is first and chief, as the only available solution to the problem of the good and evil of our mortal state. At the instant of this discovery by Asia, Demogorgon becomes capable of answering the sole question to which he can give a decisive and unambiguous reply, and that merely by a gesture: "When shall the destined hour arrive?" "Behold!" For the destined hour has at that instant arrived.

Taking up her journey back to Prometheus in the car driven by the Spirit of the Hour, Asia in a great lyric describes the correlative inner journey in which her soul, like an enchanted boat, moves up and back through age, manhood, youth, infancy, and "Through Death and Birth, to a diviner day;/ A paradise of vaulted bowers" (II, v. 72–110). This spiritual dying to be reborn is equated, on the mythical level, with her visible outer change back to the pristine form she had manifested when she had risen as Aphrodite from the sea, while "love . . . filling the living world,/ Burst from thee"; her transfiguration matches that of Prometheus back to his primal form at the moment when, suspended on the cliff, he had repealed his hate (II, i. 56 ff.). Jupiter is hurled by Demogorgon into "the dark void" (III, ii. 10); that is, the projection of man's self-isolating and domineering hate reverts to its original state of potentiality in the human psyche, whence it will reconsolidate and reemerge if man ceases to sustain his integrity by the cohesive force of love. The condition of a reintegrated humanity is signified by the reunion of Prometheus and Asia, which is exactly simultaneous with the annihilation of Jupiter. Mary Shelley's interpretation of the event is too exclusive to be adequate, but it makes salient the parallel between the conclusion of Shelley's myth and the figure of the culminating marriage in Wordsworth and other Romantic writers. Asia, says Mrs. Shelley, in some mythological interpretations was

> the same as Venus and Nature. When the benefactor of mankind is liberated, Nature resumes the beauty of her prime, and is united to her husband, the emblem of the human race, in perfect and happy union.[87]

This marital reunion coincides with the sounding of the conch shell by the Spirit of the Hour (Shelley's version of the last trump in the Book of Revelation), at which "All things . . . put their evil nature off" and man, having become what he might always have been, "made earth like heaven" and, "equal, unclassed, tribeless, and nationless," takes up residence in his achieved paradise. Unlike Grasmere Vale—Wordsworth's "earthly counterpart" of heaven, whose inhabitants differ "but little from the Man elsewhere" in their guilt and suffering—Shelley's envisioned state is one in which man will be "free from guilt or pain . . . for his will made or suffered them." Like Wordsworth's, however, Shelley's is a paradise of this earth, in which man remains inescapably conditioned by passion and by "chance, and death, and mutability"; otherwise he would not be earthly man but a disembodied idea in a Platonic heaven: these mortal conditions are

> The clogs of that which else might oversoar
> The loftiest star of unascended heaven,
> Pinnacled dim in the intense inane.
> (III, iv. 54–204)

Shelley added to *Prometheus Unbound* a fourth act in the traditional form of a nuptial masque. The act constitutes an immense epithalamion in which the elements of the human mind and of the outer cosmos celebrate the triumph of love and participate, in song, dance, and ritual mimicry, in the union of Prometheus and Asia taking place behind the scenes.

The thematic word is "Unite!" and this concept is enacted in the fantastic, yet beautiful, episode of the wooing and love union between the masculine earth and the feminine moon—possibly, Shelley's adaptation of the alchemical marriage between the male and female contraries (symbolically represented as sun and moon, as well as king and queen) which consummates the Hermetic quest for the principle that will transmute all elements to gold and all mankind to the age of gold. Held in its circular course by the embrace of the earth, the cold and sterile moon bursts into restored life and fertility, as the earth's enhanced energy manifests itself in a heightening of its electromagnetic forces and its radiated heat and light—those attributes which in Shelley's spiritual physics are material correlates of the attractive and life-giving powers of universal love. Such dramatic episodes are merely emblematic, however, of the primary union, in which all men are assimilated by love into a unitary mankind. This fulfillment Shelley describes in a statement which is his metaphorical equivalent to the myth of the reintegration of the Universal Man:

> Man, oh, not men! A chain of linkèd thought,
> Of love and might to be divided not. . . .
> Man, one harmonious soul of many a soul,
> Whose nature is its own divine control,
> Where all things flow to all, as rivers to the sea.
>
> (IV, 394–402)

5. CARLYLE AND HIS CONTEMPORARIES

The successive writings of Thomas Carlyle mark the stages of transition in England from the Romantic to the Victorian preoccupation with alienation and community. His essay "Characteristics" (1831), which puts forward most of the leading topics of his mature work, rests mainly on German views of cultural history, especially as represented in the writings of Schiller, whose life Carlyle had published in 1825. Man's primitive happiness and psychic health consisted in his instinctual unity with himself; "consciousness," because it strikes a division between the knowing self and its fragmented objects and between the thinking self and its activities, is equatable to evil and disease; and the replacement of "unconsciousness" by these modes of self-consciousness, in the first stages of philosophy and science, is the historical truth embodied in the fable of Adam's loss of paradise:

> The beginning of Inquiry is Disease: All Science . . . is and continues to be but Division, Dismemberment, and partial healing of the wrong. Thus, as was of old written, the Tree of Knowledge springs from a root of evil, and bears fruits of good and evil. Had Adam remained in Paradise, there had been no Anatomy and no Metaphysics. . . . The memory of that first state of Freedom and paradisaic Unconsciousness has faded away into an ideal poetic dream. We stand here too conscious of many things.[88]

Man's inner unity is also a prerequisite for social community. Only the early stage of human society, accordingly, "was what we can call *whole,* in both senses of the word. The individual man was in himself a whole, or complete union; and could combine with his fellows as the living member of a greater whole" (p. 15). The modern age, unhappily, has moved to the very extremity of dividedness, for "never since the beginning of Time was there . . . so intensely self-conscious a Society" (pp. 18–9). Carlyle echoes Schiller's assertion that the culture which had inflicted this wound must heal it, and like his predecessor, he suggests that the fall of man was a happy division that will lead to a greater good. Is not "the symptom of universal disease, yet also the symptom and sole means of restoration and cure? The effort of Nature, exerting her medicative force to cast out foreign impediments, and once more become One, become whole?" "Metaphysical Speculation, if a necessary evil, is the forerunner of much good" (pp. 32, 40).

Carlyle wove this theme of lost and recovered unity into the design of the biographical section of his contemporary work *Sartor Resartus.* Teufelsdroeckh is a foundling, deposited by a "mysterious stranger" with the good old couple, the Futterals. When in his youth he is rejected by his beloved Blumine for a more advantageous marriage, "he quietly lifts his *Pilgerstab*

(Pilgrim-staff) . . . and begins a perambulation and circumambulation of the terraqueous Globe!" Teufelsdroeckh's circular pilgrimage thenceforth serves as a sustained metaphor for the growth of the philosopher's mind: in "his mad Pilgrimings, and general solution into aimless Discontinuity," as Carlyle says, "his spiritual nature is nevertheless progressive, and growing." [89] Recurrently his painful wanderings are compared to those of standard guilt-ridden sinners. "Thus must he, in the temper of ancient Cain, or of the modern Wandering Jew,— save only that he feels himself not guilty and but suffering the pains of guilt,—wend to and fro with aimless speed." [90] The apparently aimless wanderings, however, are in deep spiritual truth a pilgrimage in quest of the foundling's unknown father and home.

> Ever, in my distresses and my loneliness, has Fantasy turned, full of longing (*sehnsuchtsvoll*), to that unknown Father, who perhaps far from me, perhaps near, either way invisible, might have taken me to his paternal bosom, there to be screened from many a woe. (p. 85)

The seeming disorder of the biography of Teufelsdroeckh is thus structured on the familiar Romantic model of a self-formative educational journey, which moves through division, exile, and solitariness toward the goal of a recovered home and restored familial relationship.

In an early stage of his wanderings Teufelsdroeckh is the very type of the Romantic poet who flies "into the wilds of Nature; as if in her mother-bosom he would seek healing." He climbs a mountain and experiences a Wordsworthian (and Hölderlinian) revelation of community with the feminine and maternal landscape.

> Never till this hour had he known Nature, that she was One, that she was his Mother and divine. . . . He felt as if Death and Life were one, as if the Earth were not dead, as if the Spirit of the Earth had its throne in that splendour, and his own spirit were therewith holding communion.

But in *Sartor* this experience of the one life is premature and unstable: Blumine drives by in "a gay Barouche-and-four" on her honeymoon with Herr Towgood and shatters the mood, leaving him "alone, behind them, with the Night" (pp. 149–51). His "world-pilgrimage" of life then takes Teufelsdroeckh, as it had Wordsworth (and Hegel's protagonist in the *Phenomenology*), through the stage of eighteenth-century rationalism and analysis, which leads to a crisis in which he finds himself triply divided: within himself, from other men, and from nature. Carlyle's presentation of this state of mind is a classic description of social and cosmic alienation. "It is all a grim Desert, this once-fair world of his; wherein is heard . . . the shrieks of despairing, hate-filled men. . . . To such length has the spirit of Inquiry carried him." He was

> a feeble unit in the middle of a threatening Infinitude. . . . Invisible yet impenetrable walls, as of Enchantment, divided me from all living. . . . It was a strange isolation I then lived in. . . . In the midst of their crowded streets and assemblages, I walked solitary. . . . To me the Universe was all void of Life, of Purpose, of Volition, even of Hostility: it was one huge, dead, immeasurable Steam-engine.   (pp. 161, 163–4)

"The Everlasting No had said: 'Behold, thou art fatherless, outcast.' " But suddenly came the breakthrough, the "date of my Spiritual Newbirth," a rebirth which marks his passage over the threshold to maturity; "perhaps I directly thereupon began to be a Man." This transition is marked by the turn in his "pilgriming" from his exclusive concern with the self to the "NOT-ME for wholesomer food." And only after his selfhood has been utterly canceled is he able, in the stage of maturity called "The Everlasting Yea," to achieve the goal of his life's quest. "The first preliminary moral Act, Annihilation of Self (*Selbst-tödtung*), had been happily accomplished; and my mind's eyes were now unsealed" (pp. 167–70, 186). What is revealed to him is the recognition that home was where he had been all along without his knowing it. Divisive self-concern having given way to affiliative love, the dead and alien world comes alive as his natural dwelling, where (in a secular echo of the description of the New Jerusalem in Revelation) he lives as a member of the family of mankind:

Ah, like the mother's voice to her little child that strays bewildered . . . came that Evangel. The Universe is not dead and demoniacal, a charnel-house with spectres; but godlike and my Father's!

With other eyes, too, could I now look upon my fellow-man: with an infinite Love, an infinite Pity. . . . O my Brother, my Brother, why cannot I shelter thee in my bosom, and wipe away all tears from thy eyes! . . . The poor Earth, with her poor joys, was now my needy Mother, not my cruel Stepdame; Man . . . had become dearer to me; and even for his sufferings and his sins, I now first named him Brother.[91]

A decade later, in *Past and Present* (1843), Carlyle applied the general Romantic categories of alienation and reintegration to the specific diagnosis of the human condition in an industrial and laissez-faire economy. As early as 1767 Carlyle's countryman, Adam Ferguson, had warned that in a "commercial state . . . man is sometimes found a detached and a solitary being" who deals with his fellow men "for the sake of the profits they bring." [92] Carlyle assimilates this economic insight into his earlier paradigm of unity lost and unity to be regained. In the conceptual understructure of *Past and Present* the highest good is integrity, which is dependent on the power of love, and the essential evil is division and isolation, which is effected by a turn from love to "Egoism." "Our present system of individual Mammonism, and Government by Laissez-faire" is one in which men, only half-alive, live in severance from a world which has become a lifeless other, and in severance also from other human beings within a social order in which "cash payment is . . . the sole nexus of man with man." But there is a unitive condition of familial relationship with his fellow beings and the environing world which man once possessed and which, by means of a reformation that is at once psychological, moral, and economic, man can recover, and without sacrifice of his industrial advancement.

Love of men cannot be bought by cash-payment; and without love men cannot endure to be together. . . . Your gallant battle-hosts and work-hosts, as the others did . . . must and

will be . . . joined with you in veritable brotherhood, son-
hood, by quite other and deeper ties than those of temporary
days' wages! . . . Isolation is the sum-total of wretchedness
to man. To be cut off, to be left solitary: to have a world
alien, not your world; all a hostile camp for you; not a home
at all, of hearts and faces who are yours, whose you are! It is
the frightfulest enchantment; too truly a work of the Evil
One. To have neither superior, nor inferior, nor equal, united
manlike to you. Without father, without child, without
brother. Man knows no sadder destiny.[93]

The Victorian plaint, "alone, alone, all all alone," is no less
prominent in Pater's sensationist solipsism and Arnold's cultural humanism than in Carlyle's economic corporativism. Experience, said Pater in the Conclusion to *The Renaissance,* "is
ringed round for each one of us by that thick wall of personality through which no real voice has ever pierced," and every
impression "is the impression of the individual in his isolation,
each mind keeping as a solitary prisoner its own dream of a
world." For Matthew Arnold modern life is a "strange disease"
with "its sick hurry, its divided aims," and with no place for
men to pitch their tents except on the "poor fragments of a
broken world." Arnold's reiterative figure for modern man is
that of a disoriented voyager without a haven, "still bent to
make some port he knows not where," or of a traveler without
a home,

> Wandering between two worlds, one dead,
> The other powerless to be born,
> With nowhere yet to rest my head.

Most unendurably, "We mortal millions live *alone.*" We were
all once a piece of the continent, but it has been shattered,
and every man is become an island.

> For surely once, they feel, we were
> Parts of a single continent! . . .
>
> A God, a God their severance ruled!
> And bade betwixt their shores to be
> The unplumb'd, salt, estranging sea.[94]

6. FOUR VERSIONS OF THE CIRCUITOUS RETURN: MARX, NIETZSCHE, ELIOT, LAWRENCE

We in our time are thus the heirs of a very old and expanding tradition—pagan and Christian, mythical and metaphysical, religious and secular—that it is the lot of man to be fragmented and cut off, but haunted in his exile and solitariness by the presentiment of a lost condition of wholeness and community. The alienated hero, or alienated anti-hero, in an inhuman universe and a disintegrated social order; the maimed and disinherited mind in search of a spiritual father or mother or home; the *Angst* of the solitary and self-divided consciousness in its faintly hopeful, or despairing, or absurdly persisting quest for connection, community, or even communication—these themes, predominant in our literature since World War I, have become obsessive in the philosophers, poets, novelists, and dramatists of the last two or three decades.

The old images and structural patterns survive, as well as the concepts. To conclude this section I shall cite passages from four writers to indicate how persistent and widespread is the vision of life and history that I have described, but also how extraordinarily diverse are its applications, ranging from a return to Christian orthodoxy to secular forms of explosive social and political consequences.

For Karl Marx the course of history has been an inevitable movement from a prehistoric stage of primitive communism through progressive stages, determined by altering modes of production, of the division and conflict of classes. This movement will terminate (after the penultimate stage of capitalism shall have played out its fate in total revolution) in a return to communism, but in a mature form which will preserve the productive values achieved during the intervening stages of development. The abstract design (although not the "material" emphasis on the means of production) is the Romantic, and specifically the Hegelian, spiral movement of history compelled by an immanent dialectic, but with this difference: Marx reverts to the Biblical version of the culmination of history, in which the final stage will be abruptly inaugurated, and apocalyptic violence is the inescapable precondition for the advent of the last, best things.[95]

Marx's early *Economic and Philosophic Manuscripts* of 1844 reveals the matrix of ideas out of which developed his mature social theory. These documents had been composed only a year after Carlyle's *Past and Present,* and Marx's overlap with Carlyle indicates the general currency, by that time, of the concept of the fragmentation and isolation of men in modern society.[96] In his *Manuscripts* Marx's outlook on man and on history is primarily moral, not economic, and his ideal for mankind embodies the essential values of Romantic humanism. The movement of history is toward realizing the highest good of the individual man, and that good Marx defines, very much as Schiller had defined it, as the creative self-realization of the "whole man," who by "the complete *emancipation* of all the human qualities and senses" has achieved "all the plenitude of his being" and lives as an integral part of a community in which love, replacing acquisitive "egoism" and purely monetary bonds between individuals, has become the natural form of relationship.[97] Radical evil is not private property or capitalism as such; for Marx, as for other thinkers in this tradition, evil is essentially separation, the division of the integral man and society into self-centered, isolated, and hostile parts. The basic malady of capitalism, whatever its productive gains, is that it leads to an increasing and many-dimensioned alienation and estrangement (*Entäusserung* and *Entfremdung*), as the inescapable and pervasive consequence of its mode of production. For to be fully human is to work, and to work is to transform natural things ("the inorganic body of man") into human things and so, by psychological extension, to humanize all of nature and to integrate material nature with human nature. In capitalism, however, working men survive only by doing specialized productive work in a condition of servitude to other men. As a result modern man has become alienated from the product of his labor which, since it is an object made under duress for somebody else, has become to him "an alien object which dominates him"; and by an inevitable diffusion of attitude from the made object to the entire objective universe, all the "sensuous external world" of "natural objects" has been transformed into "an alien and hostile world." Man also feels that "the act of production itself" is "something alien and not belonging to him," so that when "at work he feels homeless" and in alienation "from himself, from his own active function, his life activity." And in parallel with his alienation from nature and from himself, man is also "alienated from other men," with whom he stands in the relation either of object to object, or of servitor to master.[98] Communism, conversely, even in its "crude" form, Marx says, "is already aware of being the reintegration of man, his return to himself, the supersession of man's self-alienation."

Here is Marx's description, in his proto-Marxist period, of the perfected communist state, as that culminating stage of human and social reintegration in which there will be the total "abolition of *private property*, of *human self-alienation*":

It is, therefore, the return of man himself as a *social*, i.e., really human being, a complete and conscious return which assimilates all the wealth of previous development. Communism as a fully-developed naturalism is humanism and as a fully-developed humanism is naturalism. It is the *definitive* resolution of the antagonism between man and nature, and between man and man. . . . It is the solution of the riddle of history and knows itself to be this solution. . . .

The *human* significance of nature only exists for *social* man, because only in this case is nature a *bond* with other *men*. . . . Only then is nature the *basis* of his own *human* experience and a vital element of human reality. The *natural* existence of man has here become his *human* existence and nature itself has become human for him. Thus *society* is the accomplished union of man with nature, the veritable resurrection of nature, the realized naturalism of man and the realized humanism of nature.[99]

The voice is the voice of Marx, but the purport and very vocabulary of this humanistic naturalism we have heard often before: the expectation of a future state which is "the solution of the riddle of history" because it serves as a secular theodicy, justifying the sufferings of human history by the felicity of its earthly end; the conception of that end as a "return" to the beginning, but at a higher level which has converted to "conscious" knowledge, hence preserved, the values achieved during all preceding stages; and the view of that final stage as one in which each man, having been fragmented, has become whole again, is rejoined with other men, and is also reunited to a nature which is no longer dead and alien but has been resurrected and has assumed a companionable, because a human, form.

The consonance-in-difference of Marx's views with those of his Romantic predecessors becomes clearer if we set his last two sentences beside statements which Coleridge had written some twenty-five years earlier. Art, said Coleridge, is "the mediatress between, and reconciler of, nature and man. . . . It is, therefore, the power of humanizing nature. . . . [It is] the union and reconciliation of that which is nature with that which is exclusively human." [100] The difference is that the reconciling and integrative role which, in their various ways, Schiller, Schelling, Hegel, Coleridge, Wordsworth, and Blake had assigned to the imaginative work of the artist, Marx expands to include all the work of men's hands—provided, that is, that this work is performed in the social ambiance of free communal enterprise.

In *The Birth of Tragedy* (1872) Friedrich Nietzsche expresses his contempt for the Marxian view—the "optimistic glorification of man as such" on which "contemporary socialistic movements" base their "paradisiacal prospects." He reasserts instead the Romantic conviction "that art is the highest task and the proper metaphysical activity of this life." [101] The historical process of art exemplifies the interplay of a polarity, the Apollonian and Dionysian principles; and more patently even than his Romantic predecessors, Nietzsche bases the dialectic of generative contraries on the prototype of sexual opposition, conflict, and procreative union:

> The continuous development of art is bound up with the *Apollonian* and *Dionysian* duality: just as procreation depends on the duality of the sexes, involving perpetual strife with only periodically intervening reconciliations. . . . These

two distinct tendencies . . . at last, by a metaphysical miracle of Hellenic will . . . appear coupled with each other, and through this coupling eventually generate the art-product, equally Dionysian and Apollonian, of Attic tragedy.

The "mysterious union" and "glorious consummation in this child" of the two hostile principles, he declares, constitute the immanent teleology, "the *final goal* of [the] development and processes," of Hellenic art (pp. 167–8, 189).

Nietzsche's Apollonian-Dionysian duality, in the final analysis, reduces to the distinction between the divided many and the primogenial one. For Apollo represents the *principium individuationis* of the phenomenal world of sense and mere appearance, while Dionysus represents the "mysterious Primordial Unity" which is the "mysterious substratum," the "thing-in-itself of every phenomenon." The opposition between these two principles, accordingly, is correlative with the conflict within man between the desire to sustain his divided individuality and the impulse to return to the one life which is its substrate (pp. 171–4, 178, 185, 271–2). Nietzsche regards tragic drama as a re-presentation of the myth of Dionysus, and he interprets the Dionysian myth on the model of the cosmic myth of the Universal Man whose dismemberment constituted the primal evil and effected the creation of the world of individual beings, and whose coming resurrection into unity will mark the consummation of all things. The individual protagonist in tragic drama, he says, is merely the type of the true hero, and this hero is always

the suffering Dionysus of the mysteries, the god experiencing in himself the agonies of individuation, of whom wonderful myths tell us that as a boy he was torn to pieces by the Titans and has been worshiped in this state as Zagreus: whereby is intimated that this dismemberment, the properly Dionysian *suffering*, is like a transformation into air, water, earth, and fire, that we are therefore to regard the state of individuation as the origin and prime cause of all suffering, as something objectionable in itself.

The hope of "a new birth of Dionysus," signifying "the end of individuation," is the one thing which "casts a gleam of joy upon the features of a world torn asunder and shattered into individuals"; and the "mystery doctrine of tragedy" is "the fundamental knowledge of the oneness of everything existent, the conception of individuation as the prime cause of evil, and of art as the joyous hope that the bonds of individuation may be broken in augury of a restored oneness" (pp. 230–1).

Nietzsche cites Schiller's views on man's self-division and the reintegrative function of art no less often than he does Schopenhauer, his immediate predessor in metaphysics. But Nietzsche is an archetypal myth-critic, and in this one aspect his theory of art is closer in outline to Blake and Shelley than to Schiller. In true Greek tragedy, he says, "Dionysus never once ceased to be the tragic hero," for all tragic protagonists are "but masks of this original hero" (p. 229). And the poet in creating the tragedy, the actors in performing it, and the audience in observing it, all lose their own identities in a participation with the Dionysian-Apollonian synthesis of a "dissolution of the individual and his unification with primordial experience" which is at the same time a "redemption" of the individual "in appearance" (p. 216; see also 279, 321–2). But it is the Dionysian intoxication which is at the heart of the mystery of reintegration, in that ultimate state—not, as in Marx, a social state, but a psychic state—in which man is reunited into a "higher community," not only with other men, but also with alienated nature, to which (once again in the familiar figure) he returns as a Prodigal Son:

> Under the charm of the Dionysian not only is the union between man and man reaffirmed, but Nature which has become estranged [*entfremdete*], hostile, or subjugated, celebrates once more her reconciliation with her prodigal son, man. . . . Now the slave is free; now all the stubborn, hostile barriers, which necessity, caprice or "shameless fashion" have erected between man and man, are broken down. Now, with the gospel of universal harmony, each one feels himself not only united, reconciled, blended with his neighbor, but as one with him. . . . In song and in dance man expresses himself as a member of a higher community.
>
> (pp. 172–3; see also p. 208)

Even after a quarter-century, T. S. Eliot's *Four Quartets* has not lost its status as a strikingly "modern" poem; its evolving meditations, however, merely play complex variations upon the design and motifs of Romantic representations of the poet's educational progress. The meditations open, in *Burnt Norton*, with footfalls which

> echo in the memory
> Down the passage which we did not take
> Towards the door we never opened
> Into the rose-garden.

As in Wordsworth's *Prelude* "time past" is rendered, in the mode of a double consciousness, as it impinges on the poet's mature awareness in "time present." [102] The rose garden is associated with laughing children and birdsong, and the insistent solicitation is to follow, follow,

> Through the first gate,
> Into our first world, shall we follow
> The deception of the thrush? Into our first world [103]

—the garden world of the peace, innocence, and gaiety of our individual and generic infancy, before the beginning of the adult and fallen man's divided and unhappy consciousness. The rest of *Four Quartets* is the exploration of the multiple significance of this obsessive image, figured as a spiritual quest, by land and sea and underground, for the lost but unforgotten garden.

The second movement of *Burnt Norton* reveals that this quest is also for a reconciliation of the divided and warring contraries that constitute the world of motion in time. These contraries are represented (as the epigraphs and various allusions indicate) in accordance with the view of a unity which is divided by strife, yet also sustained by strife, that was put forward by Heraclitus, ancestor of the metaphysics of polarity. Garlic and sapphires mingle in the mud; "below inveterate scars" a trilling wire "reconciles forgotten wars"; the strife of "the boarhound and the boar" are "reconciled among the stars"; and in the union of contraries "at the still point of the turning

world" we find a new world, which is no other than the old
world, fully understood—

> both a new world
> And the old made explicit, understood
> In the completion of its partial ecstasy,
> The resolution of its partial horror.

The fifth movement of the first quartet, like the corresponding movement in the three later quartets, deals with the poet's
own art, and discloses that the poet's spiritual quest is coinci-
dent with the writing of the poem itself, which is the seemingly
hopeless quest to achieve, in a temporal and mutable medium,
the perpetual motion-in-stillness of "the form, the pattern"
which is the perfected work of art. The entire poem, therefore,
in its constitution as in its subject matter, is the search for that
condition in which the conflicting contraries of temporal experience are reconciled in a timeless experience, of which we
have a presentiment in the recurrences of the vanished yet
eternally present garden, when

> There rises the hidden laughter
> Of children in the foliage
> Quick now, here, now, always. . . .

"In my beginning is my end": the opening line of *East
Coker,* the second quartet, reveals that the poet's pilgrimage
is a circular one. And the origin which is its destination, we
are soon told, is home. "Home is where one starts from"—in
the poet's literal as well as figurative journey, for East Coker,
to which the poet has now returned, is the ancestral English
home of the Eliot family. More patently even than its predecessors in the lineage of the poet's *Bildungsreise, East Coker*
manifests the pattern that it describes (in Coleridge's image
for the perfect shape of a poem, it is a "snake with its Tail in
its Mouth"), for it ends by stating what it has achieved, in a
sentence which reiterates, with the elements reversed, the sentence with which it began: "In my end is my beginning."

But on the larger scale too "the way forward is the way back"
(p. 134), so that the structure of the *Quartets* in its entirety
also enacts its statement. Its concluding poem, *Little Gidding,*

specifies the ultimate "purification of the motive," man's liberation from divisive and acquisitive selfhood that occurs in the commonalty of a love which (as Wordsworth had said of the "love more intellectual" in which "we begin and end") is more than human merely; and this moral triumph coincides with the artist's necessary detachment from worldly things. The "liberation" from "attachment to self and to things and to persons," says Eliot, lies in a love which is "not less of love but expanding/ Of love beyond desire." Then "all shall be well," and all men who, like the Englishmen in the civil wars, were once "united in the strife which divided them," will be "folded in a single party" (pp. 142–3). In the opening presentation of the rose garden in *Burnt Norton* it had been said that "What might have been and what has been/ Point to one end, which is always present." This end is at once the redemptive end of man, the end of the poet's spiritual journey in the return home, and simply, the end of the poem. As Eliot says in the concluding movement,

> The end is where we start from. And every phrase
> And sentence that is right (where every word is at home) . . .
> Every phrase and every sentence is an end and a beginning,
> Every poem an epitaph.[104]

Accordingly this last movement of the last quartet rounds back, in the circle of its evolution, to the rose garden at the beginning of the first quartet; the garden, however, is now for the first time recognized as the home and unitary simplicity from which in the beginning the poet had strayed. But the recognition of what was always there has now been triply earned: by the poet's journey of life, by his recollection of that life in this meditative exploration of its significance, and by the imaginative act of composing the poem itself.

> We shall not cease from exploration
> And the end of all our exploring
> Will be to arrive where we started
> And know the place for the first time.
> Through the unknown, remembered gate . . .
> The voice of the hidden waterfall

> And the children in the apple-tree
> Not known, because not looked for
> But heard, half-heard, in the stillness. . . .
> Quick now, here, now, always—
> A condition of complete simplicity
> (Costing not less than everything)
> And all shall be well.   (p. 145)

"The last of earth left to discover," Eliot remarks, "Is that which was the beginning" (p. 145). This figure, we know, had been the veriest commonplace by the time Kleist wrote in 1810: "Now paradise is bolted shut, and the angel stands behind us. We must journey around the world and see whether perhaps it is open again somewhere on the yonder side." Yet Eliot's is a remarkably inventive rerendering of the genre and *topoi* of the poet's circuitous journey through his remembered past, which ends in the recognition of the garden and home he had started from, is told in the manner of a double awareness, is preoccupied with what is permanent in passing time, incorporates the discussion of its own poetic, and (by returning at the end to its beginning) involves the process of its own composition. The conspicuous difference, of course, is that Eliot's version of the Romantic genre of the artist's self-formative progress is also a reversion to its Christian prototype, the Augustinian *peregrinatio vitae*.[105] Hence in the concluding movement on his own poetic art in *Little Gidding*, when the poet discovers and acknowledges his calling—"With the drawing of this Love and the voice of this Calling"—the word (with a punning allusion to the call of the bird to follow into the rose garden) fuses the derivative sense of the artist's vocation with its original religious meaning. And the simplicity of total reconciliation in the garden of our first world, a condition glimpsed as "hints and guesses" in epiphanies of "the moment in and out of time," turns on the sole event in time which signifies for Eliot (what the landscape below Simplon Pass had symbolized for Wordsworth) the coincidence of all oppositions:

> The hint half guessed, the gift half understood, is Incarnation.
> Here the impossible union
> Of spheres of existence is actual,

Here the past and future
Are conquered, and reconciled.   (p. 136)

My last example of the circuitous return is that put forward
by a recent poet-prophet, D. H. Lawrence, and I take his statement from his book *Apocalypse*. We thus conclude this ex-
cursus from Wordsworth's figure of the marriage between
mind and nature with a commentary on the primary source of
the figure, the Book of Revelation itself.

"We and the cosmos," Lawrence announces, "are one. The
cosmos is a vast living body, of which we are still parts. . . .
Now all this is *literally* true, as men knew in the great past, and
as they will know again." [106] Lawrence finds this circular pattern of history—which he opposes to our modern "idea of time
as a continuity in an eternal straight line"—in the pagan remnants which, he contends, show through the many distortions
imposed by Jewish and Christian redactors of the original text
of the Book of Revelation:

> The old method of the Apocalypse is to set forth the image,
> make a world, and then suddenly depart from this world in a
> cycle of time and movement and event, an *epos;* and then re-
> turn again to a world not quite like the original one, but on
> another level.   (pp. 87–8)

The Biblical fable of the fall of man signifies an historical
truth, man's falling-out of his original unity with the universal
all; and this event occurred at the onset of man's divisive
knowledge and self-consciousness. "It was not till the individual began to feel separated off, not till he fell into awareness
of himself, and hence into apartness; not, mythologically, till
he ate of the Tree of Knowledge instead of the Tree of Life,
and knew himself *apart* and separate, that the conception of a
God arose, to intervene between man and the cosmos" (p. 160).
The wages of such separation is the death of the component
parts, in a process which reached a crisis after the Reformation,
when Protestants and scientists "substituted the non-vital universe of forces and mechanistic order . . . and the long, slow
death of the human being set in" (p. 48). Modern, democratic,
economic men are thus only *"fragmentary* beings" in a society

held together primarily by a pecuniary relationship, whose inevitable failures in their attempts at individual fulfillment make them "envious, grudging, spiteful." The root of our civilized ills is our desperate clinging to the principle of self, which frustrates the redemptive principle of integration that Lawrence, like his Romantic predecessors, calls "love." "The individual *cannot* love," since "to yield entirely to love"— whether as *eros* or *caritas*—"would be to be absorbed, which is the death of the individual." "We *cannot bear connection*. That is our malady." But neither can we escape our indefeasible yearning for a resurrection which will be a return to total unity with ourselves, with other men, and with the natural world.

> What man most passionately wants is his living wholeness and his living unison. . . . We ought to dance with rapture that we should be alive and in the flesh, and part of the living, incarnate cosmos. I am part of the sun as my eye is part of me. That I am part of the earth my feet know perfectly, and my blood is part of the sea. My soul knows that I am part of the human race. . . .

> What we want is to destroy our false, inorganic connections, especially those related to money, and re-establish the living organic connections, with the cosmos, the sun and earth, with mankind and nation and family. Start with the sun, and the rest will slowly, slowly happen. (pp. 190, 196–200)

What Lawrence has done, in his unique and haunting rhetoric, is to revise the Scriptural account of the fall and apocalypse, as Blake had done before him, by accepting, as a literal truth of the imagination, the myth of the catastrophic division of the Primal Man who once did, and will again, incorporate heaven and earth and god and man—a myth from which the metaphysics, psychology, aesthetics, economics, and sociology of alienation has been an elaborate but, as human history goes, a quite recent derivative.

SIX

Revelation, Revolution, Imagination, and Cognition

I have long been convinced of the eventual omnipotence of mind over matter; adequacy of motive is sufficient to anything, & *my* golden age is when the present potence will become omnipotence: this will be the millenium of Xtians "when lion shall lay down with the lamb" tho' neither will it be accomplished to complete a prophesy, or by the intervention of a *miracle*.

Shelley (aged 19) to Elizabeth Hitchener

It is surely not difficult to see that our time is a time of birth and transition to a new period. The spirit has broken with what was hitherto the world of its existence and imagination. . . . This gradual crumbling which did not alter the physiognomy of the whole is interrupted by the break of day that, like lightning, all at once reveals the edifice of the new world.

—Hegel, Preface, *Phenomenology of the Spirit*

I answered. All that we saw was owing to your metaphysics.

Blake, *The Marriage of Heaven and Hell*

The astral and Shelleyan lights are not going to alter the structure of nature. Apples will always be apples, and whoever is a ploughman hereafter will be what the ploughman has always been. For all that, the astral and the Shelleyan will have transformed the world.

—Wallace Stevens, 27 August 1940

SIX

A PASSAGE near the opening of the Prospectus to *The Recluse* opens out an important dimension of Wordsworth's scheme for poetry. He will sing

> Of truth, of Grandeur, Beauty, Love, and Hope,
> And melancholy Fear subdued by Faith;
> Of blessèd consolations in distress. . . .

The opposing terms "fear" and "hope," "distress" and "consolation," have for Wordsworth a particular historical relevance. Their bearing on a central problem of his age is indicated in a letter Coleridge wrote to Wordsworth in September of 1799, probably only a year or so before Wordsworth drafted his Prospectus:

> My dear friend. . . . I wish you would write a poem, in blank verse, addressed to those, who, in consequence of the complete failure of the French Revolution, have thrown up all hopes of the amelioration of mankind, and are sinking into an almost epicurean selfishness, disguising the same under the soft titles of domestic attachment and contempt for visionary *philosophes*. It would do great good, and might form a part of "The Recluse." [1]

Wordsworth took this advice. In 1804 he recast and greatly expanded his manuscript of *The Prelude,* making the poem pivot on his experience of the French Revolution in order to show how he, as the exemplary poet "in these times of fear,/ This melancholy waste of hopes o'erthrown," had been restored in imagination and had succeeded in reconstituting the grounds for hope (II, 448 ff.). And he designed *The Excursion,* the central book of *The Recluse* proper, in order to demonstrate to his demoralized age, through the example of the Solitary—the representative Romantic intellectual who has been plunged into dejection and apathy by the failure of the Revolution—the way from "Despondency" to "Despondency Corrected."

Not only to Coleridge and Wordsworth but to most of their contemporaries, whether poets, philosophers, or social and political thinkers, the promise and tragedy of the French Revolution was a dominant, indeed an obsessive concern—"the master theme," Shelley called it, "of the epoch in which we live." [2] And after the succession of disasters that began with the Reign of Terror, many writers undertook to establish an alternative base for the hope in high human possibility that had been shattered by the course of events in France. In his Preface to *The Revolt of Islam* (1817), Shelley described the immediately preceding decades as "an age of despair." The Revolution had aroused in "every bosom" such expectations "of unmingled good as it was impossible to realize," and the revulsion from French excesses, atrocities, and successive tyrannies had been a "terrible" one. "Many of the most ardent . . . worshippers of public good have been morally ruined," so that "gloom and misanthropy" have "tainted the literature of the age" (including "metaphysics and inquiries into moral and political science," as well as "our works of fiction and poetry") with "the hopelessness of the mind from which it flows." Writing in this climate of despair, Shelley attributes to his *Revolt of Islam* an aim very like that with which Coleridge had charged Wordsworth almost two decades before. "It is," Shelley says, "an experiment on the temper of the public mind as how far a thirst for a happier condition of moral and political society survives among the enlightened and refined the tempests which have shaken the age in which we live." [3]

1. APOCALYPSE BY REVOLUTION

Wordsworth's *Prelude,* Coleridge wrote upon first hearing the completed poem, recounts the poet's response to the events in France,

> When from the general heart of human kind
> Hope sprang forth like a full-born Deity!

It goes on to tell "Of that dear Hope afflicted and struck down," but then of how the "Bard," after he had been "summoned homeward" to "the dread watch-tower of man's absolute self," had regained the power of "action and joy." [4] "Hope" and "joy," as against "despair" and "dejection," was a central and recurrent antithesis in Romantic poetry, and the reference is often, whether directly or derivatively, to the promise and failure of the French Revolution. We need to grasp the special nature of the hope evoked by the Revolution which, as Coleridge describes it, was sudden, universal, and absolute, in order to understand how cataclysmic was the collapse of that hope in the mid-1790's and later. In an essay on *The Poetical Talent of the Present Age* (1815), Thomas Noon Talfourd repeated a common observation—which has close parallels in statements by Hazlitt, Shelley, Francis Jeffrey, De Quincey, and other contemporary observers—when he claimed that the French Revolution was not only a political and social crisis but also an intellectual, moral, and imaginative one, and that this crisis interpenetrated and shaped the great new literature of the age:

> Every faculty of the mind was awakened, every feeling raised to an intenseness of interest, every principle and passion called into superhuman exertions. At one moment, all was hope and joy and rapture; the corruption and iniquity of ages seemed to vanish like a dream; the unclouded heavens seemed once more to ring with the exulting chorus of peace on earth and good-will to men; and the spirit of a mighty and puissant

nation . . . seemed rising in native majesty to draw new inspiration from the rejoicing heavens. The most brilliant hopes
were cherished . . . and fresh prospects were daily opening,
which . . . filled us with painful delight and with giddy rapture.

But "on a sudden all was changed" and the "sublime expectations were swept away" in "the terrible changes of this august
spectacle." And one immediate effect "of this moral hurricane,
this breaking up of the surface of society, this rending of the
general heart" was "to raise and darken the imagination," and
so to contribute "to form that great age of poetry which is now
flourishing around us." The Revolution, Talfourd says, "completed the regeneration of our poetry." [5]

The outbreak and easy initial successes of the French Revolution, hard upon the conclusion of the American Revolution,
shattered the limits of what had been thought to be humanly
possible and raised the hope that, after its long agony, the race
was at the point of entering upon enduring felicity in a renovated world.[6] As Southey said, even though he was looking
back upon his radical youth from the hard Toryism of his
middle age, "few persons but those who have lived" through
the Revolution "can conceive or comprehend . . . what a visionary world seemed to open upon those who were just entering it. Old things seemed passing away, and nothing was
dreamt of but the regeneration of the human race." [7] Southey's
phrasing, like Talfourd's, is theological; it brings out the likeness of the early revolutionary excitement to a religious movement and points to its component of explicit millennial hope.
In Catholic France the Revolution, conceived mainly in terms
of the rationalism of the Enlightenment, had been grounded on
a supposedly empirical science of history and of man, with the
result that apocalyptic interpretations of contemporary events
were confined largely to the Illuminists, who were the heirs of
the occult tradition of a coming transformation of man and
his world; [8] even in France, however, Volney's *The Ruins*
(1791) and Condorcet's *Progress of the Human Spirit* (1795)
expressed the confident expectation of an imminent, abrupt,
and total turn to perfection. Most English radicals, on the

other hand, were Protestant Nonconformists, and for them the portent of the Revolution reactivated the millennialism of their left-wing Puritan ancestors in the English civil war—expectations of an impending kingdom which for a time had been shared even by moderates such as Oliver Cromwell and John Milton. The Unitarian leaders Richard Price and Joseph Priestly (who combined the careers of chemist and preacher) led a chorus of prophets who invested the political events in France with the explosive power of the great Western myth of apocalypse, and so expanded a local phenomenon into the perfervid expectation that man everywhere was at the threshold of an earthly paradise restored. As Hazlitt described the mental temper of the early 1790's, in the recurrent contemporary metaphors, it was "that glad dawn of the day-star of liberty; that spring-time of the world, in which the hopes and expectations of the human race seemed opening in the same gay career with our own." [9]

In his *Excursion* Wordsworth modeled his description of the early career of the Solitary, the type of the revolutionary fellow traveler, on one of the most popular of these enthusiasts, Joseph Fawcett, who was both a Unitarian preacher and a poet. In expressing the response of the Solitary to the "unlooked-for dawn" of "a new world of hope" in France, Wordsworth set forth the turbulent expectations (compounded of elements from Isaiah, Revelation, and Virgil's fourth eclogue) of the English radicals of the day, himself included:

> The potent shock
> I felt: the transformation I perceived.
>   . . . I beheld
> Glory—beyond all glory ever seen,
> Confusion infinite of heaven and earth,
> Dazzling the soul. Meanwhile, prophetic harps
> In every grove were ringing, "War shall cease."
>   . . . The powers of song
> I left not uninvoked; and, in still groves,
> Where mild enthusiasts tuned a pensive lay
> Of thanks and expectation, in accord
> With their belief, I sang Saturnian rule
> Returned,—a progeny of golden years

> Permitted to descend, and bless mankind.
> —With promises the Hebrew Scriptures teem:
> . . . the glowing phrase
> Of ancient inspiration serving me,
> I promised also,—with undaunted trust
> Foretold, and added prayer to prophecy.
>
> (II, 210–18; III, 716–65)

As the reference to other tuneful enthusiasts indicates, this manic mood was shared by a number of English poets who were beginning their careers in the 1790's, and it had a vigorous recrudescence, a generation later, in young Percy Shelley. A similar mood was manifested in Germany, especially by Hölderlin, a theological student in a Protestant country which had its own strong and persistent tradition of chiliastic revolutionaries, and in which the current Pietist theology stressed eschatological violence and renewal.[10] These poets responded imaginatively to a common revolutionary experience, within a similar intellectual and theological climate of opinion, in ways that are notably parallel. Blake's *The French Revolution, Song of Liberty, America,* and *Europe,* Southey's *Joan of Arc,* Coleridge's *Destiny of Nations* and *Religious Musings,* Wordsworth's conclusion to *Descriptive Sketches,* Shelley's *Queen Mab,* and a number of Hölderlin's early odes resemble one another in subject, design, poetic voice, and a number of symbolic details. They are written in the persona of the visionary poet-prophet, "the Bard," who present, past, and future sees; they incorporate the great political events of their age in suitably grandiose literary forms, especially the epic and "the greater Ode"; they present a panoramic view of history in a cosmic setting, in which the agents are in part historical and in part allegorical or mythological and the overall design is apocalyptic; they envision a dark past, a violent present, and an immediately impending future which will justify the history of suffering man by its culmination in an absolute good; and they represent the French Revolution (or else a coming revolution which will improve upon the French model) as the critical event which signals the emergence of a regenerate man who will inhabit a new world uniting the features of a restored paradise and a recovered Golden Age.

The hard shocks delivered by the procession of events in France, England, and Europe led to recantation, or at least to disillusionment and growing fatigue, in all but a few of the most obdurate radicals. Even Joseph Priestly was daunted: "Melioration of mankind by means of political revolutions is, indeed, a noble subject of speculation . . . but, for my own part, I have only the *wish* left—the *confidence* is gone." [11] For most poets and intellectuals, the emotional reaction was equal to the inordinate early hope. In *The Prelude* Wordsworth described the intoxication of the early years of "hope and joy," when "Bliss was it in that dawn to be alive," with

> France standing on the top of golden hours,
> And human nature seeming born again.
>> (X, 690–3; VI, 353–4)

But his state of mind, as it "Gave way to over-pressure of the times/ And their disastrous issues," came to be that of

> Confusion of opinion, zeal decay'd
> And lastly, utter loss of hope itself,
> And things to hope for.
>> (XI, 47–8, 5–8)

W. H. Auden's wry comment on the course of events in his *New Year Letter* is factually accurate:

> Thus WORDSWORTH fell into temptation
> In France during a long vacation,
> Saw in the fall of the Bastille
> The Parousia of liberty . . .
> A liberal fellow-traveller ran
> With Sans-culotte and Jacobin,
> Nor guessed what circles he was in,
> But ended as the Devil knew
> An earnest Englishman would do,
> Left by Napoleon in the lurch
> Supporting the Established Church.

Herschel Baker has rightly said that Wordsworth's *Prelude* recorded "the spiritual biography of his generation." Auden, writing in 1940, reminds us that it also anticipated remarkably the spiritual biography of Auden's own generation, and mine:

> We hoped; we waited for the day
> The State would wither clean away,
> Expecting the Millennium
> That theory promised us would come,
> It didn't.[12]

For Wordsworth and his contemporaries, too, the millennium didn't come. The millennial pattern of thinking, however, persisted, with this difference: the external means was replaced by an internal means for transforming the world. Such a substitution had a precedent early in the Christian era when, the assurance of an immediate Second Coming having been disappointed, Biblical exegetes postponed the literal millennium to an indefinite future and interpreted the prophecies of an earthly kingdom as metaphors for a present and entirely spiritual change in the true believer. Sixteen hundred years later Milton turned from his frustrated hope that a literal Kingdom of God would emerge from the Puritan Revolution to the possibility of an earthly paradise in a different realm of being—the possibility of "A paradise within thee, happier far." [13] Romantic literature, however, differs from these theological precedents in that its recourse is from one secular means of renovating the world to another. To put the matter with the sharpness of drastic simplification: faith in an apocalypse by revelation had been replaced by faith in an apocalypse by revolution, and this now gave way to faith in an apocalypse by imagination or cognition. In the ruling two-term frame of Romantic thought, the mind of man confronts the old heaven and earth and possesses within itself the power, if it will but recognize and avail itself of the power, to transform them into a new heaven and new earth, by means of a total revolution of consciousness. This, as we know, is the high Romantic argument, and it is no accident that it took shape during the age of revolutions.

2. APOCALYPSE BY IMAGINATION

Writing in 1819 Shelley answered the charge of an anonymous reviewer that he had imitated Wordsworth in his *Revolt of Islam,* by claiming that the major poets of his day all derive

> from the new springs of thought and feeling, which the great events of our age have exposed to view, a similar tone of sentiment, imagery, and expression. A certain similarity all the best writers of any particular age inevitably are marked with, from the spirit of that age acting on all.[14]

Like a number of his contemporaries Shelley identified a distinctive "spirit" in the literature of the age and attributed this common quality mainly to the pervasive influence of the French Revolution. An essential attribute of this revolution, as a cultural influence, is that it was a revolution which had failed. The great Romantic works were not written at the height of revolutionary hope but out of the experience of partial or total disenchantment with the revolutionary promise. The striking fact is that a number of these works nonetheless retain, but translate into a different dimension of experience, the design, the ideas, and the imagery of the callower works their authors had composed in a mood of millennial excitement.

When Wordsworth published his *Descriptive Sketches* of 1793, describing his first walking tour in France and the Alps, he ended it with an oracular vision of the new earth that was to emerge from the violence and flames of the French Revolution. Very much like the poems which, in *The Excursion,* were attributed to his youthful Solitary, Wordsworth's passage fuses Virgil's fourth eclogue with echoes of Revelation and with the apocalyptic prophecy in 2 Peter 3:10–13 of the day in which "the earth . . . shall be burned up" and give way to "new heavens and a new earth."

> Tho' Liberty shall soon, indignant, raise
> Red on his hills his beacon's comet blaze . . .
> Yet, yet rejoice, tho' Pride's perverted ire

> Rouze Hell's own aid, and wrap thy hills in fire.
> Lo! from th' innocuous flames, a lovely birth!
> With it's own Virtues springs another earth:
> Nature, as in her prime, her virgin reign
> Begins, and Love and Truth compose her train;
> With pulseless hand, and fix'd unwearied gaze,
> Unbreathing Justice her still beam surveys:
> No more, along thy vales and viny groves . . .
> On his pale horse shall fell Consumption go.[15]

So late as 1808 news of the Spanish rising against Napoleon rekindled Wordsworth's millennial imaginings which, even in the sober vehicle of a political pamphlet, are expressed still in a union of Biblical and pagan allusion—Paul's prophecy of the events "at the last trump" in 1 Corinthians 15:52–3, and Virgil's anticipation of the return of the Saturnian reign:

> There was a mighty change . . . and from that moment the contest assumed the dignity, which it is not in the power of any thing but hope to bestow . . . from that moment "this corruptible put on incorruption, and this mortal put on immortality." . . .
>   Yes! . . . a bright appearance . . . emboldened the wise to say—We trust that Regeneration is at hand: these are works of recovered innocence and wisdom:
>> Magnus ab integro seclorum nascitur ordo;
>> *Jam* redit et Virgo, redeunt Saturnia regna;
>> *Jam* nova progenies coelo demittitur alto.[16]

My next example is a passage in *The Prelude* in which Wordsworth describes how, on his second sojourn in France in 1792, he had turned eagerly to "arguments of civil polity" and to plans for the "management of Nations"; that is, to drawing up blueprints for the post-revolutionary political and social order. He and his fellow schemers looked upon this coming order, he tells us, as the actuality in this life and world of what had earlier been myths and fantasies of human felicity. "O pleasant exercise of hope and joy!" when "the whole earth/ The beauty wore of promise," and schemers found

> Stuff at hand, plastic as they could wish,
> Were call'd upon to exercise their skill,

Not in Utopia, subterraneous Fields,
Or some secreted Island, Heaven knows where,
But in the very world which is the world
Of all of us, the place in which, in the end,
We find our happiness, or not at all.

(X, 660–728)

Wordsworth goes on to relate how the course of the Revolution, the war with England, his desperate efforts to rationalize these disasters, and finally "the utter loss of hope itself," had "impaired" his imagination. But after his imagination had been "restored," he seemed again "to have sight/ Of a new world." Now, however, this is neither the vision of a coming terrestrial paradise nor of a political order which will be the real equivalent to the myth of Elysium. This "new world" is simply the ordinary world of "life's every-day appearances," which has been renovated by the interplay of mind and nature in the act of perception itself—in Wordsworth's terms, by an "interchange/ Of action from within and from without" between "the object seen, and eye that sees" (XII, 368–79).

When through this perspective we reexamine Wordsworth's announcement in the Prospectus of the "Vision" which was to be the controlling idea of his great poetic undertaking, we recognize that this manifesto of his poetic maturity recapitulates but drastically alters Wordsworth's earlier millennial thinking. In the passage of *Home at Grasmere* that leads to the Prospectus, he had dismissed as wishful fantasies "all Arcadian dreams,/ All golden fancies of the golden Age" which are located "before all time, or are to be/ Ere time expire" (lines 625–32). Yet in the Prospectus itself, after a flourish of "thunder, and the choir/ Of shouting Angels, and the empyreal thrones" (echoed from God's proclamation in *Paradise Lost* of Christ's Second Coming, when "the World shall burn, and from her ashes spring/ New Heav'n and Earth" [17]), Wordsworth reintroduces the promise of a recoverable age of gold, whether conceived in pagan or in Christian terms:

Paradise, and groves
Elysian, Fortunate Fields. . . .
For the discerning intellect of Man,

When wedded to this goodly universe
In love and holy passion, shall find these
A simple produce of the common day.

Wordsworth, it is evident, has salvaged his earlier millennial
hope by a turn both from political revolution and from uto-
pian social planning to a process which, in the phrase from the
Prospectus, is available to "the individual Mind that keeps her
own/ Inviolate retirement." The recourse is from mass action
to individual quietism, and from outer revolution to a revolutionary mode of imaginative perception which accomplishes
nothing less than the "creation" of a new world. And this
re-creative way of seeing will perhaps in the course of time
become available to "the progressive power . . . of the whole
species." To proclaim this discovery is the task which, in the
closing passage of *The Prelude,* Wordsworth calls upon Coleridge to share with him, as "joint-labourers in a work/ Of
[men's] redemption." In an age of demoralization, they will
together teach this evangel of the power-in-union of "the
mind of man" and "the earth/ On which he dwells," which
(and the metaphor in this context is weighty) " 'mid all *revolutions* in the hopes/ And fears of men, doth still remain
unchanged" (XIII, 431–50).

As in Wordsworth, so in a number of his poetic contemporaries, preoccupation with a renovated world survived from
youth into maturity, and with a parallel shift in the agency
that would bring it about. We can follow this shift, for example, in the sequence of Coleridge's odes. His vatic *Religious
Musings,* first written in 1794, presents "a Vision" of all human
history, as it moves through evil to a "blest future" that will
match the delights of "Paradise." Coleridge specifies the event
that will effect this consummation in his prose argument: "The
present State of Society. The French Revolution. Millennium.
Universal Redemption. Conclusion." In both text and lengthy
footnotes the details of the Revolution are represented as fulfilling the violent prophecies of the apocalypse of St. John, and
the poem is climaxed by the trumpet announcing the new
earth, which is blown by Milton, the prophetic bard, in the

presence of three later interpreters of the Book of Revelation
—Isaac Newton, David Hartley, and Joseph Priestley:

> To Milton's trump
> The high groves of the renovated Earth
> Unbosom their glad echoes.[18]

Four years later, when Coleridge's lingering hope in the Revolution had been shattered by the French invasion of Switzerland, he wrote *France: An Ode,* originally entitled *The Recantation.* The hope and joy evoked by a "delivered France"
had aroused the expectation of a universal alteration, in which
"Love and Joy look round, and call the Earth their own." But
this was a vain dream; now the harsh lesson has been enforced
on him that liberty is not to be found "in forms of human
power," but only in the communion of the individual mind
with the "earth, sea, and air" of the natural world.[19] Four
years later still, in *Dejection: An Ode* (1802), Coleridge, like
Wordsworth in the Prospectus, adopted the marital figure
which signalizes the new earth and heaven in the Apocalypse,
but transferred the power of renovating the earth to an imaginative act of creative perception. Dejection and the failure of
"hope" have suspended his "shaping spirit of Imagination."
But if we are to behold anything higher than an "inanimate
cold world," we need to sustain the state of "joy," for joy

> is the spirit and the power,
> Which, wedding Nature to us, gives in dower
> A new Earth and new Heaven.

The poems of revolution which William Blake wrote in the
early 1790s expressed the millennial interpretation of the great
events in America and France which the author shared with
the religious radicals of his day, as well as with his fellow poets,
Wordsworth, Coleridge, and Southey. These poems announce
the impending dawn when "the happy earth" will "sing in its
course,/ The mild peaceable nations be opened to heav'n, and
men walk with their fathers in bliss." Orc, the spirit of human
desire which, under intolerable repression, breaks out into rev-

olutionary violence, proclaims the imminent consummation ("The times are ended . . . the morning 'gins to break") and the advent of an Isaian new earth: "For Empire is no more, and now the Lion and Wolf shall cease." [20] Or as he wrote in *The Marriage of Heaven and Hell* (Plate 3), referring to Biblical texts which prophesy "the day of the Lord's vengeance" and the redeemed world that is to follow (Edom signifies revolutionary France):

> A new heaven is begun. . . . Now is the dominion of Edom, & the return of Adam into Paradise; see Isaiah xxxiv & XXXV Chap.

As late as 1801 a short-lived peace with Napoleon seems to have revived Blake's hope for an earthly kingdom.

> The Kingdoms of this World are now become the Kingdoms Of God & his Christ, & we shall reign with him for ever & ever. The Reign of Literature & the Arts Commences.[21]

But the disastrous events that followed quickly destroyed whatever confidence he may still have retained in a literal millennium. "Many persons," he wrote in *A Vision of the Last Judgment* (1810)

> say . . . we will live in Paradise & Liberty. You may do so in Spirit but not in the Mortal Body as you pretend till after the Last Judgment . . . while we are in the world of Mortality we Must Suffer.

Yet, he proclaims in this same document, his argument continues to be that of the Golden Age restored in a renewal of the world. These things are to be accomplished, however, not by revolution but by the redemptive imagination—not as an enterprise of the revolutionary Orc but as the work of Los, who is the power of imagination in this fallen world and who, in his risen form, is Urthona, the power of the fully liberated vision:

> The Nature of my Work is Visionary or Imaginative; it is an Endeavour to Restore what the Ancients called the Golden Age. . . .

The Old Heaven & old Earth are passing away & the New Heaven & New Earth descending. . . .

Error or Creation will be Burned Up & then & not till then Truth or Eternity will appear.

Like Wordsworth in his early *Descriptive Sketches,* Blake alludes here to the prophecy in Peter of the last conflagration which will annihilate the old earth and make it anew. But this transformation, Blake goes on to say, is to be effected simply by a radical change of vision: "It is Burnt up the Moment Men cease to behold it." [22] There immediately follows that which marks off Blake's account from what, to Blake's thinking, was Wordsworth's all-too-naturalistic concept of a mode of vision which is to be effected by a union of the mind with the given world:

I assert for My self that I do not behold the Outward Creation & that to me it is hindrance & not Action it is as the Dirt upon my feet No part of Me.[23]

In Blake's *Four Zoas* and other prophecies, as we know, the basic myth is that of "the Universal Man" who has fallen into divided beings and a separate material world but will be restored to his primal unity. Blake, however, freely interchanges the forms and events of this myth with a correlative account of the fall as a catastrophic alteration in man's power of perception. From a flexible, "expanded," or imaginative mode of vision—capable both of seeing the one as many and the many as one, and all as human—man has lapsed into a fixed and "narrowed" mode of "single vision" by means of the physical eye alone, which sees reality as a multitude of isolated individuals in a dehumanized world. As Robert Gleckner puts it, "fragmented vision yields a fragmented humanity." [24] In man's unfallen state in Eden, as the Savior announces to Los in *Jerusalem,*

We live as One Man; for contracting our infinite senses
We behold multitude; or expanding: we behold as one,
As One Man all the Universal Family; and that One Man
We call Jesus the Christ.

Later we are told that "Jerusalem is cast forth from Albion"; or in Blake's alternative account of the fall in terms of man's contracted and divisive eyesight,

> The Visions of Eternity, by reason of narrowed perceptions,
> Are become weak Visions of Time & Space, fix'd into furrows
>   of death. . . .
> The Eye of Man, a little narrow orb, clos'd up & dark.

Accordantly, in the apocalypse which concludes *Jerusalem,* the recovery by the mythical man of his fourfold unity is equated with every individual man's recovery of his flexible, imaginative, and creative power of unifying vision, which once again sees all the world as "Human Forms identified," and is once again capable of distinguishing without dividing, alternately perceiving the many as a multeity-in-unity and the one as a unity-in-multeity. "And every Man stood Fourfold,"

>   rejoicing in Unity
> In the Four Senses in the Outline the Circumference &
>   Form. . . .
> And they conversed together in Visionary forms dramatic . . .
> Creating Space, Creating Time according to the wonders Divine
> Of Human Imagination.
>   . . . & every Word & Every Character
> Was Human according to the Expansion or Contraction, the
>   Translucence or
> Opakeness of Nervous fibres, such was the variation of Time &
>   Space
> Which vary according as the Organs of Perception vary, & they
>   walked
> To & fro in Eternity as One Man reflecting each in each &
>   clearly seen
> And seeing: according to fitness & order.[25]

Shelley's poetic career was a delayed instance of a parallel evolution of thought. His first long poem, *Queen Mab,* after a panoramic view of past and present human evils, ends in the preview of "A garden . . . / Surpassing fabled Eden," which is inevitable and imminent, and which exhibits the features of the earthly paradise in Biblical eschatology. "All things are re-created," and the lion "in the sun/ Beside the dreadless kid" dwells in a "Paradise of peace" on a "happy Earth, reality of Heaven," which is the "consummation of all mortal hope." [26] *Queen Mab,* however, was the work of a twenty-year-old poet; and Shelley, as he meditated upon what he called "the cause of the failure of the French Revolution," [27] came to the conclusion that political revolution, given the present moral and intellectual condition of mankind, merely brings back many old evils, and adds new ones as well. Shelley's imagination remained stubbornly apocalyptic, in the sense that his public works (as distinguished from many of his personal lyrics) continued to body forth the vision of a total and enduring transformation in man and his world; but he shifted the initiative and agency for this transformation from outer revolution to an inner revolution in man's moral, intellectual, and imaginative economy. Shelley worked this altered view (with ever diminishing assurance as to the certainty of its advent) into the long poems evoked by the later waves of revolution in Europe, including *The Revolt of Islam* (1817) and *Hellas* (1821). Writing as a member of the company of "bards," he described the latter work as his equivalent to the prophecies of Isaiah and Virgil. Such prophecies, he says, do not presume to predict an inevitable future but only to hold up before mankind "a period of regeneration and happiness" as a vision of "the possible and perhaps approaching state of society in which the *'lion shall lie down with the lamb,'* and 'omnis feret omnia tellus.' " [28]

Shelley's highest and most finished achievement in this bardic mode was *Prometheus Unbound* (1818). The drama crosses Greek myth with Christian chiliasm, but translates the coming of a literal millennium or Golden Age into terms of man's spiritual conversion into a new creature to whom, as Paul had said, old things are become new. Its climax is the transfiguration and reunion of Prometheus and Asia, the mythical event that signifies the transformation of the old world into a new world. Shelley presents the transformation itself from a double perspective. In causal historical terms, Shelley clearly indicates, man's moral conversion from self-concern and hate to imaginative fellow-feeling and love will liberate his full powers of scientific, technological, and artistic creativity, by means of which he will in the course of time remake his physical and social environment into a form adequate to human needs (III, iii. 47–56; IV, 164–5, 412–23). But Shelley's ruling figure for the advent of the renovated world is that of an instantaneous and radical alteration of sight: man's imaginative vision, suddenly liberated, penetrates to the inner forms, both of man and his world, which had been there all the time, beneath the veil. When the Spirit of the Hour (that is, of the apocalyptic hour) blows the last trump, the "foul masks" fall away, "and those/ From whom they passed seemed mild and lovely forms/ After some foul disguise had fallen" (III, iv. 44–69). "My vision," reports the Spirit, "grew clear," enabling him to see men and women as "gentle radiant forms," so changed that it "made earth like heaven" (III, iv. 104–60). "The painted veil . . . is torn aside;/ The loathsome mask has fallen" (III, iv. 190–3).[29] What Coleridge and Wordsworth had said in their metaphors of creative perception, Shelley, like Blake, puts in a dramatic form: man's outlook does not merely reflect but alters his world, so that it is the state of man's mind, after his recovery of "human love," which "makes all it gazes on Paradise" (IV, 127–8), just as it had all along been man's moral and imaginative astigmatism that had made him see his fair universe awry:

> Man . . . was a many-sided mirror,
> Which could distort to many a shape of error,
> This true fair world of things, a sea reflecting love.
> (IV, 382–4)

At the height of his intoxication with the promise of France, Hölderlin, like Coleridge, assumed an oracular persona, in odes which combined classical and Biblical imagery with grandiose personifications in the eighteenth-century sublime style, in order to proclaim that the revolutionary consummation of history is at hand. So in 1791, in his *Hymne an die Menschheit:*

> Endlich ist gelungen,
> Was in Aeonen keiner Kraft gelang—

Vom Grab' ersteh'n der alten Väter Heere . . .
Und zur Vollendung geht die Menschheit ein.

[Finally there has been achieved,
What through aeons no power achieved before—
The hosts of the ancient fathers arise from the grave . . .
And mankind enters upon its consummation.]

And in *Hymne an die Freiheit* (1792) the poet, inspired by joy, chants his vision of the original "paradise" of love, innocence, and freedom, which had long before been annihilated by a "curse," but stands on the verge of redemption by the Goddess Freedom, who (like Astraea in the pagan myth of the loss of the Golden Age) had abandoned the earth, but is now drawn back by the irresistible force of love. Now "begins the hour of the new creation," that long anticipated "consummation" in which "the ancient infamy is cancelled" and "the great day of the harvest begins." [30]

Hölderlin's romance *Hyperion,* which he wrote in the late 1790s, reflects the author's own experience, evoked by the course of the French Revolution, of transition from limitless hope to bitter disappointment. Diotima reveals to her young lover Hyperion that the shifting objects of his perfervid enthusiasm had all along been symbolic displacements for the one object of his ultimate desire: a new earth which will be a recovered Golden Age.

"Do you know, then," she went on in a stronger voice, "do you know what you are starving for, the one thing that you lack? . . . It is a better age that you are seeking, a more beautiful world. It was that world alone that you embraced in your friends. . . . It was no man that you wanted; believe me, you wanted a world. The loss of all the golden centuries . . . the spirit of all spirits of a better age—you wanted a single person, one man, to take their place for you." [31]

When Diotima persuades him to enter the life of action on behalf of his native Greeks, suffering under the "shameful power that weighs them down," Hyperion kindles to the vision of such a renovated earth, couched in Isaiah's figure of a marriage between men and the land: "For the Lord delighteth in thee, and thy land shall be married. For as a young man marrieth a virgin, so shall thy sons marry thee" (62:4–5; also 65:17). In Hölderlin's version this prophecy is translated into a marriage between rejuvenated men and nature:

> Let all be changed from its foundations! Let a new world sprout from the root of humanity! . . .
>
> Thou callest for men, Nature? . . . They will come, thy men, Nature! A rejuvenated people will make thee young again too, and thou wilt be as its bride, and the old union of spirits will renew itself with thee.
>
> There will be only one beauty, and man and nature will unite in one all-embracing divinity.   (III, 88–90)

In the attempt to effect such a world by force of arms, Hyperion plunges into Hölderlin's equivalent for the French Revolution, the Greek revolution against the Turks. When this millennial hope is shattered by the brutal reality of murder, plunder, and rapine perpetrated by his own revolutionary troops, and he is left totally alone by the death of his beloved Diotima, Hyperion falls into the apathy of despair. From this condition he recovers in those passages of experience when, confronting the natural scene, he is able to escape from the confines of his sole self into a union with nature as a bride. Only in such states of being, effected by an altered relation between the perceiving mind and its objects, does he achieve a renewal of the unitary world of peace and beauty that he has hitherto sought in vain.

> O blessed Nature! I know not how it is with me when I lift my eyes before thy beauty . . . the loved one before his beloved. . . . Lost in the wide blue, I often look up into the aether and down into the sacred sea, and it seems as though a kindred spirit were opening its arms to me. . . .
>
> To be one with all, that is the life of divinity, that is the heaven of mankind. To be one with all that lives, to return in blessed self-forgetfulness into the all of Nature, this is the peak of thoughts and joys . . . the place of eternal rest. . . . Death vanishes from the union of beings, and indivisibility and eternal youth bless, beautify the world.   (III, 8–9)

Hyperion cannot sustain these high moments, but Hölderlin implies that they hold out promise of development toward a more enduring approximation to an experiential paradise which is a produce of the common day.

Novalis' ardor for the French Revolution was of lesser intensity and shorter duration than Hölderlin's, but his writings continued to be almost obsessively concerned with the bringing into being of "a new world" which will constitute a recovered Golden Age. The vision of the poet-seer, Novalis indicates in his Fragments, portends the future experience of all mankind and demonstrates the power of imagination to effect a perceptual apocalypse by a process that he calls "magical idealism" or "the magic of imagination" [32]—phrases which indicate his characteristic fusion of current metaphysics and the operations of the Magus in Illuminist occultism. It is in this sense of man's power to redeem the world of standard experience by the triumph of imaginative vision that we are to interpret his comment that man "proclaims himself and his evangel of nature. He is the Messias of nature." [33]

We can end this survey with Carlyle, who had read his English predecessors and a number of the Germans as well. In *Sartor Resartus* the protagonist's sudden break-out from his spiritual crisis is represented as an inner apocalypse in which the regenerate man himself, in Carlyle's echo of Novalis, functions as "the Messias of Nature." "And I awoke," says Teufelsdroeckh, "to a new Heaven and a new Earth." [34] But the new earth is simply the old earth, which has been re-created by a substitution of the "Imaginative" faculty for "our Logical, Mensurative faculty," or "Understanding." Were "Thy eyesight unsealed," he cries, "then sawest thou that this fair Universe . . . is in very deed the star-domed City of God." [35] Writing in the early 1830's, Carlyle recapitulates the endeavor of a generation to sustain the hope for a New Jerusalem in this very world of all of us, but to bring it about not by changing the world, but by changing our world view. A later essay expresses the lowest common denominator of the high Romantic arguments: what "the Vates Poet" achieves, says Carlyle, is a "melodious Apocalypse of Nature." [36]

3. APOCALYPSE BY COGNITION

The imagination of the young German philosophers, no less than that of the young poets, had been captured by the vision of a new man in a new world which is not hereafter, and like the poets, they translated such expectations into the realm of mind in a mode that, adopting a phrase from Kant, we can call "philosophical chiliasm." ("One sees," Kant said, that "philosophy too can have its chiliasm . . . which is nothing less than visionary." [37]) Richard Kroner has commented on "the breathtaking speed" and "explosive character" of the development of post-Kantian Idealism, which was without parallel in the history of philosophy. "There passed through the epoch something of the breath of the eschatological hopes of the era of emergent Christianity; now or never must dawn the day of truth, it is near, we are called to bring it to being." [38] Philosophers at the time were aware of the parallel between their philosophical enterprise and apocalyptic expectation; they were aware, in addition, of the relation of this mood of philosophical chiliasm to the revolutionary spirit of their age.

Within a year after the fall of the Bastille the philosopher C. L. Reinhold asserted that "the most striking and distinctive characteristics of the spirit of our age [*von dem Geiste unsers Zeitalters*] is a convulsion of all hitherto known systems, theories, and modes of conception, of an inclusiveness and depth unexampled in the history of the human spirit." The varied manifestations of this spirit of drastic change can be viewed as "sure heralds of one of the grandest and most beneficial revolutions which has ever come to pass, alike in the intellectual and in the moral world." [39] "This convulsion," he says, "extends over all of European culture," and the passage of time will reveal the degree to which all the great political as well as spiritual events of the time, including "the North American, the French, and the Netherlandish revolutions . . . are effects of one and the same cause" (pp. 14–16). And just as some decades later Shelley, Hazlitt, and other Englishmen were to describe the great new literature as a manifestation of "the spirit of the age," and to explain that spirit primarily as a response to an era of revolution, so Reinhold describes and explains the revolution in philosophy which Kant inaugurated. In Germany the present "convulsion of modes of conception" manifests itself not in the form of external revolution but preeminently

> in the arena of knowledge [*auf den Feldern der Wissenschaften*], where its genesis in the power of thought, by virtue of which it is in the strictest sense a phenomenon of the spirit, is less ambiguous. [For] Germany, of all European countries, is most inclined to revolutions of the spirit, least inclined to political revolutions. (p. 16)

Four years passed before the appearance of the first major work of post-Kantian Idealism, Fichte's *Wissenschaftslehre* (1794). Fichte composed the work just after he had published two documents in defense of the French Revolution against the reaction aroused by its excesses. By Fichte's own testimony in a letter of 1795, the Revolution provided him with the intellectual model and the burst of psychic energy for conceiving his system, which is, in fact, no other than the equivalent of the political revolution in the realm of metaphysics:

> My system is the first system of freedom; just as that nation [the French] are tearing man loose from his outer chains, so my system tears him loose from the fetters of the *Ding an sich,* from any external influence, and establishes him in his first principle as an autonomous being. In those years when [the French] fought to win political freedom with external power, my system came into being by means of an inner fight with myself, against all rooted prejudices; not without their collaboration—it was their *valeur* which set my aim still higher and released that energy in me which was required in order to conceive it. In the process of writing about that Revolution, there came to me as though by way of reward the first hints and presentiments of this system.[40]

Very slowly and reluctantly Fichte yielded up his faith in the merit of the French people and the promise of their revolutionary enterprise, leaving the burden of effecting a new life in a new world to the realm of the spirit, in man's struggle to achieve freedom by a triumph of will and of cognition. As he said in his *Lectures* of 1806: "The True Life and its Blessedness" consists in the achievement of "the new world which rises before us" and "the new life which begins within us." This new life and world "consists in a union with the Unchangeable and Eternal; but the Eternal can be apprehended only by Thought, and is in no other way approachable by us. . . . And therefore a Doctrine of Blessedness can be nothing else than a Doctrine of Knowledge." [41]

Schiller wrote the first version of his letters *On the Aesthetic Education of Man* in 1793, during the Reign of Terror, as a contribution toward resolving what he saw as the crisis of modern civilization. Throughout the treatise the French Revolution and the drastic problems which it posed for European politics and culture are both the explicit and implicit frame of Schiller's reference. His systematic procedure is to internalize the political concepts and ideals, as well as the millennial hope of the Revolution, by translating them into mental, moral, and cognitive terms. "If man is ever to solve that problem of politics in practice," as Schiller explains his enterprise, "he will have to approach it through the problem of the aesthetic, because it is only through Beauty that man makes his way to Freedom." [42] His cardinal undertaking is to put the present crisis into the general context of the nature and evolution of man, so as to demonstrate that, although mankind has not gone far enough in his educational progress to be ready for the achievement of the highest political values by violent means, the "aesthetic state" offers him an alternative realm in which he can even now achieve the great revolutionary aims of liberty, equality, and fraternity. He sets out to demonstrate also that such an aesthetic state (since it incorporates moral and political norms) constitutes a necessary educational stage through which man must pass before he will be ready to achieve equivalent aims in the realm of politics. The resulting work, in its subtle deployment of an ever expanding range of reference, is, with Shelley's *Defence of Poetry*, our greatest general statement about the indispensable role of art and of imagination in achieving the highest values in life, civilization, and the modern political and economic state.

"Man," Schiller says, "has roused himself from his long indolence and self-deception and . . . is demanding restitution
of his inalienable rights."

> But he is not just demanding this; over there, and over here
> [*i.e.*, in the American and French Revolution], he is rising up to
> seize by force what, in his opinion, has been wrongfully denied
> him. . . . Vain hope! The moral possibility is lacking, and a
> moment so prodigal of opportunity finds a generation unpre-
> pared to receive it.   (p. 25)

In his concluding letter Schiller says that, in the midst of the
"kingdom of forces" and the "kingdom of laws" in this world,
the aesthetic impulse is silently at work "on the building of a
third joyous kingdom of play and of semblance, in which man
is . . . released from all that might be called constraint" (p.
215). Schiller's *drittes Reich,* as Professors Wilkinson and Willoughby point out (p. 296), is an unmistakable allusion to the
apocalyptic "third kingdom" which had been prophesied by
Joachim of Flora, that "new age" in which mankind will
achieve on earth the fullness of freedom, community, joy, and
intellect. Schiller denominates his third kingdom "the aesthetic
state." The constitution of this state—which is both a mental
state (the organization and free play of all the human faculties)
and the model for a new social order—Schiller defines, in large
part, by a sustained strategy of serious punning, through the
use of terms which are literal for politics and metaphorical for
aesthetics. Man must inaugurate this aesthetic state by a revolution of consciousness, for before he can liberate aesthetic
semblance from subordination to his utilitarian aims and
allow it "autonomous existence . . . a complete revolution
[*Revolution*] in his whole way of feeling is required" (p. 205).
And when it is fully achieved, "to bestow freedom by means
of freedom is the fundamental law of this kingdom." "No privilege, no autocracy of any kind, is tolerated where taste rules,
and the realm of aesthetic semblance extends its sway." The
aesthetic state is one of genuine fraternity (in that while "all
other forms of communication divide society . . . only the aesthetic mode of communication unites society"), as well as of
genuine liberty and equality; and it serves both as prelude and

model, in the course of mankind's long educational journey, for the achievement of the same ideals in all the practical spheres of his existence:

> The fetters of serfdom fall away from the lifeless and the living alike. In the Aesthetic State everything—even the tool which serves—is a free citizen, having equal rights with the noblest; and the mind, which would force the patient mass beneath the yoke of its purposes, must here first obtain its assent. Here, therefore, in the realm of Aesthetic Semblance, we find that ideal of equality fulfilled which the Enthusiast would fain see realized in substance.   (pp. 215–19)

Hegel, like his fellow students at Tübingen, Schelling and Hölderlin, followed with passionate involvement the early stages of the French Revolution. Looking back from his conservative later age, Hegel described in apocalyptic terms the excitement that this "world-historical" event had aroused:

> It was a glorious dawn. All thinking beings shared in the jubilation of the epoch. A sublime emotion ruled that age, an enthusiasm of the spirit thrilled through the world, as though the time were now come of the actual reconciliation of God with the world.[43]

Hegel himself had abandoned such millennial expectations long before he wrote his *Phenomenology of the Spirit* in 1807. In that account of the self-educative development of the spirit, the Revolution plays much the same role that it does in other spiritual histories of the time, including Hölderlin's *Hyperion* and Wordsworth's *Prelude*—and also Coleridge's account of the growth of a poet-critic's mind, his *Biographia Literaria*.[44] That is, in the *Phenomenology* the events of the Revolution and the Reign of Terror are translated into the major *crise de conscience* both of Hegel as an individual and of the collective mind of mankind. These events are the dark night of the Hegelian spirit, recovery from which sets it on the way toward fulfillment in the total discovery of its identity and destiny. The stage of the Revolution, Hegel says, is "spirit in the form of absolute freedom," the extreme point of the "interaction of consciousness with itself." Hegel adopted and greatly expanded the technique of multiple reference by serious punning which Schiller had developed in his *Aesthetic Education of Man;* and in Hegel's account of this stage of the spirit we recognize, translated into his special terminology and dialectic, the political and social ideals of the French Revolution, fused both with the description of the *dies irae* in the Biblical Apocalypse and with the Augustinian description of the inner war to the death between his two opponent selves. "In this absolute freedom all social classes . . . are annihilated," after which the destructive rage turns in against itself. For, Hegel declares, at this stage there is left for the spirit "only negative action; it is merely the fury of annihilation." "The sole work and deed accomplished by the universal freedom is therefore death." "All determinate elements disappear in the loss which the self experiences in its absolute freedom; its negation is meaningless death, the sheer horror of the negative." But this death is at the same time a rebirth, wherein the spirit breaks out of "the circle of necessity," in which it would otherwise be forced "continually to repeat and traverse anew" an eternally recurrent cycle of experience. Instead, at this crisis in its development, the "self-alienated spirit, driven to the acme of its opposition . . . reduces that opposition to its transparent form, and therein finds itself." [45]

At the conclusion of the *Phenomenology,* Hegel describes the stage which the evolving spirit has reached in his own philosophical work as one in which its "former being" has been "sublimated," in that it is "new-born out of knowledge," and so is a "new being, a new world and form of the spirit [*eine neue Welt und Geistesgestalt*]" (p. 564). And in the Preface to this book, he makes explicit the reference of his figure of the *neue Welt* to his own revolutionary age:

It is surely not difficult to see that our time is a time of birth and transition to a new period. The spirit has broken with what was hitherto the world of its existence and imagination and . . . is at work giving itself a new form . . . dissolving one particle of the edifice of its previous world after another. . . . This gradual crumbling . . . is interrupted by the break of day that, like lightning, all at once reveals the edifice of the new world.[46]

But the glad dawn of this new world which at a stroke replaces the old world is an apocalypse not of revolution but of cognition; for this event is the philosophy of Hegel's era, culminating in Hegel's own *Wissenschaft,* in which evolving consciousness at last comes to recognize everything it knows as its own absolute self. At the conclusion to his *History of Philosophy* Hegel describes this consummation, in his characteristic mode of oblique allusiveness, as the historical truth embodied in the apocalyptic kingdom which had been prophesied in the image-language of Biblical eschatology:

> A new epoch has arisen in the world. It appears that the world-spirit has now succeeded in stripping off from itself all alien objective existence and in apprehending itself at last as absolute spirit. . . . The war of the finite self-consciousness against the absolute self-consciousness, in which the latter seemed to the former to exist outside of itself, now comes to an end. . . . This is the total history of the world in general up to the present time, and the history of philosophy in particular, of which the sole work is to portray this war. Now, indeed, it seems to have reached its goal. . . .
>
> I have tried to develop and to bring before your thoughts this series of the spiritual forms of philosophy in its progress, and to indicate the connection between them. This series is the true Kingdom of Spirits [*Geisterreich*], the only Kingdom of Spirits that there is.[47]

The only kingdom is a cognitive kingdom of this world, and it is a peaceable kingdom which brings to an end all the wars of consciousness in a victory of absolute knowledge. "It is my desire," Hegel exhorts his audience, "that this history of philosophy shall hold for you a challenge to grasp the spirit of the age [*den Geist der Zeit*] and, . . . each in his own place, conciously to bring it into the light of day." We recognize the revolutionary "spirit of the age" that Reinhold, Shelley, and Hazlitt also identified. We recognize also the displacement of revolution from the field of battle to the field of what Blake, in the concluding lines of *The Four Zoas,* called "intellectual

War," whereby the reign of religion gives way to the kingdom of ultimate knowledge: "The war of swords departed now/ The dark Religions are departed and sweet Science reigns."

In the Preface to his treatise, *On the Ego as the Principle of Philosophy* (1795), young Friedrich Schelling declares that his philosophy aims "not merely at a reform of knowledge [*Wissenschaft*], but at a total reversal of its principles; that is to say, it aims at a revolution [*Revolution*] of knowledge." And such a revolution will not be restricted in its influence to philosophy proper, but will transform the conditions of human life and action. For the cognitive revolution undertakes nothing less than "to liberate mankind and to eliminate the fear of the objective world"; it "sets up as its first principle the claim, that the essence of man subsists entirely in absolute freedom." If the "spirit of the age" is a timorous one, such a philosophy can hope to make but little headway.

> But it would be a despair unworthy of philosophy if it did not hope, by the great new course on which it is itself setting out, also to point out to the human spirit a new road . . . to give courage and inner strength to bruised and battered spirits, to shock those who are slaves of objective truth by the presentiment of freedom, and to teach man . . . that he can save himself only by the unity of his mode of action and by the strict pursuit of his principles.

The course of human history is from unity as a "regulative" idea at its beginning to unity as "a constitutive law" at its end; and this course is a circuitous one, in which man, who has been divided, will be reunited: all the "varied ways and byways, through which the human race has passed up to the present time, will ultimately run together in a single point, at which mankind will again gather itself together and, as a single perfected person, will again obey the same law of freedom." Schelling hints that this glad new day of liberated, reintegrated, and perfected man awaits its philosophical Messiah, for whom he himself serves as a philosophical John the Baptist:

> If there is a light of dawn, the sun cannot be far behind. Actually to bring about this more beautiful day of knowledge

[*Wissenschaft*] is a deed reserved for very few—perhaps only for one man—but may it nonetheless be granted to the individual, who has a presentiment of the coming day, to rejoice in it by anticipation.

A passage that Schelling wrote later, in 1804, differentiates the consummation to which his philosophy points both from progressive and millennial theories of history:

The sudden awareness, after long groping about, that one has eternity within himself, is like a sudden clarification and illumination of consciousness, which we can explain only by reference to the Eternal, that is to God Himself. . . . Nothing is farther from this way of thinking than the restless striving . . . of so many men who wish to precipitate the progress of mankind. . . .

The philanthropic ideas of a future golden age, of an eternal peace, etc., for the most part lose their meaning from this point of view. The golden age . . . is to be sought, not by an endless and restless progress and external activity, but rather by a return to that point from which each of us has set out—to the inner identity with the Absolute. . . . This will not be a gradual progress, it will be the true revolution [*Revolution*], the idea of which is utterly different from that which has been called by that name.[48]

That is, the pilgrimage and quest of mankind has been internalized; and the Golden Age will be achieved not by gradual progress but abruptly, and not by outer political action but by a radical transformation of consciousness, in a process which is a "revolution" in the sense that it is a circuitous return of consciousness to the unifying vision from which it had originally departed.

4. THE POLITICS OF VISION: MASTERY, SERVITUDE, AND FREEDOM

A central and persistent concern of Wordsworth's *Prelude* is to investigate the cardinal value he calls "genuine freedom," which he opposes to the state of mastery, tyranny, thraldom, and servitude—a mastery exerted by the physical eye and its material objects, which hold in servitude the perceiving mind. Inquiry into the background and rationale of this Wordsworthian *topos* introduces a prominent aspect of the role of contemporary political concerns in Romantic thought and imagination. In the folklore which has accumulated around Romantic literature, it has been a frequent claim that Romantic writers evaded the political and social crises of their era by ignoring them, or by escaping into a fantasy world. Wordsworth in fact insisted, with only moderate exaggeration, that he "had given twelve hours thought to the conditions and prospects of society, for one to poetry," [49] and he, together with most of his fellow poets, delivered himself of direct commentaries and exhortations on the great affairs of his day, both in prose and in verse. Moreover, many of the major philosophical and imaginative works are permeated with political and social issues; what obscures this fact is that these issues are often submerged, manifesting their presence only by indirection and allusion. A striking example is the degree to which the key concepts in the political theories of the Enlightenment, together with the events and the ideals of the French Revolution—equality, fraternity, and above all liberty—are transposed into nonpolitical areas, as metaphors of mind which pervade the discussion of perception, intellection, and imagination.

I have already pointed out that Schiller's letters *On the Aesthetic Education of Man* are a sustained equivoque on political states and states of the human mind. Many other writings of the period, literary as well as philosophical, manifest a similar metaphoric duplexity, in a procedure that differs from Schiller's *Aesthetic Letters* in degree rather than in kind. This subject is huge in scope, and I shall merely touch upon the role of political power-metaphors in Romantic treatments of the relation between subject and object, mind and nature, in the primary cognitive act of perception. And since in these writers sight is the primary sense and serves as paradigm for all other modes of sense perception, I have borrowed for this section Mark Schorer's apt subtitle for his book on William Blake, "The Politics of Vision."

A notable document in this development is Fichte's *Wissenschaftslehre*. I have already cited Fichte's letter of 1795, which testifies that the essential idea of his philosophy came to him while he was writing a defense of the French Revolution, and that his system, as "the first system of freedom," is the epistemological equivalent of that external Revolution, in that it tears man "loose from the fetters of the *Ding an sich,* from any external influence, and establishes him in his first principle as an autonomous being." To Fichte's view of the mind in its primal act of knowing, any entity or condition which is external to and independent of the mind's own constitution and activity—even Kant's stripped-down postulate of an unknowable *Ding an sich*—is an insupportable limitation which must be metaphysically eliminated if man is at last to come into his estate of essential freedom.

His own system, as Fichte says, "is from beginning to end no other than an analysis of the concept of freedom." [50] The absolute ego (which manifests itself through all individual egos, or consciousnesses) is "an act" which brings into being the non-ego, merely that the latter may serve as a field of resistance, an opposing limit and set of forces for the ego to strive against. The "opposition" between subject and object is thus not only a logical opposition but also a dynamic one. As Fichte puts it, an "object" [*Gegenstand*] means something which is set over against us, and that which is against us is in opposition [*Widerstand*] to us. Throughout Fichte's system, accordingly, the relation of the ego to the non-ego is couched in metaphors of *Machtpolitik*—a power language of challenge, conflict, and the struggle for mastery between two hostile forces—in which the ego cannot rest content short of achieving absolute freedom, in the conquest and annihilation of the adversary which it has itself set up. Here, however, the ego is faced with a dilemma, for to gain total victory over the non-ego would be to eliminate the antagonist against which the ego must continue to strive if it is to realize itself. Fichte solves this dilemma by representing the activity of the ego as an *unendliches Streben* against the non-ego, or "nature," toward an ever approachable but never-quite-achievable victory. As he summarized his view in *The Vocation of the Scholar:*

To subjugate [*unterwerfen*] all non-rational nature to himself,
to rule over it [*es zu beherrschen*] freely and according to his
own law, is the ultimate goal of man—an ultimate goal which
is utterly unattainable. . . . His way to it must be endless . . .
and therefore his true vocation as *man,* that is as a rational
but finite and as a sensuous but free being, is to approximate
this goal unto infinity.[51]

Such terms as master and servant, or liberty and bondage,
in spiritual as well as in literal applications, are common in
the Bible. And the detailed representation of man's mind as
the analogue to a political organization is as old as Plato, in
whose *Republic,* as Coleridge remarked, "the perfect frame of
a man is the perfect frame of a state." [52] In his moral discourses
Plato often applied the terms "master" and "slave" metaphorically, to represent the soul, or mind, as the lord and master
which ought properly to rule the body as its slave, since the
body is the locus of the passions and the sensuous pleasures,
which distract the soul from the good.[53] In accordance with
both Biblical and classical precedents, it became entirely traditional in Western moral philosophy to import from the social into the moral order of experience the contraries of freedom and submission, mastery and servitude, in reference to
the act of the human will in choosing between the good and
the bad, and also in reference to the relation of man's mind
and reason to their opponent powers, man's "natural" passions
and appetites and the solicitations of his bodily senses. In addition, with the emergence of the new science in the Renaissance, it became common to speak of man, or of the human
mind, as undertaking to "control" or "master" nature by
means of scientific knowledge and technology; as Bacon had
put this relationship, man must learn to obey nature before
he can be her master. Fichte incorporates these various applications, moral and intellectual, in representing the master-servant relation between the ego and the other. But he also goes
much further, for he extends the concept to the total stance of
man in the world, and includes the primary act of the mind
by which it comes to know the outer world. In Fichte, accordingly, the basic relation of mind to nature, even in the process
of perceiving nature, is one of irremissive conflict, the striving

to win mastery over an antagonist. This is the metaphysical attitude Coleridge had in mind when, in his *Biographia Literaria*, he described Fichte's system as "a crude egoismus, a boastful and hyperstoic hostility to NATURE, as lifeless, godless, and altogether unholy." [54]

In the treatise on the French Revolution that he published in 1793, Fichte had grounded his inquiry into "the basic right of property generally, and of landed property in particular," on the principle that

> originally we are ourselves our own property. No one is our master [*Herr*], and no one can become our master. We carry our charter of freedom, given and sealed by God, deep in our bosom. He himself has set us free and said: "from now on be no one's slave [*Sklave*]." [55]

In the metaphysical writings that followed, Fichte translated this social class-relation of master and slave into a metaphor for the normative relationship between subject and object, man and nature. Against the apparent demonstration by logic that man, in will and action, is entirely subject to the alien laws of nature, he sets forth, as the ground on which he rests his contrary argument, the demand of the ego: "I will be the master [*Herr*] of nature; and she shall be my servant [*Diener*]; I will have an influence over her according to the measure of my power, but she will have no influence over me." And even when we shall all achieve "the goal of our earthly life," in that future state of universal and enduring peace in which "selfish aims no longer have the power to divide mankind and to cause them to wear out their own powers in mutual conflict," men will join together and "turn their united might against the single common opponent [*Gegner*] remaining to them—brute, resisting nature." [56]

Friedrich Hölderlin, who like many of his young contemporaries studied ardently Fichte's bold construction of an absolute idealism, followed Fichte's lead by applying metaphors of conflict, and of the societal class-relationship which Hölderlin calls "mastery and servitude," to the cognitive relation of the mind to the outer world. Hölderlin, however, altered drastically Fichte's concept of the ideal power-relationship between mind and nature. In Hölderlin's Preface to the version of *Hyperion* which he composed in 1795, the highest, never quite attainable, human aim is not to subjugate nature, but to return, on a higher level, to that unity of the self and nature from which civilized man has departed. The ultimate state of enduring peace after conflict, as Hölderlin represents it, is thus a union of ontological equals:

> We have fallen out with nature, and what was once one . . . is now in conflict with itself, and each side alternates between mastery and servitude [*Herrschaft und Knechtschaft*]. Often it appears to us as though the world were everything and we nothing, but also often as though we were everything and the world nothing. . . .
>
> To end that eternal conflict between our self and the world, to restore that peace that passeth all understanding, to unite ourselves with nature so as to form one endless whole, that is the goal of all our striving . . . although one that is achievable only in infinite approximation.[57]

And in other early versions of *Hyperion*, Hölderlin deploys a rich variety of social and political metaphors and power terms to characterize both the malaise and well-being of the mind in its perceptual and cognitive, as well as in its practical and moral, relations to nature. For example:

> The school of fate and of custom had made me, although innocently, unjust and tyrannical against nature. The total unbelief which I entertained with respect to everything that I received from her hands permitted no love to flourish in me. I believed that the pure free mind [*Geist*] could never be reconciled with the senses and their world, and that no joys were possible except those of victory. Angrily I often demanded from fate the return of the original freedom of our being; I often took joy in the conflict that the reason wages with the non-rational, because secretly it mattered more to me to win in victory the feeling of superiority than to impart the beauty of unity to the lawless powers that agitate the human breast. . . . I did not accept the readiness with which nature offers reason her hands, for I wanted to be her master [*sie beherrschen*].

"At the very point," he writes, "at which the beautiful world came into being for us, when we achieved consciousness, did we become finite"; the result is that "we feel deeply the restraint upon our being, and our fettered power struggles impatiently against its chains." The risk, as he says in an implicit rectification of Fichte's basic metaphysical attitude, is that "embittered over the resistance of nature, we fight against her not in order to establish peace and unity in her, hence between her and the divine element in us, but instead in order to annihilate her; and in this way we tear asunder the beautiful bond which unites us to other minds and transform the world around us into a desert." [58] It would follow that the contrary psychic action, the reconciliation between the self and nature as a union of equals, will bind all minds into a social confraternity and effect the perceptual transformation of the desert into a garden.

The famed section of Hegel's *Phenomenology of the Spirit* on *Herrschaft und Knechtschaft* derives in part from Fichte and in part, no doubt, from Hegel's friend Hölderlin as well. In one stage in the evolution of consciousness, two self-conscious beings confront one another and "prove themselves and each other by means of a life and death struggle." The opponent that is weaker in purpose and in daring succumbs, so that "one becomes the master, the other the servant." But a master who, by his very nature, is dependent upon a servant is not truly free, and in the course of things there inevitably ensues an ironic reversal of relationship in which the condition of "servitude, when completed, passes into the opposite of what it immediately is" by "reversing itself into the condition of true independence." That is, the servant becomes the freeman because, unlike his idle master, he has the function of working upon the resisting external world and shaping it into enduring objects in which he recognizes his own reflection: "the working consciousness arrives by this means to the awareness of the independently existing being as itself." [59]

Hegel's primary reference in this section is to the relations between individuals and between the master class and the servant class in the social and economic order. His dialectical treatment of these relations suggested to Marx the central concept of his materialist dialectic: the *Communist Manifesto* begins, "The history of all hitherto existing society is the history of class struggles. Freeman and slave, patrician and plebeian, lord and serf . . . oppressor and oppressed—." But Hegel's *Phenomenology* is persistently polysemantic, with a sustained inner as well as outer reference, so that the altering master-servant relationship also defines a necessary stage in the cognitive and moral development both of the collective minds of men and of each individual human mind, on the long educative journey toward a consummation of consciousness. And this spiritual course, Hegel discloses, is in fact the evolution toward realization of the idea of perfect freedom. Thus Hegel brings his *Lectures on the Philosophy of History* to their conclusion, after discussing the abortive attempt by the French to achieve freedom by violent outer revolution, with the achievement of genuine freedom in the absolute self-knowledge of the thinking and perceiving mind:

> Philosophy is concerned only with the gleam of the Idea which mirrors itself in world-history. . . . Her interest is, to recognize the evolutionary course of the self-realizing Idea; and this, indeed, is the Idea of freedom, which is nothing other than consciousness of freedom. That the history of the world is this evolutionary course and coming to realization of the spirit . . . this is the true theodicy, the justification of God in history.[60]

A striking phenomenon in literary history is the degree to which English writers, collaterally with their German contemporaries, imported such societal terms as "conflict," "mastery," "tyranny," "submission," "slavery," "equality," and "freedom" into the cognitive realm, to represent the relations between the mind and the natural world, or between the mind and the physical senses, in the act of perception. William Blake wrote *A Song of Liberty* at the height of his millennial expectation from the French Revolution; but after he had lost this faith, he incorporated the events of the revolution and its aftermath of wars, reaction, and tyranny into the mythical forms and actions of his Prophetic Books. Blake applies the concepts of liberty and servitude to all aspects of human experience, but especially to the domain of sight and vision. The primal division within the human mind leads at once to a sustained struggle for dominance among its component faculties. Urizen, the isolated and self-centered reason, representing the stance of the natural scientist, says to Los, "Lo these starry hosts/ They are they servants if thou wilt obey my awful Law." To which Los, the fallen imaginative power, replies: "If you are such Lo! I am also such./ One must be master. Try thy Arts I also will try mine." [61] The achieved mastery of Urizen is correlative with a drastic change in human perception—a shrinking of "all the vast of Nature . . . / Before their shrunken eyes," and a "binding" of men "more/ And more to Earth: closing and restraining," to the point at which man's submission to the "Philosophy of Five Senses was complete." [62] The reintegration and harmonious ordering of the mental faculties, as we know, marks the liberation of that freely expansive, or "multiple," vision which delivers to human consciousness a new world which is the free state of the mind that Blake calls the New Jerusalem. "In Great Eternity," Blake says, "the Form is the Divine Vision. . . . This is Jerusalem in every Man . . . / And Jerusalem is called Liberty among the Children of Albion." [63] Similarly, in Shelley's *Prometheus Unbound* the central myth represents a conflict within the mind between the tyrant-power and its victim, whose enslavement results in the perception of distorting fantasies in place of reality; thus the victory of Prometheus over himself is manifested simultaneously in the annulment of the divisive passions of hate and vengefulness and in the emancipation of man's vision from the distortions it had imposed on the world.

Coleridge and Wordsworth embody their politics of vision in the metaphors with which they describe man's relation to the world that he sees, and both poets identify the failure of the revolutionary aims in France as the occasion which had caused them to transfer their quest for freedom from revolution and wars of liberation to the mind's experience in perception. This radical shift of reference is itself the subject of Coleridge's *France: An Ode*, the "Recantation" or "Palinodia" of his revolutionary enthusiasm [64] which he wrote early in 1798, before he had read German philosophy. The resolution of this poem is intelligible only if we recognize that it turns on the conversion of the political concepts, slavery and liberty, into metaphors of the mind in its relation to nature.

The *Ode* opens with an invocation to the clouds, waves, forests, sun, and sky, "imperious" elements of the natural scene which, since they "yield homage only to eternal laws," and so are independent of all "controul" outside their own being, serve as the type of "every thing that is and will be free"; they are thus qualified to "bear witness" to the poet's unintermitted worship of "the spirit of divinest Liberty." "When France in wrath her giant-limbs upreared,/ . . . and said she would be free," he had vested in her and her "tyrant-quelling lance" his hopes of universal liberty; and even through the British war against France and the Reign of Terror, he had sustained his faith in the imminence of a new earth of freedom, love, and joy. "Soon," I said,

> Conquering by her happiness alone,
> Shall France compel the nations to be free,
> Till Love and Joy look round, and call the Earth their own.

But now France has herself invaded Switzerland, in a war of conquest directed against the "bloodless freedom of the moun-taineer," and this event has finally brought him to recognize that freedom cannot be won or imposed by external power, and that revolution by a people who are perceptually enslaved— that is, whose minds are confined by the limits of their own physical senses—merely replaces slavery by slavery.

> The Sensual and the Dark rebel in vain,
> Slaves by their own compulsion! In mad game
> They burst their manacles and wear the name
> Of Freedom, graven on a heavier chain!
> O Liberty! . . .
> But thou nor swell'st the victor's strain, nor ever
> Didst breath thy soul in forms of human power.

The poem closes in an exemplary Romantic situation: the speaker alone on a windy cliff, fronting the open landscape, and experiencing essential liberty in the power of his being to unite

with, and so to repossess, the scene before him, in an act of
enfranchised perception which is an act of spontaneous love:

> And there I felt thee!—on that sea-cliff's verge . . .
> Yes, while I stood and gazed, my temples bare,
> And shot my being through earth, sea, and air,
> Possessing all things with intensest love,
> O Liberty! My spirit felt thee there.

In his later writings Coleridge, much like Blake, came to
identify that condition in which the mind is a slave and the
physical eye its master—the inner state that he called the
"despotism of the eye," or "the despotism of outward impressions," or the "Slavery of the Mind to the Eye and [to] the
visual Imagination, or Fancy" [65]—as the index and prime
cause of the intellectual, moral, political, and aesthetic errors
of post-Lockean sensationist philosophy. Coleridge's position is
entirely different from what he called Fichte's "hyperstoic hostility to nature"; his aim is the mastery of the mind not over
nature, but over that minimal physical thing, abstracted from
the living totality of nature, which is all that is perceptible to
the sensuous eye, and which constantly threatens to enslave
the mind and to inhibit the free play of the imagination
and other faculties. By an abuse of the abstractive function of
"his understanding and fancy," which plays a necessary, but
properly limited role in "experience and intellectual growth,"
man is tempted "to break and scatter the one divine and invisible life of nature into countless idols of the sense," and so
"is himself sensualized, and becomes a slave to the things of
which he was formed to be the conqueror and sovereign"; of
this mastery of the mind by the eye, the results are "selfishness,
hate and servitude." The beginning of genuine freedom, therefore, is to break free from the tyrant eye: "to emancipate the
mind from the despotism of the eye is the first step towards its
emancipation from the influences and intrusions of the senses,
sensations and passions generally." [66]

We return to Wordsworth's dialectic of freedom and servitude. In the Prospectus to his major poetry Wordsworth, having announced his argument of the creation which the mind

and the external world "with blended might/ Accomplish,"
invokes the "prophetic Spirit" to "nurse/ My Heart in genuine freedom." The role of freedom is no less salient in Wordsworth's *Prelude* than it is in the metaphysics of German Idealism, for it serves as a principal thematic element in his education as a poet: his early achievement of freedom, his error in
looking to the wrong means for universalizing freedom, his fall
into servitude, his gradual recovery of freedom, and his discovery of what genuine freedom is.[67] *The Prelude* in fact begins, as Coleridge's *France: An Ode* concludes, with the poet
alone in an open landscape, blown upon by the wind and
chanting a paean to liberty regained:

> A captive greets thee, coming from a house
> Of bondage, from yon City's walls set free,
> A prison where he hath been long immured.
> Now I am free, enfrancis'd and at large.
>   . . . With a heart
> Joyous, nor scar'd at its own liberty,
> I look about. . . .
> Enough that I am free.   (I, 6–33)

The "bondage," of which the nameless city is the figural type,
has been spiritual rather than physical—"'tis shaken off,/ That
burden of my own unnatural self"—and his liberated spirit
can now respond to the outer breeze by "a corresponding mild
creative breeze" which is inspiration, its power of poetic
creativity.

Throughout *The Prelude* freedom and bondage (together
with a variety of synonymous and related words) are key references in Wordsworth's narrative of the growth of his mind
through perception, and are used to represent a complex evolution in the relation of his mind to its senses and to the outer
world. The base is established in the "infant sensibility" of
the babe in his mother's arms who, since he perceives a world
altered by a pervasive awareness of his mother's love, inhabits
an "active universe" that his mind has in part created, in a
perceptual alliance of inner and outer powers. His mind, that
is,

> Creates, creator and receiver both,
> Working but in alliance with the works
> Which it beholds.—Such, verily, is the first
> Poetic spirit of our human life.
>
> (II, 255–76)

In later youth he retained this "first creative sensibility," so that his soul remained "unsubdu'd" by the "regular action of the world," and his perception continued to be an activity in which his mind and outer objects freely interchanged the roles of master and servant. As Wordsworth puts it, although his "plastic power" was at times "rebellious," it was for the most part "subservient strictly to the external things/ With which it commun'd," and the external things in their turn, irradiated by the "auxiliar light" shed by his mind, "obey'd/ A like dominion" (II, 377–92). And in describing his retention of this sensibility during his college years, Wordsworth identifies the power to sustain the alliance and reciprocative action between the mind and the world as, in its essential sense, freedom:

> For hither I had come with holy powers . . .
> To apprehend all passions and all moods
> Which time, and place, and season do impress
> Upon the visible universe, and work
> Like changes there by force of my own mind.
> I was a Freeman; in the purest sense
> Was free, and to majestic ends was strong.
>
> (III, 83–90)

The experience which shattered the free and creative play of his mind in perception was his error in fixing upon an external political means, the French Revolution, his hopes for achieving universal freedom and equality. The disastrous course of outer events, and especially the war between England and France, reenacts itself, metaphorically, in the "change," "subversion," "shock," "revolution," and "war" which take place within the precinct of his mind:

> Not in my single self alone I found,
> But in the minds of all ingenuous Youth,

Change and subversion from this hour. No shock
Given to my moral nature had I known
Down to that very moment; neither lapse
Nor turn of sentiment that might be nam'd
A revolution, save at this one time,
All else was progress on the self-same path.

(X, 232–9)

"Thus strangely," he later recapitulates, "did I war against myself" (XI, 74). And when his "natural graciousness of mind" —the harmonious order and interplay of "intellectual power," "love," "joy," and "imagination"—"gave way to over-pressure of the times/ And their disastrous issues," the immediate result of this crack-up was a conflict of the faculties, in which the eye was the victor and assumed the role of tyrant over the subservient mind:

The state to which I now allude was one
In which the eye was master of the heart,
When that which is in every stage of life
The most despotic of our senses gain'd
Such strength in me as often held my mind
In absolute dominion.   (XI, 42–8, 171–5)

Like Coleridge, Wordsworth is careful to differentiate between "nature" and the world we perceive by the unaided eye. Nature is a great deal more than its component physical objects, and that to which the mind becomes enslaved is the material thing which is the residuum of nature after it has been filtered through the merely physical eye. In fact, "Nature," as Wordsworth at once goes on to say, tries "to thwart/ This tyranny" of the eye, by summoning all the senses "to counteract" each other, and also by making all the senses and their external objects "subservient in their turn/ To the great ends," explicitly, "of Liberty and Power"; while the pleasures by which we are solicited to "such thraldom" of sight are those "of the outward sense,/ Not of the mind" (XI, 176–98).[68] Happily, however, this enslavement was for him a transient stage, for

> I had felt
> Too forcibly, too early in my life,
> Visitings of imaginative power
> For this to last: I shook the habit off
> Entirely and for ever, and again
> In Nature's presence stood, as I stand now
> A sensitive, and a creative Soul.
>
> (XI, 251–7)

It is precisely at this juncture, in order to explain the means by which he recovered his freedom, that Wordsworth introduces his discussion of the "spots of time" by which "our minds/ Are nourished and invisibly repair'd"; for the spots of time testify to earlier perceptual experiences in which the present master-servant relation between the physical senses and the mind had been reversed. Wordsworth could not be more explicit on this point:

> This efficacious spirit chiefly lurks
> Among those passages of life in which
> We have had deepest feeling that the mind
> Is lord and master, and that outward sense
> Is but the obedient servant of her will.
>
> (XI, 258–77)

The overall tenor of *The Prelude* indicates that Wordsworth means to represent such absolute dominion of the mind over outward sense not as the ideal of perceptual experience, but as an occasional extreme that helps rescue him from the disastrous opposite extreme. The perceptual ideal is put forward in the passage of the next book in which he describes his "sight/ Of a new world" as the product of a balance of equal powers which (in his persistent exploitation of the political analogue) ennobles both the eye and the visible object—

> A balance, an ennobling interchange
> Of action from within and from without,
> The excellence, pure spirit, and best power
> Both of the object seen, and eye that sees.[69]

This is for Wordsworth the normative balance of power in perception; although, as he recognized, it was a state he was able to achieve only in privileged and unsustainable moments of experience.

Like so many of the cardinal topics of *The Prelude,* Wordsworth's politics of vision is epitomized and resolved in the last book, in his recognition on Mount Snowdon of the landscape as "the perfect image of a mighty Mind." In that usurpation upon the dominion of the kingly sea—when the moonlit mists project seeming headlands and promontories

> Into the sea, the real Sea, that seem'd
> To dwindle and give up its majesty,
> Usurp'd upon as far as sight could reach—

the poet recognizes the symbol of the power of the mind to achieve dominance over the visible given:

> Above all
> One function of such mind had Nature there
> Exhibited by putting forth . . .
> That domination which she oftentimes
> Exerts upon the outward face of things.

And this "Power . . . which Nature thus/ Thrusts forth upon the senses, is the express/ Resemblance" and "genuine Counterpart" of the "glorious faculty" of "higher minds"—that is, of the creative perceptual power of the human imagination (XIII, 47–51, 73–90).

Wordsworth later clarified his intention by revising "domination" to read the "mutual domination" of mind and outward things "with interchangeable supremacy"; but even the initial version goes on to make it plain that the power relation between mind and not-mind, as symbolized in this ideal instance, is both reciprocative and interchangeable. Upon "all the objects of the universe," high imaginative minds "can send abroad/ Like transformation," but they also, "whene'er it is/ Created for them, catch it by an instinct," willing both "to work and to be wrought upon" (XIII, 93–100). And whereas, he adds, the effect of submitting to the potent tendency "of habit to enslave the mind, I mean/ Oppress it by the laws of vulgar sense" is to deliver "a universe of death" (XIII, 138–41), the product of an interplay between mind and outward things, without sacrifice of autonomy on either side, is a universe which is living and active:

> In a world of life they live,
> By sensible impressions not enthrall'd,
> But quicken'd, rouz'd.

"Hence," Wordsworth declares, "sovereignty within and peace at will." And this sovereignty and peace, translated from the political state to the state of the perceiving mind, is the essential human freedom:

> Oh! who is he that hath his whole life long
> Preserved, enlarged this freedom in himself?
> For this alone is genuine Liberty.
>
> (XIII, 102–23)

We have at last arrived at the concept of "genuine freedom" which Wordsworth invokes in the Prospectus to his poetry. This conclusion is also another of the diverse thematic elements which bend the end of *The Prelude* back to its beginning; for it has taken the entire experience of his life, recollected in tranquillity and rendered in the artistic form of the completed poem, to clarify the condition which he only now fully defines, but whose recovery he had celebrated in the "glad preamble" to this account of the growth of a poet's mind: "Now I am free. . . . Enough that I am free."

SEVEN

The Poet's Vision:
The New Earth
and the Old

To combine the child's sense of wonder and novelty with
the appearances, which every day for perhaps forty years
had rendered familiar . . . this is the character and privilege of genius.

Coleridge, *Biographia Literaria*

To see the things in a new way that is really difficult,
everything prevents one, habits, schools, daily life, reason,
necessities of daily life, indolence, everything prevents one,
in fact there are very few geniuses in the world.

—Gertrude Stein, *Picasso*

Voltaire, Shelley, Wordsworth, Byron, Rousseau . . . established a *new* connection between mankind and the universe, and the result was a vast release of energy. The
sun was reborn to man and so was the moon. To man, the
very sun goes stale, becomes a habit. Comes a saviour, a seer,
and the very sun dances new in heaven.

—D. H. Lawrence, *Aristocracy*

If I want to fix my mind on what I mean by absolute or
ethical value . . . one particular experience presents itself
to me. . . . I believe the best way of describing it is to say
that when I have it *I wonder at the existence of the world.*
. . . It is the experience of seeing the world as a miracle.

—Ludwig Wittgenstein, *Lecture on Ethics*

SEVEN

WHETHER a man shall live his old life or a new one, in a universe of death or of life, cut off and alien or affiliated and at home, in a state of servitude or of genuine freedom—to the Romantic poet, all depends on his mind as it engages with the world in the act of perceiving. Hence the extraordinary emphasis throughout this era on the eye and the object and the relation between them. Whatever their philosophical differences about what is and what only seems to be, the major poets coincide with Blake's view that "As a man is, So he Sees," that "As the Eye—Such the Object," and that "the Eye altering alters all"; [1] therefore, that to see the world wrongly is to see the wrong world, but to see it aright is to create a new earth and new heaven.

Carlyle's discussion of "The Hero as Poet" is mainly a large expansion of the triple significance of the Latin term *vates* as poet, prophet, and seer. "May we not say that intellect altogether expresses itself in this power of discerning what an object is?" "A calmly *seeing* eye; a great intellect, in short." "The seeing eye! . . . To the Poet, as to every other, we say first of all, *See*." But since to see the world anew is equivalent to making a new world, the Latin *vates* and the Greek *poeta* (maker) fall together. "Creative, we said: poetic creation, what is this too but *seeing* the thing sufficiently?" "The *Vates* Poet" presents us with a "melodious Apocalypse of Nature." [2] As Ruskin, who in this respect was Carlyle's disciple, put it: "The greatest thing a human soul ever does in this world is to *see* something, and tell what it *saw* in a plain way. . . . To see clearly is poetry, prophecy, and religion,—all in one"; it is to be a "Seer." [3]

A number of shorter poems, like the longer works of imaginative apocalypse I discussed earlier, turn on optical imagery. The poet, confronting the world, sees what he has failed to see, or no longer sees what he once saw, or sees what he once saw in a new way. Wordsworth's *Intimations Ode* is initiated by the disquieting discovery that "the things which I have seen I now can see no more," and concludes in the comfort that he now sees old things in a new light, through an "eye/ That hath kept watch o'er man's mortality." Coleridge defines his accidie in *Dejection: An Ode* by the fact that, when he gazes on the sky, the clouds, the stars, and the moon, "I see, not feel, how beautiful they are!" In Shelley's *Hymn to Intellectual Beauty*, the unseen power sheds a transforming but inconstant light and color on the world, and in *The Zucca* something, an "I know not what," appears and disappears "in flowers and leaves, and in the grass fresh-shorn." The index to Peter Bell's inner depravity, in Wordsworth's poem, is a visual deficiency—

> A primrose by a river's brim
> A yellow primrose was to him,
> And it was nothing more.

Coleridge's Mariner, on the other hand, manifests his spiritual change by a visual peripety; he had hitherto looked upon the water snakes as loathsome, but he now sees them to be beautiful: "O happy living things! No tongue/ Their beauty might declare." In the great version of Wordsworth's *The Ruined Cottage* recently retrieved from the manuscript, the Pedlar's reconcilement with the brute fact of undeserved and unrationalizable human suffering is signified by a similar alteration of the eye. Early in the poem the Pedlar had seen the abandoned and ruined cottage as offering to the wind "A cold bare wall whose earthy top is tricked/ With weeds and the rank spear grass." But he says at the close,

> Those weeds, and the high spear grass on that wall,
> By mist and silent raindrops silvered o'er,
> As once I passed, did to my mind convey

So still an image of tranquility,
So calm and still, and looked so beautiful.
    . . . I turned away
And walked along my road in happiness.[4]

The preoccupation is with a radical opposition in ways of seeing the world, and the need to turn from one way to the other,
which is very difficult, but works wonders. "Single vision," the
reliance on the "bodily," "physical," "vegetable," "corporeal,"
or "outward eye," which results in a slavery of the mind to
merely material objects, a spiritual sleep of death, and a sensual
death-in-life—to this way of seeing poets opposed the liberated,
creative, and resurrective mode of sight "thro', and not with the
eye," or of sight by means of the "inward eye," the "intellectual eye," the "imaginative eye," or simply, "the imagination." The shift is from physical optics to what Carlyle in the
title of one of his essays called "Spiritual Optics," [5] and what
Blake and others often called "Vision."

Since the perception of a new world was the criterion of success in life—the condition of experience which writers who
retained the traditional vocabulary called "redemption"—it
will be useful to identify the principal ways in which this triumph of vision over optics was said to manifest itself. In preceding chapters I discussed the major and inclusive way, the
transformation of a discrete, dead, and alien milieu into a human, integral, and companionable milieu in which man finds
himself thoroughly at home. But there are several supplementary ways in which the eye, altering, was said to yield, at least
momentarily, a re-created world. These are not always sharply
distinct either in theory or practice, but for convenience I shall
treat separately three modes of renovative perception: freshness of sensation, "moments" of illumination, and visual transvaluations.

1. FRESHNESS OF SENSATION

Literary historians have been so occupied with Wordsworth's
claim, in his Preface to *Lyrical Ballads,* to have written the

language really spoken by men, that they neglect Coleridge's testimony that Wordsworth's primary motive had in fact been to exemplify a new way of perceiving the world, by investing it with "the modifying colors of imagination." Wordsworth's aim in these poems, Coleridge declared in the *Biographia Literaria,* was

> to give the charm of novelty to things of every day, and to excite a feeling analogous to the supernatural, by awakening the mind's attention from the lethargy of custom, and directing it to the loveliness and the wonders of the world before us; an inexhaustible treasure, but for which, in consequence of the film of familiarity and selfish solicitude we have eyes, yet see not, ears that hear not, and hearts that neither feel nor understand.

Only upon publication, Coleridge adds, did Wordsworth represent the *Ballads* (in the Advertisement of 1798) "as an *experiment* . . . in the language of ordinary life." [6] In the expanded Preface of 1802, Wordsworth himself supplemented his earlier statement by saying that his "principal object" had indeed been, in part, to throw over common incidents and situations "a certain colouring of imagination, whereby ordinary things should be presented to the mind in an unusual way." [7]

In an earlier chapter of the *Biographia* Coleridge tells us that in 1796, when for the first time he heard Wordsworth read one of his poems aloud, what had immediately and profoundly impressed him was precisely the exhibition of a way of seeing which renovated reality without distorting it—the "fine balance of truth in observing, with the imaginative faculty in modifying the objects observed," and the projection of the *"atmosphere* . . . of the ideal world around forms, incidents, and situations, of which, for the common view, custom had bedimmed all the lustre."

> To find no contradiction in the union of old and new; to contemplate the ANCIENT of days and all his works with feelings as fresh, as if all had then sprang forth at the first creative fiat; characterizes the mind that feels the riddle of the world, and may help to unravel it. To carry on the feelings of childhood into the powers of manhood; to combine the child's

sense of wonder and novelty with the appearances, which every day for perhaps forty years had rendered familiar . . . this is the character and privilege of genius. . . . And therefore it is the prime merit of genius . . . so to represent familiar objects as to awaken in the minds of others . . . that freshness of sensation which is the constant accompaniment of mental, no less than of bodily, convalescence.[8]

Meditation on this characteristic power of Wordsworth, Coleridge goes on to say, is what led him, initially, to recognize that there is a distinction between imagination and fancy, and ultimately, to define imagination as the faculty which balances or reconciles "the sense of novelty and freshness, with old and familiar objects," as part of the total operation by which it creates, out of the materials of primary and standard perception, a new world: the imagination "dissolves, diffuses, dissipates, in order to recreate." Wordsworth's imagination, as he puts it elsewhere, is "the *modifying* Power in that highest sense of the word . . . in which it is a dim Analogue of Creation . . . all that we can *conceive* of creation." [9]

Coleridge's passages in the *Biographia* incorporate, in precise summation, the key terms in the Romantic lexicon of creative perception. The persistent enterprise is to make the old world new not by distorting it, but by defamiliarizing the familiar through a refreshed way of looking upon it. The prime opponent-power is "custom"—what Wordsworth in *The Prelude* repeatedly condemns as "habit," "use and custom," "the regular action of the world" [10]—which works insidiously and relentlessly to assimilate the unique existent to general perceptual categories. The result of overcoming this "lethargy of custom," Coleridge says, is to disimprison the "wonder" in the "familiar"; or in Wordsworth's alternative term, to reveal the miracle in the sheer existence of an object:

> And the world's native produce, as it meets
> The sense with less habitual stretch of mind,
> Is ponder'd as a miracle.[11]

The criterion for such freshness of sensation is "the child's sense of wonder and novelty," and it is assumed that as a child sees now, so did all mankind see in the childhood of the human race. "You look round on your Mother Earth," in Wordsworth's half-ironic self-description,

> As if you were her first-born birth,
> And none had lived before you! [12]

Among early men, Novalis said, "there was freshness and originality in all their perceptions"; and "what are children but the first men? The fresh gaze of the child is richer in significance than the presentiment of the most indubitable Seer." [13] Usually we find also an equation, implicit or overt, between the infancy of the individual and the condition of Adam in Eden, so that to restore the fresh and wondering vision of the child is to recover the pristine experience of paradise: "as if all," Coleridge put it, "had then sprang forth at the first creative fiat."

In the age of Blake and Wordsworth, as Peter Coveney says in *The Image of Childhood,* "the child emerges from comparative unimportance to become the focus of an unprecedented literary interest," both for what he is in himself and as a standard reference in defining valid adult experience.[14] It is a mistake, however, to claim, as some critics do, that the Romantic resort to the child is a regressive norm which celebrates infantilism. Here as elsewhere, the typical view is represented by Schiller, who interprets the power of our nostalgia for the state of childhood as a sign that this is "what we were" and "what we shall become again," but only by carrying on "to our coming of age," when we shall incorporate the early simplicity in "the higher harmony" of maturity.[15] "The most highly developed earthly man," in Novalis' version of the prevailing concept of development as a spiral return, "is very like the child," but in preserving the "thesis" and "antithesis" of the process of his evolution, he "is the highest synthetic degree of the child." [16] "The harmoniousness of childhood," according to Hegel, "is a gift from the hand of nature: the second harmony must spring from the labour and culture of the spirit. And so the words of Christ, 'Except ye *become* as little children,' etc., are very far from telling us that we must always remain children." [17] Although Wordsworth finds the roots of his "creative sensibility" in his infant condition in his mother's arms, and despite his evident nostalgia for the stage of childhood, he stresses that his growth to maturity involves "the discipline/ And consummation of the Poet's mind." [18] Coleridge's description of freshness of sensation in the *Biographia* is informed by the concept of growth as a spiral progress which preserves the values of its earlier stages: "To find no contradiction in the union of old and new" in perception is the mark of success in carrying on "the *feelings* of childhood into the *powers* of manhood." The norm is to sustain the responsiveness of the child in what Blake calls the "organized" vision of the developed imagination.

These Romantic formulations are rooted in Biblical and theological commonplaces. Coleridge's allusion, "the AN-CIENT of days and all his works," for example, is to the apocalyptic vision described in the seventh chapter of the Book of Daniel. And his statement about liberating the mind from custom to direct it to the "wonders of the world before us," for which "we have eyes, yet see not, ears that hear not," echoes Christ's words to those who are obtuse to the significance of his miracles: "Having eyes, see ye not? and having ears, hear ye not?"—words which Coleridge translates into a purely perceptual miraculism. [19] And for St. Augustine, as for many writers thirteen hundred years later, it had been man's habitual mode of sensation which, by chaining him to his fallen condition, is the enemy of a redeeming vision. "With my bodily senses I surveyed the external world."

> And sometimes You admit me to a state of mind that I am not ordinarily in, a kind of delight which could it ever be made permanent in me would be hard to distinguish from the life to come. But by the weight of my imperfections I fall back again, and I am swallowed up by things customary. . . . So much does the burden of custom count for. [20]

Modern preoccupation with the experiences of childhood has usually, and with some justification, been traced primarily to Rousseau, who wrote, for example, in *Émile:* "Nature wants children to be children before they are men. . . . Childhood has ways of seeing, thinking, and feeling peculiar to itself; nothing can be more foolish than to substitute our ways for them." [21] Reference to the child as norm, however, antedated Rousseau by some seventeen centuries. As Hegel reminds us, it was not a Romantic primitivist, but Christ who posited the return to the state of a child as the condition for entering the apocalyptic kingdom: "Except ye be converted, and become as children, ye shall not enter into the kingdom of heaven." And by the seventeenth century the traditional parallel between the new world perceived by the regenerate adult and the new earth awaiting the redeemed in the fullness of time had been extended back—against the strong pressure of the doctrine of inherited corruption—to establish a parallel, at the other end of the temporal span, between the perception of the newborn child and that of Adam when all creation was new. Francis Bacon, who regarded the fall of man, in its cognitive aspect, as a corruption of the perfect "commerce between the mind of man and the nature of things" in Eden, represented our coming "entrance into the kingdom of man, founded on the sciences," as "not much other than the entrance into the kingdom of heaven, whereunto none may enter except as a little child." Thomas Traherne equated his visual experience in childhood to the perception of Adam before the fall:

> Certainly Adam in Paradice had not more sweet and Curious Apprehensions of the World, then I when I was a child. . . . All appeared New, and Strange at the first, inexpressibly rare, and Delightfull, and Beautifull. . . . I seemed as one Brought into the Estate of Innocence. . . . The Green trees . . . Transported and Ravished me; their Sweetnes and unusual Beauty made my Heart to leap.[22]

This "first Light which shined in my Infancy," however, was "totally ecclypsed" by the habitual categories of standard adult perception (by "the Customs and maners of Men"); and this constituted his personal fall from original innocence: "I was quickly tainted and fell by others." As later in Coleridge and Wordsworth, so in Traherne, custom rather than depravity is the tyrant that holds our innocent senses in bondage: "Our Misery proceedeth ten thousand times more from the outward

Bondage of Opinion and Custom then from any inward corruption or Depravation of Nature: And . . . it is not our Parents Loyns, so much as our Parents lives, that Enthrals and Blinds us" (III. 7–8). The world is in truth so beautiful that "Were we to see it only once, that first Appearance would amaze us. But being daily seen, we observ it not" (II. 21). The state of mind and mode of perception of the child, however, remain for the adult accessible ideals. Now, Traherne says, "I unlearn, and becom as it were a little Child again, that I may enter into the Kingdom of GOD" (III. 3). For the eye altering alters all; or as Traherne puts it, "it did not so much concern us what Objects were before us, as with what Eys we beheld them" (III. 68).

The "splendor in the grass" and the "glory in the flower" whose loss Wordsworth elegizes in his *Intimations Ode*—that "celestial light" perceived by the child which is darkened, then obliterated, by "custom . . . with a weight,/ Heavy as frost"—had been the veriest commonplace in the evangelical tradition. Traherne, who in childhood had seen "the Works of GOD in their Splendor and Glory," in his late maturity broke free from the bonds of habit to perceive again that "evry Spire of Grass is the Work of His Hand" (III. 2, 62). Henry Vaughan, a poet who shared Traherne's concept of the prelapsarian eye of the child, sang:

> Happy those early dayes! When I
> Shin'd in my Angell-infancy. . . .
> When on some *gilded Cloud,* or *flowre*
> My gazing soul would dwell an houre,
> And in those weaker glories spy
> Some shadows of eternity.

The result of Jacob Boehme's descent "through the gates of hell" to the spiritual experience of an apocalyptic marriage, when he was "embraced with love, as the bridegroom embraces his beloved bride," was a freshness of perception which enabled him to recognize "God in all the creatures, and also in the herbs and grass." [23] In America Jonathan Edwards, the instant he accepted fully the doctrine of God's justice in preelection, experienced "a wonderful alteration in my mind" which effected a correspondent alteration of sensation: "the appearance of everything was altered; there seemed to be . . . [an] appearance of divine glory, in almost every thing"—in the "clouds, and blue sky; in the grass, flowers, trees; in the water, and all nature." [24]

The theological prototype of fall, redemption, and the creation of a new earth manifests itself, metaphorically, in almost all Romantic statements about freshness of visual experience. "Poetry," Shelley said in his *Defence of Poetry,* "makes familiar objects be as if they were not familiar."

> Poetry defeats the curse which binds us to be subjected to the accident of surrounding impressions. . . . It reproduces the common Universe of which we are portions and percipients, and it purges from our inward sight the film of familiarity which obscures from us the wonder of our being. . . . It creates anew the universe, after it has been annihilated in our minds by the recurrence of impressions blunted by reiteration. It justifies the bold and true word of Tasso: *Non merita nome di creatore, se non Iddio ed il Poeta.*[25]

Carlyle's *Sartor Resartus* brings into high visibility the inherited formulae within the Romantic doctrine. Carlyle's "Natural Supernaturalism," by means of an unassisted transaction between the ordinary object and the dishabituated eye, effects authentic miracles. "Custom blinds us to the miraculousness of daily-recurring miracles." "What is Philosophy throughout but a continual battle against Custom," and against "the Thought-forms, Space and Time" which "blind us to the wonder everywhere lying close on us." "The true use" of his book, he reveals at its end, has been "to exhibit the Wonder of daily life and common things." His hero, when his "mind's eyes were . . . unsealed, and its hands ungyved," had awakened "to a new Heaven and a new Earth." Now if the reader would only "sweep away the Illusion of Time," "how were thy eyesight unsealed, and thy heart set flaming in the Light-sea of celestial wonder!" Then all would be brought to the enduring vision of the glory in the grass—the recognition that "through every grass-blade . . . the glory of a present God still beams." [26]

2. M O M E N T S

Many Romantic writers testified to a deeply significant experience in which an instant of consciousness, or else an ordinary object or event, suddenly blazes into revelation; the unsustainable moment seems to arrest what is passing, and is often described as an intersection of eternity with time. In this instance also, Augustine's *Confessions* provides the theological prototype. "I was now studying," he says, "the ground of my admiration for the beauty of bodies" in a mode of existence which is neither created nor mutable, when

> in the thrust of a trembling glance [*in ictu trepidantis aspectus*] my mind arrived at That Which Is. Then indeed I saw clearly Your *invisible things which are understood by the things that are made;* but I lacked the strength to hold my gaze fixed, and my weakness was beaten back again, so that I returned to my old habits.   (VII. xvii)

At another time, while he conversed with his mother about the "eternal Light" and that Wisdom which "is not made" but which "simply is, for it is eternal," "with all the effort of our heart we did for one instant attain to touch it." We "in a flash of the mind [*rapida cogitatione*] attained to touch the eternal Wisdom."

> Then sighing . . . we return to the sound of our own tongue, in which a word has both beginning and ending. . . . And if this could continue . . . that [one's] life should eternally be such as that one moment [*momentum*] of understanding for which all had been sighing—would not this be: *Enter Thou into the joy of Thy Lord?* But when shall it be? Shall it be when *we shall all rise again* and *shall not all be changed?*
>   (IX. x)

This experience of eternity in a moment, Augustine suggests, anticipates the translation of all time into eternity at the apocalypse.

Over the Christian centuries revelations of the eternal within the passing, or else the sudden flare from the source of all light into the darkness of the fallen consciousness—what Jonathan Edwards, in the title of one of his sermons, called "A Divine and Supernatural Light Immediately Imparted to the Soul by the Spirit of God"—were of common report in devotional life. Rousseau, in his *Rêveries du promeneur solitaire,* naturalized these traditional apices of experience by describing them not as the breakthrough to an eternity that exists otherwhere and afterward, but in purely empirical terms; the illumination becomes self-effecting, self-warranting, self-sufficient, and manifests timelessness as a quality of the experiential moment. In certain states of mind during his reveries on the Île de Saint-Pierre, Rousseau tells us, he discovered "the supreme felicity," in which "time means nothing" and "the present lasts forever, yet without indicating its duration and without any trace of successiveness"; and "so long as this state endures one is sufficient unto himself, like God." [27]

Such experiences, with or without reference to an extramental light source and a nontemporal realm of being, were of common report among the philosophers and poets of the Romantic generation. The name for the phenomenon was then, as it has largely remained, the "moment" (in Augustine's *Confessions, momentum,* and in German writers, *der Augenblick,* or *der Moment*), which stresses its paradoxical attribute of timeless time; I shall signify this specialized use of the word "Moment" by capitalizing it. Schelling identified a condition which "sets absolute eternity into the middle of time," like "a sudden brightening and illumination of consciousness" which must seem "the effect of grace." [28] Hölderlin repeatedly celebrated "the Moments [*Augenblicke*] in which the imperishable is present in us," those "Moments of liberation . . . in which it seems to us that the unfettered spirit, its sorrows and servitude forgotten, returns in triumph to the halls of the sun." [29] Goethe's poem *Die Weisen und die Leute* describes a revelation "in Blitzes Nu"—in the flash of a now—and in *Vermächtnis* (Testament) Goethe gave witness to the Moment of finding "the center":

Dann ist Vergangenheit beständig,
Das Künftige voraus lebendig,
Der Augenblick ist Ewigkeit.

Related in kind is Blake's saving Moment—the "Moment in each Day that Satan cannot find" which "renovates every Moment of the Day if rightly placed"; or the timeless revelation "Within a Moment: a Pulsation of the Artery" when "the Poets Work is Done" (*Milton* 35. 42–5, 29. 1–3). Related also, although rendered in a different philosophical idiom, are Shelley's "best and happiest moments . . . arising unforeseen and departing unbidden," which are "as it were the interpenetration of a diviner nature through our own"—"vanishing apparitions" that poetry "arrests" and "visitations of the divinity" that poetry "redeems from decay." Shelley adds the distinction that these "evanescent visitations" are "sometimes associated with place or person, sometimes [regard] our own mind alone." [30] That is, there is a charged Moment and also a momentarily charged object, an unlocalized irradiation of consciousness and an incandescent item of sense perception. As Novalis describes the latter type (which he calls alternately the *Augenblick* and *Moment*), such experiences "are especially striking at the glimpse of many a human form and face . . . at the hearing of certain words, at the reading of particular passages," as well as at sight of "many incidents and occurrences in the natural scene." [31]

Wordsworth is preeminently a poet of the revelatory and luminous Moment, of the "gentle shock of mild surprise," of "flashes, as it were," of "objects recognis'd/ In flashes," of outer "gleams like the flashing of a shield," as well as of "attendant gleams/ Of soul-illumination." [32] In some few instances the revelation occurs when the visible scene, present or recollected, is entirely obliterated. In *Tintern Abbey,* for example, "we are laid asleep/ In body" in order with another eye to "see into the life of things"; but no sooner does Wordsworth propose this possibility than he half retracts it: "If this/ Be but a vain belief. . . ." [33] At other times an external scene evokes a sense of revelation which is ascribed to the accompanying state of mind. In the literal *rite de passage* in *The Prelude* (when "on the roof/ Of an itinerant Vehicle" the naive country boy for the first time crosses the "threshold" into London, and so into adult experience), he suddenly experiences the thrust of the divine into time. At "the very moment"—the word "moment" occurs four times in the short passage—

> that I seem'd to know
> The threshold now is overpass'd, Great God!
> That aught *external* to the living mind
> Should have such mighty sway! yet so it was
> A weight of Ages did at once descend
> Upon my heart; no thought embodied, no
> Distinct remembrances; but weight and power,
> Power growing with the weight . . .
>   'twas a moment's pause.
> All that took place within me, came and went
> As in a moment, and I only now
> Remember that it was a thing divine.
>   (VIII, 693–710)

Most frequent, however, are the instances in which, while Wordsworth's eye is fixed on the object without being mastered by it, the object itself suddenly becomes charged with revelation. To two complex Moments of this sort, as we know, Wordsworth applied the name "spots of time"; but as he goes on to remark, "Such moments . . . are scatter'd everywhere" in his life (XI, 274–5), and they are celebrated everywhere in his poems. They typically occur when the poet, solitary, is confronted by a single thing; his imagination is triggered by an assertive *Gestalt* whose attendant circumstances fall back to serve, Wordsworth says, "as solemn back-ground, or relief,/ To single forms and objects" (1850; VII, 622–3). So amid the amorphous crowd of passersby in London, he was "abruptly . . . smitten with the view/Of a blind Beggar," wearing on his chest a paper that set forth his identity.

> My mind did at this spectacle turn round
> As with the might of waters . . .
> And, on the shape of the unmoving man,
> His fixèd face and sightless eyes, I look'd,

As if admonish'd from another world.
                    (VII, 610–22)

The typical Wordsworthian "as if" quietly absorbs the world beyond time and place into the world of the apprehended here-and-now.

In the fact that Wordsworth is a poet of the Moment lies, I believe, the key to the literary mystery, why a man capable of a *gravitas* and sublimity equal to Milton's should have written what Robert Frost once called, in real if ironic admiration, the "sweet, insipid" poems in his *Lyrical Ballads* and related pieces.[34] In such poems Wordsworth nakedly puts before us an ordinary circumstance and his inordinate response, and leaves us to be startled into sharing the revelation. Sometimes he succeeds, as in the Moment recorded in *The Two April Mornings:*

> Matthew is in his grave, yet now,
> Methinks, I see him stand,
> As at that moment, with a bough
> Of wilding in his hand.

The risk, however, is that he will communicate the ordinariness but not the epiphany, and then we get the untransformed "matter-of-factness" to which Coleridge objected, and to which less perceptive readers have applied harsher terms; [35] and sometimes, as in *We Are Seven,* Wordsworth wavers just on the edge of bathos. But behind even the least successful ballads lies the intention that resulted in the lyric triumphs of several of the Lucy poems, of *The Solitary Reaper,* and of *Stepping Westward.*

The Moment which constitutes the whole of many of Wordsworth's shorter poems plays a major structural role in *The Prelude;* in *To William Wordsworth,* Coleridge remarks on the occurrence in that poem

> of moments awful
> Now in thy inner life, and now abroad,
> When power streamed from thee, and thy soul received
> The light reflected as a light bestowed.

The early manuscripts of *The Prelude* are mainly collections of spots of time, so that the final version, as Geoffrey Hartman says, can be regarded as developing out of this "one type of experience which is the nuclear cell of the whole." [36] In the completed poem of 1805 the overall plot of mental growth moves in leaps of discovery, at encounters when a natural or human object unexpectedly shows forth a meaning beyond propositional statement. These experiences range from the earliest "gleams like the flashing of a shield" in the opening book (I, 614) to the occasion on Snowdon when the mist-shrouded landscape flares into hierophany, at that Moment when the light of the moon "upon the turf/ Fell like a flash" (XIII, 39–41).

3. TRANSVALUATIONS

A number of Romantic descriptions of the breakthrough from sensual into imaginative seeing stress the radical elevation in the status of the object. The visiting of an "I know not what," says Shelley in *The Zucca,* his unfinished version of the *Intimations Ode,* makes "divine the loftiest and the lowest," and shows itself in "all things common." Carlyle cites Tieck's comment about Novalis, that he saw "the commonest and nearest as a wonder" and "men's every-day life" as "a wondrous fable"; and we recall that Diogenes Teufelsdroeckh (whose name incarnates divinity in devil's dung) undertook to reveal "the Wonder of daily life and common things" and to show "were it in the meanest province . . . the star-domed City of God." [37] A similar reversal of value is a familiar element in the literature of religious experience. His faith in God's goodness, said Traherne, led him "to the Study of the most Obvious and Common Things," for "it is most consonant and Agreeable with His nature, that the Best Things should be most Common. . . . Air, Light . . . Trees, Men and Women" (*Centuries* III. 53). William James cites a convert at a rural revival meeting who testified to the sudden perception of a glory in his hogs: "When I came to myself . . .

oh, how I was changed, and everything became new. My horses and hogs and even everybody seemed changed." [38]

Wordsworth's perceptual transvaluations, however, are distinctive, both in the quality with which he invests such experiences and in the crucial part they play in his theory and practice of poetry. All readers of Wordsworth are aware of his brooding concern with the banal, and of the gravity, the reverence, the extraordinary pathos with which he charges terms that, in both social and aesthetic discourse, had earlier been used mainly to derogate or contemn: "low," "humble," "common," "ordinary," "everyday," "trivial," "vulgar," "mean"; "the earth/ And common face of Nature," "all the sweetness of a common dawn," "the common haunts of the green earth,/ And ordinary interests of man," "vulgar men . . . trivial forms . . . mean shapes," "it was, in truth/ An ordinary sight," "the meanest flower that blows."

> The common growth of mother-earth
> Suffices me—her tears, her mirth,
> Her humblest mirth and tears. . . .
> If I along that lowly way
> With sympathetic heart may stray,
> And with a soul of power. . . .
> What nobler marvels than the mind
> May in life's daily prospect find,
> May find or there create? [39]

Wordsworth was keenly aware of the novelty of this poetic mode, of the boldness of its departure from the reigning standards for serious poetry, and of the risks of neglect or contempt that he ran by adopting it as his special province. He adverts to these matters repeatedly, not only in the Prefaces to *Lyrical Ballads*, but also in his quasi-autobiographical description of the Pedlar in *The Ruined Cottage*, in *Home at Grasmere*, in *The Prelude*, in the *Essay* he added to his *Poems* of 1815, and in various letters. In sum, this is what Wordsworth claims: in his ability to perceive the inherent sublimity in the common and lowly, and the charismatic power in the trivial and the mean, lies his essential originality as a poet; his poetry of the lowly-sublime and of the heroism of meekness and fortitude will replace, and transcend, the traditional epic of heroic prowess; to express this vision of life and the world constitutes his particular mission as a chosen son, a poet-prophet for his age; his discovery of this mission was essential to his recovery from despair after the French Revolution, and served to replace his faith in the promise of the Revolution by more solid and durable grounds for hope; and in giving up his role as a political radical he had assumed the role of a poetic radical, with the task of subverting the corrupted values which his readers had inherited from a class-divided and class-conscious past. Wordsworth also tells us that to accomplish his poetic enterprise will require no less a feat than the absolute redemption of his upper-class readers, by liberating their sensibilities from bondage to unnatural social-aesthetic norms and so opening their eyes to his own imaginative vision of a new world, in which men who are equal in the dignity of their common humanity are at home in a nature which, even in its humblest or most trivial aspect, is instinct with power and grandeur.

In the course of his exposition, Wordsworth shows his awareness that his insight into the grandeur of the lowly and into the heroic values in ordinary life derives from the religious tradition, and ultimately from the Bible. The reigning European poetic, from the Renaissance through the eighteenth century, had been based primarily on classical models and adapted mainly to an aristocratic audience, and Wordsworth emphasizes that the incursion into poetry of Biblical concepts and values is deeply subversive of these established hierarchies, decorums, and tastes. The document in which Wordsworth expounds in most explicit detail the relations of his poetic mission to Scriptural values is his *Essay, Supplementary to the Preface* of 1815. This essay is a complex and rather obscurely argued *apologia pro vita sua poetica,* in which Wordsworth's primary aim is to defend the kind of poety he had inaugurated in *Lyrical Ballads* against the "senseless outcry," "the unremitting hostility," and "the slight, the aversion, and even the contempt, with which these Poems have been received." [40] In the original Prefaces to *Lyrical Ballads* Wordsworth had justified his innovations mainly in terms of prevailing critical norms, by claiming that the subjects and language of his poems exemplify universal and permanent "nature" as against the passing fashions of a current "art" which he identified with the "artificial." [41] In the *Essay* of 1815, however, he shifts the justification for his poetic practice to entirely different grounds—to the nature of original genius, the radical consequences for poetry of his particular kind of originality, and the paradoxical attributes which are inevitable in an original kind of poetry which has its roots both in the pagan literary tradition and in the essential values of traditional Christianity.

Wordsworth's argument in this essay centers on his claim that he is a poet fated for a long time to suffer misunderstanding and hostility by the very fact that he is "an original Writer." The originality of genius manifests itself by doing well "what was never done before," through applying "powers to objects on which they had not before been exercised" and so producing "effects hitherto unknown"; as a consequence Wordsworth, like his great innovative predecessors, is faced with the supremely difficult "task of *creating* the taste by which he is to be enjoyed." [42] He is in fact a poet whose appointed office is nothing less than revolutionary: he must claim from the reader "emotions of the pathetic . . . that are complex and revolutionary . . . against which [the heart] struggles with pride"; and as for the emotions of "the sublime," "can it be wondered that there is little existing preparation for a Poet charged with a new mission to extend its kingdom, and to augment and spread its enjoyments?" Wordsworth specifies that his extension of the traditional sublime to new objects has a double and diverse origin—in the pagan heroic on the one side and in Christian humility on the other; in his words, it is "the instinctive wisdom of antiquity and her heroic passions uniting, in the heart of the Poet, with the meditative wisdom of later ages" which "have produced that accord of sublimated humanity" (pp. 185–6). This is a paradoxical union; but as Wordsworth remarks, "the higher poetry" always combines "the wisdom of the heart and the grandeur of the imagination," and so unites "magnificence" and "simplicity." And it is the essential quality of Christianity itself to baffle "the calculating understanding" by what Wordsworth calls its "contradictions"; that is, its paradoxical fusion of the humblest with the highest:

> For when Christianity, the religion of humility, is founded upon the proudest quality of our nature [i.e., the imagination], what can be expected but contradictions? [43]

Wordsworth goes on to detail "affinities between religion and poetry" which account for the fact that the Scriptural revelations and the highest poetry manifest similar contradictions. What he calls the "community of nature" between poetry and Christianity is rooted in the attribute of God which theologians termed His "condescension," or "accommodation." This concept had evolved through centuries of Christian speculation, and had been especially prominent in the Pietist and evangelical movements of the preceding century. It signifies the paradox at the heart of revelation, in that the infinite and supreme Being had accommodated Himself to man's finite capacities for understanding, especially by condescending to manifest His divinity through lowly human agents and trivial objects and events. As Wordsworth very precisely defines the traditional *accomodatio:*

> The commerce between Man and his Maker cannot be carried on but by a process where much is represented in little, and the infinite Being accommodates himself to a finite capacity.
> (p. 163)

The central and supreme instance had been God's consent to what Gerard Manley Hopkins later called the "incredible condescension of the Incarnation," which does away, as Hopkins put it, with "the trivialness of life." [44] The initial definition of this founding paradox of Christianity was Paul's statement in Philippians 2:7–9, that Christ "took upon him the form of a servant . . . in the likeness of men," and "humbled himself" even unto "the death of the cross. Wherefore God also hath highly exalted him. . . ." This inversion of the highest into the lowest, Paul said, which is "unto the Jews a stumbling block," is to the classical sensibility the ultimate absurdity— "unto the Greeks foolishness." But such is God's standard procedure—to confound man's pride in his rationality and in his worldly status by inverting all secular hierarchies:

> But God hath chosen the foolish things of the world to confound the wise; and God hath chosen the weak things of the world to confound the things which are mighty; And base things of the world, and things which are despised, hath God chosen . . . That no flesh should glory in his presence.
>
> (1 Corinthians 1:23–9)

Unmistakably, though in cautious circumlocution, Wordsworth extends the "community of nature" between Christianity and poetry to include the supreme condescension of the Incarnation. There is an affinity, as he puts it, "between religion—whose element is infinitude . . . submitting herself to circumscription and reconciled to substitutions; and poetry—etherial and transcendant, yet incapable to sustain her existence without sensuous incarnation" (p. 163).

Wordsworth, then, regarded it as his special mission to employ his originality of vision, which subverts the conventional rank of the objects it perceives, in order to effect a revolution in the poetic sources of pathos and sublimity, and so to "extend the domain of sensibility for the delight, the honor, and the benefit of human nature" (p. 187). The insistent transvaluations of Scripture—"blessed are the meek: for they shall inherit the earth," "many that are first shall be last, and the last first"—translated into the literary domain, reappear in Wordsworth's characteristic oxymorons: the glory of the commonplace, the loftiness of the lowly and mean, the supreme import of the trivial, and the heroic grandeur of the meek and the oppressed. But it is evident that this new poetry and poetic, put forward in a revolutionary age, also has political and social parallels and implications, as William Hazlitt discerned in his brilliant essay on the sociology of Wordsworth's poetry. "Mr. Wordsworth's genius," Hazlitt said, "is a pure emanation of the Spirit of the Age," and "one of the innovations of the time."

> It partakes of, and is carried along with, the revolutionary movement of our age: the political changes of the day were

the model on which he formed and conducted his poetical experiments. His Muse . . . is a levelling one. It proceeds on a
principle of equality, and strives to reduce all things to the
same standard. It is distinguished by a proud humility. . . .
It takes the commonest events and objects, as a test to prove
that nature is always interesting from its inherent truth and
beauty. . . . Fools have laughed at, wise men scarcely understand them. . . .

His popular, inartificial style gets rid (at a blow) of all the
trappings of verse, of all the high places of poetry. . . . We
begin *de novo.* . . . Kings, queens, priests . . . the distinctions of rank, birth, wealth, power . . . are not to be found
here. . . . He elevates the mean by the strength of his own
aspirations. . . . [He] has struck into the sequestered vale of
humble life . . . and endeavoured (not in vain) to aggrandise
the trivial and add the charm of novelty to the familiar. No
one has shown the same imagination in raising trifles into importance.[45]

In sum, Hazlitt says, Wordsworth "has given a new view or
aspect of nature," and "is in this sense the most original poet
now living."

The early Wordsworth was indeed, in genre, subjects, and
style, the poetical Jacobin of his generation; more radical, in
this important aspect, than Shelley or even Blake. By exploiting the implications for secular literature of what, to readers
trained in Neoclassic decorum, seemed the drastic impropriety
of the literature of the Bible, he accomplished an egalitarian
revolution in poetry, deleting the traditional hierarchy and
decorums of literary kinds, subjects, protagonists, and styles,
with their built-in class structure and inherent scale of aristocratic values. And by an ultimate subversion, Wordsworth did
not merely level the Neoclassic order, but turned it upside
down, by preferring in his subjects the last over the first and
by transforming the humble and the passive into the heroic,
the low into the sublime, and the petty into the numinous.
Hence the deliberate absurdities (or in his term, "contradictions") of subjects and language in Wordsworth's earlier poetry, which outraged the sensitivities of many of his middle-
class reviewers—the extraordinary protagonists, for example,
of his serious or tragic narratives, who speak and are described

in a language replete with Biblical overtones—not demigods, kings, noblemen, warriors, or even members of the middle classes, nor only peasants, pedlars, and wagoners, but also the ignominious, the disinherited, the criminal, and the outcast; superannuated soldiers, beggars, convicts, murderers, abandoned mothers, infanticides, holy idiots, and stoical leechgatherers threatened with technological unemployment, who move through his poems with a sacramental dignity and unknowingly exert a charismatic power. Hence also Wordsworth's brooding concern with the meanest flower that blows. His favorite flowers are "the small celandine," to which he addressed three poems, and the daisy, on which he composed four lyrics—an "unassuming Common-place/ Of Nature, with that homely face,/ And yet with something of a grace," which to the gaze of the poet takes on a "function apostolical." [46]

In the *Essay* of 1815 from which I have been quoting, Wordsworth himself points up the fact that his particular mission as a poet has a social as well as a religio-aesthetic dimension. For if his new poetry of the common man and the commonplace is to create the taste by which it is to be enjoyed, it must utterly reform his readers' characters and sensibilities, which have been permeated with class consciousness and social prejudices. Part of the difficulty, as he puts it, lies in "breaking the bonds of custom, in overcoming the prejudices of false refinement . . . in divesting the Reader of the pride that induces him to dwell upon those points wherein Men differ from each other, to the exclusion of those in which all Men are alike, or the same; and in making him ashamed of the vanity that renders him insensible of the appropriate excellence . . . conferred on Men who may stand below him in the scale of society." He must therefore as poet establish "that dominion over the spirits of Readers by which they are to be humbled and humanized, in order that they may be purified and exalted." (This last sentence echoes Luke 14:11—"For whosoever exalteth himself shall be abased; and he that humbleth himself shall be exalted.") But above all, Wordsworth says, his task is difficult because his poetry cannot appeal to a ready-made, hence passive, sensibility, but must communicate to the reader an active *"power"* to cooperate with the "powers" of the poet as applied "to objects on which they had not before been exercised." "*There* lies the true difficulty," and it is for this reason that he, as the kind of original poet it has been given to him to be, "must reconcile himself for a season to few and scattered hearers." [47]

Wordsworth's new poetry from the beginning had its champions; and in 1815 Thomas Noon Talfourd attributed to his writing a sacred character (approaching "Mr. Wordsworth's sublimities," he said, we feel "that we are entering upon holy ground") precisely because it converts the last into the first: it links the "humblest" and "the lowliest" to "the loftiest sublimities of our nature," and makes us perceive "the universal workings of the great Spirit" in "the meanest and most disgusting of all earthly objects." [48] Other critics, however, gave Wordsworth substantial grounds for his complaint about the failure of contemporary taste to meet the drastic demands he placed upon it.

The issue between Wordsworth and his readers had close and venerable precedents in a duplex European culture, in which the Biblical and classical elements pointed in opposite directions and generated opposing values. Very early in the Christian era Augustine and other theologians, who had themselves been trained in the strict decorums of traditional rhetoric, had felt compelled to justify the seeming absurdity and barbarousness in the *humilitas-sublimitas* of the Biblical subjects and style.[49] And even well into the eighteenth century, critics of the Bible as literature found it necessary to decry the Neoclassic taste which responded to the Biblical conflation of the lowest with the highest as a breach of social and literary decorum. In his *Lectures on the Sacred Poetry of the Hebrews,* published in 1753, Robert Lowth identified as the paradoxical quality "almost peculiar to the sacred poets" of the Old Testament a use of imagery which invests "the most common and familiar with the greatest dignity." The effect is that of a *humilitas-sublimitas;* or as Lowth puts it, "the meanness of the image" and "the plainness and inelegance of the expression" are used with such "consistency" and "propriety" that "I do not scruple to pronounce it sublime." Such imagery and language derive from "a simple and uncultivated (or rather uncorrupted) state of life," and to consider the present state and values of society as a superior stage of development is to fall into the error of taking "luxury, levity, and pride" as criteria of a "superior civilization." The cause of an adverse response to the high virtues of the Biblical style lies in the false refinement of the reader: "If any person of more nicety than judgment should esteem some of these rustic images grovelling or vulgar," Lowth declares, "such an effect can only result from the ignorance" and "peculiar prejudices" of the modern critic.[50]

A half-century later Wordsworth found it necessary to defend the transvaluations in his secular poems against similar charges, in which, as he saw it, class snobbery operated in the mode of aesthetic sensibility.[51] And even so late as 1844 R. H. Horne, although a warm admirer of Wordsworth, continued to lament the gross violations of "taste" in his deliberate and persistent inversion of the class status both of men and of things. In Wordsworth's poems, he says,

> by carrying a great principle to a ridiculous extreme, are gravely "exalted" garden-spades, common streets, small celandines, wagoners, beggars, household common places, and matter-of-fact details . . . forced upon the attention as pre-eminently claiming profound admiration or reverence.

"These deliberate outrages upon true taste, judgment, and the ideality of poetry," in Horne's judgment, are the defects which have "cost a great poet twenty years of abuse and laughter." [52]

4. HAMANN AND WORDSWORTH: SOME PARALLELS IN SPIRITUAL DISCOVERY

In Book XII of *The Prelude* Wordsworth narrates the biographical circumstances of his discovery of his "new mission" as a poet who will revolutionize the pathetic and extend the kingdom of the sublime—circumstances to which he adverts in his *apologia* in the *Essay* of 1815 that he wrote a decade later. It will, I think, clarify the tradition that lies behind Wordsworth's discovery of vocation if we set the relevant pas-

sages in *The Prelude* beside the spiritual autobiography of a
German writer, Johann Georg Hamann, who was entirely unknown to Wordsworth. The two accounts serve as an addi-
tional instance of the similarities-in-difference among authors
in the lineage of Augustine's *Confessions.*

In a diary he wrote at white heat in 1758, Hamann describes
the event which was the turning point of his life. At the age
of twenty-eight he had been sent to London to transact some
business. The enterprise ended in ludicrous failure and he
plunged into frantic dissipation, which soon precipitated a
crisis of "aridity" and "affliction." In a desperate search for
relief from the sense of "emptiness and darkness and wilderness" in his heart, he pored over the Bible (the authorized
English version) and abruptly underwent a conversion, after
the prototype of Augustine's experience in the Garden at
Milan:

> In the evening of 31 March I read the fifth chapter of Deu-
> teronomy, and fell into deep thought. . . . I felt my heart
> throb, I heard a voice sigh in its depths. . . . All at once I
> felt my heart swell, and pour out in tears, and I could no
> longer—I could no longer conceal from my God that I was
> the fratricide, the murderer of his only begotten Son. The
> Spirit of God went on . . . to reveal to me more and more
> the mystery of the divine love.

He read rapidly through the Bible, and when he had finished
he found his heart at rest in the experience of a consolation
"which swallowed up all fear, all sadness, all mistrust." [53]

The key to Hamann's recovery was his discovery of a pair
of basic and interrelated truths: that God is an author who
has revealed himself in two parallel symbol-systems—the Book
of Scripture and the Book of Nature—and that the primal attribute manifested in both systems of revelation is the "condescension" by which God expresses his boundless love for
mankind:

> God an author!—The inspiration of this Book is just as great
> a self-humbling and condescension of God [*Erniedrigung und
> Herunterlassung Gottes*] as the Father's creation and the In-
> carnation of the Son.

God has revealed himself to man in nature and in His word. . . . Both revelations explain and support each other, and cannot contradict each other.

God reveals himself—the Creator of the world an author!

God condescended as much as He could to man's disposition and ideas, even to his prejudices and weaknesses.

As deep as is His condescension . . . so high does He surpass our powers of thought.[54]

At the heart of Hamann's concept of divine condescension is Paul's statement that God inverted worldly status in order to subvert worldly wisdom and pride of place. Hamann says:

What man would be bold enough to speak as Paul does of the folly of God, of the weakness of God (1 Corinthians 1:25) . . . that the mighty God willed to reveal His wisdom and power in that He hath chosen the foolish things of the world to confound the wise . . . the weak things of the world . . . the base things of the world, and things which are despised . . . yea and things which are not, to bring to nought things that are, and that can pride themselves on their existence.

"I repeat this observation to myself so often," says Hamann, "because it has been for me a masterkey." [55]

Hamann's writing is directed against eighteenth-century intellectualism and sensibility; in both realms alike, as he sees it, pride of reason and pride of class recoil from the rational absurdities and social improprieties of the Scriptural revelation. God's loving condescension, "of which all of Scripture is full, gives grounds for mockery to weak minds, who presuppose in the divine Word . . . a consonance with the taste of the age in which they live" (I, 10). The Holy Spirit "like a fool and a madman . . . made for our proud reason childish stories and contemptible events into the history of heaven and God" (II, 48). "A philosophical book for children," he wrote to Kant, in a letter which is an ironic episode in the history of eighteenth-century rationalism, "would need to appear as simple, foolish, and in bad taste [*abgeschmackt*] as a divine book which was written for men" (II, 372).

From the dual premise of God's loving condescension and his self-manifestation in the symbols of natural objects, Hamann deduces a variety of consequences. There is a radical difference between Hamann's flamboyant irrationalism and Wordsworth's quiet testimony about his altering vision of the world, but the substance of Hamann's claims has a familiar ring to readers who know Wordsworth's asserted role as a poet-prophet, his communings, by means of "the language of the sense," with "the speaking face of earth and heaven," and his mission to reveal the grandeur of the lowly and trivial and the miraculousness of the ordinary. "We are all capable of being prophets," Hamann says, for "all the phenomena of nature are dreams, visions, riddles, which have their meaning, their secret sense" (I, 308). To the prophetic vision, equipped with the "key" to the divine intention, is revealed the absolute equality—in fact, the reversal of customary status—in both things and men; for before the Lord "nothing is little, nothing great, and if He deals with things relatively, it is by an inverted relation: the little is for Him great, and the great is little" (I, 102). "Indeed the whole Bible seems to have been written to teach us the providence of God in trivial things" (II, 46). To the eye freed from habit, "what is there in nature, in its most common and natural events, which is not for us a miracle, in the strictest sense a miracle?" (I, 24). For "God enters into every little circumstance and prefers to reveal His providence in the common events of human life rather than in the rare and extraordinary ones" (I, 36). And by the circumstances of his own spiritual recovery, Hamann is assured that he has been elected for a special literary mission. For God "has bestowed on me many proofs . . . of his choice of me, as pledge and earnest of His divine calling," and "my present calling is now like Adam's in Paradise" (I, 252–3).

Hamann's editor, Joseph Nadler, comments that the *Diary of a Christian* attests "that the spiritual root of the great eighteenth century—of [German] Classicism as well as Romanticism, both of which Hamann fathered—is religious in origin" (I, 321). Hamann's *Diary* also sharpens our sensitivity to the religious understructure of Wordsworth's characteristic forms of experience. To Hamann a crucial discovery was that "the

Book of Nature," and all of human history, is "no other than ciphers, hidden signs, which require the same key that unlocks Holy Scripture"—the key, that is, of the *Regierung Gottes in Kleinigkeiten* (I, 308). In Wordsworth's biography of the Pedlar in *The Ruined Cottage* of 1798, in which he embodied "chiefly an idea of what I fancied my own character might have become in his circumstances," [56] Wordsworth had said very much the same thing. The Pedlar, reading his Bible in an isolated rural schoolhouse, "had early learned/ To reverence the volume which displays/ The mystery, the life which cannot die"; but only later did the deep meaning of that revelation come home to him, when he learned to decipher the parallel script of natural phenomena:

> But in the mountains did he *feel* his faith
> There did he see the writing—All things there
> Looked immortality, revolving life,
> And greatness still revolving, infinite. . . .

The cardinal doctrine which he read in the language of nature was that of the magnitude of the most trivial things, and the moral effect of this way of seeing was to inform his own being with a sublime humility:

> There littleness was not, the least of things
> Seemed infinite, and there his spirit shaped
> Her prospects, nor did he *believe*—he saw,
> What wonder if his being thus became
> Sublime and comprehensive.
>   . . . Yet was his heart
> Lowly; for he was meek in gratitude.[57]

For the Pedlar, Wordsworth goes on to say (lines 272–81), "was a chosen son" whose eye could unriddle what Hamann had called the "ciphers, hidden signs," and "secret sense" of the Book of Nature. In Wordsworth's statement:

>   In all shapes
> He found a secret and mysterious soul,
> A fragrance and a spirit of strange meaning.

In his first-person account of his spiritual crisis in *The Prelude,* Wordsworth tells us in the twelfth book that the recovery involved the disclosure of his identity as a poet rather than as a man of action, and a poet whose mission is to reveal the grandeur implicit in the common, the humble, and the despised. In Wordsworth's narrative, unlike Hamann's, the reversal in his spiritual history is gradual rather than abrupt, and his revelation is described in a way that emphasizes the political and social elements but submerges and mutes the religious element; for Wordsworth's mentor in this process is not Hamann's Holy Spirit, but the Spirit of Nature.

> Above all
> Did Nature bring again that wiser mood
> More deeply re-establish'd in my soul,
> Which, seeing little worthy or sublime
> In what we blazon with the pompous names
> Of power and action, early tutor'd me
> To look with feelings of fraternal love
> Upon those unassuming things, that hold
> A silent station in this beauteous world.

He had earlier succumbed, he had said in the preceding book, to the "tyranny" of the merely physical eye. But now "again I took the intellectual eye/ For my instructor," and thus was able to see validly. The result was the transfer of his hopes for a better future from revolutionary activism to the possibilities inherent in ordinary life.

> The promise of the present time retired
> Into its true proportion; sanguine schemes,
> Ambitious virtues pleased me less, I sought
> For good in the familiar face of life
> And built thereon my hopes of good to come.
>   (XII, 44–68)

He turned, accordingly, from men who thrust themselves upon us "as Rulers of the world," as well as from the abstractions of doctrinaire "modern Statists," in order to explore "the dignity of individual Man . . . the man whom we behold/ With our own eyes," and to investigate the "real worth" of the oppressed rural proletariat: "those who liv'd/ By bodily labour . . . under all the weight/ Of that injustice" entailed "by composition of society." He turned away also from "the throes/ And mighty hopes of Nations" to "lonely Roads" and "naked Moors," and there discovered the "grandeur" that invests "the Wanderers of the Earth," and was "awed . . . by strolling Bedlamites" and "uncouth Vagrants," and heard "from mouths of lowly men and of obscure/ A tale of honour." Listening to such men, he also found that "strong affections" and "love" do not require a "language purified/ By manners thoughtful and elaborate," and so came to recognize how misleading are those books which are adapted to the "judgments of the wealthy Few, who see/ By artificial lights," and which flatter "our self-conceit" by exploiting the superficial signs of caste,

> the outside marks by which
> Society has parted man from man,
> Neglectful of the universal heart.
> (XII, 73–219)

Here Wordsworth also discovers (or in his elected terms, nature discloses to him) his destined poetic enterprise; and it is plain that this enterprise is the one that he also set forth in the Prefaces to *Lyrical Ballads* and later justified, from a different perspective, in the *Essay* of 1815:

> Of these, said I, shall be my Song; of these . . .
> Will I record the praises . . . speak of these
> That justice may be done, obeisance paid
> Where it is due: thus haply shall I teach,
> Inspire. . . .

His subject, that is, will be "men as they are men within themselves" though "rude in shew," and who, in place of the rhetoric of artifice, utter the spontaneous overflow of powerful feelings: "Expressing liveliest thoughts in lively words/ As native passion dictates." In this undertaking he shall move "with no timid step," but with the boldness of a man chosen for a sacred but unpopular mission:

> It shall be my pride
> That I have dared to tread this holy ground,
> Speaking no dream but things oracular.
>
> (XII, 223–77)

Central to his vision is his recognition of the sublimity of the lowliest and the meanest things, natural and human.

> Nature through all conditions hath a power
> To consecrate, if we have eyes to see,
> The outside of her creatures, and to breathe
> Grandeur upon the very humblest face
> Of human life;

and, in their continuous interchange with the passions of the perceiving mind,

> the forms
> Of Nature have a passion in themselves
> That intermingles with those works of man
> To which she summons him; although the works
> Be mean, have nothing lofty of their own.

That he has been granted this originality of insight provides the grounds for Wordsworth's claim (which he at this point puts forward) that he possesses that "genius of the Poet" which gives him a place, though as "the meanest of this Band," in the visionary company of "Poets" who,

> even as Prophets, each with each
> Connected in a mighty scheme of truth,
> Have each for his peculiar dower, a sense
> By which he is enabled to perceive
> Something unseen before.
>
> (XII, 278–312)

Such persistent visual references express Wordsworth's conception that the elected poet is literally a seer, a man who sees in a new way, and that his particular vocation is to liberate the vision of his readers from bondage to the physical eye, habitual categories, social custom, and caste prejudice, so that they may see the world that he has come to see.

In discussing Wordsworth's "freshness of sensation" in the *Biographia Literaria*, Coleridge says that upon first hearing Wordsworth recite a poem in 1796, he had at once recognized Wordsworth's power to renew the old world, by virtue of a balance of "truth in observing" with the modifying "imagination." Wordsworth's account of his imaginative recovery in Book XII of *The Prelude* has brought him to that point in his life at which, during a walking tour on Salisbury Plain, he had composed the very poem (an early version of *Guilt and Sorrow*) to which Coleridge was to allude in this passage.[58] Wordsworth ends his account by recalling to his friend what he had told Wordsworth about that poem: thou "hast said, perusing some imperfect verse/ Which in that lonesome journey was composed,"

> That also then I must have exercised
> Upon the vulgar forms of present things
> And actual world of our familiar days,
> A higher power, have caught from them a tone,
> An image, and a character, by books
> Not hitherto reflected.

Wordsworth humbly submits that his new way of seeing, which Coleridge had inferred from his verses, had indeed been a fact of his perceptual experience:

> The mind is to herself
> Witness and judge, and I remember well
> That in life's every-day appearances
> I seem'd about this period to have sight
> Of a new world, a world, too, that was fit
> To be transmitted and made visible
> To other eyes

—a new world that is the product of "a balance, an ennobling interchange" which involves both "the object seen, and eye that sees" (XII, 360–79).

Thus Wordsworth's narrative in *The Prelude* XII of his discovery of what he was born to do ends in his experience of what was to be the "high argument" of his major poetry—the power-in-union of mind and nature to create, out of the "vulgar forms" of the "actual world," by an apocalyptic act of imaginative vision, "a new world" which is capable of being "made visible to other eyes," and which (as he adds in the Prospectus) is man's only available paradise. In the last hundred lines of *Home at Grasmere* that lead up to the definitive statement of this argument in the Prospectus, Wordsworth summarizes the process of discovery which he details in Book XII of *The Prelude.* The index of his destined "office," he there tells us, is his possession of "an internal brightness" which is "solely mine," but which can and must be communicated. He had been endowed at birth with "wild appetites and blind desires/ Motions of savage instinct"; but nature, later sanctioned by his reason, had tamed him and taught him to "be mild and cleave to gentle things,/ Thy glory and thy happiness be there."

Accordingly, he bids "farewell to the Warrior's schemes" and also to "that other hope, long mine . . . to fill/ The heroic trumpet with the Muse's breath." That is, he gives up both the life of militant action and his earlier plan to write a Miltonic epic—the genre in which Milton had adapted the new matter of Christian fortitude-in-meekness to the traditional pomp and decorum of the heroic mode. But in his new poetry, Wordsworth claims in the Prospectus, he will need "a greater Muse" than Milton's; for as he had explained in *Home at Grasmere* (lines 737–44), in surrendering heroic militancy for poetic radicalism he has merely shifted to a new province the challenge to his audacity. No need to fear, he says,

> a want
> Of aspirations that have been, of foes
> To wrestle with, and victory to complete,
> Bounds to be leapt, darkness to be explored.
> All that inflamed thy infant heart, the love,
> The longing, the contempt, the dauntless quest,
> All shall survive—though changed their office, all
> Shall live,—it is not in their power to die.

EIGHT

The Poet's Vision:
Romantic and Post-Romantic

I saw this familiar—too *familiar*—fact at a different
angle, and I was charmed and haunted by it. . . . I had
seen into paradisaic regions, with their air and sky, and I
was no longer wholly or merely a denizen of this vulgar
earth.

—Thoreau, *Journal*

Le Paradis est toujours à refaire; il n'est point en quelque
lointaine Thulé. Il demeure sous l'apparence. . . .
Le Poète est celui qui regarde. Et que voit-il?—Le Paradis.
—André Gide, *Le Traité du Narcisse*

The eye believes and its communion takes. . . .
To have satisfied the mind and turn to see,
(That being as much belief as we may have,)
And turn to look and say there is no more
Than this, in this alone I may believe,
Whatever it may be; then one's belief
Resists each past apocalypse.
—Wallace Stevens, *Extracts from
Addresses to the Academy of Fine Ideas*

EIGHT

"LE POÈTE," said André Gide, "est celui qui regarde." "Someone who looks"—of all Romantic innovations, none has so preempted the attention of poets, novelists, and painters (and the critics of poetry, novels, and painting) as the concern with the eye and the object and the need for a revolution in seeing which will make the object new. And to our own day the chief definitions of transforming vision have continued to be recognizable, if sometimes distorted, variations on the Romantic categories of freshness of sensation, revelatory Moments, and the rectified outlook which inverts the status of the lowly, the trivial, and the mean.

American literature, beyond all others, has stressed the first category—the fresh sensation of the child—as the norm for a valid relation to the universe. In *The Reign of Wonder* Tony Tanner has recently demonstrated the persistence, from Emerson and Thoreau through Mark Twain and Henry James to J. D. Salinger, of the ideal of the child's innocent eye which, by freeing perception from habit and prejudice and sustaining the sense of wonder, transforms the old world into a new Eden.[1] Historical reasons for this American preoccupation are not far to seek. From the time of its discovery, and beginning with the writings of Columbus himself, the geographical New World had been identified with the new earth prophesied in Revelation, and the belief that America was the locale of the promised millennial kingdom had been brought to these shores both by Franciscan missionaries and by the Puritan fathers. This way of thinking was rearoused by the American Revolution, and to some extent again by the Civil War—singers of the *Battle Hymn of the Republic* echoed the millennial expectation of their Puritan ancestors in the English Civil War: "Mine eyes have seen the glory of the coming of the Lord." The doctrine of Manifest Destiny in the 1840's and later decades derived its impetus from the continuing myth of America as the elected theater for the fulfillment of eschatological prophecy. As William Gilpin wrote in 1846:

> The *untransacted* destiny of the American people is to subdue the continent—to rush over this vast field to the Pacific Ocean . . . to regenerate superannuated nations . . . to confirm the destiny of the human race—to carry the career of mankind to its culminating point . . . to cause a stagnant people to be reborn . . . to absolve the curse that weighs down humanity, and to shed blessings round the world! [2]

From its early period, much New World writing represented the American as a new Adam, emancipated from the burden of history and the corruptions of the Old World, and inhabiting, if he would but open his eyes to the fact, a pristine garden-land like Eden.[3] And in American churches and revival meetings, Jonathan Edwards and many evangelical preachers stressed the experience of a conversion which redeems man's corrupted eye and makes all creation new. In this unique climate of Edenic and millennial imagination, in its various theological and secular versions, the American Transcendentalists, beginning in the 1830's, seized upon and expanded the assertions by Coleridge, Wordsworth, Carlyle, and their German contemporaries concerning the power of renewal in the eye of a man who sees as a child sees, on the assumption that to become as a child again is to see as Adam saw.

1. FRESHNESS OF SENSATION AND THE DISORDERING OF THE SENSES

"We distrust and deny inwardly," Emerson said, "our sympathy with nature," but "infancy is the perpetual Messiah, which comes into the arms of fallen men, and pleads with them to return to paradise." [4] Or in unmistakably Coleridgean terms, "Few adult persons can see nature. . . . The lover of nature is he . . . who has retained the spirit of infancy even into the era of manhood." In other passages his phrasing echoed Carlyle: "all wonder" is prevented by "the coarse mattings of custom," but "the wise man wonders at the usual" and sees "the miraculous in the common." Like Wordsworth, Emerson asserted the absolute equality of natural phenomena: "The distinctions which we make . . . of low and high, honest and base, disappear when nature is used as a symbol." He recognized the Biblical prototype for the subversion of stylistic decorum—in the Hebrew prophets, he remarked, "small and mean things serve as well as great symbols"; and he also recognized, as had Hazlitt, the relation of such literary radicalism to the spirit of the age, hailing the evidences in poetry of an "Age of Revolution" which, in the realm of politics, "effected the elevation of what was called the lowest class in the state."

> Instead of the sublime and beautiful, the near, the low, the common, was explored and poetized. . . . I embrace the common, I explore and sit at the feet of the familiar, the low.

A shift in vision, he adds, can be an adequate alternative to a forfeited Golden Age and a millennial hereafter: "Give me insight into to-day, and you may have the antique and future worlds." [5] And for the Moment of revelation in the trivial fact Emerson introduces a term which, to the modern ear, is portentous. "The aroused intellect," he says, when it confronts "facts, dull, strange, despised things," finds "that a fact is an Epiphany of God." [6]

More radically even than Emerson, Thoreau defined the primary values of life in terms of the relation between the eye and its objects. "How much virtue there is in simply seeing! . . . We are as much as we see." "Every child," he remarks, "begins the world again." The height of his own experience had occurred in childhood, "before I lost any of my senses" and "my life was ecstasy." And in the adult, to re-achieve freshness of sensation suffices to redeem the familiar and trivial world:

I saw this familiar—too *familiar*—fact at a different angle, and I was charmed and haunted by it. . . . I had seen into paradisaic regions, with their air and sky, and I was no longer wholly or merely a denizen of this vulgar earth. . . . Only what we have touched and worn is trivial,—our scurf, repetition, tradition, conformity. To perceive freshly, with fresh senses, is to be inspired. . . . The age of miracles is each moment thus returned.[7]

Recourse to the vision of the child was not limited to English and American writers. In 1863 Baudelaire discovered in Constantin Guys, "the painter of modern life," exactly those characteristics of genius which Coleridge had discovered in Wordsworth's poetry more than a half-century earlier: the child's freshness of sensation surviving in the powers of the man, which is an index to mental convalescence and manifests itself in the perception of novelty in old and familiar appearances. Guys, Baudelaire says, can be regarded as "un éternel convalescent . . . un homme-enfant," "that is to say, a genius for whom no aspect of life has become stale."

Now, convalescence is like a return to childhood. The convalescent, like the child, enjoys to the highest degree the power to take a lively interest in all things, even those which seem to be the most trivial. . . . The child sees everything as *new;* he is always *intoxicated.* . . . But genius is no other than *childhood recovered* at will, childhood now endowed, in order to express itself, with the powers of manhood [*d'organes virils*] and with that analytic mind which enables him to order the sum of the materials which he has involuntarily accumulated. This deep and joyous curiosity is the explanation of the fixed and animal-like ecstatic eye of the child confronted by the *new,* whatever it may be, face or landscape. . . .

The passage in Baudelaire, however, has overtones which signalize a new turn in the aesthetics of the innocent eye. The genius is "an eternal convalescent" because he suffers from an incurable disease; artistic inspiration is something like a cerebral stroke; and the sustained sense of novelty in perception is a result of hyperasthesia: "I dare to press farther; I declare that inspiration has some relation with a cerebral congestion, and that every sublime thought is accompanied by a nervous shock . . . which reverberates up to the cerebellum." The born artist is an *artiste maudit,* for when as a child he showed himself to be "obsessed and possessed" by external objects and forms, "predestination" manifested itself in him and "la *damnation* était faite." [8]

In his poem *Moesta et errabunda* Baudelaire expresses the longing for a voyage back to the "green paradise" of infancy; but infancy to Baudelaire is both more Augustinian and more Freudian than the Edenic childhood posited by Traherne, Wordsworth, and Emerson—it is "le vert paradis des amours enfantines/ L'innocent paradis, plein de plaisirs furtifs." And if the artist is an eternal convalescent, he inhabits a world which, Baudelaire says in a prose-poem, "is a hospital where every patient is possessed by the desire to change his bed"; and Baudelaire's goaded soul "explodes" in a cry of desire for a voyage, "N'importe où! n'importe où! pourvu que ce soit hors de ce monde!" [9] This indefinite destination is the goal of *Le Voyage,* Baudelaire's distinctive version of that ancient genre, the spiritual pilgrimage of life, which concludes *Les Fleurs du mal.* The poem begins with "l'enfant, amoureux de cartes et d'estampes" for whom the world is adequate to his desires, moves through the adult's ennui and disgust with a world which has become all too familiar, and ends with a tactic of desperation in quest of something new:

> Plonger au fond du gouffre, Enfer ou Ciel, qu'importe?
> Au fond de l'Inconnu pour trouver du *nouveau!*

"Let us require of the *poet* something *new,*" Arthur Rimbaud cried in his two letters on the poet as *voyant.* "The first Romantics were *seers* without understanding it very well," but "Baudelaire is the first seer, the king of poets, *a real God.*" [10] By making explicit and pressing to the extreme elements which in Baudelaire had remained submerged or qualified, the sixteen-year-old Rimbaud reshaped a Romantic concept—the visionary poet who perceives the world as a new heaven and earth—into the rudiments of that rarity in aesthetic history, a genuinely new poetic. The implications of Rimbaud's theory of art are still being assiduously explored by writers in our own generation.

Rimbaud's emphasis on drugs as a means for achieving a new poetic world, like his other devices toward the same end, had been anticipated by Baudelaire. Baudelaire had said that hashish provides the experience of a recovered paradise—an "artificial paradise," however, which is the product of "a distortion of the senses." [11] Baudelaire's involuntary predecessors in drug addiction, Coleridge and De Quincy, had looked upon the novelty of experience made possible by opium as a temporary result, for which the penalty is enslavement of the will and the destruction not only of human autonomy and dignity but of creativity as well. Baudelaire too warned that the *paradis par la pharmacie* is evanescent, but that its price is enduring slavery to "a poison." Man, wanting "to be God," falls "lower than his actual nature," and "what is a paradise that one buys at the cost of his eternal salvation?" [12] In Rimbaud this cost becomes the martyrdom of a man predestined to the damnation of the poet's sacred calling. For the way to vision is the way of the Christian mystic, turned inside out—a discipline which consists in the systematic violation of both the moral sensibilities and the sensory system by means of dissipation, drugs, and perversity.

Rimbaud's poetic is new only as a specifically aesthetic theory and program; its component ideas are familiar enough to the student of the variegated history of Christian thought. The prototype of Rimbaud's poet as *voyant* is to be found in an extravagant, harshly repressed, yet stubbornly recurrent Christian heresy. This way of thinking was developed in the second and third century by the Carpocratians and other fringe groups among the Christian Gnostics, who regarded the world as a creation not of God but of a spirit of evil; it turned up in the movement of the Spiritual Libertines, or "Brethren of the Free Spirit," which from the fourteenth century through the sixteenth century spread over a vast area of Europe, including France; it had a recrudescence in the English Ranters of the age of Cromwell; and it manifested itself in the eighteenth century as a Judaic heresy, in the movement led by Joseph Frank, the follower of the apostate Messiah, Sabbatai

Zevi.[13] Common to the diverse forms of the heresy is an extreme type of antinomian doctrine which asserts not merely the permissibility of sin but also the holiness of sin. For those elect who, in an ecstasy of illumination, have entered the new world of the pure spirit, the law of commandments and prohibitions which governs the fallen world is totally abrogated. And the way to the redeeming vision is often represented as the deliberate and systematic flouting of all moral restraints and denials, especially through participating in forbidden forms of sexuality. These acts are not performed for the purpose of sensual gratification, but as a harsh discipline for rooting out the fear, shame, and remorse which are the appurtenances of fallen man in his world of evil, in order to achieve that identity with the One Spirit which makes man into a godlike new creature who is endowed with the power of creative, or thaumaturgic, vision, and who dwells in a new reality beyond good and evil.

Such is the formula which Rimbaud translated into a regimen for the discipline and consummation of the poet's mind. His use of the term "Savant" for the poet who has achieved *gnosis*—the revelation of absolute novelty—indicates the probable source of his ideas in the strain of libertine doctrines which survived among the *Illuminés* of mid-nineteenth-century Europe:

> Now I am debauching myself as much as I can. Why? I want to be a poet, and I am working to make myself a *seer*. . . . The sufferings are enormous, but one must be strong, must be born a poet, and I have recognized myself to be a poet. That is not in the least my fault. . . .
>
> What is needed is to make the soul monstrous. . . .
>
> The poet makes himself a *seer* by a long, immense, and calculated *disordering* of *all his senses* [*dérèglement* de *tous les sens*]. All the forms of love, of suffering, of madness; he himself experiments, he exhausts within himself every poison, in order to retain only its quintessence. Ineffable torture wherein he needs the utmost faith, the utmost superhuman strength, wherein he becomes supremely the great diseased one, the great criminal, the great accursed—and the supreme Savant!— For he reaches the *unknown!* . . . He reaches the unknown,

and even though, made mad, he should end by losing the understanding of his visions, he has at any rate seen them! [14]

These extraordinary letters, and Rimbaud's consonant practice in his life and writings, point forward to prominent aspects of French Symbolism and the Decadence; to Alfred Jarry
and *les Pataphysiciens;* as well as to Surrealism, free fantasy,
automatic writing, and other modes of composition in which
control is surrendered to the unconscious mind.[15] For Rimbaud had written in his letters, "It is false to say: I think.
One ought to say: I am thought." "For I is an other [*Je est
un autre*]. If the brass is roused to a bugle call, that is none
of its doing. . . . I attend at the blossoming of my thought:
I look at it, I listen." Rimbaud also points the way to another
conspicuous movement in the literature of our day. Wordsworth, as we know, had found in Scripture the precedent for
his violation of conventional decorums in elevating the lowly
and the outcast into the protagonists of his serious or tragic
poems. Modern writers, however, by an absolute act of moral
as well as social inversion, transform the base, the pathological,
and the perverse not merely into the heroes, but also into the
sacred figures of fiction, poetry, and drama. Rimbaud's "le
grand malade, le grand criminel, le grand maudit,—et le su-
prême Savant!" have become familiar personages in the age
of Jean Genet—*Saint Genet: Comédien et Martyr* as, by a
typical inversion, he is represented by Jean-Paul Sartre.

2. VARIETIES OF THE MODERN MOMENT

The Romantic Moment in which, as Frank Kermode puts it,
chronos suddenly becomes *kairos*,[16] has had an enduring and
multiform literary life. The illuminated phenomenal object,
if transparent to a significance beyond itself, reappears as the
symbol of the Symbolists, but if opaque, as the image of the
Imagists; in both cases, however, the Romantic object is usually cut off from its context in the ordinary world and in
common experience and assigned an isolated existence in the
self-limited and self-sufficing work of art. And the Moment of

consciousness, the abrupt illumination in an arrest of time, has become a familiar component in modern fiction, where it sometimes functions, like Wordsworth's spots of time, as a principle of literary organization, by signalizing the essential discoveries or precipitating the narrative resolution. We recognize the familiar traits not only in Proust's *moments privilégiés,* but also in Henry James's act of imagination which "converts the very pulses of the air into revelations"; in Joseph Conrad's "moment of vision" that reveals "all the truth of life"; in Virginia Woolf's "moments of vision," the "little daily miracles, illuminations, matches struck unexpectedly in the dark"; in Thomas Wolfe's attempt "to fix eternally . . . a single moment of man's living . . . that passes, flames and goes"; in William Faulkner's "instant of sublimation . . . a flash, a glare." [17]

The modern Moment is frequently connected with the concept of freshness of sensation, as well as with the discovery of the charismatic virtue of a trivial object or event, and it is expounded both in secular and in religious frames of reference. In his Conclusion to *The Renaissance,* Walter Pater defined all of human experience as constituted by successive "moments" of sensation in consciousness; there is no realm of existence either outside the sphere of sense-data or after the death of the senses. "Every moment some form grows perfect . . . some tone . . . some mood . . . for that moment only," and to maintain an "ecstasy" of intense moments "is success in life." "Our failure," correspondingly, "is to form habits: for, after all, habit is relative to a stereotyped world"; and to maximize the ecstasy of our sensuous existence, art has the most to offer, "for art comes to you proposing frankly to give nothing but the highest quality to your moments as they pass, and simply for those moments' sake." Gerard Manley Hopkins, with the help of Duns Scotus, undertook to retrieve the refreshed sensation and the intense Moment from Pater, his pagan schoolteacher, and to give them back to their original Author. Hopkins' poems of "inscape," in which a stale phenomenon abruptly "will flame out, like shining from shook foil" to reveal "the dearest freshness deep down things," typically end with the attribution: "Because the Holy Ghost over the bent/ World broods," or, "He fathers-forth whose beauty is past change." [18] For Hopkins, everything that seems trivial in the perceptual world has, to the eye of faith, been redeemed by a single event in past time: "I think that the trivialness of life is, and personally to each one, ought to be seen to be, done away with by . . . the incredible condescension of the Incarnation." [19] And in *That Nature Is a Heraclitean Fire,* the poet's Moment of renewal at the last trump of an inner apocalypse reverts from its immediate precedent, the Romantic poems of dejection versus joy, to their theological prototype:

> Away grief's gasping, joyless days, dejection. . . .
> In a flash, at a trumpet crash,
> I am all at once what Christ is, since he was what I am, and
> This Jack, joke, poor potsherd, patch, matchwood,
>   immortal diamond,
>   Is immortal diamond.

As in Hopkins' poems, so in Eliot's *Four Quartets,* the poet's experience of the still center is represented as something more than Pater's Moment of pure sensation—in Eliot's description, it is "not the intense moment/ Isolated, with no before and after." [20] Eliot's own "moments of happiness . . . the sudden illumination," which we vainly seek by magic, psychoanalysis, and barbiturates (the "usual/ Pastimes and drugs"), are again described, as they had been by Augustine, as "the point of intersection of the timeless/ With time," of which "the hint half guessed, the gift half understood, is Incarnation" (pp. 132–3, 135–6). And Eliot's Moment of Moments, "the moment in the rose-garden," represents at the same time the individual's glimpse of his own lost garden and his foresight of a generic garden to be regained (pp. 119, 125). In most of our recent writers, however, preoccupation with the Moment rescued from time saves the traditional experience without subscribing to its traditional premise. In *Stream and Sun at Glendalough* Yeats's account of a sudden illumination is put in the form of a question that involves an as-if:

> Through intricate motions ran
> Stream and gliding sun
> And all my heart seemed gay. . . .

> What motion of the sun or stream
> Or eyelid shot the gleam
> That pierced my body through?
> What made me live like those that seem
> Self-born, born anew?

Emerson long ago said that to an "aroused intellect," "facts, dull . . . despised things" are "an Epiphany of God." It was James Joyce, however, who by deliberately transferring the theological term into a naturalistic aesthetic, affixed to the Moment what seems destined to become its standard name. It is noteworthy that in a précis of English literary history which he composed in the spring of 1905, Joyce gave "the highest palms" to Wordsworth, together with Shakespeare and Shelley; and a few months later he wrote to Stanislaus Joyce, "I think Wordsworth of all English men of letters best deserves your word 'genius.' " [21] This is the very time when Joyce was working on *Stephen Hero,* wherein he identified and analyzed "moments" of epiphany; and although Joyce refers only to Aquinas, his epiphanies share attributes with the Wordsworthian Moment (the charismatic revelation in the commonplace or trivial object) which are lacking both in Aquinas' analysis of *claritas* in beauty and in his description of the "quiddity or nature existing in corporeal matter" through which the human intellect "rises to a certain knowledge of things invisible." [22] An epiphany, Joyce specifically notes, may appear in "a trivial incident," at the instant when the "spiritual eye" adjusts "to an exact focus."

> By an epiphany [Stephen] meant a sudden spiritual manifestation, whether in the vulgarity of speech or of gesture or in a memorable phase of the mind itself. He believed that it was for the man of letters to record these epiphanies with extreme care, seeing that they themselves are the most delicate and evanescent of moments. . . .

> For a long time I couldn't make out what Aquinas meant . . . but I have solved it. *Claritas* is *quidditas.* . . . Its soul, its whatness, leaps to us from the vestment of its appearance. The soul of the commonest object . . . seems to us radiant. The object achieves its epiphany.[23]

Although Joyce quickly gave up using the name, he clearly used the thing as an important element in his later writings. "It is my idea of the significance of trivial things," he told his brother, "that I want to give the two or three unfortunate wretches who may eventually read me." [24] The *Portrait of the Artist,* like Wordsworth's *Prelude,* marks the stages of the artist's development by a sequence of discoveries which are climaxed by the Moment on the strand in which Stephen Dedalus, solitary, suddenly confronts an isolated human being in a natural setting. In its structural function Joyce's scene is equivalent to the climactic Moment in which the landscape below Snowdon suddenly discloses to Wordsworth his great poetic subject, the workings of the mind and imagination of man:

> He was alone . . . amid a waste of wild air and brackish waters and the seaharvest of shells and tangle and veiled grey sunlight and gayclad lightclad figures of children and girls. . . .
>
> A girl stood before him in midstream, alone and still, gazing out to sea. She seemed like one whom magic had changed into the likeness of a strange and beautiful seabird. . . .
>
> —Heavenly God! cried Stephen's soul, in an outburst of profane joy. . . .
>
> Her image had passed into his soul for ever and no word had broken the holy silence of his ecstasy. . . . To live, to err, to fall, to triumph, to recreate life out of life! A wild angel had appeared to him, the angel of mortal youth and beauty, an envoy from the fair courts of life, to throw open before him in an instant of ecstasy the gates of all the ways of error and glory.[25]

Dedalus loses his mundane life to find himself an artist. The episode is part of Joyce's systematic translation of religious formulas into a comprehensive aesthetic theory, in which the artist, or artificer, undertakes to redeem both life and the world by recreating them into a new world. Joyce's new world, however, is radically opposed to Wordsworth's, for it is no other than the work of art itself.

Another admirer of Wordsworth, Wallace Stevens, describes

his own enterprise as a poet with the rigor of his skeptical naturalism: the mind, exiling "desire/ For what is not," confronts the alien other resolved to "see the very thing and nothing else," and by an act of creative fiction in lieu of the Creator, imposes the order and values it can no longer find. Stevens' "supreme fiction" nonetheless incorporates the Romantic freshness of sensation which makes the world new:

> The freshness of transformation is
> The freshness of a world. It is our own,
> It is ourselves, the freshness of ourselves. . . .

It retains also the traditional Moments—"times of inherent excellence," he calls them, "moments of awakening" when "all/ Is well"—as occasions in which the poet as-if-reborn looks out upon a world as-if-renewed.

> Only this evening I saw again low in the sky
> The evening star, at the beginning of winter, the star
> That in spring will crown every western horizon,
> Again . . . as if it came back, as if life came back. . . .
>
> It was like sudden time in a world without time,
> This world, this place, the street in which I was,
> Without time. . . .
>
> Only this evening I saw it again,
> At the beginning of winter, and I walked and talked
> Again, and lived and was again, and breathed again
> And moved again and flashed again, time flashed again.[26]

In *Black Rook in Rainy Weather* a remarkable young poet, the late Sylvia Plath, also testified to the recurrent Moment:

> I can't honestly complain:
> A certain minor light may still
> Leap incandescent
>
> Out of kitchen table or chair
> As if a celestial burning took
> Possession of the most obtuse objects now and then.

But the traditional language is here used ironically, to identify phenomenal flare-ups that signify only themselves, in the
quiet desperation of a life that rejects all hope.

> I only know that a rook
> Ordering its black feathers can so shine
> As to seize my senses, haul
> My eyelids up, and grant
>
> A brief respite from fear
> Of total neutrality. . . .
>
> Miracles occur,
> If you care to call those spasmodic
> Tricks of radiance miracles. The wait's begun again,
> The long wait for the angel,
> For that rare, random descent.[27]

A current literary movement (if it is still current) deals obsessively with novelty of sensation, illuminated Moments, and
the visual apocalypse. The Beat generation, in the words of
Gregory Corso in *Gasoline* (1958), are writers "screaming:
Apocalypse! Apocalypse!" [28]—though, one must add, *d'une
voix lamentable*. They are heirs, in the age of the internal
combustion engine, urban decay, Disestablishmentarianism,
collapsing social and international order, and the apocalyptic
bomb, of the *fin de siècle* writers who, in rebellion against the
horror and the boredom of an earlier stage of the modern
world, sought for something new by following Rimbaud's pre-
scription for a calculated disordering of all the senses through
direct assault upon the moral and nervous system. "Angel-
headed hipsters," Allen Ginsberg described them, in a strident
parody of the Romantic vocabulary of the transforming vision,

> burning for the ancient heavenly connection
>   to the starry dynamo in the machinery of night,
> who poverty and tatters and hollow-eyed and high sat up
>   smoking in the supernatural darkness of cold-water flats
>   floating across the tops of cities contemplating jazz,
> who bared their brains to Heaven under the El and saw

> Mohammedan angels staggering on tenement roofs
>   illuminated . . .
> who ate fire in paint hotels or drank turpentine in
>   Paradise Alley, death, or purgatoried their torsos night
>   after night
> with dreams, with drugs, with waking nightmares,
>   alcohol and cock and endless balls . . .
> who chained themselves to subways for the endless ride
>   from Battery to holy Bronx on benzedrine . . .
> who studied Plotinus Poe St. John of the Cross telepathy
>   and bop kaballa because the cosmos instinctively
>   vibrated at their feet in Kansas,
> who loned it through the streets of Idaho seeking visionary
>   indian angels who were visionary indian angels,
> who thought they were only mad when Baltimore gleamed
>   in supernatural ecstasy. . . .
> They broke their backs lifting Moloch to Heaven! Pavements,
>   trees, radios, tons! lifting the city to Heaven which
>   exists and is everywhere about us!
> Visions! omens! hallucinations! miracles! ecstasies!
>   gone down the American river! [29]

"Gone down the American river!" In a final irony Ginsberg uses the long verse-line of Walt Whitman, poet of the redeemed vision and elected prophet of the party of hope—

> I, chanter of Adamic songs,
> Through the new garden the West, the great cities calling

—to express the dead end of the dream of the New World as the recovered Eden in the prophecies.[30] But the ever incipient despair of America is simply equal and opposite to the inordinateness of its millennial expectations, as Herman Melville had recognized even in 1876:

> How far beyond the scope
> Of elder Europe's saddest thought
> Might be the New World's sudden brought
> In youth to share old age's pains—
> To feel the arrest of hope's advance,

And squandered last inheritance;
And cry—"To Terminus build fanes!
Columbus ended earth's romance:
No New World to mankind remains!" [31]

We also possess contemporary versions of the spiritual autobiography in which the established climax is the revelation,
to the regenerate eye, of a new heaven and earth. Jack Kerouac,
who has been hailed by Allen Ginsberg as the "new Buddha
of American prose," [32] ends *The Dharma Bums* (1958) with
his epiphany on a mountain, in the lineage (apparent through
the verbal coloring of a Westernized Buddhism) of Moses on
Horeb, Petrarch on Mont Ventoux, Rousseau's St. Preux in
the Valois, and Wordsworth on Mount Snowdon. Kerouac's
mountain is Desolation Peak in the Pacific Northwest, where
he has completed a solitary summer as a fire ranger, and the
timeless Moment in which the author becomes as a child again
involves a commonplace little animal:

> There he was, my chipmunk, in the bright clear windy sunny
> air staring on the rock. . . . The vision of the freedom of
> eternity was mine forever. The chipmunk ran into the rocks
> and a butterfly came out. It was as simple as that. . . . Down
> on the lake rosy reflections of celestial vapor appeared, and I
> said "God, I love you" and looked up to the sky and really
> meant it. "I have fallen in love with you, God. Take care of
> us all, one way or the other."
> To the children and the innocent it's all the same. . . .
> As I was hiking down the mountain with my pack I turned
> and knelt on the trail and said "Thank you, shack." Then I
> added "Blah," with a little grin, because I knew that shack and
> that mountain would understand what that meant, and turned
> and went on down the trail back to this world.[33]

Kerouac's revelation of a new world, all gratulant, is the
traditional interior apocalypse, gone soft. More representative
of recent decades is a reversion to the savagery and destructiveness of the original Biblical paradigm, but without its sanction
in a transcendent other world. Much of our literature of absurdity and black comedy is a form of black apocalypse—gro-
tesque visions of an ultimate violence which destroys not to

renew but simply to annihilate a world which is regarded as an affront to being, revealing behind its disintegrating fabric not a new heaven and earth but *le Néant,* nothing at all.

3.   THE ROMANTIC POSITIVES

In this, as in earlier chapters, I have stressed analogues in post-Romantic literature to the ideas and forms that were developed during that period of astonishing creativity, the several decades after the French Revolution. Such an emphasis may appear to align my point of view with the recent tendency to break down the traditional opposition between what is Romantic and what seems to us distinctively "modern" in literature. Characteristic of this tendency is Frank Kermode's interesting and influential book, *The Romantic Image.* Professor Kermode undertakes to trace back to the generation of Coleridge and Wordsworth what he identifies as the premises of the modern movement: the concept of the self-sufficient image or symbol; the concept of the poem as an object which, insulated from the world and from ordinary human concerns, exists only for its own perfection; and the related concept of the alienated and anguished artist whose priestly vocation entails the renunciation of this life and of this contemptible world in favor of that other world which is the work of his art. We may agree that these are central and recurrent ideas in much of the major literature from Baudelaire to the recent past. And there are discernible similarities, as well as some direct causal connections, between Professor Kermode's categories and a number of the Romantic ideas with which we have been concerned. The fact is, however, that many of the chief figures in the modernist movement —including, in England and America, Hulme, Pound, and Eliot—identified themselves as, explicitly, counter-Romantic; and from any comprehensive view of their basic premises and literary practice, it seems to me that in this judgment they were manifestly right.[34]

To make a valid distinction between post-Romantic and anti-Romantic, we need to decide what can properly be called Romantic. Can we identify among the major Romantic poets, whatever their philosophical differences, a set of assumptions and values so basic and so widely shared as to constitute a distinctive outlook on life and art and the relations between them? I propose to look for these attitudes especially among the poets who came to literary maturity during the crisis precipitated by the course of the French Revolution, which for them was an intellectual, moral, and aesthetic as well as political crisis: in England Wordsworth, Blake, and Coleridge, and in Germany Schiller and Hölderlin, who was the heir to Schiller's humanism. I shall emphasize the writings of that period when these poets had not lost the assurance of their youth, yet could join it to the fullness of their poetic power; and I shall add to this list Shelley, who, although he belonged to the post-Revolutionary generation, recapitulated to a remarkable degree the evolution of his predecessors from political to imaginative radicalism.

We know that these poets envisioned their role in quasi-religious terms. But when Wordsworth at the beginning of *The Prelude* describes the sudden access of power which testified to his election—

> to the open fields I told
> A prophecy: poetic numbers came
> Spontaneously, and cloth'd in priestly robe
> My spirit, thus singled out, as it might seem,
> For holy services

—he did not mean that he had died to this life to become a novitiate in the religion of art. He donned his "priestly robe" as a poet-prophet who remained, as he said in the great Preface, a responsible human spokesman—"a man speaking to men." Having begun *The Prelude* with the confirmation of his identity, Wordsworth ends it by girding himself for the task the vocation imposes, "in a work/ Of [men's] redemption." So Shelley, when he describes his major poetic contemporaries as "the priests of an unapprehended aspiration," goes on to say that they thereby become "the unacknowledged legislators of the world," for they are the authors "to others of the highest wisdom, pleasure, virtue, and glory." [35] These poets, like their German counterparts, had inherited the severe and conscientious spirit of radical Protestantism, which fostered views at an extreme from the later French development of art for art's sake and of life for art's sake. The Romantic aesthetic was of art for man's sake, and for life's sake. Poetry, like all art, Coleridge said, "is purely human; for all its materials are from the mind, and all its products are for the mind"; and in Wordsworth's view, the poet "is the rock of defence for human nature; an upholder and preserver." [36] Keats was as certain as Shelley that "Great spirits now on earth are sojourning" and that "these will give the world another heart,/ And other pulses." In some passages read out of context, Keats seems to come closer than any of his contemporaries to a religion of beauty. Yet in his first major poem about poetry he bound himself to press on through the pastoral realm of Flora and Old Pan to "a nobler life" of "the agonies, the strife/ Of human hearts"; and in his last poem on the same subject, *The Fall of Hyperion,* the Induction represents him in the very act of passage to that stage, when, having demonstrated his acquired awareness that "a poet is a sage;/ A humanist, Physician to all men," he is reborn as a poet of suffering humanity.[37] These writers, whatever their religious creed or lack of creed, were all, in Keats's term, humanists. They posited the central importance and essential dignity of man (including, Wordsworth especially insisted, the lowly, helpless, and outcast man); they set as the aim of man an abundant life in this world, in which he may give play to all his creative powers; they estimated poetry by the extent to which it contributes toward this aim; and their poetic imagination was a moral imagination and their vision of the world a moral vision.

Raymond Williams has reminded us that in England the "ideas that we call Romantic have to be understood in terms of the problems of experience with which they were advanced to deal"; that the "mould in which general experience was cast" consisted of the social conflicts and dislocations, and the disintegration of inherited certainties, that followed the French Revolution and accompanied the Industrial Revolution; and that the great writers "were, as men and poets, passionately committed to the tragedy of their period." [38] To ignore this historical context is to overlook the grounds and to underestimate the seriousness of the claims that Romantic writers made for their role as poets and for the efficacy of all great poetry. When they assumed a vatic identity, what they signified was that—like their forbears at the crises of civilization, from the Old Testament prophets to Milton after the failure of an earlier Revolution—they had something to say which urgently needed saying to "this time/ Of dereliction and dismay" (in Wordsworth's somber diagnosis),

> these times of fear,
> This melancholy waste of hopes o'erthrown,
> . . . 'mid indifference and apathy
> And wicked exultation, when good men,
> On every side fall off we know not how,
> To selfishness, disguis'd in gentle names
> Of peace, and quiet, and domestic love,
> Yet mingled, not unwillingly, with sneers
> On visionary minds.   (II, 448–56)

Their conviction was that these "visionary minds" are alone capable of reconstituting the grounds for hope in what man may yet become.

In our own age a number of the most talented authors have turned against the traditional values of the civilized order, to voice the negatives of what Lionel Trilling has called an "adversary culture." Some envision the end of our world as an apocalyptic bang, others as a plaintive whimper; in the latter version, an anti-hero plays out the moves of the end-game of civilization in a non-work which, in some instances, approaches the abolition of meaningfulness in language itself. The Romantic writers neither sought to demolish their life in this world in a desperate search for something new nor lashed out in despair against the inherited culture. The burden of what they had to say was that contemporary man can redeem himself and his world, and that his only way to this end is to reclaim and to bring to realization the great positives of the Western past. When, therefore, they assumed the visionary persona, they spoke as members of what Wordsworth called the "One great Society . . ./ The noble Living and the noble Dead," [39] whose mission was to assure the continuance of civilization by reinterpreting to their drastically altered condition the enduring humane values, making whatever changes were required in the theological systems by which these values had earlier been sanctioned. Chief among these values were life, love, liberty, hope, and joy. These are the high Romantic words, the interrelated norms which always turn up when the poets get down to the first principles of life and of art, which they proclaim without unease and with no sense that these commonplaces may have outworn their relevance.

The ground-concept is life. Life is itself the highest good, the residence and measure of other goods, and the generator of the controlling categories of Romantic thought. Love, as we have seen, expresses the confraternity of the one life shared not only with other men but also with a milieu in which man can feel fully at home; while liberty signifies not only a political circumstance, but also the deliverance of mind and imagination from the mortmain of custom and the slavery of sense so that they may transform the dull and lifeless world into a new world instinct with the life and joy it reciprocates with the perceiving mind. Hope (with its related value, fortitude) is essential for sustaining the possibility of the triumph of life, love, and liberty. And the norm of life is joy— by which is meant not that joy is the standard state of man, but that joy is what man is born for: it is the sign that an individual, in the free exercise of all his faculties, is completely alive; it is the necessary condition for a full community of life and love; and it is both the precondition and the end of the highest art.

4. THE WORLD'S SONG OF LIFE
AND JOY

Life is the premise and paradigm for what is most innovative and distinctive in Romantic thinkers. Hence their vitalism: the celebration of that which lives, moves, and evolves by an internal energy, over whatever is lifeless, inert, and unchanging. As Friedrich Schlegel stated this idea, we must put aside "the concept of an eternal, unchanging, constant being and put in its place the opposing concept of that which is eternally living and becoming."

> True philosophy . . . finds the highest reality only in an eternal becoming, in an eternally living and moving activity which, under ever changing forms and shapes, engenders an endless fullness and diversity.[40]

Hence also their organicism: the metaphorical translation into the categories and norms of intellection of the attributes of a growing thing, which unfolds its inner form and assimilates to itself alien elements, until it reaches the fullness of its complex, organic unity. We can observe Hegel transposing the growth of a plant into the controlling ideas of his philosophy. The pure idea, he says, is "essentially concrete, like a flower," which is "a unity of leaves, of form, of color, of smell, something which lives and grows."

> The true, thus self-determined, has the drive to *develop*. Only the living, that which is spirit, sets its own self in motion and develops. The idea, concrete in itself and developing, is thus an organic system, a totality, which *contains in itself a wealth of stages and moments.*
>
> Philosophy is the knowing for itself of this development and, as thought which comprehends, is itself this thinking development. . . .
>
> Thus a mature philosophy . . . is a single idea in its whole and in all its members, just as in a living individual *one* life, *one* pulse beats through all its members. . . . All these particular parts are but mirrors and images of this *one* life.[41]

In the ending of his Preface to *The Philosophy of Right,* Hegel follows out the implication of this celebration of life; the living process of philosophy is a lesser thing than life itself, for philosophy can only conceptualize the actual thing, and only after the fact. "When philosophy paints its gray on gray, a form of life has grown old, and this gray on gray cannot rejuvenate it, only understand it. The owl of Minerva begins its flight only at twilight." [42]

In this passage Hegel echoes Goethe's *Faust:* "Grau . . . ist

alle Theorie/ Grün des Lebens goldner Baum." "Is there not,"
Wordsworth cried, a poetry so authentic that it is life itself—

> An art, a music, a strain of words
> That shall be life, the acknowledged voice of life? [43]

The poet "is a man speaking to men," but a man who has in
him more life, therefore more joy and creative power—"who
rejoices more than other men in the spirit of life that is
in him; delighting to contemplate similar volitions and passions as manifested in the goings-on of the Universe, and
habitually impelled to create them where he does not find
them." [44] And as it is his delight in the fullness of his life
which compels the poet to express and represent and create
life, so it is the importance of his poetry that it enhances the
life of the reader by effecting pleasure, which is the elemental
driving principle of all living beings:

> Nor let this necessity of producing immediate pleasure be
> considered as a degradation of the Poet's art. It is far other-
> wise. . . . It is a homage paid to the native and naked dig-
> nity of man, to the grand elementary principle of pleasure,
> by which he knows, and feels, and lives, and moves. [45]

With this judgment Schiller, in an essay he wrote the following year, is in agreement; and as in Wordsworth, so in Schiller,
pleasure conduces to joy, and joy at its highest is the sign in
our consciousness of the free play of all our vital powers. The
auditor of art, Schiller wrote in 1803, properly "seeks pleasure,"
for

> all art is dedicated to joy, and there is no higher and no more
> serious undertaking, than to make man happy. The right art
> is that alone which creates the highest enjoyment. But the
> highest enjoyment is the freedom of the spirit in the living
> play of all its powers. [46]

And Schiller was the poet who wrote the ode *An Die Freude*
—on the joy, compelling all living process, that binds male to
female, man to men, and all to the natural world—which

Beethoven, deaf and ailing, set to music as the last movement of his last symphony.

"What," Shelley inquired, "are changes of empires," "the revolutions of the globe . . . and the operations of the elements," "the universe of stars, and suns . . . compared with life? Life, the great miracle, we admire not, because it is so miraculous." [47] There is a metaphysical gulf between Shelley's skeptically qualified idealism and Wordsworth's idealized naturalism, yet Shelley's *Defence of Poetry* coincides with Wordsworth's Preface to *Lyrical Ballads* in its essential values: life, love, pleasure, joy. "The end of social corruption is to destroy all sensibility to pleasure; and, therefore, it is corruption"; but "poetry ever communicates all the pleasure which men are capable of receiving; it is ever still the light of life," whose influence "connects, animates, and sustains the life of all." "The delight of love and friendship . . . the joy of the perception and still more of the creation of poetry is often wholly unalloyed." Shelley is often singled out as the prime Romantic instance of the poetry of anguish, alienation, and revulsion from life. What he himself claimed, on the contrary, was that "poetry is the record of the best and happiest moments of the happiest and best minds," bearing "sweet news of kindred joy" to its auditors and revealing to us "the wonder of our being." [48]

Coleridge signalizes the moral conversion of his Ancient Mariner by his spontaneous response of love to the recognition of the joy of sheer vitality even in the lowliest form of life—"O happy living things! . . . A spring of love gushed from my heart." It was not until his own sad middle age that Coleridge interpolated in *The Eolian Harp* the lines that best epitomize the Romantic constellation of joy, love, and the shared life:

> O! the one Life within us and abroad . . .
> Rhythm in all thought, and joyance every where—
> Methinks, it should have been impossible
> Not to love all things in a world so fill'd.

In *The Friend* Coleridge incorporated these elements into a central concept of his metaphysics: "that intuition of things

. . . when we possess ourselves, as one with the whole . . . with a joy unfathomable, with a love all-comprehensive." [49]

"Every thing that lives is holy," Blake wrote again and again at the height of the buoyant vitalism of his middle thirties. Orc sang the renewal of "the fiery joy,"

> For everything that lives is holy, life delights in life;
> Because the soul of sweet delight can never be defil'd;

and the Fairy who dictated *Europe: A Prophecy* to Blake undertook to show him "all alive/ The world, where every particle of dust breathes forth its joy." [50] In Blake's late epic, *Milton*, these attributes survive; although, as he now puts it, they remain only marginally apparent until we break out of the constriction of the physical eye into the imaginative vision which apprehends all things as "Sons of Los," hence as participants in the song and joyous dance of life:

> Thou seest the gorgeous clothed Flies that dance & sport
>   in summer
> Upon the sunny brooks & meadows; every one the dance
> Knows in its intricate mazes of delight artful to weave:
> Each one to sound his instruments of music in the dance,
> To touch each other & recede; to cross & change & return.
> . . . These are the Sons of Los! These the Visions of Eternity
> But we see only as it were the hem of their garments
> When with our vegetable eyes we view these wond'rous Visions.
>   (Plate 26, lines 2–12)

We do not think of Wordsworth as a poet of exuberance, yet he has expressed incomparably his response to the plenitude of jocund and boisterous life in the world. "The pulse of Being everywhere was felt . . ./ One galaxy of life and joy." And again:

>   I was only then
> Contented when with bliss ineffable
> I felt the sentiment of Being spread
> O'er all that moves, and all that seemeth still . . .
> O'er all that leaps, and runs, and shouts, and sings,
> Or beats the gladsome air, o'er all that glides

> Beneath the wave, yea, in the wave itself
> And mighty depth of waters. Wonder not
> If such my transports were; for in all things
> I saw one life, and felt that it was joy.

Some recent critics of Wordsworth interpret his penchant for "mystic" experiences, when the light of sense goes out, as a symptom of his unconscious revulsion from life and nature. What Wordsworth goes on to say, to the contrary, is that he is moved to such an ecstasy beyond sense through the very fullness of his participation in what Hölderlin (in a metaphor he shared with Wordsworth and other contemporaries) called "the world's song of life":

> One song they sang, and it was audible,
> Most audible then when the fleshly ear,
> O'ercome by grosser prelude of that strain,
> Forgot its functions, and slept undisturb'd.[51]

"Wer das Tiefste gedacht, liebt das Lebendigste"—who has thought most deeply loves what is most alive—Hölderlin has Socrates say, in a most un-Socratic line.[52] His young Hyperion experiences a transport like that of young Wordsworth in unison with the leaping, running, flying, swimming, teeming life of the natural world.

> Each living thing flew and leaped and struggled out into the divine air, and beetles and swallows and doves and storks wheeled and mingled in joyous confusion in the depths and heights, and the steps of those who were bound to earth turned into flight, over the furrows charged the horse and over the hedges the roe, and out of the depths of the sea the fish rose and leaped over its surface. . . .
>
> So didst thou lie poured forth, sweet Life, so didst thou look up, arise, and stand there in slender fullness, divinely calm, thy heavenly face still full of the serene delight in which I interrupted thee.[53]

Hölderlin's poems repeatedly express the joyous sentiment of being that he shares with prolific nature in its abundance. "Von Dorfe zu Dorf jauchzt es, von Tage zu Tag. . . . Gross

ist das Werden umher. . . . Darum wächset uns auch fast
über das Haupt die gewaltge/ Fülle." "The jubilation spreads
from village to village, from day to day. . . . Vast is the
growth going on all around us. . . . Thus the mighty abundance springs higher almost than our heads." *Wie wenn am
Feiertage* celebrates the explosion of outer life after a storm,
and the consonant upsurge of creative power in the spirit of
the observer.

> Die Natur ist jetzt mit Waffenklang erwacht,
> Und hoch vom Aether bis zum Abgrund nieder
> Nach vestem Gesetze, wie einst, aus heiligem
>   Chaos gezeugt,
> Fühlt neu die Begeisterung sich,
> Die Allerschaffende wieder.
>   . . . Sie sind erkannt,
> Die Allebendigen, die Kräfte der Götter.[54]

> [Now Nature with a clash of arms awakens,
> And from the height of the aether to the depth of the abyss
> According to steadfast law, as when once it was begotten
>   from sacred chaos,
> The inspiration, the all-creative power
> Is felt anew.
>   . . . They are recognized,
> The one Life within us and abroad, the powers of the Gods.]

5. THE ROMANTIC "REVERDIE"

One of the most characteristic Romantic motifs is as old as
Western poetry itself; this is the *reverdie,* the celebration of
the regreening earth in springtime.[55] Wordsworth's passage
out of the winter of his spirit occurs in consonance with the
seasonal rebirth:

> Spring returns,
> I saw the Spring return, when I was dead
> To deeper hope, yet had I joy for her . . .
> In common with the Children of her Love,
> Plants, insects, beasts in field, and birds in bower.
>   (XI, 23–8)

Goethe's Faust, at the opening of Part II, awakens to his new life on an earth which resounds and flames with its own renewal:

> Des Lebens Pulse schlagen frisch lebendig. . . .
> Der Wald ertönt von tausendstimmigem Leben. . . .
> Nun aber bricht aus jenen ewigen Gründen
> Ein Flammenübermass, wir stehn betroffen;
> Des Lebens Fackel wollten wir entzünden,
> Ein Feuermeer umschlingt uns. . . .
>
> [The pulses of life beat strongly once again. . . .
> The wood rings with the thousand voices of life. . . .
> Now bursts from those eternal depths
> An excess of flame, we stand astounded;
> We wanted to kindle the torch of life—
> A sea of fire embraces us. . . .]

What is unprecedented in the Romantic versions of this ancient *topos* is the power and exultation of the poet's response to the resurgent life in nature when, in Hölderlin's phrase, "All' die gesammelte Kraft aufflammt in üppigem Frühling"—[56] "All the concentrated power blazes up in exuberant springtime."

Hölderlin's *Hyperion* concludes in his protagonist's recovery from the dark night of the spirit, in harmony with *das Lebenslied der Welt* in spring:

> I had never so fully experienced the old unchanging decree of fate that a new joy springs up in the heart when it perseveres and endures through the midnight of suffering, and that, like the song of the nightingale in the darkness, only then, in our deep pain, does the world's song of life sound out divinely to us. . . .
>
> And when often in the morning . . . I climbed to the mountain's top . . . near me the dear birds, sated with sweet sleep, flew out of the thickets reeling in the half-light and greedy for the day . . . and now the high light, divinely joyous, followed its customary path, enchanting the Earth with undying life so that her heart grew warm and all her children once more felt their being.

And it is the thoroughness with which he participates in the revival of nature that leads Hyperion to accept death not only as the inevitable consequence, but as the defining condition of life. Let men perish, "for thus they return to thy root; and so may I too, O tree of life, that I may grow green again with thee"; for "all is one eternal, burning life." [57]

The most exuberant of Romantic *reverdies* occurs at the moment of imaginative apocalypse in Night the ninth of Blake's *Four Zoas:*

> For Lo the winter melted away upon the distant hills
> And all the black mould sings. She speaks to her infant
>   race, her milk
> Descends down on the sand. The thirsty sand drinks &
>   rejoices. . . .
> The roots shoot thick thro the solid rocks bursting their way
> They cry out in joys of existence.
>   . . . The bats burst from the hardend slime crying
> To one another, What are we & whence is our joy & delight? . . .
> Herds throng up the Valley, wild beasts fill the forests;
> Joy thrilld thro all the Furious form of Tharmas humanizing.

And at the culmination of the apocalypse, the liberated and "Expanding Eyes of Man" behold the earth as a recovered Eden, in the form of one vast and prolific garden:

> The Sun arises from his dewy bed & the fresh airs
> Play in his smiling beams giving the seeds of life to grow
> And the fresh Earth beams forth ten thousand thousand springs
>   of life.[58]

In the poems of Shelley's maturity we hear two voices, sometimes separately and sometimes in counterpoint within a single poem. One is the public, vatic voice, in the manner of Isaiah and of Virgil in the fourth eclogue; as Shelley explained, less than a year before he died, he has deliberately assumed the voice of such "bards," who, by the use of a faculty which they either "possess or feign," announce their vision of the human utmost—"the possible and perhaps approaching state" of social regeneration and happiness.[59] The other is the private voice of Shelley in his own person, who is "a Power girt round with weakness" (like others of Shelley's self-descriptions, this is an adaptation of a New Testament paradox, "for my strength is made perfect in weakness"). When he speaks in this latter voice, Shelley does not sustain the assurance of the prophet, but expresses sharp oscillations of mood; and at times, exhausted by rejection, isolation, failure to reach an audience, and the repeated blows of private disasters, he exhibits himself as more than half in love with easeful death.

Both the great poems of the last two darkening years of Shelley's life were written in the Italian springtime and incorporate that season as their setting. In *Adonais* the elegiac peripety, with its traditional claim that its subject is better off dead, evokes from Shelley an abrupt application to his private circumstance. "Thy hopes are gone before . . . thou shouldst now depart!" (lines 470–1). Yet the Romantic response to the earth's upsurge of life, joy, and generative urgency has never been more puissantly registered than in this poem which concludes in a personal *laus mortis:*

> The amorous birds now pair in every brake,
>   And build their mossy homes in field and brere;
>   And the green lizard and the golden snake,
> Like unimprisoned flames, out of their trance awake.

> Through wood and stream and field and hill and Ocean
>   A quickening life from the Earth's heart has burst
>   As it has ever done, with change and motion,
> From the great morning of the world when first
> God dawned on Chaos; in its stream immersed,
>   The lamps of Heaven flash with a softer light;
> All baser things pant with life's sacred thirst;
>   Diffuse themselves; and spend in love's delight,
> The beauty and the joy of their renewèd might.

In terms of the Neoplatonic world-view that Shelley elected for his poem, he describes the one spirit, "the burning fountain," as wielding "the world with never-wearied love," ceaselessly working to force all things "to its own likeness,"

> And bursting in its beauty and its might
>   From trees and beasts and men into the Heaven's light.

And even while Shelley as individual succumbs to the attraction of an immediate return to "the fire for which all thirst," he describes the spirit as "That Light whose smile kindles the Universe,/ That Beauty in which all things work and move,/ That Benediction . . . that sustaining Love." We should not read the transport of Shelley's imagined escape from his own circumstances at the end as revoking the celebration of the life force against which it is deliberately counterpoised. Harold Bloom finely describes Shelley's balance in the closing stanzas: "His final cry affirms the vision, but denies the efficacy of himself as seer." [60]

Shelley's last poem, *The Triumph of Life,* is in the familiar Romantic form of the education of the poet; like Keats's *The Fall of Hyperion,* it is represented as a Dantean dream-vision, and its crisis is the revelation of the human tragedy. Both terms of the ironic title are used in a special sense. The "Triumph" is the Roman *triumphus,* the entrance into the city of a victorious general in a procession with his prisoners of war, and the "Life" is not the "quickening life" which in *Adonais* bursts out in beauty and joy, but those material and sensual conditions of everyday existence which solicit, depress, and corrupt the aspiring human spirit. The procession of captives includes, in an order of classes apportioned to the degree of their failure, all who have compromised their fidelity to their imagination of uttermost human possibility, and these turn out to be all men except a "sacred few." The bleak facts, however, are narrated with the verve of a poet who has tapped new sources of creative strength, and Shelley's dream-vision is set in the frame of a joyous morning in spring. The poem leaps into being, at once adducing a simile which is far from despairing:

> Swift as a spirit hastening to his task
> Of glory & of good, the Sun sprang forth
> Rejoicing in his splendour, & the mask
>
> Of darkness fell from the awakened Earth.
> The smokeless altars of the mountain snows
> Flamed above crimson clouds, & at the birth
>
> Of light, the Ocean's orison arose

To which the birds tempered their matin lay. . . .

And in succession due, did Continent,

Isle, Ocean, & all things that in them wear
The form & character of mortal mould,
Rise as the Sun their father rose. . . .[61]

This is Shelley's version of the antique convention of the
Natureingang, but no other spring opening matches the power
and assurance of Shelley's forty-line induction, as the rejoicing
sun springs to his work of glory, to be greeted with the quiet
ceremonies of natural worship by the mortal creatures of the
revolving earth to whom the sun brings light, heat, and
awakened life—to all except the solitary poet who, having
waked while the world slept in darkness, now composes himself to sleep as the world revives, to undergo, in the transparent darkness of a trance, his vision of history as the almost
unrelieved tragedy of the defeat of human potentiality. What
was to have been the outcome of this crisis we can only specu-
late; the poet died before he could tell us.

6. HOPE AND DEJECTION

As for hope: It is true that this term, ever recurrent in
Wordsworth, Coleridge, Hölderlin, Shelley, is often linked in
their poetry to its contrary, "dejection," "despondency," or
what Wordsworth, in treating the cycle of hope and disillusion,
called the "utter loss of hope itself/ And things to hope for"
(*Prelude,* XI, 6–7). These poets, however, did not write about
dejection because they considered *Angst* to be the native and
inalienable state of man or the necessary condition of artistic creativity, but precisely for the opposite reason—because
they felt intensely the strength of the temptation to hopelessness and apathy which is chief (in Wordsworth's phrase in
the *Intimations Ode*) among "all that is at enmity with joy,"
hence with life and creativity. Their point about hope is that it
must be proof against the acid bath of counter-evidence in

personal experience, human history, and their particular age
of reversion "to old idolatry . . . to servitude . . . to ignom-
iny and shame" (*Prelude*, XIII, 432–4). Schiller wrote in 1801:

> Let us confront evil destiny face to face. Not in ignorance of
> the dangers that lie in ambush for us . . . but only in *knowl-
> edge* of them is there salvation for us. To such knowledge we
> are helped by the terrifyingly splendid drama of all-destroy-
> ing, recreating, and again destroying vicissitude—of now slow-
> sapping, now fast-striking ruin . . . of men struggling against
> fate, of the ineluctable flight of fortune, of security betrayed,
> injustice triumphant, and innocence overcome, which history
> presents in abundant measure and tragic art by its mimicry
> brings before our eyes.[62]

More puzzling even than the charge that the Romantics
evaded the realities of their age is the charge that they scanted
the fact of human suffering and the problem of evil. The Romantic poets were not *complete* poets, in that they represent
little of the social dimension of human experience; for although they insist on the importance of community, they express this matter largely as a profound need of the individual
consciousness. The fact is, however, that these poets were almost obsessively occupied with the reality and rationale of the
agonies of the human condition. Arnold's statement that
"Wordsworth's eyes avert their ken/ From half of human fate"
has become a cliché or literary history. Wordsworth himself
claimed, in the Prospectus, that his high argument of the imaginative possibility of a recovered paradise entailed the need,
as a poet of human truth, to utter "authentic comment" on
"madding passions mutually inflamed," humanity piping "solitary anguish," and "the fierce confederate storm of sorrow."
The subjects of Wordsworth's narrative poems are man's in-
humanity to man, gross social injustice, destitute and helpless
old age, guilt and sorrow, seduction and abandonment, in-
fanticide, the steady deterioration of character under the pressure of unmerited and immitigable suffering, the fortitude of
men who possess no other recourse against bitter circumstance,
the sudden loss of a beloved child, and Lucy in her grave.

From these Wordsworthian preoccupations Arnold averted his ken, perhaps because, unlike traditional tragedy, they had to do with "humble and rustic life."

As for what is called "the problem of evil"—in broadest terms, the question of what kind of intellectual and emotional sense we can make of a world in which such things constantly happen—that, as I tried to show in earlier chapters, was precisely the central and pervasive concern of the major Romantic philosophers. Finding no longer tenable the justification of earthly suffering as a divine plan for sorting out those beings who will be translated to a better world, they undertook to justify the experience of suffering within the limits of experience itself. We have seen that what Keats, following Wordsworth, called "the Burden of the Mystery" was also the paramount theme of most of the long imaginative works of the age, autobiographic and fictional, realistic and mythic, and in novelistic, epic, dramatic, or lyric form. These writers, like the philosophers, set out to demonstrate that suffering plays an indispensable role in making the man and the poet more fully, consciously, integrally, and maturely human. A critic's charge that Romantic writers neglected the problem of evil is probably only a way of saying that he does not approve of their solution to the problem.

These Romantic affirmations do not eliminate nor, taken in their full context, do they minimize the agony and the strife of human hearts. To justify evil by placing it in a larger conceptual overview is not to annul it, or to lessen the pain of suffering; an excess of suffering does not foster character but destroys it; and the tragic paradox is that the values of life are valuable precisely because they are limited and defined by death. In the philosophy of Schelling's maturity, the course of individual and racial history enacts the pattern of Christ's passion; and although Hegel justifies the spirit's evolution toward self-fulfillment in history as "the true theodicy," he describes the history through which the spirit evolves as a vast "slaughter-bench," and characterizes his narration of that history as "the recollection and Golgotha of the absolute spirit." [63] Wordsworth's *Tintern Abbey* and the *Intimations Ode,* which, like *The Prelude,* are poems of what it means to grow to

maturity, resound with a Virgilian sense of *lachrimae rerum*.
Life is growth, but growth means loss, and the loss deeply matters; so that, although Wordsworth finds in the attributes of
maturity "abundant recompense," the ode's conclusion is that
to have a "human heart" is to find in the meanest of mortal
things "thoughts that do often lie too deep for tears." And
before this life, and beneath it, and after it, is the dark; as A. C.
Bradley has said, to Wordsworth " 'Our being rests' on 'dark
foundations,' and 'our haughty life is crowned with darkness.' " [64] Shelley's projection in *Prometheus Unbound* of the
best of all humanly possible worlds leaves man subject to passion and to "chance, and death, and mutability" (III, iv. 197–
204); and even this imaginable but very uncertain possibility
can not be final, for it hangs on a poise of the mind that can
readily be thrown again into disorder (IV, 562–7). Nor does
Shelley understate the sinister compulsions which man must
face up to and overcome if he is to move toward this qualified
earthly paradise. The Furies tempt Prometheus to despair
by revealing the foulness beneath the threshold of consciousness
in every mind, and especially the corruption of the erotic
instinct by the death instinct which expresses itself in a lust
for destruction (I, 445–91).

Salient in our own time is a kind of literary Manichaeism—
secular versions of the radical *contemptus mundi et vitae* of
heretical Christian dualism—whose manifestations in literature
extend back through Mallarmé and other French Symbolists
to Rimbaud and Baudelaire. A number of our writers and
artists have turned away, in revulsion or despair, not only from
the culture of Western humanism but from the biological conditions of life itself, and from all life-affirming values. They
devote themselves to a new Byzantinism, which T. E. Hulme
explicitly opposed to the Romantic celebration of life and
admiringly defined as an art which, in its geometrized abstractness, is "entirely independent of vital things," expresses
"disgust with the trivial and accidental characteristics of living
shapes," and so possesses the supreme virtue of being "anti-
vital," "non-humanistic," and "world-rejecting." [65] Alternatively, the new Manichaeans project a vision of the vileness,
or else the blank nothingness of life, and if they celebrate Eros,

it is often an Eros *à rebours*—perverse, hence sterile and life-negating. And to some critics, looking back at earlier literature through the gloomy contemporary perspective, it has seemed that Romantic writers could not really have meant what they claimed, hence that they must have been self-divided, or even unconsciously committed to the negations of the positives they so confidently asserted.

One contemporary scholar, for example, has applied to Wordsworth a mode of analysis which assumes that "the apparent subject matter" of his poems is "a kind of cipher or hieroglyph for meanings which reject or devaluate the very experiences which express them." It turns out that, under the ostensible surface, Wordsworth in reality felt "a hatred" against "the mortal limitations of man"; that in his character as a "mystic" (defined as one for whom "nature . . . must be destroyed, obliterated absolutely") he was also "a hater of temporal nature"; that he harbored a "hatred and fear of the ordinary experiences of men"; and that, in fact, Wordsworth's essential genius as a great poet "was his enmity to man, which he mistook for love." [66] Another commentator on the Romantic poets uses a similar strategy to detect, beneath "the placid surface" of even Wordsworth's earlier poetry, "an uneasy fear and distrust of nature"; this critic, however, tends to view such ambivalence toward man and nature as an expression of Romantic neurosis rather than of genius. Shelley, above all, "in mistaking the neuroses of the man for the infirmities of genius . . . was led into an extravagant indulgence in the neuroses which was almost fatal to the poet." Throughout Shelley's poetry there is a "fundamental contradiction" between "the tone of affirmation" and the underlying truth of his "renunciation of the world and society"; even the conclusion of *Prometheus Unbound,* under its surface assurance, expresses "a morbid antipathy and revulsion against society in any form . . . an indifference to, even a dislike of, human beings" in the concrete.[67]

One virtue, at any rate, of this ingenious exegetic is that it directs attention to the scope and complexity of Romantic attitudes, lacking which these writers would have indeed been the one-eyed optimists of the Neo-Humanist's earlier and

exactly opposite caricature. I cannot accept the ruling premise, however, that these poets grossly mistook their own deepest
inclinations and values. Like the great writers they most
revered, Dante, Shakespeare, and Milton, they were deeply
aware of the powers of darkness in man and the universe, and
like the religious minds of all ages, they had their doubts and
terrors and knew the strength of the impulse to give up.
Against the accumulated evidence of public and private experience—"terror, madness, crime, remorse," in Asia's grim
catalogue of moral and physical evil in *Prometheus Unbound*
(II, iv. 19–27), under which "each one reels . . . towards the
pit of death,"

> Abandoned hope, and love that turns to hate;
> And self-contempt . . .
> Pain, whose unheeded and familiar speech
> Is howling, and keen shrieks

—these poets deliberately elected their stance, not of optimism, but of qualified hope. As in the traditional creed *deiectio,*
sloth, accidie had verged on the unredeemable sin of despair
of grace, so in the Romantic view dejection breeds sterility,
and to persist in a state of apathy and hopelessness is to live
what Coleridge called a "death-in-life"; while to commit oneself to hope ("the vitality & cohesion of our Being," as Coleridge defined it [68]) is an essential obligation—a moral obligation, without which we are indeed doomed. For while hope,
by holding open a possibility, releases man's powers of imagination and action, despair is self-fulfilling, because it guarantees
the condition to which it surrenders. "Let us," Shelley said,
"believe in a kind of optimism in which we are our own gods,"
and then went on to define the serious residuum within his
ironic exaggeration:

> It is best that we should think all this for the best even though
> it be not, because Hope, as Coleridge says is a solemn duty
> which we owe alike to ourselves & to the world—a worship
> to the spirit of good within, which requires before it sends
> that inspiration forth, which impresses its likeness upon all
> that it creates, devoted & disinterested homage.[69]

One of the darkest of Romantic poems, Coleridge's *Dejection: An Ode,* sets forth the poet's personal failure under the emotional stresses and physical "afflictions" of his life. The poem, however, is another Romantic *reverdie* set in reviving April, which in Coleridge's employment is not the cruelest month, but the seasonal correlative of the renewal of hope, joy, and life, which are the norms by which the poet measures his own losses. The speaker's dejection marks his insulation from other men and from the outer world. In a later aesthetic theory, such alienation became the condition for artistic creativity; in Coleridge's poem, its effect is artistic sterility—the suspension of the poet's "shaping spirit of imagination." For hope (in Coleridge's recapitulation of the Romantic complex of interrelated values) is reciprocal with joy; joy is itself "Life, and Life's effluence" (in one version it is the "Life of our life"); and the free and joyous abundance of the inner life, by making "all things live, from pole to pole" in the "eddying of [our] living soul," is what effects the experience of a "new Earth and new Heaven" commensurate with human needs. Coleridge's confession of his own irreparable loss of joy and creativity ends in an undaunted optative to the person to whom the poem is addressed (who in one version had been Wordsworth): "Thus mayest thou ever, evermore rejoice."

7. THE EAGLE AND THE ABYSS

"O the mind, mind has mountains," Gerard Manley Hopkins wrote,

> cliffs of fall
> Frightful, sheer, no-man-fathomed. Hold them cheap
> May who ne'er hung there.

In his Prospectus Wordsworth tells us that his poetic journey through the mind of man will ascend higher than "the heaven of heavens." But Wordsworth's landscape of the mind, like Hopkins', has its abysses too. In his description (I cite the version in a manuscript of the Prospectus),

Not chaos, not
The darkest Pit of the profoundest hell
Nor aught of [blinder] vacancy scoop'd out
By help of dreams can breed such fear and awe
As fall upon us often when we look
Into our minds, into the mind of Man.[70]

The most remarkable sequence in the spiritual journey of *The Prelude* tells of two occasions when Wordsworth trembled on the brink of the inner abyss, but found consolation. These passages are a central instance of the counterplay of hope against the temptation to despair, and they reveal the relation of this persistent Romantic opposition to the prototypical experience of shattered hope in what Shelley called "the master theme of the epoch in which we live—the French Revolution." [71]

Book VI of *The Prelude* recounts Wordsworth's walking tour of France and the Alps with Robert Jones in the summer of 1790. The two young men land at Calais on the eve of the first anniversary of the Quatorze Juillet, at the euphoric height of millennial expectation,

a time when Europe was rejoiced,
France standing on the top of golden hours,
And human nature seeming born again.
(VI, 352–4)

"Joy of one" was "joy of tens of millions," and all France was one great festival of renewal. The pilgrims "found benevolence and blessedness/ Spread like a fragrance everywhere, like Spring," and everywhere saw "dances of Liberty" that continued far into the night. In a patently ritual incident the Englishmen, while sailing down the Rhone, fall in with a wildly joyous group of delegates returning from the Federation fete in Paris and partake of their supper, "guests welcome almost as the Angels were/ To Abraham," after which all "form'd a ring/ And, hand in hand, danced round and round the Board." Immediately after "this glad Rout," the two travelers ascend the mountain to the Convent of the Chartreuse (VI, 357–423).

A few years after he had completed the first version of *The Prelude* in 1805, Wordsworth inserted into the narrative a passage which transfers to this occasion an event which, in historical fact, did not occur until two years later—the forceful dispossession of the inhabitants of the ancient convent by French revolutionary troops.

> Ours eyes beheld,
> As we approached the Convent, flash of arms
> And military glare of riotous men
> Commissioned to expel and overturn
> With senseless rapine.[72]

This is the narrator's first experience of revolutionary violence and its indiscriminate destruction of what is good as well as evil in the inherited past, and the shock of the discovery is profound and enduring. He hears nature vainly cry out against this impiety under the great cross of the Chartreuse, and even after this "trance" ended, "my mind/ Continued still to heave within herself." As he attends to the murmur of "the sister streams of Life and Death"—in the literal reality behind this symbol, the mountain streams are the *Guiers vif* and the *Guiers mort*—he hears mingled with it the sound of an inner voice which, in the cause of "new-born Liberty," accepts the contradictions in the "mighty passions of the time,/ The vengeance and the transport and the hope," yet implores that this convent at least be spared, "if past and future" are to continue jointly to support the moving "Spirit of human knowledge." Let it be saved for the sake of faith resting on religious revelation, and also for the sake of the "humbler claim" based on the natural symbols of duration—"that imaginative impulse sent/ From these majestic floods—those shining cliffs." Abruptly, the natural precipice modulates into a mental abyss from whose brink the poet, momentarily lost, peers trembling into the void:

> those shining cliffs . . .
> These forests unapproachable by death,
> That shall endure, as long as man endures
> To think, to hope, to worship and to feel,

To struggle, to be lost within himself
In trepidation, from the blank abyss
To look with bodily eyes and be consoled.

Leaving this "desecrated spot," Wordsworth and his companion hasten on into Switzerland, to experience a second instance of disillusion at the disparity between the ideal and the actual:

> That day we first
> Beheld the summit of Mont Blanc, and griev'd
> To have a soulless image on the eye
> Which had usurp'd upon a living thought
> That never more could be.

But he tells us, they were "reconcil'd . . . to realities" by the human and natural aspects of the Vale of Chamouni, including the birds nearby and an eagle in the distance:

> There small birds warble from the leafy trees,
> The Eagle soareth in the element.
>   (VI, 452–63)

Wordsworth then goes on to describe a third and climactic experience of the gulf separating expectation from reality, which this time effected a deep "dejection," a "dull and heavy slackening." The "two brother Pilgrims," while traversing the Simplon Pass, had left their guide and were eagerly climbing upward, when a chance-met peasant told them what at first they refused to believe—"for still we had hopes that pointed to the clouds"—that they had already crossed the Alps and "that thenceforward all our course/ Was downwards."

Suddenly, in the process of reliving this experience while narrating it, Wordsworth is again lost within himself, as in a mist that rises from an abyss in the mind across his poetic path. The revised version of this passage makes clearer Wordsworth's double use of a journey, which is literal for the tour he is describing and metaphorical for the process of composing the poem:

> Imagination. . . .
> That awful Power rose from the mind's abyss
> Like an unfathered vapour that enwraps,
> At once, some lonely traveller. I was lost;
> Halted without an effort to break through.
>
> (1850 ed.; VI, 591–7)

But after an interval, "now recovering, to my Soul I say/ I
recognize thy glory." Only now in retrospect, in a revelation
"when the light of sense/ Goes out in flashes that have shewn
to us/ The invisible world," does Wordsworth discover the
significance of his hitherto inexplicable dejection at finding
that, while he thought he was still ascending, his actual way lay
downward. The context makes plain the relation of this event
and its significance to his preceding experiences on the tour,[73]
as well as to his experience of the course of the French Revolution which was still to come. Occurring as it did at the height
of millennial expectation at the advent of the Revolution, but
after the shocks of disillusionment at the Chartreuse and at
Mont Blanc, Wordsworth's sudden dejection at having crossed
the Alps (he now recognizes) had in fact portended what succeeding events would amply confirm: that between man's boundless expectations from the French Revolution and its harsh
reality lies a gap no less wide than that between the journeyer's
"hopes that pointed to the clouds" and the material apex of
the Simplon Pass. But the flash of vision also discloses the general truth which his experience in the pass had typified: "To
my Soul I say/ I recognize thy glory"—

> Our destiny, our nature, and our home
> Is with infinitude, and only there;
> With hope it is, hope that can never die,
> Effort, and expectation, and desire,
> And something evermore about to be.

From the vantage of his poetic maturity, Wordsworth thus
achieves a central Romantic discovery.[74] Man is not born for
ultimate satisfactions, but in his power to sustain an aspiration
that is commensurate with desire, rather than with things as
they are, consists man's tragic dignity; and in this recognition of

the glory of a hope beyond possibility, Wordsworth goes on to say, the mind finds strength and a fertilizing joy: "Strong in itself, and in the access of joy/ Which hides it like the overflowing Nile." Immediately thereupon in *The Prelude* (VI, 549 ff.) Wordsworth hurries down into the ravine below the Alpine pass to confront, in its unified opposition of the ghastly and the beautiful, the passing and the enduring, "Tumult and peace, the darkness and the light," the ineluctable contraries that make up human life.

In the Vale of Chamouni Wordsworth, grieving at the discrepancy between the prior notion and the fact of Mont Blanc, had been reconciled to realities by the sight of an eagle: "The Eagle soareth in his element." The image of soaring (*schweben*), as Professor Matthijs Jolles has noted, was a favorite one of Friedrich Schiller, in application both to life and to art,[75] and his long lyric *Der Spaziergang* (1795) turns on the sudden apparition of a soaring eagle. The poet, alone on a mountainous cliff and desolated by a vision of the destructive violence that has issued from the French Revolution, is lost in trepidation at the verge of a mental abyss, but looks with bodily eyes and is consoled by seeing an eagle, emblem of the poise of human aspiration between impossibility and despair.

Shelley, as we know, asserted the similarities in poetic "sentiment, imagery, and expression" which derive from "the new springs of thought and feeling" attending "the great events of our age." [76] Schiller's *The Walk* exemplifies the extent to which Shelley's claim is valid for German as well as for English poetry. So many tendencies of the age intersect in this remarkable poem of two hundred lines that it can serve as a résumé of much that I have been detailing in this book about design, imagery, and ideas in works of the Romantic imagination. It is in the first instance what I have called a greater Romantic lyric, written in the same year as Coleridge's *Eolian Harp*, which initiated the English vogue for that form.[77] That is, *Der Spaziergang* represents a solitary speaker confronting a particularized landscape, moves through a sustained meditation which is stimulated by the altering visual details, then rounds back to a close which echoes the opening description, but with a difference effected by all that has intervened. The poet's literal walk up a winding mountain path, moreover, is the sustained trope for a self-educative journey, both of the lyric speaker and of the human race, moving from a natural and happy unity, through progressive division, estrangement, and conflict, to a crisis which eventuates in a new and complex integrity. In both poetic form and intellectual content Schiller's poem is thus, as Professor Jolles has remarked, "a great circular journey"; and in the course of this journey (as in those later and longer *Bildungsreisen,* Wordsworth's *Prelude,* Hölderlin's *Hyperion,* and Hegel's *Phenomenology of the Spirit*), the crisis, both of history and of the poet's inner life, is the French Revolution and its aftermath. This crisis is resolved on the higher level of comprehensive and unillusioned awareness which is the correlative, whether in a developed culture or a mature consciousness, to the extended prospect from the mountain height to which the traveler, despite the ever wilder and more terrifying terrain, has won his way.

In the *Natureingang* to Schiller's poem the lyric speaker, like Wordsworth in his "glad preamble," has escaped from imprisoning walls into the freedom of the open fields ("entflohn des Zimmers Gefängnis . . ./ Frei empfängt mich die Wiese"); and like *The Prelude,* the poem goes on to explore natural and cultural modes of liberty and law in quest of the condition of genuine freedom. The walker is greeted by the newly risen sun, lovingly irradiating the peak of the mountain to which he is about to ascend, and by "the serene blue" which pours "over the greening wood"; and, again like Wordsworth in the preamble to *The Prelude,* he finds himself animated by a vital outer breeze: "Deiner Lüfte balsamischer Strom durchrinnt mich erquickend." His path first traverses a level meadow, an instance of complete natural harmony in which "the delightful strife" of the varying colors "resolves in grace" [*löset in Anmut sich auf*]. It then winds up the hill, opening out to view the pastoral countryside where, despite the divisions of rural property which bespeak the reign of manmade laws, man himself, "not yet awakened to freedom," lives in neighborly harmony both with other men and with the soil; for here the manmade road binds the cultivated fields to the wood and hill and the trees embrace with their branches the dwellings of men.

As the narrator climbs on, the prospect suddenly widens to reveal the sundering of harmony into oppositions:

> Spröde sondert sich ab, was kaum noch liebend sich mischte,
> Und das Gleiche nur ist's, was an das Gleiche sich reiht.

> [Coldly those things separate which have just lovingly mingled,
> And now it is only like which arrays itself with like.]

Great estates with their proud retinues of poplars announce rule, privilege, and the class division between master and servant ("Dieses Dienergefolg' meldet den Herrscher mir an"). A city with its domes and towers rises into view, from which "the wood-fauns have been forced out into the wilderness." As men are packed closer together, their inner world becomes more intense and active, and patriotism provides the bond which holds together a society of which the motive forces are competition and the rivalry of divided powers. Specialization of function effects the immense development of science, technology, commerce, and the arts. The rapid increase and spread of knowledge leads mankind into the Enlightenment, but the concomitant dissipation of earlier illusions drives him inexorably on into revolution:

> Da zerrint vor dem wundernden Blick der Nebel des Wahnes,
> Und die Gebilde der Nacht weichen dem tagenden Licht.
> Seine Fesseln zerbricht der Mensch. . . .

> [The mist of delusion dissolves before man's wondering gaze,
> And the images of night give way to the dawning light.
> Man shatters his chains. . . .]

Simultaneously, however, the substratum of wild nature within human nature, which has been suppressed by the progress of civilization, explodes into antinomian license. " 'Freedom!' man's reason cries out," but at the same time " 'Freedom!' cry out his savage desires./ Greedily they tear themselves loose from sacred nature."

The critical point of the meditation is the poet's nightmare vision of the French Revolution transformed into what Hegel in the *Phenomenology* was to call the "absolute freedom and terror" which is "merely the fury of annihilation"—the shocking revelation, at the height of the hope for human possibility, of the abyss of primordial savagery and destructiveness beneath the civilized surface of the human mind. The poem ends with a recovery of the "mood of hopeful youth," after the darkness of this "dream which seized me, trembling, with its terrifying image of life." The speaker apprehends, in contradistinction to the explosive violence of a divided, suppressed, and savage nature, the constancy and lawfulness of another nature, *fromme Natur,* which serves to bind the days of the race, as of the individual, each to each by natural piety:

Immer dieselbe, bewahrst du in treuen Händen dem Manne
Was dir das gaukelnde Kind, was dir der Jungling vertraut.

[Ever unchanging, thou preservest in thy faithful hands
        for the adult man
That which the frolicsome child, that which the youth has
        entrusted to thee.]

Schiller's concluding lines, after his dark fantasy, are a reprise of the serene blue sky, the green woods, and the glorious sun of the opening description; these details are now imbued, however, with added resonance as the enduring and unifying elements in the course of human history, and the natural sun is apprehended as Apollo, the mentor of the modern as he was of the ancient poet:

Unter demselben Blau, über dem nämlichen Grün
Wandeln die nahen und wandeln vereint die fernen Geschlechter,
Und die Sonne Homers, siehe! sie lächelt auch uns.

[Beneath the same blue, over that very green
Walk the present and the distant generations, united,
And the sun of Homer—Look! it smiles also upon us.]

Throughout this meditation the speaker's mind has been engaged, in a give and take of influence and interpretation, not only with the ever enlarging prospect but also with the increasingly wilder condition of the track up which he has been climbing. When he had left the idyllic plain, the hill had dropped abruptly away.

Endlos unter mir seh' ich den Äther, über mir endlos,
Blicke mit Schwindeln hinauf, blicke mit Schaudern hinab.

His way, however, had at this stage been well marked and secure:

Aber zwischen der ewigen Höh' und der ewigen Tiefe
Trägt ein geländerter Steig sicher den Wandrer dahin.

[Endless below me I see the ether, endless above me,
Look giddily up, look shuddering down.
But between the eternal height and the eternal depth
A railed path bears the traveler safely along.]

But at the crisis of his vision of human savagery and of civilization crumbling into chaos, the speaker finds himself lost, halted on a trackless height at the brink of an abyss.

Aber wo bin ich? Es birgt sich der Pfad. Abschüssige Gründe
Hemmen mit gähnender Kluft hinter mir, vor mir den Schritt. . . .
Wild ist es hier und schauerlich öd'! . . .

[But where am I? The path has disappeared. Precipitous slopes
Halt my steps behind me, before me, by a yawning abyss. . . .
It is savage here, and terrifyingly desolate! . . .]

At this point, in mid-line, occurs the lyric reversal. An eagle soars into view, suspended in serene assurance between the inaccessible heaven and the immeasurable abyss: "In lonely space/ Hangs only the eagle and fastens the world to the clouds."

Im einsamen Luftraum
Hängt nur der Adler und knüpft an das Gewölke die Welt.

In summarizing the plot of *The Prelude* in his ode *To William Wordsworth,* Coleridge recapitulated Wordsworth's account of the "moments awful" of mind-nature interchange in his youth, "When power streamed from thee," then the burst of hope during the jubilant early days of the French Revolution, and how, after that "Hope" had been "afflicted and struck down," it had been "summoned homeward" to stand "calm and sure" in "the dread watch-tower of man's absolute self." In this last statement Coleridge recalled the passage, which he had just heard Wordsworth read aloud in the concluding book of *The Prelude,* describing how in his crisis of shattered hope, and against the insidious tendency of "vulgar sense" to "enslave the mind," the poet had managed to preserve the power of his imagination to redeem "a universe of death":

> Here must thou be, O Man!
> Strength to thyself; no Helper has thou here;
> Here keepest thou thy individual state. . . .
>
> (XIII, 120–89)

For the mind, unaided, thus to confront the world and, by an act of imagination empowered by love and joy, to experience it as a sufficient paradise, is a demanding enterprise. To sustain this stance and way of seeing no doubt requires the buoyancy and resilience of youth, as Wordsworth himself at one point recognized, in the very process of recalling an early instance of just such a transforming moment, when his mind had been "lord and master" and outer sense "the obedient servant." Once again, at this instant of bleak insight, he is lost within himself:

> Oh! mystery of Man, from what a depth
> Proceed thy honours! I am lost.
>   . . . The days gone by
> Come back upon me from the dawn almost
> Of life: the hiding places of my power
> Seem open; I approach, and then they close;
> I see by glimpses now; when age comes on,
> May scarcely see at all.
>
> (XI, 271–3, 330–49)

At the age of fifty-three Coleridge wrote to James Gillman a wry summary of the history of his own mental life in which, through the self-ironic raillery, we recognize the tragedy of personal defeat. Coleridge's narrative is formulated in the elemental Romantic duality of subject and object, mind and nature; the altering perceptual relations between these two protagonists are projected in the persistent Romantic metaphor of the power-politics of vision; and the tragedy consists in that reversal whereby his mind, having once been the master, has become the slave. "My Dear Friend," Coleridge wrote:

> In youth and early manhood the mind and nature are, as it were, two rival artists both potent magicians, and engaged . . . in sharp conflict of conjuration, each having for its object to turn the other into canvas to paint on, clay to mould, or cabinet to contain. For a while the mind seems to have the better in the contest, and makes of Nature what it likes . . . transforms her summer gales into harps and harpers, lovers' sighs and sighing lovers, and her winter blasts into Pindaric Odes, Christabels, and Ancient Mariners set to music by Beethoven, and in the insolence of triumph conjures her clouds into whales and walruses with palanquins on their backs, and chases the dodging stars in a sky-hunt! But alas! alas! that Nature is a wary wily long-breathed old witch, tough-lived as a turtle and divisible as the polyp. . . .[78]

The passage becomes even more poignant when we realize that Coleridge implicitly describes his having succumbed, with the passage of time, to the actuality in his own experience of a concept of the mind in perception against which his own philosophy of the active, projective, and creative mind had been a sustained refutation. This is Locke's concept, as Coleridge understood Locke, that the mind is passive and receptive in the process of perceiving the outer world—a concept Locke had represented in his repeated metaphors of the mind as a *tabula rasa,* or dark cabinet, or waxed tablet, into which the ideas of sense write or project or impress themselves.[79] Coleridge goes on to restate his version, grounded in his latter-day experience, of these Lockean metaphors of mind; and he ends,

characteristically, by rounding back to his point of departure.
Nature, he says,

> is sure to get the better of Lady *Mind* in the long run and to
> take her revenge too; transforms our to-day into a canvas dead-
> coloured to receive the dull, featureless portrait of yesterday
> . . . turns . . . the ci-devant sculptress . . . into clay . . .
> and lastly (to end with that which suggested the beginning)
> she mocks the mind with its own metaphor, metamorphosing
> the memory into a *lignum vitae* escritoire. . . . Finis!

With the passage of time Coleridge's contemporaries also
showed a diminution of the assurance and buoyancy of their
radical youth, and some of them (Coleridge earliest) cast out
toward a being beyond temporal existence, from whom the
values in experience are derivative and by whom they are
guaranteed. Yet their attempt to salvage traditional values and
the traditional hope for a new earth from the dissolving creeds
which had hitherto been their source and sanction had been
a bold and deliberate enterprise; and if their confidence in the
efficacy of the human imagination was to various degrees
eroded by the world, and life, and time, the defeat was not
unheroic. They were not, at any rate, demoralized into turning upon what they had earlier found most valuable, much
less into inverting these values into the negatives of an adversary culture.

The distinctive Romantic ethos, however, is that which these
writers put forward in the assurance of their innovative prime.
This outlook was succinctly and powerfully stated at the close
of the last act of *Prometheus Unbound*. One by one Demogorgon summons everyone and everything to hear his reaffirmation
of the elementary positives of Western humanism; and since,
over the preceding eighteen centuries, this had been a Christian humanism, Demogorgon's summation repeatedly echoes
the book Shelley knew almost by heart, translated to a human
center of reference "in the wise heart." [80] In his concluding
statement Demogorgon recalls a central doctrine: "Charity
. . . beareth all things, believeth all things, hopeth all things,
endureth all things. . . . And now abideth faith, hope, charity, these three; but the greatest of these is charity." These

cardinal virtues Demogorgon assimilates into the cardinal values of his radical humanism: hope, love, freedom, life, and joy. Faith, since its object is transferred to man's destiny in this world, falls into coincidence with hope, which endureth all things, even at the very brink of the abyss in Shelley's landscape of the mind—"the slippery, steep,/ And narrow verge of crag-like agony."

> To suffer woes which Hope thinks infinite;
> To forgive wrongs darker than death or night;
> To defy Power, which seems omnipotent;
> To love, and bear; to hope till Hope creates
> From its own wreck the thing it contemplates;
> Neither to change, nor falter, nor repent;
> This, like thy glory, Titan, is to be
> Good, great and joyous, beautiful and free;
> This is alone Life, Joy, Empire, and Victory.

But if in this testament Shelley echoes the Bible ultimately, he echoes more proximately Wordsworth, about whom he could be devastatingly ironic, yet as Mary Shelley said, "No man ever admired Wordsworth's poetry more;—he read it perpetually." [81] Of Wordsworth's writings *The Excursion* was the major long poem known to his contemporaries; and though Shelley was disappointed at its retreat from both political and imaginative radicalism, *The Excursion* was nonetheless for him, as for Keats, a pervasive influence; especially the long verse passage from *The Recluse,* written at the full tide of his powers some fourteen years earlier, which Wordsworth had reproduced in his Preface to *The Excursion* "as a kind of *Prospectus* of the design and scope of the whole Poem."

We end this exploration of Romantic thought and imagination then, as Coleridge in his letter to Gillman stated the circuitous Romantic design, "with that which suggested the beginning," and I trust, on a somewhat higher point of vantage. In the Prospectus, as prologue to the high argument of his poetry, Wordsworth tallied the primary values informing his meditations "on Man, on Nature, and on Human Life," which he represented as a translation to his age of the values embodied in Milton's religious epic. "I sing," he said,

> Of Truth, of Grandeur, Beauty, Love, and Hope,
> And melancholy Fear subdued by Faith;
> Of blessèd consolations in distress;
> Of moral strength, and intellectual Power;
> Of joy in widest commonalty spread

—a catalogue which in the early manuscripts ends with the value of values, "being limitless, the one great Life." These are the positives investing what Shelley called "the spirit of the age" in the "new birth" that he recognized in the literature of the immediate past,[82] and they define the moral dimension of what has the best historical claim to be called the English Romantic tradition. If such affirmations strike a contemporary ear as deluded or outworn, that may be the index of their relevance to an age of profounder dereliction and dismay than Shelley and Wordsworth knew.

Wordsworth's Prospectus for "The Recluse"

Wordsworth's Prospectus: the initial page of MS 2 (at the conclusion of *Home at Grasmere*, MS B)

Wordsworth's Prospectus: MS 3

1.   IN THE PREFACE TO
THE EXCURSION

Wordsworth published the program for his poetry that he called the "Prospectus" as the conclusion of his Preface to *The Excursion* (1814). The text below is an exact reprint of this version, except that I have added line-numbers in the right margin.

The text of the Preface and Prospectus printed by de Selincourt and Darbishire (*The Poetical Works of William Wordsworth*, V, 1–6) is the revised form that Wordsworth included in his *Poetical Works* of 1849–50. This latter version includes, in addition to a number of alterations in capitalization and punctuation, two substantive changes from the Prospectus of 1814: (1) In line 25, "Holiest of Men" becomes "In holiest mood." (2) In line 83, "—Come thou prophetic Spirit" becomes "Descend, prophetic Spirit!"

In this Preface Wordsworth discusses the relation of his autobiographical "preparatory Poem" (that is, *The Prelude*) to his projected masterwork, *The Recluse;* describes the position of *The Excursion* as the second part of *The Recluse;* and then goes on, in the final prose paragraph, to introduce the versified Prospectus, as follows:

It is not the Author's intention formally to announce a system: it was more animating to him to proceed in a different course; and if he shall succeed in conveying to the mind clear thoughts, lively images, and strong feelings, the Reader will have no difficulty in extracting the system for himself. And in the mean time the following passage, taken from the conclusion of the first Book of the Recluse, may be acceptable as a kind of *Prospectus* of the design and scope of the whole Poem.

> *"On Man, on Nature, and on Human Life*
> *Musing in Solitude, I oft perceive*
> *Fair trains of imagery before me rise,*
> *Accompanied by feelings of delight*
> *Pure, or with no unpleasing sadness mixed;*   5
> *And I am conscious of affecting thoughts*
> *And dear remembrances, whose presence soothes*
> *Or elevates the Mind, intent to weigh*
> *The good and evil of our mortal state.*
> *—To these emotions, whencesoe'er they come,*   10
> *Whether from breath of outward circumstance,*
> *Or from the Soul—an impulse to herself,*
> *I would give utterance in numerous Verse.*
> *—Of Truth, of Grandeur, Beauty, Love, and Hope—*
> *And melancholy Fear subdued by Faith;*   15
> *Of blessed consolations in distress;*
> *Of moral strength, and intellectual power;*
> *Of joy in widest commonalty spread;*
> *Of the individual Mind that keeps her own*
> *Inviolate retirement, subject there*   20
> *To Conscience only, and the law supreme*
> *Of that Intelligence which governs all;*
> *I sing:—"fit audience let me find though few!"*
>
> *So prayed, more gaining than he asked, the Bard,*
> *Holiest of Men.—Urania, I shall need*   25
> *Thy guidance, or a greater Muse, if such*
> *Descend to earth or dwell in highest heaven!*
> *For I must tread on shadowy ground, must sink*
> *Deep—and, aloft ascending, breathe in worlds*
> *To which the heaven of heavens is but a veil.*   30

All strength—all terror, single or in bands,
That ever was put forth in personal form;
Jehovah—with his thunder, and the choir
Of shouting Angels, and the empyreal thrones,
I pass them, unalarmed. Not Chaos, not   35
The darkest pit of lowest Erebus,
Nor aught of blinder vacancy—scooped out
By help of dreams, can breed such fear and awe
As fall upon us often when we look
Into our Minds, into the Mind of Man,   40
My haunt, and the main region of my Song.
—Beauty—a living Presence of the earth,
Surpassing the most fair ideal Forms
Which craft of delicate Spirits hath composed
From earth's materials—waits upon my steps;   45
Pitches her tents before me as I move,
An hourly neighbour. Paradise, and groves
Elysian, Fortunate Fields—like those of old
Sought in the Atlantic Main, why should they be
A history only of departed things,   50
Or a mere fiction of what never was?
For the discerning intellect of Man,
When wedded to this goodly universe
In love and holy passion, shall find these
A simple produce of the common day.   55
—I, long before the blissful hour arrives,
Would chaunt, in lonely peace, the spousal verse
Of this great consummation:—and, by words
Which speak of nothing more than what we are,
Would I arouse the sensual from their sleep   60
Of Death, and win the vacant and the vain
To noble raptures; while my voice proclaims
How exquisitely the individual Mind
(And the progressive powers perhaps no less
Of the whole species) to the external World   65
Is fitted:—and how exquisitely, too,

Theme this but little heard of among Men,
The external world is fitted to the Mind;
And the creation (by no lower name
Can it be called) which they with blended might   70
Accomplish:—this is our high argument.
—Such grateful haunts foregoing, if I oft
Must turn elsewhere—to travel near the tribes
And fellowships of men, and see ill sights
Of madding passions mutually inflamed;   75
Must hear Humanity in fields and groves
Pipe solitary anguish; or must hang
Brooding above the fierce confederate storm
Of sorrow, barricadoed evermore
Within the walls of Cities; may these sounds   80
Have their authentic comment,—that, even these
Hearing, I be not downcast or forlorn!
—Come thou prophetic Spirit, that inspir'st
The human Soul of universal earth,
Dreaming on things to come; and dost possess   85
A metropolitan Temple in the hearts
Of mighty Poets; upon me bestow
A gift of genuine insight; that my Song
With star-like virtue in its place may shine;
Shedding benignant influence,—and secure,   90
Itself, from all malevolent effect
Of those mutations that extend their sway
Throughout the nether sphere!—And if with this
I mix more lowly matter; with the thing
Contemplated, describe the Mind and Man   95
Contemplating; and who, and what he was,
The transitory Being that beheld
This Vision,—when and where, and how he lived;—
Be not this labour useless. If such theme
May sort with highest objects, then, dread Power,   100
Whose gracious favour is the primal source
Of all illumination, may my Life

Express the image of a better time,
More wise desires, and simpler manners;—nurse
My Heart in genuine freedom:—all pure thoughts   105
Be with me;—so shall thy unfailing love
Guide, and support, and cheer me to the end!"

2. THE MANUSCRIPTS OF THE PROSPECTUS

The three extant manuscripts are described by de Selincourt and Darbishire in *The Poetical Works,* V, 372. To avoid confusion, I conform to the precedent of these editors in labeling them MS1, MS2, and MS3. However, comparison of these texts with each other, and with the later version of the Prospectus published in 1814, makes it altogether certain that the actual order of composition was MS1, then MS3, then MS2. De Selincourt and Darbishire incorporated some variants from these manuscripts in their footnotes to the published version (*The Poetical Works,* V, 3–6), and also printed separately an incomplete and somewhat inaccurate transcript of MS2 (V, 338–9).

MS1 is found in a small notebook similar to those used for drafts of parts of *The Prelude.* MS2 is the conclusion to MS B of Part I, Book I of *The Recluse,* named *Home at Grasmere.* MS3 is a fragment written on a loose leaf out of an octavo notebook. The editors of *The Poetical Works* say that MS1 is "quite likely a fair copy of a draft . . . written as early as 1798, at Alfoxden," and that MSS 2 and 3 seem to be contemporary and date "probably . . . from the early months of 1800" (V, 372). It should be emphasized that both these dates are conjectural. It is possible that none of the MSS was written before 1804, or even 1806.* A more certain dating of these

---

* John Finch presents evidence for dating some parts of the MS B version of *Home at Grasmere* (possibly including the section which constitutes MS2 of the Prospectus) in July, 1806. See "On the Dating of *Home at Grasmere:* A New Approach," in *Bicentenary Wordsworth Studies in Memory of John*

documents must await a detailed study and sorting out of the tangled profusion of Wordsworth's literary remains.

The transcriptions below follow the holographs as exactly as is possible in print.* Inserted lines, words, or letters are printed in smaller type, in the places in which they occur in the manuscript. A gap in the printed text indicates a blank space in the manuscript. A bracketed word and query—[sink?] —signifies an uncertain reading. A bracketed query—[?]—signifies an illegible word or sequence of words. A part of a word followed by a query—tha[?]—signifies that the remainder of the word is illegible.

For convenience of intercomparison, I have added in the right margin the number of the line in the published Prospectus of 1814 with which the manuscript line coincides, or to which it approximates.

Alban Finch, ed. Jonathan Wordsworth, to be published by Cornell University Press, 1971. Professor Mark L. Reed writes to me that his investigations make it seem likely, but far from certain, that all three MSS of the Prospectus date between late March, 1804, and early September, 1806.

* I reprint these manuscripts with the generous permission of the Trustees of the Wordsworth Library at Dove Cottage, Grasmere. I wish also to thank Professor George Healey, Curator of the Cornell Wordsworth Collection, for access to the photographic reproductions of the manuscripts in the Wordsworth Library at Dove Cottage.

THE PROSPECTUS: MS 1

On Man, on Nature, and on human Life	1
Thinking in solitude, from time to time	2
I find sweet passions traversing my soul	—
Like music: unto these, where'er I may	—
I would give utterance in numerous verse.	13
Of Truth, of Grandeur, Beauty, Love, and Hope;	14
Of joy in various commonalty spread;	18
Of th' individual mind that keeps its own	19
Inviolate retirement, and consists	20
With being limitless, the one great Life,	—
I sing; fit audience let me find though few.	23
Fit audience find though few! Thus prayd the Bard	24
Holiest of Men. Urania I shall need	25
Thy guidance, or a greater Muse, if such	26
Descend to earth, or dwell in highest heaven.	27
For I must tread on Shadowy ground, must [sink?]	28
Deep, and ascend aloft, and worlds	29
To which the Heaven of heavens is but a veil.	30
All strength, all terror, single, or in bands	31
That ever was put forth by personal Form	32
Jehovah, with his thunder, and the choir	33
Of shouting Angels, and th' empyreal thrones	34
I pass them unalarm'd. The darkest pit	35
Of the profoundest hell, night, chaos, death	36
Nor aught of blinder vacancy scoop'd out	37
By help of dreams, can breed such fear and awe	38
As fall upon me often when I look	39
Into my soul, into the soul of man	40
My haunt, and the main region of my song.	41
Beauty, whose living home is the green earth	42
Surpassing far what hath by special craft	43
Of delicate Poets, been call'd forth, & shap'd	44
From earths materials, waits upon my steps	45
Pitches her tents before as I move	46

My hourly neighbour. Paradise, & groves 47

Elysian, blessed island in the deep 48

Of choice seclusion, wherefore need they be 49

A history, or but a dream, when minds 50

Once wedded to this outward frame of things 53

In love, finds these the growth of common day. 54/55

Such pleasant haunts foregoing, if my Song 72

Must turn elswhere, & travel near the tribes 73

And Fellowships of men, and see ill sights 74

Of passions ravenous from each others rage, 75

Insult & injury & wrong and strife —

~~Wisdom be thou my Guide, and if so [?]~~ —

must

I hear humanity in fields & groves 76

Pipe solitary anguish, or must hang 77

Brooding above the fierce confederate storm 78

Of sorrow, barricadoed ever more 79

Within the walls of Cities; to these sounds 80

Let me find

~~Give meaning~~

~~Do thou~~ give meaning more akin to that —

Which to Gods ear they carry, that even these 81

Hearing, I be not heartless, or forlorn. 82

Come Thou, prophetic Spirit, soul of Man 83

Thou human Soul of the wide earth, that hast 84

Thy metropolitan temple in the hearts 86

Of mighty Poets, unto me vouchsafe 87

Thy foresight, teach me to discern, & part 88

Inherent things from casual, what is fixd —

From fleeting, that my song may live, & be 88

Even as a light hung up in heaven to chear —

The world in times to come. And if this 93

I mingle humbler matter, with [this?] the thing 94

Contemplated describe the mind & man 95

Contemplating & who he was & what 96

~~The [solitary?] being tha[?]~~

The transitory being that beheld 97

~~when & where & how~~
~~This vision, how he lived, & when, & where~~

This vision, when & where & how he lived   98

With all his little realties of life   —

In part a Fellow citizen, in part   —

   [fugitive?]   —
An outlaw, and a borderer of his age

Be not this labour useless. O great God *   99

To less than thee I cannot make this prayer   —

Innocent mighty Spirit let my life   102

Express the image of a better time   103

Desires more wise & simpler manners, nurse   104

My heart in genuine freedom, all pure thoughts   105

Be with me & uphold me to the end.   107

---

* On the facing page:

such
If ~~this~~ theme

   not unworthy
Be ~~also~~ worthy then Eternal God

THE PROSPECTUS: MS 2

On Man on Nature & on human Life   1

I often
Thinking in solitude, from time to time   2

Delightful
~~I feel sweet~~ passions traversing my Soul   —

Like Music, unto these, whereer I may   —

I would give utterance in numerous verse   13

Of truth of grandeur beauty love & hope   14

~~Hope for this earth & hope beyond the grave~~   —

~~Of [virtue?] & of inellectual power~~   —

Of moral [strength?] & intellectual Power   17

Of blessed consolations in distress   16

Of joy in widest commonalty spread   18

Of the individual mind that keeps its own   19

Inviolate retirement, & consists   20

With being limitless the one great Life   —

I sing, fit audience let me find though few   23

asked
So pray'd, more gaining than wish'd   24

Fit ~~audience find tho'~~ few thus pray'd the Bard   24

Holiest of Men Urania I shall need   25

Thy guidance or a greater Muse if such   26

Descend to earth or dwell in highest heaven   27

For I must tread on shadowy ground must sink   28

Deep, & aloft ascending breathe in worlds   29

To which the Heaven of heavens is but a veil   30

All strength all terror single or in bands   31

That ever was put forth in personal forms   32

Jehovah with his thunder & the quire   33

Of shouting angels & the empyreal thron   34

Not chaos, not
I pass them unalarmed. ~~The darkest Pit~~   35

The darkest Pit of the profoundest hell,   36
~~Of the profoundest Hell, chaos night~~
    The ~~lowes~~ darkest Pit of lowest Erebus
Nor aught of   vacancy scoop'd out   37
By help of dreams can breed such fear & awe   38
As fall upon us often when we look   39
Into our minds into the mind of Man   40
My haunt & the main region of my song.   41
    a living Presence of the Earth
Beauty ~~whose Living home is the green~~ earth   42
Surpassing the most fair ideal Forms   43
   Which
~~The~~ craft of delicate spirits hath compos'd   44
From earths materials waits upon my steps   45
Pitches her tents before me where I move   46
An hourly Neighbour. Paradise, & groves   47
Elysian fortunate ~~islands,~~ fields like those of old   48
    main
In the ~~deep~~ ocean wherefore should they be   49
A History or but a dream when minds   50
Once wedded to this outward frame of things   53
In love find these the growth of common day   54/55
I long before the bless'd hour arrives   56
            1000
  ~~chant~~
Would sing in solitude the spousal verse   57
Of this great consummation, would proclaim   58
(Speaking of nothing more than what we are)   59
How exquisitely the individual Mind   63
And the progressive powers perhaps no less   64
Of the whole species to the external world   65
Is fitted; & how exquisitely too   66
Theme this but little heard of among men   67
The external world is fitted to the mind   68
And the creation (by no lower name   69
Can it be call'd) which they with blended might   70
Accomplish: this is my great argument.   71

Such	foregoing if I oft	72

Must turn elswhere & travel near the tribes   73
And fellowships of men & see ill sights   74
Of passions ravenous from each other's rage   75
Must hear humanity in fields & groves   76
Pipe solitary anguish or must hang   77
Brooding above the fierce confederate Storm   78

Of Sorrow barricadoed evermore   79
₁₀₂₀
Within the walls of Cities may these sounds   80
Have their authentic comment that even these   81
Hearing, I be not heartless or forlorn.   82
Come thou prophetic Spirit, Soul of Man   83
Thou human Soul of the wide earth that hast   84
Thy metropolitan Temple in the hearts   86
Of mighty Poets unto me vouchsafe   87

succour
Thy ~~guidance~~ teach me to [discern?] & part   —
Inherent things from casual, what is fixed   —
From fleeting that my verse may live & be   —
Even as a light hung up in heaven to chear   —

with
Mankind in times to come. And if ʌ this   93
I blend more lowly matter with the thing   94
Contemplated describe the mind & man   95
Contemplating & who & what he was   96
The transitory Being that beheld   97
This vision when & where & how he lived   98
[His?] [joys?] [?] hopes & fears

With all his ~~little~~ realties of life   —
small

Be not this labour useless: if such theme   99
1040
May sort with highest things, then gratious god
Perfect
~~With highest things may   then great~~ God   100
Thou who art breath & being way & guide   —

       soul

And ~~power~~ & understanding may my life   102

Express the image of a better time   103

More wise desires & simple manners nurse   104

My heart in genuine freedom all pure thoughts   105

Be with me & uphold me to the end   107

          1047

                verse a [few?] [?   ]

       That my ~~verse may live & shine~~   —

With [undecaying?] [properties?] may [live?]

Untouched * by the mutation of the [world?]   92/93

            that the body of my verse   —

Un[?]

By the mutation of the world untouchd   92/93

And by its ferments undisturbed may shine   89

      as a

Even ~~like~~ a light hung up in heaven to chear   —

---

* The "Un" in "Untouched" is written over the word "By."

THE PROSPECTUS: MS 3

st hear humanity in fiels and groves *	76
e solitary or anguish or must hang	77
ding above the fierce confederate Storm	78
w barricadoed evermore	79
the walls of cities may such sounds	80
their authentic comment that even these	81
Hearing I be not heartless or forlorn.	82
Come thou Prophetic Spirit Soul of { ? } Man	83
Thou human Soul of the wide earth that hast	84
Thy metropolitan Temple in the hearts	86
Of mighty Poets unto me voutchsafe	87
Thy guidance teach me to discern and part	—
Inherent things from casual, what is fixd	—
From fleeting that my verse may live, and be	—
Even as a light hung up in heavn to chear	—
Mankind in times to come. And if this	93
I blend more lowly matter with the thing	94
Contemplated describe the mind and Man	95
Contemplating & who & what he was	96
The transitory Being that beheld	97
This Vision when & where & how he lived	98
With all ~~its~~ his little realties of life	—
Be not this labour useless: if such theme	99
With highest things may mingle then great God	100

Thou who art breath & being way & guide
~~Almighty being thou who art light & law~~   —
    power

And ~~strength~~ & understanding may my life	102
Express the image of a better time	103
More wise desire, & simple manners nurse	104
My heart in genuine freedom all pure thoughts	105
Be with me and ~~to~~ uphold me to the end.	107

Recluse **
   Innocent mighty Spirit

---

* The upper left corner of the MS is torn off.
** This word is not in Wordsworth's hand.

Notes

ONE / *"This Is Our High Argument"*

1. To Thomas De Quincey, 6 March 1804; *The Letters of William and Dorothy Wordsworth: The Early Years 1787–1805,* ed. E. de Selincourt and Chester L. Shaver (2d ed.; Oxford, 1967), p. 454.

2. Preface to *The Excursion, The Poetical Works of William Wordsworth,* ed. E. de Selincourt and Helen Darbishire (5 vols.; Oxford, 1940–9), V, 2. For evidence that *The Excursion* is incomplete, and for an estimate of the length of the projected *The Recluse,* see Lionel Stevenson, "The Unfinished Gothic Cathedral," *University of Toronto Quarterly,* XXXII (1963), 170–83.

3. Summary accounts of the history of *The Recluse* are given in *The Poetical Works,* V, 363–72; and in *The Prelude,* ed. de Selincourt and Darbishire (2d ed.; Oxford, 1959), pp. xxxiii–xl. A detailed discussion of its tangled problems is to be found in John Finch's doctoral thesis, *Wordsworth, Coleridge, and "The Recluse," 1798–1814,* Cornell University, 1964.

4. See the Appendix to this book for the various drafts of Wordsworth's Prospectus, and the question as to their dating.

5. *Poetical Works,* V, 2. In a letter to Sir George Beaumont, 3 June 1805 (*Letters: The Early Years,* p. 594), Wordsworth had described *The Prelude* as "a sort of portico to *The Recluse,* part of the same building."

6. Preface to the *Poems* of 1815, *Literary Criticism of William Wordsworth,* ed. Paul M. Zall (Lincoln, Nebraska, 1966), p. 143. See also p. 140, where Wordsworth describes his "minor Poems" as having a "connection with each other," as well as a "subordination" to *The Recluse.*

7. The importance of the Prospectus was noted early by an anonymous reviewer of Wordsworth's *Complete Poetical Works* of 1837, in *The New York Review,* VII (1839), p. 28: "The extract from 'The Recluse' introduced in the preface to 'The Excursion,' is, perhaps, the fullest exposition of the general argument of Wordsworth's poetry." As we shall see in chapter VII, Wordsworth's *Essay, Supplementary to the Preface* of 1815 expands upon certain parts of the program announced in the Prospectus, published the year before.

8. A. C. Bradley, "Wordsworth," *Oxford Lectures on Poetry* (London, reprinted 1950), p. 101.

9. *Home at Grasmere,* in *The Poetical Works,* V, 335–8 (ll. 664 ff.).

10. *The Poetical Works,* V, 3, 11. 23–4. I shall cite the Prospectus in the version of 1814, noting as the occasion arises significant differences in the earlier manuscripts.

11. *Paradise Lost,* VII, 23–31.

12. *The Prelude,* ed. de Selincourt and Darbishire, p. 75, note. Relevant to Wordsworth's view of the bardic and prophetic poet is *The Prelude* (1805) V, 41 ("The consecrated works of Bard and Sage") and XII, 301 ff. ("Poets, even as Prophets, each with each/ Connected in a mighty scheme of truth"). In his ode *To William Wordsworth* Coleridge, upon hearing Wordsworth read *The Prelude,* hailed him as a "Great Bard! . . . viewed . . . in the choir/ Of ever-enduring men."

13. *Henry Crabb Robinson on Books and Their Writers,* ed. Edith J. Morley (3 vols.; London, 1938), II, 776.

14. Preface to *Poems* of 1815, *Literary Criticism of William Wordsworth,* pp. 150–1.

15. *The Letters of Charles and Mary Lamb,* ed. E. V. Lucas (3 vols.; London, 1935), I, 246. In Coleridge's letter to Thomas Poole, 31 Mar. 1800, he calls Wordsworth "a greater poet than any since Milton," and parallels him to

Milton "at the age of thirty." *Collected Letters of Samuel Taylor Coleridge,* ed. E. L. Griggs (Oxford, 1956 ff.), I, 584.

16. To Thomas Poole, 28 Apr. 1814; *The Letters of William and Dorothy Wordsworth, The Middle Years 1806–20,* ed. E. de Selincourt (2 vols.; Oxford, 1937), II, 596. On the extent of Wordsworth's identification with Milton, in his life and views as well as his poetry, see Lionel Stevenson, "The Unfinished Gothic Cathedral," pp. 174–5, and Brian Wilkie, *Romantic Poets and Epic Tradition* (Madison and Milwaukee, 1965), p. 67 and p. 240, note 17.

17. Writing to Wordsworth on 30 May 1815, Coleridge reminded him that *The Recluse* was "to have affirmed a Fall in some sense, as a fact," and "to point out . . . a manifest Scheme of Redemption" (*Collected Letters,* IV, 574–5). On 21 July 1832 Coleridge described the plan of *The Recluse* as including "a redemptive process in operation." *The Table Talk and Omniana,* ed. H. N. Coleridge (London, 1917), p. 189.

18. *Paradise Lost,* I, 6–17; VII, 1–12, 39–40; IX, 13–43; also *Paradise Regained,* I, 8–17.

19. Milton used the Biblical phrase "the heaven of heavens" (I Kings 8:27; Psalm 148:4) in the way Augustine had defined it, as the first-created and eternal heaven, the "dwelling place" of the Lord and of "the citizens of Your City which is in heaven far above the heavens we see" (Augustine, *Confessions,* XII, ii–xi).

20. Henry Crabb Robinson, letter to Dorothy Wordsworth, Feb., 1826, in *Blake, Coleridge, Wordsworth, Lamb, Etc.,* ed. Edith J. Morley (Manchester, 1922), p. 15; and *H. C. Robinson on Books and their Writers,* I, 327. See also Blake's marginal annotations on Wordsworth's *Poems* of 1815 and on the Prospectus, in *The Poetry and Prose of William Blake,* ed. David Erdman and Harold Bloom (New York, 1965), pp. 654–6.

21. H. C. Robinson, *Blake, Coleridge, Wordsworth, Lamb, Etc.,* p. 6; *H. C. Robinson on Books and Their Writers,* I, 327. Other contemporaries worried about the heretical arrogance of the passage in Wordsworth's Prospectus. Flaxman, Robinson tells us, "took umbrage at some mystical expressions in the fragment in the preface in which Wordsworth talks of seeing *Jehovah* unalarmed. 'If my brother had written that,' said Flaxman, 'I should say burn it.' But he admitted that Wordsworth could not mean anything impious in it." "Indeed," Robinson adds, "I was unable, and am still, to explain the passage. And Lamb's explanation is unsatisfactory, viz. that there are deeper sufferings in the mind of man than in any imagined hell." *H. C. Robinson on Books and Their Writers,* I, 156–7.

22. Also *Paradise Lost,* I, 249: "Farewell happy Fields/ Where Joy for ever dwells. . . ." The view that the pagan fables of the golden age, Elysium, and the Islands of the Blest were a distant and distorted reflection of the true paradise had been a commonplace among Christian commentators and poets. See Arthur O. Lovejoy and George Boas, *Primitivism and Related Ideas in Antiquity* (Baltimore, 1935), pp. 290–303; and Hans-Joachim Mähl, *Die Idee des goldenen Zeitalters im Werk des Novalis* (Heidelberg, 1965), pp. 11–145.

23. In his earlier writings Wordsworth also had joined pagan fable with the Christian paradise, in a context in which he looks forward to a restored Golden Age. See, e.g., *Descriptive Sketches* (1793), ll.774 ff.; and *The Convention of Cintra,* ed. A. V. Dicey (London, 1915), pp. 10–11, 122; cf. *The Excursion,* III, 752–65.

24. For the "sleep of death" see Psalm 13:3–5.

25. This statement can be supplemented by a passage in MS. JJ of *The Prelude* that de Selincourt dates 1798–9:

> Those first born affinities which fit
> Our new existence to existing things
> And in our dawn of being constitute
> The bond of union betwixt life and joy.

See *The Prelude*, ed. de Selincourt and Darbishire, pp. 636–7; for the dating, see p. xxvi.

26. *The Prelude* (1805), III, 82–185. An early version of lines 82–167 was written in February, 1798, as part of *The Ruined Cottage; see Poetical Works*, V, 388.

27. This stanza also constituted part of Coleridge's first version of this poem, *A Letter to [Asra]*, written April, 1802.

28. Blake, *Jerusalem*, Plates 77, 97–9.

29. Hölderlin, *Sämtliche Werke*, ed. Friedrich Beissner (6 vols.; Stuttgart, 1946 ff.), III, 89–90.

30. Novalis, *Henry von Ofterdingen*, translated by Palmer Hilty (New York, 1964), pp. 143–8.

31. Novalis, *Briefe und Werke* (3 vols.; Berlin, 1943); III, 375.

32. F. W. J. von Schelling, *The Ages of the World*, trans. Frederick de Wolfe Bolman, Jr. (New York, 1942), pp. 84, 90–1.

33. Preface to *Poems* of 1815, *Literary Criticism*, ed. Zall, p. 150.

34. Blake, *Milton*, Plate 16. 47–50; 20. 4–14. See the anthology, *The Romantics on Milton*, ed. J. A. Wittreich, Jr. (Cleveland and London, 1970).

35. H. C. Robinson, *Blake, Coleridge, Wordsworth, Lamb, Etc.*, p. 12; *The Laocoön*, in *The Poetry and Prose of William Blake*, p. 271.

36. To J. H. Reynolds, May 3, 1818, and to George and Georgiana Keats, Feb. 14–May 3, 1819; *The Letters of John Keats*, ed. Hyder E. Rollins (2 vols.; Cambridge, Mass., 1958), I, 278–9, 282; II, 103.

37. Preface to *Prometheus Unbound, Shelley's Prose*, ed. David Lee Clark (Albuquerque, New Mexico, 1954), p. 328; Thomas Medwin, *The Life of Percy Bysshe Shelley*, ed. H. Buxton Forman (London, 1913), p. 262.

38. Mary Shelley, "Notes on Poems of 1817," in *The Complete Poetical Works of Shelley*, ed. Thomas Hutchinson (London, 1948), p. 551. In "Note on the Revolt of Islam," *ibid.*, p. 156, Mary speaks of Shelley's "constant perusal" of "the Psalms, the Book of Job, the Prophet Isaiah," and other parts of the Old Testament, "the sublime poetry of which filled him with delight." On Shelley's use of the Bible in his poems see Bennett Weaver, *Toward the Understanding of Shelley* (Ann Arbor, Michigan, 1932); and for his intensive study of the Bible, as recorded in Mary Shelley's *Journal* and Shelley's letters, see *The Letters of Percy Bysshe Shelley*, ed. Frederick L. Jones (2 vols.; Oxford, 1964), Appendix VIII, "Shelley's Reading."

39. Medwin, *The Life of Shelley*, p. 255.

40. Quoted by Arthur O. Lovejoy and George Boas, *Primitivism and Related Ideas in Antiquity* (Baltimore, 1935), p. 84; this book is a comprehensive analysis and anthology of Greek and Roman primitivism and cyclism. See also W. K. C. Guthrie, *In the Beginning* (Ithaca, New York, 1957), chap. IV.

41. Augustine, *The City of God*, XII. 13; see also XII.14–19.

42. Thomas Burnet, *The Sacred Theory of the Earth* (6th ed.; 2 vols., London, 1726) I, 143. The primitive text of this endlessly recurrent concept is Paul's Epistle to the Romans, 1:20. "For the invisible things of Him from the creation of the world are clearly seen, being understood by the things that are made." (Throughout this book I cite the Bible in the Authorized Version which was read by the English Romantic poets.)

43. As Milton, in *On the Morning of Christ's Nativity*, said of the relative im-

port for human felicity of the Incarnation as against the final Advent: before "Time will run back and fetch the age of gold," the Babe new born must redeem us on the cross, and afterward return for the Last Judgment:

> And then at last our bliss
> Full and perfect is,
> But now begins. . . .

44. Hence Milton's statement, at the beginning of *Paradise Lost*, that his story moves from the "loss of Eden" to the regaining of "the blissful Seat." For the retrospective and prospective paradises in Christian writings—the same term being commonly applied to the primal earthly residence of Adam and Eve, to the new Kingdom on earth to be established at the millennium, and also to the ultimate Kingdom of Heaven—see Jean Daniélou, "Terre et paradis chez les pères de l'église," *Eranos-Jahrbuch*, XXII (1953); also Harry Levin, "Paradises, Heavenly and Earthly," *The Huntington Library Quarterly*, XXIX (1966), 305–24.

45. Karl Löwith, *Meaning in History* (Chicago, 1949), p. 183.

46. Isaac Newton, *Observations upon the Prophecies of Daniel, and the Apocalypse of St. John*, ed. Benjamin Smith (2 parts; London, 1733); Joseph Priestley, *The Present State of Europe Compared with Antient Prophecies* (London, 1794); D. H. Lawrence, *Apocalypse* (New York, 1932); *Paul Claudel interroge l'Apocalypse* (Paris, 1952).

47. Lawrence, *Apocalypse*, pp. 7, 10.

48. Michael Fixler, *Milton and the Kingdoms of God* (Evanston, 1964), p. 71. For Milton's images from Revelation and the Gospels, see Theodore Banks, *Milton's Imagery* (New York, 1950), pp. 176–7.

49. On the development of prophecy into apocalyptic and the nature of apocalyptic writings see, e.g., F. C. Burkett, *Jewish and Christian Apocalypses* (London, 1914); Christopher R. North, *The Old Testament Interpretation of History* (London, 1946); Stanley Brice Frost, *Old Testament Apocalyptic, Its Origins and Growth* (London, 1952); Martin Buber, "Prophecy, Apocalyptic, and the Historical Hour," in *Pointing the Way* (New York, 1957); H. H. Rowley, *The Relevance of Apocalyptic* (3d ed.; New York, 1964).

50. Rufus M. Jones, *The Eternal Gospel* (New York, 1938), p. 5.

51. The non-Biblical Apocalypse, Secrets of Enoch, written in the first century, envisions a new day, or Sabbath, of one thousand years which will come at the end of the six-thousand-year history of the world (32:2–33:2). The equation of one thousand years with each day of God's week of creation is based on Psalm 90:4, "For a thousand years in thy sight are but as yesterday when it is past." Cf. 2 Peter 3:8, "One day is with the Lord as a thousand years, and a thousand years as one day."

52. For the phrase "new heavens and new earth" as it occurs in various Biblical and apocryphal apocalypses, see R. H. Charles, *A Critical and Exegetical Commentary on the Revelation of St. John* (2 vols.; Edinburgh, 1920), II, 184, 187, 193, 199, 203.

53. In *The Christian Doctrine*, I.xxxiii, Milton had said that whether by "*its final conflagration . . .* is meant the destruction of the substance of the world itself, or only a change in the nature of its constituent parts, is uncertain, and of no importance to determine. . . . Our glorification will be accompanied by the renovation of heaven and earth, and of all things therein adopted to our service or delight, to be possessed by us in perpetuity." To illustrate this interpretation of the New Testament promise, Milton then cites Isaiah 65:17 on "I create new heavens and a new earth." See also *Paradise Lost*, III, 333–8; X, 638–40; XI, 900–1; XII, 547–51.

54. These views are summarized and discussed by S. H. Hooke, *The Siege Perilous* (London, 1956).

55. For the tradition of the transfiguration of the promised land and of the holy city of Jerusalem in the last days, see Jean Daniélou, "Terre et paradis," pp. 438 ff. In the first-century apocalypse, 2 Esdras 7:26, the bride, as in the Book of Revelation, is a city: "The bride shall appear, even the city coming forth, and she shall be seen that now is withdrawn from the earth." Austin Farrer, *A Rebirth of Images* (Boston, 1963), pp. 65–8, proposes that the description of the end of the world in Revelation, including the holy marriage, is designed to recapitulate and fulfill the promise of the beginning of the world as described in Genesis: as "the new heavens and new earth" replace and fulfill the creation of heaven and earth on the first day, so Christ and the New Jerusalem, a second Adam and Eve, replace and fulfill the work of the sixth day when "male and female created he them" (Genesis 1:27).

56. Matthew 9:15, 25:1–13; also Matthew 22:2 ff.; Mark 2:19–20; Luke 5:34–5; John 2:1–3; 3:29; Ephesians 5:23–32. See Claude Chavasse, *The Bride of Christ* (London, 1940).

57. Augustine, *Sermo suppositus*, cxx. 8, in *Patrologia Latina*, ed. Migne, XXXIX, col. 1986 f. A probable bridge between the Old Testament promise of a remarriage between God and Israel and the doctrine of Christ's consummation on the cross of His marriage to the children of Adam is Paul's preaching on the Agape of the Cross, Romans 5:6–10; e.g., "But God commendeth his love toward us, in that, while we were yet sinners, Christ died for us." See also Jean Daniélou, *The Bible and the Liturgy* (Notre Dame, Indiana, 1956), pp. 206–7; and Erich Auerbach, "Rising to Christ on the Cross," *Modern Language Notes*, LXIV (1949). The ancient conception of the Passion as the consummation of a marriage is still viable in Coventry Patmore's *The Unknown Eros*; even the reversal of sexual roles had exegetical precedents:

> In season due, on His sweet-fearful bed,
> Rock'd by an earthquake, curtain'd by eclipse,
> Thou shared'st the spousal rapture of the sharp spear's head
> And thy bliss pale
> Wrought for our boon what Eve's did for our bale.

58. Frederic W. Farrar, *History of Interpretation* (London, 1886), pp. 32–3, lists nineteen diverse allegorical interpretations of Canticles.

59. A number of Church Fathers established a tradition of coherent symbolism which viewed the apocalyptic marriage as initiated by the creation of Adam and Eve; predicted by the prophets; prefigured by a number of historical events in the Old Testament; detailedly imaged forth in Canticles; achieved in the Incarnation; consummated by the Passion; celebrated in the ritual sacraments (not only of matrimony, but also of baptism and the Eucharist, which were looked upon as nuptial mysteries); and awaiting its fulfillment and fruition in the marriage of the Lamb at the end of the world. See, e.g., Jean Daniélou, *The Bible and the Liturgy*, pp. 191–220.

60. The basis is Revelation 14:1–5, where the author beholds 144,000 virgins who, even before Christ's second Advent, have been "redeemed from among men" to dwell with the Lamb.

61. John 5:24–5; also 11:25–6. See C. H. Dodd, *The Interpretation of the Fourth Gospel* (Cambridge, England, 1953).

62. Romans 7:1–4; also Galatians 6:15. See Rudolf Bultmann, *History and Eschatology* (New York, 1957), pp. 40–7.

63. For the role in Augustine's conversion of Anthanasius' *Vita Antonii* (to

which Augustine himself refers), see Pierre Courcelle, *Recherches sur les Confessions de Saint Augustin* (Paris, 1950), pp. 181 ff.

64. Erich Auerbach's analysis of the characteristic psychological pattern in Augustine's description of the temptation of Alypius at the gladiatorial show (*Confessions* VI. viii) is relevant here; see *Mimesis* (Princeton, New Jersey, 1953), pp. 66–72. A. D. Nock discusses the important differences, under their similarities, between the distinctively Christian experience of conversion and the resurrection rituals of Orphism and other mystery cults in antiquity: *Conversion* (Oxford, 1933), pp. 12 ff.; 138 ff.

65. *The Confessions of Saint Augustine*, trans. F. J. Sheed (London, 1944), Book VIII, pp. 130, 133, 138–42.

66. On the theory of Scriptural polysemantics see, e.g., Beryl Smalley, *The Study of the Bible in the Middle Ages* (Oxford, 1952), and H. Flanders Dunbar, *Symbolism in Medieval Thought* (New York, 1961).

67. For Wordsworth's judgments of "the divine Spenser," see Markham L. Peacock, *The Critical Opinions of William Wordsworth*, pp. 360–1.

68. In the poem *Personal Talk*, lines 37–42, Wordsworth says that "pre-eminently dear" to him, among books which deal with "personal themes," are *Othello* and "The heavenly Una with her milk-white Lamb." See also Wordsworth's extended comment on the first book of *The Faerie Queene* in his Dedication to *The White Doe of Rylstone, Poetical Works*, III, 281–3.

69. See Josephine Waters Bennett, *The Evolution of "The Faerie Queene"* (Chicago, 1942), pp. 108–22.

70. Evelyn Underhill's *Mysticism* (New York, 1955) is a readily accessible compendium of relevant passages; see, e.g., pp. 136–9, 369–79.

71. The violence of the experience of spiritual union with God was sometimes described as a rape of the soul by the mystics. "And as well this is called a ravishing as the other," wrote Richard Rolle, "for with a violence it is done, and as it were against nature." See Evelyn Underhill, *Mysticism*, pp. 369, 377.

72. For earlier statements than Milton's of a correspondence to hell within the microcosm of man, see Merritt Y. Hughes, "'Myself Am Hell,'" *Modern Philology*, LIV (1956–7), pp. 80–9; and on the inner correspondence to Paradise see Jean Daniélou, "Terre et paradis," pp. 467–8, 470, and Louis L. Martz, *The Paradise Within* (New Haven, 1964), pp. 35–9.

73. See George H. Sabine, ed., *The Works of Gerrard Winstanley* (Ithaca, N. Y., 1941), Introduction, pp. 5–21.

74. *Ibid.*, pp. 493–4.

75. *Ibid.*, p. 214. John Donne expressed the central view of the age, in which both Anglicans and the chief Puritan sects were in agreement, when he accepted a controlled spiritual or allegorical reading of Scripture, but emphasized the primacy of the literal and historical sense. "Though it be ever lawfull, and often times very usefull . . . to induce the *diverse senses* that the Scriptures doe admit, yet this may not be admitted, if there may be danger thereby, to neglect or weaken the *literall* sense it selfe." "But the literall sense of every place, is the principall intention of the Holy Ghost, in that place. . . ." See Helen Gardner, *The Limits of Literary Criticism* (London, 1956), pp. 47–51.

76. "To Nobodaddy," and *The Marriage of Heaven and Hell*, Plate 14.

77. H. C. Robinson, *Blake, Coleridge, Wordsworth, Lamb, Etc.*, p. 12. "Both read the Bible day & night/ But thou readst black where I read white," Blake declared in *The Everlasting Gospel* (*Poetry and Prose*, p. 516).

78. Revelation, chaps. 4–5; also 10:1–4 and 14:1–3; and see *Paradise Lost*, III, 56–64, 323–49.

79. For the possibility that Hebrew eschatology assimilated elements from early Zoroastrian myths of the final triumph of the forces of good over the forces

of evil, see A. D. Nock, *Conversion*, pp. 242–4. R. C. Zaehner, however, in *The Dawn and Twilight of Zoroastrianism* (New York, 1961), pp. 57–8, denies that there is any solid evidence for such influence. Virgil's prediction in his Fourth Eclogue that the lost Golden Age will return was widely quoted by exegetes and poets as a pagan premonition of the Christian truth, and it has been proposed by some more recent scholars that in this Eclogue Virgil was influenced by Hebrew prophecy. Notice, however, that Virgil's description of the return of the age of gold is entirely consonant with—in fact, is entailed by—the classical view of history as an endless sequence of cyclical recurrences:

> Magnus ab integro saeclorum nascitur ordo.
> Iam redit et Virgo, redeunt Saturnia regna—

"The great succession of the ages begins anew. Now the Virgin [i.e., Astraea] returns, and the Saturnian reign returns. . . . Then there will be a second Tiphys, and a second Argo to carry the chosen heroes; there will also be a second war, and once again shall great Achilles be sent to Troy." The difference from Biblical prophecy is made clear by Shelley's great lyric, "The world's great age begins anew," which echoes the Fourth Eclogue. In his conclusion Shelley (like Blake in his Introduction to *Songs of Experience:* "Turn away no more:/ Why wilt thou turn away") calls upon history to square off at the top of its revolving cycles, and to terminate there:

> Oh, cease! must hate and death return?
> Cease! must men kill and die?
> Cease! drain not to its dregs the urn
> Of bitter prophecy.
> The world is weary of the past,
> Oh, might it die or rest at last!

In effect these poets cry out for a transformation of history from the shape of eternal recurrence to the shape of apocalyptic prophecy, in which history reaches its highest point and then stops.

80. Hans Conzelmann interprets the eschatology in the Gospel of St. Luke as already based on the view that the Parousia will not occur until the distant and indefinite future: *The Theology of St. Luke*, trans. Geoffrey Buswell (London, 1960), Part II, "Luke's Eschatology." And see 2 Peter 3:3–4:

81. J. B. Bury, *The Idea of Progress* (1920). See also, e.g., the Introduction by Charles A. Beard in the Dover reprint of Bury (New York, 1955); Arthur O. Lovejoy, Foreword to Lois Whitney, *Primitivism and the Idea of Progress* (Baltimore, 1934), pp. xvii–xix; George H. Hildebrand, ed., *The Idea of Progress* (Berkeley and Los Angeles, 1949), Introduction.

A number of Greek and Roman writers presented views of past and future human progress, but differed from post-Renaissance theorists by setting limits to the scope of human activities in which progress manifests itself, the degree of advance which is possible, and the length of time in which progress can continue, before the inevitable downturn of the historical cycle. See the examples collected by Ludwig Edelstein, *The Idea of Progress in Classical Antiquity* (Baltimore, 1967).

82. Carl Becker, "Progress," in *The Encyclopedia of the Social Sciences* (1934), vol. XII; R. S. Crane, "Anglican Apologetics and the Idea of Progress, 1699–1745," *The Idea of the Humanities and Other Essays* (2 vols.; Chicago, 1967), I, 214–87; Ernest Tuveson, *Millennium and Utopia* (Berkeley and Los Angeles, 1949). See also John Baillie, *The Belief in Progress* (New York, 1951). As early as the twelfth century Joachim of Flora had translated Biblical history and eschatology into a theory of historical eras,

adapted to the reign of the Father, the Son, and the Holy Spirit, each re-
capitulating a parallel cycle of events but on a successively higher plane,
until the third and final earthly stage of a classless, institutionless, monas-
tic brotherhood of all mankind. See Karl Löwith, *Meaning in History*,
chap. VIII, and Morton Bloomfield, "Joachim of Flora," *Traditio*, XIII
(1957), 249–311. As we shall see in chapter IV, in the 1790's and later the
major German philosophers, including Herder, Kant, Schiller, Fichte, and
Hegel, continued explicitly to link their particular versions of human progress with Biblical eschatology in the mode of rationalized theology that
Kant called "philosophical chiliasm."

83. "Answer to the Letter of Mathetes," *The Prose Works of William Wordsworth*, ed. Alexander B. Grosart (3 vols.; London, 1876), I, 312. See also
M. L. Peacock, Jr., *The Critical Opinions of William Wordsworth*, pp. 179–
80, 314. For comparable judgments of Bacon's genius see *Coleridge on the
Seventeenth Century*, ed. Roberta Florence Brinkley (Durham, North Caro-
lina, 1955), pp. 5, 41–58; and *Shelley's Prose*, ed. David Lee Clark (Albuquerque, New Mexico, 1954), pp. 231, 233, 251, 280, 292, 318, 328.

84. Francis Bacon, *The New Organon*, Aphorisms I.xcii–iii, in *The New Organon and Related Writings*, ed. Fulton H. Anderson (New York, 1960),
pp. 90–2.

85. Aphorisms II.lii, *ibid.*, p. 267.

86. *The Great Instauration, ibid.*, pp. 15, 3, 14.

87. Aphorisms, I.lxviii, *ibid.*, p. 66; see also *The Natural and Experimental
History for the Foundation of Philosophy*, in *The Works of Francis Bacon*,
ed. James Spedding, Robert Leslie Ellis, and Douglas Dennon Heath (15
vols.; Boston, 1863), IX, 370–71. For a striking example of the degree to
which the theory of historical progress and human perfectibility continued
to be couched in Biblical terms of the fall and the coming redemption of
man in an earthly paradise, even in the nineteenth century and by a pro-
fessed atheist, see Pierre Proudhon, *Système des contradictions économiques*, ed. Roger Picard (2 vols.; Paris, 1923), I, 353 ff.

88. As translated in *The New Organon*, ed. Fulton H. Anderson, pp. 22–3.
The key terms in Bacon's Latin are: "thalamum Mentis et Universi";
"Epithalamii autem votum sit, ut ex eo connubio. . . ." In *Francesco
Bacone* (Bari, 1957), Paolo Rossi argues that Bacon adapted to empirical
science the procedure for obtaining mastery over nature proposed for the
illuminated Magus in Renaissance magic. We shall see in the third chapter how widespread in Renaissance occultism was Bacon's interpretation of
the fall of man as a division both among the powers of the mind and between the mind and nature, and his interpretation of the redemption of
man as a reintegration of the mental faculties and a recovered unity with
nature.

89. *Ibid.*, p. 29. In the Latin: "Atque in eo sunt omnia, siquis oculos mentis
a rebus ipsis nunquam dejiciens, earum imagines plane ut sunt excipiat."
Cf. Wordsworth: "I have at all times endeavoured to look steadily at my
subject; consequently I hope it will be found that there is in these Poems
little falsehood of description." ". . . the eye of the Poet had been steadily
fixed upon his object." *Literary Criticism of William Wordsworth*, ed. Paul
M. Zall, pp. 22, 173; cf. p. 140. See also the sudden revelation to Wordsworth of the landscape in an Alpine ravine as "Characters of the great
Apocalypse,/ The types and symbols of Eternity" (*The Prelude*, VI, 570–3).

90. See Isaiah Berlin, *Historical Inevitability* (London, 1954); and on the concept of total revolution, Karl Mannheim, *Ideology and Utopia*, trans. Louis
Wirth and Edward Shils (New York, 1936).

91. Norman Cohn, *The Pursuit of the Millennium* (London, 1957). On Jewish
messianic movements see Abba Hillel Silver, *A History of Messianic Speculation in Israel from the First through the Seventeenth Centuries* (Boston,

1959); and Gershom Scholem, "Zum Verständnis der messianischen Idee im Judentum," *Judaica* (Frankfurt am Main, 1963).

92. Cohn, *The Pursuit of the Millennium*, chaps. X–XII. Vittorio Lanternari chronicles the violent millenarian cults fostered outside European civilization by the Biblical teachings of Christian missionaries, in *Movimenti religiosi di libertà e di salvezza dei popoli oppressi* (Milan, 1961).

93. See Louise Fargo Brown, *The Political Activities of the Baptists and Fifth Monarchy Men in England during the Interregnum* (Washington, D.C., 1912). On the millenarian beliefs and movements of the time see also William Haller, *The Rise of Puritanism* (New York, 1938), especially pp. 269–71.

94. *The Clarke Papers*, ed. C. H. Firth, The Camden Society, New Series XLIX (1891), pp. 378–9. See also Arthur Barker, *Milton and the Puritan Dilemma, 1641–1660* (Toronto, 1942), p. 197.

95. Milton, *Of Reformation in England* (1641), *The Complete Prose Works*, (3 vols.; New Haven, 1953–62), I, 616; *Animadversions* (1641), *ibid.*, p. 707. For a full account of Milton's apocalyptic expectations and disappointments, see Michael Fixler, *Milton and the Kingdoms of God* (London, 1964).

96. Pierre Proudhon, *Système des contradictions économiques* (1846), ed. Roger Picard (2 vols.; Paris, 1923), I, 53, 55–6.

97. Friedrich Schlegel, *Gespräch über die Poesie* (1800), in *Kunstanschauung der Frühromantik*, ed. Andreas Müller (Leipzig, 1931), pp. 184–90.

98. F. W. J. Schelling, *Philosophie der Kunst, Sämtliche Werke*, Pt. I, Vol. V, p. 446. On the call for a "new mythology" by German writers of the period see Fritz Strich, *Die Mythologie in der deutschen Literatur* (2 vols.; Halle, 1910).

99. *A Defence of Poetry, Shelley's Prose*, p. 290.

100. *The Letters of John Keats*, ed. Rollins, II, 103.

101. Carlyle, *Sartor Resartus*, ed. Charles Frederick Harrold (New York, 1937), pp. 194, 254; see also Introduction, p. xxiv.

102. T. E. Hulme, "Romanticism and Classicism," *Speculations*, ed. Herbert Read (London, 1936), p. 118.

103. *Home at Grasmere*, ll.700–1, 738–40. In *To William Wordsworth*, ll.1–11, Coleridge declared that in *The Prelude* "thou hast dared to tell/ What may be told, to the understanding mind . . . Theme hard as high!"

104. *Of Modern Poetry*, in *The Collected Poems of Wallace Stevens* (New York, 1961), pp. 239–40. In one of Stevens' prose renderings of this concept: "The major poetic idea in the world is and always has been the idea of God. One of the visible movements of the modern imagination is the movement away from the idea of God. The poetry that created the idea of God will either adapt it to our different intelligence, or create a substitute for it, or make it unnecessary. These alternatives probably mean the same thing." *Opus Posthumous*, ed. Samuel French Morse (New York, 1957), p. xv.

105. *Home at Grasmere*, ll.747–50. Brian Wilkie has discussed the relation of *The Prelude* to the epic in *Romantic Poets and Epic Tradition* (Madison, Wisconsin, 1965).

106. *Chocorua to Its Neighbor, Collected Poems*, p. 300.

T W O / *Wordsworth's "Prelude" and the Crisis-Autobiography*

1. To DeQuincey, 6 March 1804, *Letters: The Early Years*, p. 454; to Beaumont, 3 June 1805, *ibid.*, p. 594.

2. To Wordsworth, 30 May 1815, *Collected Letters*, IV, 573.

3. *Home at Grasmere*, ll.686–91, preceding the Prospectus.

4. "Essay, Supplementary to the Preface of 1815," *Literary Criticism of Wordsworth*, ed. Zall, p. 184. See also *The Prelude*, XII, 298–312. Upon first hearing the complete *Prelude*, Coleridge specified the bold novelty of the "high theme by thee first sung aright," which is the "foundations and building up/ Of a Human Spirit" (*To William Wordsworth*, ll.4–8).

5. To Beaumont, 25 Dec. 1804, *Letters: The Early Years*, p. 518; and the Isabella Fenwick note to *The Norman Boy, Poetical Works*, I, 365.

6. Isabella Fenwick note to *There Was a Boy*, and *The Prelude*, XIII, 408; my italics. K. P. Moritz's *Anton Reiser* was published in 1785, J. J. Heinse's *Ardinghello* in 1789, Goethe's *Wilhelm Meister's Lehrjahre* in 1795-6, and Hölderlin's *Hyperion* in 1797-9. On the later evolution of the novel about the development of the artist, see Maurice Beebe, *Ivory Towers and Sacred Founts* (New York, 1964).

7. The opening "preamble" to *The Prelude* has, on no valid evidence, been widely attributed to Wordsworth's walk from Bristol to Racedown in September, 1795. John Finch, however, presents convincing evidence that the chief prototype in Wordsworth's life was his walk to Grasmere in the fall of 1799; see his essay, "Wordsworth's Two-Handed Engine," *Bicentenary Wordsworth Studies, in Memory of John Alban Finch*, ed. Jonathan Wordsworth (Ithaca, N.Y.; 1970). It is probable, as de Selincourt and Darbishire suggest (*The Prelude*, p. 512), that Wordsworth deliberately telescoped aspects of his arrival at Racedown with his later walk to Grasmere Vale in order to make the induction to *The Prelude* the typological instance of a change of venue which signifies a new stage in his spiritual history. Mary Lynn Woolley deals with Wordsworth's fusion of separate places and incidents into a single typical valley, in "Wordsworth's Symbolic Vale as It Functions in *The Prelude*," *Studies in Romanticism*, VII (1968), 176–89. See also Mark L. Reed, *Wordsworth, The Chronology of the Early Years* (Cambridge, Mass., 1967), pp. 30, 170-1. That *The Prelude* concludes in time with Wordsworth's residence at Grasmere is indicated in XIII, 338–9.

8. E.g., *The Prelude*, VII, 1–56; XI, 1–12.

9. IV, 247–64. See also the early MS JJ, *The Prelude*, p. 641, on the "visible scene" of "recollected hours," "islands in the unnavigable depth/ Of our departed time."

10. In a passage in *The Friend* (Essay V, 10 Aug. 1809) Coleridge described the ability of men "to contemplate the past in the present" so as to produce that "continuity in their self-consciousness" without which "they exist in fragments." He cited Wordsworth's *My Heart Leaps Up* to illustrate the concept; *The Friend*, ed. Barbara E. Rooke (2 vols.; London, 1969), I, 40. Herbert Lindenberger, *On Wordsworth's "Prelude"* (Princeton, 1963), chap. V, has emphasized Wordsworth's "time-consciousness," and identified *The Prelude* as an ancestor of modern "time-books."

11. A detailed account of the evolution of *The Prelude*, both in its overall scheme and its constituent passages, is to be found in John Finch, *Wordsworth, Coleridge, and "The Recluse," 1789–1814*, doctoral thesis (Cornell University, 1964) chaps. IV, VI.

12. MS B, *Poetical Works*, V, 339; for the age of dereliction and dismay see *The Prelude*, II, 448–57.

13. *The Prelude*, XIII, 269–79: Though "much hath been omitted, as need was," the "discipline/ And consummation of the Poet's mind/ In everything that stood most prominent/ Have faithfully been pictured."

14. In the deviations from its true line of development at Cambridge, for example, "the mind/ Drooped not; but there into herself returning,/ With prompt rebound seemed fresh as heretofore" (1850 ed., III, 95–8).

15. *The Prelude*, XII, 44–76, 112–16. Cf. *Home at Grasmere*, ll.664–752.
16. On the date of Wordsworth's ascent of Snowdon see Raymond Dexter Havens, *The Mind of a Poet* (2 vols.; Baltimore, 1941), II, 607–8. Wordsworth deleted from *The Prelude* the apologetic acknowledgement in MS W that "I must premise that several years/ Are overleap'd to reach this incident" (*Prelude*, p. 478).
17. It is surprising that the *Prelude* should sometimes be said—even by admirers who express insightful things about its component parts—to be formless and aggregative in the whole and to end in a perfunctory conclusion in which nothing is concluded. Wordsworth was one of the great masters of complex poetic structure. *Tintern Abbey*, for example—in which the conclusion (anticipating his sister's future memories of the present time) turns back upon itself to assimilate the elements of the entire poem, until it closes by echoing the opening description—has a circular structure which is similar to that of *The Prelude* and, on its smaller scale, equally intricate. Moreover, as Wordsworth told Miss Fenwick, *Tintern Abbey* was composed in its entirety before a word was committed to paper. In contrast to the economy of the lyric, the capaciousness of an epic-length autobiography permits, and requires, excursions and details which mask its architectonics; but there is no reason to think that Wordsworth's shaping skill deserted him when, at the height of his powers, he worked and reworked this "ante-chapel" to the great "gothic church" that was to be his monument as a poet.
18. *A la recherche du temps perdu* (3 vols.; Bibliothèque de la Pléiade, Paris, 1954), III, 866.
19. *Ibid.*, I, 45; see III, 866–7.
20. *Ibid.*, III, 899.
21. *Ibid.*, III, 870, 880.
22. *Ibid.*, III, 904–6, 1044.
23. *Ibid.*, III, 1032–3, 1035, 1040.
24. *Ibid.*, III, 1044–46.
25. Edmund Wilson, *Axel's Castle* (New York, 1936), p. 163.
26. On the relation of the *Confessions* to classical traditions, see Georg Misch, *A History of Autobiography in Antiquity* (2 vols.; Cambridge, Mass., 1951), especially Part III, chap. iii.
27. Augustine, *Confessions*, X. iii–iv. The translation is that of F. J. Sheed (London, 1944).
28. *Ibid.*, X. viii. And XI. xviii: "Thus for example my boyhood, which no longer exists; but the likeness of my boyhood, when I recall it and talk of it, I look upon in time present, because it is still present in my memory." See also John Freccero's discussion of the role of the two selves in the narratives of Dante, whose old life has been transformed into a "new life" by the profound experience of conversion. In the *Vita Nuova* "the Dante who *is* tells the story of the Dante who *was*"; and the *Divine Comedy* "recapitulates the whole of the poet's life in retrospect"—a life in which Christianity and poetry are "not separable vocations." *Dante: A Collection of Critical Essays* (Prentice-Hall, 1965), "Introduction," pp. 4–5.
29. See the account in Pierre Courcelle, *Recherches sur les Confessions de Saint Augustin* (Paris, 1950), pp. 7–12, 257–8. See also Courcelle's *Les Confessions de Saint Augustin dans la tradition littéraire* (Paris, 1963).
30. *Confessions*, VIII. vi–xii. For the conventional elements in Augustine's conversion see Courcelle, *Recherches sur les Confessions*, pp. 181 ff.
31. Norman Malcolm, *Ludwig Wittgenstein, A Memoir* (London, 1958), p. 71: Wittgenstein "revered the writings of St. Augustine," and decided to begin his *Philosophical Investigations* with a quotation from the *Confessions* because "the conception *must* be important if so great a mind held it."
32. *Confessions*, XIII. xxxv, xxxvii. In a subtle rhetorical turn which rounds

the end back to the beginning, Augustine's plea in the opening paragraph of the induction, "Those that seek shall find. . . . Let me seek thee, Lord, by praying thy aid" (Quaerentes enim invenient eum. . . . Quaeram te, domine, invocans te), is echoed and completed in the last words of the closing paragraph: "Of You we must ask, in You we must seek, at You we must knock. Thus only shall we receive, thus shall we find, thus will it be opened to us." (A te petatur, in te quaeratur, ad te pulsetur: sic, sic accipietur, sic invenietur, sic aperietur.) On the concept of time in Augustine and other writers to the present day, see Georges Poulet, *Studies in Human Time* (Baltimore, 1956).

33. This concept was based on the Psalms—"The heavens declare the glory of God; and the firmament sheweth his handiwork"—and on a passage in St. Paul which was one of Augustine's favorite quotations (Romans 1:20): "For the invisible things of him from the creation of the world are clearly seen, being understood by the things that are made, even his eternal power and Godhead." For Augustine's echoes of this passage in the *Confessions* see, e.g., VII. x, xvii, xx, and (immediately following the colloquy with nature I quote in the text) X. vi.

34. On Wordsworth's religious beliefs, the most detailed treatment is Hoxie N. Fairchild's *Religious Trends in English Poetry*, vol. III (New York, 1949), chap. IV.

35. Wordsworth's major revisions in passages referring to the deity are discussed in *The Prelude*, ed. de Selincourt and Darbishire, pp. lxxi–iv, and in Helen Darbishire, *The Poet Wordsworth* (Oxford, 1950), pp. 133–43. Wordsworth similarly pietized the early versions of the Prospectus to *The Recluse* when he published it in 1814 in the Preface to *The Excursion;* e.g., he added lines 20–2: "subject there/ To Conscience only, and the law supreme/ Of that Intelligence which governs all."

36. Hazlitt, review of *The Excursion, Complete Works*, ed. P. P. Howe (21 vols.; London, 1930–4), IV, 113.

37. Henry Crabb Robinson, who was versed in contemporary German philosophy and also knew intimately Wordsworth and his poetry, recognized the common tendency toward a secular analogue to Christianity: "I believe [Wordsworth's] religion to be like [that] of the German metaphysicians, a sentimental and metaphysical mysticism in which the language of Christianity is used, which is a sort of analogy to this poetical and philosophical religion" (*On Books and Their Writers*, ed. Morley, 3 Jan. 1815; I, 158).

38. Hegel, *Lectures on the Philosophy of Religion*, trans. E. B. Speirs and J. B. Sanderson (3 vols.; New York, 1962), I, 20. As Frederick Copleston has remarked in his *History of Philosophy*, vol. VII (London, 1963), p. 241: In Hegel "absolute idealism is presented as esoteric Christianity and Christianity as exoteric Hegelianism."

39. On the nature and history of this lyric form, and on Coleridge's rationale for it in terms of a subject-object philosophy, see M. H. Abrams, "Structure and Style in the Greater Romantic Lyric," *From Sensibility to Romanticism*, ed. Frederick W. Hilles and Harold Bloom (New York, 1965).

40. MS JJ (1798–9), in *The Prelude*, pp. 638, 640. Brian Wilkie suggests that the agencies and powers which Wordsworth attributes to nature are equivalent to the "machinery" of the traditional epic: *Romantic Poets and Epic Tradition*, pp. 80 ff. It is at any rate misleading to read Wordsworth's references, alternately, to the "Soul" and "Souls," the "Spirit" and "Spirits" of Nature, as propositional statements of his religion of nature—as though the poet could not make up his mind whether he was a natural monotheist or a natural polytheist. Such passages are grounded, indeed, in what Coleridge called "a fact of mind"—the poet's deeply-felt sense of communion with a living, reciprocative universe. Their function, however, is

not to affirm a creed, but to serve as a literary means, of very ancient origin, which helps Wordsworth to conduct his poem, on one of its levels, as a continuing discourse between his mind and the "speaking face of heaven and earth."

41. *The Prelude*, IV, 200–44. So in *Tintern Abbey*, ll.88 ff., the growth of the poet's mind since his earlier visit to the same scene manifests itself as a musical chord, "the still, sad music of humanity," which now sounds its accompaniment as he looks "on nature"; and in the *Intimations Ode* the mind's accumulated experience of suffering and mortality translates itself into a change in the radiance and color which invests the natural world.

42. *The Prelude*, III, 171–7. So also in IV, 156–8: "the immortal Soul with God-like power/ Informs, creates, and thaws the deepest sleep/ That time can lay upon her." And see II, 379–8.

43. *The Prelude*, XII, 3–4; and p. 571.

44. See *ibid.*, I, 362–71, 439–41, 490–501, 630–40; II, 320–6, 341–8, 389–93; III, 131–6; XII, 1–14; and the MS passages, pp. 572, 577–8.

45. *Ibid.*, I, 573, and the 1850 version, I, 546. Also I, 635–6, "scenes . . . beauteous and majestic"; p. 578, "familiar things and awful, the minute/ And grand"; and VI, 672–6: "whate'er/ I saw, or heard, or felt . . . did administer/ To grandeur and to tenderness."

46. Samuel H. Monk, *The Sublime: A Study of Critical Theories in XVIII–Century England* (New York, 1935), pp. 227–32. See also Herbert Lindenberger, *On Wordsworth's Prelude* (Princeton, 1963), pp. 23–39.

47. Marjorie Hope Nicolson, *Mountain Gloom and Mountain Glory* (Ithaca, N. Y. 1959), p. 83; and see chap. II.

48. Coleridge's annotation in Pepys' Diary, in *Coleridge on the Seventeenth Century*, ed. Roberta Florence Brinkley (Durham, N. C., 1955), p. 492. He classed Burnet's *Theoria Sacra* with the writings of Plato and Bishop Taylor as "undeniable proofs that poetry of the highest kind may exist without metre" *(Biographia Literaria*, II, 11). For Coleridge's high admiration for Burnet in the 1790's, see J. L. Lowes, *The Road to Xanadu* (Boston and New York, 1927), p. 16, and Index, "Burnet."

49. *The Sacred Theory of the Earth* (6th edition; 2 vols., London, 1726), I, 142–4.

50. *Ibid.*, I, 240; see also I, 349. A variant in a MS of the Prospectus is even closer to Burnet: "Paradise, and groves/ Elysian, fortunate islands like those/ In the deep ocean. . . ."

51. Edmund Burke, *A Philosophical Enquiry into the Origin of Our Ideas of the Sublime and Beautiful*, ed. J. T. Boulton (London, 1958), Part I, Sections 6–18.

52. *Ibid.*, II, 1–13.

53. As early as the *Descriptive Sketches* of 1793 Wordsworth included a long note on the attributes of the sublime: *Poetical Works*, I, 62. See also his careful discrimination between beautiful and sublime scenes in his *Guide to the Lakes*, ed. Ernest de Selincourt (London, 1906), e.g., pp. 21–6, 36, 69, 99, 102.

54. *Poetical Works*, V, 373 [my italics].

55. *The Ruined Cottage*, MS B, *Poetical Works*, V, 384–8 (ll.220–81).

56. *Ibid.*, pp. 386–7. Like the Pedlar, Wordsworth in *The Prelude* underwent the natural discipline of terror "ere I had seen/ Nine summers" (I, 310–11).

57. *Ibid.*, p. 384; the last five lines of this passage are written on the verso of the MS page.

58. See, e.g., *The Prelude*, p. 53 (variant in MS B), and the editorial note, p. 522; also, p. 77 (variant in MS A)—an apparent recollection of Burnet's view that the ruined world in which fallen mankind lives retains traces of the beauty of its prime.

59. *The Sacred Theory of the Earth*, I, 190–2. Burnet asks the reader to imagine the prospect he had seen from an Alpine mountain, "a Multitude of vast Bodies thrown together in Confusion . . . Rocks standing naked round about him; and the hollow valleys gaping under him," listening to "the Thunder come from below." On Wordsworth's route through the Simplon Pass and the ravine of Gondo, and his treatment of his experience in *Descriptive Sketches* as well as *The Prelude*, see Max Wildi, "Wordsworth and the Simplon Pass," *English Studies*, XL (1959), 224–32, and XLIII (1962), 359–77.

60. Thomas Gray, *Works*, ed. Edmund Gosse (4 vols.; New York, 1885), II, 45. For an account of eighteenth-century Alpine travelogues see Marjorie Nicolson, *Mountain Gloom and Mountain Glory*, pp. 276–9, 289–90, 304–7, 354–8. While actually on the tour he later reworked in accordance with his idea of *The Prelude*, Wordsworth in a letter to his sister had alluded to his Simplon crossing in the standard theological-aesthetic language of the natural sublime: Among the more awful scenes of the Alps . . . my whole soul was turned to him who produced the terrible majesty before me" (*Letters: The Early Years*, p. 34).

61. See Revelation 1:8, 11, 17–18; 21:6; 22:13. Wordsworth may be recalling also the morning hymn of Adam and Eve, who praise in the qualities of the creation the "goodnesss beyond thought, and Power Divine" of "him first, him last, him midst, and without end" (*Paradise Lost*, V, 153–65).

62. Cf. *Paradise Lost*, IX, 1–12, with *The Prelude*, IX, 1–17, as well as the MS variant, pp. 314–15. De Selincourt and Darbishire remarked this significant parallel in *The Prelude*, p. 584.

63. *The Prelude*, X, 873–902; and in the edition of 1850, XI, 306–7.

64. See Martin Price, "The Picturesque Moment," in *From Sensibility to Romanticism*, ed. F. W. Hilles and Harold Bloom (New York, 1965), pp. 288–9.

65. The implicit parallel to Milton's invocation to Book III of *Paradise Lost* continues through Milton's plangent lament for his blindness, which no longer permits him to read in God's book of nature the symbolic significance of the return of day and of the revolving seasons. In Wordsworth's account, "The morning shines,/ Nor heedeth Man's perverseness; Spring returns,/ I *saw* the Spring return, when I was dead/ To deeper hope"; so that, unlike Milton, being able to see, he found in nature's symbolism "a counterpoise . . . / Which, when the spirit of evil was at height/ Maintain'd for me a secret happiness." Cf. *Paradise Lost*, III, 40–50 and *The Prelude*, XI, 22–34; also *Paradise Lost*, III, 26–38 and *The Prelude*, XI, 12–22.

66. *The Prelude*, X, 922–7, and MS version, p. 420.

67. *Inferno*, III, 5–6. T. S. Eliot's formulation, in the theodicy which concludes his *Four Quartets*, is even more succinct: "Who then devised the torment? Love" (*Little Gidding*, IV).

68. John Jones, *The Egotistical Sublime* (London, 1954), pp. 126–9.

69. A striking theological parallel to Wordsworth's secular form of experience is described in Jonathan Edwards' spiritual history, the *Narrative of His Conversion*. From childhood, he says, "the doctrine of God's sovereignty" in preelecting whom he pleased "eternally to perish, and be everlastingly tormented in hell," had appeared "like a horrible doctrine to me." But then he happened to read the text of I Tim. 1:17, and it brought him to "not only a conviction, but a *delightful* conviction" of the absolute sovereignty of God; and this inner conversion effected a correlative transformation of the external world: "The appearance of everything was altered; there seemed to be, as it were, a calm, sweet cast, or appearance of divine glory, in almost everything," and in "all nature."

Edwards' experience of a glory in the landscape then led him, three-quarters of a century before Wordsworth, to solitary communings with the speaking face of nature. Jonathan Edwards, *Representative Selections*, ed. C. H. Faust and T. Johnson (New York, 1935), pp. 58–60.

70. Francis Christensen, "Intellectual Love: The Second Theme of *The Prelude*," PMLA, LXXX (1965), p. 70.

71. *The Prelude*, XIII, 370–85. Wordsworth, who tells us that he had memorized hundreds of lines of Pope's verse, may here be recalling the key statement in the theodicy of *The Essay on Man:*

> All Discord, Harmony not understood;
> All partial Evil, universal Good.
>
> (I, 291–2)

72. Elizabeth Sewell, *The Orphic Voice* (New Haven, 1960), p. 342.

73. XIII, 166–80. Also XIII, 289–90: "having track'd the main essential Power,/ Imagination, up her way sublime."

74. *Henry Crabb Robinson on Books and Their Writers*, ed. Edith Morley; I conjoin the details of Robinson's two reports of this same conversation, in I, 87 and I, 158. The Reverend Christopher Wordsworth, although circumspectly, makes the same point about his uncle's not feeling the need for a Redeemer at the time of the crisis described in *The Prelude:* "He had a good deal of Stoical pride, mingled with not a little of Pelagian self-confidence. Having an inadequate perception of the necessity of divine good, he placed his hopes where they could not stand" (*Memoirs of William Wordsworth* [London, 1851], I, 89).

75. "The New Law of Righteousness," *The Works of Gerrard Winstanley*, pp. 162, 214–15.

76. Blake, *Jerusalem*, 5. 58–9; see also 24. 23, 60. 57, 74. 13; and *Milton*, 3.4–5.

77. Novalis, *Briefe und Werke* (Berlin, 1943), III, 265–6.

78. Goethe, *Dichtung und Wahrheit*, III, xii, in *Goethes Werke* (Weimar ed.), Part I, Vol. XXVIII (1890), p. 120.

79. As quoted in Bertrand Russell, *History of Western Philosophy* (2nd ed.; London, 1961), p. 719; and *Morgenröte*, No. 79, in Nietzsche's *Werke*, ed. Karl Schlechta (3 vols.; Munich, 1954), I, 1066.

80. *Of Modern Poetry*, in *The Collected Poems of Wallace Stevens* (New York, 1961), p. 239; *Opus Posthumous* (New York, 1957), p. 158; *Final Soliloquy of the Interior Paramour, Collected Poems*, p. 524.

81. Introduction, *The Oxford Book of Modern Verse*, ed. W. B. Yeats (Oxford, 1936), p. xxxiii.

82. Yeats, *Prayer for My Daughter*, and *A Dialogue of Self and Soul, Collected Poems* (New York, 1945), pp. 218, 272–3.

83. *The Life of Frederick Denison Maurice*, ed. Frederick Maurice (2 vols.; New York, 1884), II, 59. The passage has been quoted by John Lindenberger, *On Wordsworth's "Prelude,"* p. 276.

84. To J. H. Reynolds, 3 May 1818, *The Letters of John Keats*, ed. Hyder E. Rollins (2 vols.; Cambridge, Mass., 1958), I, 278–82.

85. To George and Georgiana Keats, 21 April 1819, *ibid.*, II, 101–3.

86. To Reynolds, *ibid.*, I, 281.

87. As early as *Sleep and Poetry* (1816) Keats had announced his sense of vocation and mapped out his program for poetry, which was to start in the realm of "Flora, and old Pan" and within ten years was to achieve the "nobler life" of tragic poetry, "Where I may find the agonies, the strife/ Of human hearts." Like *The Prelude* and various other portraits of the developing artist, *Sleep and Poetry* is a poem which ends with the circumstance of its own beginning:

> And up I rose refresh'd, and glad, and gay,
> Resolving to begin that very day
> These lines. . . .

Sleep and Poetry has as epigraph a quotation from *The Flowre and the Leafe* (which Keats believed to be Chaucer's), and its circular form may well reflect that of this poem, which ends with the author's decision to "put al that I had seen in wryting." Also at the close of Chaucer's own *Book of the Duchess*, the dreamer awakens and decides to put his dream in rhyme " 'As I kan best, and that anoon.'/ This was my sweven; now hit ys doon." Apropos of *The Fall of Hyperion*, it should be noted that the greatest of confessional dream-visions was granted its poet as induction to the poem that embodies it; for within Dante's vision, Cacciaguida charges Dante to publicize his vision in a poem: "tutta tua vision fa manifesta." *Paradiso*, XVII, 128.

88. For the prevalence of the Christian confession in the seventeenth century and later, see L. D. Lerner, "Puritanism and the Spiritual Autobiography," *The Hibbert Journal* (LV, 1956–7), 373–86; G. A. Starr, *Defoe and Spiritual Autobiography* (Princeton, 1965); and John N. Morris, *Versions of the Self* (New York, 1966). In his brief introduction Morris insightfully aligns *The Prelude*, as well as *Sartor Resartus*, with the religious confessions from Bunyan's *Grace Abounding* to Cowper's *Memoir*. Both nineteenth-century works, however, are much closer in content and construction to Augustine's philosophically sophisticated and deliberately artful *Confessions* than to the vigorous, but purposely simple autobiographies of the Puritan and evangelical writers.

89. Thomas Carlyle, *Sartor Resartus*, ed. Charles Frederick Harrold (New York, 1937), p. 194.

90. Harry Levin, *James Joyce* (Norfolk, Conn., 1941), p. 42. G. B. Tennyson's *"Sartor" Called "Resartus"* (Princeton, 1965) is an extended analysis of the structure of Carlyle's book. William Blake preceded Carlyle as an author of the self-reflexive semi-parody. In *The Marriage of Heaven and Hell*, for example (an inverted form of Swedenborg's prophetic visions), he describes his vision of his own "diabolic" self, reflected in the copper plate on which he is etching, with corrosive acid, the very passage which represents this vision:

> On the abyss of the five senses, where a flat sided steep frowns over the present world, I saw a mighty Devil folded in black clouds, hovering on the sides of the rock; with corroding fires he wrote the following sentence now perceived by the minds of men, & read by them on earth. . . .
>
> (Plates 6–7; see also Plates 14–15)

91. As with Augustine's *Confessions* and Wordsworth's *Prelude*, the discrepancy between the narrated conversion of Teufelsdröckh and Carlyle's accounts of his own spiritual crisis has led to debate about the autobiographical authenticity of *Sartor*; see, e.g., Carlisle Moore, "*Sartor Resartus* and the Problem of Carlyle's 'Conversion,'" PMLA, LXX (1955). Carlyle was fully aware that the central experience of the crisis-autobiography is culture bound—that "conversion" is a "spiritual attainment peculiar to the modern [i.e. the Christian] Era" (p. 198)—and that he was adapting Christian conventions to his own secular "mythus."

92. *Sartor Resartus*, pp. 53, 188, 217, 258.

93. MS fragment, *The Prelude*, p. 566; cf. VI, 543–8, and the lyric, *Expostulation and Reply*. The extreme statement of Wordsworth's quietism is

the long narrative poem *The White Doe of Rylstone* (1807–8). The quotations from *Sartor Resartus* are on pp. 183, 197.

94. Prospectus, 1.16, and variant of ll.87 ff. Wordsworth wrote to Sir George Beaumont in 1808: "Every great Poet is a Teacher; I wish either to be considered as a Teacher, or as nothing" (*The Letters of William and Dorothy Wordsworth: The Middle Years*, I, 170).

95. Leslie Stephen, "Wordsworth's Ethics," *Hours in a Library*, 3rd Series (London, 1879), pp. 218–19; John Morley, ed., *The Complete Poetical Works of William Wordsworth* (London, 1895), Introduction, pp. lxvi–ii.

96. *The Prelude*, III, 196–201.

97. Newton P. Stallknecht, *Strange Seas of Thought* (2nd ed.; Bloomington, 1962), p. xi.

98. *Autobiography of John Stuart Mill*, ed. John Jacob Coss (New York, 1924), pp. 93–105.

99. Richard Henry Dana, Preface to *The Idle Man*, in *Poems and Prose Writings* (2 vols.: New York, 1850), I, 150–1.

100. William Hale White, *The Autobiography of Mark Rutherford* (London, 1923), pp. 18–19. The German writer Karl Gutzkow has left testimony of a similar effect upon him of Hegel's lectures, in which Hegel deliberately translated the Christian story into metaphysical dialectic. The lectures were "lame, dragging . . . interrupted by eternal repetitions and irrelevant filler words. . . . But to be truthful, I confess that in Hegel's lectures the Damascus miracle (in reverse, I might say: the conversion from a theological Paul to a philosophizing Saul), which I had experienced in the park in the winter, was repeated for me hourly." *Lebensbilder* (1870), as quoted by Walter Kaufmann, *Hegel* (New York, 1965), p. 360.

101. *Autobiography of J. S. Mill*, p. 103.

102. Ralph Barton Perry, *The Thought and Character of William James* (2 vols.; Boston, 1935), I, 337. For an analysis of James's crisis as a struggle to discover his identity and vocation, see Cushing Strout, "William James and the Twice-Born Sick Soul," *Daedalus* (1968), pp. 1062–79.

103. *Ibid.*, I, 320, 322, 339; on Wordsworth's *Excursion*, see also p. 355.

104. Bede Griffiths, *The Golden String* (New York, 1954), pp. 9–10, 31.

105. *Ibid.*, pp. 30, 52, 15–16.

THREE / *The Circuitous Journey: Pilgrims and Prodigals*

1. Cited by Thomas DeQuincey, "On Wordsworth's Poetry," *The Collected Writings*, ed. David Masson (14 vols.; Edinburgh, 1889–90), XI, 300.

2. 30 May 1815; *Collected Letters of S. T. Coleridge*, IV, 574–5. In *Table Talk* for July 21, 1832, Coleridge said that the plan of *The Recluse*, as he had discussed it with Wordsworth, was to have demonstrated "the whole state of man and society being subject to, and illustrative of, a redemptive process in operation, showing how this idea reconciled all anomalies, and promised future glory and restoration." He added: "It is in substance, what I have been all my life doing in my system of philosophy." We remember that Wordsworth concluded *The Prelude* with the call to Coleridge to join him as joint-laborer "in a work . . . / Of [man's] redemption, surely yet to come" (XIII, 439–41).

3. Coleridge uses "sensual" to signify one whose knowledge and values are limited to the testimony of the senses; e.g., in *France: An Ode:* "The Sensual and the Dark rebel in vain."

4. *The Friend*, ed. Barbara E. Rooke, I, 520.

5. E.g., *Man Alone: Alienation in Modern Society*, ed. Eric and Mary Josephson (New York, 1962); *Alienation: The Cultural Climate of Our Time*, ed. Gerald Sykes (2 vols.; New York, 1964).

6. Plotinus, *The Six Enneads*, trans. Stephen MacKenna and B. S. Page (Chicago, 1952), II. ix. 1.

7. The second Ennead, Book IX, is addressed "against the Gnostics," or "those who say that the Demiurge is bad and the world is evil." On Gnostic views, and especially on the Gnostic concept of the "alien life" and the "alien man," totally and ineradicably estranged from the essentially evil world in which he finds himself, see Hans Jonas, *The Gnostic Religion* (Boston, 1958).

8. Proclus, *The Elements of Theology*, ed. and trans. E. R. Dodds (Oxford, 1933), Props. 33 and 146. For the continuous and unending circulation of each soul out into the temporal order and back to being, see Props. 199 and 206.

9. *Ibid.*, Prop. 13. ". . . the Good unqualified and the One unqualified merge in a single principle, a principle which makes things one and in doing so makes them good. Hence it is that things which in some fashion have fallen away from their good are at the same stroke deprived of participation of unity; and in like manner things which have lost their portion in unity, being infected with division, are deprived of their good." In a variant form of the cosmic geometry of the circle, the One which is the beginning and the end is conceived, not as the point on the circumference of the circle from which everything issues and circles back, but as the point at the center of the circle which pulsates out to the circumference, then contracts again into a point. See John Freccero, "Donne's 'Valediction: Forbidding Mourning,'" *ELH*, XXX (1963), 335–41. Georges Poulet, in *Les Metamorphoses du cercle* (Paris, 1961), provides a detailed history of the varying theological and metaphysical applications of a very different kind of circle—that peculiar circle of which the center is everywhere and the circumference nowhere. See also Hans Leisegang's analysis of circular thought-forms in his book *Denkformen* (2d ed.; Berlin, 1951).

10. Dionysius the Areopagite, *On the Divine Names*, trans. C. E. Rolt (New York, 1920), pp. 92, 107 (IV. iv and IV. xiv). This concept of the great circle of being is to be distinguished from the cyclical concept of history. The theory of cycles is a temporal theory, in the sense that in the world's unending process of change from better to worse to better again, the same stage of human well-being and the same kinds of events will recur when the passage of time brings the world back to a particular position on the chronological cycle. The great circle, however, is atemporal; all stages in the eternal rotation of emanation and return to the undifferentiated One, and therefore all degrees of approximation to reality, goodness, and felicity, are simultaneously present in the universe of existing things.

11. Leone Ebreo, *The Philosophy of Love*, trans. F. Friedeberg-Seeley and Jean H. Barnes (London, 1937), p. 351.

12. E.g., Boethius, *The Consolation of Philosophy*, IV.vi; trans. H. F. Stewart and E. K. Rand (Loeb Classical Library; London, 1962), p. 356:

> This powerful love
> Is common unto all,
> Which for desire of good do move
> Back to the springs from whence they first did fall.
> No worldly thing

Can a continuance have,
Unless love back again it bring
Unto the cause which first the essence gave.

In the version of Marsilio Ficino, *De amore*, II. 2: "There is one continuous attraction, beginning with God, going to the world and ending at last in God; an attraction which returns to the same place from which it began as though in a kind of circle."

13. *De Principiis*, I.vi.1–4, in *The Writings of Origen*, trans. Frederick Crombie (Edinburgh, 1869), pp. 53–9. See also II.i.1–3, and III.vi. 4–6, pp. 72–4 and 266–70. David Hume, writing in the assumed character of a "Platonist," deftly summarized the circular human course: "The Divinity is a boundless ocean of bliss and glory: human minds are smaller streams, which, arising at first from this ocean, seek still, amid all their wanderings, to return to it, and to lose themselves in that immensity of perfection." "The Platonist," in *"Of the Standard of Taste" and Other Essays*, ed. John W. Lenz (Indianapolis, 1965), p. 115.

14. John Scotus Erigena, *De divisione naturae*, II. 2; in *Patrologia Latina*, ed. Migne, CXXII, 528 B.

15. E.g., *ibid.*, V. 20; 893 B–C: "In quo, videlicet homine, omnis creatura visibilis et invisibilis condita est. Ideoque *officina omnium* dicitur, quoniam in eo omnia, quae post Deum sunt, continentur. . . . Proinde ex adunatione divisionis hominis in duplicem sexum praedictarum divisionum incipit ascensus et adunatio. In resurrectione enim sexus aufferetur, et natura adunabitur. . . ."

16. See, e.g., G. Quispel, "Der gnostische Anthropos und die jüdische Tradition," *Eranos-Jahrbuch*, XXII (1953).

17. Ernst Benz, *Adam: Der Mythus vom Urmenschen* (Munich, 1955), is a convenient anthology of passages on the splintering and reintegration of the primal androgyne, from Leone Ebreo to Nikolaj Berdjajev. André Gide's *Le Traité du Narcisse* (1891) represents this ancient plot. For recent claims for the valid rationale underlying the myth of the androgyne, see Suzanne Lilar, *Le Couple* (Paris, 1963), trans. Jonathan Griffin as *Aspects of Love in Western Society* (London, 1965), and Norman O. Brown, *Love's Body* (New York, 1966).

18. The classic commentary on Kabbalism is Gershom G. Scholem, *Major Trends in Jewish Mysticism* (New York, 1961). For Neoplatonic and Gnostic elements in Kabbalism, see also Professor Scholem's *Ursprung und Anfänge der Kabbala* (Berlin, 1962).

19. The primal man had also been bisexual: "Observe that at the creation of Adam the Holy One, blessed be He, made him male and female together, female behind and male before. Then He sawed them asunder and tricked out the woman and brought her to Adam." *The Zohar*, trans. Harry Sperling, Maurice Simon, and others (5 vols.; London and Bournemouth, 1949), IV, 288.

20. Scholem, *Major Trends in Jewish Mysticism*, p. 236.

21. See *ibid.*, pp. 232–5.

22. *The Zohar*, III. 260b and III. 77b; as trans. by Sperling, Simon, and others, Vol. V, 343–4 and 83–4. The literal translations I have inserted in brackets were supplied by my colleague Isaac Rabinowitz.

23. See, e.g., F. Sherwood Taylor, *The Alchemists* (New York, 1962); Alexandre Koyré *Mystiques, spirituels, alchimistes* (Paris, 1955); Titus Burckhardt, *Alchemie, Sinn und Weltbild* (Olten and Freiburg, 1960). C. G. Jung's *Psychology and Alchemy* (Bollingen Series; London, 1953), though organized around a special thesis, is a useful repository of quotations and pictorial illustrations from a great variety of Hermetic texts.

24. *Hermetica*, trans. and ed. Walter Scott (4 vols.; Oxford, 1924–36), I, 117–29; see also *Asclepius, ibid.*, pp. 327 ff.
25. For the cosmology of Paracelsus see Koyré, *Mystiques*, pp. 61–77; Walter Pagel, *Paracelsus, An Introduction to Philosophical Medicine in the Era of the Renaissance* (Basel and New York, 1958), pp. 50–125.
26. Paracelsus, *Secretum magicum*, in *Opera, Bücher, und Schriften*, ed. John Huser (2 vols.; Strasbourg, 1603), II, 677.
27. Quoted by Koyré, *Mystiques*, pp. 76–7.
28. F. S. Taylor, *The Alchemists*, p. 116.
29. See *ibid.*, pp. 119–20; and Burckhardt, *Alchemie*, pp. 166 ff.
30. A number of such illustrations of the marital *coniunctio* are reproduced in C. G. Jung, *Psychology and Alchemy*. On the prevalence and centrality of the concept see also C. G. Jung, *Mysterium Coniunctionis*, trans. R. G. C. Hull (Bollingen Series; New York, 1963).
31. For the dissemination of Kabbalist doctrine in Christian Europe, see François Secret, *Le Zohar chez les Kabbalistes Chrétiens de la Renaissance* (Paris, 1958); and for the prevalence of Hermetic thought in the Renaissance see Frances A. Yates, *Giordano Bruno and the Hermetic Tradition* (Chicago, 1964); on page ix the author reviews recent scholarship in this area.
32. On Bruno see Frances Yates, *Bruno and the Hermetic Tradition*. On Boehme see Alexandre Koyré's lucid and detailed commentary, *La philosophie de Jacob Boehme* (Paris, 1929). Herbert Deinert's article, "Die Entfaltung des Bösen in Böhme's *Mysterium Magnum*," *PMLA*, LXXIX (1964), 401–10, is an excellent commentary on Boehme's last major book, written in 1623.
33. A number of Boehme's passages on the androgyne are collected in Benz, *Adam, Der Mythus vom Urmenschen*, pp. 51–77.
34. E.g., Boehme, *Mysterium Pansophicum* (1620), in *Jacob Boehmes sämtliche Werke*, ed. K. W. Schiebler (7 vols.; Leipzig, 1832–64), VI, 413: "Der Ungrund ist ein ewig Nichts, und machet aber einen ewigen Anfang, als eine *Sucht;* denn das Nichts ist eine Sucht nach Etwas: und da doch auch Nichts ist, das Etwas gebe. . . . So denn also eine Sucht im Nichts ist, so machet sie in ihr selber den Willen zu Etwas, und derselbe Wille ist ein Geist, als ein Gedanke, der gehet aus der Sucht, und ist der Sucht Sucher." See also the summary of the creation in *Mysterium Magnum* (1623), *ibid.*, V, 701–4.
35. *Mysterium Magnum*, VIII. 24, in *Sämtliche Werke*, V, 38.
36. E.g., *Theosophische Fragen* (1624), III, 2–3; *ibid.*, VI, 597–8: "The reader should know that all things consist in Yes and No, whether these things are divine, devilish, earthly, or whatever else might be mentioned . . . . The No is an opponent of the Yes, or of truth, in order that the truth may become apparent. . . . Except for these two things, which nonetheless remain in constant conflict, all things would be a nothing, and would stand still and motionless." In short, without contraries there is no progression.
37. *Psychologia Vera* (1620), 74–8; *ibid.*, VI, 18–19.
38. *Mysterium Pansophicum*, VI, 4; *ibid.*, VI, 418. And *Mysterium Magnum*, V, 703: "No thing can rest in itself, unless it returns into the one out of which it has come."
39. *Psychologia Vera*, 83; *ibid.*, VI, 20.
40. *The Works of Gerrard Winstanley*, ed. Sabine, pp. 155–7. On the currency of Boehme's works in English translations, beginning in 1645, see R. M. Jones, *Spiritual Reformers in the Sixteenth and Seventeenth Centuries* (London, 1914).
41. *The City of God*, IX. xvii; trans. Marcus Dodds (New York, 1950), p. 296.

The editor remarks that Augustine, apparently quoting from memory, conflates "two passages of the *Enneades*, I. vi. 8, and ii. 3."

42. In this passage Paul probably echoes Leviticus 25:23 and Psalm 39:12.
43. For the figure of the *peregrinatio* in the ecclesiastical tradition see Morton W. Bloomfield, *Piers Plowman as a Fourteenth-Century Apocalypse* (New Brunswick, N.J., 1962), p. 194, n. 43; and G. V. Smithers, "The Meaning of *The Seafarer* and *The Wanderer*," *Medium Aevum*, XXVI–VII (1957–8), 145–51. Evelyn Underhill deals with the application of this image to the mystical journey of the soul in *Mysticism* (12th ed.; New York, 1955), pp. 129 ff.; Samuel Chew describes the currency of the allegorical pilgrimage in the literature and other arts of the Renaissance, in *The Pilgrimage of Life* (New Haven and London, 1962); and G. R. Owst cites examples of the detailed use of the figure in medieval sermons, in *Literature and Pulpit in Medieval England* (2d ed.; New York, 1961), pp. 102–8.
44. See the references in Richard Chevenix Trench, *Notes on the Parables of Our Lord* (New York, 1867), pp. 322–35.
45. Erigena, *De divisione naturae*, V. xxxviii.
46. *A Companion to the Study of St. Augustine*, ed. Roy Battenhouse (New York, 1955), p. 15.
47. Spenser, Prefatory Letter to Sir Walter Raleigh.
48. See chapter II, above, note 88. In *Aurora*, chap. XIX, Boehme represents his own spiritual quest, crisis, and conversion, in the vehicle of a journey culminating in a lover's meeting: after a deep depression and agonized struggle, his spirit descended "through the gates of hell to the most secret birth of the divinity, and there was embraced with love, as a fiancé embraces his beloved"—an ecstatic experience which he says is "like the birth of life in the midst of death." *Sämtliche Werke*, II, 212–13.
49. *The Pilgrim's Progress* (London, 1902), pp. 151–2.
50. Paul F. Reiff, *Die Aesthetik der deutschen Frühromantik*, Illinois Studies in Language and Literature, XXXI (1946), 61.
51. Schelling, *Philosophie der Offenbarung, Sämtliche Werke*, Pt. II, Vol. III, p. 123.
52. Coleridge, *Biographia Literaria*, ed. J. Shawcross (2 vols.; Oxford, 1907), I, 95, 97.
53. *Ibid.*, I, 98. On the continued currency, in Priestley, Erasmus Darwin, and other scientists in the latter eighteenth century, of the anti-mechanist view that all matter is vital and imbued with immanent forces, see H. W. Piper, *The Active Universe: Pantheism and the Concept of Imagination in the English Romantic Poets* (London, 1962), chaps. I and II.
54. E.g., L. Pearce Williams, in *Michael Faraday* (New York, 1954), has shown that Faraday and other pioneers of electromagnetic theory profited from *Naturphilosophie* in developing the concepts of polarity, lines of force, and fields of force, which they opposed to the mechanistic views inherited from eighteenth-century Newtonianism, and which constituted the historical starting point of modern field-theory.
55. Schelling, *The Ages of the World* (1811), trans. Frederick de Wolfe Bolman, Jr. (New York, 1942), pp. 230, 210. "True philosophy," Friedrich Schlegel said, "can nowhere affirm a constant substance, something which is motionless and unchanging; it finds the highest reality only in an eternal becoming, an eternally living and moving activity which begets out of itself, under constantly altering forms and shapes, an infinite fullness and manifoldness." *Philosophische Vorlesungen aus den Jahren 1804 bis 1806*, ed. C. J. H. Windischmann (Bonn, 1846), I, 112.
56. *Biographia Literaria*, I, 101.
57. Schelling, *System des transcendentalen Idealismus* (1800), *Sämtliche Werke* (14 vols.; Stuttgart, 1856–61), Pt. I, Vol. III, p. 340.
58. *Ibid.*, pp. 615–29.

59. Hegel, Preface to *The Phenomenology of Spirit*, trans. Walter Kaufmann, in *Hegel: Reinterpretation, Texts, and Commentary* (New York, 1965), pp. 410, 442. And *The Science of Logic*, trans. W. H. Johnston and L. G. Struthers (2 vols.; London, 1929), II, 468: "Method is no more than the movement of the notion [*Begriff*, "concept"] itself. . . . Its movement is . . . the self-determining and self-realizing movement."

60. *Grundlinien der Philosophie des Rechts*, ed. Georg Lasson (3d ed.; Leipzig, 1930), p. 44; and *The Logic of Hegel*, trans. William Wallace (2d ed.; Oxford, 1892), pp. 148–50.

61. Preface to *The Phenomenology*, Sect. 13; trans. Kaufmann, p. 424. Cf. Coleridge's description of the motion-in-stillness of the self-generated development of a living plant: "Lo!—how upholding the ceaseless plastic motion of the parts in the profoundest rest of the whole it becomes the visible *organismus* of the entire silent or elementary life of nature," yet serves at the same time as the correlative and symbol of the opposite extreme on the scale of being, "the natural symbol of that higher life of reason, in which the whole series . . . is perfected." *The Statesman's Manual*, Appendix B, in *Lay Sermons*, ed. Derwent Coleridge (3d ed.; London, 1852), pp. 77–8.

62. Hegel, *Einleitung: System und Geschichte der Philosophie*, ed. Johannes Hoffmeister (Leipzig, 1940), pp. 31–2.

63. Schelling, *The Ages of the World*, p. 212. See also pp. 213–17 for Schelling's explicit translation into philosophical concepts of both the physical and psychological details of sexual attraction, union, and generation. For Novalis, H. J. Mähl has said, "the polarity of the sexes appeared the prototype of all polarity": the union of opposites has its phenomenal model in the "embrace" of male and female, and the synthesis of opposites has its model in the child which is conceived in that embrace. See *Die Idee des goldenen Zeitalters im Werk des Novalis*, pp. 365–6.

64. Coleridge to C. A. Tulk, 12 Jan. 1818, *Collected Letters*, ed. Earl Leslie Griggs (Oxford), IV (1959), 806.

65. Hegel, "Love" (1797 or 1798), in *On Christianity: Early Theological Writings*, trans. and ed. T. M. Knox and Richard Kroner (New York, 1961), pp. 307–8. And see *Phänomenologie des Geistes*, pp. 535–6. For the bisexual prototype underlying the dialectic of creative antitheses in Nietzsche, see chap. V, sect. 6.

66. *The Logic of Hegel*, trans. Wallace, Sect. 24, p. 46; and *Phänomenologie des Geistes*, pp. 561–3.

67. Novalis, *Briefe und Werke*, III, 702.

68. As Hegel put it, when "the merely external, or abstract spirit becomes an other to itself, or enters into existence . . . it *creates* a world. This 'creation' is the word of pictorial representation [*Vorstellung*]" for the process by which pure thought becomes "opposed to itself, or the other." He goes on similarly to analyze the crucial Biblical events of the fall of man, the Incarnation, the Passion and Resurrection, and the universal redemption as representations, in the limited mode of a figurative language "taken from nature," of "moments" in the sustained transactions of the spirit with itself. *Phänomenologie des Geistes*, pp. 536–44.

69. Frederick Copleston, S.J., *A History of Philosophy* (London), VII (1963), 12.

70. *The Logic of Hegel*, trans. Wallace, Sect. 24, p. 54. Also *The Science of Logic*, trans. Johnston and Struthers, II, 466: "Philosophy has the same content and end as art and religion, but it is the highest manner of comprehending the Absolute Idea, because its manner is the highest—the Notion [*Begriff*, "concept"]." On this topic see J. N. Findlay, *Hegel: A Reexamination* (New York, 1962), pp. 130–2, 141–2.

71. Fichte, *Grundriss des Eigenthümlichen der Wissenschaftslehre, Sämtliche Werke*, ed. J. H. Fichte (8 vols.; Berlin, 1845), I, 332–3.

72. *Grundlage der gesammten Wissenschaftslehre, ibid.*, I, 326–7.

73. Schelling, *Sämtliche Werke*, Pt. I, Vol. I, p. 54, and Pt. I, Vol. III, pp. 349, 628. See also *Ideen zu einer Philosophie der Natur, ibid.*, Pt. I, Vol. II, pp. 56–61.

74. Preface to *The Phenomenology of the Spirit*, trans. Kaufmann, p. 388. In his *Lectures on the History of Philosophy, Sämtliche Werke*, ed. Hermann Glockner, XIX, 239, Hegel quotes the Renaissance Neoplatonist Giordano Bruno: "'Thus One Being is in all. That process downwards is the same as this return,' and it forms a Circle."

75. For Hegel's criticism of the "formalism" of Schelling's imperfect dialectic, see also the Preface to *The Phenomenology of the Spirit*, trans. Kaufmann, pp. 384–6.

76. *The Logic of Hegel*, trans. Wallace, Sect. 17, pp. 27–8. "Knowledge," said Hegel, in a statement which emphasizes that the circular movement of the conceptual system is inherent in the concepts themselves, "consists in the seeming inactivity which merely observes how the element that is distinguished moves by its own nature and returns again into its unity." *Phänomenologie des Geistes*, p. 561.

77. *Ideen zu einer Philosophie der Natur, Sämtliche Werke*, Pt. I, Vol. II, pp. 57–8.

78. Preface to *The Phenomenology*, trans. Kaufmann, pp. 406–8. See also Hegel's *Early Theological Writings*, pp. 309–11, and his *Differences of the Fichtean and Schellingian System of Philosophy*, in Kaufmann, p. 74.

79. Novalis, *Briefe und Werke*, III, 630.

80. Schelling, *Ideen zu einer Philosophie der Natur, Sämtliche Werke*, Pt. I, Vol. II, pp. 13–14. Compare Hegel, in Kaufmann, *Hegel*, p. 74.

81. *Allgemeine Deduktion des dynamischen Processes, ibid.*, Pt. I, Vol. IV, p. 77.

82. *The Friend*, ed. Rooke, I, 520.

83. Preface to *The Phenomenology*, trans. Kaufmann, p. 412. In Hegel's philosophy, W. T. Stace has said, "the whole development of spirit from its earliest stages has been motivated by this one impulse—to bridge the gulf between subject and object," and in its ultimate stage as Absolute Idea this process "is now complete, and with this the development of spirit is complete. Subject and object are now identical. Absolute reconciliation is reached." *The Philosophy of Hegel* (Dover Publications, 1955), p. 516. See also Jean Hyppolite, *Genèse et structure de la Phénoménologie de l'Esprit de Hegel* (Paris, 1946), pp. 67 ff.

84. *The Logic of Hegel*, p. 379.

85. As cited by Robert L. Kahn, "Some Recent Definitions of German Romanticism," *Rice University Studies*, L (1964), 8.

86. *Zur Naturwissenschaft*, in *Goethes Werke* (Weimar), Pt. II, Vol. XI (1893), pp. 11, 166. Matthijs Jolles has shown the degree to which this concept is operative in Goethe's general thought and in the design of his literary creations, as well as in his scientific investigations, in *Goethes Kunstanschauung* (Bern, 1957), chap. IV. For an indication of the relation of Goethe's views to the occult concept of the divided androgyne and bisexual polarity and union see, e.g., *Zur Morphologie, Goethes Werke*, Pt. II, Vol. VII, pp. 67–8. "You are no chemist," Novalis remarked, "or you would know that through genuine combination there ensues a third thing which is both at the same time, and more than both" (*Briefe und Werke*, III, 20). On Schiller's complex use of the concept of the "third thing" which both mediates and preserves differentiations and contraries, see Elizabeth M.

Wilkinson and L. Willoughby, trans. and eds., Schiller's *On the Aesthetic Education of Man* (Oxford, 1967); e.g., pp. li–ii, xciii–iv, 349–50.

87. *Hints towards the Formation of a more Comprehensive Theory of Life*, ed. Seth B. Watson (London, 1848), p. 63.

88. Preface to *The Phenomenology*, trans. Kaufmann, p. 434; and *Vorlesungen über die Geschichte der Philosophie, Sämtliche Werke*, XIX, 685.

89. *Essays in Radical Empiricism*, and *A Pluralistic Universe*, ed. Ralph Barton Perry (New York, 1943), II, 48.

90. *The Great Chain of Being* (Cambridge, Mass., 1936), pp. 293–8. This passage, incidentally, indicates how mistaken it is to reduce Lovejoy's position on "Romanticism" to a simple "nominalism" which denies validity to any application of the term to a period of human thought and culture.

91. *The Friend*, ed. Rooke, I, 522. Compare Hegel in Kaufmann, *Hegel*, p. 74: "Necessary bifurcation [*Entzweiung*] is a factor of life which forms itself through eternal opposing, and totality is possible in the highest liveliness only through restoration out of the highest separation. Reason is only against the absolute fixation of bifurcation by the understanding."

92. Schiller, *On the Aesthetic Education of Man*, ed. Wilkinson and Willoughby, pp. 87–9, 125. On this concept see M. H. Abrams, *The Mirror and the Lamp* (New York, 1953), pp. 220–2.

93. *Denkmal der Schrift . . . des Herrn F. H. Jacobi, Sämtliche Werke*, Pt. I, Vol. VIII, pp. 59, 81.

94. Preface to *The Phenomenology*, trans. Kaufmann, pp. 388–90. Again Hegel adduces a biological analogue, p. 392: "While the embryo is surely in itself human, it still is not human for itself: human for itself is only the educated reason which has made itself that which it is in itself."

95. See Hegel, *Phänomenologie des Geistes*, ed. Johannes Hoffmeister (6th ed.; Hamburg, 1952), pp. xxiv, xxxvii, 67.

96. Schelling, *Sämtliche Werke*, Part I, Vol. VII, p. 32.

97. *Vorlesungen über die Philosophie der Weltgeschichte*, ed. Georg Lasson (2 vols.; Leipzig, 1920) II, 936. See also *Die Vernunft in der Geschichte*, ed. Johannes Hoffmeister (5th ed.; Hamburg, 1955), pp. 48, 61–2.

98. Preface to *The Phenomenology*, trans. Kaufmann, pp. 402–4.

99. Schelling, *Sämtliche Werke*, Pt. I, Vol. V, p. 290.

100. *Ibid.*, Pt. I, Vol. I, p. 38.

101. *The Ages of the World*, trans. Frederick de Wolfe Bolman, Jr. (New York, 1942), pp. 225–6.

102. *Die Vernunft in der Geschichte*, ed. Hoffmeister, pp. 79–80; and *Phänomenologie des Geistes*, pp. 67, 564.

103. *Sämtliche Werke*, Pt. I, Vol. VI, p. 57; also III, 628.

104. *The Friend*, ed. Rooke, I, 508–9.

105. Preface to *The Phenomenology*, trans. Kaufmann, pp. 400–2.

106. Lessing, *Die Erziehung des Menschengeschlechts, Sämtliche Schriften*, ed. Karl Lachmann and Franz Muncker, (Leipzig), XIII (1897), Sect. 93; see also Sects. 91–2.

107. Hegel, *Phänomenologie des Geistes*, p. 549. "The circle," Goethe said, "which mankind must pass through is determinate enough, and . . . it has already traveled over its path of life more than once. If we also want to ascribe to mankind a spiral movement, it still turns back always to that region through which it has already passed." Cited by Hans Leisegang, *Denkformen*, p. 140.

108. Bernard Blackstone, *The Lost Travellers* (London, 1962), p. 106. On the quest-plot see also Georg Roppen and Richard Sommer, *Strangers and Pilgrims* (Norwegian University Press, 1964), and Northrop Frye, *A Study of English Romanticism* (New York, 1968).

109. Novalis' remarks apply to much of the philosophy and literature of his lifetime: "Each science becomes poetry—after it has become philosophy"; and "Poetry is the hero of philosophy. Philosophy elevates poetry into its own basic principle." *Briefe und Werke*, III, 173–4.

110. For the currency in German Pietist literature of the figures of the pilgrimage back home, and of *Heimweh* for the father and the fatherland, see August Langen, *Der Wortschatz des deutschen Pietismus* (Tübingen, 1954), pp. 138–9. On Romantic *Heimweh* see W. Rehm, *Orpheus: Der Dichter und die Toten* (Düsseldorf, 1950), p. 20.

111. Blake, *To the Accuser Who Is the God of This World* and *Ah! Sunflower*.

112. Novalis, *Briefe und Werke*, III, 172, 375.

F O U R / *The Circuitous Journey: Through Alienation to Reintegration*

1. On the Pietist theologians in the Württemberg of Schiller's youth see Benno von Wiese, *Friedrich Schiller* (Stuttgart, 1959), especially chap. IV. On the probable influence of Oetinger see also Schiller's *On the Aesthetic Education of Man*, ed. Wilkinson and Willoughby, pp. lxxxi, 254, 315. Oetinger's comments on the primal androgyne are reprinted in Ernst Benz, *Adam, der Mythus vom Urmenschen*, 22, 163–70.

2. Kant, *Critique of Practical Reason*, trans. Lewis White Beck (New York, 1956), pp. 90, 126–7.

3. Isaiah Berlin, "Herder and the Enlightenment," in *Aspects of the Eighteenth Century*, ed. Earl R. Wasserman (Baltimore, 1965), pp. 87–9.

4. Blaise Pascal, Preface to *Le Traité du vide*, *Opuscules et lettres*, ed. Louis Lafuma (Éditions Montaigne, 1955), p. 54.

5. Lessing, *Die Erziehung des Menschengeschlechts*, Sect. 1. R. S. Crane's "Anglican Apologetics and the Idea of Progress, 1699–1745," in *The Idea of the Humanities*, I, 214–87, reveals the currency of most of Lessing's key ideas in eighteenth-century England. That God (in the technical term) "accommodates" the revelation of religious and moral truths to the stages in the intellectual growth of mankind from infancy to maturity, and that history therefore represents the progressive theological education of the human race, had been proposed by Tertullian in the third century; and these ideas were expanded by various later Church Fathers and scholastic theologians. See Crane, *ibid.*, I, 216–21.

6. Herder, *Sämtliche Werke*, ed. Bernhard Suphan (33 vols.; Berlin, 1877–1913), VII, 5, 130. See also *Auch eine Philosophie der Geschichte zur Bildung der Menschheit* (1774), *ibid.*, V.

7. *Ibid.*, XIII, 189–92.

8. *Kant's gesammelte Schriften* (Akademie Ausgabe; Berlin, 1902 ff.), VIII, 109–10. See also Kant's *Idee zu einer allgemeinen Geschichte in weltbürgerlicher Absicht* (1784).

9. For Kant on "der philosophische Chiliasmus," see his *Gesammelte Schriften*, VI, 34, 134–6; VIII, 27.

10. Schiller, *Sämtliche Werke*, ed. Otto Güntter and Georg Witkowski (20 vols.; Leipzig, n.d.), XVI, 142–4.

11. *Patrologia Latina*, ed. Migne, XIV, 1065; cited by A. O. Lovejoy in his classic study of "Milton and the Paradox of the Fortunate Fall," *Essays in the History of Ideas* (Baltimore, 1948), p. 288.

12. *Paradise Lost*, XII, 458–78. See also *Paradise Regained*, IV, 612 ff.: "For though that seat of earthly bliss be fail'd,/ A fairer Paradise is founded now/ For *Adam* and his chosen Sons. . . ."

13. *Sämtliche Werke*, XVI, 144.

14. Schiller, *On the Aesthetic Education of Man*, trans. Wilkinson and Willoughby, Introduction, p. li; see this introduction for a penetrating analysis of the structure and dialectical process of Schiller's thought. I am grateful to Professor Wilkinson for having allowed me to read this Introduction in proof.

15. *On the Aesthetic Education of Man*, ibid., pp. 11, 31, 23.

16. Adam Ferguson, *An Essay on the History of Civil Society*, 1767 edition, ed. Duncan Forbes (Edinburgh, 1966), p. 19. This work was translated into German the year after its publication (Leipzig, 1768). Ferguson's friend Adam Smith, in lectures he delivered at the University of Glasgow in 1763, had earlier analyzed the "commercial spirit" of a developed economy and the progressive division of labor necessary to increase efficiency in industrial production, and had indicated the "disadvantages" of these events in "contracting" the mind of the workman and in dampening courage and the martial spirit. These lectures, however, were not published until 1896, from a student's notes; see Adam Smith, *Lectures on Justice, Police, Revenue and Arms*, ed. Edwin Cannan (Oxford, 1896), pp. 255–9. Smith later incorporated his analysis in *An Enquiry into . . . the Wealth of Nations* (1776); see e.g., the edition by Edwin Cannan (New York, 1937), pp. 3–21, 734–40. Wilkinson and Willoughby, in Schiller's *On the Aesthetic Education of Man*, pp. 231–3, cite parallels to some elements in Schiller's descriptions of fragmented man in Herder's *Vom Erkennen und Empfinden der Menschlichen Seele* (1778) and in Rousseau's *Discourses* (1750–4).

17. For Schiller's early and close study of Adam Ferguson, see Benno von Wiese, *Friedrich Schiller*, pp. 76–82; and for the influence of Ferguson's *Essay on Civil Society* on Schiller, as well as on Herder and other German thinkers, see Roy Pascal, " 'Bildung' and the Division of Labour," in *German Studies Presented to Walter Horace Bruford* (London, 1962), pp. 14–28, and his "Herder and the Scottish Historical School," *Publications of the English Goethe Society*, New Series, XIV (1938–9), 23–42.

18. Schiller, *Sämtliche Werke*, XVII, 479–81.

19. Kant, *Critique of Practical Reason*, trans. Beck, pp. 126–7; Fichte, *Sämtliche Werke*, VI, 299–300; Schiller, *Aesthetic Letters*, p. 59; Hölderlin, *Hyperion's Jugend*, *Sämtliche Werke*, III, 204; Wordsworth, *The Prelude*, VI, 531–42; Coleridge, *Shakespearian Criticism*, ed. T. M. Raysor (2 vols.; Cambridge, Mass., 1930), II, 262–3.

20. 30 Aug. 1795; *Friedrich Heinrich Jacobi's auserlesener Briefwechsel* (2 vols.; Leipzig, 1825–7), II, 208–10. In his *Lectures on the Vocation of the Scholar* (1794), Fichte had said that "Rousseau, under the name of the state of Nature" and the "ancient poets . . . under the title of the golden age" had both placed "behind us" what in fact "lies before us!" Man must inevitably leave his peaceful animal state; "he plucks at all hazards the apple of knowledge, for the drive is ineradicably planted in him to be like God," even though "the first step out of this state leads him to sorrow and toil." *Sämtliche Werke*, VI, 342–3.

21. Fichte, *Die Grundzüge des gegenwärtigen Zeitalters* (1804–5), *Sämtliche Werke*, VII, 5–12. These lectures, as well as those *On the Vocation of the Scholar*, are available in a translation by William Smith, *The Popular Works of J. G. Fichte* (2 vols.; London, 1889).

22. Schelling, *De prima malorum humanorum origine*, *Sämtliche Werke*, Pt. 1, Vol. 1, pp. 32–3.

23. *Ibid.*, pp. 38–9.

24. *Ideen zu einer Philosophie der Natur* (1797), *Sämtliche Werke*, Pt. 1, Vol. II, pp. 12–14.
25. *The Logic of Hegel*, trans. Wallace, Sect. 24, pp. 52–4. For Hegel's close study of the ideas of Schiller, see Walter Kaufmann, *Hegel*, pp. 48–58.
26. *The Logic of Hegel*, trans. Wallace, pp. 54–7. See also Schelling, *Sämtliche Werke*, Pt. II, Vol. III, pp. 364–5: "Philosophy has as its highest aim to repair that rent consciousness [*zerissene Bewusstsein*]. . . . The philosopher . . . is the physician who again binds up and with gentle, slow hand seeks to heal the deep wounds of human consciousness." For Hegel's earlier discussion of the Biblical story of man's expulsion from paradise as a "pictorial" representation of the spirit's act of self-division by which it becomes "an other to itself," see his *Phänomenologie des Geistes*, ed. Hoffmeister, pp. 536 ff.
27. Schiller had said, e.g., that a purely voluntary human action "can never show grace." *Über Anmut und Würde* (1793), *Sämtliche Werke*, XVII, 329.
28. *Über das Marionettentheater*, in *Heinrich von Kleist's Werke*, ed. Wilhelm Waetzoldt (6 parts; Berlin, n.d.), V, 76–9. See Helmut Sembdner, ed., *Kleist's Aufsatz über das Marionettentheater: Studien und Interpretationen* (Berlin, 1967).
29. *Darlegung des wahren Verhältnisses der Naturphilosophie zu der verbesserten Fichteschen Lehre* (1806), *Sämtliche Werke*, Pt. I, Vol. VII, pp. 58–9, 81–2.
30. For various parallels between the philosophy of Schelling and the poetry of Wordsworth, see E. D. Hirsch, Jr., *Wordsworth and Schelling: A Typological Study of Romanticism* (New Haven, 1960).
31. *Sämtliche Werke*, Pt. I, Vol. III, pp. 628, 341.
32. *Ibid.*, VI, 42, 57.
33. *The Ages of the World*, trans. Frederick de Wolfe Bolman, Jr. (New York, 1942), pp. 84–5, 88, 90–2. Cf. Walt Whitman's anticipation of the poet-seer who will redeem all division, including the primal division between man and nature, in *Passage to India*, Sect. 5:

> All these separations and gaps shall be taken up and hook'd and
>   linked together,
> The whole earth, this cold, impassive, voiceless earth, shall be
>   completely justified,
> Trinitas divine shall be gloriously accomplish'd and compacted by
>   the true son of God, the poet . . .
> Nature and Man shall be disjoin'd and diffused no more,
> The true son of God shall absolutely fuse them.

34. For a discussion of Schelling's abortive epic poem, see Fritz Strich, *Die Mythologie in der deutschen Literatur von Klopstock bis Wagner* (2 vols.; Halle, 1910), II, 31–9.
35. *The Logic of Hegel*, trans. Wallace, Sect. 17, p. 28.
36. *Ibid.*, Sect. 15, p. 24. Cf. Proclus, *The Elements of Theology*, Props. 33 and 146. As Hegel put it in his "longer Logic" (*The Science of Logic*, trans. Johnston and Struthers, II, 483–4):

> Each step in the progress of further determination in advancing from the indeterminate beginning is also a rearward approach to it. . . . The Science [*die Wissenschaft*] is seen to be a circle which returns upon itself, for mediation bends back its end into its beginning or simple ground. Further, this circle is a circle of circles; for each member . . . is intro-Reflection which, returning to the beginning, is at the same time the beginning of a new member.

Also in *Vorlesungen über die Geschichte der Philosophie, Sämtliche Werke,*
XVII, 56:

> This activity . . . must be represented not as a straight line extended
> into abstract infinity, but as a circle, as a return into itself. This circle
> has for its periphery a great many circles; the whole is a large sequence
> of developments which turn back upon themselves.

37. Preface to *The Phenomenology*, trans. Kaufmann, *Hegel*, p. 410; see also
     pp. 434, 448.
38. *The Logic of Hegel*, trans. Wallace, Sect. 244, p. 379. Cf. *The Science of
     Logic*, II, 484–6; also, II, 483: "The concept, in its dialectical progress not
     only loses nothing and leaves nothing behind, but carries with it all that
     it has acquired."
39. *Ibid.*, Sect. 17–18, pp. 27–9. Cf. *The Science of Logic*, II, 485–6.
40. See, e.g., *Phänomenologie des Geistes*, ed. Hoffmeister, pp. 558–9; in the
     translation by J. B. Baillie, *The Phenomenology of Mind* (Harper Torch-
     books, New York, 1967), pp. 800–1. (The Preface to Hegel's *Phenomenology*
     I quote from Walter Kaufmann's accurate translation in his book, *Hegel*.
     Quotations from the body of the *Phenomenology* are my own translation,
     with the page references to Hoffmeister's German edition. For the con-
     venience of the English reader, I follow this with a page reference, in pa-
     rentheses, to Baillie's rather loose translation, indicated by the initial "B.")
41. Preface to the *Phenomenology*, in Kaufmann, pp. 380–400.
42. *Ibid.*, pp. 402–4. Also p. 452: "the long path of education and the move-
     ment, as rich as it is profound, through which the spirit reaches knowl-
     edge. . . ."
43. *Phänomenologie des Geistes*, pp. 66–7 (B., 135–6).
44. *Ibid.*, p. xxxviii.
45. *Lectures on Modern Idealism* (New Haven, Conn., 1919), pp. 147 ff. On the
     analogue to the *Bildungsroman* see also Kaufmann, *Hegel*, pp. 158, 381.
46. *Phänomenologie des Geistes*, p. 549 (B., 789–90). As Hegel summarizes the
     sequence, in the author's advertisement of the book: In the consecutive
     "appearances of the spirit . . . the imperfect ones dissolve and pass over
     into higher ones, which are their next truth. They find their final truth
     first in religion, and then in science, as the result of the whole." *Phäno-
     menologie*, p. xxxviii.
47. *Vorlesungen über die Geschichte der Philosophie, Sämtliche Werke*, XVII,
     51–2. See also *Phänomenologie*, p. 557: In absolute knowledge, "Ich in
     seinem Anderssein [ist] bei sich selbst."
48. G. R. G. Mure, *The Philosophy of Hegel* (London, 1965), pp. 62–3.
49. "Vorrede" to the "Vorletzte Fassung," *Sämtliche Werke*, ed. Friedrich
     Beissner (Stuttgart), III (1957), 236. The earlier version of the Preface, pub-
     lished in 1794 with the Hyperion-Fragment in Schiller's periodical, *Neue
     Thalia*, is closer to Schiller's formulation of the educational course both
     of the individual and of mankind, for it describes the way as a movement
     out from the simple unity of nature, up and around to the complex unity
     of culture:

> There are two ideals of our existence: a condition of the highest sim-
> plicity, in which our needs—by the mere organization of nature, and
> without any assistance from us—are in mutual consonance with each
> other, with our powers, and with everything to which we are related;
> and a condition of the highest culture [*Bildung*] where the same thing
> would ensue, with our needs and powers endlessly multiplied and
> strengthened, by means of the organization that we are capable of
> accomplishing for ourselves. The eccentric path which man, both ge-
> nerically and as an individual, passes through, from one point (of a

more or less pure simplicity) to another point (of more or less perfected culture [*vollendeten Bildung*]) appears, in its essential tendencies, always to be the same.   (*Ibid.*, III, 163)

The *Thalia* fragment also makes patent Hölderlin's identification of the
fall from simplicity into separation with the Biblical story of the paradise
lost and to be regained.

> The simplicity and innocence of the primal time dies so that it may
> return in a perfected culture [*Bildung*], and the holy peace of para-
> dise is destroyed so that what was only a gift of nature may flourish
> again as the earned possession of mankind. . . .
>   "But perfection will only come," said Melite, "in the distant land
> . . . of eternal youth. . . . There will we too all find each other again,
> at the great reunion of all things severed."   (*Ibid.*, III, 180–1)

50. Wolfgang Schadewaldt discusses the probable astronomic origins of the
    term in "Das Bild der exzentrischen Bahn bei Hölderlin," *Hölderlin-Jahr-
    buch* (1952), pp. 1–16. For the "eccentric circle" in Ptolemaic astronomy
    see Thomas S. Kuhn, *The Copernican Revolution* (New York, 1959), pp.
    69–70; and for a discussion of the term contemporary with the writing of
    Hyperion, see Charles Hutton, *A Mathematical and Philosophical Diction-
    ary* (London, 1796), I, 454. In *Hölderlin's "Hyperion": Exzentrische Bahn
    und Dichterberuf* (Stuttgart, 1965), pp. 12–15, Lawrence Ryan proposes the
    alternative view that "eccentric" refers to a shift of the center of the cir-
    cuitous path from the true point of unity outside oneself, in the *en kai pan*
    of the world, to a point within the individual self; see, however, the ob-
    jections to this interpretation by Ulrich Gaier in his review of Ryan's work
    in *The German Quarterly*, XXXIX (1966), 244–9. On the cyclical structure
    of the final version of *Hyperion* see also Paul de Man, "Keats and Hölder-
    lin," *Comparative Literature*, VIII (1956), 28–45.

51. For the widespread Romantic concern with the relation of "mastery and
    servitude" between the self and nature, see chap. VI, sect. 4.

52. Hölderlin, *Sämtliche Werke*, III, 10. *Hyperion* is now available in a good
    English translation by Willard R. Trask (Signet Classics; New York, 1965).

53. *Ibid.*, III, 157, 159. Cf. Hölderlin's lyric, *Lebenslauf*, on suffering and the
    circuitous course of life:

    > Grössers wolltest auch du, aber die Liebe zwingt
    >   All uns nieder, das Laid beuget gewaltiger,
    >   Doch es kehret umsonst nicht
    >   Unser Bogen, woher er kommt.

54. *Ibid.*, III, 158–9. Cf. the passage, similar even in many details, in *The Pre-
    lude* (1805), XI, 1 ff., where Wordsworth announces the beginning of re-
    covery from his crisis of despair in a reviving spring landscape.

55. Ryan, *Hölderlin's "Hyperion*," pp. 215–16.

56. *Sämtliche Werke*, III, 158. Cf. p. 51: "If only we can become again like
    children, so that the golden age of innocence returns, the age of peace and
    freedom, so that there is one joy, one resting place on earth!"

57. *Hölderlin's "Hyperion*," pp. 223 ff.

58. *Hyperion's Jugend, Sämtliche Werke*, III, 204.

59. Novalis, *Schriften*, ed. Paul Kluckhohn, Richard Samuel, Heinz Ritter,
    Gerhard Schulz (Stuttgart), I (1960), 79–82. There is an English translation
    of the romance by Ralph Manheim, *The Novices of Sais* (New York, 1949).
    Novalis' statements that "Mannigfache Wege gehen die Menschen" and
    that "jeder [Weg] endlich . . . zu dieser heiligen Heimat wieder führet"
    echoes an ancient topos in connection with man's spiritual journey, based
    on Jeremiah 6:16. In Chaucer's version at the opening of *The Parson's*

Tale: "Manye been the weyes espirituels that leden folk to oure Lord Jhesu Crist, and to the regne of glorie. Of whiche weyes, ther is . . . the righte wey of Jerusalem celestial."

60. *Schriften,* I, 82–8. Novalis wrote, in his notes for his intended *Enzyklopädie:* "Everything evil and wicked is isolating (it is the principle of separation). . . ." *Briefe und Werke* (Berlin, 1943), III, 630.

61. *Schriften,* I, 100; and p. 101: "A new bond between the Thou and the I."

62. *Ibid.,* I, 104–6.

63. *Ibid.,* I, 93–5.

64. *Ibid.,* I, 110–11.

65. *Henry von Ofterdingen,* trans. Palmer Hilty (New York, 1964), pp. 26–7.

66. *Ibid.,* pp. 48, 92; see also p. 75.

67. *Briefe und Werke* (Berlin, 1943), Fragmente, III, 632.

68. To Friedrich Schlegel, 18 June 1800, *ibid.,* I, 455.

69. *Henry von Ofterdingen,* pp. 120–48.

70. *Schriften,* ed. Kluckhohn and others, I, 345, 347.

71. *Confessions,* XII. xvi; XIII. xiii.

F I V E / *The Circuitous Journey: From Blake to D. H. Lawrence*

1. *The Ages of the World,* trans. Bolman, p. 91.

2. Introduction to *Songs of Experience; Jerusalem,* 15. 5–9. All my quotations of Blake's text are from *The Poetry and Prose of William Blake,* ed. David V. Erdman and Harold Bloom (New York, 1965); I have in some instances altered Blake's punctuation, for readier intelligibility.

3. Schelling, *Philosophie der Kunst, Sämtliche Werke,* Pt. I, Vol. V, p. 446; Blake, *Jerusalem,* 10. 20.

4. To Dr. Trusler, 23 Aug. 1799; *The Poetry and Prose,* p. 676.

5. [*The Laocoön*], *ibid.,* p. 271.

6. Addressing "the Jews" in his *Jerusalem,* Plate 27, Blake points to the aspect of truth in the Adam Kadmon of the Kabbala: "You have a tradition, that Man anciently contained in his mighty limbs all things in Heaven & Earth; this you received from the Druids. . . . Albion was the parent of the Druids."

7. *The Four Zoas,* VII [A], 87, ll.33–4.

8. *A Vision of the Last Judgment, The Poetry and Prose,* p. 545. Los, as Blake says in *Jerusalem,* 95. 18–20, even in his fallen form as "Urthonas Spectre," had "kept the Divine Vision in time of trouble."

9. *The Four Zoas,* VIII, 110, ll.6–7, 26–7; IX, 122, ll.16–18; 132, ll.23–8.

10. *Fearful Symmetry* (Princeton, 1947), p. 386.

11. E.g., in *The Four Zoas,* I, 5, ll.8–12.

12. *Jerusalem,* 17. 33–44.

13. *Milton,* 30. 1–14; On Blake's "Beulah," see Harold Bloom, *Blake's Apocalypse* (New York, 1963), pp. 341–7.

14. *Fearful Symmetry,* p. 91.

15. *The Four Zoas,* IX, 139, ll.4–10.

16. See chap. I, sect. 1.

17. *Jerusalem,* 29–30.

18. E.g., *Jerusalem,* 32. 28–9; 39. 38–40.

19. *Ibid.,* 99. 1–5. Earlier in the poem (34. 46–8) Blake had interrupted the narrative to cry out, when he himself suddenly beheld "the Visions of Albion":

for Cities
Are Men, fathers of multitudes, and Rivers & Mountains
Are also Men; everything is Human, mighty! sublime!

20. To H. F. Cary, 6 Feb. 1818; *Collected Letters*, IV, 833–4. For Coleridge's evaluation of the individual poems and illustrations in the *Songs of Innocence and of Experience*, see his letter to C. A. Tulk, 12 Feb. 1818, *ibid.*, pp. 836–8.

21. *Religious Musings*, in *The Complete Poetical Works*, ed. E. H. Coleridge (2 vols.; Oxford, 1912), I, 108–25, ll.226–48.

22. *Ibid.*, ll.66–7 (variant), 215–18.

23. To John Thelwall, 14 Oct. 1797, *Collected Letters*, I, 349. As Hölderlin's *Hyperion* had said: "Wo finden wir das Eine, das uns Ruhe giebt, Ruhe?" *Sämtliche Werke*, III, 164.

24. *Anima Poetae*, ed. E. H. Coleridge (Boston, 1895), p. 156; *The Friend*, ed. Rooke, I, 494, 520; and *The Statesman's Manual*, Appendix D, in *Lay Sermons* (London, 1852), p. 105. "The natural alien of their negative eye" is Coleridge's quotation from his own poem, "Limbo," in *Complete Poetical Works*, I, 429–30. To "become a soul-less fixed Star," Coleridge said, "receiving no rays nor influences into my Being," is "a Solitude which I so tremble at, that I cannot attribute it even to the Divine Nature." *Inquiring Spirit*, ed. Kathleen Coburn (London, 1951), p. 34.

25. *The Friend*, III, 263.

26. "On Poesy or Art," in *Biographia Literaria*, II, 262.

27. *The Theory of Life*, ed. Seth B. Watson (London, 1848), pp. 50–2. See also *The Friend*, I, 94, note, where Coleridge attributes the first statement of the "universal Law of Polarity" to Heraclitus, and assigns its development into "the foundation both of Logic, of Physics, and of Metaphysics" to Giordano Bruno.

28. Appendix B, *The Statesman's Manual* in *Lay Sermons*, pp. 94–5.

29. *Biographia Literaria*, I, 183–5, 196–8, 202; II, 12.

30. Appendix B, *The Statesman's Manual* in *Lay Sermons*, p. 64.

31. *Collected Letters*, IV, 575; and see, e.g., *Biographia Literaria*, I, 183–5.

32. *The Friend*, I, 508–9.

33. "On Poesy or Art," in *Biographia Literaria*, II, 253, 258. Coleridge's essay is based upon, but greatly elaborates and sharpens, ideas in Schelling's "On the Relation of the Formative Arts to Nature."

34. Appendix B, *The Statesman's Manual* in *Lay Sermons*, pp. 75–6, 77–8.

35. *The Philosophical Lectures*, ed. Kathleen Coburn (New York, 1949), p. 358; and see *Collected Letters*, IV, 769.

36. *The Friend*, III, 263.

37. *Biographia Literaria*, I, 202.

38. William Hazlitt, "The Drama: XI" (Dec. 1820), in *The Complete Works*, ed. P. P. Howe (London, 1933), XVIII, 371. On Coleridge's use of the serpent as a symbol see J. B. Beer, *Coleridge the Visionary* (New York, 1962), pp. 74–6.

39. To Joseph Cottle, 7 Mar. 1815; *Collected Letters*, IV, 545.

40. *Ibid.*

41. There is a close parallel in Hölderlin's *Empedokles* in which the philosopher, having signified his adequacy to live for himself, independently of nature and nature's gods, suffers to the full the isolation he has pridefully chosen: "Weh! einsam! einsam! einsam!" Hölderlin, *Sämtliche Werke*, IV, Pt. I, p. 103.

42. On Coleridge's role in developing this lyric form, and its relations to his philosophy of the reconciliation of subject and object, see M. H. Abrams, "Structure and Style in the Greater Romantic Lyric," in *From Sensibility*

to *Romanticism*, ed. F. W. Hilles and Harold Bloom (New York, 1965).

43. *The Philosophical Lectures*, p. 179.

44. For the Neoplatonic circulation from and to the soul which "links the end to its beginning," so that "the movement is one and continuous," see e.g., Proclus, *Elements of Theology*, ed. Dodds, Props. 33, 199, 206. Coleridge himself, in an essay *On the Principles of Genial Criticism*, indicated the relevance of the philosophy of Plotinus to his own presentation of divided and reunified mind and nature in *Dejection: An Ode*. Discussing his theory of beauty as "the reduction of many to one," Coleridge cites a long section from a manuscript version of his *Ode* (including "I see, not feel, how beautiful they are," as well as the passage on "Joy . . . wedding Nature to us"), in order to remark the relevance of a passage he quotes from the *Enneads*, I. vi. 3. In it, Plotinus characterizes beauty as a perception which unifies the fragments of a splintered outer world, and so renders them concordant, companionable, and assimilable to mind:

> So with the perceptive faculty: discerning in certain objects the Ideal-Form which has bound and controlled shapeless matter . . . it gathers into unity what still remains fragmentary, catches it up and carries it within, no longer a thing of parts, and presents it to the Ideal-Principle as something concordant and congenial, a natural friend.

(In *Biographia Literaria*, II, 239–41. I have given the Stephen Mackenna translation of the passage Coleridge cites in Greek.)

45. *The Correspondence of Henry Crabb Robinson with the Wordsworth Circle*, ed. Edith J. Morley (2 vols.; Oxford, 1927), I, 401.

46. *The Prelude*, II, 220–6, 395–434, and MS RV, p. 525.

47. Variant of *The Ruined Cottage, Poetical Works*, V, 402. Wordsworth reworked part of this passage into *The Excursion*, IV, 957 ff.

48. John Jones, *The Egotistical Sublime*, chap. II.

49. *Poetical Works*, V, 338.

50. *Ibid.*, p. 2.

51. "The Contrarieties: Wordsworth's Dualistic Imagery," *PMLA*, LXIX (1954), 1181.

52. *The Prelude*, XI, 393–6. In a noteworthy passage Wordsworth describes how he, the man, incomplete in himself, is perfected by conjunction with his feminine counterpowers: *The Prelude*, XIII, 200–10. Here Wordsworth seemingly expresses in metaphor the union with the feminine contrary that Novalis, Blake, and Shelley put forward in the form of myth.

53. Wordsworth so described his *Prelude* to Isabella Fenwick; see her note on *There Was a Boy*. To my earlier parallels between Wordsworth's *Prelude* and *A la recherche du temps perdu* it is relevant to add here Harry Levin's observation about the madeleine which evokes all of Marcel's past life: "Proust would not have us forget that the name and shape of that little tea-cake are traceable to the shells that pilgrims wore on their hats as badges of their vocation. Let us make no mistake; we are at the commencement of a religious pilgrimage." *The Gates of Horn* (New York, 1966), p. 390.

54. *The Orphic Voice: Poetry and Natural History* (New Haven, 1960), pp. 338–9. On Wordsworth's use of the journey as a structural metaphor in *The Prelude*, see also, e.g., R. A. Foakes, *The Romantic Assertion* (London, 1958), chap. IV, and Georg Roppen and Richard Sommer, *Strangers and Pilgrims* (Oslo, Norway, 1964), Pt. II, chap. I.

55. *The Prelude*, XII, 156; in this context, Wordsworth describes the enduring "power o'er my imagination" of lonely roads and the wayfarers who traverse them.

56. *Ibid.*, XI, 43–4; X, 239–42; XIII, 270–1.

57. *Ibid.*, XI, 48–56; see also I, 35–8.

58. *Ibid.*, (1850), IX, 1–22; see also the variant, pp. 314–15, and the footnote, p. 584.

59. As de Selincourt points out (*Wordsworth's Poetical Works*, V, 365), the opening book of *The Recluse* "is in fact a continuation of his poetical autobiography from the place where *The Prelude* leaves off." This place, as we have seen, is also the place from which *The Prelude* has set out.

60. *Home at Grasmere*, *Wordsworth's Poetical Works*, V, 313–14, ll.1–59.

61. *Ibid.*, ll.60 ff., MS variant, pp. 315–16.

62. *Ibid.*, ll.103–9. As late as in a poem of 1811 Wordsworth parallels his "Departure from the Vale of Grasmere" to that of a tenant of "Elysian plains" or of "celestial Paradise," whom it might please to absent himself from felicity long enough to take a round trip to a lower realm.

> O pleasant transit, Grasmere! to resign
> Such happy fields, abodes so calm as thine. . . .
> Ne'er can the way be irksome or forlorn
> That winds into itself for sweet return.
> *(Poetical Works*, III, 64)

63. Hegel, *Phänomenologie*, pp. 347, 376; Coleridge, *Religious Musings*, ll.146–9; Wordsworth, *The Prelude*, II, 448–57; Shelley, *Prometheus Unbound*, I, 625–8.

64. Anders Nygren, *Agape and Eros*, trans. Philip Watson (London, 1953), pp. 574, 578. The use of "love" for the universal cohesive and unifying force is as old as Presocratic philosophy. Empedocles, for example, described things as "at one time all coming together, through Love, into one, at another each borne apart from the others through Strife." Kirk and Raven, *The Presocratic Philosophers*, pp. 326–7.

65. Erigena, *De divisione naturae*, I. lxxiv. "Love" remained the name for the general integrative force in occult philosophy. For the role of "Amour" in Boehme, e.g., see Alexandre Koyré, *La Philosophie de Jacob Boehme*, pp. 139–42.

66. "Essay on Love," *Shelley's Prose*, ed. David Lee Clark (Albuquerque, 1954), p. 170.

67. Hegel, "Love," *Early Theological Writings*, pp. 304–5; and see Schiller, "Liebe," in *Philosophische Briefe*, *Sämtliche Werke*, ed. Güntter and Witkowski, XVII, 198 ff.

68. *Milton and Wordsworth* (New York and Cambridge, 1937), p. 176.

69. The version of 1802, in *Literary Criticism of William Wordsworth*, ed. Zall, p. 52.

70. Juan Luis Vives, *On Education*, trans. Foster Watson (Cambridge, 1913), p. 28. I am indebted for this passage to Mrs. Caroline Bloomfield.

71. Hegel, *Phänomenologie des Geistes*, p. 542. For my references to Plotinus, Boehme, Winstanley, and Schelling, see above, chapter III, sects. 1 and 2, and chapter IV, sect. 2.

72. *Jerusalem*, 5. 21; *The Four Zoas*, IX. 133, ll. 22–5; *Jerusalem*, 96. 14–21. Gerrard Winstanley had said that the fallen Adam in every man is the "selfish power," or "self-love," but that "the law of love flowing forth to every creature, is Christ in you." *Works*, ed. Sabine, pp. 157, 174–5.

73. *Religious Musings*, ll.148–56. See also Coleridge's *Statesman's Manual*, in *Lay Sermons*, pp. 95–6.

74. *The Revolt of Islam*, VIII. xxii; *Prometheus Unbound*, III, iv. 134–6; *The Defence of Poetry*, in *Shelley's Prose*, ed. D. L. Clark, pp. 293, 277, 282–3.

75. *Endymion*, I. 777–811. See also the letter to John Taylor, 30 Jan. 1818,

where Keats said of this passage on the ascent from the self to selfless love: "My having written that Argument will perhaps be of the greatest Service to me of anything I ever did."

76. Schelling, *Sämtliche Werke*, Pt. I, Vol. VII, p. 62; Wordsworth, *To My Sister*. In a version of *The Ruined Cottage* (*Poetical Works*, V, 382) Wordsworth described

> the pure joy of love,
> By sound diffused, or by the breathing air . . .
> Or flowing from the universal face
> Of earth and sky.

77. Ronald Peacock, *Hölderlin* (London, 1938), p. 46.
78. For instances of Novalis' erotic figures for universal relationships see above, chapter IV, sect. 4.
79. "On the Manners of the Ancient Greeks," *Shelley's Prose*, p. 220.
80. As quoted from a Bodleian MS by Earl Wasserman, *Shelley's "Prometheus Unbound"* (Baltimore, 1965), p. 90n.
81. *Shelley's Prose*, p. 327.
82. *Shelley's "Prometheus Unbound,"* pp. 195, 30–1.
83. *Shelley's Prose*, p. 170.
84. See Harold Bloom's insightful discussion of the divided Prometheus in *The Visionary Company*, pp. 298 ff. Wasserman in *Shelley's "Prometheus Unbound"* also suggests that various characters and events of the dramas are "the symbolic externalizing of mental acts and powers"; see, e.g., pp. 2–3.
85. *Religious Trends in English Poetry* (4 vols.; New York, 1939–57), III, 350.
86. *Jerusalem*, VII. 57–61.
87. *Complete Poetical Works of P. B. Shelley*, ed. Thomas Hutchinson (London, 1939), p. 272.
88. *The Works of Thomas Carlyle*, XXVIII, 2–3.
89. *Sartor Resartus*, ed. C. F. Harrold, pp. 81, 147, 157–8.
90. *Ibid.*, p. 156. On the motif of the Wandering Jew see G. B. Tennyson, *Sartor Called Resartus* (Princeton, N. J., 1965), pp. 201–12.
91. *Ibid.*, pp. 188–9. In Revelation 21:4 it is God who "shall wipe away all tears from their eyes; and there shall be no more death" nor "any more pain." In a later section of *Sartor* called "Organic Filaments," Carlyle's metaphors patently reflect the myth of the Primal Man: "Yes, truly, if Nature is one, and a living indivisible whole, much more is Mankind, the Image that reflects and creates Nature, without which Nature were not"; palpable lifestreams flow "in that wondrous Individual Mankind. . ." (pp. 246–7). An interesting American instance of the circuitous form is Hawthorne's *The Marble Faun* (1860). See Cushing Strout, "Hawthorne's International Novel," *Nineteenth-Century Fiction*, XXIV (1969), 169–81. Strout analyzes the work as a novel of self-formation, whose structure mimics its theme: a spiral movement from home and innocence, into the discipline of exile and the experience of evil, then back home.
92. *An Essay on the History of Civil Society*, p. 19; see above, chapter IV, sect. 1.
93. *Past and Present, The Works of Thomas Carlyle* (Centenary Edition), X, 257, 186, 272–4.
94. Arnold, *The Scholar Gypsy, Obermann Once More, A Summer Night, Stanzas from the Grand Chartreuse, To Marguerite—Continued*. Reference to Arnold's *Obermann Once More* (he wrote another poem, as well as an essay, on Senancour's *Obermann*) provides occasion to mention this early instance of the native French tradition of existential isolation, disgust, and the sense of *le néant*. Senancour wrote *Obermann*, an epistolary quasi-autobiography, in 1804. A relevant passage:

I am alone. . . . Here I am in the world, wandering, lonely in the middle of the crowd which means nothing to me; like a man struck with an ancient deafness. . . . In the midst of the world's noise he hears a universal silence; amid a world of living beings, he is an absentee.

See Robert M. Adams, *Nil* (New York, 1966), pp. 23–4.

95. However in the *Phenomenology of the Spirit* (the work by Hegel which most influenced Marx's thought), the "absolute freedom and terror" which is "merely the fury of destruction" (the stage of evolving spirit, manifested historically in the era of the French Revolution, which precedes its culmination as "absolute knowledge") obviously is Hegel's conceptual version of the *dies irae* in the "image-representation" of Biblical apocalypse. See the *Phänomenologie*, ed. Hoffmeister, pp. 414–22.

96. For example, the French Socialist, Pierre-Joseph Proudhon, in a book published in 1846 which shows the influence both of German thought and of the social theories of Saint-Simon, described "the antagonism of society . . . the state of separation, of isolation, of hostility against his fellow-creatures in which man has lived to the present time; in a word, this alienation of his heart." His remedy for this individual and social fragmentation is love: "When man, reconciled with himself, will cease regarding his neighbor and nature as hostile powers, only then will he love. . . . Then, love [will become] in fact and without division the law of mankind." *Système des contradictions économiques,* ed. Roger Picard (2 vols.; Paris, 1923), I, 367–8.

97. *Economic and Philosophical Manuscripts* of 1844, trans. T. B. Bottomore, in Erich Fromm, *Marx's Concept of Man* (New York, 1961), pp. 131–2, 135. For Marx on the relationship of love, see pp. 126–7, 168. "The relation of man to woman," he says, "is the *most natural* relation of human being to human being," and its qualitative character at any time reveals to what extent "man has become . . . a *species-being,* a *human being,*" and "in his individual existence at the same time a social being."

98. *Ibid.,* pp. 98–105.

99. *Ibid.,* pp. 127, 129. The translation of the myth of fragmented and reunified man (assimilated to the Biblical design of history) into economic, and specifically into communistic, terms goes back at least as far as Gerrard Winstanley, the religious philosopher of the small society of Diggers during the English civil wars. When "man began to fall out of his Maker," said Winstanley, he "sought content from creatures and outward objects," which then "fell out of him," with the result that all became "selfish." This curse of the self, or "covetousnesse," was "the beginner of particular interest," or private property, with men "buying and selling the earth from one particular hand to another, saying, *This is mine,* upholding this particular propriety by a law of government of his own making." The result of this division of communal into private property was that universal liberty was destroyed and the entire creation brought "under the curse of bondage, sorrow, and tears." But the redemptive power of universal love in man is even now at the point of restoring the earth to "a common treasury as it was in the beginning . . . making the earth one store-house, and every man and woman to live in the law of Righteousnesse and peace as members of one household." And this culminating stage of man's communal life in a familial equality of work and of possessions will fulfill the prophecy in Revelation of "a new heaven, and a new earth, wherein dwells righteousnesse." *The New Law of Righteousnes* (1649), *Works,* ed. Sabine, pp. 156, 158–9, 184.

100. Coleridge, "On Poesy or Art," *Biographia Literaria,* II, 253–5. To Hegel,

also, art helps the spirit to recognize and repossess its own alienated self. E.g., in *Vorlesungen über die Aesthetik, Sämtliche Werke,* ed. Glockner, XII, 34: Works of art are "an estrangement" [*Entfremdung*] of thoughts and concepts "into the sensuous," and in such works the spirit shows its power "of recognizing itself once more in its externalization to sensation and the sensuous, of grasping itself in its other, in that it transforms the alienated to thought, and so leads it back to itself."

101. *The Birth of Tragedy,* trans. Clifton Fadiman, in *The Philosophy of Nietzsche* (The Modern Library, New York), pp. 296–7, 166.

102. As Robert D. Wagner has said, the event is reported "from two points of view," the simple vision of the child and "the superimposed vision of the poet for whom the experience has become a memory modified by 'mature reflection.'" "The Meaning of Eliot's Rose Garden," *PMLA,* LXIX (1954), 24; see also Leonard Unger, "T. S. Eliot's Rose Garden," in *T. S. Eliot: A Selected Critique,* ed. Unger (New York, 1948), pp. 374–94.

103. In T. S. Eliot, *The Complete Poems and Plays* (New York, 1952), pp. 117–18.

104. *Ibid.,* p. 145. Compare Augustine's analysis, in the *Confessions,* XI. xxviii, of the altering role of expectation and memory, and the evolving play of past, present, and future, in the process of reciting a psalm; and his statement that "it is the same for the whole life of man . . . and likewise for the whole history of the human race."

105. Bede Griffith's recent autobiography, *The Golden String* (1954), p. 15, in representing the spiritual journey of his life, reverts to Augustine's chief type for the circular return, the parable of the Prodigal Son: "Every step in advance is a return to the beginning, and we shall not really know him as he is, until we have returned to the beginning, and learned to know him as both the beginning and end of the journey. We are all, like the Prodigal Son, seeking our home, waiting to hear the Father's voice."

106. D. H. Lawrence, *Apocalypse* (New York, 1932), p. 45. Frank Kermode discusses the apocalyptic structure, episodes, and imagery in Lawrence's own novels, in "Lawrence and the Apocalyptic Types," *Word in the Desert,* ed. C. B. Cox and A. E. Dyson (London, 1968), pp. 14–38.

s i x / *Revelation, Revolution, Imagination, and Cognition*

1. Circa 10 September 1799; *Collected Letters,* I, 527.

2. To Lord Byron, 8 Sept. 1816, *Letters of P. B. Shelley,* ed. F. L. Jones, I, 504.

3. Preface to *Laon and Cythna,* 1817 (reissued in 1818 as *The Revolt of Islam*), *Shelley's Prose,* ed. D. L. Clark, pp. 315–17.

4. *To William Wordsworth,* ll.38–45.

5. Thomas Noon Talfourd, "An Attempt to Estimate the Poetical Talent of the Present Age," *The Pamphleteer,* V (1815), 432–3. Cf. Hazlitt, *Complete Works,* V, 161; XI, 86–7; *Shelley's Prose,* pp. 239–40; Francis Jeffrey, *Contributions to the Edinburgh Review* (4 vols.; London, 1844), I, 158–67; *The Collected Writings of Thomas DeQuincey,* ed. David Masson, II, 273–4.

6. See M. H. Abrams, "English Romanticism: The Spirit of the Age," *Romanticism Reconsidered,* ed. Northrop Frye (New York, 1963), pp. 26–53.

7. *The Correspondence of Robert Southey with Caroline Bowles,* ed. Edward Dowden (Dublin, 1881), p. 52.

8. See, e.g., Auguste Viatte, *Les Sources occultes du romantisme* (2 vols.; Paris, 1928), especially I, 41, 98–103, 128–9, 232–69; II, 83–5, 199–201.

9. *The Complete Works of William Hazlitt*, ed. P. P. Howe (21 vols.; London, 1930–4), IV, 119–20.

10. For apocalyptic revolutionary movements in Germany, see Norman Cohn, *The Pursuit of the Millennium* (London, 1957). As Alexandre Koyré has pointed out (*La Philosophie de Jacob Boehme*, pp. 7–9), Boehme lived in a period of eschatological expectations, and himself anticipated the near advent, after drastic calamities, of a new age of felicity. For the preoccupation with the apocalyptic last days in eighteenth-century German Pietism, see Hans-Joachim Mähl, *Die Idee des goldenen Zeitalters im Werk des Novalis* (Heidelberg, 1965), pp. 232–45. Herder wrote in the early period of the French Revolution: "What say you to the present times and the times to come? . . . Do we not live in strange times, and must we not almost believe in the apocalypse? To what end will the higher economy of things unfold all these events?" To Gleim, 12 Nov. 1792; *Von und an Herder*, ed. Heinrich Düntzer and Ferdinand Gottfried von Herder (3 vols.; Leipzig, 1861), I, 152.

It is relevant also that, as Gershom Scholem points out, faith in the boundless promise of the Revolution was most current among those Jews who were descended from the radical sect of the latter seventeenth century which had accepted Sabbatai Zevi as the Messiah. At the outbreak of the French Revolution, Scholem says, "no great change was needed for them to become the apostles of an unbounded political apocalypse." One of these Jews, Junius Frey, was guillotined together with Danton. See Scholem, *Major Trends in Jewish Mysticism*, pp. 287 ff., especially p. 320.

11. As quoted by Geoffrey Carnall, *Robert Southey and His Age* (Oxford, 1960), p. 41. Thomas Holcroft, though remaining staunchly Republican, conceded in 1798 "that political revolutions are not so well calculated to better man's condition, as during a certain period I, with almost all the thinking men in Europe, had been led to suppose." *Memoirs of Thomas Holcroft* (London, 1926), p. 269.

12. Herschel Baker, *William Hazlitt* (Cambridge, Mass., 1962), p. 66; *The Collected Poetry of W. H. Auden* (New York, 1945), pp. 284–5, 288.

13. *Paradise Lost*, XII. On Milton's internalization of the earthly paradise see Michael Fixler, *Milton and the Kingdoms of God* (London, 1964), and Northrop Frye, *The Return of Eden* (Toronto, 1965), chap. IV.

14. To Charles Ollier, Oct. 15, 1819, in *The Letters of Percy Bysshe Shelley*, ed. Jones, II, 127. For Shelley on "the spirit of the age" as a product of an age of revolution, see also *Shelley's Prose*, ed. D. L. Clark, pp. 239–40, 296–7, 327–8; and Hazlitt's *The Spirit of the Age*, in *The Complete Works*, XI.

15. *Descriptive Sketches*, ll.774–91, in *Wordsworth's Poetical Works*, I, 88. In the revised version of 1849 Wordsworth made more explicit his echo of the Biblical prophecy of "a new heaven and a new earth," at the same time that he retracted his earlier assurance of an impending terrestrial paradise by means of political revolution. Note, however, that even so late Wordsworth asserted a pragmatic value in his having once entertained these impossible hopes:

> Lo, from the flames a great and glorious birth;
> As if a new-made heaven were hailing a new earth!
> —All cannot be; the promise is too fair
> For creatures doomed to breathe terrestrial air:
> Yet not for this will sober reason frown
> Upon that promise, nor the hope disown;

> She knows that only from high aims ensue
> Rich guerdons, and to them alone are due.

In *The Prelude* of 1805, X, 371–414, Wordsworth says that he was able to look even upon the "enormities" and "atrocities" of the Reign of Terror with "some portion of [the] spirit" of "the ancient Prophets," as the condign and cleansing violence of the *dies irae*—"the consummation of the wrath of Heaven."

16. Wordsworth, *The Convention of Cintra*, ed. A. V. Dicey (London, 1915), pp. 10, 122.
17. See *Paradise Lost*, III, 56–8, 323–49.
18. Coleridge, *The Complete Poetical Works*, I, 108–23. See also the apocalyptic allusions in Coleridge's notebook of 1796; *The Notebooks of S. T. Coleridge*, ed. Kathleen Coburn (New York, 1957 ff.), I, 273.
19. *Ibid.*, pp. 243–7. On the background of *France: An Ode*, see Carl Woodring, *Politics in the Poetry of Coleridge* (Madison, 1961), pp. 180–7.
20. *The French Revolution*, pp. 11–12, in *Poetry and Prose*, ed. Erdman and Bloom, pp. 292–3; *America*, Plates 6–8 (p. 52); see also *A Song of Liberty*, Plate 25 (pp. 43–4).
21. To John Flaxman, 19 Oct. 1801, *ibid.*, p. 686.
22. *A Vision of the Last Judgment, ibid.*, pp. 554, 545, 555.
23. *Ibid.*, p. 555. In his early *Marriage of Heaven and Hell*, Blake had interpreted the apocalyptic conflagration in terms of a heightening of the power of the senses:

> The whole creation will be consumed, and appear infinite and holy whereas it now appears finite & corrupt.
> This will come to pass by an improvement of sensual enjoyment. . . .
> If the doors of perception were cleansed everything would appear to man as it is, infinite.   (Plate 14; *ibid.*, pp. 38–9)

24. Robert Gleckner, "Blake and the Senses," *Studies in Romanticism*, V (1965), 14.
25. *Jerusalem*, Plates 33, 49, 98–9, in *Poetry and Prose*, pp. 178, 196, 254–6. See also *The Four Zoas*, 21, in *Poetry and Prose*, p. 306. In a poem enclosed in a letter to Butts of 2 Oct. 1800, Blake describes his "first Vision of Light"; that is, his initial experience (which occurred while he was walking on the beach at Felpham) of his sight gradually opening out to the ultimate state of vision, in which it saw all things as human and as one. As Blake put it, "My Eyes did Expand," and he saw all natural objects—rocks, hills, fountain, sea, stars—as human ("For each was a Man/ Human formd"); by his altering perception, he also saw the natural scene as a woman embracing "in her fair arms/ My Shadow . . . / And my wife's shadow too/ And My Sister & Friend." After this, "My Eyes more & more . . . Expanding," all these men "Appeard as One Man," who proceeded to enfold in his beams the purged form of Blake himself. *Poetry and Prose*, pp. 683–4.
26. *Queen Mab*, IV, 88–9; VIII, 107, 124–6, 238; IX, 1, 4.
27. For Shelley's preoccupation with the failure of the French Revolution see Ross Woodman, *The Apocalyptic Vision in the Poetry of Shelley* (Toronto, 1964), pp. ix, 4, 24.
28. Notes to *Hellas*, *The Complete Poetical Works*, pp. 479–80.
29. That Shelley is translating into secular terms the traditional Christian rendering of a spiritual apocalypse is evident from his echoes in these passages from Dante's *Paradiso*. Beatrice tells Dante that the objects he sees—river, sparks of light, flowers—are but "shadowy forecasts of their truth; not that these things are imperfect in themselves, but the defect is in thyself, that thy vision is not yet so exalted." The instant, however,

that Dante leans over and lets his eyes "drink" of the sight of the River of Grace, "then, like people who have been under masks and seem other than before if they put off the semblance not their own in which they were hid, the flowers and the sparks changed for me into a greater festival, so that I saw both the courts of heaven made plain . . . the high triumph of the true kingdom" (*Paradiso*, XXX, 77–99, trans. J. D. Sinclair).

30. *Sämtliche Werke*, ed. Beissner, I, i, 148, 139–42.

31. *Hyperion, ibid.*, III, 66–7. For Hölderlin's altering attitude toward the French Revolution see Maurice Delorme, *Hölderlin et la révolution française* (Monaco, 1959).

32. E.g., Novalis, *Schriften*, ed. Kluckhohn (1929), II, 338; III, 123, 147, 159, 228. See Hans-Joachim Mähl, *Die Idee des goldenen Zeitalters im Werk des Novalis*, Pt. II. Wilfried Malsch, *"Europa": Poetische Rede des Novalis* (Stuttgart, 1965), discusses the role of the French Revolution in shaping the design of Novalis' *Die Christenheit oder Europa* (1799).

33. *Schriften*, ed. Kluckhohn and Samuel (1960), I, 110–11.

34. *Sartor Resartus*, ed. Harrold, pp. 220, 186.

35. *Ibid.*, pp. 222, 264.

36. *On Heroes, Hero-Worship, and the Heroic in History, Works*, V, 84.

37. *Kant's gesammelte Schriften* (Akademie Ausgabe), VIII, 27; see also VI, 34, 134–6.

38. Richard Kroner, *Von Kant bis Hegel* (2d. ed.; 2 vols.; Tübingen, 1961), I, 1–2.

39. Carl Leonhard Reinhold, *Briefe über die Kantische Philosophie* (2 vols.; Leipzig, 1790), I, 12, 9. For Reinhold's later parallel between the contemporary revolutions in politics and metaphysics, see his essay "Ueber die teutschen Beurtheilungen der französischen Revoluzion," *Neue teutsche Merkur*, April, 1793, especially p. 396.

40. To Baggesen, April 1795, in J. G. Fichte, *Briefwechsel*, ed. Hans Schulz (2 vols.; Leipzig, 1925), I, 449–50. On Fichte's judgments of the Revolution, see M. Gueroult, "Fichte et la révolution française," *Revue Philosophique* (Sept.–Dec., 1939), 226–320. Friedrich Schlegel wrote in the *Athenaeum* (1798): "The French Revolution, Fichte's 'Wissenschaftslehre,' and Goethe's 'Meister' are the greatest tendencies of this age. Anyone who takes offense at this juxtaposition, to whom no revolution can appear important which is not noisy and material, has not yet risen to the high and inclusive standpoint of the history of mankind." (Schlegel, *Kritische Schriften*, ed. Wolfdietrich Rasch [Munich, 1964], p. 48.) In 1804 Schlegel declared that the French Revolution was "far less important than another greater, more rapid, and more comprehensive revolution which has at the same time taken place in the depth of the human spirit"—that is, "the invention of [philosophical] Idealism" (*Lessing's Geist aus seinen Schriften, ibid.*, pp. 444–5).

41. *The Way towards the Blessed Life*, in *The Popular Works of J. G. Fichte*, trans. William Smith (2 vols.; London, 1889), II, 306, 309. See also *The Vocation of Man, ibid.*, I, 441–2, 470.

42. Schiller, *On the Aesthetic Education of Man*, trans. Wilkinson and Willoughby, p. 9.

43. *Vorlesungen über die Philosophie der Weltgeschichte*, ed. Georg Lasson (Leipzig, 1919), II, 926.

44. The tenth chapter of Coleridge's literary life gives a muted narrative of his reactions to the French Revolution, from the "hey-day of hope" to the time when "my mind sank into a state of thorough disgust and despondency." Like Wordsworth in *The Prelude*, he tells us that he then devoted his "thoughts and studies to the foundations of religion and morals," only to find himself "all afloat. Doubts rushed in; broke upon me

'from the fountains of the great deep,' " and "it was long ere my ark touched on an Ararat, and rested" (*Biographia Literaria*, I, 132–3).

45. *Phänomenologie des Geistes*, ed. Hoffmeister, pp. 415–18, 420–2; in Baillie's translation, pp. 600–1, 603–5, 607–8.

46. Preface to the *Phenomenology*, trans. Kaufmann, *Hegel*, p. 380. And see J. Hippolyte, "La Signification de la révolution française dans la *Phénoménologie* de Hegel," *Revue Philosophique* (1939), pp. 321–52.

47. *Vorlesungen über die Geschichte der Philosophie*, *Sämtliche Werke*, XIX, 689–91.

48. *Vom Ich als Princip der Philosophie*, *Sämtliche Werke*, Pt. I, Vol. I, 156–9; and *System der gesammten Philosophie und der Naturphilosophie insbesondere*, Pt. I, Vol. VI, 562–4.

49. Cited by F. M. Todd, *Politics and the Poet: A Study of Wordsworth* (London, 1957), p. 11.

50. Letter to Reinhold, cited by Theodor Ballauf and Ignaz Klein, editors, *Fichte's Freiheitslehre* (Düsseldorf, 1956), p. 9. I have already cited Schelling's parallel claim, in 1795, that his "revolution of knowledge" sets up as its first principle "that the essence of man subsists entirely in absolute freedom." As Emile Bréhier remarks, "the idealist revolution, like the French Revolution, proclaims liberty," but an inner liberty, which "consists essentially in autonomy," in the sense that the mind obeys only laws which it has itself originated. Emile Bréhier, *Schelling* (Paris, 1912), p. 17.

51. *Fichte's Sämtliche Werke*, ed. J. H. Fichte, VI, 299–300.

52. Appendix B of *Statesman's Manual*, in *Lay Sermons*, ed. Derwent Coleridge, p. 66.

53. See Gregory Vlastos, "Slavery in Plato's Thought," *The Philosophical Review*, L (1941); especially pp. 294–5, 301, on Plato's application of the terms "master" and "slave" to the body-soul relationship in the moral dimension of experience. In discussing the cognitive quest of the soul for truth, rather then virtue, Plato also represents the soul as in conflict with the body, because the bodily senses are inaccurate and unreliable, and also because the body distracts the soul from its quest for truth by its intrusive desires, fears, and fantasies. The ideal in cognition, however, Plato specifies not as the mastery of the soul over the body, but as the achievement by the soul of the greatest possible detachment from the errorful and distracting body. See, e.g., *Plato's "Phaedo,"* trans. R. Hackforth (Cambridge, England, 1955), 64C–67B, and the commentary, pp. 48–51.

54. *Biographia Literaria*, I, 101–2.

55. *Beiträge . . . über die französiche Revolution*, *Sämtliche Werke*, VI, 117.

56. *Die Bestimmung des Menschen* (1800), *ibid.*, II, 191–3, 277.

57. Vorrede, *Die vorletzte Fassung*, *Sämtliche Werke*, ed. Beissner, III, 236. In the Preface to his earlier *Fragment von Hyperion*, Hölderlin had posited two tendencies in the human mind vis-à-vis nature: the acquisitive drive, which he calls *Bedürfnisse*, and the power-drive, which he calls *Kräfte*. When one or the other of these tendencies becomes excessive, man shows his "dangerous side," in either "desiring everything or enslaving everything." The stage of man's "highest self-development," however, will consist in his achieving an "organization" of these opponent powers "in infinitely multiplied and strengthened form" (*ibid.*, p. 163). On this concept in Hölderlin see Ulrich Gaier, review of Ryan's *Hölderlin's "Hyperion"*, *German Quarterly*, XXXIX (1966), 246.

58. Prose version of *Die Metrische Fassung* of Hyperion (1794–5), *Sämtliche Werke*, III, 186–94; see also *Hyperion's Jugend* (1795), *ibid.*, 199–205. The relations of the passages I have cited to the doctrines of Fichte are clarified

by Hölderlin's comments on Fichte in his letters of that time; see, e.g., to Hegel, 26 Jan. 1795; and to his brother, 13 Apr. 1795 and 24 Dec. 1798.

59. *Phänomenologie des Geistes*, ed. Hoffmeister, pp. 141–50; in Baillie's translation, pp. 228–40.

60. *Vorlesungen über die Philosophie der Weltgeschichte*, ed. Lasson, p. 938. Also in Hegel's Introduction to his *History of Philosophy*: Spirit passes through "division" and "alienation," "but only so that it can find itself, so that it can return to itself. Only this is freedom; for that is free which is not connected with nor dependent on an other. . . . In nothing else but in thought does the mind achieve this freedom. . . . Only in thought does all alien matter become transparent; here the mind is, in an absolute fashion, free." *Sämtliche Werke*, XVII, 52.

61. *The Four Zoas*, 12. 16–20; ed. Erdman and Bloom, pp. 302–3. Cf. Asia's repeated question to Demogorgon, in Shelley's dialectic of reversible mental power-relations, *Prometheus Unbound*, II, iv. 106–14: "Who is the master of the slave?"

62. *The Song of Los*, 4. 11–16; *ibid.*, p. 66.

63. *Jerusalem*, Plate 54, ll.1–5; *ibid.*, p. 201.

64. *The Complete Poetical Works of S. T. Coleridge*, I, 168, 243, notes; see also Coleridge's contemporary letter to his brother George, circa 10 Mar. 1798, *Collected Letters*, I, 394–8.

65. *Biographia Literaria*, I, 74, 77; *Philosophical Lectures*, ed. Kathleen Coburn (New York, 1949), p. 434.

66. *The Friend* (ed. Rooke), I, 517–18; Alice D. Snyder, *Coleridge on Logic and Learning* (New Haven, 1929), pp. 126–7.

67. Various recent commentators have discussed the theme of freedom in Wordsworth; see, e.g., Carl R. Woodring, "On Liberty in the Poetry of Wordsworth," *PMLA*, LXX (1955), 1033–48; Karl Kroeber, *The Artifice of Eternity* (Madison and Milwaukee, 1964), chap. II; Richard Stang, "The False Dawn: A Study of the Opening of Wordsworth's *The Prelude*," *ELH*, XXXIII (1966), 58–65.

68. In his prose criticism Wordsworth affirmed that to write with the eye on the object is a necessary but insufficient condition for poetry, since it is a mode of perception in which the visible object is master of the mind: it is a "power, though indispensable to a Poet . . . which he employs only in submission to necessity, and never for a continuance of time: as its exercise supposes all the higher qualities of mind to be passive, and in a state of subjection to external objects." Preface to the *Poems* (1815), *Literary Criticism of William Wordsworth*, ed. Zall, p. 140; see also pp. 160, 173. In the poem *Personal Talk (II)* Wordsworth says, "Whose mind is but the mind of his own eyes,/ He is a Slave"; and in *The Excursion* he alludes to that false science whose "dull eye" hangs "chained to its object in brute slavery." *Poetical Works*, IV, 74; V, 149.

69. *The Prelude*, XII, 370–9. In a manuscript draft which describes Wordsworth's "second birth" as a "redemption of his mind" from "submission and a slavish world," the mind and the outer universe are represented as equals, in that the aspiration of the one is matched by the possibilities of the other:

> He feels that, be his mind however great
> In aspiration, the universe in which
> He lives is equal to his mind, that each
> Is worthy of the other; if the one
> Be insatiate, the other is inexhaustible.

The Prelude, ed. de Selincourt and Darbishire, pp. 575–6.

SEVEN / *The Poet's Vision: The New Earth and the Old*

1. Blake, *Poetry and Prose*, ed. Erdman and Bloom, pp. 677, 634, 476.
2. Carlyle, *On Heroes, Hero-Worship, and the Heroic in History*, *Works* (Centenary edition), V, 93, 104–5, 84. See also Carlyle's *Sartor Resartus*, p. 197, and "Burns," *Works*, XXVI, 273: "It is not the dark *place* that hinders, but the dim *eye.*"
3. Ruskin, *Modern Painters* (New York, 1856), III, 268.
4. Lines 106–8, 513–25; see Jonathan Wordsworth, *The Music of Humanity: A Critical Study of Wordsworth's "Ruined Cottage"* (London, 1969).
5. Printed from manuscript by James Anthony Froude, *Thomas Carlyle 1795–1835* (2 vols.; New York, 1882), II, 7–12.
6. *Biographia Literaria*, II, 6.
7. *Literary Criticism of William Wordsworth*, ed. Zall, p. 40. Later Wordsworth told Isabella Fenwick, without mentioning the question of diction, that *Lyrical Ballads* had originated in a discussion with Coleridge of the possibility of a volume of poems "chiefly on natural subjects taken from common life, but looked at, as much as might be, through an imaginative medium" (Note to *We Are Seven*, *Poetical Works*, I, 361).
8. *Biographia Literaria*, I, 59–60. Coleridge quotes the passage beginning "To find no contradiction in the union of old and new," with some changes, from his earlier essay in *The Friend*, No. 5 (Sept. 14, 1809). He thought this statement so central to his view of the powers of the mind as to cite it repeatedly; see, e.g., *The Statesman's Manual* in *Lay Sermons*, pp. 27–8.
9. *Biographia Literaria*, I, 60; II, 12; I, 202; and to Richard Sharp, 15 Jan. 1804, *Collected Letters*, II, 1034.
10. *The Prelude* (1805), XIII, 139; (1850), XIV, 158; (1805), II, 380. The poet, Coleridge says elsewhere, "carries the simplicity of childhood into the powers of manhood" and "with a soul unsubdued by habit, unshackled by custom, contemplates all things with the freshness and wonder of a child." *Coleridge's Shakespearean Criticism*, ed. T. M. Raysor (2 vols.; Cambridge, Mass., 1930), II, 148.
11. *The Prelude*, MS Y, p. 572, ll.56–8. Wordsworth's sense that for a thing to exist is a sufficient miracle underlies what Helen Darbishire calls "the potency of the verb to be" in Wordsworth's "most memorable lines." *The Poet Wordsworth* (Oxford, 1950), p. 171.
12. *Expostulation and Reply*, ll.9–12. Rousseau wrote, "I tried to put myself completely in the state of a man who is just beginning to live"; and in his *Rêveries* he describes his recovery of consciousness after a fall, and his first awareness of "the sky, some stars, and a little greenery": "This first sensation was a delightful moment. . . . I was born that instant to life." See Georges Poulet, *Studies in Human Time* (Baltimore, 1956), pp. 168–9.
13. Novalis, *The Novices of Sais*, trans. Mannheim, p. 21; and *Fragmente*, in *Schriften*, ed. Kluckhohn and Samuel (4 vols.; Leipzig, 1929), II, 352. On the role of the child as norm in Novalis see Mähl, *Die Idee des goldenen Zeitalters*, pp. 362–71.
14. Peter Coveney, *The Image of Childhood* (Penguin Books, 1967), pp. 29–31.
15. Schiller, *Über naive und sentimentalische Dichtung*, *Sämtliche Werke*, ed. Güntter and Witkowski, XVII, 479–81, 495.
16. Novalis, *Schriften* (1929), II, 23; III, 192.

17. *The Logic of Hegel,* trans. Wallace, Sect. 24, p. 55. See also Hölderlin, Thalia-Fragment of *Hyperion, Sämtliche Werke,* III, 180.

18. When in the *Intimations Ode* Wordsworth's adopted scheme of a quasi-Platonic preexistence of the soul leads him to address the child as "thou best philosopher . . . Mighty Prophet! Seer blest!" Coleridge objects vigorously to this seeming cultural primitivism: "In what sense can [these] magnificent attributes be appropriated to a *child,* which would not make them equally suitable to a *bee,* or a *dog,* or a *field of corn* . . . ?" *Biographia Literaria,* II, 113.

19. Mark 8:18; also Isaiah 6:9–10, Jeremiah 5:21, Ezekiel 12:2.

20. *Confessions,* X.xl; see also VIII.v.

21. See, e.g., Coveney, *The Image of Childhood,* pp. 42–6.

22. Francis Bacon, *The New Organon and Related Writings,* ed. Fulton H. Anderson (New York, 1960), pp. 3, 15, 66; Thomas Traherne, *Centuries, Poems, and Thanksgivings,* ed. H. M. Margoliouth (2 vols.; Oxford, 1958), *Centuries,* III. 1–3; see also Traherne's poems "Wonder" and "Walking." *The Centuries of Meditation* remained in manuscript until 1908. "A childe that is new borne," said Winstanley, "or till he growes up to some few yeares . . . is innocent, harmelesse, humble, patient, gentle. . . . And this is *Adam,* or mankinde in his Innocency." Winstanley, however, unlike Traherne and Vaughan, does not attribute to the child a paradisal sense perception; for according to his view, it is at the moment that "outward objects intice him to pleasure," or to "seeke content without him," that each man "falls, and is taken captive, and falls lower and lower." *Fire in the Bush* (1649 or 1650), *The Works of Gerrard Winstanley,* pp. 493–4.

23. Vaughan, *The Retreate;* Boehme, *Aurora,* XIX. 12–13, in Koyré, *La Philosophie de Jacob Boehme,* p. 23.

24. "Personal Narrative," *Jonathan Edwards, Representative Selections,* ed. Clarence H. Faust and Thomas H. Johnson (New York, 1935), pp. 59–61.

25. *Shelley's Prose,* ed. D. L. Clark, pp. 282, 295. And p. 289: "The familiar appearance and proceedings of life became wonderful and heavenly, and a paradise was created as out of the wrecks of Eden. And as this creation itself is poetry, so its creators were poets."

26. *Sartor Resartus,* ed. Harrold, pp. 254, 259, 262, 267, 186, 264. In *Hard Times* Dickens, following Carlyle, epitomizes the death-dealing spirit of a commercial and utilitarian England by Gradgrind's stern command to his daughter, "Louisa, never wonder!"

27. *Les Rêveries du promeneur solitaire,* ed. Henri Roddier (Paris, 1960), *Cinquième Promenade,* pp. 70–1. See Poulet, *Studies in Human Time,* pp. 169–84; also his "Timelessness and Romanticism," *Journal of the History of Ideas,* XV (1954), 3–22. See also Northrop Frye's·discussion of "the point of epiphany" in *The Anatomy of Criticism* (Princeton, 1957), pp. 203–6.

28. Schelling, *Sämtliche Werke,* Pt. I, Vol. VI, 562–3.

29. Letter to Neuffer, March 1796, *Sämtliche Werke,* VI, 204; *Hyperion, ibid.,* III, 52.

30. *Defence of Poetry, Shelley's Prose,* ed. Clark, pp. 294–5.

31. *Blütenstaub, Briefe und Werke,* III, 60.

32. *Prelude,* V, 407; VII, 469; V, 628–9; I, 614; and (1850), VI, 513–14.

33. *Tintern Abbey,* ll.45–50. See also *Prelude,* II, 431–5: "Most audible then when the fleshly ear . . . / Forgot its functions, and slept undisturb'd./ If this be error . . . "; and VI, 534–6: "when the light of sense/ Goes out in flashes that have shewn to us/ The invisible world. . . ."

34. Robert Frost, "A Tribute to Wordsworth," *The Cornell Library Journal* (No. 11; Spring, 1970), 77–99.

35. Coleridge, *Biographia Literaria,* II, 101 ff. In a moment of irritation with

Wordsworth's "egotistical sublime," Keats complained even about the epiphany in *The Two April Mornings*, in a letter to J. H. Reynolds, 3 Feb. 1818: "Old Matthew spoke to him some years ago on some nothing, & because he happens in an Evening Walk to imagine the figure of the old man . . . it is henceforth sacred." Anna Seward regarded Wordsworth's "I wandered lonely as a cloud" as the product of an "egotistical manufacturer of metaphysical importance upon trivial themes." *Letters of Anna Seward* (6 vols.; Edinburgh, 1811), VI, 367.

36. Geoffrey Hartman, *Wordsworth's Poetry 1787–1814* (New Haven, 1964), pp. 211–12.

37. Carlyle, "Novalis," *Works*, XXVII, 53; *Sartor Resartus*, pp. 267, 264.

38. *The Varieties of Religious Experience* (The Modern Library, New York), p. 245.

39. Prologue to *Peter Bell*, ll.133–45. In *Personal Talk III*, Wordsworth alludes to the mood "Which with the lofty sanctifies the low." As early as 1794, in an addition to *An Evening Walk*, Wordsworth had described the sublimation of the trivial and mean which occurs for "those favoured souls" to whom "Science" and "a burning energy" have given "that other eye":

> With them the sense no trivial object knows
> Oft at its meanest touch their spirit glows.
> *(Poetical Works, I, 13, note)*

40. *Literary Criticism of William Wordsworth*, ed. Zall, pp. 158, 181–2.

41. See, e.g., M. H. Abrams, *The Mirror and the Lamp*, pp. 103–14, and W. J. B. Owen, *Wordsworth's Preface to "Lyrical Ballads"* (Copenhagen, 1957), chap. I.

42. *Literary Criticism of William Wordsworth*, ed. Zall, pp. 182, 184.

43. *Ibid.*, pp. 161, 163. That by "the proudest quality of our nature" Wordsworth refers to the imagination is indicated on p. 161, and also p. 183: "imagination . . . the faculty which is perhaps the noblest of our nature." He wrote to J. K. Miller, 17 Dec. 1831: "It is the habit of my mind inseparably to connect loftiness of imagination with that humility of mind which is best taught in Scripture." *The Letters, Later Years*, II, 592.

44. To E. H. Coleridge, 22 Jan. 1866, in *Further Letters of Gerard Manley Hopkins*, ed. Claude Colleer Abbott (London, 1938), p. 9. Karlfried Gründer, in *Figur und Geschichte* (Freiburg/Munich, 1958), chap. II, summarizes the history of *condescensio* and *accomodatio*, from the Church Fathers through the eighteenth century in Germany and England. See also Burnet, *Sacred Theory of the Earth* (ed. 1726), II, 152–3. Wordsworth's Wanderer adverts to the concept of *condescensio* in *The Excursion*, IV, 631–47: The first men heard the voice of God, and saw and talked to angels, either in "actual vision . . . or that in this sort/ Have condescendingly been shadowed forth/ Communications spiritually maintained."

45. "Mr. Wordsworth," in *The Spirit of the Age* (1825), *The Complete Works of William Hazlitt*, ed. P. P. Howe (London, 1932), XI, 86–8. Wallace Stevens' words in *The Comedian as the Letter C* (perhaps intentionally) apply precisely to Wordsworth's enterprise:

> Hence the reverberations in the words
> Of his first central hymns, the celebrants
> Of rankest trivia, tests of the strength
> Of his aesthetic, his philosophy,
> The more invidious, the more desired. . . .

The Collected Poems (New York, 1961), p. 37.

46. For the poems on the small celandine, see *Poetical Works*, II, 142, 144,

and IV, 244; for those on the daisy, II, 135–8, and IV, 67, 260. All these poems were written between 1802 and 1805.

47. *Literary Criticism of William Wordsworth*, pp. 182–4, 186. In a letter written to John Wilson early in June 1802, Wordsworth had defended *The Idiot Boy* by appealing from the literary preferences of "Gentlemen, persons of fortune, professional men, ladies," to the responses of men who "lead the simplest lives . . . who have never known false refinements." For "a great Poet" is a moral reformer who needs "to rectify men's feelings . . . to render their feelings more sane, pure, and permanent, in short more consonant to nature." *Ibid.*, pp. 71–2.

48. T. N. Talfourd, "An Attempt to Estimate the Poetical Talent of the Present Age," *The Pamphleteer*, V (1815), 462–3.

49. See Erich Auerbach, "Figurative Texts Illustrating . . . Dante's *Commedia*," *Speculum*, XXI (1946), 474–89; "Sermo Humilis," *Romanische Forschungen*, LXIV (1952), 304–64; "St. Francis of Assisi in Dante's *Commedia*," in *Scenes from the Drama of European Literature* (New York, 1959), pp. 79–98; also *Mimesis* (Princeton, 1953), pp. 72–3, 151–5.

50. Robert Lowth, *The Sacred Poetry of the Hebrews* (London, 1847), pp. 83–4, 79–80.

51. A convenient collection of comments on Wordsworth's early poetry is Elsie Smith's *An Estimate of William Wordsworth by His Contemporaries, 1793–1822* (Oxford, 1932). See also Coleridge, *Biographia Literaria*, I, 55.

52. R. H. Horne, *A New Spirit of the Age* (New York, 1884), pp. 191–2.

53. *Gedanken über den eigenen Lebenslauf, Sämtliche Werke*, ed. Josef Nadler (Vienna, 1949), II, 39–40; trans. in Ronald Gregor Smith, *J. G. Hamann 1730–1788* (London, 1960), pp. 148–54.

54. *Tagebuch eines Christen, Sämtliche Werke*, I, 5, 8–10, 13. Hamann's *Diary* in its original form included, among other parts, the *Thoughts about My Life* and *Observations upon Reading Holy Scripture;* see Nadler, *ibid.*, p. 322. For a discussion of the central role of "condescension" in all of Hamann's thought see Gründer, *Figur und Geschichte*, pp. 19 ff., and W. M. Alexander, *Johann Georg Hamann, Philosophy and Faith* (The Hague, 1966), pp. 25–37.

55. *Sämtliche Werke*, I, 6, 158. In an enlightening essay, Eric A. Blackall discusses the influence of these concepts on Hamann's prose style and characteristic irony; see "Irony and Imagery in Hamann," *Publications of the English Goethe Society*, XXVI (1957), 1–25.

56. *Poetical Works*, V, 373.

57. *The Ruined Cottage*, ll.55–9, 146–59, in *Poetical Works*, V, 380–3. In a letter of January 1815, Wordsworth said that he had "transfused" into *The Excursion* "the innumerable analogies and types of infinity . . . from the Bible of the Universe as it speaks to the ear of the intelligent, as it lies open to the eyes of the humble minded." *Literary Criticism of William Wordsworth*, ed. Zall, p. 134.

58. *The Prelude*, XII, 313–19, 356–9; also the variants, pp. 474–5. De Selincourt (*ibid.*, pp. 617–18) points out that Wordsworth and Coleridge probably "are recalling an actual conversation" of 1796 "which remained an ineffaceable memory with both."

E I G H T / *The Poet's Vision: Romantic and Post-Romantic*

1. Tony Tanner, *The Reign of Wonder: Naivety and Reality in American Literature* (Cambridge, England, 1965).

2. Quoted by Henry Nash Smith, *Virgin Land* (New York, 1957), p. 40; see also pp. 11, 12, 45, 50–1. On the millennial myth of America see, e.g., John Leddy Phelan, *The Millennial Kingdom of the Franciscans in the New World* (Berkeley and Los Angeles, 1956); F. I. Carpenter, "The American Myth: Paradise (To Be) Regained," *PMLA*, LXXIV (1959), 599–607; Charles L. Sanford, *The Quest for Paradise; Europe and the American Moral Imagination* (Urbana, 1961); Ernest L. Tuveson, *Redeemer Nation; The Idea of America's Millennial Role* (Chicago, 1968). The ancient expectation continues to be memorialized on our one-dollar bills, in the echo from Virgil's "Messianic eclogue": *Novus ordo Seclorum.*

3. See R. W. B. Lewis, *The American Adam: Innocence, Tragedy and Tradition in the Nineteenth Century* (Chicago, 1955).

4. R. W. Emerson, *The Complete Works* ("Centenary Edition"; Cambridge, Mass., 1903), I, 70–1.

5. *Ibid.*, I, 8–9; III, 285; I, 74: III, 17; I, 110–11.

6. Emerson, *Journals*, June 21, 1838, in *Selections from Ralph Waldo Emerson*, ed. Stephen Whicher (Boston, 1957), p. 90.

7. *The Writings of Henry David Thoreau* (20 vols.; Boston, 1906), VII, 247–8; VIII, 306–7; XIV, 43–4.

8. Charles Baudelaire, *Le Peintre de la vie moderne*, *Oeuvres Complètes*, ed. Y.-G. Le Dantec and Claude Pichois (Pléiade, 1963), pp. 1158–60.

9. *Le Spleen de Paris*, XLVIII, *ibid.*, pp. 303–4.

10. Rimbaud, *Oeuvres Complètes*, ed. Rolland de Renéville and Jules Mouquet (Pléiade, 1963), pp. 272–3.

11. Baudelaire, *Le Poème du haschisch*, *Oeuvres Complètes*, pp. 366, 372.

12. *Ibid.*, pp. 349, 384, 386.

13. On the libertine sects among the Gnostics, see Eugène de Faye, *Gnostiques et Gnosticisme* (Paris, 1913), pp. 391–406, and Herbert Liboron, *Die Karpokratianische Gnosis* (Leipzig, 1938). On the Spiritual Libertines in Europe and England, see Norman Cohn, *The Pursuit of the Millennium*, pp. 149–94, 315–72; and on parallel movements in late Jewish Messianism, Gershom G. Scholem, *Major Trends in Jewish Mysticism*, pp. 287–324.

14. Rimbaud, letters to Georges Izambard, 13 May 1871, and to Paul Demeny, 15 May 1871; *Oeuvres Complètes*, pp. 268, 270–71.

15. See Marcel Raymond, *From Baudelaire to Surrealism* (New York, 1950).

16. Frank Kermode, *The Sense of an Ending* (London, 1967), p. 47.

17. Henry James, *The House of Fiction*, ed. Leon Edel (London, 1957), pp. 31–2; Joseph Conrad, Preface to *The Nigger of the Narcissus* (Edinburgh and London, 1925), p. xii; Virginia Woolf, "Moments of Vision," *Times Literary Supplement*, May 23, 1918, p. 243, and *To the Lighthouse* (London, 1930), p. 249; Thomas Wolfe, *Of Time and the River* (New York, 1935), p. 551; William Faulkner, "All the Dead Pilots," in *Collected Stories* (New York, 1950), p. 531. These passages are quoted in Morris Beja's study of *Evanescent Moments: The Epiphany in the Modern Novel* (doctoral thesis, Cornell University, 1963).

18. *God's Grandeur, Pied Beauty.*

19. To E. H. Coleridge, 22 Jan. 1866; *Further Letters of Gerard Manley Hopkins*, ed. C. C. Abbott (London, 1938), p. 9.

20. T. S. Eliot, *Four Quartets*, in *The Complete Poems and Plays* (New York, 1952), p. 129.

21. To Stanislaus Joyce, 2 or 3 May [?], 1905 and 11 June, 1905; *Letters of James Joyce*, ed. Richard Ellman (New York, 1966), pp. 90, 91.

22. Thomas Aquinas, *Summa Theologica*, I. Q. 84. Art. 7.3.

23. *Stephen Hero*, ed. Theodore Spencer (New York, 1944), pp. 211–13. On Joyce's concept and use of epiphanies see Robert Scholes, "Joyce and the Epiphany," *Sewanee Review*, LXII (1964).

24. Quoted from Joyce's Diary by Richard Ellman, *James Joyce* (New York, 1959), p. 169; Joyce parallels this transvaluation of the trivial to the Christian mystery of the Eucharist.

25. *A Portrait of the Artist as a Young Man*, in *The Portable James Joyce*, ed. Harry Levin (New York, 1947), pp. 431–3. Joyce's culminating spot of time resembles the Wordsworthian Moment which involves a solitary person or thing, when, as he comments in *The Prelude*, attendant circumstances drop back to serve "as a solemn background, or relief,/ To single forms and objects" (1850 ed.; VII, 622–3). In a similar fashion, Joyce described the preliminary stage of the epiphany (to which he applies Aquinas' term, *integritas*) as "the performance of your . . . mind when confronted with an object," in which it "divides the entire universe into two parts, the object, and the void which is not the object" (*Stephen Hero*, p. 212).

26. *Credences of Summer, Notes toward a Supreme Fiction, Martial Cadenza*, in *The Collected Poems of Wallace Stevens* (New York, 1961), pp. 373, 397–8, 386, 237–8. As Stevens put it in *Notes toward a Supreme Fiction*, pp. 398–9, in such an "irrational moment . . . / These are not things transformed./ Yet we are shaken by them as if 'they were."

27. Sylvia Plath, in *The Colossus* (London, 1960), pp. 42–3. Eugène Ionesco, dramatist of the absurd, also describes his experience of secular Moments of grace:

> When I wake up, on a morning of grace, from my nocturnal sleep as well as from the mental sleep of routine, and I suddenly become aware of my existence and of the universal presence, so that everything appears strange, and at the same time familiar to me, when the astonishment of being invades me—these sentiments, this intuition belong to all men, of all times.

Cited by Martin Esslin, *The Theatre of the Absurd* (Anchor Books, 1961), p. 137.

28. Gregory Corso, *Selected Poems* (London, 1962), p. 17.

29. Allen Ginsberg, *Howl and Other Poems* (San Francisco, 1956), pp. 9–11, 18.

30. *Ages and Ages Returning*, ll.4–5. Whitman had also given poetic expression to the latter-day revival of American millennialism, the manifest destiny of American imperialism to regenerate the old world and the ancient races of man:

> I chant the new empire grander than any before, as in a vision it comes to me,
> I chant America the mistress, I chant a greater supremacy . . .
> Commerce opening, the sleep of ages having done its work, races reborn, refresh'd,
> . . . the old, the Asiatic renew'd as it must be.
>
> (*A Broadway Pageant*)

31. *Clarel*, in *The Works of Herman Melville* (London, 1924), XV, 250.

32. *Howl and Other Poems*, "Dedication."

33. Jack Kerouac, *The Dharma Bums* (New York, 1958), pp. 243–4.

34. I have discussed some aspects of this issue in "Coleridge, Baudelaire, and Modernist Poetics," *Immanente Ästhetik, Ästhetische Reflexion: Lyrik als Paradigma der Moderne*, ed. W. Iser (Munich, 1966).

35. *Shelley's Prose*, ed. D. L. Clark, pp. 240, 295; see also p. 297.

36. Coleridge, "On Poesy or Art," in *Biographia Literaria*, ed. Shawcross, II, 254; Wordsworth, Preface to *Lyrical Ballads*, *Literary Criticism*, ed. Zall, p. 52.

37. Keats, *Second Sonnet to Hayden* (1816); *Sleep and Poetry* (1816), ll.101–25; *The Fall of Hyperion* (1819), I, 141–9, 189–201.

38. Raymond Williams, *Culture and Society, 1780–1850* (New York, 1960), pp. 36, 31.

39. *The Prelude*, X, 969–70.

40. *Friedrich Schlegel's philosophische Vorlesungen aus den Jahren 1804 bis 1806*, ed. C. J. H. Windischmann (Bonn, 1846), I, 111–12.

41. Hegel, *Einleitung: System und Geschichte der Philosophie*, ed. Hoffmeister, pp. 32–3.

42. *Philosophie des Rechts*, ed. Hoffmeister (4th ed.; Hamburg, 1955), p. 17.

43. *Home at Grasmere*, ll.401–3.

44. Preface to *Lyrical Ballads*, *Literary Criticism*, ed. Zall, pp. 48–9.

45. *Ibid.*, p. 51 (a passage added in 1802). Lionel Trilling remarks that Wordsworth's statement "is bold to the point of being shocking, for it echoes and controverts St. Paul's sentence which tells us that 'we live, and move, and have our being' in God (Acts 17:28)." *Beyond Culture* (New York, 1965), p. 58.

46. Preface to *Die Braut von Messina*, *Sämtliche Werke*, ed. Güntter and Witkowski, XX, 252. The passage brings to mind Coleridge's statement that "the poet, described in *ideal* perfection, brings the whole soul of man into activity," *Biographia Literaria*, II, 12.

47. "Essay on Life," *Shelley's Prose*, ed. D. L. Clark, p. 172.

48. *A Defence of Poetry*, *ibid.*, pp. 286–7, 292, 294–5.

49. *The Eolian Harp*, ll.26–31 (added in the edition of 1817); *The Friend* (ed. Rooke), I, 520. In his *Hymn before Sunrise* Coleridge describes Mont Blanc as "blending with my Thought,/ Yea, with my Life and Life's own secret joy." See also *Collected Letters*, ed. Griggs, I, 397–8.

50. Blake, *Poetry and Prose*, ed. Erdman and Bloom, pp. 53, 59; see also pp. 44, 50.

51. *Prelude*, VIII, 627–31; II, 418–34. For Wordsworth's persistent complex of life, joy, and the union of self and nature, see also I, 580–5; XIII, 253–63. Hölderlin uses the phrase, "das Lebenslied der Welt," in *Hyperion*, *Sämtliche Werke*, III, 157.

52. Hölderlin, "Sokrates und Alcibiades," *Sämtliche Werke*, I, i, 260.

53. *Hyperion*, *ibid.*, III, 49–51.

54. *Stuttgart*, ll.16, 59, 67–8, in *Sämtliche Werke*, II, i, 86–8; *Wie wenn am Feiertage*, ll.23–7, 35–6, *ibid.*, II, i, 118–19.

55. For an account of the *topos* of spring in classical and medieval love poetry see James J. Wilhelm, *The Cruelest Month* (New Haven and London, 1965).

56. Hölderlin, *Der Wanderer*, line 35, *Sämtliche Werke*, II, i, 81.

57. *Hyperion*, *ibid.*, III, 157–60.

58. *The Four Zoas*, 132. 23–36; 138. 25; 139. 1–3. See also the lovely *reverdie* in Blake's *Milton*, Book II, 31. 28–45: even lamentations in the land of Beulah, when they attain to the senses of man in this world of generation, are apprehended as the mild song and orderly dance of life in joyous spring.

59. Note on *Hellas*, *Complete Poetical Works*, pp. 479–80.

60. Harold Bloom, *The Visionary Company*, p. xv.

61. *Shelley's "The Triumph of Life,"* ed. Donald H. Reiman (Urbana, Illinois, 1965), ll.1–18.

62. *Über das Erhabene*, *Sämtliche Werke*, ed. Güntter and Witkowski, XVII, 632.

63. Hegel, *Vorlesungen über die Philosophie der Geschichte*, ed. Lasson, II, 938; *Die Vernunft in der Geschichte*, ed. Hoffmeister, pp. 79–80; *Phänomenologie des Geistes*, ed. Hoffmeister, p. 564.

64. A. C. Bradley, "Wordsworth," *Oxford Lectures on Poetry* (London, 1950), p. 125. On Shelley's acute sense of the evil propensities in human nature,

see C. S. Lewis, "Shelley, Dryden, and Mr. Eliot," in *English Romantic Poets: Modern Essays in Criticism*, ed. M. H. Abrams (New York, 1960), pp. 255–8.
65. *Speculations* (London, 1936), pp. 8–9, 53–5, 92–3.
66. David Ferry, *The Limits of Mortality* (Middletown, Conn., 1959), pp. 52, 4, 32, 53, 173.
67. Edward E. Bostetter, *The Romantic Ventriloquists* (Seattle, 1963), pp. 33, 235, 236–7, 218.
68. To Humphry Davy, 2 Dec. 1800; *Collected Letters*, I, 649.
69. To Maria Gisborne, 13 or 15 Oct. 1819, *The Letters of P. B. Shelley*, ed. F. L. Jones (2 vols.; Oxford, 1964), II, 125. Three years earlier Shelley, after referring to the French Revolution, had also cited Coleridge's statement that "Hope is a most awful duty"; *ibid.*, I, 504. See also Wordsworth's sonnet (*Poetical Works*, III, 140), written in 1811 with reference To the Spanish uprising against Napoleon: singing of liberty, the poet

> did not shrink from hope
> In the worst moment of these evil days;
> From hope, the paramount *duty* that Heaven lays,
> For its own honour, on man's suffering heart.

70. Hopkins' sonnet, *No worst, there is none;* and Wordsworth's Prospectus, from MS B in Dove Cottage. Coleridge too knew what it was to confront *le Néant*—what he called "positive Negation," "the mere horror of blank Naught-at-all"; see the poem *Limbo*, in *Complete Poetical Works*, pp. 429–31.
71. *The Letters of P. B. Shelley*, I, 504.
72. *The Prelude*, pp. 198, 200; and see the notes, pp. 556–7. De Selincourt, following Legouis, suggests that Wordsworth mistook a domiciliary visit by French troops at the time of his trip to the Chartreuse in 1790 for the armed occupation which did not take place until 1792.
73. Wordsworth's earlier account of this same tour of France and Switzerland in *Descriptive Sketches*—which he wrote in 1791–2, soon after completion of the tour, and before the Reign of Terror—underlines the significance of this revelation. For that earlier narrative had ended with the confident prediction that the flame of the Revolution was a purifying apocalyptic fire from which would be born "another earth" that would be a restored Golden Age. See *Poetical Works*, I, 88, ll.774–91.
74. See above, Chapter IV, pp. 215–17.
75. Matthijs Jolles, *Dichtkunst und Lebenskunst: Studien zum Problem der Sprache und Dichtung bei Friedrich Schiller*. I had the privilege of reading the chapter of my late colleague's manuscript entitled "Der schwebende Adler." His book is being prepared for posthumous publication.
76. To Charles Ollier, 15 Oct. 1819, in *The Letters of P. B. Shelley*, II, 127.
77. Schiller's *Spaziergang*, like Wordsworth's *Tintern Abbey*, is a hill poem. Unlike Wordsworth's poem and other English instances of the greater lyric, however, it retains the formula (frequent in eighteenth-century "topographical poetry") of a sustained climb, in the course of which the altering prospect evokes appropriate changes in the accompanying meditation; see, e.g., John Dyer's *Grongar Hill* (1726).
78. To James Gillman, 10 Oct. 1825, in *The Letters of S. T. Coleridge*, ed. E. H. Coleridge (2 vols.; Boston and New York, 1895), II, 742–3.
79. For the ruling metaphors of the passive and receptive mind (vis-à-vis the objects of the external world) in Locke and other empirical sensationists, as opposed to the metaphors of the active and projective mind in Coleridge and his contemporaries, see M. H. Abrams, *The Mirror and the Lamp*, pp. 57–69.

80. E.g., Paul had said in Ephesians 4:8 (cf. Psalms 68:18, and *Paradise Lost* X, 185–8), "When he ascended up on high, he led captivity captive." In Demogorgon's echo (IV, 556), "And Conquest is dragged captive through the deep," the reversal of direction signifies also a reversal of reference. For "the deep" is the depths of man's own nature, by whose opposing promptings and projections man becomes at the same time "a despot and a slave" to himself (IV, 549). And it is from "its awful throne of patient power/ In the wise heart" (the internal mirror-image of the now empty throne of Jupiter in "Heaven's despotism") that "Love . . . springs/ And folds over the world its healing wings" (IV, 557–61).

81. Note on *Peter Bell the Third,* in *The Complete Poetical Works of P. B. Shelley,* p. 362.

82. *A Defence of Poetry* (1821), *Shelley's Prose,* pp. 296–7; also *ibid.,* pp. 239–40. Cf. William Hazlitt, *The Spirit of the Age* (1825), *The Complete Works,* XI, especially pp. 86–7.

Index

Index

Books cited frequently in the text are listed at the end of the entry under the author's name. The reference that follows is to the note identifying the edition cited.